IMMANUEL KANT

Theoretical Philosophy after 1781

The purpose of the Cambridge edition is to offer translations of the best modern German editions of Kant's work in a uniform format suitable for Kant scholars. When complete (fifteen volumes are currently envisioned) the edition will include all of Kant's published works and a generous selection of his unpublished writings, such as the *Opus postumum, handschriftliche Nachlass,* lectures, and correspondence.

This volume is the first to assemble in historical sequence the writings that Kant issued or projected between 1783 and 1796 to popularize, summarize, amplify, and defend the doctrines of his masterwork, the *Critique of Pure Reason* of 1781. The best known of them, the *Prolegomena,* is often recommended to beginning students, but the other texts are also vintage Kant and important sources for a fully rounded picture of his intellectual development.

As with other volumes in the series there are copious linguistic notes and a glossary of key terms. The editorial introductions and explanatory notes shed light on the hostile reception accorded Kant by the metaphysicians of his day and on Kant's own efforts to derail his opponents.

THE CAMBRIDGE EDITION OF THE WORKS OF IMMANUEL KANT

IMMANUEL KANT

Theoretical Philosophy after 1781

EDITED BY

HENRY ALLISON
Boston University

PETER HEATH
University of Virginia

TRANSLATED BY

GARY HATFIELD
University of Pennsylvania

MICHAEL FRIEDMAN
Indiana University

HENRY ALLISON

PETER HEATH

CAMBRIDGE
UNIVERSITY PRESS

CAMBRIDGE UNIVERSITY PRESS
Cambridge, New York, Melbourne, Madrid, Cape Town, Singapore,
São Paulo, Delhi, Dubai, Tokyo

Cambridge University Press
The Edinburgh Building, Cambridge CB2 8RU, UK

Published in the United States of America by Cambridge University Press, New York

www.cambridge.org
Information on this title: www.cambridge.org/9780521147644

First published 2002
This digitally printed version 2010

A catalogue record for this publication is available from the British Library

Library of Congress Cataloguing in Publication data
Kant, Immanuel, 1724–1804.
[Selections. English. 2002]
Theoretical philosophy after 1781 / edited by Henry Allison, Peter Heath.
p.   cm. – (The Cambridge edition of the works of Immanuel Kant)
Includes bibliographical references and indexes.
ISBN 0-521-46097-2 (hardcover)
1. Philosophy.   I. Allison, Henry E.   II. Heath, Peter Lauchlan, 1922–   III. Title.
B2758.A4513   2002
193 – dc21   2001037551

ISBN 978-0-521-46097-2 Hardback
ISBN 978-0-521-14764-4 Paperback

Dedicated to the memory of Norman Kemp Smith (1872–1958).

In old age a friend to one of the present editors,
and in all ages a friend to would-be
translators of Kant.

Contents

General editors' preface

Within a few years of the publication of his *Critique of Pure Reason* in 1781, Immanuel Kant (1724–1804) was recognized by his contemporaries as one of the seminal philosophers of modern times – indeed as one of the great philosophers of all time. This renown soon spread beyond German-speaking lands, and translations of Kant's work into English were published even before 1800. Since then, interpretations of Kant's views have come and gone and loyalty to his positions has waxed and waned, but his importance has not diminished. Generations of scholars have devoted their efforts to producing reliable translations of Kant into English as well as into other languages.

There are four main reasons for the present edition of Kant's writings:

1. *Completeness.* Although most of the works published in Kant's lifetime have been translated before, the most important ones more than once, only fragments of Kant's many important unpublished works have ever been translated. These include the *Opus postumum*, Kant's unfinished *magnum opus* on the transition from philosophy to physics; transcriptions of his classroom lectures; his correspondence; and his marginalia and other notes. One aim of this edition is to make a comprehensive sampling of these materials available in English for the first time.

2. *Availability.* Many English translations of Kant's works, especially those that have not individually played a large role in the subsequent development of philosophy, have long been inaccessible or out of print. Many of them, however, are crucial for the understanding of Kant's philosophical development, and the absence of some from English-language bibliographies may be responsible for erroneous or blinkered traditional interpretations of his doctrines by English-speaking philosophers.

3. *Organization.* Another aim of the present edition is to make all Kant's published work, both major and minor, available in comprehensive volumes organized both chronologically and topically, so as to facilitate the serious study of his philosophy by English-speaking readers.

4. *Consistency of translation.* Although many of Kant's major works have been translated by the most distinguished scholars of their day, some of these translations are now dated, and there is considerable terminological disparity among them. Our aim has been to enlist some of the most accomplished Kant scholars and translators to produce new translations,

freeing readers from both the philosophical and literary preconceptions of previous generations and allowing them to approach texts, as far as possible, with the same directness as present-day readers of the German or Latin originals.

In pursuit of these goals, our editors and translators attempt to follow several fundamental principles:

1. As far as seems advisable, the edition employs a single general glossary, especially for Kant's technical terms. Although we have not attempted to restrict the prerogative of editors and translators in choice of terminology, we have maximized consistency by putting a single editor or editorial team in charge of each of the main groupings of Kant's writings, such as his work in practical philosophy, philosophy of religion, or natural science, so that there will be a high degree of terminological consistency, at least in dealing with the same subject matter.

2. Our translators try to avoid sacrificing literalness to readability. We hope to produce translations that approximate the originals in the sense that they leave as much of the interpretive work as possible to the reader.

3. The paragraph, and even more the sentence, is often Kant's unit of argument, and one can easily transform what Kant intends as a continuous argument into a mere series of assertions by breaking up a sentence so as to make it more readable. Therefore, we try to preserve Kant's own divisions of sentences and paragraphs wherever possible.

4. Earlier editions often attempted to improve Kant's texts on the basis of controversial conceptions about their proper interpretation. In our translations, emendation or improvement of the original edition is kept to the minimum necessary to correct obvious typographical errors.

5. Our editors and translators try to minimize interpretation in other ways as well, for example, by rigorously segregating Kant's own footnotes, the editors' purely linguistic notes, and their more explanatory or informational notes; notes in this last category are treated as endnotes rather than footnotes.

We have not attempted to standardize completely the format of individual volumes. Each, however, includes information about the context in which Kant wrote the translated works, a German–English glossary, an English–German glossary, an index, and other aids to comprehension. The general introduction to each volume includes an explanation of specific principles of translation and, where necessary, principles of selection of works included in that volume. The pagination of the standard German edition of Kant's works, *Kant's Gesammelte Schriften*, edited by the Royal Prussian (later German) Academy of Sciences (Berlin: Georg Reimer, later Walter de Gruyter & Co., 1900–), is indicated throughout by means of marginal numbers.

Our aim is to produce a comprehensive edition of Kant's writings, embodying and displaying the high standards attained by Kant scholarship in the English-speaking world during the second half of the twentieth century, and serving as both an instrument and a stimulus for the further development of Kant studies by English-speaking readers in the century to come. Because of our emphasis on literalness of translation and on information rather than interpretation in editorial practices, we hope our edition will continue to be usable despite the inevitable evolution and occasional revolutions in Kant scholarship.

PAUL GUYER
ALLEN W. WOOD

General introduction

This volume, which is devoted to Kant's theoretical writings after 1781 (the time of the publication of the first edition of the *Critique of Pure Reason*), contains the following works: *Prolegomena to Any Future Metaphysics* (1783) [to be referred to as *Prolegomena*]; *Metaphysical Foundations of Natural Science* (1786) [to be referred to as *Metaphysical Foundations*]; *On a Discovery whereby Any New Critique of Pure Reason Is to Be Made Superfluous by an Older One* (1790) [to be referred to as *On a Discovery*]; *What Real Progress Has Metaphysics Made in Germany since the Time of Leibniz and Wolff?* (written during 1793–4, but only published after Kant's death in 1804) [to be referred to as *Progress*]; and the companion pieces: "On a Recently Prominent Tone of Superiority in Philosophy" and "Proclamation of the Imminent Conclusion of a Treaty of Perpetual Peace in Philosophy" (1796) [to be referred to as *Tone* and *Proclamation*, respectively].

Together these writings constitute only a small portion of Kant's total output after 1781, which includes the *Groundwork to the Metaphysics of Morals* (1785), the *Critique of Practical Reason* (1788), the *Critique of Judgment* (1790), *Religion within the Boundaries of Mere Reason* (1793), *Perpetual Peace* (1795), and the *Metaphysics of Morals* (1797), as well as many other writings (both substantive and occasional) dealing with religious, historical, political, and scientific issues. Nevertheless, at least the first four of the works translated in this volume constitute an important segment of Kant's overall production during this period, since they are the texts in which we find him both developing and refining points initially made in the *Critique of Pure Reason* and defending his views against attacks from a number of directions. Clearly, the second edition of the *Critique of Pure Reason* (1787) belongs to this category as well; but since it is contained in the volume devoted to the *Critique* itself, it will not be discussed here in any detail.[1]

If one is to understand Kant's philosophical writings that fall between the two editions of the *Critique*, however, it is necessary to see them against the backdrop of the first edition and his initial view of the scope and function of that work, particularly with respect to metaphysics. Accordingly, the first portion of this General Introduction, which is divided into three parts, is concerned with some of the central themes of that work, insofar as they bear on later developments in Kant's thought. The second part discusses the two works that are more or less the immediate offshoots of the first edition of the *Critique* and its initial reception, namely the *Prolegomena* and the *Metaphysical Foundations*. The third and final part deals with the four texts from the 1790s, all of which are essentially polemical in nature. After a brief consideration of the relevance of the second and third *Critiques* to the understanding of Kant's philosophical views after 1790, it discusses each of them in turn. As we shall see, these four texts fall into two groups: the first pair, *On a Discovery* and *Progress*, represent Kant's response to the Wolffian challenge that reached its pinnacle in the late 1780s; while the second, *Tone* and *Proclamation*, contain his reply to a rather inept attack on reason (and the critique thereof) in the name of feeling and intuition. Although the latter two brief essays cannot be said to contribute significantly to our understanding of the major tenets of Kant's thought, they provide graphic illustrations of the persistence of his polemical abilities at an advanced age and the enduring nature of his defense of reason, even while limiting its theoretical pretensions. For further information regarding the composition, content, and context of these works, the reader is referred to the introductions preceding each of them.

I

The fundamental question underlying the *Critique of Pure Reason* is the possibility of metaphysics, understood as philosophical (as distinct from mathematical) knowledge that transcends the bounds of experience. And, as the title suggests, the means for answering this question once and for all was to be a "critique of pure reason," by which Kant understood a critical examination of the faculty of reason itself and of its capacity to acquire knowledge independently of experience or *a priori*. But already in the Preface to the first edition of the *Critique*, Kant distinguishes sharply between such a critique, whose task is to determine the possibility and limits of metaphysics, and a "system of pure (speculative) reason," which he states that he hopes to deliver subsequently under the title "*Metaphysics of Nature*" (A xxi). Thus, the *Critique* is initially presented as distinct from, and as a propaedeutic to, metaphysics, which remains the ultimate goal of philosophical enquiry, and which is itself defined as "nothing but the *inventory* of all we possess through *pure reason*, ordered systematically" (A xx). In a frequently cited passage from a letter to Marcus Herz, which traditionally has been dated on or about May 11, 1781, Kant makes the point regarding the propaedeutic function of the *Critique* by remarking that it includes "the *metaphysics of metaphysics*."[2]

The basic outlines of the relationship between the *Critique of Pure Reason* and the metaphysics to which it is intended as propaedeutic or "metaphysics" are further articulated near the very end of the *Critique* in the third chapter of the Transcendental Doctrine of Method: "The

Architectonic of Pure Reason." In essential agreement with the scheme set forth in the Preface, Kant divides what he terms the "philosophy of pure reason" into two parts. One is the propaedeutic, which "investigates the faculty of reason in regard to all pure *a priori* cognition, and is called **critique**." The other is the "system of pure reason (science)," which is identified with **metaphysics** (A 841/B 869). Thus, critique is again distinguished from metaphysics and presented as its necessary preparation. This time, however, Kant offers a more expanded definition of metaphysics, according to which it encompasses all "pure philosophy," including the critique (which presumably explains his comment in the previously cited letter to Herz). Metaphysics in this expanded sense is contrasted with empirical and mathematical knowledge. It is distinguished from the former by being *a priori*, and from the latter by being based on concepts rather than on the construction of concepts. As Kant puts it in the beginning of the Transcendental Doctrine of Method, "**Philosophical** cognition [i.e., metaphysics in this expanded sense] is rational **cognition** from **concepts**, mathematical cognition that from the **construction** of concepts" (A 713/B 741). Ever since his 1764 essay, *Inquiry concerning the Distinctness of the Principles of Natural Theology and Morals*, Kant had emphasized this distinction between mathematical and philosophical cognition and used it to attack the forms of rationalism that assumed a common ground between them. We shall see that he returns to this theme in his later polemical writings; but for the present the main point to note is that Kant held that the fact that mathematics can demonstrate its propositions by constructing its objects in pure intuition protects it from the doubts that naturally arise regarding metaphysical claims, which have no such possibility of construction. Consequently, with respect to the first edition of the *Critique* at least, it is primarily metaphysics that stands in need of an account of its possibility and therefore a critique.

It is also important for understanding the future development of Kant's thought to note that metaphysics (in the first of the above-mentioned senses) is now divided into a metaphysics of the **speculative** and of the **practical** use of pure reason. The former is a **metaphysics of nature** and contains all *a priori* theoretical cognition of things outside of mathematics. The latter is a **metaphysics of morals** and contains "pure morality," that is, the basic principles of morality that are independent of anthropology or, more generally, of any empirical conditions (A 841–2/B 869–70). Although Kant notes that his immediate concern is with the former, it should be kept in mind that he initially envisaged the *Critique* as providing the sufficient foundation for both branches of metaphysics. Thus, with the *Critique* in place, the plan was to produce both a metaphysics of nature and a metaphysics of morals, the original ideas for both of which long antedated the *Critique*.[3]

As was to happen frequently during the decade following the initial publication of the *Critique*, which was easily the most fruitful period of his philosophical career, Kant's plans and even his conception of his critical philosophy underwent profound changes. In the realm of moral theory, which lies beyond the scope of this volume, this involved the abandonment of the original scheme of proceeding directly to the composition of a metaphysics of morals based on the foundations laid in the first *Critique*. Presumably recognizing that the latter did not provide a sufficient foundation for a moral theory grounded in the principle of the autonomy of the will, Kant published in 1785 the *Groundwork to the Metaphysics of Morals*, a brief but highly influential work whose task is to search for and establish the supreme principle of morality (Ak 4:392), which is there located in the autonomy of the will. Even this did not prove sufficient, however, since Kant's next major contribution to moral theory was the *Critique of Practical Reason*; and he waited another nine years before finally delivering the long-promised *Metaphysics of Morals*.[4]

There is a roughly parallel story regarding the theoretical side of Kant's thought, and this story is our main concern. According to the original plan sketched in the *Critique*, the metaphysics of nature encompasses all *a priori* theoretical cognition outside of mathematics. This, in turn, is divided into transcendental philosophy or ontology (traditionally called *metaphysica generalis*) and what Kant terms the "physiology of pure reason." The former considers only principles of understanding and reason that relate to "objects in general," without assuming that they are in any way given to us. The latter considers the sum-total of given objects, which is identified with nature, but without considering whether they are given to the senses or perhaps to another kind of intuition (A 845/ B 873).[5] The latter is further divided into an immanent and a transcendent physiology of pure reason, depending on the use of reason involved. Since the transcendent use of reason, that is, its use beyond the bounds of possible experience, was shown to be illegitimate in the Transcendental Dialectic, this leaves us with an immanent physiology of pure reason (its use within possible experience) as the appropriate sphere for the metaphysics of nature built on the foundations provided by the *Critique*.

In spite of its connection with experience, "immanent physiology" still counts as part of metaphysics because its claims are *a priori*. Such an immanent metaphysics is possible, according to Kant, because the *Critique* had shown in the Transcendental Aesthetic and Transcendental Analytic that the objects of human cognition (phenomena) are cognized on the basis of certain *a priori* forms or conditions, viz., space and time as conditions of sensibility and the pure concepts of the understanding or categories as conditions of the thought of an object, which derive respectively from the nature of human sensibility and understanding. Consequently, according to the argument of the *Critique*, it follows that we can know *a priori* that every object of a possible human experience will conform to the above-mentioned conditions. What we cannot know on this account (but can merely think) is how objects may be independently of these conditions of our experience of them. Expressed in Kantian terms, we know things only as they appear to us (under these conditions), not as they may be in themselves (i.e., as thought by some "pure understanding").[6]

Moreover, since there are two forms of experience (outer and inner), there are likewise two sorts of objects encountered in experience: bodies, or objects of outer sense, and souls, or objects of inner sense. The former collectively constitute corporeal and the latter thinking nature. The science of the former is physics – and since the knowledge in question is *a priori*, "rational physics" – while that of the latter is "rational psychology" (A 846/B 874).

Given Kant's trenchant critique of the pretensions of rational psychology, understood as the attempt to derive substantive conclusions about the nature of the self by the mere analysis of the capacity to think, in the "Paralogism" chapter in the Transcendental Dialectic, it is certainly surprising to find him here including it, together with rational physics, within the immanent physiology of pure reason that supposedly contains legitimate metaphysical knowledge claims. It appears, however, that what Kant here has in mind is not equivalent to the illusory science criticized in the Dialectic. For as species of "immanent physiology," both rational physics and rational psychology have a necessary relation to experience.[7] What preserves their rational (i.e., *a priori*) character, Kant now suggests, is that "[w]e take from experience nothing more than is necessary to **give** ourselves an object, partly of outer and partly of inner sense." The former, he goes on to add, "is accomplished through the mere concept of matter (impenetrable lifeless extension), the latter through the concept of a thinking being (in the empirically inner representation 'I think')" (A 848/B 876). In other words, according to Kant's original plan sketched in the first *Critique*, the projected metaphysics of nature was to include both a rational physics and a rational psychology, each of which contain *a priori* conditions of our empirical knowledge: of bodies in the one case and of souls or minds in the other. Moreover, Kant makes it clear that this immanent rational psychology is also to be distinguished from empirical psychology (which is basically an account of thought and the emotions). The latter was assigned a separate chapter in the metaphysical systems of Wolff and Baumgarten, but Kant makes it clear that he includes it within metaphysics only because of this customary usage (A 848/B 876).

II

Kant first became sidetracked from the project of this metaphysics of nature by the decision to write the *Prolegomena*. Although details concerning the genesis of this work remain murky and controversial, the relevant points are noted by Gary Hatfield in the introduction to his translation. For our purposes, perhaps the most important point is that in the previously mentioned letter to Herz, that is, at the time of the initial publication of the *Critique*, Kant indicates that he was already planning to write a more popular work, which could make his novel results comprehensible to a wider audience (Ak 10:269). It is also clear from the same letter, however, that this projected popular work cannot be identified with the eventual *Prolegomena*, since Kant suggested that it would begin, unlike the latter, with a discussion of the antinomies (Ak 10:270).

What seems to have led Kant to modify his initial plan to produce a truly popular work and to write the *Prolegomena* instead – which, as he tells us in the Preface, was intended not for apprentices but for future teachers of philosophy (Ak 4:255), was his increasing disappointment with the early reception of the *Critique*. Already in the same letter to Herz, Kant had expressed his disappointment in the fact that Mendelssohn, who had been given an advance copy and was one of those on whose understanding he was counting, had "put the book aside" (Ak 10:270).[8] And this disappointment was no doubt increased by reports from his friends and correspondents that readers had found the work unintelligible as well as by the lack of any serious early reviews.[9]

Moreover, the situation was not improved by the first significant review, which appeared on January 19, 1782, in the *Göttingische Gelehrte Anzeigen*, by which time Kant was already working on the *Prolegomena*. Although published anonymously, it was known to have been written by Christian Garve, albeit with some heavy-handed contributions by the editor, J. G. H. Feder (hence the notorious "Garve–Feder review").[10] In addition to the fact that it completely ignored the whole problematic of the synthetic *a priori* and of the Transcendental Deduction, what seems to have particularly irked Kant about the review was the gross misunderstanding of his central term 'transcendental' and the accusation that he presented an essentially Berkeleyan form of subjective idealism, which, as such, provides no criteria for distinguishing truth from illusion Thus, Kant explicitly addresses these issues in the Appendix to the *Prolegomena*, where, in order to avoid future misunderstanding, he retracts the label 'transcendental' and declares that he wishes his brand of idealism to be characterized as 'formal', or better 'critical', so as to distinguish it from both the dogmatic idealism of Berkeley and the skeptical idealism of Descartes (Ak 4:375).

Not content to limit his discussion of the question of idealism to the Appendix, he also takes it up in the main body of the work in two lengthy notes added to Part One, where he deals with the nature of space and time (Ak 4:288–94). In both the Appendix and the notes, the main point is that the idealism of the *Critique*, whether it be called "transcendental," "formal," or "critical," is concerned with the *a priori* conditions of our cognition of things (particularly the sensory conditions) rather than with the existence of the things known; and in this respect it differs decisively from the subjective idealism of Berkeley. Accordingly, it seems reasonable to suggest that one of the major contributions of the *Prolegomena* is a clarification of the nature of Kant's idealism.[11]

Perhaps the most distinctive features of the *Prolegomena* vis-à-vis the *Critique*, however, are its use (at least in the first three parts) of the analytic rather than the synthetic method and its sharp focus on what is termed "Hume's problem" concerning causality as the key to the possibility of metaphysics. But since both of these topics are skillfully treated by Hatfield in his introduction, I shall again be quite brief.

In essence, by the analytic method Kant understood a regressive procedure that moves from some given fact or datum (the conditioned) to its conditions. This is contrasted with the synthetic or progressive procedure of the *Critique*, which moves from the elements of human cognition (sensibility and understanding), understood as the conditions, to the basic normative principles or laws governing such cognition and the determination of their domain as that of possible experience, which is the conditioned. The very idea of a critique of pure reason entails the synthetic method, since it consists in a self-examination of reason, particularly with respect to its pretensions to synthetic *a priori* knowledge. Consequently, such a critique cannot, without begging the essential question, assume any species of such knowledge to be given as a "fact." But once this critique is completed, its results can be presented in an analytic form by showing that the possibility of certain generally accepted bodies of *a priori* knowledge can be accounted for only on the basis of principles laid down in the critique. And while such an analytical procedure cannot of itself establish the conclusions of the critique, Kant thought that it is nonetheless extremely useful in making these conclusions comprehensible, particularly since it puts the reader "in the position to survey the whole" (Ak 4:263).

This, then, is the task of the *Prolegomena*, which Kant also characterized as "preparatory exercises" and which he hoped would lead to a better understanding of the teachings of the *Critique* itself (Ak 4:261). But Kant's awareness of the gulf between the *Prolegomena* and a genuinely popular work, such as he had envisaged in the letter to Herz, is reflected in his remark at the end of the Preface that those who find this work still obscure "may consider that it is simply not necessary for everyone to study metaphysics, that there are some talents that proceed perfectly well in fundamental and even deep sciences that are closer to intuition, but will not succeed in the investigation of purely abstract concepts . . ." (Ak 4:263–4).

As part of his effort to put those who do study metaphysics in "the position to survey the whole," Kant famously organizes his Preface around Hume's skeptical analysis of causality. And perhaps more than anything else, this has led to the interpretation of Kant's theoretical philosophy, at least in the English-speaking philosophical world, as at bottom a response to Humean skepticism. Not only does Kant "freely admit that the remembrance of David Hume was the very thing that . . . first interrupted my dogmatic slumber" (Ak 4:260); he also describes the *Critique of Pure Reason* as "the elaboration of the Humean problem in its greatest possible amplification" (Ak 4:261). The latter is because, when so amplified or generalized, Hume's worry about the grounds for the belief in a necessary connection between cause and effect becomes the general problem of the synthetic *a priori*. Thus, the "answer to Hume" becomes, in effect, the main task of transcendental philosophy, since such an answer is tantamount to the vindication of the synthetic *a priori*. Moreover, this conception of the task is evident from Kant's division of "the main transcendental question," which serves as the organizing principle of the *Prolegomena*, into the four subquestions: (1) How is pure mathematics possible? (2) How is pure natural science possible? (3) How is metaphysics in general possible? (4) How is metaphysics as science possible? (Ak 4:280)

To a reader of the first edition of the *Critique*, it is probably the first of these questions that would have seemed most puzzling. It is not that Kant did not affirm the synthetic *a priori* nature of pure mathematics in the first edition. Indeed, he did, and he also attempted to account for its possibility in the Transcendental Doctrine of Method by showing that it relies on construction in pure intuition (A 713/B 741–A 719/B 747).[12] But rather than constituting part of the transcendental problem as Kant then conceived it, the example of mathematics was used mainly to underscore what he took to be the true problem, namely that "transcendental propositions," that is, those that are the concern of metaphysics, "can never be given through construction of concepts, but only in accordance with *a priori* concepts" (A 720/B 749). In other words, the problem concerns precisely the *nonmathematical* synthetic *a priori*, since no appeal to construction in intuition is there available.

All this changes in the *Prolegomena*, however, and the change may be seen as a direct consequence of the presentation of the main transcendental question as the generalization of Hume's problem.[13] For now mathematics itself becomes problematic and stands in need of a transcendental critique precisely because of its synthetic *a priori* nature. Indeed,

Kant even suggests that if Hume had been aware of the true nature of mathematics, instead of mistakenly regarding its claims as analytic, he would have rethought his wholesale rejection of metaphysics and have been led to a line of thought similar to that of the critical philosophy (Ak 4:272–3).[14] Thus, whereas in the first edition the emphasis was on the distinction between mathematical and metaphysical claims (the fact that the former but not the latter can verify its propositions through construction in pure intuition), the emphasis is now placed on their commonality as synthetic *a priori*. To be sure, their difference is not denied; but it is now used as the occasion for a reflection on the possibility of the pure intuition on which mathematical construction supposedly rests. Moreover, rather than limiting this analysis to the *Prolegomena*, with its essentially analytic procedure, Kant incorporated this whole line of thought into the second edition of the *Critique*, particularly in the Introduction and the Transcendental Aesthetic, thereby not only blurring the sharp distinction between the analytic and synthetic procedures drawn in the *Prolegomena*, but giving a significant new turn to the critical philosophy as well.[15]

A final noteworthy feature of the *Prolegomena* is its treatment of the Transcendental Deduction, which Kant acknowledges in the A Preface to be the investigation that cost him the most effort (A xvii). Instead of this deduction, with its appeal to the unity of apperception, the threefold synthesis, and all of the apparatus of what Strawson has disparagingly termed "the imaginary subject of transcendental psychology,"[16] Kant introduces in the second part of this work, which is concerned with questions of the conditions of the possibility of a "pure natural science," the distinction between judgments of experience and judgments of perception. These are presented as two species of empirical judgment, only the first of which supposedly involves the categories. And parallel to this distinction between the two types of judgment, Kant also distinguishes between two forms of consciousness: "consciousness in general" and the consciousness of one's particular mental state (Ak 4:297–305). Whereas the former is a normative conception, which goes together with judgments of experience and presumably plays the role assigned to transcendental apperception in the *Critique*, the latter is a merely de facto consciousness, which goes together with judgments of perception and seems to be intended as the analogue of the non-normative empirical apperception of the *Critique*.

Reduced to its simplest terms, the problem that Kant poses in this portion of the *Prolegomena* is how experience (understood as objectively valid empirical knowledge consisting of judgments of experience) can arise from mere perception, which, as such, has only subjective validity. And the answer given is that this is possible only by means of the subsumption of the intuitively given content of perception under the categories, which is also described as its connection in the normative "consciousness in general," as contrasted with the connection of the same content in the merely de facto consciousness of one's particular mental state. The former mode of connection takes place through categoreally determined judgments of experience and the latter through judgments of perception, which supposedly do not involve any use of the categories. Roughly, one might think of the contrast as between claims about how things "really are" (in the realm of phenomena) or, equivalently, how they are judged to be according to the norms of an objectively valid empirical science, and how they appear to a particular observer under contingent perceptual conditions. Since experience is defined in terms of the former kind of judgment, and since that is claimed to require the categories, it supposedly follows that the categories are necessary conditions of the possibility of experience.

This distinction between the two kinds of empirical judgment, which is not found in either edition of the *Critique* (though it is contained in the lectures on logic),[17] has been the topic of considerable discussion in the literature and remains highly controversial. Particularly problematic in this regard is the compatibility of the conception of a judgment of perception with the text of the B Deduction, where Kant appears to argue (in contrast to the *Prolegomena*) that judgment as such has objective validity and is therefore subject to the categories.[18] Setting that whole issue aside, however, what is most striking about Kant's treatment of the Transcendental Deduction in the *Prolegomena* is his virtual repudiation of the original argument of the *Critique*. This is to be found near the end of the Appendix, where Kant expresses dissatisfaction with the presentation of his views (though not with the views themselves) because of its excessive prolixity in both the Transcendental Deduction and the Paralogisms. And, more importantly, he suggests that these discussions can be replaced by the *Prolegomena*'s accounts of the topics with which they deal (Ak 4:381). Thus, while he does not actually recant his argument in either of these chapters of the *Critique*, he does clearly state that the accounts in the *Prolegomena* are to be viewed as authoritative.

This view of the Paralogism chapter is hardly surprising, since the first edition discussion is extremely prolix, and both the succinct account in the *Prolegomena* (Ak 4:333–7) and the later version in the second edition of the *Critique* are distinct improvements in this regard. Nevertheless, given the systematic importance attributed to it, this is certainly a remarkable claim for Kant to make about the Transcendental Deduction. Indeed, it calls to mind Hume's notorious disowning of the *Treatise* in favor of the *Enquiries*, which was similarly based on a frustration over being generally misunderstood.[19] In Kant's case, however, it poses a significant problem, since it is, to say the least, difficult to reconcile with the claim that the *Prolegomena* contains merely "preparatory exercises."

How, one might ask, can such an "exercise," conducted in the analytic manner, be substituted for the synthetic procedure of the *Critique* at its most important point? Kant never addresses this question; but his willingness to substitute the *Prolegomena's* counterpart to the Transcendental Deduction for that of the *Critique* can be understood only as the reflection of a deep ambivalence on his part regarding what was supposedly the very heart of his transcendental project. Moreover, we shall see that evidence of this ambivalence is still to be found in his next work.

That work is the *Metaphysical Foundations* (1786), and it marks a return to the original project of a metaphysics of nature. At the same time, however, this return involved a considerable modification of the initial plan of the *Critique*. Moreover, this modification can be understood only in light of the transformations in the organization, formulation, and emphases of Kant's critical theory that were already present in the *Prolegomena* and that were, at least in part, brought about by his attempt to respond to the objections posed in the Garve–Feder review and the misunderstandings of his views that underlay them.

The most fundamental of these changes is already indicated in the title of the work. Although he had not abandoned the goal of eventually providing a full-fledged metaphysics of nature, Kant now offers instead a metaphysical foundations of *natural science*, which was to serve as a preparation for the former.[20] Nevertheless, as Michael Friedman points out in his introduction to his translation, these metaphysical foundations constitute Kant's most explicit answer to the question of the possibility of a pure natural science that was first posed in the second part of the *Prolegomena*.

By "pure natural science" Kant understood the *a priori* component of natural science, which he now claims to pertain only to physics or the doctrine of body. Thus, both the "immanent" version of a rational psychology, which he seemed to entertain as a possibility in the Architectonic chapter of the *Critique*, and the strictly universal pure natural science (one pertaining to nature in general) whose actuality he affirms in the *Prolegomena*, are summarily dropped from the metaphysical program.[21] In fact, Kant not only rejects the possibility of anything like a rational (i.e., *a priori*) doctrine of the mind corresponding to the "pure" part of the doctrine of body; he also denies the possibility of an empirical science of the mind or, as he terms it, "doctrine of the soul." This denial is based on two grounds. The first is the general principle that science in the "proper" sense requires *a priori* certainty, that is to say, a "pure part" (Ak 4:469), which is itself linked to the possibility of a mathematical treatment (Ak 4:470). Since there is no such knowledge concerning the mind, it follows that empirical claims about it lack genuine scientific status. This principle applies, however, not only to psychology, but also to other putatively empirical sciences such as chemistry. Accordingly, Kant adds a second reason that applies uniquely to the former, namely that it does not allow for the possibility of the kind of observation available in chemistry and other empirical disciplines. And because of this second defect, Kant insists that, unlike them, psychology cannot even become an experimental doctrine, but must remain merely an "historical doctrine of nature" (of inner sense) or a "natural description of the soul" (Ak 4:471).[22]

Kant's concern in the *Metaphysical Foundations* is, therefore, exclusively with the *a priori* component of the doctrine of body, which consists of two parts: one is mathematical and involves the application of mathematics to appearances; and the other, which is concerned with the conditions underlying the possibility of such an application, is discursive or conceptual, that is to say, metaphysical. This division reflects Kant's adherence to the view that, on the one hand, with regard to a "special doctrine of nature [of which the doctrine of body is the only available specimen] there can be only as much *proper* science as there is mathematics therein" (Ak 4:470), while, on the other hand, the applicability of mathematics to appearances, which is simply taken for granted by the practicing scientist, itself requires a philosophical grounding. Both of these points are emphasized in the Preface to the *Metaphysical Foundations*. Indeed, although much of its early portion focuses on the importance of mathematics, Kant ends by remarking in connection with Newton's *Mathematical First Principles of Natural Science* that "[s]ince mathematics must here necessarily borrow from metaphysics, it must also not be ashamed to let itself be seen in community with the latter" (Ak 4:479).

Not surprisingly, Kant maintains that the foundation of the metaphysics from which mathematics must "borrow" is laid in the Analytic of Principles of the *Critique*. Of themselves, however, the Transcendental Principles of the Analytic are too general to be immediately useful for the task in hand. This is because, as the Architectonic indicates, they belong to general metaphysics or ontology insofar as they are concerned with objects in general or, in the critical version, objects of possible experience in general (both inner and outer). Thus, the *Metaphysical Foundations* proceeds by way of a specification of these perfectly general transcendental principles by relating them to a subset of the objects of possible experience, namely those of outer sense or bodies. In terms of the traditional distinctions to which Kant appeals, this means that these "foundations" pertain to the "special metaphysics" of corporeal nature.

For Kant, such a metaphysics proceeds by introducing the supposedly "intrinsically empirical" concept of matter into what had been a purely transcendental story. Although the introduction of an empirical component certainly compromises the "purity" of the resulting metaphysics, Kant insists that it does not undermine its apriority and therefore genuinely metaphysical status. This is justified on the basis of the perfect generality of the concept. Rather than any particular kind of matter – and without appealing to any particular experiences – the *Metaphysical Foundations* is concerned merely with "matter in general," that is, with what is necessarily involved in being an object of outer sense, assuming only the spatiotemporal form of human experience and the transcendental laws regarding nature in general established in the first *Critique* (Ak 4:472).

With its appeal to a generic concept of matter, Kant's procedure here accords with the one sketched in the Architectonic, wherein rational physics "borrowed" from experience only enough to give itself an object of outer sense. There is, however, a significant difference in the way in which this concept of matter is characterized in the two texts. In the *Critique*, as we have already seen, it is understood to involve simply "impenetrable, lifeless extension," whereas in the *Metaphysical Foundations* its most fundamental designation is as the "movable in space" (Ak 4:480). Thus, even though impenetrability and inertia (or "lifeless extension") turn out to be essential features of the concept of matter that is eventually "constructed," movability proves to be basic and the key to developing a metaphysics of body or corporeal nature.

Kant's explicit justification for privileging the concept of motion is that it is the means whereby the senses are affected by material objects, thereby providing the data for outer experience. As he puts it, "The basic determination of something that is to be an object of the outer senses had to be motion, because only thereby can these senses be affected" (Ak 4:476). It seems clear, however, that Kant's deeper reason lies in the connection between motion and mathematizability. Since motion can be analyzed in terms of spatiotemporal coordinates, it is itself directly mathematizable and provides the basis for a mathematical treatment of all the other general properties or predicates of matter (e.g., forces), all of which are themselves traceable back to motion. And given Kant's views about the connection between "science proper" and mathematization, it follows that "natural science is either a pure or applied *doctrine of motion* throughout" (Ak 4:476).

But if it is the motion of matter in general that provides the content or subject matter of a pure science of nature, it is the categories that provide the form. Moreover, this form turns out to be crucial for Kant, who holds that "all true metaphysics is drawn from the essence of the faculty of thinking itself" (Ak 4:472). Thus, the method Kant adopts in the *Metaphysical Foundations* is to bring the concept of matter successively under each of the four headings of the table of categories: quantity, quality, relation, and modality, thereby producing a set of increasingly rich determinations of the motion that necessarily pertains to matter as such.

The first, **phoronomy**, considers motion as a pure quantum, without any consideration of the quality of what is movable. Thus, it is here that matter is defined simply as the "movable in space" (Ak 4:480). The second, **dynamics**, introduces the qualitative feature pertaining to matter as such, namely the filling of space, and analyzes the motion of matter, so conceived, under the name of an original moving force. The basic claim is that matter fills space by virtue of its inherent attractive and repulsive forces, which provides the basis for Kant's so-called "dynamic theory of matter."[23] The third, **mechanics**, investigates the motion of matter, so conceived, in relation to other portions of movable matter. It is here that Kant presents his three "laws of mechanics": (1) the principle of the conservation of mass or quantity of matter; (2) the law of inertia; and (3) the principle of the equality of action and reaction. These are of particular interest to students of Kant because they closely correspond to the three Analogies of Experience in the *Critique of Pure Reason*. Finally, **phenomenology** is concerned with the modality of claims about motion; but its specific aim is to ground the distinction between real and apparent motion, which is itself a specification of the fundamental critical distinction between mere appearance and experience.[24]

Since this supposedly exhausts what can be claimed about matter *a priori*, independently of an appeal to either experience or explicitly mathematical principles (the second part of pure natural science), Kant thinks that the resulting doctrine constitutes a self-contained whole that can be articulated separately from the remainder of physics. And, of equal importance for an understanding of the development of Kant's views on metaphysics, he also insists that these *Metaphysical Foundations* can be separated from the remainder of metaphysics. As he puts it:

[M]etaphysics has busied so many heads until now (and will continue to busy so many), not in order thereby to extend natural knowledge ... but rather so as to attain cognition of that which lies wholly beyond all boundaries of experience: God, freedom, and immortality. Then one gains in the advancement of this goal if one frees this science [general metaphysics] from an offshoot that certainly springs from its root but nonetheless only hinders its regular growth, and one plants this offshoot specially ... without, however, failing to appreciate the origin of this offshoot from the science [general metaphysics] and without omitting the mature plant from the system of general metaphysics. (Ak 4:477)

Although Kant here retains the doctrine of the *Critique* that the *a priori* principles in question have their roots in general metaphysics or transcendental philosophy, he here breaks with the original plan according to which this system of special metaphysics was to be presented in terms of its organic connection with general metaphysics. Moreover, this separation of the offshoot from its natural root is presented as benefitting not only physics, but general metaphysics as well; indeed, it is the benefit to the latter that is emphasized. As Kant makes clear, this is because the true concern of the latter is not with the foundations of physics, but with God, freedom, and immortality, that is, with the super-sensible. Presumably, this reflects Kant's increasing emphasis on what is termed in the *Critique of Practical Reason* the "primacy of practical reason," or, more generally, on the exclusively moral foundations of any metaphysical claims regarding these three super-sensible objects of pure reason. The basic idea, which Kant will develop further in his later writings, is that segregating these conceptions from any connection with theoretical or "speculative" claims is essential to their preservation and defense. In the Preface to the second edition of the *Critique of Pure Reason* Kant makes this point by means of his famous pronouncement that he "had to deny **knowledge** in order to make room for **faith**" (B xxx).

This is not, however, the only service that a separate *Metaphysical Foundations* performs for metaphysics in general. For the latter, as Kant conceives it, is itself divided into two parts: one, as noted above, is concerned with the super-sensible and the traditional metaphysical questions regarding God, freedom, and immortality; the other is concerned with *a priori* concepts to which corresponding objects can be given in experience. In the Preface to the second edition of the *Critique*, Kant referred to the latter as the first part of metaphysics and the former as the second part (B xviii–xix).[25] Usually they are referred to as transcendent and immanent metaphysics, respectively. And while the separation of the offshoot of the *Metaphysical Foundations* serves the transcendent part of metaphysics (which remains the part of main interest) indirectly by making apparent its true home in practical reason, it serves the immanent part more directly by providing the sensible intuitions necessary for the realization of its claims. For, as Kant remarks in a continuation of the passage cited above:

It is also indeed very remarkable... that general metaphysics, in all instances where it requires examples (intuitions) in order to provide meaning for its pure concepts of the understanding, must always take them from the general doctrine of body – and thus from the form and principles of outer intuition. And, if these are not exhibited completely, it gropes uncertainly and unsteadily among mere meaningless concepts. (Ak 4:478)

Here Kant is pointing ahead to some of the changes he will make in the second edition of the *Critique*, where he emphasizes the epistemic primacy of outer experience. As Michael Friedman points out in his introduction, this is signaled in the General Observation to the System of Principles (B 228–94), where Kant insists for the first time that the determination of the objective reality of the categories requires not merely sensory intuition, but specifically outer, that is, spatial intuition. Thus, only the intuition of something in space (matter) can provide the permanent that corresponds to the category of substance, and only motion as the alteration of something in space provides the alteration corresponding to the concept of causality (B 291). And this, of course, reinforces the rejection of both the immanent rational psychology of the Architectonic chapter of the *Critique* and the strictly universal pure science of nature of the *Prolegomena*, which, as we have seen, was already effectively accomplished in the *Metaphysical Foundations*. Kant's most important expression of this privileging of outer experience, however, is the new Refutation of Idealism (B 274–9). Appealing to the principle that only outer experience can provide the intuition of something permanent, Kant there argues against the "problematic idealism" of Descartes, for whom only the inner experience of the 'I' is indubitable, that the very self-consciousness that the Cartesian skeptic assumes presupposes the existence of objects in space external to the self.

Although it stands apart from the systematic concern of the work, the *Metaphysical Foundations* is also of considerable importance for understanding the development of Kant's views on the Transcendental Deduction. As we have seen, already in the *Prolegomena* Kant expressed dissatisfaction with his exposition of the argument of the Deduction in the first edition of the *Critique* (though not with its conclusions) and requested that the reader replace it with what he says there. He returns to this topic in a lengthy and important footnote in the Preface to the *Metaphysical Foundations*, which is devoted explicitly to a review of Johann August Heinrich Ulrich's *Institutiones Logicae et Metaphysicae*. A Wolffian philosopher and professor at Jena, Ulrich attempted in this work to reconcile the main positive results of the *Critique* (e.g., the ideality of space and time and the validity of the Principles) with a Leibnizian metaphysics by arguing that, given its own premises, the *Critique* should not limit knowledge to objects of possible experience.[26] Kant's concern in the note, however, is not so much with Ulrich's work itself as it is with the favorable review it received in the *Allgemeine Literaturzeitung*. Apparently, what particularly irked Kant about the review was that, despite its anonymity, he knew that it had been written by his close friend and disciple Johann Schultz, who was also the author of the first commentary on the *Critique*.[27] While expressing agreement with Ulrich on numerous points, Schultz criticizes him for neglecting the Transcendental Deduction, which, like a good Kantian, he takes to be the heart of the *Critique* and the place where Kant makes his case for the limitation of the categories to objects of possible experience. At the same time, however, Schultz excuses Ulrich's neglect of the Deduction on the familiar grounds of its obscurity. And this objection, coming from so close to home, was certainly not something that Kant could afford to ignore.

Kant's response in the note consists of two parts. The first amounts to an apparent minimization of the importance of the Transcendental Deduction to the overall critical project. In the spirit of the *Prolegomena*, but undoubtedly much to the surprise of Schultz (and, indeed, of any reader of the first edition of the *Critique*), Kant rejects the latter's claim that "*without an entirely clear and sufficient deduction of the categories* the system of the *Critique of Pure Reason* totters on its foundation." Instead, he insists that "the system of the *Critique* must carry apodeictic certainty for whoever subscribes ... to my propositions concerning the sensible character of all our intuition and the adequacy of the table of categories, as determinations of our consciousness derived from the logical functions of judgments in general" (Ak 4:474). In other words, Kant seems to be saying here that the truly essential parts of the *Critique* are the Transcendental Aesthetic and the Metaphysical Deduction. By contrast, the Transcendental Deduction, whose task is to show *how* the categories make experience possible, is said to be, "with respect to the principal end of the system" (here identified with the determination of the limits of pure reason) "in no way *compulsory* but merely *meritorious*" (Ak 4:470).

This appears to stand in direct contradiction with the *Critique*'s unequivocal insistence on the indispensability of a Deduction; and this fact was called to Kant's attention by Reinhold.[28] Kant's response is be found in a note appended to the end of *On the Use of Teleological Principles in Philosophy* (1788), where he remarks that his comment about the importance of the Transcendental Deduction concerned only its negative function of limiting knowledge and was not to be construed as minimizing its positive role in determining the validity of the categories with respect to objects of possible experience (Ak 8:184).

Although this distinction enables Kant to avoid the charge of self-contradiction and is certainly consistent with the contents of the note, his response is nevertheless problematic. For it suggests a continued commitment to the claim of the note that the "principal end of the system" (for which the Transcendental Deduction is not absolutely necessary) is to be understood in essentially negative terms as the limitation of knowledge to objects of possible experience. And while this may serve to define the issue between himself and Ulrich, it remains, to say the least, difficult to reconcile with Kant's avowed concern to "lay the foundations for a future metaphysics" or to provide a "metaphysics of metaphysics."

The second part of Kant's discussion in the note is of interest because of what it tells us about his views on the structure of the argument of the Transcendental Deduction, construed as the attempt to show how experience is possible only on the basis of the categories. In a much-cited passage, Kant states that, as he now understands this problem, "it can be solved with just as much ease [as the problem of the limitation of knowledge], since it can almost be accomplished through a single inference from the precisely determined definition of a *judgment* in general" (Ak 4:475). This anticipates the revision of the Deduction contained in the second edition, where the first part of a two-part proof focuses precisely on the connection between the categories and judgment. And, depending on how one understands the "almost," it might also be taken to anticipate the second part as well, where Kant goes beyond the connection between the categories and judgment and attempts to relate them to the objects of human intuition.[29]

Finally, although it is impossible to discuss the issue here in any detail, it should at least be noted that the importance of the *Metaphysical Foundations* stems not only from its relation to the doctrines of the *Critique*, but also from its close connection to the work known as the *Opus postumum*. The latter has come down to us as a fragmentary manuscript on which Kant was working during the last decade of his life, in which he sketches (though never completes) a fundamental reformulation of the critical philosophy. What is of particular interest to us here, however, is the fact that Kant initially entitled this projected work *Transition from the Metaphysical Foundations of Natural Science to Physics*. Thus, it turns out that some apparently narrow and technical concerns regarding the connection between the *Metaphysical Foundations* and the empirical science of physics led Kant at the very end of his career to a fundamental re-examination of his whole philosophical position.[30]

III

After the publication of the *Metaphysical Foundations* in 1786 and the second edition of the *Critique* one year later, the main focus of Kant's concern shifted from theoretical philosophy first back to practical philosophy (with the publication of the *Critique of Practical Reason* in 1788), and then to the so-called "critical synthesis" of the *Critique of Judgment* (1790), in which both aesthetic judgment and teleology are subjected to a critical examination. Since these writings, unlike the *Opus postumum*, are not directly concerned with theoretical philosophy, they fall outside of the scope of this volume and therefore cannot be considered here in any detail. But since it is impossible to understand the orientation and concerns of Kant's later writings in theoretical philosophy apart from them, it is necessary at least to note some of their main themes.

As far as the *Critique of Practical Reason* is concerned, two closely related points are of fundamental importance in this context. The first is the conception of the "fact of reason" and the understanding of the relationship between the moral law and freedom that it involves. In the first *Critique*, freedom, in the "strict" or transcendental sense that involves an independence from all natural causality, is treated essentially as a problematic idea, whose logical possibility is assured by the resolution of the Third Antinomy, but whose objective reality remains incapable of determination by theoretical reason. In the *Groundwork*, Kant assumes this result; but starting with the necessity of presupposing the *idea* of freedom insofar as one takes oneself to be a rational agent, he attempts to provide a "deduction" of the moral law as the supreme practical principle to which anyone taking himself to be free is subject. In the second *Critique*, however, Kant reverses the latter procedure, asserting that "the moral law is given, as an apodeictically certain fact as it were of pure reason of which we are *a priori* conscious" (Ak 5:42). And he also asserts that it is this law that alone assures us of the reality of freedom.[31] This not only establishes freedom (from a practical point of view) by grounding it directly in our consciousness of standing under the moral law; it also privileges freedom among the ideas of reason by virtue of its immediate connection with morality.

The second essential feature is the doctrine of the "primacy of practical reason," which is articulated in the second *Critique* in connection with the concept of the highest good (the union of virtue and happiness), and the closely associated postulates of practical reason. Although both the concept of the highest good, and the need to postulate God and immortality as conditions of its attainability, are found in the "Canon of Pure Reason" in the first *Critique*, they hardly figure prominently in the overall argument of the work. More importantly, these postulates are there only related tangentially to morality, since they are introduced in connection with the question **"What may I hope?"** (assuming that I act morally) rather than **"What should I do?"**[32] By contrast, in the second *Critique* these postulates are directly related to the latter question, since the realization (or at least promotion) of the highest good is itself commanded by the moral law. And this grounds the postulation of God, immortality, and freedom as necessary conditions of the possibility of fulfilling this duty (Ak 5:122–34).[33] This, in turn, enables Kant to claim that it is the connection with duty, and therefore with pure practical reason, that grounds the objective reality of these ideas, which themselves belong originally to speculative reason.[34] Kant also insists, however, that their reality is established only from a "practical point of view," that is, as necessary presuppositions of the possibility of an end (the highest good) that we are morally required to pursue. Nevertheless, speculative reason is itself constrained to accept these practical results, which address its own perennial concerns, but which are beyond its capacity to establish. And the latter is the basic meaning of the "primacy of practical reason."[35]

The significance of the *Critique of Judgment* for Kant's theoretical writings in the 1790s stems not so much from its accounts of taste and teleology as from its underlying conception of the purposiveness of nature as an *a priori* principle unique to judgment, and the closely related claim that judgment, on the basis of this principle, makes possible a transition from nature to freedom, or, as Kant henceforth tends to characterize these two "realms," from the sensible to the super-sensible. The initial question, posed in the Introduction to the work, is how judgment, which together with understanding and reason, constitute the three "higher cognitive faculties," could have its own *a priori* principle and therefore become subject to a critique. The problem is that this appears to be precluded by the results of the first two *Critiques*, which established *a priori* principles for understanding and reason (now identified with practical reason) respectively, with the former legislating to nature (the sensible) and the latter to freedom (the super-sensible). Since, as was already maintained in the *Critique of Pure Reason*, these constitute the only two "domains" of *a priori* legislation, this appears to leave judgment, which in its logical capacity mediates between understanding and reason, without any autonomous transcendental function of its own.[36] Kant's solution, which gave birth to the *Critique of Judgment*, turns on the introduction of a new (radically subjective) kind of *a priori* principle (the purposiveness of nature), which pertains to judgment in its reflective capacity, and through which it legislates neither to nature nor to freedom, but to itself.

To say that with the principle of the purposiveness of nature judgment legislates merely to itself is to say that it does not claim that nature *is* purposive (i.e., ordered by an intelligent, "more-than-human" mind), but rather that, given the discursive, finite nature of our intellects, we are rationally constrained to consider it *as if* it were. As Kant maintains in the Introduction to the third *Critique*, this necessity applies both to cognition (as a condition of the attainment of empirical knowledge) and to practice (as a condition of the pursuit of the ends dictated by the moral law). What is of primary importance for the understanding of Kant's later theoretical writings, however, is that this conception makes possible the required transition from the sensible to the super-sensible, since it provides rational credentials (not amounting to knowledge) for a way of thinking about the sensible (nature) that sees it as grounded in a super-sensible intelligence, without violating critical strictures on the limits of knowledge.

To varying degrees, these themes from the second and third *Critiques* underlie the four writings from the 1790s included in this volume. In particular, all are centrally concerned in one way or another with the relation between the sensible and the super-sensible. An equally prominent feature of these works, however, is an insistence on the absolute necessity of a critique of pure reason as a precondition of any ascent in thought from the sensible to the super-sensible. In fact, in each of them Kant responds to an attempt either to minimize the significance (or originality) of such a critique or to deny completely the need for one. Thus, each of them has an essentially polemical thrust.

The first of these writings, *On a Discovery*, was published simultaneously with the *Critique of Judgment* and contains an important allusion to it at the end. It is also Kant's most bitterly polemical work, composed in response to the critique of the influential Wolffian philosopher, Johann

August Eberhard. The latter, together with a small group of colleagues of a similar philosophical persuasion, founded in 1788 a journal called the *Philosophisches Magazin*, in which they attacked the Kantian philosophy from the standpoint of Leibniz and Wolff. Thus, whereas Kant's earlier opponents, as reflected in the Garve–Feder review, represented a broadly empiricistic, commonsensical standpoint, his new opponents stood at the opposite end of the philosophical spectrum and represented the rationalistic metaphysics, which Kant had supposedly discredited in the first *Critique* as ungrounded dogmatism. Nevertheless, Eberhard's attack was directed not so much at the idea of a critique of pure reason as against Kant's claim of originality on its behalf and the negative implications for speculative metaphysics that he derived from it. Appealing largely to Leibniz's epistemological reflections that were directed against Locke in his *New Essays Concerning Human Understanding* (which was first published in 1765), Eberhard in effect argues that these reflections amount to a critique of pure reason and, indeed, in contrast to the Kantian version, one that grounds the possibility of rational knowledge of a super-sensible reality. The essence of Eberhard's position is clearly expressed in this passage from the first issue of his journal:

The Leibnizian philosophy contains just as much of a critique of reason as the new philosophy, while at the same time it still introduces a dogmatism based on a precise analysis of the faculties of knowledge. It therefore contains all that is true in the new philosophy and, in addition, a well-grounded extension of the sphere of the understanding.[37]

As the full title of his response indicates, Kant was particularly irked by this claim, since it constitutes a direct challenge to both the originality and the validity of the central teachings of the *Critique of Pure Reason* regarding metaphysics and the limits of human knowledge. Accordingly, in his response Kant emphasizes both, while also accusing Eberhard not merely of faulty reasoning, but also of deliberate obfuscation and misrepresentation of the teachings of the *Critique*. And he ends the work with a rhetorical flourish, suggesting that it is not the writings of Eberhard and his colleagues, but rather the *Critique of Pure Reason* that constitutes the genuine apology for Leibniz (Ak 8:250).

The reader is referred to the introduction to this work for more information concerning its background and content. Here it must suffice to note that its entire first part is devoted to a detailed and devastating critique of Eberhard's attempt to demonstrate the possibility of ascending from the sensible world to its super-sensible grounds by means of an appeal to the Leibnizian principle of sufficient reason, and that its second part is concerned with a defense of the originality and importance of the distinction between analytic and synthetic judgments. In both parts Kant claims that Eberhard is a fundamentally dishonest thinker, who willfully misrepresents not only Kant's own position, but at crucial points Leibniz's as well. Although it does not go materially beyond the accounts given in the *Critique of Pure Reason* and the *Prolegomena*, Kant's discussion of the analytic–synthetic distinction is of particular interest because of the light it sheds on his understanding of the originality of this distinction and its relation to the distinction between sensibility and understanding.

Kant's next attempt to define his philosophy against the rationalism of Leibniz and Wolff remained unfinished and was published by his editor, Rink, only after his death in 1804. It consists of a projected reply to an essay contest announced by the Royal Academy in Berlin in 1790 on the topic: "What real progress has metaphysics made in Germany since the time of Leibniz and Wolff?" Kant correctly saw that this question was directed precisely at the issues raised by Eberhard, namely the significance of his critical philosophy and its role in the development of German thought. Accordingly, he planned a response, which, for reasons that remain obscure, was never completed and therefore was not submitted to the competition.

Once again, the reader is referred to the introduction to the translation of this work for details concerning its historical background, content, and structure. From the point of view of the overall development of Kant's theoretical philosophy after the initial publication of the *Critique*, however, the most noteworthy feature of this fragmentary work is its reconceptualization of metaphysics and reformulation of the relationship between it and the critical philosophy in light of the results of the second and third *Critiques*. It thus provides the reader with an illuminating retrospective of Kant's conception of his philosophy as a whole as it relates to the traditional concerns of metaphysics.

First, metaphysics is now viewed as composed of various stages. These are sometimes characterized in a putatively historical fashion as dogmatism, skepticism, and criticism, and sometimes more systematically as ontology, a "doctrine of doubt," which reflects the critique of traditional metaphysics contained in the Transcendental Dialectic of the first *Critique*, and a "doctrine of wisdom." But the essence and task of metaphysics is formulated in terms of the language of the third *Critique* as the transition from the sensible to the super-sensible. Accordingly, it is not surprising that Kant assigns an important role to the third *Critique*'s principle of purposiveness in effecting this transition.

Second, instead of locating his major accomplishment in providing a propaedeutic or prolegomenon to a "future metaphysics" that is to be completed by a metaphysics of nature and of freedom, Kant now suggests that the critical philosophy (understood as including the contents of all three *Critiques*) itself contains the completion of metaphysics. Moreover, this is not because of the results obtained in the *Metaphysical Foundations*, which is, after all, concerned merely with *a priori* conditions of the experience of matter in motion (and therefore the sensible). It is rather that it provides all that is required for a transition to the super-sensible, understood in terms of the ideas of God, freedom, and the soul, that is, for a "doctrine of wisdom." In line with the teachings of the second *Critique*, however, the grounding of these ideas that marks the completion of metaphysics is by way of practical rather than theoretical reason and is now described as "practico-dogmatic."

The last two essays in this volume, *Tone* and *Proclamation*, both of which were published in 1796, constitute a pair, since they are addressed primarily to the same opponent, namely one Johann Georg Schlosser, an amateur philosopher and translator of Plato's letters. Together with a small group of sympathizers, Schlosser advocated an esoteric form of Christianized Neo-Platonism, according to which feeling and intuition (rather than reason) are the proper means for apprehending ultimate reality. As before, the reader is referred to the translator's introduction for further historical and biographical information concerning the background of the controversy. Our concern here is with the central philosophical themes of these brief essays, insofar as they can be formulated in abstraction from the pervasive and occasionally heavy-handed irony to which Kant resorts in both texts.

As its title indicates, the first of these essays is above all an attack on philosophical esotericism, that is, any view which sees philosophy as containing secret doctrines expressed in a mysterious language that are accessible only to a few adepts by means of some special power of intuition. Not only is any such view, which is often connected with the Platonic epistles translated by Schlosser and his associates, completely antithetical to the very idea of a critique of pure reason, it is also anathema to Kant's political republicanism.[38] Accordingly, a good portion of the essay is devoted to a discussion of Plato, in which Kant contrasts favorably the exoteric Plato of the Academy, who emphasized the importance of geometry, where rigorous demonstration is required, and whose concern is ultimately with the moral (justice and the idea of the good), with the esoteric Plato of the epistles, whose teachings are favored by Schlosser and his associates.

This discussion reflects Kant's long-standing and deep-seated ambivalence toward Plato. On the one hand, there is the Plato to whom Kant pays homage in the first *Critique* as the first to recognize the true nature of ideas as archetypes and who emphasized their indispensability for morality (A 314/B 370/A 319/B 375). On the other hand, there is the mystical Plato, whom, also in the *Critique*, Kant accuses of having "abandoned the world of the senses because it posed so many hindrances for the understanding, and dared to go beyond it on the wings of the ideas, in the empty space of the pure understanding" (A 5/B 9). It is this latter Plato whose name is attached to the dogmatic intellectualism of the theses of the four antinomies, while that of Epicurus is connected to the equally dogmatic empiricism of the antitheses (A 471/B 500).[39]

In the present essay, as elsewhere, Kant tends to explain (and in part excuse) the excesses of the Platonic philosophy (its misguided appeal to an intellectual intuition of ideas as they exist in the divine understanding) as the result of a failure to recognize that mathematics achieves its rigorous demonstrations and extension of knowledge independently of experience by means of a reference to pure (though sensible) intuition. Kant's claim is that because of his understandable failure to recognize this essential feature of mathematical demonstration, Plato had no recourse but to appeal to the famous doctrine of recollection, which Kant construes as involving a past intellectual intuition of the ideas in the divine understanding that becomes obscured at birth through the connection of the soul with the body (Ak 8:391).[40] A further noteworthy feature of this discussion, which reflects the teachings of the third *Critique*, is Kant's introduction of the idea of purposiveness in connection with mathematics. Basically, Kant suggests that Plato, who was "no less a mathematician than he was a philosopher," was seduced by the apparent purposiveness of certain geometrical figures, such as the circle – that is, by the fact that they appear to be designed with the solution of mathematical problems in view – into the belief that they were created with that end in view by some superhuman understanding (Ak 8:391). But as he had done in the *Critique of Judgment*, Kant suggests that no genuine purposiveness is involved here, since the properties of a circle (or any geometrical figure) follow necessarily from the conditions of its construction.[41]

A second important theme of this essay is the role of feeling in philosophy. The view that Kant is attacking proclaims that feeling is the instrument through which the mind has access to the divine or, in Kantian terms, the super-sensible. Kant remarks that "[t]he principle of wishing to philosophize by influence of a higher *feeling* is the most suitable of all for the tone of superiority" (Ak 8:395). And, not surprisingly, he characterizes such a view, and the visionary enthusiasm it involves, as the "death of all philosophy" (Ak 8:405). More interestingly, however, Kant also contrasts what he terms the "summons of the latest German wisdom, *to philosophize through feeling*," with the "view of a few years ago, *to employ philosophy to put* the moral *feeling* into *force* and motion" (Ak 8:400). The latter, of course, refers to the standpoint of the *Critique of Practical Reason*, which had been published some eight years earlier. Moreover, in light of this contrast, Kant takes up Schlosser's challenge that "[t]he surest mark of authenticity in human philosophy is not that it should make us more certain, but that it should make us better" (Ak 8:400).

In accepting Schlosser's challenge, Kant turns the remainder of the discussion decidedly in the direction of the morally-practical, and particularly toward the central concept of freedom in its connection with moral feeling. Kant's main point here seems to be that moral feeling, which for him is nothing mystical but is inseparable from our consciousness of the moral law as the "fact of reason," is thereby also linked directly with the consciousness of freedom, understood as the awareness of a capacity to do one's duty in the face of all the threats and allurements that the sensible world has to offer. Freedom, so conceived, is described as the Archimedean point, "to which reason can apply its lever to move the human will, even when the whole of nature resists" (Ak 8:403). It is, then, this "feeling" of freedom, which Kant suggests is arrived at only through the laborious development of concepts of the understanding rather than by means of a sudden and effortless illumination, that is the "secret" or "mystery" that both makes us better and provides a transition to the super-sensible (though only from a practical point of view). Kant uses the esoteric vocabulary of "secret" and "mystery" here both to emphasize the point that freedom, so conceived, remains theoretically inexplicable and to call attention to the sharp difference between this "secret," which has its foundation in practical reason and reflects the epistemic modesty of the critical philosophy, and the mysterious doctrine to which Schlosser and his associates appeal in their "superior tone."

A final noteworthy feature of this essay is its insistence on the importance of the concept of form in philosophy. This is brought into the discussion in response to Schlosser's characterization of a concern for form and the *formal* in our knowledge as "a pedantry, under the name of a 'pattern factory'" (Ak 8:404). Given the central emphasis placed on the concept of "form" in all three *Critiques*, it is hardly surprising that Kant reacted strongly to such a sentiment. And in response he cites the scholastic dictum, "In form resides the essence of the matter" (*forma dat esse rei*), to which he adds the significant qualification, "so far as this is to be known by reason" (Ak 8:404). This qualification is important because it links form directly to reason, and (by implication) the denial of the significance of form to a rejection of reason. Moreover, Kant supports this claim by noting how form is crucial for empirical knowledge, for mathematics, for metaphysics understood as "pure philosophy" – that is, ontology, which is concerned with the *forms of thought* – and even for the transition to the super-sensible. The latter is the case because this transition can be accomplished only from a morally-practical point of view, which involves reference to practical laws, the principle of which is the purely formal categorical imperative.

In spite of all of this, Kant ends the essay by making what amounts to a peace offering, suggesting that the difference between the two parties is due to a misunderstanding, since both are motivated by the intention to make men wise and honest. And, in light of this, he holds out the prospect of a "treaty," which would amount to an agreement to disagree. Such a treaty would be possible, Kant suggests, because the two parties agree on the main point, namely that "[t]he veiled goddess, before whom we both bow the knee, is the moral law within us in its inviolable majesty." Where they disagree, according to Kant's account, is over the question of the source of this law: "whether it comes from man himself, out of the absolute authority of his own reason, or whether it proceeds from another being, whose nature is unknown to him, and which speaks to man through this, his own reason" (Ak 8:405).

Although this way of framing the difference really points to the vast gulf between the two positions, one based on the principle of autonomy and the primacy of practical reason, the other on a theological version of heteronomy, Kant initially indicates that this difference is of little significance, since it concerns mere speculation and does not extend to the practical question of our duty. But rather than leaving it at this point, which might have brought the controversy to an end, Kant goes on to point out that the latter way of understanding the foundations of morality leads to that "visionary enthusiasm, which is the death of all philosophy."

Our final text, *Proclamation*, is perhaps most notable for the unmistakable allusion in its full title to Kant's famous work, *Toward Perpetual Peace: A Philosophical Project*, which had been published one year earlier (1795). Unlike the latter, it is clearly not something that Kant had planned to write, but was occasioned by Schlosser's somewhat unexpected and harsh reply to his initial essay, which contained gross misrepresentations of Kant's views.[42] The basic thesis of Kant's response to this new and misguided foray by Schlosser is that only the critical philosophy is compatible with a permanent state of peace in philosophy because it alone is capable of ending the perennial conflict between dogmatism and skepticism to the satisfaction of the true interests of both sides. In full agreement with the works previously discussed, Kant suggests that his philosophy has this capability because it preserves and vindicates the traditional concerns of metaphysics with God, freedom, and immortality by grounding them in practical reason, while, at the same time, limiting the claims of theoretical reason. Thus, although Kant does not put it in this way, it may be said to recognize the moment of truth in both dogmatism and skepticism (the traditional protagonists). This is contrasted with the reconciliation proposed by Schlosser under the name of "*Moderatism.*" The latter proceeds largely on the basis of probabilities, which, as Kant had long insisted, have no place in metaphysics, since it is concerned solely with *a priori* claims. Moreover, Kant suggests that because of his "unexpected sally on to the battlefield of *metaphysics*" (Ak 8:419), and the misrepresentations of the critical philosophy which he has affirmed (particularly concerning the categorical imperative), it is Schlosser who stands in the way of the advent of a state of peace in philosophy.

Finally, even though this brief essay contains nothing really new in terms of doctrine, it is of interest for the therapeutic conception of philosophy that it advocates. The concern (or effect) of philosophy, understood as a doctrine of wisdom, is nothing less than the "health of reason" (Ak 8:414). And the clear message is that the superiority of the critical philosophy lies in its capacity to preserve a state of health (which seems to be equivalent to a state of peace in philosophy). It turns out, however, that the kind of peace (or health) attainable by philosophy differs in at least one significant respect from the peace that Kant envisioned in the political realm in the original essay on *Perpetual Peace*. For there Kant emphasized that it is the very fact that states find themselves in an armed condition that inclines and invariably leads them to war. Thus, the third of the preliminary articles for perpetual peace among states that Kant proposes is that "[s]tanding armies (*miles perpetuus*) shall in time be abandoned altogether" (Ak 8:345). By contrast, in the realm of philosophy, no such abolition is recommended. On the contrary, Kant insists that the critical philosophy is "an outlook ever-armed (against those who perversely confound appearances with things-in-themselves)," and he suggests that precisely because this "armed state" (*bewaffneter Zustand*) "unceasingly accompanies the activity of reason," it "offers the prospect of a perpetual peace among philosophers" (Ak 8:416).[43] At least in philosophy, then, it appears that the key to perpetual peace (and the health of reason) lies in an eternal vigilance rather than the laying down of arms. And as the very existence of this essay shows, Kant maintained this vigilance to the end.

Prolegomena to any future metaphysics
that will be able to come forward as science

Translator's introduction

The *Prolegomena to Any Future Metaphysics* is the preeminent synopsis in the history of philosophy. Kant completed it about fifteen months after the *Critique of Pure Reason* was published. He wanted to present his critical philosophy concisely and accessibly, for "future teachers" of metaphysics. He also wanted to convince his fellow metaphysicians "that it is unavoidably necessary to suspend their work for the present," until they have determined "whether such a thing as metaphysics is even possible at all" (4:255).[1] Although the *Critique* "always remains the foundation to which the *Prolegomena* refer only as preparatory exercises" (4:261), Kant nonetheless hoped that the shorter work would be used to assess the critical philosophy "piece by piece from its foundation," serving "as a general synopsis, with which the work itself could then be compared on occasion" (4:380).

In the *Prolegomena*, Kant distilled his critical inquiry into the General Question, "Is metaphysics possible at all?" (4:271), which he in turn interpreted as a question about the possibility of synthetic *a priori* cognition (4:275–6), or cognition through pure reason (that is, independent of sensory experience). To answer the General Question, Kant first asked how synthetic *a priori* cognition is possible in two areas where he considered it actual: pure mathematics and pure natural science. He found that this possibility (and actuality) could be explained only by positing cognitive structures that the subject brings to cognition, as forms of sensory intuition and categories of the understanding. But this explanation can hold only for synthetic *a priori* cognition of objects of possible experience. Kant could not see how forms of intuition or categories grounded in the knowing subject could yield *a priori* cognition of items beyond sensory experience, such as God, the human soul, and the world as it is in itself, which were the objects of traditional metaphysics. Since he could see no other way to achieve synthetic *a priori* cognition of such things, he concluded that traditional metaphysics is impossible. Its objects lie beyond the boundary of human knowledge. Yet Kant also held that such objects, while not determinately cognizable, are in some way thinkable. A boundary line implies a space beyond it, in this case, a region of unknowable intelligible beings, perhaps including a freely acting human soul that spontaneously initiates causal sequences.

Many consider the *Prolegomena* the best introduction to Kant's philosophy. Kant so liked parts of the Preamble and the General Questions that he introduced them, with little modification, into the Introduction to the second or B edition of the *Critique*. Nonetheless, some commentators doubt that the *Prolegomena* captures the main points of the *Critique*, arguing that it begs the question against Humean skepticism.[2] Others counter by asking whether Kant's arguments were actually directed toward a general skeptical challenge of the sort attributed to Hume.[3] Such questions will be raised but not settled in this Introduction, which examines the origin of the *Prolegomena*, outlines its method of exposition, surveys its structure in relation to the first *Critique*, provides a context for Kant's statements about Hume, describes the work's reception, and discusses texts and translation.

I

ORIGIN AND PURPOSE OF THE *PROLEGOMENA*

Kant completed the Preface to the *Critique of Pure Reason* in April, 1781, and on July 22 he presented a bound volume to his friend and former student Johann Georg Hamann.[4] By August he had sent his publisher a proposal for an abstract or summary of the big book. This shorter work was intended to make his challenge to metaphysics accessible to a wider audience than the *Critique* was reaching.

The *Critique* was the product of nine years of sustained labor, and the fulfillment of a project to evaluate metaphysical cognition that Kant had mentioned in 1765.[5] In it, Kant sought to decide "the possibility or impossibility of a metaphysics in general," and to determine its "sources," "extent," and "boundaries" by evaluating the ability of human cognition to answer traditional metaphysical questions (A xii). If he succeeded, "there should not be a single metaphysical problem that has not been solved here, or at least for whose solution the key has not been offered" (A xiii).

Kant was disappointed by the *Critique*'s reception. In the April Preface he described the work as "dry" and "scholastic" (A xviii). Presumably he had already had complaints from Hamann, who was reading the book in proof and with whom he spoke often. On April 8, Hamann wrote to Kant's publisher, Johann Friedrich Hartknoch, that after reading the first thirty signatures he believed "few readers would be equal to the scholastic content." On April 20 he wrote to Kant's former student J. G. Herder that the book "all comes down to pedantry and empty verbiage."[6] Kant soon learned that other readers were having difficulty. On May 1, Kant had written to Marcus Herz in Berlin, asking him to arrange presentation copies for Moses Mendelssohn, C. G. Selle, and Herz himself, and a dedicatory copy for Karl Abraham von Zedlitz, the Prussian minister of education. Sometime after June 8 he wrote to thank Herz for his efforts, expressing regret at the news that Mendelssohn had "put the book aside," since he was relying on Mendelssohn, J. N. Tetens, and Herz himself to explain his theory to the rest of the world.[7] Kant predicted that at first "very few readers" would study his *Critique* thoroughly, and that few would understand it.[8] As he explained, "this kind of inquiry will always remain difficult; for it includes the *metaphysics of metaphysics*."

In this same letter Kant mentioned a plan "according to which even *popularity* can be gained" for his results.[9] On August 18, 1781, Kant sent his publisher Hartknoch a proposal for an *Auszug*, that is, an abstract or epitome, of the *Critique*. The letter is lost, but Kant's plan can be reconstructed. Writing in August and September, Hamann describes Kant's willingness to "bring out a popular abstract of his *Critique*, even for laypersons," and his talk of "an abstract of his *Critique* to popular taste" and a "brief abstract" of a "few printed sheets." On October 23, Hamann reported to Hartknoch that some, including Kant, described the new project as an "abstract," others as a "reader on metaphysics." He continued to inquire about Kant's "abstract," "reader," or "textbook."[10] On November 19, 1781, Hartknoch, replying to Kant's lost letter, instructed that "if the abstract of the *Critique* should, as I doubt not, be finished, please send it to the printer Grunert in Halle, who printed the big work. And kindly notify me as soon as the manuscript has been sent" (Ak 10:279).

On January 11, 1782, Hamann reported that Kant thought the "small work" would be finished by Easter. In the following week's *Göttingen gelehrte Anzeigen*, for January 19, 1782, there appeared an anonymous review of the *Critique*. Kant was upset by it. In response he wrote an Appendix to the *Prolegomena* (4:372–80) and made other additions – including at least Notes II and III to the First Part, which distinguish Kant's transcendental idealism from Berkeley's idealism. On February 8, Hamann asked after the "small supplement" to the *Critique*, and on April 22, 1782, reported the title "Prolegomena for a still to be written metaphysics."[11] Kant was nearly finished when a second review, more to his liking, appeared in the *Gothaische gelehrte Zeitungen* for August 24, 1782. He had seen it by mid-September, and his brief response in the Appendix (4:380) presumably caused little delay in sending the final copy to the printer. The work appeared in the spring of 1783. Hartknoch later acknowledged that the printer had been slow.[12]

The materials reviewed thus far establish that Kant began his new work between August, 1781, and January, 1782, but they do not reveal which work it was. Do the various descriptions refer to a single work as it evolved, or did Kant have three separate works in mind – a popular presentation, an abstract for contemporary metaphysicians and future teachers, and a textbook of metaphysics – only one of which appeared in 1783?

The reported "textbook" or "reader" on metaphysics was not the abstract or *Prolegomena*. The intervening title reported by Hamann, "*Prolegomena einer noch zu schreibenden Metaphysik*," suggests that Kant thought of it as prolegomena to his own projected metaphysics. In the A Preface Kant said he was planning a "metaphysics of nature," that is, a "system of pure (speculative) reason" (A 21).[13] Not long after the *Prolegomena* appeared, Kant wrote to Mendelssohn that he still hoped to complete "a textbook of metaphysics according to the critical principles mentioned, having all the brevity of a handbook, for use in academic lectures" (August 16, 1783, Ak 10:346). His correspondents pressed for the "metaphysics of nature," and in 1786 Kant published the *Metaphysical Foundations of Natural Science*, which he considered preparatory.[14] Kant's full metaphysics of nature never appeared, but in 1785 C. G. Schütz suggested that the first *Critique* contained future textbooks of metaphysics "virtually."[15]

The relation of the *Prolegomena* to the rumored "popular abstract" is less clear. In 1878 and 1904, Benno Erdmann argued, on epistolary and internal textual grounds, that by the summer of 1781, Kant had decided to write, and perhaps started, a popular presentation of his views, but that he soon abandoned popularity in favor of a work directed at philosophers and teachers of philosophy.[16] Erdmann held that a draft of this "abstract" was complete when the Göttingen review appeared in January, 1782, after which Kant found two reasons to revise it. First, in response to the review itself, he wanted to refute the charge of Berkeleyan idealism. Second, Erdmann contended that since at this time Hamann was emphasizing Hume's influence on the critical philosophy, Kant wanted to distinguish his contribution from Hume's.[17]

Erdmann believed that he could differentiate the additions made in response to these factors from the original draft, and his 1878 edition of the *Prolegomena* set the presumed additions in smaller type, enclosed by brackets.[18] These portions contain every mention of Hume. On Erdmann's hypothesis, Kant's remarks on Hume through the Second Part responded to Hamann's labeling him a "Prussian Hume" due to his negative conclusions about metaphysics.[19] Kant wanted to show that beyond agreeing with Hume about dogmatic metaphysics, he alone had seen that a survey of the boundaries of human reason was needed and could be achieved by examining the possibility of synthetic *a priori* cognition. Kant's comments on Hume's *Dialogues* in the Third Part were added to show that despite granting Hume's arguments against theism, his philosophy did not prohibit thought of God as cause of the world.[20]

The Kant philologist Emil Arnoldt wrote a scathing response to Erdmann's 1878 work, denying that Kant had written anything before January, 1782, and asserting that Kant started work only in response to the Göttingen review.[21] A young Hans Vaihinger soon revealed crucial defects in Arnoldt's evidence, leaving no clear indication of what Kant might have written prior to January, though Hamann's reports make it likely he was at work in 1781.[22]

In any event, we may agree with both Erdmann and Arnoldt that what-ever Kant's intentions about a popular work, the *Prolegomena* was written for fellow philosophers. Kant himself says the work was meant to allow "future teachers" of metaphysics (4:255, 383) not only to understand and assess the critical philosophy, but also to discover metaphysics itself "for the first time" (4:255). It would do so by remedying the obscurity of the large book. He feared that the *Critique* would be misunderstood because readers would skim through rather than thinking through it, and be-cause of its dryness, obscurity, prolixity, and opposition to "all familiar concepts" (4:261). He dismissed complaints of "lack of popularity, enter-tainment, and ease," but confessed to a "certain obscurity" partly stem-ming from the "expansiveness" of the *Critique*. The *Prolegomena* would "redress" this obscurity, with the *Critique* remaining the "foundation" to which it would refer as "preparatory exercises" (4:261, see also 274). The short work is a "plan" of the larger work, allowing one "to survey the whole" and "to test one by one the main points at issue" in the new science of critique, and allowing Kant to improve his exposition (4:263). It follows the "analytic method" as opposed to the synthetic method of the *Critique* (4:263, 274–5, 278–9). Despite the difference in method, Kant (as already noted) offered the *Prolegomena* as a "general synopsis, with which the work itself could then be compared on occasion" (4:380). It could serve as a "plan and guide for the investigation" of the *Critique* (4:381), and as a replacement for the Deduction and Paralogisms.[23]

Kant intended the *Prolegomena* "to present the essential content of the *Critique*" (4:280). It was not to be truly popular, "for laypersons," but was to reach a wider audience of philosophers. While writing it, Kant confessed that he was unable to "give ease" to his presentation.[24] Shortly after publication, he wrote to Garve that "popularity cannot be attempted in studies of such high abstraction" (August 7, 1783, Ak 10:339). An early reviewer correctly judged the intended audience of the *Prolegomena* to be that of the *Critique* itself, that is, "speculative thinkers," especially those "who concern themselves with metaphysics" or "who intend to write a metaphysics."[25]

II
THE ANALYTIC METHOD

According to Kant, the most fundamental difference between the *Prolegomena* and the A *Critique* is that the first follows the analytic method, the second the synthetic method (4:263, 274–5, 278–9). A contrast between analytic and synthetic methods (or regressive and progressive methods) was regularly discussed in medieval and early modern philosophy, in connection with mathematics, natural philos-ophy, and metaphysics. These discussions did not yield uniform, precise definitions.[26] The features widely attributed to each method were that analysis proceeds from consequent to ground, or from whole to part, and synthesis from ground to consequent, or part to whole. Analysis may start from something given in experience, or merely assumed as given, and seek its proof or explanation, while synthesis starts from abstract definitions and principles. Analysis and synthesis were described as, respectively, methods of discovery and of proof, and as contrasting methods of exposition.

In the *Prolegomena*, Kant attributed two features of the synthetic method to the *Critique*. First, as regards method of exposition, the big book "had to be composed according to the *synthetic method*, so that the science [viz., transcendental philosophy] might present all of its articulations, as the structural organization of a quite peculiar faculty of cognition, in their natural connection" (4:263). It examined first the "elements" of pure reason and then the "laws of its pure use" (4:274), moving from parts to whole and from ground to consequent. Second, as regards the source of conviction, he could accept nothing as given "except reason itself" and so had to "develop cognition out of its original seeds without relying on any fact whatever" (4:274). He had to argue directly for his account of the elements and laws of pure reason. The analytic method of the *Prolegomena* proceeded differently on both counts, starting from something known and familiar and proceeding to discover its elements or grounds. The method was nonetheless intended to justify the discovered elements or grounds, in this case by showing that Kant's theory of synthetic *a priori* cognition is the only possible account of the knowledge we actually possess.

The applicability of this methodological distinction to the *Prolegomena* might be challenged. If the *Prolegomena* were fully analytic, it would "ascend" to the distinction between analytic and synthetic judgments by starting from actual instances of judgment. But instead it lays out definitions and distinctions in the Preamble, including those between analytic and synthetic judgments and between *a priori* and *a posteriori* cognition.

In order to evaluate Kant's use of this methodological distinction, one must determine what was being synthetically articulated or analytically discovered. In the Preface to the *Prolegomena* Kant mentions two projects immediately before introducing the phrase "analytic method": settling the "possibility of metaphysics" (4:260), and presenting the "new science" of critique (4:262). These projects are related, for the latter science was to settle the former question. According to Kant, metaphysics is possible only if its objects can be cognized through pure reason. To assess this possibility in the *Critique*, he constructed an elaborate theory of cognition involving the senses, understanding, and reason, their relations, and the associated classes of representation (intuitions, concepts, and ideas). It is this theory of cognition, and its implications for the possibility of metaphysics, that is to be "ascended to" (and thereby justified) in the *Prolegomena*. The shorter work will "rely on something already known to be dependable, from which we can go forward with confidence and ascend to the sources, which are not yet known, and whose discovery will not only explain what is known already, but will also exhibit an area with many cognitions that all arise from these same sources" (4:275). It will start with mathematics and natural science as bodies of actual, given, dependable, and uncontested synthetic cognition *a priori*. With respect to these, the question is not *whether* such cognition is possible, but *how* it is possible (4:275), or indeed how "alone" it is possible (4:276, note). The *Prolegomena* is to establish analytically the main outlines of Kant's theory of cognition and the main results of his transcendental philosophy: the theory that space and time are forms of intuition, the necessity of the categories for the experience of objects, the limitation of synthetic *a priori* cognition to the domain of experience, the role of ideas in transcendental illusion, and the notion of noumena lying beyond the boundary of possible knowledge, thinkable but unknowable. These results are then used to evaluate the possibility of metaphysical cognition according to the previous analysis of its structure (as synthetic *a priori* cognition), set out (synthetically) in the Preamble.

Kant organized the *Prolegomena* around four questions. The first two ask how pure mathematics and pure natural science are possible. The third examines the possibility of "metaphysics in general" – not the science of metaphysics, but the natural inclination of the human mind to pursue metaphysics (4:279). The fourth question asks, "How is metaphysics as a science possible?" (4:280).

Only the first three parts of the *Prolegomena*, corresponding to the first three questions, follow the analytic method. Kant signaled the close of his "analytic" treatment in the Third Part (4:365), offering his subsequent response to the fourth question as a "Solution to the General Question of the Prolegomena." To match the first three questions, Kant took three things to be "actual" in his investigations. The first two, pure mathematics and pure natural science, provide the basis for his discovery of how (alone) synthetic *a priori* cognition is possible – that is, only if the forms of intuition and the categories serve as conditions for all possible experience. Consequently, synthetic *a priori* cognition is not possible for the transcendent objects of metaphysics. The third thing that Kant took to be actual was the "natural disposition" to metaphysics (4:279), that is, the naturally given tendency of human beings to pose metaphysical questions concerning the putative objects of pure reason. Here, Kant sought to explain reason's natural tendency to claim synthetic *a priori* knowledge, even when unjustified, and to show how reason is able to form ideas, however problematic, of God, the soul, and the world as a whole.[27] The finding that cognition or knowledge does not extend beyond the boundary of possible experience does not preclude the thought (or existence) of objects beyond that boundary. The ideas of reason allow intelligible beings – including God as necessary cause of the sensible world and the soul as a freely acting simple substance – to be thought, even if they cannot be cognized as objects (4:344–7, 351–6). Finally, having completed his "analytic" argument, Kant "solves" the question of how metaphysics is possible as a science – namely, through study of the critical philosophy (4:365).

III
STRUCTURE OF THE WORK IN RELATION
TO THE FIRST *CRITIQUES*

In the twentieth century, little work was done on the *Prolegomena* and its relation to the first *Critiques*.[28] Nonetheless, Kant himself intended the *Prolegomena* to summarize and improve upon the main results of the A *Critique*, and he incorporated parts of it into the B *Critique*.

The Preface to the *Prolegomena* sets the task of evaluating the possibility of metaphysics and contains Kant's most celebrated allusions to Hume (4:257, 260). The Preamble and General Questions lay out fundamental Kantian distinctions and introduce the analytic method. These three sections correspond to parts of the Preface, Introduction, and Method of the A *Critique*. Discussions of the relations among analytic judgments, the principle of contradiction, and the synthetic foundations of metaphysics and mathematics, which appeared far into the A *Critique* (in the Analytic of Principles, A 149–54, 159–60, 163–4/B 188–93, 198–9, 204–5), are helpfully brought forward into the Preamble.

The First, Second, and Third Parts of the *Prolegomena* correspond respectively to the Transcendental Aesthetic, the Transcendental Analytic, and the Transcendental Dialectic. The First Part focuses on the possibility of pure mathematical cognition *a priori*. Since mathematics is fundamentally intuitive rather than discursive, and since its results are apodictic, it can be founded only on synthetic *a priori* construction in intuition, in accordance with the human forms of intuition, space and time. Consequently, pure mathematics is restricted to possible objects of experience. Notes I–III in the *Prolegomena* seek to show the advantages of Kant's transcendental idealism for explaining the objective validity of geometry (see A 46–9/B 63–6), and to distinguish his form of idealism from the skeptical idealism of Descartes and the visionary idealism of Berkeley (see B 69–71).

The Second Part offers a newly formulated argument for the conclusions of the Deduction, using terminology not found in either edition of the *Critique*, including the notion of "consciousness in general" and a distinction between "judgments of perception" and "judgments of experience." It draws on the Analytic of Principles (A 155–60/B 195–9), the Amphiboly, the Distinction between Phenomena and Noumena, and the Doctrine of Method (A 760–9/B 788–97).

In §§14–26, Kant asks how pure natural scientific cognition, that is, cognition of universal natural laws, is possible. Such cognition could not apply to things in themselves, he reasons, because these could not be cognized *a priori* without any contact with them; but if we had contact with them through experience, that could provide only *a posteriori* cognition and so could not yield the necessity required of laws of nature. Focusing on the law of cause, he restates the problem as that of explaining the possibility of objectively valid experience of objects. He contends that such experience presupposes that the law of cause (and others) hold *a priori* for all possible experience. Using a contrast between merely subjective judgments of perception (such as, that we see the sun shining on the stone and then the stone feels warm) and universally valid judgments of experience (such as, that the sun warms the stone), he argues that the universal validity demanded by the latter can be achieved only if the categories (as derived from the logical table of judgments) are brought to experience by the subject, so as to render the judgment not merely subjectively valid, but valid for "consciousness in general," that is, not just here and now and for me, but for everyone and at all times. The categories serve as conditions for all possible (objectively valid) experience. This account of the possibility of *a priori* cognition of universal laws of nature restricts such cognition to objects of experience as opposed to things in themselves (see A 155–60/B 195–9). Kant then makes some observations on the tables of judgments, categories, and principles (§§21–6, 39).

In §§27–31, Kant takes up "Hume's doubt," that is, Hume's challenge to reason to give an account of "by what right she thinks: that something could be so constituted that, if it is posited, something else necessarily must thereby be posited as well" (Preface, 4:257). Kant agrees with Hume that reason cannot see how the concept of cause (or substance, or community) could apply to things in themselves. But he claims to have discovered that both the concept and the law of cause can be cognized *a priori* if they are restricted to the domain of possible experience, to phenomena as opposed to noumena. The understanding, by its nature, tries to extend the categories beyond possible experience; only a scientific (i.e., systematic) self-knowledge of reason can show where the understanding can apply the law of cause *a priori* and where it cannot, and so prevent it from being led into dogmatic assertions about things in themselves of the sort that Kant (as Hume) wanted to undermine (see A 760–9/B 788–97). The results of these sections are then extended via the distinction between phenomena and noumena (§§32–5) and discussion of the relation between the principles of experience and the laws of nature (§§36–8; see A 126–8, and subsequently B 159–65).

The Third Part provides a brief survey of the main parts of the Dialectic, summarizing the Paralogisms and the Antinomies, and simply referring to the Ideal of Pure Reason for the critique of theology. In §56, General Note, and §§57–60, Conclusion, Kant argues that a successful critique of pure reason reveals the boundaries of pure reason and the proper use of reason beyond them. Critique limits the understanding to possible experience. It shows that reason cannot decisively answer questions about the ultimate constituents of the world (whether they are simple or not), its spatial and temporal boundaries, or the existence and nature of the soul and God. But reason is permitted to seek *systematic unity* in the appearances as a whole, and *to think* God and the soul – though not determinately, and so not as proper objects of cognition. Reason, being convinced that materialism is inadequate to explain the appearances, is permitted to "adopt the concept" of the soul as an immaterial being (4:352). In an extended discussion of Hume's *Dialogues*, Kant argues that Hume is right that we cannot know the theistic concept, but denies that this precludes us from using that concept to view the world as if it were created by an all-wise being. Kant permits analogical application of the concept of cause in this case. The value of Hume's skepticism as a response to dogmatism, and the need for the critical philosophy to determine the true boundary of reason, had been discussed in the Method (A 758–69/B 786–97).

The Solution and programmatic parts of the Appendix assert that genuine metaphysical cognition is possible only through Kant's critical results. These discussions correspond to parts of the Discipline of Pure Reason (A 738–57/B 766–85) and are reflected in the B Preface (B xxiv–xxxvii).

Despite such correspondences, the *Prolegomena* differs significantly from the *Critique*, if only because of its brevity. There are also differences in emphasis, due in part to adoption of the analytic method and in part to the clarity that comes with restatement. The *Prolegomena* provided a more forceful statement of Kant's project to evaluate the claims of metaphysics than had the A edition. Nonetheless, in the A Preface Kant had set the task of evaluating the claims of metaphysics to achieve cognition apart from experience (A xii), and in the A Introduction he had emphasized the importance of discovering "the ground of the possibility of synthetic *a priori* judgments" (A 10/B 23). Further, while the *Prolegomena*, in accordance with the analytic method, assumed the actuality of geometrical cognition, it had previously been asserted in the A *Critique*. Kant there argued from the need to account for the apodictic certainty of geometry to his conclusion that space is a subjective form of intuition

(A 24, A 38–41/B 55–8, A 46–9/B 64–6).[29] As is well known, Kant reorganized the B Aesthetic to expand and emphasize this discussion, creating a separate section on geometry (B 40–1). Given the foreshadowing of the argument in A, its subsequent expansion in B need not be seen as a distortion of the original argument. Rather, Kant may have decided that the argument from the actuality of geometry deserved greater emphasis.

Kant drew on the General Questions in restating his critical aims in the B Introduction (B 19–22). In doing so, he silently introduced the analytic method into parts of the B *Critique*. Thus, the Introduction contained the four Main Transcendental Questions (not labeled as such), together with the assumption that pure mathematics and pure natural science are actual (B 20). Further, Kant ended the revised Aesthetic by recalling the General Question on the possibility of synthetic *a priori* propositions (B 73). And in material added to the First Section of the Deduction in B, he rejected the "empirical" derivation of the categories attributed to Locke and Hume because it "cannot be reconciled with the reality of the scientific cognition *a priori* that we possess, that namely of *pure mathematics* and *pure natural science*, and is therefore refuted by the fact" (B 127–8). The question of whether this change in strategy "begs the question" against the Humean skeptic depends on what Kant believed Hume to have challenged, as is broached in the next section.

Much of the extant philosophical work on the relation between the *Prolegomena* and the first *Critiques* has addressed the relation between the A and B Transcendental Deductions and the Second Part of the *Prolegomena*. In that part, Kant started from the supposition that we have *a priori* knowledge of universal laws of nature, including the causal law and the law that substance persists, and then treated the question of the possibility of such laws as a question about the conditions for universally valid judgments of experience. Interpreters have wondered whether the resultant argument, its distinction between judgments of perception and judgments of experience, and its appeal to "consciousness in general" in relation to universal validity, provide insight into the Deductions themselves.[30] Some things are clear. The argument in the Second Part avoids the details of cognitive processes as discussed in the "subjective" portion of the A Deduction. The argument is cast entirely in terms of the necessary conditions for experience and the role of categories therein. The search for the conditions of experience is found in both the A and B Deductions. Neither includes the precise terminology of the *Prolegomena*, but both argue that the categories are necessary for universally valid experience. The technical terminology of a "unity of apperception," found in both Deductions, receives only scant (and unexplained) use in the *Prolegomena* (4:318; also 4:335, note). But talk of "connection" or "unification" in a "consciousness in general" plays a corresponding role (4:300, 304–5, 312). While neither Deduction includes a terminological contrast between (merely subjective) "judgments of per-ception" and (universally valid, objective) "judgments of experience," both try to show how merely subjective sensory appearances, or percep-tions, can be rendered objective (A 89–90/B 122–3; B 159–61). To decide how well the Second Part captures the point of either Deduction, one would need to specify the intended functions of the Deductions in Kant's philosophy, something on which there is no agreement.

IV
KANT'S RELATION TO HUME

The most celebrated sentence in the *Prolegomena* is: "I freely admit that the remembrance of *David Hume* was the very thing that many years ago first interrupted my dogmatic slumber and gave a completely dif-ferent direction to my researches in the field of speculative philoso-phy" (4:260). This sentence, together with Kant's description of "Hume's problem" concerning causation, were constant signposts for Kant inter-pretation in the twentieth century. All the same, there is no agreement on what Kant remembered, when he did so, or how he understood Hume's challenge.

Some things are known about Kant's relation to Hume.[31] Hume's *Enquiries* and essays were translated into German in the mid-1750s by Johann Georg Sulzer in Berlin, and Kant had read them by the early 1760s. It is unlikely that this initial reading was what interrupted his slumber. Although Kant was alive to empiricist and skeptical challenges to metaphysics during the 1760s, in his *Inaugural Dissertation* (1770) he held that intellectual cognition of an intelligible world – the sort of cog-nition claimed by traditional metaphysics – was possible. In that work Kant asserted the ideality of space and time as forms of intuition, a po-sition he took over into the Transcendental Aesthetic. But he also held that an intelligible world of things in themselves might be cognized through its form, the causal relation. This use of the causal relation to think intelligible beings as a ground for the sensible world would seem to be what Hume's challenge interrupted. Indeed, within a year of his *Inaugural Dissertation* Kant presumably read Hamann's partial transla-tion of the conclusion to Book I of Hume's *Treatise*, published in the *Königsberger Zeitung* for July 5, 1771. In 1772 there appeared a German translation of Beattie's attack on Hume, with ample quotations from the *Treatise*.[32]

Kant's "remembrance" has received more attention than his later read-ing of Hume while writing the A *Critique* and the *Prolegomena*. In late summer of 1780, Hamann gave Kant a draft of his abbreviated translation of Hume's *Dialogues Concerning Natural Religion*. Kant looked through it immediately and soon asked to read it again.[33] Having nearly completed the *Critique*, he was prepared to appreciate Hume's skeptical challenge to the argument from design, particularly the problems with theological anthropomorphism and with using the principle "like effects prove like causes" to infer a being outside experience. Hamann suppressed his translation when he learned of a rival one, by Karl Schreiter with annotations by Ernst Platner, which appeared at the Leipzig book fair for Michaelmas, 1781. Kant owned a copy by December.[34]

Kant clearly took a new interest in Hume during this time. In the A *Critique*, Hume's name occurs only six times, all in the Doctrine of Method (A 745–6/B 773–4; A 760–9/B 788–97; A 856/B 884). In the *Prolegomena* it appears twenty-seven times. Hume is portrayed as inspiring the critical philosophy through his challenge to dogmatic metaphysics. The B *Critique* contains three new references to Hume, in the Introduction (B 5, 19–20) and the Deduction (B 127–8).

It is often assumed that Kant regarded Hume not only as challenging the causal concept in metaphysics, but also as skeptically attacking natural science and even ordinary perception. This interpretation relies heavily on Kant's statements in the *Prolegomena*. It is not suggested by the A *Critique*, where the skeptical idealist is described as a "benefactor" of human reason who forces acceptance of transcendental idealism (A 377–8), where Hume is portrayed as attacking application of the causal concept in theistic metaphysics (A 760/B 788), and where skeptical challenges to dogmatic metaphysics are helpful preparation for critique (A 761/B 789; A 769/B 797).[35] Further, even in the *Prolegomena* Hume is seen as presenting his challenge specifically to metaphysics, and the new passages in the B *Critique* have Hume rightly questioning metaphysical attempts to use causal reasoning to transcend experience (B 119–20) and failing to realize that his account of cognition is refuted by the synthetic *a priori* cognition we actually possess (B 5, 19–20). Of course, in the Second Part of the *Prolegomena* Kant speaks of "removing" Hume's doubt. Though Kant is sometimes portrayed as here "replying to the skeptic" in a general way, he might instead be seen as specifically answering Hume's challenge to reason's right to use the concept of cause *a priori*. Did Kant think of Hume's challenge as posing a general skeptical threat to knowledge, including natural science? Or did he see Hume as posing a challenge primarily to metaphysical cognition, a challenge upon which Kant would build? Was Hume Kant's ally in attacking dogmatic metaphysics, and his inspiration toward providing a more adequate theory of the conditions and boundaries of experience, or was he a skeptical enemy to be thwarted? Upon these questions turns an understanding not only of Kant's relation to Hume, but also of the motivation and goal of the critical philosophy itself, in its speculative branch. One thing is certain. The *Prolegomena* must figure largely in any study of Kant's perception of and response to Hume.

V

RECEPTION OF THE *PROLEGOMENA*

In the Solution, Kant expressed hope "that these *Prolegomena* will perhaps excite investigation in the field of critique" (4:367). He subsequently suggested to Garve that the work might make clear some main points of the *Critique*, which would shed light on other points, until eventually the whole was understood (August 7, 1783, Ak 10:338). His hopes were soon fulfilled.

The most negative early assessment of the *Prolegomena* was by Johann Schultz, who wanted to clarify Kant's philosophy through his own *Exposition of Kant's Critique of Pure Reason* of 1784. Schultz allowed that the *Prolegomena* contained "an estimable elucidation of [Kant's] *Critique*" and that it "spread much welcome light over the system of the author," but he reported that "it almost seems that one hardly recoils any less from the *Prolegomena* than from the *Critique*."[36] The first published review of the *Prolegomena*, by Johann Christian Lossius, was also mixed. It contained a largely accurate overview of the work, along with some critical remarks that revealed a failure to understand Kant's argument for the synthetic status of metaphysics. Lossius complained of the long sentences and suggested that Kant might have written more clearly in Latin or French, since his German required translation even for German speakers. But he allowed that Kant had "fully reached his aim that through these *Prolegomena* the overview of the whole, and the understanding of that quite remarkable and deeply thought work, be markedly facilitated," and he granted that both works "belong among the most remarkable of our time."[37]

Also in 1784, H. A. Pistorius published a thorough and accurate review of the *Prolegomena* in the *Allgemeine deutsche Bibliothek*. At first hesitant "to make an abstract from an abstract," Pistorius proceeded because of the work's "rare importance," its "analytic method," its comparative clarity, and its responses to objections.[38] The review captured the purpose of Kant's argument, recognizing that transcendental idealism was a consequence of his critical investigation, the main point of which concerned the possibility of metaphysics and the boundary of pure reason. Pistorius suspected that Kant was resting his claim that the table of categories was complete on the de facto results of previous logic, an empirical source that could not support an allegedly *a priori* result. He also questioned the "derivation" of the ideas of pure reason from the three forms of the syllogism.[39]

By 1785 it could no longer be said that the learned public was "honoring" the critical philosophy with its silence (4:380). The appearance of the *Groundwork of the Metaphysics of Morals* spurred interest in Kant, but work on his critique of reason was already in motion, stirred by the

Prolegomena. Johann August Heinrich Ulrich's *Institutiones logicae et meta-physicae* appeared at the Easter book fair and soon attracted notice. Although Ulrich was not seeking to develop a Kantian metaphysics, he did want to acquaint students more closely with Kantian ideas.[40] He adopted and explained the distinction between analytic and synthetic propositions, the existence of synthetic *a priori* propositions, the distinctions among sensibility, understanding, and reason, the doctrine that space is the form of outer sense, and the distinction between mathematical and philosophical methods.[41] While accepting the categories as pure concepts of the understanding, he challenged the completeness of Kant's table and denied that the categories are limited to possible experience.[42] Also in 1785, Tiedemann evaluated and rejected Kant's limits on metaphysics, drawing liberally from the *Prolegomena* as well as the *Critique*.[43] Schütz, who helped found the pro-Kantian *Allgemeine Literatur-Zeitung* in Jena, used his review of Schultz's *Exposition* to focus on the *Critique* itself, with reference to the *Prolegomena*. By the 1790s, Kant interpretation was a regular industry, spawning handbooks, dictionaries, and monographs. The *Prolegomena* received due attention in these works.[44] Although receiving only intermittent attention from subsequent scholars, it remains the standard introduction to Kant's theoretical philosophy.

VI
NOTE ON TEXTS AND TRANSLATIONS

The translation has been made using a reprint of the original *Prolegomena zu einer jeden künftigen Metaphysik die als Wissenschaft wird auftreten können* (Riga: Hartknoch, 1783; reprint, Erlangen: Harald Fischer Verlag, 1988) and Karl Vorländer's edition, as revised (Hamburg: Felix Meiner Verlag, 1976); on occasion, Benno Erdmann's edition in Ak, vol. 4, has been consulted. As is customary, the page numbers of Ak are shown in the margins of the translation. Vorländer's edition, completed after Ak, collects significant textual variants from many previous editions (and provides other useful information). Vorländer followed the Vaihinger-Sitzler "galley switching" thesis in reorganizing the text of the Preamble and the first General Question. Vaihinger argued, on internal grounds and by comparison to the B *Critique*, that a portion of text was transposed from §2 into §4 during the printing of the Preamble and the first General Question; Sitzler further argued that two galleys of 100 lines were switched.[45] The emended text is not without minor problems (in response to which a paragraph break has been added), but it is much improved over editions without the emendation.

Previous translations of the *Prolegomena* fall into three lines. The first translation, by John Richardson (London: Simpkin and Marshall, 1819), is uniformly disparaged and was not consulted. John P. Mahaffy and

John H. Bernard (2nd ed., London: Macmillan, 1889) relied somewhat on Richardson. Paul Carus (3rd ed., Chicago: Open Court, 1912) revised Mahaffy; Lewis White Beck (Indianapolis: Bobbs-Merrill, 1950) revised Carus; and James W. Ellington (Indianapolis: Hackett, 1977) revised Beck. Ernest Belfort Bax (2nd ed., London: Bell and Sons, 1891) made an independent translation, as did Peter G. Lucas (Manchester: Manchester University Press, 1953), achieving admirable quality. I have also made a new translation, sometimes consulting the earlier works, especially Lucas and Beck.[46]

The original editions of the *Prolegomena*, like the B *Critique*, contained no table of contents. Later German editions reconstructed the table from the section headings embedded in the text, which otherwise was printed in continuous fashion without page breaks to mark divisions (save between Preface and Preamble). Bax and Carus provided no table; Mahaffy, Beck, Lucas, and Ellington offered reconstructions. Their tables agree in structure, with the following exceptions. Mahaffy, Beck, and Ellington place the two sections headed General Question (§§4–5) within the Preambles; and Beck and Ellington treat the Conclusion: On Determining the Boundary of Pure Reason as a major division, while all others include it within the Third Part. From study of an original edition and consideration of the functions of the parts, I agree with Ak, Vorländer, and Lucas in rendering the General Questions as a major division and placing the Conclusion in the Third Part.

The present version is a variant of my edition in the Cambridge Texts in the History of Philosophy. It contains more extensive critical apparatus than would have been useful in that edition. I have revised my translation of *schwärmerisch* and related words in descriptions of Berkeley's idealism, adopting "visionary" as the adjective, and I have rendered *Bedeutung* as "significance" or "signification" when used to describe the lack of application for the categories outside possible experience. When supplying German words, I show declination and follow original orthography.

I have departed from some translators in rendering *sinnliche Anschauung* as "sensory intuition," rather than "sensible intuition." This choice accords with Kant's own advice about the related terms *intelligibel* and *intellectuel* (below, §34n), the first of which he restricted to "intelligible" objects (those able to be cognized by the intellect), as opposed to "intellectual" cognitions (cognitions belonging to the intellect as a faculty). Although "sensual intuition" would be the most literal translation for *sinnliche Anschauung*, it brings its own ambiguities, so I have used "sensory" when the adjective *sinnlich* is used to indicate the kind of cognition rather than to describe an object as being capable of being sensed (i.e., "sensible"). I have followed standard practice in rendering *Sinnlichkeit* as "sensibility." It might as well or better be translated as "sense," or "faculty of sense." "Sense" was used in eighteenth-century English-language philosophical writings to refer to the senses as a cognitive faculty or power.

In many cases there are similarities in word roots that Kant could play upon, but that do not carry over to English. Thus, in translating *Vernunftschluss* (literally, "inference of reason") as "syllogism," the connection between the faculty of reason and the syllogism is lost. The word *Satz* is particularly rich in such connections. It is typically rendered as "proposition," but in connection with the antinomies as "thesis," and in *Satz des Widerspruch* as "principle" (in the phrase "principle of contradiction"). The word *Grundsatz* is often translated as "principle," although "fundamental proposition" or "basic principle" would be more literal. Because Kant sometimes classifies *Grundsätze* as a subclass of *Principien*, a relation elided by translating both as "principles," I sometimes use the more literal alternatives. A similar problem arises with *gesunder Menschenverstand* and related terms. Kant sometimes played on its literal meaning, "healthy human understanding." But in Kant's time (as now) it was translated as "common sense," which is how I have rendered it.

I have followed as much as possible Kant's original punctuation for giving propositions, marking foreign words, and showing emphasis. Kant set propositions off with colons, as in, "the proposition: that substance remains and persists,..."; in such cases, the proposition usually ends at the first comma, semicolon, or period. On rare occasions when he used quotation marks I have followed; these have been found to be word-for-word quotations from a source only in §56 (Kant's note) and the Appendix (quoting the Garve–Feder review). In the first edition, Latin and French words were set in roman type, against the gothic of the German; I have used italics for Latin, French, and Greek words, against the roman of the main text. Italics also show emphasis, where Kant used bold type and letter spacing. For book titles, the italics have usually been added. Kant rarely marked book titles typographically, and he played on the fact that the German counterparts to "critique of pure reason" and "prolegomena" can be used both as ordinary nouns for a type of critical activity or a kind of written work, and as titles for his own writings. Other emphasis follows the first edition. Vorländer and Ak, following current German typography, emphasize all names of persons; the first edition did not, and it has been followed without further note. Bold font shows Kant's double stress, and his stress on *Noumena* in its germanized form (originally printed in gothic rather than roman), found in the Third Part.

Prolegomena to any future metaphysics
that will be able to come forward as science

Contents[a]

---

[a] This table of contents has been constructed from the section titles. The original editions
did not contain a table of contents.

These prolegomena are not for the use of apprentices, but of future teachers, and indeed are not to help them to organize the presentation of an already existing science, but to discover this science itself for the first time.

There are scholars for whom the history of philosophy (ancient as well as modern) is itself their philosophy; the present prolegomena have not been written for them. They must wait until those who endeavor to draw from the wellsprings of reason itself have finished their business, and then it will be their turn to bring news of these events to the world. Otherwise, in their opinion nothing can be said that has not already been said before; and in fact this opinion can stand for all time as an infallible prediction, for since the human understanding has wandered over countless subjects in various ways through many centuries, it can hardly fail that for anything new something old should be found that has some similarity to it.

My intention is to convince all of those who find it worthwhile to occupy themselves with metaphysics that it is unavoidably necessary to suspend their work for the present, to consider all that has happened until now as if it had not happened, and before all else to pose the question: "whether such a thing as metaphysics is even possible at all."

If metaphysics is a science, why is it that it cannot, like other sciences, attain universal and lasting acclaim? If it is not, how does it happen that, under the pretense of a science it incessantly shows off, and strings along the human understanding with hopes that never dim but are never fulfilled? Whether, therefore, we demonstrate our knowledge or our ignorance, for once we must arrive at something certain concerning the nature of this self-proclaimed science; for things cannot possibly remain on their present footing. It seems almost laughable that, while every other science makes continuous progress, metaphysics, which desires to be wisdom itself, and which everyone consults as an oracle, perpetually turns round on the same spot without coming a step further. Furthermore, it has lost a great many of its adherents, and one does not find that those who feel strong enough to shine in other sciences wish to risk their reputations in this one, where anyone, usually ignorant in all other things, lays claim to a decisive opinion, since in this region there are

4: 256

---

[a] Section heading supplied, with Vorländer, by analogy with *Vorrede* in A/B.

in fact still no reliable weights and measures with which to distinguish profundity from shallow babble.

It is, after all, not completely unheard of, after long cultivation of a science, that in considering with wonder how much progress has been made someone should finally allow the question to arise: whether and how such a science is possible at all. For human reason is so keen on building that more than once it has previously erected a tower, but has afterwards torn it down again in order to see how well constituted its foundation may have been. It is never too late to grow reasonable and wise; but if the insight comes late, it is always harder to bring it into play.

To ask whether a science might in fact be possible assumes a doubt about its actuality.[a] Such a doubt, though, offends everyone whose entire belongings may perhaps consist in this supposed jewel; hence he who allows this doubt to develop had better prepare for opposition from all sides. Some, with their metaphysical compendia in hand, will look down on him with scorn, in proud consciousness of their ancient, and hence ostensibly legitimate, possession; others, who nowhere see anything that is not similar to something they have seen somewhere else before, will not understand him; and for a time everything will remain as if nothing at all had happened that might yield fear or hope of an impending change.

Nevertheless I venture to predict that the reader of these prolegomena who thinks for himself will not only come to doubt his previous science, but subsequently will be fully convinced that there can be no such science unless the requirements expressed here, on which its possibility rests, are met, and, as this has never yet been done, that there is as yet no metaphysics at all. Since, however, the demand for it can never be exhausted,[*] because the interest of human reason in general is much too intimately interwoven with it, the reader will admit that a complete reform or rather a rebirth of metaphysics, according to a plan completely unknown before now, is inevitably approaching, however much it may be resisted in the meantime.[1]

Since the Essays of *Locke*[2] and *Leibniz*,[3] or rather since the rise of metaphysics as far as the history of it reaches, no event has occurred that could have been more decisive with respect to the fate of this science than the attack made upon it by *David Hume*.[4] He brought no light to this kind of knowledge,[c] but he certainly struck a spark from which a

---

* Rusticus exspectat, dum defluat amnis, at ille
  Labitur et labetur in omne volubilis aevum. Horace.[b]

[a] *Wirklichkeit*
[b] "A rustic waits for the river to flow away, but it flows on, and will so flow for all eternity."
   Horace, *Epistles*, I.ii.42–3.
[c] *Erkenntniss*

light could well have been kindled, if it had hit some welcoming tinder whose glow had then been carefully kept going and made to grow.

Hume started mainly from a single but important concept in metaphysics, namely, that of the *connection*[a] *of cause and effect* (and of course also its derivative concepts, of force and action, etc.), and called upon reason, which pretends to have generated this concept in her womb, to give him an account of by what right she thinks: that something could be so constituted that, if it is posited, something else necessarily must thereby be posited as well; for that is what the concept of cause says. He undisputably proved that it is wholly impossible for reason to think such a connection[b] *a priori* and from concepts, because this connection contains necessity; and it is simply not to be seen how it could be, that because something is, something else necessarily must also be, and therefore how the concept of such a connection[c] could be introduced *a priori*. From this he concluded that reason completely and fully deceives herself with this concept, falsely taking it for her own child, when it is really nothing but a bastard of the imagination, which, impregnated by experience, and having brought certain representations under the law of association, passes off the resulting subjective necessity (i.e., habit) for an objective necessity (from insight).[5] From which he concluded that reason has no power at all to think such connections, not even merely in general, because its concepts would then be bare fictions, and all of its cognitions allegedly established *a priori* would be nothing but falsely marked ordinary experiences; which is as much as to say that there is no metaphysics at all, and cannot be any.*

4: 258

As premature and erroneous as his conclusion was, nevertheless it was at least founded on inquiry, and this inquiry was of sufficient value, that the best minds of his time might have come together to solve (more happily if possible) the problem in the sense in which he presented it, from which a complete reform of the science must soon have arisen.

---

* All the same, *Hume* named this destructive philosophy itself metaphysics and placed great value on it. "Metaphysics and morals," he said (*Essays*, 4th pt., p. 214, German translation), "are the most important branches of science; mathematics and natural science are not worth half so much."[6] The acute man was, however, looking only to the negative benefit that curbing the excessive claims of speculative reason would have, in completely abolishing so many endless and continual conflicts that perplex the human species; he meanwhile lost sight of the positive harm that results if reason is deprived of the most important vistas, from which alone it can stake out for the will the highest goal of all the will's endeavors.

[a] *Verknüpfung*
[b] *Verbindung*
[c] *Verknüpfung*

But fate, ever ill-disposed toward metaphysics, would have it that Hume was[a] understood by no one. One cannot, without feeling a certain pain, behold how utterly and completely his opponents, *Reid, Oswald, Beattie*, and finally *Priestley*,[7] missed the point of his problem, and misjudged his hints for improvement – constantly taking for granted just what he doubted, and, conversely, proving with vehemence and, more often than not, with great insolence exactly what it had never entered his mind to doubt – so that everything remained in its old condition, as if nothing had happened. The question was not, whether the concept of cause is right, useful, and, with respect to all cognition of nature, indispensable, for this Hume had never put in doubt; it was rather whether it is thought through reason *a priori*, and in this way has an inner truth independent of all experience, and therefore also a much more widely extended use which is not limited merely to objects of experience: regarding this *Hume* awaited enlightenment.[b] The discussion was only about the origin of this concept, not about its indispensability in use; if the former were only discovered, the conditions of its use and the sphere in which it can be valid would already be given.

In order to do justice to the problem, however, the opponents of this celebrated man would have had to penetrate very deeply into the nature of reason so far as it is occupied solely with pure thought, something that did not suit them. They therefore found a more expedient means to be obstinate without any insight, namely, the appeal to *ordinary common sense*.[c] It is in fact a great gift from heaven to possess right (or, as it has recently been called, plain)[c] common sense. But it must be proven through deeds, by the considered and reasonable things one thinks and says, and not by appealing to it as an oracle when one knows of nothing clever to advance in one's defense. To appeal to ordinary common sense when insight and science run short, and not before, is one of the subtle discoveries of recent times, whereby the dullest windbag can confidently take on the most profound thinker and hold his own with him. So long as a small residue of insight remains, however, one would do well to avoid resorting to this emergency help. And seen in the light of day, this appeal is nothing other than a call to the judgment of the multitude; applause at which the philosopher blushes, but at which the popular wag becomes triumphant and defiant. I should think, however, that *Hume* could lay just as much claim to sound common sense[d] as *Beattie*, and on top of this to something that the latter certainly did not possess, namely, a critical reason, which keeps ordinary common sense in check, so that

4: 259

---

[a] Reading *wurde* for *würde*, with Ak.
[b] *Eröffnung*
[c] *gemeinen Menschenverstand*
[d] *gesunden Verstand*

it doesn't lose itself in speculations, or, if these are the sole topic of discussion, doesn't want to decide anything, since it doesn't understand the justification for its own principles; for only so will it remain sound common sense. Hammer and chisel are perfectly fine for working raw lumber, but for copperplate one must use an etching needle.[9] Likewise, sound common sense and speculative understanding are both useful, but each in its own way; the one, when it is a matter of judgments that find their immediate application in experience, the other, however, when judgments are to be made in a universal mode, out of mere concepts, as in metaphysics, where what calls itself (but often *per antiphrasin*)[a] sound common sense has no judgment whatsoever.

4: 260

I freely admit that the remembrance of *David Hume* was the very thing that many years ago first interrupted my dogmatic slumber[10] and gave a completely different direction to my researches in the field of speculative philosophy. I was very far from listening to him with respect to his conclusions, which arose solely because he did not completely set out his problem but only touched on a part of it, which, without the whole being taken into account, can provide no enlightenment.[b] If we begin from a well-grounded though undeveloped thought that another bequeaths us, then we can well hope, by continued reflection, to take it further than could the sagacious man whom one has to thank for the first spark of this light.

So I tried first whether *Hume's* objection might not be presented in a general manner, and I soon found that the concept of the connection of cause and effect is far from being the only concept through which the understanding thinks connections of things *a priori*; rather, metaphysics consists wholly of such concepts. I sought to ascertain their number, and once I had successfully attained this in the way I wished, namely from a single principle, I proceeded to the deduction of these concepts, from which I henceforth became assured that they were not, as *Hume* had feared, derived from experience, but had arisen from the pure understanding. This deduction, which appeared impossible to my sagacious predecessor, and which had never even occurred to anyone but him, even though everyone confidently made use of these concepts without asking what their objective validity is based on – this deduction, I say, was the most difficult thing that could ever be undertaken on behalf of metaphysics; and the worst thing about it is that metaphysics, as much of it as might be present anywhere at all, could not give me the slightest help with this, because this very deduction must first settle the possibility of a metaphysics. As I had now succeeded in the solution of the Humean problem not only in a single case but with respect to the entire faculty of

[a] "by way of expression through the opposite"
[b] *Auskunft*

4: 261 pure reason, I could therefore take sure, if still always slow, steps toward finally determining, completely and according to universal principles, the entire extent of pure reason with regard to its boundaries as well as its content, which was indeed the very thing that metaphysics requires in order to build its system according to a sure plan.

But I fear that the *elaboration* of the Humean problem in its greatest possible amplification (namely, the *Critique of Pure Reason*) may well fare just as the *problem* itself fared when it was first posed. It will be judged incorrectly, because it is not understood; it will not be understood, because people will be inclined just to skim through the book, but not to think through it; and they will not want to expend this effort on it, because the work is dry, because it is obscure, because it opposes all familiar concepts and is long-winded as well. Now I admit that I do not expect to hear complaints from a philosopher regarding lack of popularity, entertainment, and ease, when the matter concerns the existence of highly prized knowledge that is indispensable to humanity, knowledge that cannot be constituted except according to the strictest rules of scholarly exactitude, and to which popularity may indeed come with time but can never be there at the start. But with regard to a certain obscurity – arising in part from the expansiveness of the plan, which makes it difficult to survey the main points upon which the investigation depends – in this respect the complaint is just; and I will redress it through the present *Prolegomena*.[a]

The previous work, which presents the faculty of pure reason in its entire extent and boundaries, thereby always remains the foundation to which the *Prolegomena* refer only as preparatory exercises; for this *Critique* must stand forth as science, systematic and complete to its smallest parts, before one can think of permitting metaphysics to come forward, or even of forming only a distant hope for metaphysics.

We have long been accustomed to seeing old, threadbare cognitions newly trimmed by being taken from their previous connections and fitted out by someone in a systematic garb of his own preferred cut, but under new titles; and most readers will beforehand expect nothing else from the *Critique*. Yet these *Prolegomena* will bring them to un-

4: 262 derstand that there exists a completely new science, of which no one had previously formed so much as the thought, of which even the bare idea was unknown, and for which nothing from all that has been provided before now could be used except the hint that *Hume's* doubts had been able to give; Hume also foresaw nothing of any such possible formal science, but deposited his ship on the beach (of skepticism) for safekeeping,[11] where it could then lie and rot, whereas it is important to me to give it a pilot, who, provided with complete sea-charts and a compass, might safely navigate the ship wherever seems good to him,

---

[a] Emphasis in original.

following sound principles of the helmsman's art drawn from a knowledge of the globe.

To approach a new science – one that is entirely isolated and is the only one of its kind – with the prejudice that it can be judged by means of one's putative cognitions already otherwise obtained, even though it is precisely the reality of those that must first be completely called into question, results only in believing that one sees everywhere something that was already otherwise known, because the expressions perhaps sound similar; except that everything must seem to be extremely deformed, contradictory, and nonsensical, because one does not thereby make the author's thoughts fundamental, but always simply one's own, made natural through long habit. Yet the copiousness of the work, insofar as it is rooted in the science itself and not in the presentation, and the inevitable dryness and scholastic exactitude that result, are qualities that indeed may be extremely advantageous to the subject matter itself, but must of course be detrimental to the book itself.

It is not given to everyone to write so subtly and yet also so alluringly as *David Hume*, or so profoundly and at the same time so elegantly as *Moses Mendelssohn*;[12] but I could well have given my presentation popularity (as I flatter myself) if all I had wanted to do was to sketch a plan and to commend its execution to others, and had I not taken to heart the well-being of the science that kept me occupied for so long; for after all it requires great perseverance and also indeed not a little self-denial to set aside the enticement of an earlier, favorable reception for the expectation of an admittedly later, but lasting approval.

To make plans is most often a presumptuous, boastful mental preoccupation, through which one presents the appearance of creative genius, in that one requires what one cannot provide oneself, censures what one cannot do better, and proposes what one does not know how to attain oneself – though merely for a sound plan for a general critique of reason, somewhat more than might be expected would already have been required if it were not, as is usual, to be merely a recitation of idle wishes. But pure reason is such an isolated domain, within itself so thoroughly connected, that no part of it can be encroached upon without disturbing all the rest, nor adjusted without having previously determined for each part its place and its influence on the others; for, since there is nothing outside of it that could correct our judgment within it, the validity and use of each part depends on the relation in which it[a] stands to the others within reason itself, and, as with the structure of an organized body, the purpose of any member can be derived only from the complete concept of the whole. That is why it can be said of such a critique, that it is never trustworthy unless it is *entirely complete* down to the least elements of

4: 263

---

[a] Reading *er* for *es*, with Ak.

pure reason, and that in the domain of this faculty one must determine and settle either *all* or *nothing*.

But although a mere plan that might precede the *Critique of Pure Reason* would be unintelligible, undependable, and useless, it is by contrast all the more useful if it comes after. For one will thereby be put in the position to survey the whole, to test one by one the main points at issue in this science, and to arrange many things in the exposition better than could be done in the first execution of the work.

Here then is such a *plan* subsequent to the completed work, which now can be laid out according to the *analytic method,[a]* whereas the *work* itself absolutely had to be composed according to the *synthetic method,[b]* so that the science might present all of its articulations, as the structural organization of a quite peculiar faculty of cognition, in their natural connection.[13] Whosoever finds this plan itself, which I send ahead as prolegomena for any future metaphysics, still obscure, may consider that it simply is not necessary for everyone to study metaphysics, that there are some talents that proceed perfectly well in fundamental and even deep sciences that are closer to intuition, but that will not succeed in the investigation of purely abstract concepts, and that in such a case one should apply one's mental gifts to another object; that, however, whosoever undertakes to judge or indeed to construct a metaphysics, must thoroughly satisfy the challenge made here, whether it happens that they accept my solution, or fundamentally reject it and replace it with another – for they cannot dismiss it; and finally, that the much decried obscurity (a familiar cloaking for one's own indolence or dimwittedness) has its use as well, since everybody, who with respect to all other sciences observes a wary silence, speaks masterfully, and boldly passes judgment in questions of metaphysics, because here to be sure their ignorance does not stand out clearly in relation to the science of others, but in relation to genuine critical principles, which therefore can be praised:

4: 264

> *Ignavum, fucos, pecus a praesepibus arcent. Virg.[c]*

[a] *analytischer Methode*
[b] *synthetischer Lehrart*
[c] "They protect the hives from the drones, an idle bunch." Virgil, *Georgica*, IV.168.

Preamble
on the
Distinguishing Feature of All
Metaphysical Cognition

---

§1
On the sources of metaphysics

If one wishes to present a body of cognition as *science*,*ᵃ* then one must first be able to determine precisely the differentia it has in common with no other science, and which is therefore its *distinguishing feature*; otherwise the boundaries of all the sciences run together, and none of them can be dealt with thoroughly according to its own nature.

Whether this distinguishing feature consists in a difference of the *object* or the *source of cognition*, or even of the *type of cognition*, or several if not all of these things together, the idea of the possible science and its territory depends first of all upon it.

First, concerning the *sources* of metaphysical cognition, it already lies in the concept of metaphysics that they cannot be empirical. The principles*ᵇ* of such cognition (which include not only its fundamental propositions,*ᶜ* but also its fundamental concepts) must therefore never be taken from experience; for the cognition is supposed to be not physical but metaphysical, i.e., lying beyond experience. Therefore it will be based upon neither outer experience, which constitutes the source of physics proper, nor inner, which provides the foundation of empirical psychology. It is therefore cognition *a priori*, or from pure understanding and pure reason.

In this, however, there would be nothing to differentiate it from pure mathematics; it must therefore be denominated *pure philosophical cognition*; but concerning the meaning of this expression I refer to the *Critique of Pure Reason*, pp. 712 f.,[14] where the distinction between these two types of use of reason has been presented clearly and sufficiently. – So much on the sources of metaphysical cognition.[15]

ᵃ *eine Erkenntniss als Wissenschaft*
ᵇ *Principien*
ᶜ *Grundsätze*

§2
On the type of cognition,
that alone can be called metaphysical
(a) On the distinction between synthetic and analytic
judgments in general

Metaphysical cognition must contain nothing but judgments *a priori*, as required by the distinguishing feature of its sources. But judgments may have any origin whatsoever, or be constituted in whatever manner according to their logical form, and yet there is nonetheless a distinction between them according to their content, by dint of which they are either merely *explicative* and add nothing to the content of the cognition, or *ampliative* and augment the given cognition; the first may be called *analytic* judgments, the second *synthetic*.

Analytic judgments say nothing in the predicate except what was actually thought already in the concept of the subject, though not so clearly nor with the same consciousness. If I say: All bodies are extended, then I have not in the least amplified my concept of body, but have merely resolved it, since extension, although not explicitly said of the former concept prior to the judgment, nevertheless was actually thought of it; the judgment is therefore analytic. By contrast, the proposition: Some bodies are heavy, contains something in the predicate that is not actually thought in the general concept of body; it therefore augments my cognition, since it adds something to my concept, and must therefore be called a synthetic judgment.[16]

4: 267

(b) The common principle[a] of all analytic judgments
is the principle of contradiction

All analytic judgments rest entirely on the principle of contradiction and are by their nature *a priori* cognitions, whether the concepts that serve for their material be empirical or not. For since the predicate of an affirmative analytic judgment is already thought beforehand in the concept of the subject, it cannot be denied of that subject without contradiction; exactly so is its opposite necessarily denied of the subject in an analytic, but negative, judgment, and indeed also according to the principle of contradiction. So it stands with the propositions: Every body is extended, and: No body is unextended (simple).

For that reason all analytic propositions are still *a priori* judgments even if their concepts are empirical, as in: Gold is a yellow metal; for in order to know this, I need no further experience outside my concept of gold, which includes that this body is yellow and a metal; for this

[a] *Princip*

constitutes my very concept, and I did not have to do anything except analyze it, without looking beyond it to something else.[17]

(c) Synthetic judgments require a principle other than the principle of contradiction

There are synthetic judgments *a posteriori* whose origin is empirical; but there are also synthetic judgments that are *a priori* certain and that arise from pure understanding and reason. Both however agree in this, that they can by no means arise solely from the principle[a] of analysis, namely the principle of contradiction; they demand yet a completely different principle,[b] though they always must be derived from some fundamental proposition,[c] whichever it may be, *in accordance with the principle of contradiction*; for nothing can run counter to this principle, even though everything cannot be derived from it. I shall first classify the synthetic judgments.

1. *Judgments of experience* are always synthetic. For it would be ab-   4: 268
surd to base an analytic judgment on experience, since I do not at all need to go beyond my concept in order to formulate the judgment and therefore have no need for any testimony from experience. That a body is extended, is a proposition that stands certain *a priori*, and not a judgment of experience. For before I go to experience, I have all the conditions for my judgment already in the concept, from which I merely extract the predicate in accordance with the principle of contradiction, and by this means can simultaneously become conscious of the *necessity* of the judgment, which experience could never teach me.

2. *Mathematical judgments* are one and all synthetic. This proposition appears to have completely escaped the observations of analysts of human reason up to the present, and indeed to be directly opposed to all of their conjectures, although it is incontrovertibly certain and very important in its consequences. Because they found that the inferences of the mathematicians all proceed in accordance with the principle of contradiction (which, by nature, is required of any apodictic certainty), they were persuaded that even the fundamental propositions were known through the principle of contradiction, in which they were very mistaken; for a synthetic proposition can of course be discerned in accordance with the principle of contradiction, but only insofar as another synthetic propositions is presupposed from which the first can be deduced, never however in itself.

[a] *Grundsatze*
[b] *Princip*
[c] *Grundsatze*

First of all it must be observed: that properly mathematical propositions are always *a priori* and not empirical judgments, because they carry
necessity with them, which cannot be taken from experience. But if this
will not be granted me, very well, I will restrict my proposition to *pure
mathematics*, the concept of which already conveys that it contains not
empirical but only pure cognition *a priori*.

One might well at first think: that the proposition $7 + 5 = 12$ is a
purely analytical proposition that follows from the concept of a sum
of seven and five according to the principle of contradiction. However,
upon closer inspection, one finds that the concept of the sum of 7 and
5 contains nothing further than the unification of the two numbers into
one, through which by no means is thought what this single number may
be that combines the two. The concept of twelve is in no way already
thought because I merely think to myself this unification of seven and
five, and I may analyze my concept of such a possible sum for as long as
4: 269   may be, still I will not meet with twelve therein. One must go beyond
these concepts, in making use of the intuition that corresponds to one of
the two, such as one's five fingers, or (like *Segner* in his arithmetic)[18] five
points, and in that manner adding the units of the five given in intuition
step by step to the concept of seven. One therefore truly amplifies one's
concept through this proposition $7 + 5 = 12$ and adds to the first concept
a new one that was not thought in it; that is, an arithmetical proposition
is always synthetic, which can be seen all the more plainly in the case
of somewhat larger numbers, for it is then clearly evident that, though
we may turn and twist our concept as we like, we could never find the
sum through the mere analysis of our concepts, without making use of
intuition.

Nor is any fundamental proposition of pure geometry analytic. That
the straight line between two points is the shortest is a synthetic proposition. For my concept of the straight contains nothing of magnitude,[a]
but only a quality. The concept of the shortest is therefore wholly an
addition and cannot be extracted by any analysis from the concept of the
straight line. Intuition must therefore be made use of here, by means of
which alone the synthesis is possible.

Some other fundamental propositions that geometers presuppose
are indeed actually analytic and rest on the principle of contradiction; however, they serve only, like identical propositions, as links in
the chain of method and not as[b] principles: e.g., a = a, the whole is
equal to itself, or (a + b) > a, i.e., the whole is greater than its part.
And indeed even these, although they are valid from concepts alone,

---

[a] *Grösse*
[b] Reading *als* for *aus*, with Ak (and B 17).

are admitted into mathematics only because they can be exhibited in intuition.[a]

It is merely ambiguity of expression which makes us commonly believe here that the predicate of such apodictic judgments already lies in our concept and that the judgment is therefore analytic. Namely, we *are re-quired*[b] to add in thought a particular predicate to a given concept, and this necessity is already attached to the concepts. But the question is not, what we *are required to add in thought* to a given concept, but what we *actually think* in it,[c] even if only obscurely, and then it becomes evident that the predicate attaches to such concepts indeed necessarily, though not immediately, but rather through an intuition that has to be added.[d]

The essential feature of pure *mathematical* cognition, differentiating it from all other *a priori* cognition, is that it must throughout proceed *not from concepts*, but always and only through the construction of concepts (*Critique*, p. 713).[19] Because pure mathematical cognition, in its propositions, must therefore go beyond the concept to that which is contained in the intuition corresponding to it, its propositions can and must never arise through the analysis of concepts, i.e., analytically, and so are one and all synthetic.[20]

4: 272

I cannot, however, refrain from noting the damage that neglect of this otherwise seemingly insignificant and unimportant observation has brought upon philosophy. *Hume*, when he felt the call, worthy of a philosopher, to cast his gaze over the entire field of pure *a priori* cognition, in which the human understanding claims such vast holdings, inadvertently lopped off a whole (and indeed the most considerable) province of the same, namely pure mathematics, by imagining that the nature and so to speak the legal constitution of this province rested on completely different principles, namely solely on the principle of contradiction; and although he had by no means made a classification of propositions so formally and generally, or with such nomenclature, as I have here, it was nonetheless just as if he had said: Pure mathematics contains only *analytic* propositions, but metaphysics contains synthetic propositions *a priori*. Now he erred severely in this, and this error had decisively damaging consequences for his entire conception. For had he not done this, he would have expanded his question about the origin of our synthetic judgments far beyond his metaphysical concept of causality and extended

---

[a] Paragraph break added to reflect continuity of the new paragraph with the three paragraphs prior to the preceding two sentences.

[b] *sollen*

[c] Reading *ihm* for *ihnen*, with Ak (and B 17).

[d] The following five paragraphs are taken from §4 in accordance with the Vaihinger-Sitzler galley-switching thesis (see Translator's Introduction).

it also to the possibility of *a priori* mathematics; for he would have had to accept mathematics as synthetic as well. But then he would by no means have been able to found his metaphysical propositions on mere experience, for otherwise he would have had to subject the axioms of pure mathematics to experience as well, which he was much too reasonable to do.[21] The good company in which metaphysics would then have come to be situated would have secured it against the danger of scornful mistreatment; for the blows that were intended for the latter would have had to strike the former as well, which was not his intention, and could not have been; and so the acute man would have been drawn into reflections which must have been similar to those with which we are now occupied, but which would have gained infinitely from his inimitably fine presentation.[22]

3.[a] *Properly metaphysical* judgments are one and all synthetic. Judgments belonging *to metaphysics* must be distinguished from properly *metaphysical* judgments. Very many among the former are analytic, but they merely provide the means to metaphysical judgments, toward which the aim of the science is completely directed, and which are always synthetic. For if concepts belong to metaphysics, e.g., that of substance, then necessarily the judgments arising from their mere analysis belong to metaphysics as well, e.g., substance is that which exists only as subject, etc., and through several such analytic judgments we try to approach the definition of those concepts. Since, however, the analysis of a pure concept of the understanding (such as metaphysics contains) does not proceed in a different manner from the analysis of any other, even empirical, concept which does not belong to metaphysics (e.g., air is an elastic fluid, the elasticity of which is not lost with any known degree of cold), therefore the concept may indeed be properly metaphysical, but not the analytic judgment; for this science possesses something special and proper to it in the generation of its *a priori* cognitions, which generation must therefore be distinguished from what this science has in common with all other cognitions of the understanding; thus, e.g., the proposition: All that is substance in things persists, is a synthetic and properly metaphysical proposition.

If one has previously assembled, according to fixed principles, the *a priori* concepts that constitute the material of metaphysics and its tools, then the analysis of these concepts is of great value; it can even be pre-

sented apart from all the synthetic propositions that constitute metaphysics itself, as a special part (as it were a *philosophia definitiva*)[23] containing nothing but analytic propositions belonging to metaphysics. For in fact such analyses do not have much use anywhere except in metaphysics,

---

[a] The numeral three is added in accordance with the Vaihinger–Sitzler thesis.

i.e., with a view toward the synthetic propositions that are to be generated from such previously analyzed concepts.

The conclusion of this section is therefore: that metaphysics properly has to do with synthetic propositions *a priori*, and these alone constitute its aim, for which it indeed requires many analyses of its concepts (therefore many analytic judgments), in which analyses, though, the procedure is no different from that in any other type of cognition when one seeks simply to make its concepts clear through analysis. But the *generation* of cognition *a priori* in accordance with both intuition and concepts, ultimately of synthetic propositions *a priori* as well, and specifically in philosophical cognition, forms[a] the essential content of metaphysics.

§3
Note on the general division of judgments into analytic and synthetic

4: 270

This division is indispensable with regard to the critique of human understanding, and therefore deserves to be *classical* in it; other than that I don't know that it has much utility anywhere else. And in this I find the reason why dogmatic philosophers (who always sought the sources of metaphysical judgments only in metaphysics itself, and not outside it in the pure laws of reason in general) neglected this division, which appears to come forward of itself, and, like the famous *Wolf*, or the acute *Baumgarten* following in his footsteps, could try to find the proof of the principle of sufficient reason, which obviously is synthetic, in the principle of contradiction.[24] By contrast I find a hint of this division already in *Locke's* essays on human understanding. For in Book IV, Chapter III, §9 f., after he had already discussed the various connections of representations[b] in judgments and the sources of the connections, of which he located the one in identity or contradiction (analytic judgments) but the other in the existence of representations in a subject (synthetic judgments), he then acknowledges in §10 that our cognition (*a priori*) of these last is very constricted and almost nothing at all.[25] But there is so little that is definite and reduced to rules in what he says about this type of cognition, that it is no wonder if no one, and in particular not even *Hume*, was prompted by it to contemplate propositions of this type.[26] For such general yet nonetheless definite principles are not easily learned from others who have only had them floating obscurely before them. One must first have

---

[a] Reading *macht* for *machen*, with Vorländer.
[b] *Vorstellungen*, translated as "representations" here as elsewhere, even though corresponding to Locke's word "ideas." German translators of philosophy at this time tended to avoid the loan word "*Idee*," usually rendering the English "idea" as *Begriff* (on which, see Poley's translation of the *Essay*, his n. 6, on p. 8).

come to them oneself through one's own reflection, after which one also finds them elsewhere, where one certainly would not have found them before, because the authors did not even know themselves that their own remarks were grounded on such an idea. Those who never think for themselves in this way nevertheless possess the quick-sightedness to spy everything, after it has been shown to them, in what has already been said elsewhere, where no one at all could see it before.

§4

If a metaphysics that could assert itself as science were actual, if one could say: here is metaphysics, you need only to learn it, and it will convince you of its truth irresistibly and immutably, then this question would be unnecessary, and there would remain only that question which would pertain more to a test of our acuteness than to a proof of the existence of the subject matter itself, namely: *how it is possible*, and how reason should set about attaining it. Now it has not gone so well for human reason in this case. One can point to no single book, as for instance one presents a *Euclid*, and say: this is metaphysics, here you will find the highest aim of this science, knowledge*ᵃ* of a supreme being and a future life, proven from principles of pure reason. For one can indeed show us many propositions that are apodictically certain and have never been disputed; but they are one and all analytic and pertain more to the materials and implements of metaphysics than to the expansion of knowledge, which after all ought to be our real aim for it. (§2c) But although you present synthetic propositions as well (e.g., the principle of sufficient reason), which you have never proven from bare reason and consequently *a priori*, as was indeed your obligation, and which are gladly ceded to you all the same: then if you want to use them toward your main goal, you still fall into assertions so illicit and precarious that one metaphysics has always contradicted the other, either in regard to the assertions themselves or their proofs, and thereby metaphysics has itself destroyed its claim to lasting approbation. The very attempts to bring such a science into existence were without doubt the original cause of the skepticism that arose so early,²⁷ a mode of thinking in which reason moves against itself with such violence that it never could have arisen except in complete despair as regards satisfaction of reason's most important aims. For long before we began to question nature methodically, we questioned just our iso-   4: 272
lated reason, which already was practiced to a certain extent through common experience: for reason surely is present to us always, but laws of nature must normally be sought out painstakingly; and so metaphysics

ᵃ Erkenntniss

69

was floating at the top like foam, though in such a way that as soon as what had been drawn off had dissolved, more showed itself on the surface, which some always gathered up eagerly, while others, instead of seeking the cause of this phenomenon in the depths, thought themselves wise in mocking the fruitless toil of the former.[a]

4: 274 Weary therefore of dogmatism, which teaches us nothing, and also of skepticism, which promises us absolutely nothing at all, not even the tranquility of a permitted ignorance; summoned by the importance of the knowledge[b] that we need, and made mistrustful, through long experience, with respect to any knowledge that we believe we possess or that offers itself to us under the title of pure reason, there remains left for us but one critical question, the answer to which can regulate our future conduct: *Is metaphysics possible at all?* But this question must not be answered by skeptical objections to particular assertions of an actual metaphysics (for at present we still allow none to be valid), but out of the still *problematic* concept of such a science.

In the *Critique of Pure Reason*[c] I worked on this question *synthetically,*[d] namely by inquiring within pure reason itself, and seeking to determine within this source both the elements and the laws of its pure use, according to principles. This work is difficult and requires a resolute reader to think himself little by little into a system that takes no foundation as given except reason itself, and that therefore tries to develop cognition out of its original seeds without relying on any fact whatever. *Prolegomena*[e] should by contrast be preparatory exercises; they ought more to indicate what needs to be done in order to bring a science into existence if possible,

4: 275 than to present the science itself. They must therefore rely on something already known to be dependable, from which we can go forward with confidence and ascend to the sources, which are not yet known, and whose discovery not only will explain what is known already, but will also exhibit an area with many cognitions that all arise from these same sources. The methodological procedure of prolegomena, and especially of those that are to prepare for a future metaphysics, will therefore be *analytic.*

Fortunately, it happens that, even though we cannot assume that metaphysics as science is *actual*, we can confidently say that some pure synthetic cognition *a priori* is actual and given, namely, *pure mathematics*

---

[a] Here followed the five paragraphs that have been placed in §2 (pp. 65–7), following the Vaihinger–Sitzler thesis.
[b] *Erkenntniss*
[c] Emphasis in original.
[d] Emphasis added.
[e] Emphasis in original.

and *pure natural science*; for both contain propositions that are fully acknowledged, some as apodictically certain through bare reason, some from universal agreement with experience (though these are still recognized as independent of experience). We have therefore some at least *uncontested* synthetic cognition *a priori*, and we do not need to ask whether it is possible (for it is actual), but only: *how it is possible*, in order to be able to derive, from the principle of the possibility of the given cognition, the possibility of all other synthetic cognition *a priori*.

Prolegomena
General Question
How is cognition from pure reason possible?

§5

We have seen above the vast difference between analytic and synthetic judgments. The possibility of analytic propositions could be comprehended very easily; for it is founded solely upon the principle of contradiction. The possibility of synthetic propositions *a posteriori*, i.e., of such as are drawn from experience, also requires no special explanation; for experience itself is nothing other than a continual conjoining (synthesis) of perceptions. There remain for us therefore only synthetic propositions *a priori*, whose possibility must be sought or investigated, since it must rest on principles other than the principle of contradiction.

4: 276 Here, however, we do not need first to seek the *possibility* of such propositions, i.e., to ask whether they are possible. For there are plenty of them actually given, and indeed with indisputable certainty, and since the method we are now following is to be analytic, we will consequently start from the position: that such synthetic but pure rational cognition is actual; but we must nonetheless next *investigate* the ground of this possibility, and ask: *how* this cognition is possible, so that we put ourselves in a position to determine, from the principles of its possibility, the conditions of its use and the extent and boundaries of the same.[28] Expressed with scholastic precision, the exact problem on which everything hinges is therefore:

How are synthetic propositions a priori *possible?*

For the sake of popularity I have expressed this problem somewhat differently above, namely as a question about cognition from pure reason which I could well have done on this occasion without disadvantage for the desired insight; for, since we assuredly have to do here only with metaphysics and its sources, it will, I hope, always be kept in mind, following the earlier reminders, that when we here speak of cognition from pure reason, the discussion is never about analytic cognition, but only synthetic.*

Whether metaphysics is to stand or fall, and hence its existence, now depends entirely on the solving of this problem. Anyone may present his contentions on the matter with ever so great a likelihood, piling conclusion on conclusion to the point of suffocation; if he has not been able beforehand to answer this question satisfactorily then I have the right to say: it is all empty, baseless philosophy and false wisdom. You speak through pure reason and pretend as it were to create *a priori* cognitions, not only by analyzing given concepts, but by alleging new connections that are not based on the principle of contradiction and that you nonetheless presume to understand completely independently of all experience; now how do you come to this, and how will you justify such pretenses? You cannot be allowed to call on the concurrence of general common sense;[b] for that is a witness whose standing is based solely on public rumor. *Quodcunque ostendis mihi sic, incredulus odi.*[c] *Horat.*

4: 277

As indispensable as it is, however, to answer this question, at the same time it is just as difficult; and although the principal reason why the answer has not long since been sought rests in the fact that it had occurred to no one that such a thing could be asked, nonetheless a second reason is that a satisfactory answer to this one question requires more assiduous, deeper, and more painstaking reflection than the most prolix work of metaphysics ever did, which promised its author immortality on its first appearance. Also, every perceptive reader, if he carefully ponders what this problem demands, being frightened at first by its difficulty, is bound to consider it insoluble and, if such pure synthetic cognitions *a*

---

* When knowledge[a] moves forward little by little, it cannot be helped that certain expressions which have already become classical, having been present from the very infancy of science, subsequently should be found insufficient and badly suited, and that a certain newer and more apt usage should fall into danger of being confused with the old one. The analytic method, insofar as it is opposed to the synthetic, is something completely different from a collection of analytic propositions; it signifies only that one proceeds from that which is sought as if it were given, and ascends to the conditions under which alone it is possible. In this method one often uses nothing but synthetic propositions, as mathematical analysis exemplifies, and it might better be called the *regressive* method to distinguish it from the synthetic or *progressive* method. Again the name analytic is also found as a principal division of logic, and there it is the logic of truth and is opposed to dialectic, without actually looking to see whether the cognitions belonging to that logic are analytic or synthetic.

[a] *Erkenntniss*
[b] *allgemeinen Menschenvernunft*
[c] "Whatsoever you show me thusly, unbelieving, I hate it." Horace, *Epistles*, II.3.188.

priori were not actual, altogether impossible; which is what actually befell *David Hume*, although he was far from conceiving the question in such universality as it is here, and as it must be if the reply is to be decisive for all metaphysics. For how is it possible, asked the acute man, that when I am given one concept I can go beyond it and connect another one to it that is not contained in it, and can indeed do so, as though the latter *necessarily* belonged to the former? Only experience can provide us with such connections (so he concluded from this difficulty, which he took for an impossibility), and all of this supposed necessity – or, what is the same – this cognition taken for *a priori*, is nothing but a long-standing habit of finding something to be true and consequently of taking subjective necessity to be objective.

4: 278 　If the reader complains about the toil and trouble that I shall give him with the solution to this problem, he need only make the attempt to solve it more easily himself. Perhaps he will then feel himself obliged to the one who has taken on a task of such profound inquiry for him, and will rather allow himself to express some amazement over the ease with which the solution could still be given, considering the nature of the matter; for indeed it cost years of toil to solve this problem in its full universality[a] (as this word is understood by the mathematicians, namely, as sufficient for all cases), and also ultimately to be able to present it in analytic form, as the reader will find it here.

All metaphysicians are therefore solemnly and lawfully suspended from their occupations until such time as they shall have satisfactorily answered the question: *How are synthetic cognitions* a priori *possible?* For in this answer alone consists the credential which they must present if they have something to advance to us in the name of pure reason; in default of which, however, they can expect only that reasonable persons, who have been deceived so often already, will reject their offerings without any further investigation.

If, on the contrary, they want to put forth their occupation not as *science*, but as an *art* of beneficial persuasions accommodated to general common sense, then they cannot justly be barred from this trade. They will then use the modest language of reasonable belief, they will acknowledge that it is not allowed them even once *to guess*, let alone to *know*,[b] something about that which lies beyond the boundaries of all possible experience, but only *to assume* something about it (not for speculative use, for they must renounce that, but solely for practical use), as is possible and even indispensable for the guidance of the understanding and will in life. Only thus will they be able to call themselves useful and wise men, the more so, the more they renounce the name of metaphysicians;

[a] *Allgemeinheit*
[b] *wissen*

for metaphysicians want to be speculative philosophers, and since one cannot aim for vapid probabilities when judgments *a priori* are at stake (for what is alleged to be cognized *a priori* is thereby announced as necessary), it cannot be permitted them to play with guesses, but rather their assertions must be science or they are nothing at all. 4: 279

It can be said that the whole of transcendental philosophy, which necessarily precedes all of metaphysics, is itself nothing other than simply the complete solution of the question presented here, but in systematic order and detail, and that until now there has therefore been no transcendental philosophy; for what goes under this name is really a part of metaphysics, but this science is to settle the possibility of metaphysics in the first place, and therefore must precede all metaphysics. Hence there need be no surprise because a science is needed that is utterly deprived of assistance from other sciences and hence is in itself completely new, in order just to answer a single question adequately, when the solution to it is conjoined with trouble and difficulty and even with some obscurity.

In now setting to work on this solution – and indeed following the analytic method, in which we presuppose that such cognitions from pure reason are actual – we can appeal to only two *sciences* of theoretical knowledge (which alone is being discussed here), namely, *pure mathematics* and *pure natural science*; for only these can present objects to us in intuition, and consequently, if they happen to contain an *a priori* cognition, can show its truth or correspondence with the object *in concreto*, i.e., *its actuality*, from which one could then proceed along the analytic path to the ground of its possibility. This greatly facilitates the work, in which general considerations are not only applied to facts, but even start from them, instead of, as in the synthetic procedure, having to be derived wholly *in abstracto* from concepts.

But in order to ascend from these pure *a priori* cognitions (which are not only actual but also well-founded) to a possible cognition that we seek – namely, a metaphysics as science – we need to comprehend under our main question that which gives rise to metaphysics and which underlies its purely naturally given (though not above suspicion as regards truth) cognition *a priori* (which cognition, when pursued without any critical investigation of its possibility, is normally called metaphysics already) – in a word, the natural disposition to such a science; and so the main transcendental question, divided into four other questions, will be answered step by step: 4: 280

1. How is pure mathematics possible?
2. How is pure natural science possible?
3. How is metaphysics in general possible?
4. How is metaphysics as science possible?

It can be seen that even if the solution to these problems is intended principally to present the essential content of the *Critique*, still it also possesses something distinctive that is worthy of attention in its own right, namely, the search for the sources of given sciences in reason itself, in order to investigate and to measure out for reason, by way of the deed itself, its power to cognize something *a priori*; whereby these sciences themselves then benefit, if not with respect to their content, nonetheless as regards their proper practice, and, while bringing light to a higher question regarding their common origin, they simultaneously provide occasion for a better explanation of their own nature.

Main Transcendental Question,
First Part
How is pure mathematics possible?

§6

Here now is a great and proven body of cognition,[a] which is already of admirable extent and promises unlimited expansion in the future, which carries with it thoroughly apodictic certainty (i.e., absolute necessity), hence rests on no grounds of experience, and so is a pure product of reason, but beyond this is thoroughly synthetic. "How is it possible then for human reason to achieve such cognition wholly *a priori*?" Does not this capacity, since it is not, and cannot be, based on experience, presuppose some *a priori* basis for cognition, which lies deeply hidden, but which might reveal itself through these its effects, if their first beginnings were but diligently tracked down?

§7

4: 281

We find, however, that all mathematical cognition has this distinguishing feature, that it must present its concept beforehand *in intuition* and indeed *a priori*, consequently in an intuition that is not empirical but pure, without which means it cannot take a single step; therefore its judgments are always *intuitive*,[b] in the place of which philosophy can content itself with *discursive* judgments *from mere concepts*, and can indeed exemplify its apodictic teachings through intuition[c] but can never derive them from it. This observation with respect to the nature of mathematics already guides us toward the first and highest condition of its possibility; namely, it must be grounded in some *pure intuition* or other, in which it can present, or, as one calls it, *construct* all of its concepts *in concreto* yet *a priori*.* If we could discover this pure intuition and its possibility, then from there it could easily be explained how synthetic *a priori* propositions are possible in pure mathematics, and consequently also how this science

---

* See *Critique* p. 713.[29]

[a] *eine grosse und bewährte Erkenntniss*
[b] *intuitiv*
[c] *Anschauung*

itself is possible; for just as empirical intuition makes it possible for us, without difficulty, to amplify (synthetically in experience) the concept we form of an object of intuition through new predicates that are presented by intuition itself, so too will pure intuition do the same only with this difference: that in the latter case the synthetic judgment will be *a priori* certain and apodictic, but in the former only *a posteriori* and empirically certain, because the former contains only what is met with in contingent empirical intuition, while the latter contains what necessarily must be met with in pure intuition, since it is, as intuition *a priori*, inseparably bound with the concept *before all experience* or individual perception.

§8

But with this step the difficulty seems to grow rather than to diminish. For now the question runs: *How is it possible to intuit something* a priori? An intuition is a representation of the sort which would depend immediately on the presence of an object. It therefore seems impossible *originally* to intuit *a priori*, since then the intuition would have to occur without an object being present, either previously or now, to which it could refer, and so it could not be an intuition. Concepts are indeed of the kind that we can quite well form some of them for ourselves *a priori* (namely, those that contain only the thinking of an object in general) without our being in an immediate relation to an object, e.g., the concept of quantity, of cause, etc.; but even these still require, in order to provide them with signification and sense, a certain use *in concreto*, i.e., application to some intuition or other, by which an object for them is given to us. But how can the *intuition* of an object precede the object itself?

4: 282

§9

If our intuition had to be of the kind that represented things *as they are in themselves*, then absolutely no intuition *a priori* would take place, but it would always be empirical. For I can only know what may be contained in the object in itself if the object is present and given to me. Of course, even then it is incomprehensible how the intuition of a thing that is present should allow me to cognize it the way it is in itself, since its properties cannot migrate over into my power of representation; but even granting such a possibility, the intuition still would not take place *a priori*, i.e., before the object were presented to me, for without that no basis for the relation of my representation to the object can be conceived; so it would have to be based on inspiration. There is therefore only one way possible for my intuition to precede the actuality of the object and occur as an *a priori* cognition, *namely if it contains nothing else except the form of sensibility, which in me as subject precedes all actual impressions through which*

I am affected by objects. For I can know *a priori* that the objects of the senses can be intuited only in accordance with this form of sensibility. From this it follows: that propositions which relate merely to this form of sensory intuition will be possible and valid for objects of the senses; also, conversely, that intuitions which are possible *a priori* can never relate to things other than objects of our senses.

§10

4: 283

Therefore it is only by means of the form of sensory intuition that we can intuit things *a priori*, though by this means we can cognize objects only as they *appear* to us (to our senses), not as they may be in themselves; and this supposition is utterly necessary, if synthetic propositions *a priori* are to be granted as possible, or, in case they are actually encountered, if their possibility is to be conceived and determined in advance.

Now space and time are the intuitions upon which pure mathematics bases all its cognitions and judgments, which come forward as at once apodictic and necessary; for mathematics must first exhibit all of its concepts in intuition – and pure mathematics in pure intuition – i.e., it must first construct them, failing which (since mathematics cannot proceed analytically, namely, through the analysis of concepts, but only*a* synthetically) it is impossible for it to advance a step, that is, as long as it lacks pure intuition, in which alone the material*b* for synthetic judgments *a priori* can be given. Geometry bases itself on the pure intuition of space. Even arithmetic forms its concepts of numbers through successive addition of units in time, but above all pure mechanics can form its concepts of motion only by means of the representation of time.[30] Both representations are, however, merely intuitions; for, if one eliminates from the empirical intuitions of bodies and their alterations (motion) everything empirical, that is, that which belongs to sensation, then space and time still remain, which are therefore pure intuitions that underlie *a priori* the empirical intuitions, and for that reason can never themselves be eliminated; but, by the very fact that they are pure intuitions *a priori*, they prove that they are mere forms of our sensibility that must precede all empirical intuition (i.e., the perception of actual objects), and in accordance with which objects can be cognized *a priori*, though of course only as they appear to us.

§11

The problem of the present section is therefore solved. Pure mathematics, as synthetic cognition *a priori*, is possible only because it refers to

a Adding *nur*, with Vorländer.
b *Stoff*

4: 284 no other objects than mere objects of the senses, the empirical intuition of which is based on a pure and indeed *a priori* intuition (of space and time), and can be so based because this pure intuition is nothing but the mere form of sensibility, which precedes the actual appearance of objects, since it in fact first makes this appearance possible. This faculty of intuiting *a priori* does not, however, concern the matter of appearance – i.e., that which is sensation in the appearance, for that constitutes the empirical – but only the form of appearance, space and time. If anyone wishes to doubt in the slightest that the two are[a] not determinations inhering in things in themselves but only mere determinations inhering in the relation of those things to sensibility, I would very much like to know how he can find it possible to know, *a priori* and therefore before all acquaintance with things, how their intuition must be constituted – which certainly is the case here with space and time. But this is completely comprehensible as soon as the two are taken for nothing more than formal conditions of our sensibility, and objects are taken merely for appearances; for then the form of appearance, i.e., the pure intuition, certainly can be represented from ourselves, i.e., *a priori*.

§12

In order to add something by way of illustration and confirmation, we need only to consider the usual and unavoidably necessary procedure of the geometers. All proofs of the thoroughgoing equality of two given figures (that one can in all parts be put in the place of the other) ultimately come down to this: that they are congruent with one another; which plainly is nothing other than a synthetic proposition based upon immediate intuition; and this intuition must be given pure and *a priori*, for otherwise that proposition could not be granted as apodictically certain but would have only empirical certainty. It would only mean: we observe it always to be so and the proposition holds only as far as our perception has reached until now. That full-standing space (a space that is itself not the boundary of another space)[31] has three dimensions, and that space in general cannot have more, is built upon the proposition that not more than three lines can cut each other at right angles in one point; this proposition can, however, by no means be proven from con-

4: 285 cepts, but rests immediately upon intuition, and indeed on pure *a priori* intuition, because it is apodictically certain; indeed, that we can require that a line should be drawn to infinity (*in indefinitum*), or that a series of changes (e.g., spaces traversed through motion) should be continued to infinity, presupposes a representation of space and of time that can only inhere in intuition, that is, insofar as the latter is not in itself bounded

[a] Reading *sind* for *seyn*, with Ak.

by anything;[32] for this could never be concluded from concepts. Therefore pure intuitions *a priori* indeed actually do underlie mathematics, and make possible its synthetic and apodictically valid propositions; and consequently our transcendental deduction of the concepts of[a] space and time[33] at the same time explains the possibility of a pure mathematics, a possibility which, without such a deduction, and without our assuming that "everything which our senses may be given (the outer in space, the inner in time) is only intuited by us as it appears to us, not as it is in itself," could indeed be granted, but into which we could have no insight at all.

§13

All those who cannot yet get free of the conception, as if space and time were actual qualities attaching to things in themselves, can exercise their acuity on the following paradox, and, if they have sought its solution in vain, can then, free of prejudice at least for a few moments, suppose that perhaps the demotion of space and of time to mere forms of our sensory intuition may indeed have foundation.

If two things are fully the same (in all determinations belonging to magnitude and quality) in all the parts of each that can always be cognized by itself alone, it should indeed then follow that one, in all cases and respects, can be put in the place of the other, without this exchange causing the least recognizable difference. In fact this is how things stand with plane figures in geometry; yet various spherical figures,[34] notwithstanding this sort of complete inner agreement, nonetheless reveal such a difference[b] in outer relation that one cannot in any case be put in the place of the other; e.g., two spherical triangles from each of the hemispheres, which have an arc of the equator for a common base, can be fully equal with respect to their sides as well as their angles, so that nothing will be found in either, when it is fully described by itself, that is not also in the description of the other, and still one cannot be put in the place of the other (that is, in the opposite hemisphere); and here is then after all an *inner* difference between the triangles that no understanding can specify as inner, and that reveals itself only through the outer relation in space. But I will cite more familiar instances that can be taken from ordinary life.

4: 286

What indeed can be more similar to, and in all parts more equal to, my hand or my ear than its image in the mirror? And yet I cannot put such a hand as is seen in the mirror in the place of its original; for if the one was a right hand, then the other in the mirror is a left, and the image of the right ear is a left one, which can never take the place of the former. Now there

---

[a] Reading *von* for *im*, with Vorländer.
[b] Adding *Verschiedenheit*, with Vorländer.

are no inner differences here that any understanding could merely think; and yet the differences are inner as far as the senses teach, for the left hand cannot, after all, be enclosed within the same boundaries as the right (they cannot be made congruent), despite all reciprocal equality and similarity; one hand's glove cannot be used on the other. What then is the solution? These objects are surely not representations of things as they are in themselves, and as the pure understanding would cognize them, rather, they are sensory intuitions, i.e., appearances, whose possibility rests on the relation of certain things, unknown in themselves, to something else, namely our sensibility. Now, space is the form of outer intuition of this sensibility, and the inner determination of any space is possible only through the determination of the outer relation to the whole space of which the space is a part (the relation to outer sense); that is, the part is possible only through the whole, which never occurs with things in themselves as objects of the understanding alone, but well occurs with mere appearances. We can therefore make the difference between similar and equal but nonetheless incongruent things (e.g., oppositely spiralled snails) intelligible through no concept alone, but only through the relation to right-hand and left-hand, which refers immediately to intuition.

Note I

4: 287

Pure mathematics, and especially pure geometry, can have objective reality only under the single condition that it refers merely to objects of the senses, with regard to which objects, however, the principle remains fixed, that our sensory representation is by no means a representation of things in themselves, but only of the way in which they appear to us. From this it follows, not at all that the propositions of geometry are[a] determinations of a mere figment of our poetic phantasy,[35] and therefore could not with certainty be referred to actual objects, but rather, that they are valid necessarily for space and consequently for everything that may be found in space, because space is nothing other than the form of all outer appearances, under which alone objects of the senses can be given to us. Sensibility, whose form lies at the foundation of geometry, is that upon which the possibility of outer appearances rests; these, therefore, can never contain anything other than what geometry prescribes to them. It would be completely different if the senses had to represent objects as they are in themselves. For then it absolutely would not follow from the representation of space, a representation that serves *a priori*, with all the various properties of space, as foundation for the geometer, that all of this, together with what is deduced from it, must be exactly so

---

[a] Adding *sind*, with Ak.

in nature. The space of the geometer would be taken for mere fabrication and would be credited with no objective validity, because it is simply not to be seen how things would have to agree necessarily with the image that we form of them by ourselves and in advance. If, however, this image – or, better, this formal intuition – is the essential property of our sensibility by means of which alone objects are given to us, and if this sensibility represents not things in themselves but only their appearances, then it is very easy to comprehend, and at the same time to prove incontrovertibly: that all outer objects of our sensible world must necessarily agree, in complete exactitude, with the propositions of geometry, because sensibility itself, through its form of outer intuition (space), with which the geometer deals, first makes those objects possible, as mere appearances. It will forever remain a remarkable phenomenon in the history of philosophy that there was a time when even mathematicians who were at the same time philosophers began to doubt, not, indeed, the correctness of their geometrical propositions insofar as they related merely to space, but the objective validity and application to nature of this concept itself and all its geometrical determinations, since they were concerned that a line in nature might indeed be composed of physical points, consequently that true space in objects might be composed of simple parts, notwithstanding that the space which the geometer holds in thought can by no means be composed of such things.[36] They did not realize that this space in thought itself makes possible physical space, i.e., the extension of matter; that this space is by no means a property of things in themselves, but only a form of our power of sensory representation; that all objects in space are mere appearances, i.e., not things in themselves but representations of our sensory intuition; and that, since space as the geometer thinks it is precisely the form of sensory intuition which we find in ourselves *a priori* and which contains the ground of the possibility of all outer appearances (with respect to their form), these appearances must of necessity and with the greatest precision harmonize with the propositions of the geometer, which he extracts not from any fabricated concept, but from the subjective foundation of all outer appearances, namely sensibility itself. In this and no other way can the geometer be secured, regarding the indubitable objective reality of his propositions, against all the chicaneries of a shallow metaphysics, however strange this way must seem to such a metaphysics because it does not go back to the sources of its concepts.

4: 288

Note II

Everything that is to be given to us as object must be given to us in intuition. But all our intuition happens only by means of the senses; the understanding intuits nothing, but only reflects. Now since, in accordance with what has just been proven, the senses never and in no single instance enable us to cognize things in themselves, but only their appearances, and as these are mere representations of sensibility, "consequently all bodies together with the space in which they are found must be taken for nothing but mere representations in us, and exist nowhere else than merely in our thoughts." Now is this not manifest idealism?[37]

4: 289   Idealism consists in the claim that there are none other than thinking beings; the other things that we believe we perceive in intuition are only representations in thinking beings, to which in fact no object existing outside these beings corresponds. I say in opposition: There are things given to us as objects of our senses existing outside us, yet we know[a] nothing of them as they may be in themselves, but are acquainted[b] only with their appearances, i.e., with the representations that they produce in us because they affect our senses. Accordingly, I by all means avow that there are bodies outside us, i.e., things which, though completely unknown[c] to us as to what they may be in themselves, we know[d] through the representations which their influence on our sensibility provides for us, and to which we give the name of a body – which word therefore merely signifies the appearance of this object that is unknown to us but is nonetheless real. Can this be called idealism? It is the very opposite of it.

That one could, without detracting from the actual existence of outer things, say of a great many of their predicates: they belong not to these things in themselves, but only to their appearances and have no existence of their own outside our representation, is something that was generally accepted and acknowledged long before *Locke's* time, though more commonly thereafter. To these predicates belong warmth, color, taste, etc. That I, however, even beyond these, include (for weighty reasons) also among mere appearances the remaining qualities of bodies, which are called *primarias*: extension, place, and more generally space along with everything that depends on it (impenetrability or materiality, shape, etc.), is something against which not the least ground for uncertainty can be raised; and as little as someone can be called an idealist because he wants to admit colors as properties that attach not to the object in itself, but only to the sense of vision as modifications, just as little can my system be called idealist simply because I find that even more of, *nay, all of the properties that make up the intuition of a body* belong merely to its appearance: for the existence of the thing that appears is not thereby nullified, as with real idealism, but it is only shown that through the senses we cannot cognize it at all as it is in itself.

[a] *wissen*
[b] *kennen*
[c] *unbekannt*
[d] *kennen*

I would very much like to know how then my claims must be framed so as not to contain any idealism. Without doubt I would have to say: that the representation of space not only is perfectly in accordance with the relation that our sensibility has to objects, for I have said that, but that it is even fully similar to the object; an assertion to which I can attach no sense, any more than to the assertion that the sensation of red is similar to the property of cinnabar that excites this sensation in me.

4: 290

Note III

From this an easily foreseen but empty objection can now be quite easily rejected: "namely that through the ideality of space and time the whole sensible world would be transformed into sheer illusion."[38] After all philosophical insight into the nature of sensory cognition had previously been perverted by making sensibility into merely a confused kind of representation, through which we might still cognize things as they are but without having the ability to bring everything in this representation of ours to clear consciousness, we showed on the contrary that sensibility consists not in this logical difference of clarity or obscurity, but in the genetic difference of the origin of the cognition itself, since sensory cognition does not at all represent things as they are but only in the way in which they affect our senses, and therefore that through the senses mere appearances, not the things themselves, are given to the understanding for reflection;[39] from this necessary correction an objection arises, springing from an inexcusable and almost deliberate misinterpretation, as if my system transformed all the things of the sensible world into sheer illusion.

If an appearance is given to us, we are still completely free as to how we want to judge things from it. The former, namely the appearance, was based on the senses, but the judgment on the understanding, and the only question is whether there is truth in the determination of the object or not. The difference between truth and dream, however, is not decided through the quality of the representations that are referred to objects, for they are the same in both, but through their connection according to the rules that determine the combination of representations in the concept of an object, and how far they can or cannot stand together in one experience. And then it is not the fault of the appearances at all, if our cognition takes illusion for truth, i.e., if intuition, through which an object is given to us, is taken for the concept of the object, or even for its existence, which only the understanding can think. The course of the planets is represented to us by the senses as now progressive, now retrogressive, and herein is neither falsehood nor truth, because as long as one grants that this is as yet only appearance, one still does not judge at all the objective quality of their motion. Since,

4: 291

however, if the understanding has not taken good care to prevent this subjective mode of representation from being taken for objective, a false judgment can easily arise, one therefore says: they appear to go backwards; but the illusion is not ascribed to the senses, but to the understanding, whose lot alone it is to render an objective judgment from the appearance.

In this manner, if we do not reflect at all on the origin of our representations, and we connect our intuitions of the senses, whatever they may contain, in space and time according to rules for the combination of all cognition in one experience, then either deceptive illusion or truth can arise, according to whether we are heedless or careful; that concerns only the use of sensory representations in the understanding, and not their origin. In the same way, if I take all the representations of the senses together with their form, namely space and time, for nothing but appearances, and these last two for a mere form of sensibility that is by no means to be found outside it in the objects, and I make use of these same representations only in relation to possible experience: then in the fact that I take[a] them for mere appearances is contained not the least illusion or temptation toward error; for they nonetheless can be connected together correctly in experience according to rules of truth. In this manner all the propositions of geometry hold good for space as well as for all objects of the senses, and hence for all possible experience, whether I regard space as a mere form of sensibility or as something inhering in things themselves; though only in the first case can I comprehend how it may be possible to know those propositions *a priori* for all objects of outer intuition; otherwise, with respect to all merely possible experience, everything remains just as if I had never undertaken this departure from the common opinion.

But if I venture to go beyond all possible experience with my concepts of space and time – which is inevitable if I pass them off for qualities that attach to things in themselves (for what should then prevent me from still permitting them to hold good for the very same things, even if my senses might now be differently framed and either suited to them or not?) – then an important error can spring up which rests on an illusion, since I passed off as universally valid that which was a condition for the intuition of things (attaching merely to my subject, and surely valid for all objects of the senses, hence for all merely possible experience), because I referred it to the things in themselves and did not restrict it to conditions of experience.

Therefore, it is so greatly mistaken that my doctrine of the ideality of space and time makes the whole sensible world a mere illusion, that, on the contrary, my doctrine is the only means for securing the application

4: 292

---

[a] Reading *halte* for *enthalte*, with Ak.

to actual objects of one of the most important bodies of cognition – namely, that which mathematics expounds *a priori* – and for preventing it from being taken for nothing but mere illusion, since without this observation it would be quite impossible to make out whether the intuitions of space and time, which we do not derive from experience but which nevertheless lie *a priori* in our representations, were not mere self-produced fantasies, to which no object at all corresponds, at least not adequately, and therefore geometry itself a mere illusion, whereas we have been able to demonstrate the incontestable validity of geometry with respect to all objects of the sensible world for the very reason that the latter are mere appearances.

Second, it is so greatly mistaken that these principles of mine, because they make sensory representations into appearances, are supposed, in place of the truth of experience, to transform sensory representations into mere illusion, that, on the contrary, my principles are the only means of avoiding the transcendental illusion by which metaphysics has always been deceived and thereby tempted into the childish endeavor of chasing after soap bubbles, because appearances, which after all are mere representations, were taken for things in themselves; from which followed all those remarkable enactments of the antinomy of reason, which I will mention later on, and which is removed through this single observation: that appearance, as long as it is used in experience, brings forth truth, but as soon as it passes beyond the boundaries of experience and becomes transcendent, brings forth nothing but sheer illusion.

Since I therefore grant their reality to the things that we represent to ourselves through the senses, and limit our sensory intuition of these things only to the extent that in no instance whatsoever, not even in the pure intuitions of space and time, does it represent[a] anything more than mere appearances of these things, and never their quality in themselves, this is therefore no thoroughgoing illusion ascribed by me to nature, and my protestation against all imputation of idealism is so conclusive and clear that it would even seem superfluous if there were not unauthorized judges who, being glad to have an ancient name for every deviation from their false though common opinion, and never judging the spirit of philosophical nomenclatures but merely clinging to the letter, were ready to put their own folly in the place of well-determined concepts, and thereby to twist and deform them. For the fact that I have myself given to this theory of mine the name of transcendental idealism cannot justify anyone in confusing it with the empirical idealism of *Descartes* (although this idealism was only a problem, whose insolubility left everyone free, in *Descartes'* opinion, to deny the existence of the corporeal world, since the problem could never be answered satisfactorily) or with

4: 293

---

[a] Reading *vorstelle* for *vorstellen*, with Ak.

the mysticaland visionary[a, 40] idealism of *Berkeley* (against which, along with other similar fantasies, our *Critique*, on the contrary, contains the proper antidote).[41] For what I called idealism did not concern the existence of things (the doubting of which, however, properly constitutes idealism according to the received meaning), for it never came into my mind to doubt that, but only the sensory representation of things, to which space and time above all belong; and about these last, hence in general about all *appearances*, I have only shown: that they are not things (but mere modes of representation), nor are they determinations that belong to things in themselves. The word transcendental, however, which with me never signifies a relation of our cognition to things, but only to the *faculty of cognition*, was intended to prevent this misinterpretation. But before it prompts still more of the same,[b] I gladly withdraw this name, and I will have it called critical idealism. But if it is an in fact reprehensible idealism to transform actual things (not appearances) into mere representations,[42] with what name shall we christen that idealism which, conversely, makes mere representations into things? I think it could be named *dreaming* idealism, to distinguish it from the preceding, which may be called *visionary* idealism, both of which were to have been held off by my formerly so-called transcendental, or better, *critical* idealism.

4: 294

[a] *schwaermerischen*
[b] Reading *dieselbe* for *denselben*, with Ak.

Main Transcendental Question, Second Part
How is pure natural science possible?

§14

Nature is the *existence* of things, insofar as that existence is determined according to universal laws. If nature meant the existence of things *in themselves*, we would never be able to cognize it, either *a priori* or *a posteriori*. Not *a priori*, for how are we to know what pertains to things in themselves, inasmuch as this can never come about through the analysis of our concepts (analytical propositions), since I do not want to know what may be contained in my concept of a thing (for that belongs to its logical essence), but what would be added to this concept in the actuality of a thing, and what the thing itself would be determined by in its existence apart from my concept. My understanding, and the conditions under which alone it can connect the determinations of things in their existence, prescribes no rule to the things themselves; these do not conform to my understanding, but my understanding would have to conform to them; they would therefore have to be given to me in advance so that these determinations could be drawn from them, but then they would not be cognized *a priori*.

Such cognition of the nature of things in themselves would also be impossible *a posteriori*. For if experience were supposed to teach me *laws* to which the existence of things is subject, then these laws, insofar as they relate to things in themselves, would have to apply to them *necessarily* even apart from my experience. Now experience teaches me what there is and how it is, but never that it necessarily must be so and not otherwise. Therefore it can never teach me the nature of things in themselves.

§15

Now we are nevertheless actually in possession of a pure natural science, which, *a priori* and with all of the necessity required for apodictic propositions, propounds laws to which nature is subject. Here I need call to witness only that propaedeutic to the theory of nature which, under

4: 295

the title of universal natural science, precedes all of physics (which is founded on empirical principles).[a] Therein we find mathematics applied to appearances, and also merely discursive principles[b] (from concepts), which make up the philosophical part of pure cognition of nature.[43] But indeed there is also much in it that is not completely pure and independent of sources in experience, such as the concept of *motion*, of *impenetrability* (on which the empirical concept of matter is based), of *inertia*, among others, so that it cannot be called completely pure natural science; furthermore it refers only to the objects of the outer senses, and therefore does not provide an example of a universal natural science in the strict sense; for that would have to bring nature in general – whether pertaining to an object of the outer senses or of the inner sense (the object of physics as well as psychology) – under universal laws. But among the principles of this universal physics[44] a few are found that actually have the universality we require, such as the proposition: *that substance remains* and persists, that *everything that happens* always previously *is determined by a cause* according to constant laws, and so on. These are truly universal laws of nature, that exist fully *a priori*. There is then in fact a pure natural science, and now the question is: *How is it possible?*

§16

The word *nature* assumes yet another meaning, namely one that determines the *object*, whereas in the above meaning it only signified the *conformity to law* of the determinations of the existence of things in general. Nature considered *materialiter*[45] is the *sum total of all objects of experience*. We are concerned here only with this, since otherwise things that could never become objects of an experience if they had to be cognized according to their nature would force us to concepts whose significance could never be given *in concreto* (in any example of a possible experience), and we would therefore have to make for ourselves mere concepts of the nature of those things,[c] the reality of which concepts, i.e., whether they actually relate to objects or are mere beings of thought, could not be decided at all. Cognition of that which cannot be an object of experience would be hyperphysical, and here we are not concerned with such things at all, but rather with that cognition of nature, the reality of which can be confirmed through experience, even though such cognition is possible *a priori* and precedes all experience.

4: 296

[a] *Principien*
[b] *Grundsätze*
[c] Reading *deren* for *dessen*, with Ak.

§17

The *formal* in nature in this narrower meaning is therefore the conformity to law of all objects of experience, and, insofar as this conformity is cognized *a priori*, the *necessary* conformity to law of those objects. But it has just been shown: that the laws of nature can never be cognized *a priori* in objects insofar as these objects are considered, not in relation to possible experience, but as things in themselves. We are here, however, concerned not with things in themselves (the properties of which we leave undetermined), but only with things as objects of a possible experience, and the sum total of such objects is properly what we here call nature. And now I ask whether, if the discussion is of the possibility of a cognition of nature *a priori*, it would be better to frame the problem in this way: How is it possible to cognize *a priori* the necessary conformity to law *of things* as objects of experience, or: How is it possible in general to cognize *a priori* the necessary conformity to law *of experience* itself with regard to all of its objects?

On closer examination, whether the question is posed one way or the other, its solution will come out absolutely the same with regard to the pure cognition of nature (which is actually the point of the question). For the subjective laws under which alone a cognition of things through experience[a] is possible also hold good for those things as objects of a possible experience (but obviously not for them as things in themselves, which, however, are not at all being considered here). It is completely the same, whether I say: A judgment of perception can never be considered as valid for experience without the law, that if an event is perceived then it is always referred to something preceding from which it follows according to a universal rule; or if I express myself in this way: Everything of which experience shows that it happens must have a cause.

It is nonetheless more appropriate to choose the first formulation. For since we can indeed, *a priori* and previous to any objects being given, have a cognition of those conditions under which alone an experience regarding objects is possible, but never of the laws to which objects may be subject in themselves without relation to possible experience, we will therefore be able to study *a priori* the nature of things in no other way than by investigating the conditions, and the universal (though subjective) laws, under which alone such a cognition is possible as experience (as regards mere form), and determining the possibility of things as objects of experience accordingly; for were I to choose the second mode of expression and to seek the *a priori* conditions under which nature is possible as an *object* of experience, I might then easily fall into misunderstanding

4: 297

---

[a] *Erfahrungserkenntniss*; not translated as "empirical cognition," which translates Kant's *empirische Erkenntniss*, which he distinguished from the former (§18).

and fancy that I had to speak about nature as a thing in itself, and in that case I would be wandering about fruitlessly in endless endeavors to find laws for things about which nothing is given to me.

We will therefore be concerned here only with experience and with the universal conditions of its possibility which are given *a priori*, and from there we will determine nature as the whole object of all possible experience. I think I will be understood: that here I do not mean the rules for the *observation* of a nature that is already given, which presuppose experience already; and so do not mean, how we can learn the laws from nature (through experience), for these would then not be laws *a priori* and would provide no pure natural science; but rather, how the *a priori* conditions of the possibility of experience are at the same time the sources out of which all universal laws of nature must be derived.

§18

We must therefore first of all note: that, although all judgments of experience are empirical, i.e., have their basis in the immediate perception of the senses, nonetheless the reverse is not the case, that all empirical judgments are therefore judgments of experience; rather, beyond the empirical and in general beyond what is given in sensory intuition, special concepts must yet be added, which have their origin completely *a priori* in the pure understanding, and under which every perception can first be subsumed and then, by means of the same concepts, transformed

4: 298   into experience.

Empirical judgments, insofar as they have objective validity, are JUDGMENTS OF EXPERIENCE; those, however, that are *only subjectively valid* I call mere JUDGMENTS OF PERCEPTION. The latter do not require a pure concept of the understanding, but only the logical connection of perceptions in a thinking subject. But the former always demand, in addition to the representations of sensory intuition, special *concepts originally generated in the understanding*, which are precisely what make the judgment of experience *objectively valid*.

All of our judgments are at first mere judgments of perception; they hold only for us, i.e., for our subject, and only afterwards do we give them a new relation, namely to an object, and intend that the judgment should also be valid at all times for us and for everyone else; for if a judgment agrees with an object, then all judgments of the same object must also agree with one another, and hence the objective validity of a judgment of experience signifies nothing other than its necessary universal validity. But also conversely, if we find cause to deem a judgment necessarily, universally valid (which is never based on the perception, but on the pure concept of the understanding under which the perception is subsumed), we must then also deem it objective, i.e., as expressing not merely a relation of a perception to a subject, but a property of an object; for there would be no reason why other judgments necessarily would have to agree with mine, if there were not the unity of the object – an object to which they all refer, with which they all agree, and, for that reason, also must all harmonize among themselves.

§19

Objective validity and necessary universal validity (for everyone) are therefore interchangeable concepts, and although we do not know the object in itself, nonetheless, if we regard a judgment as universally valid and hence necessary, objective validity is understood to be included. Through this judgment we cognize the object (even if it otherwise remains unknown as it may be in itself) by means of the universally valid and necessary connection of the given perceptions; and since this is the case for all objects of the senses, judgments of experience will not derive their objective validity from the immediate cognition of the object (for this is impossible), but merely from the condition for the universal validity of empirical judgments, which, as has been said, never rests on empirical, or indeed sensory conditions at all, but on a pure concept of the understanding. The object always remains unknown in itself; if, however, through the concept of the understanding the connection of the representations which it provides to our sensibility is determined as universally valid, then the object is determined through this relation, and the judgment is objective.

4: 299

Let us provide examples: that the room is warm, the sugar sweet, the wormwood[46] repugnant,* are merely subjectively valid judgments. I do not at all require that I should find it so at every time, or that everyone else should find it just as I do; they express only a relation of two sensations to the same subject, namely myself, and this only in my present state of perception, and are therefore not expected to be valid for the object: these I call judgments of perception. The case is completely different with judgments of experience. What experience teaches me

---

* I gladly admit that these examples do not present judgments of perception such as could ever become judgments of experience if a concept of the understanding were also added, because they refer merely to feeling – which everyone acknowledges to be merely subjective and which must therefore never be attributed to the object – and therefore can never become objective; I only wanted to give for now an example of a judgment that is merely subjectively valid and that contains in itself no basis for necessary universal validity and, thereby, for a relation to an object. An example of judgments of perception that become judgments of experience through the addition of a concept of the understanding follows in the next note.

under certain circumstances, it must teach me at every time and teach everyone else as well, and its validity is not limited to the subject or its state at that time. Therefore I express all such judgments as objectively valid; as, e.g., if I say: the air is elastic, then this judgment is to begin with only a judgment of perception; I relate two sensations in my senses only to one another. If I want it to be called a judgment of experience, I then require that this connection be subject to a condition that makes it universally valid. I want therefore that I, at every time, and also everyone else, would necessarily have to connect the same perceptions[a] under the same circumstances.

§20

We will therefore have to analyze experience in general, in order to see what is contained in this product of the senses and the understanding, and how the judgment of experience is itself possible. At bottom lies the intuition of which I am conscious, i.e., perception (*perceptio*), which belongs solely to the senses. But, secondly, judging (which pertains solely to the understanding) also belongs here. Now this judging can be of two types: first, when I merely compare the perceptions and connect them in a consciousness of my state, or, second, when I connect them in a consciousness in general. The first judgment is merely a judgment of perception and has thus far only subjective validity; it is merely a connection of perceptions within my mental state, without reference to the object. Hence it is not, as is commonly imagined, sufficient for experience to compare perceptions and to connect them in one consciousness by means of judging; from that there arises no universal validity and necessity of the judgment, on account of which alone it can be objectively valid and so can be experience.

A completely different judgment therefore occurs before experience can arise from perception. The given intuition must be subsumed under a concept that determines the form of judging in general with respect to the intuition, connects the empirical consciousness of the latter in a consciousness in general, and thereby furnishes empirical judgments with universal validity; a concept of this kind is a pure *a priori* concept of the understanding, which does nothing but simply determine for an intuition the mode in general in which it can serve for judging. The concept of cause being such a concept, it therefore determines the intuition which is subsumed under it, e.g., that of air, with respect to judging in general – namely, so that the concept of air serves, with respect to expansion, in the relation of the antecedent to the consequent in a hypothetical judgment. The concept of cause is therefore a pure concept

---

[a] Reading *Wahrnehmungen* for *Wahrnehmung*, as suggested at Ak 4:617.

of the understanding, which is completely distinct from all possible perception, and serves only, with respect to judging in general, to determine
that representation which is contained under it and so to make possible
a universally valid judgment.

Now before a judgment of experience can arise from a judgment of
perception, it is first required: that the perception be subsumed under   4: 301
a concept of the understanding of this kind; e.g., the air belongs under
the concept of cause,[a] which determines the judgment about the air as
hypothetical with respect to expansion.* This expansion is thereby represented not as belonging merely to my perception of the air in my state
of perception or in several of my states or in the state of others, but as
necessarily belonging to it, and the judgment: the air is elastic, becomes
universally valid and thereby for the first time a judgment of experience, because certain judgments occur beforehand, which subsume the
intuition of the air under the concept of cause and effect, and thereby
determine the perceptions not merely with respect to each other in my
subject, but with respect to the form of judging in general (here, the hypothetical), and in this way make the empirical judgment universally valid.

If one analyzes all of one's synthetic judgments insofar as they are objectively valid, one finds that they never consist in mere intuitions that
have, as is commonly thought, merely been connected in a[b] judgment
through comparison,[47] but rather that they would not be possible if,
over and above the concepts drawn from intuition, a pure concept of
the understanding had not been added under which these concepts had
been subsumed and in this way first combined into an objectively valid
judgment. Even the judgments of pure mathematics in its simplest axioms are not exempt from this condition. The principle: a straight line is
the shortest line between two points, presupposes that the line has been
subsumed under the concept of magnitude, which certainly is no mere
intuition, but has its seat solely in the understanding and serves to determine the intuition (of the line) with respect to such judgments as may be
passed on it as regards the quantity of these judgments, namely plurality

---

* To have a more easily understood example, consider the following: If the sun
  shines on the stone, it becomes warm. This judgment is a mere judgment of
  perception and contains no necessity, however often I and others also have
  perceived this; the perceptions are only usually found so conjoined. But if I
  say: the sun *warms* the stone, then beyond the perception is added the understanding's concept of cause, which connects *necessarily* the concept of sunshine
  with that of heat, and the synthetic judgment becomes necessarily universally
  valid, hence objective, and changes from a perception into experience.

[a] Reading *Ursache* for *Ursachen*, with Ak.
[b] Reading *einem* for *ein*, with Ak.

4: 302 (as *judicia plurativa* *), since through such judgments it is understood that in a given intuition a homogeneous plurality is contained.

§21

In order therefore to explain the possibility of experience insofar as it rests on pure *a priori* concepts of the understanding, we must first present that which belongs to[a] judgments in general, and the various moments of the understanding therein, in a complete table; for the pure concepts of the understanding – which are nothing more than concepts of intuitions in general insofar as these intuitions are, with respect to one or another of these moments, in themselves determined to judgments and therefore determined necessarily and with universal validity – will come out exactly parallel to them. By this means the *a priori* principles of the possibility of all experience as objectively valid empirical cognition will also be determined quite exactly. For they are nothing other than propositions that subsume all perception (according to certain universal conditions of intuition) under those pure concepts of the understanding.

LOGICAL TABLE
of Judgments

1.
According to Quantity

Universal
Particular
Singular

2.
According to Quality

Affirmative
Negative
Infinite

3.
According to Relation

Categorical
Hypothetical
Disjunctive

4: 303

4.
According to Modality

Problematic
Assertoric
Apodictic

---

* So I would prefer those judgments to be called, which are called *particularia* in logic. For the latter expression already contains the thought that they are not universal. If, however, I commence from unity (in singular judgments) and then continue on to the totality, I still cannot mix in any reference to the totality; I think only a plurality without totality, not the exception to the latter.[48] This is necessary, if the logical moments are to be placed under the pure concepts of the understanding; in logical usage things can remain as they were.

[a] Reading *zu* for *zum*, with Vorländer.

TRANSCENDENTAL TABLE
of Concepts of the Understanding

1.
According to Quantity

Unity (measure)
Plurality (magnitude)
Totality (the whole)

2.
According to Quality

Reality
Negation
Limitation

3.
According to Relation

Substance
Cause
Community

4.
According to Modality

Possibility
Existence
Necessity

PURE PHYSIOLOGICAL TABLE
of Universal Principles of Natural Science

1.
Axioms
of intuition

2.
Anticipations
of perception

3.
Analogies
of experience

4.
Postulates
of empirical thinking in general

§21[a][a]

4: 304

In order to comprise all the preceding in one notion, it is first of all necessary to remind the reader that the discussion here is not about the genesis of experience, but about that which lies in experience. The former belongs to empirical psychology and could never be properly developed even there without the latter, which belongs to the critique of cognition and especially of the understanding.

---

[a] Adding the letter "a," with Ak and Vorländer, to distinguish this section from the preceding one, both of which are shown as "§21" in the original edition.

Experience consists of intuitions, which belong to sensibility, and of judgments, which are solely the understanding's business. Those judgments that the understanding forms solely from sensory intuitions are, however, still not judgments of experience by a long way. For in the one[a] case the judgment would only connect perceptions as they are given in sensory intuition; but in the latter case the judgments are supposed to say what experience in general contains, therefore not what mere perception – whose validity is merely subjective – contains. The judgment of experience must still therefore, beyond the sensory intuition and its logical connection (in accordance with which the intuition has been rendered universal through comparison in a judgment), add something that determines the synthetic judgment as necessary, and thereby as universally valid; and this can be nothing but that concept which represents the intuition as in itself determined with respect to one form of judgment rather than the others,[b] i.e.,[c] a concept of that synthetic unity of intuitions which can be represented only through a given logical function of judgments.

§22

To sum this up: the business of the senses is to intuit; that of the understanding, to think. To think, however, is to unite representations in a consciousness. This unification either arises merely relative to the subject and is contingent and subjective, or it occurs without condition and is necessary or objective. The unification of representations in a consciousness is judgment. Therefore, thinking is the same as judging or as relating representations to judgments in general. Judgments are therefore either merely subjective, if representations are related to one consciousness in one subject alone and are united in it, or they are objective, if they are united in a consciousness in general, i.e., are

4: 305

united necessarily therein. The logical moments of all judgments are so many possible ways of uniting representations in a consciousness. If, however, the very same moments serve as concepts, they are concepts of the *necessary* unification of these representations in a consciousness, and so are principles[d] of objectively valid judgments. This unification in a consciousness is either analytic, through identity, or synthetic, through combination and addition of various representations with one another. Experience consists in the synthetic connection of appearances (perceptions) in a consciousness, insofar as this connection is necessary.

[a] Reading *dem einen* for *einem*, as suggested by Vorländer.
[b] Reading *anderen* for *andere*, with Ak.
[c] Reading *d. i.* for *die*, with Ak.
[d] *Principien*

Therefore pure concepts of the understanding are those under which all perceptions must first be subsumed before they can serve in judgments of experience, in which the synthetic unity of perceptions is represented as necessary and universally valid.*

§23

Judgments, insofar as they are regarded merely as the condition for the unification of given representations in a consciousness, are rules. These rules, insofar as they represent the unification as necessary, are *a priori* rules, and provided that there are none above them from which they can be derived, are principles. Now since, with respect to the possibility of all experience, if merely the form of thinking is considered in the experience, no conditions on judgments of experience are above those that bring the appearance (according to the varying form of their intuition) under pure concepts of the understanding (which make the empirical judgment objectively valid), these conditions are therefore the *a priori* principles of possible experience. 4: 306

Now the principles of possible experience are, at the same time, universal laws of nature that can be cognized *a priori*. And so the problem that lies in our second question, presently before us: *how is pure natural science*[a] *possible?* is solved. For the systematization that is required for the form of a science is here found to perfection, since beyond the aforementioned formal conditions of all judgments in general, hence of all rules whatsoever furnished by logic, no others are possible, and these form a logical system; but the concepts based thereon, which contain[b] the *a priori* conditions for all synthetic and necessary judgments, for that very reason form a transcendental system; finally, the principles by means of

---

* But how does this proposition: that judgments of experience are supposed to contain necessity in the synthesis of perceptions, square with my proposition, urged many times above: that experience, as *a posteriori* cognition, can provide merely contingent judgments? If I say: Experience teaches me something, I always mean only the perception that is in it – e.g., that upon illumination of the stone by the sun, warmth always follows – and hence the proposition from experience is, so far, always contingent. That this warming follows necessarily from illumination by the sun is indeed contained in the judgment of experience (in virtue of the concept of cause), but I do not learn it from experience; rather, conversely, experience is first generated through this addition of a concept of the understanding (of cause) to the perception. Concerning how the perception may come by this addition, the *Critique* must be consulted, in the section on transcendental judgment, pp. 137ff.[49]

[a] Reading *Naturwissenschaft* for *Vernunftwissenschaft*, with Ak.
[b] Reading *enthalten* for *erhalten*, with Ak.

which all appearances are subsumed under these concepts form a physiological system, i.e., a system of nature,^{a} which precedes all empirical cognition of nature and first makes it possible, and can therefore be called the true universal and pure natural science.

§24

The^b first* of the physiological principles subsumes all appearances, as intuitions in space and time, under the concept of *magnitude* and is to that extent a principle for the application of mathematics to experience. The^c second does not subsume the properly empirical – namely sensation, which signifies the real^d in intuitions – directly under the concept of *magnitude*, since sensation is no intuition *containing* space or time, although it does place the object corresponding to it in both; but there nonetheless is, between reality (sensory representation) and nothing, i.e., the complete emptiness of intuition in time, a difference that has a magnitude, for indeed between every given degree of light and darkness, every degree of warmth and the completely cold, every degree of heaviness and absolute lightness, every degree of the filling of space and completely empty space, ever smaller degrees can be thought, just as between consciousness and total unconsciousness (psychological darkness) ever smaller degrees occur; therefore no perception is possible that would show a complete absence, e.g., no psychological darkness is possible that could not be regarded as a consciousness that is merely outweighed by another, stronger one, and thus it is in all cases of sensation; as a result of which the understanding can anticipate even sensations, which form the proper quality of empirical representations (appearances), by means of the principle that they all without exception, hence the real in all appearance, have degrees – which is the second application of mathematics (*mathesis intensorum*) to natural science.[51]

4: 307

§25

With respect to the relation of appearances, and indeed exclusively with regard to their existence, the determination of this relation is

---

* The three subsequent sections could be difficult to understand properly, if one does not have at hand what the *Critique* says about principles as well; but they might have the advantage of making it easier to survey the general features of such principles and to attend to the main points.[50]

^{a} *Natursystem*
^{b} Reading *der* for *das*, with Ak.
^{c} Reading *der* for *das*, with Ak.
^{d} *Reale*

not mathematical but dynamical, and it can[a] never be objectively valid, hence fit for experience, if it is not subject to *a priori* principles, which first make cognition through experience possible with respect to that determination.[52] Therefore appearances must be subsumed under the concept of substance, which, as a concept of the thing itself, underlies all determination of existence; or second, insofar as a temporal sequence, i.e., an event, is met with among the appearances, they must be subsumed under the concept of an effect in relation to a[b] cause; or, insofar as coexistence is to be cognized objectively, i.e., through a judgment of experience, they must be subsumed under the concept of community (interaction): and so *a priori* principles underlie objectively valid, though empirical, judgments, i.e., they underlie the possibility of experience insofar as it is supposed to connect objects in nature according to existence. These principles are the actual laws of nature, which can be called dynamical.

Finally, there also belongs to judgments of experience the cognition of agreement and connection: not so much of the appearances among themselves in experience, but of their relation to experience in general, a relation that contains either their agreement with the formal conditions that the understanding cognizes, or their connection with the material of the senses and perception, or both[c] united in one concept, and thus possibility, existence, and necessity according to universal laws of nature; all of which would constitute the physiological theory of method (the distinction of truth and hypotheses, and the boundaries of the reliability of the latter).

4: 308

§26

Although the third table of principles, which is drawn *from the nature of the understanding itself* according to the critical method, in itself exhibits a perfection through which it raises itself far above every other that has (albeit vainly) ever been attempted or may yet be attempted in the future *from the things themselves* through the dogmatic method: namely, that in it[d] all of the synthetic principles *a priori* are exhibited completely and according to a principle,[e] namely that of the faculty for judging in general (which constitutes the essence of experience with respect to the understanding), so that one can be certain there are no more such principles (a satisfaction that the dogmatic method can never provide) – nevertheless this is still far from being its greatest merit.

[a] Adding *kann*, with Ak.
[b] Adding *eine*, with Vorländer.
[c] Reading *beides* for *beiden*, as suggested at Ak 4:617.
[d] Reading *in ihr* for *sie*, with Vorländer.
[e] *Princip*

Notice must be taken of the ground of proof that reveals the possibility of this *a priori* cognition and at the same time limits all such principles to a condition that must never be neglected if they are not to be[a] misunderstood and extended in use further than the original sense which the understanding places in them will allow: namely, that they contain only the conditions of possible experience in general, insofar as it is subject to *a priori* laws. Hence I do not say: that things *in themselves* contain[b] a magnitude, their reality a degree, their existence a connection of accidents in a substance, and so on; for that no one can prove, because such a synthetic connection out of mere concepts, in which all relation to sensory intuition on the one hand and all connection of such intuition in a possible experience on the other is lacking, is utterly impossible. Therefore the essential limitation on the concepts in these principles is: that only *as objects of experience* are all things necessarily subject *a priori* to the aforementioned conditions.

From this there follows then secondly a specifically characteristic mode of proving the same thing: that the above-mentioned principles

are not referred directly to appearances and their relation, but to the possibility of experience, for which appearances constitute only the matter but not the form, i.e., they are referred to the objectively and universally valid synthetic propositions through which judgments of experience are distinguished from mere judgments of perception. This happens because the appearances, as mere intuitions *that fill a part of space and time*, are subject to the concept of magnitude, which synthetically unifies the multiplicity of intuitions *a priori* according to rules; and because the real in the appearances must have a degree, insofar as perception contains, beyond intuition, sensation as well, between which and nothing, i.e., the complete disappearance of sensation, a transition always occurs by diminution, insofar, that is, as sensation itself *fills no part of space and time*,*

---

* Warmth, light, etc. are just as great (according to degree) in a small space as in a large one; just as the inner representations (pain, consciousness in general) are not smaller according to degree whether they last a short or a long time. Hence the magnitude here is just as great in a point and in an instant as in every space and time however large. Degrees are therefore magnitudes,[c] not, however, in intuition, but in accordance with mere sensation, or indeed with the magnitude of the ground of an intuition, and can be assessed as magnitudes only through the relation of 1 to 0, i.e., in that every sensation can proceed in a certain time to vanish through infinite intermediate degrees, or to grow from nothing to a determinate sensation through infinite moments of accretion. (*Quantitas qualitatis est gradus.*)[d]

[a] Reading *sollen* for *soll*, with Vorländer.
[b] Reading *enthalten* for *enthalte*, as suggested at Ak 4:617.
[c] Reading *Grössen* for *grösser*, with Vorländer.
[d] "The magnitude of quality is degree."

but yet the transition to sensation from empty time or space is possible only in time, with the consequence that although sensation, as the quality of empirical intuition with respect to that by which a sensation differs specifically from other sensations, can never be cognized *a priori*, it nonetheless can, in a possible experience in general, as the magnitude of perception, be distinguished intensively from every other sensation of the same kind; from which, then, the application of mathematics to nature, with respect to the sensory intuition whereby nature is given to us, is first made possible and determined.

Mostly, however, the reader must attend to the mode of proving the principles that appear under the name of the Analogies of Experience. For since these do not concern the generation of intuitions, as do the principles for applying mathematics to natural science in general, but the connection of their existence in one experience, and since this connection can be nothing[a] other than the determination of existence in time according to necessary laws, under which alone the connection is objectively valid and therefore is experience: it follows that the proof does not refer to synthetic unity in the connection *of things* in themselves, but of *perceptions*, and of these indeed not with respect to their content, but to the determination of time and to the relation of existence in time in accordance with universal laws. These universal laws contain therefore the necessity of the determination of existence in time in general (hence *a priori* according to a rule of the understanding), if the empirical determination in relative time is to be objectively valid, and therefore to be experience. For the reader who is stuck in the long habit of taking experience to be a mere empirical combining of perceptions – and who therefore has never even considered that it extends much further than these reach, that is, that it gives to empirical judgments universal validity and to do so requires a pure unity of the understanding that precedes *a priori* – I cannot adduce more here, these being prolegomena, except only to recommend: to heed well this distinction of experience from a mere aggregate of perceptions, and to judge the mode of proof from this standpoint.

4: 310

§27

Here is now the place to dispose thoroughly of the Humean doubt. He rightly affirmed: that we in no way have insight through reason into the possibility of causality, i.e., the possibility of relating the existence of one thing to the existence of some other thing that would necessarily be posited through the first one. I add to this that we have just as little insight into the concept of subsistence, i.e., of the necessity that a subject, which itself cannot be a predicate of any other thing, should

---

[a] Reading *nichts* for *nicht*, with Ak.

underlie the existence of things – nay, that we cannot frame any concept of the possibility of any such thing (although we can point out examples of its use in experience); and I also add that this very incomprehensibility affects the community of things as well, since we have no insight whatsoever into how, from the state of one thing, a consequence could be drawn about the state of completely different things outside it (and vice versa), and into how substances, each of which has its own separate existence, should depend on one another and should indeed do so

4: 311 necessarily. Nonetheless, I am very far from taking these concepts to be merely borrowed from experience, and from taking the necessity represented in them to be falsely imputed and a mere illusion through which long habit deludes us; rather, I have sufficiently shown that they and the principles taken from them stand firm *a priori* prior to all experience, and have their undoubted objective correctness, though of course only with respect to experience.

§28

Although I therefore do not have the least concept of such a connection of things in themselves, how they can exist as substances or act as causes or stand in community with others (as parts of a real whole), and though I can still less think such properties of appearances as appearances (for these concepts do not contain what lies in appearances, but what the understanding alone must think), we nonetheless do have a concept of such a connection of representations in our understanding, and indeed in judging in general, namely: that representations belong in one kind of judgments as subject in relation to predicate, in another as ground in relation to consequence, and in a third as parts that together make up a whole possible experience. Further, we cognize *a priori*: that, without regarding the representation of an object as determined with respect to one or another[a] of these moments, we could not have any cognition at all that was valid for the object; and if we were to concern ourselves with the object in itself, then no unique characteristic would be possible by which I could cognize that it[b] had been determined with respect to one or another of the above-mentioned moments, i.e., that it belonged under the concept of substance, or of cause, or (in relation to other substances) under the concept of community; for I have no concept of the possibility of such a connection of existence. The question is not, however, how things in themselves, but how the cognition of things in experience is determined with respect to said moments of judgments in general, i.e., how things as objects of experience can and should be subsumed under

---

[a] Reading *eines oder des* for *einer oder der*, with Ak.
[b] Reading *er* for *es*, with Ak.

those concepts of the understanding. And then it is clear that I have complete insight into not only the possibility but also the necessity of subsuming all appearances under these concepts, i.e., of using them as principles of the possibility of experience.

§29

For having a try at *Hume's* problematic concept (this, his *crux metaphysicorum*),[a] namely the concept of cause, there is first given to me *a priori*, by means of logic: the form of a conditioned judgment in general, that is, the use of a given cognition as ground and another as consequent. It is, however, possible that in perception a rule of relation will be found, which says this: that a certain appearance is constantly followed by another (though not the reverse); and this is a case for me to use hypothetical judgment and, e.g., to say: If a body is illuminated by the sun for long enough, then it becomes warm. Here there is of course not yet a necessity of connection, hence not yet the concept of cause. But I continue on, and say: if the above proposition, which is merely a subjective connection of perceptions, is to be a proposition of experience, then it must be regarded as necessarily and universally valid. But a proposition of this sort would be: The sun through its light is the cause of the warmth. The foregoing empirical rule is now regarded as a law, and indeed as valid not merely of appearances, but of them on behalf of a possible experience, which requires universally and therefore necessarily valid rules. I therefore have quite good insight into the concept of cause, as a concept that necessarily belongs to the mere form of experience, and into its possibility as a synthetic unification of perceptions in a consciousness in general; but I have no insight at all into the possibility of a thing in general as a cause, and that indeed because the concept of cause indicates a condition that in no way attaches to things, but only to experience, namely, that experience can be an objectively valid cognition of appearances and their sequence in time only insofar as the antecedent appearance can be connected with the subsequent one according to the rule of hypothetical judgments.

§30

Consequently, even the pure concepts of the understanding have no significance at all if they depart from objects of experience and want to be referred to things in themselves (*noumena*).[b] They serve as it were

---

[a] "cross of metaphysics"

[b] *Noumena* is a latinized Greek word (singular: *noumenon*) meaning literally "that which is thought" or "that which is conceived," but used by Kant in connection with the

only to spell out appearances, so that they can be read as experience; the principles that arise from their relation to the sensible world serve our understanding for use in experience only; beyond this there are arbitrary connections without objective reality whose possibility cannot be cognized *a priori* and whose relation to objects cannot, through any example, be confirmed or even made intelligible, since all examples can be taken only from some possible experience or other and hence the objects of these concepts can be met with nowhere else but in a possible experience.

4: 313

This complete solution of the Humean problem, though coming out contrary to the surmise of the originator, thus restores to the pure concepts of the understanding their *a priori* origin, and to the universal laws of nature their validity as laws of the understanding, but in such a way that it restricts their use to experience only, because their possibility is founded solely in the relation of the understanding to experience: not, however, in such a way that they are derived from experience, but that experience is derived from them, a completely reversed type of connection that never occurred to *Hume*.

From this now flows the following result of all the foregoing investigations: "All synthetic *a priori* principles[a] are nothing more than principles[b] of possible experience," and can never be related to things in themselves, but only to appearances as objects of experience. Therefore both pure mathematics and pure natural science can never refer to anything more than mere appearances, and they can only represent either that which makes experience in general possible, or that which, being derived from these principles,[c] must always be able to be represented in some possible experience or other.

§31

And so for once one has something determinate, and to which one can adhere in all metaphysical undertakings, which have up to now boldly enough, but always blindly, run over everything without distinction. It never occurred to dogmatic thinkers that the goal of their efforts might have been set up so close, nor even to those who, obstinate in their so-called sound common sense,[d] sallied forth to insights with concepts and principles of the pure understanding that were indeed legitimate and

philosophical meaning of *nous* as "intellect" to mean "intelligible objects," or "intelligible beings" or "beings of the understanding." In §32 he contrasts *noumena* with *phaenomena*, which he speaks of as "sensible beings" or "appearances."

[a] *Grundsätze*
[b] *Principien*
[c] *Principien*
[d] *gesunde Vernunft*

natural, but were intended for use merely in experience, and for which they neither recognized nor could recognize any determinate boundaries, because they neither had reflected on nor were able to reflect on the nature or even the possibility of such a pure understanding.

4: 314

Many a naturalist of pure reason (by which I mean he who trusts himself, without any science, to decide in matters of metaphysics) would like to pretend that already long ago, through the prophetic spirit of his sound common sense, he had not merely suspected, but had known and understood, that which is here presented with so much preparation, or, if he prefers, with such long-winded pedantic pomp: "namely that with all our reason we can never get beyond the field of experiences." But since, if someone gradually questions him on his rational principles,[a] he must indeed admit that among them there are many that he has not drawn from experience, which are therefore independent of it and valid *a priori* – how and on what grounds will he then hold within limits the dogmatist (and himself), who makes use of[b] these concepts and principles beyond all possible experience for the very reason that they are cognized independently of experience. And even he, this adept of sound common sense, is not so steadfast that, despite all of his presumed and cheaply gained wisdom, he will not stumble unawares out beyond the objects of experience into the field of chimeras. Ordinarily, he is indeed deeply enough entangled therein, although he cloaks his ill-founded claims in a popular style, since he gives everything out as mere probability, reasonable conjecture, or analogy.

§32

Already from the earliest days of philosophy, apart from the sensible beings[c] or appearances (*phaenomena*) that constitute the sensible world, investigators of pure reason have thought of special intelligible beings[d] (*noumena*), which were supposed to form an intelligible world;[e] and they have granted reality to the intelligible beings alone, because they took appearance and illusion to be one and the same thing (which may well be excused in an as yet uncultivated age).[53]

In fact, if we view the objects of the senses as mere appearances, as is fitting, then we thereby admit at the very same time that a thing in itself underlies them, although we are not acquainted with this thing as it may be constituted in itself, but only with its appearance, i.e., with the way in which our senses are affected by this unknown something. Therefore the

4: 315

[a] *Vernunftprincipien*
[b] Adding *sich*, with Ak.
[c] *Sinnenwesen*
[d] *Verstandeswesen*
[e] *Verstandeswelt*

understanding, just by the fact that it accepts appearances, also admits to the existence of things in themselves, and to that extent we can say that the representation of such beings as underlie the appearances, hence of mere intelligible beings, is not merely permitted but also unavoidable.

Our critical deduction in no way excludes things of such kind (*noumena*), but rather restricts the principles of aesthetic[54] in such a way that they are not supposed to extend to all things, whereby everything would be transformed into mere appearance, but are to be valid only for objects of a possible experience. Hence intelligible beings are thereby allowed only with the enforcement of this rule, which brooks no exception whatsoever: that we do not know and cannot know anything determinate about these intelligible beings at all, because our pure concepts of the understanding as well as our pure intuitions refer to nothing but objects of possible experience, hence to mere beings of sense, and that as soon as one departs from the latter, not the least significance remains for those concepts.

§33

There is in fact something insidious in our pure concepts of the understanding, as regards enticement toward a transcendent use; for so I call that use which goes out beyond all possible experience. It is not only that our concepts of substance, of force, of action, of reality, etc., are wholly independent of experience, likewise contain no sensory appearance whatsoever, and so in fact seem to refer to things in themselves (*noumena*); but also, which strengthens this supposition yet further, that they contain in themselves a necessity of determination which experience never equals. The concept of cause contains a rule, according to which from one state of affairs another follows with necessity; but experience can only show us that from one state of things another state often, or, at best, commonly, follows, and it can therefore furnish neither strict universality nor necessity (and so forth).

Consequently, the concepts of the understanding appear to have much more significance and content than they would if their entire vocation were exhausted by mere use in experience, and so the understanding unheededly builds onto the house of experience a much roomier wing, which it crowds with mere beings of thought, without once noticing that it has taken its otherwise legitimate concepts far beyond the boundaries of their use.

4: 316

§34

Two important, nay completely indispensable, though utterly dry investigations were therefore needed, which were carried out in the *Critique*, pp.137ff. and 235ff.[55] Through the first of these it was shown that the senses do not supply pure concepts of the understanding *in concreto*, but only the schema for their use, and that the object appropriate to this schema is found only in experience (as the product of the understanding from materials of sensibility). In the second investigation (*Critique*, p. 235) it is shown: that notwithstanding the independence from experience of our pure concepts of the understanding and principles, and even their apparently larger sphere of use, nonetheless, outside the field of experience nothing at all can be thought by means of them, because they can do nothing but merely determine the logical form of judgment with respect to given intuitions; but since beyond the field of sensibility there is no intuition at all, these pure concepts lack completely all significance, in that there are no means through which they can be exhibited *in concreto*, and so all such *noumena*, together with their aggregate – an intelligible* world – are nothing but representations of a problem, whose object is in itself perfectly possible, but whose solution, given the nature of our understanding, is completely impossible, since our understanding is no faculty of intuition but only of the connection of given intuitions in an experience; and experience therefore has to contain all the objects for our concepts, whereas apart from it all concepts will be without significance, since no intuition can be put under them.

4: 317

§35

The imagination may perhaps be excused if it daydreams[c] every now and then, i.e., if it does not cautiously hold itself inside the limits of experience; for it will at least be enlivened and strengthened through such free flight, and it will always be easier to moderate its boldness than to remedy its languor. That the understanding, however, which is supposed *to think*, should, instead of that, *daydream* – for this it can never

---

* Not (as is commonly said) an *intellectual[a]* world. For the *cognitions* through the understanding are *intellectual*, and the same sort of cognitions also refer to our sensible world; but *intelligible[b]* means *objects* insofar as they can be represented *only through the understanding*, and none of our sensory intuitions can refer to them. Since, however, to each object there must nonetheless correspond some possible intuition or other, we would therefore have to think of an understanding that intuits things immediately; of this sort of understanding, however, we have not the least concept, hence also not of the *intelligible beings* to which it is supposed to refer.

[a] *intellectuellen*
[b] *intelligibel*
[c] *schwärmt*

be forgiven; for all assistance in setting bounds, where needed, to the revelry[a] of the imagination depends on it alone.

The understanding begins all this very innocently and chastely. First, it puts in order the elementary cognitions that dwell in it prior to all experience but must nonetheless always have their application in experience. Gradually, it removes these constraints, and what is to hinder it from doing so, since the understanding has quite freely taken its principles from within itself? And now reference is made first to newly invented forces in nature, soon thereafter to beings outside nature, in a word, to a world for the furnishing of which building materials cannot fail us, since they are abundantly supplied through fertile invention, and though not indeed confirmed by experience, are also never refuted by it. That is also the reason why young thinkers so love metaphysics of the truly dogmatic sort, and often sacrifice their time and their otherwise useful talent to it.

It can, however, help nothing at all to want to curb these fruitless endeavors of pure reason by all sorts of admonitions about the difficulty of resolving such deeply obscure questions, by complaints over the limits of our reason, and by reducing assertions to mere conjectures. For if the *impossibility* of these endeavors has not been clearly demonstrated, and if reason's *knowledge of itself*[b] does not become true science, in which the sphere of its legitimate use is distinguished with geometrical certainty (so to speak) from that of its empty and fruitless use, then these futile efforts will never be fully abandoned.

§36
4: 318
How is nature itself possible?

This question, which is the highest point that transcendental philosophy can ever reach, and up to which, as its boundary and completion, it must be taken, actually contains two questions.

FIRST: How is nature possible in general in the *material* sense, namely, according to intuition, as the sum total of appearances; how are space, time, and that which fills them both, the object of sensation, possible in general? The answer is: by means of the constitution of our sensibility, in accordance with which our sensibility is affected in its characteristic way by objects that are in themselves unknown to it and that are wholly distinct from said appearances. This answer is, in the book itself, given in the Transcendental Aesthetic, but here in the *Prolegomena* through the solution of the first main question.

[a] *Schwärmerei*
[b] *Selbsterkenntniss*

SECOND: How is nature possible in the *formal*^a sense, as the sum total of the rules to which all appearances must be subject if they are to be thought as connected in one experience? The answer cannot come out otherwise than: it is possible only by means of the constitution of our understanding, in accordance with which all these representations of sensibility are necessarily referred to one consciousness, and through which, first, the characteristic mode of our thinking, namely by means of rules, is possible, and then, by means of these rules, experience is possible – which is to be wholly distinguished from insight into objects in themselves. This answer is, in the book itself, given in the Transcendental Logic,[56] but here in the *Prolegomena*, in the course of solving the second main question.

But how this characteristic property of our sensibility itself may be possible, or that of our understanding and of the necessary apperception that underlies it and all thinking, cannot be further solved and answered, because we always have need of them in turn for all answering and for all thinking of objects.

There are many laws of nature that we can know only through experience, but lawfulness in the connection of appearances, i.e., nature in general, we cannot come to know through any experience, because experience itself has need of such laws, which lie *a priori* at the basis of its possibility.

4: 319

The possibility of experience in general is thus at the same time the universal law of nature, and the principles of the former are themselves the laws of the latter. For we are not acquainted with nature except as the sum total of appearances, i.e., of the representations in us, and so we cannot get the laws of their connection from anywhere else except the principles of their connection in us, i.e., from the conditions of necessary unification in one consciousness, which unification constitutes the possibility of experience.

Even the main proposition that has been elaborated throughout this entire part, that universal laws of nature can be cognized *a priori*, already leads by itself to the proposition: that the highest legislation for nature must lie in ourselves, i.e., in our understanding, and that we must not seek the universal laws of nature from nature by means of experience, but, conversely, must seek nature, as regards its universal conformity to law, solely in the conditions of the possibility of experience that lie in our sensibility and understanding; for how would it otherwise be possible to become acquainted with these laws *a priori*, since they are surely not rules of analytic cognition, but are genuine synthetic amplifications of cognition? Such agreement, and indeed necessary agreement, between the principles^b of

---

^a Emphasis added, with Vorländer.
^b *Principien*

possible experience and the laws of the possibility of nature, can come about only from one of two causes: either these laws are taken from nature by means of experience, or, conversely, nature is derived from the laws of the possibility of experience in general and is fully identical with the mere universal lawfulness of experience. The first one contradicts itself, for the universal laws of nature can and must be cognized *a priori* (i.e., independently of all experience) and set at the foundation of all empirical use of the understanding; so only the second remains.*

4: 320 We must, however, distinguish empirical laws of nature, which always presuppose particular perceptions, from the pure or universal laws of nature, which, without having particular perceptions underlying them, contain merely the conditions for the necessary unification of such perceptions in one experience; with respect to the latter laws, nature and *possible* experience are one and the same, and since in possible experience the lawfulness rests on the necessary connection of appearances in one experience (without which we would not be able to cognize any object of the sensible world at all), and so on the original laws of the understanding, then, even though it sounds strange at first, it is nonetheless certain, if I say with respect to the universal laws of nature: *the understanding does not draw its* (a priori) *laws from nature, but prescribes them to it.*

§37

We will elucidate this seemingly daring proposition through an example, which is supposed to show: that laws which we discover in objects of sensory intuition, especially if these laws have been cognized as necessary, are already held by us to be such as have been put there by the understanding, although they are otherwise in all respects like the laws of nature that we attribute to experience.

§38

If one considers the properties of the circle by which this figure unifies in a universal rule at once so many arbitrary determinations of the space within it, one cannot refrain from ascribing a nature to this geometrical thing. Thus, in particular, two lines that intersect each other and also the

---

* Crusius[57] alone knew of a middle way: namely that a spirit who can neither err nor deceive originally implanted these natural laws in us. But, since false principles are often mixed in as well – of which this man's system itself provides not a few examples – then, with the lack of sure criteria for distinguishing an authentic origin from a spurious one, the use of such a principle looks very precarious, since one can never know for sure what the spirit of truth or the father of lies may have put into us.

circle,[58] however they happen to be drawn, nonetheless always partition each other in a regular manner such that the rectangle from the parts of one line is equal to that from the other. Now I ask: "Does this law lie in the circle, or does it lie in the understanding?" i.e., does this figure, independent of the understanding, contain the basis for this law in itself, or does the understanding, since it has itself constructed the figure in accordance with its concepts (namely, the equality of the radii), at the same time insert into it the law that chords cut one another in geometrical proportion? If one traces the proofs of this law, one soon sees that it can be derived only from the condition on which the understanding based the construction of this figure, namely, the equality of the radii. If we now expand upon this concept so as to follow up still further the unity of the manifold properties of geometrical figures under common laws, and we consider the circle as a conic section, which is therefore subject to the very same fundamental conditions of construction as other conic sections, we then find that all chords that intersect within these latter (within the ellipse, the parabola, and the hyperbola) always do so in such a way that the rectangles from their parts are[a] not indeed equal, but always stand to one another in equal proportions. If from there we go still further, namely to the fundamental doctrines of physical astronomy, there appears a physical law of reciprocal attraction, extending to all material nature, the rule of which is that these attractions[b] decrease inversely with the square of the distance from each point of attraction, exactly as the spherical surfaces into which this force spreads itself increase, something that seems to reside as necessary in the nature of the things themselves and which therefore is customarily presented as cognizable *a priori*. As simple as are the sources of this law – in that they rest merely on the relation of spherical surfaces[c] with different radii – the consequence therefrom is nonetheless so excellent with respect to the variety and regularity of its agreement that not only does it follow that all possible orbits of the celestial bodies are conic sections, but also that their mutual relations are such that no other law of attraction save that of the inverse square of the distances can be conceived as suitable for a system of the world.

4: 321

Here then is nature that rests on laws that the understanding cognizes *a priori*, and indeed chiefly from universal principles[d] of the determination of space. Now I ask: do these laws of nature lie in space, and does the understanding learn them in that it merely seeks to investigate the wealth of meaning that lies in space, or do they lie in the understanding

---

[a] Adding *sind*, with Ak.
[b] Reading *sie* as plural, with the singular antecedent *Attraction*, with Vorländer.
[c] Reading *Kugelflächen* for *Kugelfläche*, with Vorländer.
[d] *allgemeinen Principien*

and in the way in which it determines space in accordance with the conditions of the synthetic unity toward which its concepts are one and all directed? Space is something so uniform, and so indeterminate with respect to all specific properties, that certainly no one will look for a stock of natural laws within it. By contrast, that which determines space into the figure of a circle, a cone, or a sphere is the understanding, insofar as it contains the basis for the unity of the construction of these figures. The mere universal form of intuition called space is therefore certainly the substratum of all intuitions determinable upon particular objects, and, admittedly, the condition for the possibility and variety of those intuitions lies in this space; but the unity of the objects is determined solely through the understanding, and indeed according to conditions that reside in its own nature; and so the understanding is the origin of the universal order of nature; in that it comprehends all appearances under its own laws and thereby first brings about experience *a priori* (with respect to its form), in virtue of which everything that is to be cognized only through experience is necessarily subject to its laws. For we are not concerned with the nature of *the things in themselves*, which is independent of the conditions of both our senses and understanding, but with nature as an object of possible experience, and here the understanding, since it makes experience possible, at the same time makes it that the sensible world is either not an object of experience at all, or else is nature.

§39
Appendix to pure natural science
On the system of categories

Nothing can be more desirable to a philosopher than to be able to derive, *a priori* from one principle,[a] the multiplicity of concepts or basic principles[b] that previously had exhibited themselves to him piecemeal in the use he had made of them *in concreto*, and in this way to be able to unite them all in one cognition. Previously, he believed simply that what was left to him after a certain abstraction, and that appeared, through mutual comparison, to form a distinct kind of cognitions, had been completely assembled: but this was only an *aggregate*; now he knows that only precisely so many, not more, not fewer, can constitute this[c] kind of cognition, and he has understood the necessity of his division: this is a comprehending,[d] and only now does he have a *system*.

---

[a] *Princip*
[b] *Grundsätze*
[c] Reading *diese* for *die*, as suggested in Vorländer.
[d] *ein Begreifen*; contrasted with the "comparison" mentioned earlier.

To pick out from ordinary cognition the concepts that are not based on any particular experience and yet are present in all cognition from experience (for which they constitute as it were the mere form of con-   4: 323 nection) required no greater reflection or more insight than to cull from a language rules for the actual use of words in general, and so to compile the elements for a grammar (and in fact both investigations are very closely related to one another) without, for all that, even being able to give a reason why any given language should have precisely this and no other formal constitution, and still less why precisely so many, neither more nor fewer, of such formal determinations of the language can be found at all.

Aristotle had compiled ten such pure elementary concepts under the name of categories.* To these, which were also called predicaments, he later felt compelled to append five post-predicaments,** some of which (like *prius, simul, motus*) are indeed already found in the former; but this rhapsody[59] could better pass for, and be deserving of praise as, a hint for future inquirers than as an idea worked out according to rules, and so with the greater enlightenment of philosophy it too has been rejected as completely useless.

During an investigation of the pure elements of human cognition (containing nothing empirical), I was first of all able after long reflection to distinguish and separate with reliability the pure elementary concepts of sensibility (space and time) from those of the understanding. By this means the seventh, eighth, and ninth categories were now excluded from the above list. The others could be of no use to me, because no principle[c] was available whereby the understanding could be fully surveyed and all of its functions, from which its pure concepts arise, determined exhaustively and with precision.

In order, however, to discover such a principle,[d] I cast about for an act of the understanding that contains all the rest and that differentiates itself only through various modifications or moments in order to bring the multiplicity of representation under the unity of thinking in general; and there I found that this act of the understanding consists in judging. Here lay before me now, already finished though not yet wholly free of defects, the work of the logicians, through which I was put in

---

* 1. *Substantia.* 2. *Qualitas.* 3. *Quantitas.* 4. *Relatio.* 5. *Actio.* 6. *Passio.* 7. *Quando.* 8. *Ubi.* 9. *Situs.* 10. *Habitus.*[a]
** *Oppositum, Prius, Simul, Motus, Habere.*[b]

[a] Substance, quality, quantity, relation, action, affection, time, place, position, state.
[b] Opposition, priority, simultaneity, motion, possession.
[c] *Princip*
[d] *Princip*

4: 324 the position to present a complete table of pure functions of the understanding, which were however undetermined with respect to every object. Finally, I related these functions of judging to objects in general, or rather to the condition for determining judgments as objectively valid, and there arose pure concepts of the understanding, about which I could have no doubt that precisely these only, and of them only so many, neither more nor fewer, can make up our entire cognition of things out of the bare understanding. As was proper, I called them *categories*, after their ancient name, whereby I reserved for myself to append in full, under the name of *predicables*, all the concepts derivable from them – whether by connecting them with one another, or with the pure form of appearance (space and time) or its matter, provided the latter is not yet determined empirically (the object of sensation in general) – just as soon as a system of transcendental philosophy should be achieved, on behalf of which I had, at the time, been concerned only with the critique of reason itself.

The essential thing, however, in this system of categories, by which it is distinguished from that ancient rhapsody (which proceeded without any principle),[a] and in virtue of which it alone deserves to be counted as philosophy, consists in this: that through it[b] the true signification of the pure concepts of the understanding and the condition of their use could be exactly determined. For here it became apparent that the pure concepts of the understanding are, of themselves, nothing but logical functions, but that as such they do not constitute the least concept of an object in itself but rather need sensory intuition as a basis, and even then they serve only to determine empirical judgments, which are otherwise undetermined and indifferent with respect to all the functions of judging, with respect to those functions, so as to procure universal validity for them, and thereby to make *judgments of experience* possible in general.

This sort of insight into the nature of the categories, which would at the same time restrict their use merely to experience, never occurred to their first originator, or to anyone after him; but without this insight (which depends precisely on their derivation or deduction), they are completely useless and are a paltry list of names, without explanation or rule for their use. Had anything like it ever occurred to the ancients, then without doubt the entire study of cognition through pure reason, which under the name of metaphysics has ruined so many good minds over the centuries, would have come down to us in a completely different 4: 325 form and would have enlightened the human understanding, instead of, as has actually happened, exhausting it in murky and vain ruminations and making it unserviceable for true science.

[a] *Princip*
[b] Reading *desselben* for *derselben*, with Ak.

This system of categories now makes all treatment of any object of pure reason itself systematic in turn, and it yields an undoubted instruction or guiding thread as to how and through what points of inquiry any metaphysical contemplation must be directed if it is to be complete; for it exhausts all moments of the understanding, under which every other concept must be brought. Thus too has arisen the table of principles, of whose completeness we can be assured only through the system of categories; and even in the division of concepts that are supposed to go beyond the physiological use of the understanding (*Critique*, p. 344, also p. 415),[60] there is always the same guiding thread, which, since it always must be taken through the same fixed points determined *a priori* in the human understanding, forms a closed circle every time, leaving no room for doubt that the object of a pure concept of the understanding or reason, insofar as it is to be examined philosophically and according to *a priori* principles, can be cognized completely in this way. I have not even been able to refrain from making use of this guide with respect to one of the most abstract of ontological classifications, namely the manifold differentiation of the *concepts of something and nothing*, and accordingly from achieving a rule-governed and necessary table (*Critique*, p. 292). *[61]

This very system, like every true system founded on a universal principle,[c] also exhibits its inestimable usefulness in that it expels all the   4: 326

---

* All sorts of nice notes can be made on a laid-out table of categories, such as: 1. that the third arises from the first and second, conjoined into one concept, 2. that in those for quantity and quality there is merely a progression[a] from Unity to Totality, or from something to nothing (for this purpose the categories of quality must stand thus: Reality, Limitation, full Negation), without *correlata* or *opposita*, while those of relation and modality carry the latter with them, 3. that, just as in the *logical table*, categorical judgments underlie all the others, so the category of substance underlines all concepts of real things, 4. that, just as modality in a judgment is not a separate predicate, so too the modal concepts[b] do not add a determination to things, and so on. Considerations such as these all have their great utility. If beyond this all the *predicables* are enumerated – they can be extracted fairly completely from any good ontology (e.g., Baumgarten's)[62] – and if they are ordered in classes under the categories (in which one must not neglect to add as complete an analysis as possible of all these concepts), then a solely analytical part of metaphysics will arise, which as yet contains no synthetic proposition whatsoever and could precede the second (synthetic) part, and, through its determinateness and completeness, might have not only utility, but beyond that, in virtue of its systematicity, a certain beauty.[63]

[a] Reading *fortgehe* for *forgehen*, with Vorländer.
[b] Reading *Modalbegriffe* for *Modelbegriffe*, with Ak.
[c] *Princip*

extraneous concepts that might otherwise creep in among these pure concepts of the understanding, and it assigns each cognition its place. Those concepts that, under the name of *concepts of reflection*, I had also put into a table under the guidance of the categories mingle in ontology with the pure concepts of the understanding without privilege and legitimate claims, although the latter are concepts of connection and thereby of the object itself, whereas the former are only concepts of the mere comparison of already given concepts, and therefore have an entirely different nature and use; through my law-governed division (*Critique*, p. 260)[64] they are extricated from this amalgam. But the usefulness of this separated table of categories shines forth yet more brightly if, as will soon be done, we separate from the categories the table of transcendental concepts of reason, which have a completely different nature and origin than the concepts of the understanding (so that the table must also have a different form), a separation that, necessary as it is, has never occurred in any system of metaphysics, as a result of which[a] these ideas of reason and concepts of the understanding run confusedly together as if they belonged to one family, like siblings, an intermingling that also could never have been avoided in the absence of a separate system of categories.

[a] Adding *wo daher*, with Ak.

Main Transcendental Question, Third Part
How is metaphysics in general possible?

Pure mathematics and pure natural science would not have needed, *for the purpose of their own security* and certainty, a deduction of the sort that we have hitherto accomplished for them both; for the first is supported by its own evidence, whereas the second, though arising from pure sources of the understanding, is nonetheless supported from experience and thoroughgoing confirmation by it – experience being a witness that natural science cannot fully renounce and dispense with, because, as philosophy,[65] despite all its certainty it can never rival mathematics. Neither science had need of the aforementioned investigation for itself, but for another science, namely metaphysics.

Apart from concepts of nature, which always find their application in experience, metaphysics is further concerned with pure concepts of reason that are never given in any possible experience whatsoever, hence with concepts whose objective reality (that they are not mere fantasies) and with assertions whose truth or falsity cannot be confirmed or exposed by any experience; and this part of metaphysics is moreover precisely that which forms its essential end, toward which all the rest is only a means – and so this science needs such a deduction *for its own sake*. The third question, now put before us, therefore concerns as it were the core and the characteristic feature of metaphysics, namely, the preoccupation of reason simply with itself, and that acquaintance*a* with objects which is presumed to arise immediately from reason's brooding over its own concepts without its either needing mediation from experience for such an acquaintance, or being able to achieve such an acquaintance through experience at all.*

* If it can be said that a science is *actual* at least in the thought*b* of all humankind from the moment it has been determined that the problems which lead to it are set before everyone by the nature of human reason, and therefore that many (if faulty) attempts at those problems are always inevitable, it will also have to be said: Metaphysics is subjectively actual (and necessarily so); and then we will rightly ask: How is it (objectively) possible?

a *Bekanntschaft*
b *Idee*

4: 328

Without a solution to this question, reason will never be satisfied with itself. The use in experience to which reason limits the pure understanding does not entirely fulfill reason's own vocation. Each individual experience is only a part of the whole[a] sphere of the domain of experience, but the *absolute totality*[b] *of all possible experience* is not itself an experience, and yet is still a necessary problem for reason, for the mere representation of which reason needs concepts entirely different from the pure concepts of the understanding, whose use is only *immanent*, i.e., refers to experience insofar as such experience can be given, whereas the concepts of reason extend to the completeness, i.e., the collective unity of the whole of possible experience, and in that way exceed any given experience and become *transcendent*.

Hence, just as the understanding needed the categories for experience, reason contains in itself the basis for ideas, by which I mean necessary concepts whose object nevertheless *cannot* be given in any experience. The latter are just as intrinsic to the nature of reason as are the former to that of the understanding; and if the ideas carry with them an illusion that can easily mislead, this illusion is unavoidable, although it can very well be prevented "from leading us astray."

Since all illusion consists in taking the subjective basis for a judgment to be objective, pure reason's knowledge of itself in its transcendent (overreaching)[c] use will be the only prevention against the errors into which reason falls if it misconstrues its vocation and, in transcendent fashion, refers to the object in itself that which concerns only its own subject and the guidance of that subject in every use that is immanent.

§41

The distinction of *ideas*, i.e., of pure concepts of reason, from categories, or pure concepts of the understanding, as cognitions of completely different type, origin, and use, is so important a piece of the foundation of a science which is to contain a system of all these cognitions *a priori* that,

4: 329

without such a division, metaphysics is utterly impossible, or at best is a disorderly and bungling endeavor to patch together a house of cards, without knowledge of the materials with which one is preoccupied and of their suitability for one or another end. If the *Critique of Pure Reason* had done nothing but first point out this distinction, it would thereby have already contributed more to elucidating[d] our conception of, and to guiding inquiry in, the field of metaphysics, than have all the fruitless

[a] *ganzen*
[b] *absolute Ganze*
[c] *überschwenglichen*
[d] *Aufklärung*

efforts undertaken previously to satisfy the transcendent problems of pure reason, without it ever being imagined that one may have been situated in a completely different field from that of the understanding, and as a result was listing the concepts of the understanding together with those of reason as if they were of the same kind.

§42

All the pure cognitions of the understanding are such that their concepts can be given in experience and their principles confirmed through experience; by contrast, the transcendent cognitions of reason neither allow what relates to their *ideas* to be given in experience, nor their *theses*[a] ever to be confirmed or refuted through experience; hence, only pure reason itself can detect the error that perhaps creeps into them, though this is very hard to do, because this selfsame reason by nature becomes dialectical through its ideas, and this unavoidable illusion cannot be kept in check through any objective and dogmatic investigation[b] of things, but only through a subjective investigation of reason itself, as a source[c] of ideas.

§43

In the *Critique* I always gave my greatest attention not only to how I could distinguish carefully the types of cognition, but also to how I could derive all[d] the concepts belonging to each type from their common source, so that I might not only, by learning their origin, be able to determine their use with certainty, but also have the inestimable advantage (never yet imagined) of cognizing *a priori*, hence according to principles,[e] the completeness of the enumeration, classification, and specification of the concepts. Failing this, everything in metaphysics   4: 330 is nothing but rhapsody, in which one never knows whether what one has is enough, or whether and where something may still be lacking. Such an advantage is, of course, available only in pure philosophy, but it constitutes the essence of that philosophy.

Since I had found the origin of the categories in the four logical functions of all judgments of the understanding, it was completely natural to look for the origin of the ideas in the three functions of syllogisms;[f] for once such pure concepts of reason (transc. ideas) have

---

[a] *Sätze*
[b] Reading *Untersuchung* for *Untersuchungen*, as suggested in Vorländer.
[c] Reading *eines Quells* for *einem Quell*, with Ak.
[d] Reading *alle* for *allein*, with Ak.
[e] *Principien*
[f] *Vernunftschlüsse*; literally, "inferences of reason."

been granted; then, if they are not to be taken for innate, they could indeed be found nowhere else except in this very act of reason which, insofar as it relates merely to form, constitutes the logical in syllogisms, but, insofar as it represents the judgments of the understanding as determined with respect to one or another *a priori* form, constitutes the transcendental concepts of pure reason.

The formal distinction of syllogisms necessitates their division into categorical, hypothetical, and disjunctive. Therefore the concepts of reason based thereupon contain first, the idea of the complete subject (the substantial), second, the idea of the complete series of conditions, and third, the determination of all concepts in the idea of a complete sum total of the possible. * The first idea was psychological,^{c} the second cosmological, the third theological; and since all three give rise to a dialectic, but each in its own way, all this provided the basis for dividing the entire dialectic of pure reason into the paralogism, the antinomy, and finally the ideal of pure reason – through which derivation it is rendered completely certain that all claims of pure reason are represented here in full, and not one can be missing, since the faculty of reason itself, whence they all originate, is thereby fully surveyed.

§44

4:331

In this examination it is in general further noteworthy: that the ideas of reason^d are not, like the categories, helpful to us in some way in using the understanding with respect to experience, but are completely dispensable with respect to such use, nay, are contrary to and obstructive of the maxims for the cognition of nature through reason, although they are still quite necessary in another respect, yet to be determined.[66]

---

* In disjunctive judgments we consider *all possibility* as divided with respect to a certain concept. The ontological principle^a of the thoroughgoing determination of a thing in general (out of all possible opposing predicates, one is attributed to each thing), which is at the same time the principle of all disjunctive judgments, founds itself upon the sum total of all possibility, in which the possibility of each thing in general is taken to be determinable.^{b} The following helps provide a small elucidation of the above proposition: That the act of reason in disjunctive syllogisms is the same in form with that by which reason achieves the idea of a sum total of all reality, which contains in itself the positive members of all opposing predicates.

^{a} *Princip*
^{b} Reading *bestimmbar* for *bestimmter*, with Ak.
^{c} Reading *psychologisch* for *physiologisch*, with Ak.
^{d} Reading *Vernunftideen* for *Vernunftidee*, with Ak.

In explaining the appearances of the soul, we can be completely indifferent as to whether it is a simple substance or not; for we are unable through any possible experience to make the concept of a simple being sensorily intelligible, hence intelligible *in concreto*; and this concept is therefore completely empty with respect to all hoped-for insight into the cause of the appearances, and cannot serve as a principle[a] of explanation of that which supplies inner or outer experience. Just as little can the cosmological ideas of the beginning of the world or the eternity of the world (*a parte ante*)[b] help us to explain any event in the world itself. Finally, in accordance with a correct maxim of natural philosophy, we must refrain from all explanations of the organization of nature drawn from the will of a supreme being,[c] because this is no longer natural philosophy but an admission that we have come to the end of it. These ideas therefore have a completely different determination of their use from that of the categories, through which (and through the principles built upon them) experience itself first became possible. Nevertheless our laborious analytic of the understanding[67] would have been entirely superfluous, if our aim had been directed toward nothing other than mere cognition of nature insofar as such cognition can be given in experience; for reason conducts its affairs in both mathematics and natural science quite safely and quite well, even without any such subtle deduction; hence our critique of the understanding joins with the ideas of pure reason for a purpose that lies beyond the use of the understanding in experience, though we have said above that the use of the understanding in this regard is wholly impossible and without object or significance. There must nonetheless be agreement between what belongs to the nature of reason and of the understanding, and the former must contribute to the perfection of the latter and cannot possibly confuse it.[68]

The solution to this question is as follows: Pure reason does not, among its ideas, have in view particular objects that might lie beyond the field of experience, but it merely demands completeness in the use of the understanding in the connection of experience. This completeness can, however, only be a completeness of principles,[d] but not of intuitions and objects. Nonetheless, in order to represent these principles determinately, reason conceives of them as the cognition of an object, cognition of which is completely determined with respect to these rules – though the object is only an idea – so as to bring cognition through

4: 332

---

[a] *Princip*
[b] "up until now," literally, "on the side of the previous."
[c] *höchsten Wesens*
[d] *Principien*

the understanding as close as possible to the completeness that this idea signifies.

§45
Preliminary Remark
On the Dialectic of Pure Reason

We have shown above (§§33, 34): that the purity of the categories from all admixture with sensory determinations can mislead reason into extending their use entirely beyond all experience to things in themselves; and yet, because the categories are themselves unable to find any intuition that could provide them with significance and sense *in concreto*, they cannot in and of themselves provide any determinate concept of anything at all, though they can indeed, as mere logical functions, represent a thing in general. Now hyperbolical objects of this kind are what are called NOUMENA or pure beings of the understanding (better: beings of thought)[a] – such as, e.g., *substance*, but which is thought *without persistence* in time, or a *cause*, which would however *not* act *in time*, and so on – because such predicates are attributed to these objects as serve only to make the lawfulness of experience possible, and yet they are nonetheless deprived of all the conditions of intuition under which alone experience is possible, as a result of which the above concepts again lose all significance.

There is, however, no danger that the understanding will of itself wantonly stray beyond its boundaries into the field of mere beings of thought, without being urged by alien laws. But if reason, which can never be fully satisfied with any use of the rules of the understanding in experience because such use is always still conditioned, requires completion of this chain of conditions, then the understanding is driven out of its circle, in order partly to represent the objects of experience in a series stretching so far that no experience can comprise the likes of it, partly (in order to complete the series) even to look for NOUMENA entirely outside said experience to which reason can attach the chain and in that way, independent at last of the conditions of experience, nonetheless can make its hold complete. These then are the transcendental ideas, which, although in accordance with the true but hidden end of the natural determination of our reason they may be aimed not at overreaching concepts but merely at the unbounded expansion of the use of concepts in experience, may nonetheless, through an unavoidable illusion, elicit from the understanding a *transcendent* use, which, though deceitful, nonetheless cannot be curbed by any resolve to stay within the bounds of experience, but only through scientific instruction and hard work.

4: 333

---

[a] *Gedankenwesen*, contrasted with the just previous *Verstandeswesen*.

§46
I. Psychological ideas (*Critique*, pp. 341ff.)[69]

It has long been observed that in all substances the true subject – namely that which remains after all accidents (as predicates) have been removed – and hence the *substantial* itself, is unknown to us; and various complaints have been made about these limits to our insight. But it needs to be said that human understanding is not to be blamed because it does not know the substantial in things, i.e., cannot determine it by itself, but rather because it wants to cognize determinately, like an object that is given, what is only an idea. Pure reason demands that for each predicate of a thing we should seek its appropriate subject, but that for this subject, which is in turn necessarily only a predicate, we should seek its subject again, and so forth to infinity (or as far as we get). But from this it follows that we should take nothing that we can attain for a final subject, and that the substantial itself could never be thought by our ever-so-deeply penetrating understanding, even if the whole of nature were laid bare before it; for the specific nature of our understanding consists in thinking everything discursively, i.e., through concepts, hence through mere predicates, among which the absolute subject must therefore always be absent. Consequently, all real properties by which we cognize bodies are mere accidents for which we lack a subject – even impenetrability, which must always be conceived only as the effect of a force.

4: 334

Now it does appear as if we have something substantial in the consciousness of ourselves (i.e., in the thinking subject), and indeed have it in immediate intuition; for all the predicates of inner sense are referred to the *I* as subject, and this *I* cannot again be thought as the predicate of some other subject. It therefore appears that in this case completeness in referring the given concepts to a subject as predicates is not a mere idea, but that the object, namely the *absolute subject* itself, is given in experience. But this expectation is disappointed. For the I is not a concept* at all, but only a designation of the object of inner sense insofar as we do not further cognize it through any predicate; hence although it cannot itself be the predicate of any other thing, just as little can it be a determinate concept of an absolute subject, but as in all the other cases it can only be the referring of inner appearances to their unknown subject.

---

* If the representation of apperception, the *I*, were a concept through which anything might be thought, it could then be used as a predicate for other things, or contain such predicates in itself. But it is nothing more than a feeling of an existence without the least concept, and is only a representation of that to which all thinking stands in relation (*relatione accidentis*).[a]

a "relation of accident"

Nevertheless, through a wholly natural misunderstanding, this idea (which, as a regulative principle, serves perfectly well to destroy completely all materialistic explanations of the inner appearances of our soul)[a] gives rise to a seemingly plausible argument for inferring the nature of our thinking being from this presumed cognition of the substantial in it, inasmuch as knowledge of its nature falls completely outside the sum total of experience.

§47

This thinking self (the soul), as the ultimate subject of thinking, which cannot itself be represented as the predicate of another thing, may now indeed be called substance: but this concept nonetheless remains completely empty and without any consequences, if persistence (as that which renders the concept of substances fertile within experience) cannot be proven of it.

4: 335   Persistence, however, can never be proven from the concept of a substance as a thing in itself, but only for the purposes of experience. This has been sufficiently established in the first Analogy of Experience (*Critique*, p. 182);[70] and anyone who will not grant this proof can test for themselves whether they succeed in proving, from the concept of a subject that does not exist as the predicate of another thing, that the existence of that subject is persistent throughout, and that it can neither come into being nor pass away, either in itself or through any natural cause. Synthetic *a priori* propositions of this type can never be proven in themselves, but only in relation to things as objects of a possible experience.

§48

If, therefore, we want to infer the persistence of the soul from the concept of the soul as substance, this can be valid of the soul only for the purpose of possible experience, and not of the soul as a thing in itself and beyond all possible experience. But life is the subjective condition of all our possible experience: consequently, only the persistence of the soul during life can be inferred, for the death of a human being is the end of all experience as far as the soul as an object of experience is concerned (provided that the opposite has not been proven, which is the very matter in question). Therefore the persistence of the soul can be proven only during the life of a human being (which proof will doubtless be granted us), but not after death (which is actually our concern) – and indeed then only from the universal ground that the concept of substance, insofar as it is to be considered as connected necessarily with the concept of persistence,

---

[a] The original has an asterisk here, with no corresponding note.

can be so connected only in accordance with a principle of possible experience, and hence only for the purpose of the latter.*

§49

That our outer perceptions not only do correspond to something real[b] outside us, but must so correspond, also can never be proven as a connection of things in themselves, but can well be proven for the purpose of experience. This is as much as to say: it can very well be proven that there is something outside us of an empirical kind, and hence as appearance in space; for we are not concerned with objects other than those which belong to a possible experience, just because such objects cannot be given to us in any experience and therefore are nothing for us. Outside me empirically is that which is intuited in space; and because this space, together with all the appearances it contains, belongs to those representations whose connection according to laws of experience proves their objective truth, just as the connection of the appearances of the inner sense proves the reality[c] of my soul (as an object of inner sense), it follows that I am, by means of outer appearances, just as conscious of the reality of bodies

---

* It is in fact quite remarkable that metaphysicians have always slid so blithely over the principle of the persistence of substances, without ever attempting to prove it; doubtless because they found themselves completely forsaken by all grounds of proof as soon as they commenced with the concept of substance. Common sense, being well aware that without this assumption no unification of perceptions in an experience would be possible, made up for this defect with a postulate; for it could never extract this principle from experience itself, partly because experience cannot follow the materials (substances) through all their alterations and dissolutions far enough to be able to find matter always undiminished, partly because the principle contains *necessity*, which is always the sign of an *a priori* principle.[a] But the metaphysicians applied this principle confidently to the concept of the soul as a *substance* and inferred its necessary continuation after the death of a human being (principally because the simplicity of this substance, which had been inferred from the indivisibility of consciousness, saved it from destruction through dissolution). Had they found the true source of this principle, which however would have required far deeper investigations than they ever wanted to start, then they would have seen: that this law of the persistence of substances is granted only for the purpose of experience and therefore can hold good only for things insofar as they are to be cognized in experience and connected with other things, but never for things irrespective of all possible experience, hence not for the soul after death.

[a] *Princips*
[b] *Wirkliches*
[c] *Wirklichkeit*

as outer appearances in space, as I am, by means of inner experience, conscious of the existence of my soul in time – which soul I cognize[a] only as an object of inner sense through the appearances constituting an inner state, and whose being as it is in itself,[b] which underlies these appearances, is unknown to me. Cartesian idealism therefore distinguishes only outer experience from dream, and lawfulness as a criterion of the truth of the former from the disorder and false illusion of the latter.[c] In both cases it presupposes space and time as conditions for the existence of objects and merely asks whether the objects of the outer senses are actually[d] to be found in the space in which we put them while awake, in the way that the object of inner sense, the soul, actually is in time, i.e., whether experience carries with itself sure criteria to distinguish it from imagination. Here the doubt can easily be removed, and we always remove it in ordinary life by investigating the connection of appearances in both space and time according to universal laws of experience, and if the representation of outer things consistently agrees therewith, we cannot doubt that those things should not constitute truthful experience. Because appearances are considered as appearances only in accordance with their connection within experience, material idealism can therefore very easily be removed; and it is just as secure an experience that bodies exist outside us (in space) as that I myself exist in accordance with the representation of inner sense (in time) – for the concept: *outside us*, signifies only existence in space. Since, however, the I in the proposition *I am* does not signify merely the object of inner intuition (in time) but also the subject of consciousness, just as body does not signify merely outer intuition (in space) but also the thing *in itself* that underlies this appearance, accordingly the question of whether bodies (as appearances of outer sense) exist *outside my thought* as bodies in nature[e] can without hesitation be answered negatively; but here matters do not stand otherwise for the question of whether I myself *as an appearance of inner sense* (the soul according to empirical psychology) exist in time outside my power of representation, for this question must also be answered negatively. In this way everything is, when reduced to its true signification, conclusive and certain. Formal idealism (elsewhere called transcendental idealism by me) actually destroys[f] material or Cartesian idealism. For if space is nothing but a form of my sensibility, then it is, as a representation in me,

4: 337

---

[a] Reading *erkenne* for *erkennen*, with Vorländer.
[b] *Wesen an sich selbst*
[c] *der letzteren*, plural for dreams; rejecting the emendation to *des letztern* in Ak.
[d] *wirklich*
[e] Placing *in der Natur* after *ausser meinen Gedanken*, with Vorländer, as opposed to its original placement after *ohne Bedenken*.
[f] *aufhebt*

just as real*ᵃ* as I am myself, and the only question remaining concerns the empirical truth of the appearances in this space. If this is not the case, but rather space and the appearances in it are something existing outside us, then all the criteria of experience can never, outside our perception, prove the reality of these objects outside us.

§50

II. Cosmological ideas (*Critique*, pp. 405 ff.)[71]

This product of pure reason in its transcendent use is its most remarkable phenomenon, and it works the most strongly of all to awaken philosophy from its dogmatic slumber, and to prompt it toward the difficult business of the critique of reason itself.

I call this idea cosmological because it always finds its object only in the sensible world and needs no other world than that whose object*ᵇ* is an object*ᶜ* for the senses, and so, thus far, is immanent*ᵈ* and not transcendent, and therefore, up to this point, is not yet an idea; by contrast, to think of the soul as a simple substance already amounts to thinking of it as an object (the simple) the likes of which cannot be represented at all to the senses. Notwithstanding all that, the cosmological idea expands the connection of the conditioned with its condition (be it mathematical or dynamic) so greatly that experience can never match it, and therefore it is, with respect to this point, always an idea whose object can never be adequately given in any experience whatever.

§51

In the first place, the usefulness of a system of categories is here revealed so clearly and unmistakably that even if there were no further grounds of proof of that system, this alone would sufficiently establish their indispensability in the system of pure reason. There are no more than four such transcendental*ᵉ* ideas, as many as there are classes of categories; in each of them, however, they refer only to the absolute completeness of the series of conditions for a given conditioned. In accordance with these cosmological ideas there are also only four kinds of dialectical assertions of pure reason, which show themselves to be dialectical because for each such assertion a contradictory one stands in opposition in accordance

---

ᵃ *wirklich*
ᵇ *Gegenstand*
ᶜ *Object*
ᵈ *einheimisch*
ᵉ Reading *transscendentalen* for *transscendenten*, as suggested by Vorländer, and in accordance with §§45, 55–7, and 60.

129

4: 339   with equally plausible principles of pure reason, a conflict that cannot be avoided by any metaphysical art of the most subtle distinctions, but that requires the philosopher to return to the first sources of pure reason itself. This antinomy, by no means arbitrarily contrived, but grounded in the nature of human reason and so unavoidable and neverending, contains the following four theses together with their antitheses.[a]

I.[b]

Thesis
The world has, as to time and space,
a beginning (a boundary).

Antithesis
The world is, as to time and space,
infinite.

<table>
<tr>
<td>

2.

Thesis
Everything in the world
is constituted out of the
simple.

Antithesis
There is nothing simple,
but everything is
composite.

</td>
<td>

3.

Thesis
There exist in the world
causes through
freedom.

Antithesis
There is no freedom,
but everything is
nature.

</td>
</tr>
</table>

4.
Thesis
In the series of causes in the world there is a
necessary being.

Antithesis
There is nothing necessary in this series, but in it
everything is contingent.

§52a

Here is now the strangest phenomenon of human reason, no other example of which can be pointed to in any of its other uses. If (as normally happens) we think of the appearances of the sensible world as things in themselves, if we take the principles of their connection to be principles that are universally valid for things in themselves and not merely 4: 340   for experience (as is just as common, nay, is unavoidable without our

---

[a] *Sätze and Gegensätzen*; in the *Kritik*, assertion and counterassertion are labelled *These and Antithese*, terms that are used below, §§52b, 52c.

[b] Stress added to the last line of the thesis and antithesis, to parallel the typography in 2, 3, and 4.

Critique): then an unexpected conflict comes to light, which can never be settled in the usual dogmatic manner, since both thesis and antithesis can be established through equally evident, clear, and incontestable proofs – for I will vouch for the correctness of all these proofs – and therefore reason is seen to be divided against itself, a situation that makes the skeptic rejoice, but must make the critical philosopher pensive and uneasy.

§52b

One can tinker around with metaphysics in sundry ways without even suspecting that one might be venturing into untruth. For if only we do not contradict ourselves – something that is indeed entirely possible with synthetic, though completely fanciful, propositions – then we can never be refuted by experience in all such cases where the concepts we connect are mere ideas, which can by no means be given (in their entire content) in experience. For how would we decide through experience: Whether the world has existed from eternity, or has a beginning? Whether matter is infinitely divisible, or is constituted out of simple parts? Concepts such as these cannot be given in any experience (even the greatest possible), and so the falsity of the affirmative or negative thesis cannot be discovered through that touchstone.

The single possible case in which reason would reveal (against its will) its secret dialectic (which it falsely passes off as dogmatics) would be that in which it based an assertion on a universally*a* acknowledged principle, and, with the greatest propriety in the mode of inference, derived the direct opposite from another equally accredited principle. Now this case is here actual, and indeed is so with respect to four natural ideas of reason, from which there arise – each with proper consistency and from universally acknowledged principles – four assertions on one side and just as many counterassertions on the other, thereby revealing the dialectical illusion of pure reason in the use of these principles, which otherwise would have had to remain forever hidden.

Here is, therefore, a decisive test, which must necessarily disclose to us a fault that lies hidden in the presuppositions of reason.* Of two mutually   4: 341

---

* I therefore desire that the critical reader concern himself mainly with this antinomy, because nature itself seems to have set it up to make reason suspicious in its bold claims and to force a self-examination. I promise to answer for each proof I have given of both thesis*b* and antithesis,*c* and thereby to establish the certainty of the inevitable antinomy of reason. If the reader is induced, through this strange phenomenon, to reexamine the presupposition that underlies it, he will then feel constrained to investigate more deeply with me the primary foundation of all cognition through pure reason.

contradictory propositions, both cannot be false save when the concept underlying them both is itself contradictory; e.g., the two propositions: a square circle is round, and: a square circle is not round, are both false. For, as regards the first, it is false that the aforementioned circle is round, since it is square; but it is also false that it is not round, i.e., has corners, since it is a circle. The logical mark of the impossibility of a concept consists, then, in this: that under the presupposition of this concept, two contradictory propositions would be false simultaneously; and since between these two no third proposition can be thought, through this concept *nothing at all* is thought.

§52c

Now underlying the first two antinomies, which I call mathematical because they concern adding together or dividing up the homogeneous, is a contradictory concept of this type; and by this means I explain how it comes about that thesis and antithesis are false in both.

If I speak of objects in time and space, I am not speaking of things in themselves (since I know nothing of them), but only of things in appearance, i.e., of experience as a distinct mode of cognition of objects that is granted to human beings alone. I must not say of that which I think in space or time: that it is in itself in space and time, independent of this thought of mine; for then I would contradict myself, since space and time, together with the appearances in them, are nothing existing in themselves and outside my representations, but are themselves only modes of representation, and it is patently contradictory to say of a mere mode of representation that it also exists outside our representation. The objects of the senses therefore exist only in experience; by contrast, to grant them a self-subsistent existence of their own, without experience or prior to it, is as much as to imagine that experience is also real without experience or prior to it.

Now if I ask about the magnitude of the world with respect to space and time, for all of my concepts it is just as impossible to assert that it is infinite as that it is finite. For neither of these can be contained in experience, because it is not possible to have experience either of an *infinite* space or infinitely flowing time, or[d] of a *bounding* of the world by an empty space or by an earlier, empty time; these are only ideas. Therefore the magnitude of the world, determined one way or the other, must

4: 342

---

[a] Reading *allgemein* for *allgemeinen*, with Ak.
[b] *Thesis*
[c] *Antithesis*
[d] Reading *noch* for *nach*, with Ak.

lie in itself, apart from all experience. But this contradicts the concept of a sensible world, which is merely a sum total of appearance, whose existence and connection takes place only in representation, namely in experience, since it is not a thing in itself,[a] but is itself nothing but a kind of representation. From this it follows that, since the concept of a sensible world existing for itself is self-contradictory, any solution to this problem as to its magnitude will always be false, whether the attempted solution be affirmative or negative.

The same holds for the second antinomy, which concerns dividing up the appearances. For these appearances are mere representations, and the parts exist only in the representation of them, hence in the dividing, i.e., in a possible experience in which they are given, and the dividing therefore proceeds only as far as possible experience reaches. To assume that an appearance, e.g., of a body, contains within itself, before all experience, all of the parts to which possible experience can ever attain, means: to give to a mere appearance, which can exist only in experience, at the same time an existence of its own previous to experience, which is to say: that mere representations are present before they are encountered in the representational power, which contradicts itself and hence also contradicts every solution to this misunderstood problem, whether that solution asserts that bodies in themselves consist of infinitely many parts or of a finite number of simple parts.

§53

4: 343

In the first (mathematical) class of antinomy, the falsity of the presupposition consisted in the following: that something self-contradictory (namely, appearance as a thing in itself)[b] would be represented as being unifiable in a concept. But regarding the second, namely the dynamical, class of antinomy, the falsity of the presupposition consists in this: that something that is unifiable is represented as contradictory; consequently, while in the first case both of the mutually opposing assertions were false, here on the contrary the assertions, which are set in opposition to one another through mere misunderstanding, can both be true.

Specifically, mathematical combination necessarily presupposes the homogeneity of the things combined (in the concept of magnitude), but dynamical connection does not require this at all. If it is a question of the magnitude of something extended, all parts must be homogeneous among themselves and with the whole; by contrast, in the connection of cause and effect homogeneity can indeed be found, but is not necessary;

[a] *Sache an sich*
[b] *Sache an sich selbst*

for the concept of causality (whereby through one thing, something completely different from it is posited) at least does not require it.

If the objects of the sensible world were taken for things in themselves, and the previously stated natural laws for laws of things in themselves, contradiction would be unavoidable. In the same way, if the subject of freedom were represented, like the other objects, as a mere appearance, contradiction could again not be avoided, for the same thing would be simultaneously affirmed and denied of the same object in the same sense. But if natural necessity is referred only to appearances and freedom only to things in themselves, then no contradiction arises if both kinds of causality are assumed or conceded equally, however difficult or impossible it may be to make causality of the latter kind conceivable.

Within appearance, every effect is an event, or something that happens in time; the effect must, in accordance with the universal law of nature, be preceded by a determination of the causality of its cause (a state of the cause), from which the effect follows in accordance with a constant law. But this determination of the cause to causality must also be something *that* occurs or *takes place*; the cause must have *begun* to act, for otherwise no sequence in time could be thought between it and the effect. Both the effect and the causality of the cause would have always existed. Therefore the *determination* of the cause *to act* must also have arisen among the appearances, and so must, like its effect, be an event, which again must have its cause, and so on, and hence natural necessity must be the condition in accordance with which efficient causes are determined. Should, by contrast, freedom be a property of certain causes of appearances, then that freedom must, in relation to the appearances as events, be a faculty of starting those events *from itself (sponte)*,[a] i.e., without the causality of the cause itself having to begin, and hence without need for any other ground to determine its beginning. But then *the cause*, as to its causality, would not have to be subject to temporal determinations of its state, i.e., would *not* have to be *appearance* at all, i.e., would have to be taken for a thing in itself, and only the *effects* would have to be taken for *appearances*.* If this sort of influence of intelligible beings on appearances

4: 344

---

* The idea of freedom has its place solely in the relation of the *intellectual*,[b] as cause, to the *appearance*, as effect. Therefore we cannot bestow freedom upon matter in consideration of the unceasing activity by which it fills its space, even though this activity occurs through an inner principle. We can just as little find any concept of freedom to fit a purely intelligible being, e.g., God, insofar as his action is immanent. For his action, although independent of causes determining it from outside, nevertheless is determined in his eternal reason, hence in the divine *nature*. Only if *something* should *begin* through an action, hence the effect be found in the time series, and so in the sensible world (e.g., the beginning of the world), does the question arise of whether the causality of the cause must itself also have a beginning, or whether the cause

can be thought without contradiction, then natural necessity will indeed attach to every connection of cause and effect in the sensible world, and yet that cause which is itself not an appearance (though it underlies appearance) will still be entitled to freedom, and therefore nature and freedom will be attributable without contradiction to the very same thing, but in different respects, in the one case as appearance, in the other as a thing in itself.

We have in us a faculty that not only stands in connection with its subjectively determining grounds, which are the natural causes of its actions – and thus far is the faculty of a being which itself belongs to appearances – but that also is related to objective grounds that are mere ideas, insofar as these ideas can determine this faculty, a connection that is expressed by *ought*.[c] This faculty is called *reason*, and insofar as we are considering a being (the human being) solely as regards this objectively determinable reason, this being cannot be considered as a being of the senses; rather, the aforesaid property is the property of a thing in itself, and the possibility of that property – namely, how the *ought*, which has never yet happened, can determine the activity of this being and can be the cause of actions whose effect is an appearance in the sensible world – we cannot comprehend at all. Yet the casuality of reason with respect to effects in the sensible world would nonetheless be freedom, insofar as *objective grounds*, which are themselves ideas, are taken to be determining with respect to that causality. For the action of that causality would in that case not depend on any subjective, hence also not on any temporal conditions, and would therefore also not depend on the natural law that serves to determine those conditions, because grounds of reason provide the rule for actions universally, from principles, without influence from the circumstances of time or place.

What I adduce here counts only as an example, for intelligibility, and does not belong necessarily to our question, which must be decided from mere concepts independently of properties that we find in the actual world.

I can now say without contradiction: all actions of rational beings, insofar as they are appearances (are encountered in some experience or

can originate an effect without its causality itself having a beginning. In the first case the concept of this causality is a concept of natural necessity, in the second of freedom. From this the reader will see that, since I have explained freedom as the faculty to begin an event by oneself, I have exactly hit that concept which is the problem of metaphysics.

[a] "spontaneously"
[b] *des Intellektuellen*
[c] *Sollen*

other), are subject to natural necessity; but the very same actions, with respect only to the rational subject and its faculty of acting in accordance with bare reason, are free. What, then, is required for natural necessity? Nothing more than the determinability of every event in the sensible world according to constant laws, and therefore a relation to a cause within appearance; whereby the underlying thing in itself and its causality remain unknown. But I say: *the law of nature remains*, whether the rational being be a cause of effects in the sensible world through reason and hence through freedom, or whether that being does not determine such effects through rational grounds. For if the first is the case, the action takes place according to maxims whose effect within appearance will always conform

4: 346   to constant laws; if the second is the case, and the action does not take place according to principles of reason, then it is subject to the empirical laws of sensibility, and in both cases the effects are connected according to constant laws; but we require nothing more for natural necessity, and indeed know nothing more of it. In the first case, however, reason is the cause of these natural laws and is therefore free, in the second case the effects flow according to mere natural laws of sensibility, because reason exercises no influence on them; but, because of this, reason is not itself determined by sensibility (which is impossible), and it is therefore also free in this case. Therefore freedom does not impede the natural law of appearances, any more than this law interferes with the freedom of the practical use of reason, a use that stands in connection with things in themselves as determining grounds.

In this way practical freedom – namely, that freedom in which reason has causality in accordance with objective determining grounds – is rescued, without natural necessity suffering the least harm with respect to the very same effects, as appearances. This can also help elucidate what we have had to say about transcendental freedom and its unification with natural necessity (in the same subject, but not taken in one and the same respect). For, as regards transcendental freedom, any beginning of an action of a being out of objective causes is always, with respect to these determining grounds, a *first beginning*, although the same action is, in the series of appearances, only a *subalternate beginning*, which has to be preceded by a state of the cause which determines that cause, and which is itself determined in the same way by an immediately preceding cause: so that in rational beings (or in general in any beings, provided that their causality is determined in them as things in themselves) one can conceive of a faculty for beginning a series of states spontaneously, without falling into contradiction with the laws of nature. For the relation of an action to the objective grounds of reason is not a temporal relation; here, that which determines the causality does not precede the action as regards time, because such determining grounds do not represent the relation of objects to the senses (and so to causes within appearance), but rather they represent determining causes as things in themselves, which are not subject to temporal conditions. Hence the action can be regarded as a first beginning with respect to the causality of reason, but can nonetheless at the same time be seen as a mere subordinated beginning with respect to the series of appearances, and can without contradiction be considered in the former respect as free, in the latter (since the action is mere appearance) as subject to natural necessity.

4: 347

As regards the *fourth* antinomy, it is removed in a similar[a] manner as was the conflict of reason with itself in the third. For if only the *cause in the appearances* is distinguished from the *cause of the appearances* insofar as the latter cause can be thought as a *thing in itself*, then these two propositions can very well exist side by side, as follows: that there occurs no cause of the sensible world (in accordance with similar laws of causality) whose existence is absolutely necessary, as also on the other side: that this world is nonetheless connected with a necessary being as its cause (but of another kind and according to another law) – the inconsistency of these two propositions resting solely on the mistake of extending what holds merely for appearances to things in themselves, and in general of mixing the two of these up into one concept.

§54

This then is the statement and solution of the whole antinomy in which reason finds itself entangled in the application of its principles[b] to the sensible world, and of which the former (the mere statement) even by itself would already be of considerable benefit toward a knowledge[c] of human reason, even if the solution of this conflict should not yet fully satisfy[d] the reader, who has here to combat a natural illusion that has only recently been presented to him as such, after he had hitherto always taken that illusion for the truth. One consequence of all this is, indeed, unavoidable; namely, that since it is completely impossible to escape from this conflict of reason with itself as long as the objects of the sensible world are taken for things in themselves[e] – and not for what they in fact are, that is, for mere appearances – the reader is obliged, for that reason, to take up once more the deduction of all our cognition *a priori* (and the examination of that deduction which I have provided), in order to come to a decision about it. For the present I do not require more; for

---

[a] Reading *ähnliche* for *die ähnliche*, with Vorländer.
[b] *Principien*
[c] *Kenntniss*
[d] Reading *noch nicht völlig befriedigen* for *hiedurch noch nicht völlig befriedigt werden*, with Vorländer.
[e] *Sachen an sich selbst*

4: 348 if, through this pursuit, he has first thought himself deeply enough into the nature of pure reason, then the concepts by means of which alone the solution to this conflict of reason is possible will already be familiar to him, a circumstance without which I cannot expect full approbation from even the most attentive reader.

§55
III. Theological idea (*Critique*, pp. 571ff.)[72]

The third transcendental idea, which provides material for the most important among all the uses of reason – but one that, if pursued merely speculatively, is overreaching (transcendent) and thereby dialectical – is the ideal of pure reason. Here reason does not, as with the psychological and the cosmological idea, start from experience and become seduced by the ascending sequence of grounds into aspiring, if possible, to absolute completeness in their series, but instead breaks off entirely from experience and descends from bare concepts of what would constitute the absolute completeness of a thing in general – and so by means of the idea of a supremely perfect first being[a] – to determination of the possibility, hence the reality, of all other things; in consequence, here the bare presupposition of a being that, although not in the series of experiences, is nonetheless thought on behalf of experience, for the sake of comprehensibility in the connection, ordering, and unity of that experience – i.e., the *idea* – is easier to distinguish from the concept of the understanding than in the previous cases. Here therefore the dialectical illusion, which arises from our taking the subjective conditions of our thinking for objective conditions of things themselves[b] and our taking a hypothesis that is necessary for the satisfaction of our reason for a dogma, is easily exposed, and I therefore need mention nothing more about the presumptions of transcendental theology, since what the *Critique* says about them is clear, evident, and decisive.

§56
General Note
to
the Transcendental Ideas

4: 349 The objects that are given to us through experience are incomprehensible to us in many respects, and there are many questions to which natural law carries us, which, if pursued to a certain height (yet always in conformity with those laws) cannot be solved at all; e.g., how

---

[a] *höchst vollkommenen Urwesens*
[b] *der Sachen selbst*

pieces of matter attract one another. But if we completely abandon nature, or transcend[a] all possible experience in advancing the connection of nature and so lose ourselves in mere ideas, then we are unable to say that the object[b] is incomprehensible to us and that the nature of things presents us with unsolvable problems; for then we are not concerned with nature or in general with objects[c] that are given, but merely with concepts that have their origin solely in our reason, and with mere beings of thought, with respect to which all problems, which must originate from the concepts of those very beings, can be solved, since reason certainly can and must be held fully accountable for its own proceedings.* Because the psychological,[d] cosmological, and theological ideas are nothing but pure concepts of reason, which cannot be given in any experience, the questions that reason puts before us with respect to them are not set for us through objects, but rather through mere maxims of reason for the sake of its self-satisfaction, and these questions must one and all be capable of sufficient answer – which occurs by its being shown that they are principles for bringing the use of our understanding into thoroughgoing harmony, completeness, and synthetic unity, and to that extent are valid only for experience, though in the *totality* of that experience. But although an absolute totality of experience is not possible, nonetheless the idea of a totality of cognition according to principles in general is what alone can provide it with a special kind of unity, namely that of a system, without which unity our cognition is nothing but piecework and cannot be used for the highest end (which is nothing other than the system of all ends); and here I mean not only the practical use of reason, but also the highest end of its speculative use.

4: 350

---

* Herr Platner in his *Aphorisms* therefore says with astuteness (§§728–729): "If reason is a criterion, then there cannot possibly be a concept that is incomprehensible to human reason. – Only in the actual does incomprehensibility have a place. Here the incomprehensibility arises from the inadequacy of acquired ideas."[73] – It therefore only sounds paradoxical, and is otherwise not strange to say: that in nature much is incomprehensible to us (e.g., the procreative faculty), but if we rise still higher and even go out beyond nature, then once again all will be comprehensible to us; for then we entirely leave behind the *objects* that can be given to us, and concern ourselves merely with ideas, with respect to which we can very well comprehend the law that reason thereby prescribes to the understanding for its use in experience, since that law is reason's own product.

[a] *übersteigen*
[b] *Gegenstand*
[c] *Objecten*
[d] Reading *psychologischen* for *physiologische*, with Ak.

139

Therefore the transcendental ideas express the peculiar vocation of reason, namely to be a principle[a] of the systematic unity of the use of the understanding. But if one looks upon this unity of mode of cognition as if it were inhering in the object of cognition, if one takes that which really is only *regulative* to be *constitutive*, and becomes convinced that by means of these ideas one's knowledge[b] can be expanded far beyond all possible experience, hence can be expanded transcendently, even though this unity serves only to bring experience in itself as near as possible to completeness (i.e., to have its advance constrained by nothing that cannot belong to experience), then this is a mere misunderstanding in judging the true vocation of our reason and its principles, and it is a dialectic, which partly confounds the use of reason in experience, and partly divides reason against itself.

Conclusion
on
Determining the Boundary of Pure Reason
§57

After the extremely clear proofs we have given above, it would be an absurdity for us, with respect to any object, to hope to cognize more than belongs to a possible experience of it, or for us, with respect to any thing that we assume not to be an object of possible experience, to claim even the least cognition for determining it according to its nature as it is in itself; for by what means will we reach this determination, since time, space, and all the concepts of the understanding, and especially the concepts drawn from empirical intuition or *perception* in the sensible world, do not and cannot have any other use than merely to make experience possible, and if we relax this condition even for the pure concepts of the understanding, they then determine no object whatsoever, and have no significance anywhere.

But, on the other hand, it would be an even greater absurdity for us not to allow any things in themselves at all, or for us to want[c] to pass off our experience for the only possible mode of cognition of things – hence our intuition in space and time for the only possible intuition and our discursive understanding for the archetype of every possible understanding – and so to want to take principles[d] of the possibility of experience for universal conditions on things in themselves.

4: 351

---

[a] *Princips*
[b] *Kenntniss*
[c] Reading *wollten* for *wollte*, with Ak.
[d] *Principien*

Our principles,[a] which limit the use of reason to possible experience alone, could accordingly themselves become *transcendent* and could pass off the limits of our reason for limits on the possibility of things themselves (for which *Hume's* Dialogues[74] can serve as an example), if a painstaking critique did not both guard the boundaries of our reason even with respect to its empirical use, and set a limit to its pretensions. Skepticism originally arose from metaphysics and its unpoliced dialectic. At first this skepticism wanted, solely for the benefit of the use of reason in experience, to portray everything that surpasses this use as empty and deceitful; but gradually, as it came to be noticed that it was the very same *a priori* principles[b] which are employed in experience that, unnoticed, had led still further than experience reaches – and had done so, as it seemed, with the very same right – then even the principles of experience began to be doubted. There was no real trouble with this, for sound common sense[c] will always assert its rights in this domain; but there did arise a particular confusion in science, which cannot determine how far (and why only that far and not further) reason is to be trusted, and this confusion can be remedied and all future relapses prevented only through a formal determination, derived from principles, of the boundaries for the use of our reason.

It is true: we cannot provide, beyond all possible experience, any determinate concept of what things in themselves may be. But we are nevertheless not free to hold back entirely in the face of inquiries about those things; for experience never fully satisfies reason; it directs us ever further back in answering questions and leaves us unsatisfied as regards their full elucidation, as everyone can sufficiently observe in the dialectic of pure reason, which for this very reason has its good subjective ground. Who can bear being brought, as regards the nature of our soul, both to the point of a clear consciousness of the subject and to the conviction that the appearances of that subject cannot be explained *materialistically*, without asking what then the soul really is, and, if no concept of experience suffices thereto, without perchance adopting a concept of reason (that of a simple immaterial[d] being) just for this purpose, although we can by no means prove the objective reality of that concept? Who can satisfy himself with mere cognition through experience in all the cosmological questions, of the duration and size of the world, of freedom or natural necessity, since, wherever we may begin, any answer given according to principles of experience[e] always begets a new question which also

4: 352

---

[a] *Principien*
[b] *Grundsätze*
[c] *gesunde Verstand*
[d] Reading *immateriellen* for *materiellen*, with Ak.
[e] Reading *Erfahrungsgrundsätzen* for *Erfahrungsgrundgesetzen*, with Ak.

requires an answer, and for that reason clearly proves the insufficiency of all physical modes of explanation for the satisfaction of reason? Finally, who cannot see, from the throughgoing contingency and dependency of everything that he might think or assume according to principles of experience, the impossibility of stopping with these, and who does not feel compelled, regardless of all prohibition against losing himself in transcendent ideas, nevertheless to look for peace and satisfaction beyond all concepts that he can justify through experience, in the concept of a being the idea of which indeed cannot in itself be understood as regards possibility – though it cannot be refuted either, because it pertains to a mere being of the understanding – an idea without which, however, reason would always have to remain unsatisfied?[a]

Boundaries[b] (in extended things) always presuppose a space that is found outside a certain fixed location, and that encloses that location; limits[c] require nothing of the kind, but are mere negations that affect a magnitude insofar as it does not possess absolute completeness. Our reason, however, sees around itself as it were a space for the cognition of things in themselves, although it can never have determinate concepts of those things and is limited to appearances alone.

As long as reason's cognition is homogeneous, no determinate boundaries can be thought for it. In mathematics and natural science, human reason recognizes limits but not boundaries, i.e., it indeed recognizes that something lies beyond it to which it can never reach, but not that it would itself at any point ever complete its inner progression. The expansion of insight in mathematics, and the possibility of ever-new inventions, goes to infinity; so too does the discovery of new properties in nature (new forces and laws) through continued experience and the unification of that experience by reason. But limits here are nonetheless unmistakable, for mathematics refers only to *appearances*, and that which cannot be an object of sensory intuition, like the concepts of metaphysics and morals, lies entirely outside its sphere, and it can never lead there; but it also has no need whatsoever for such concepts. There is therefore no continuous progress and advancement toward those sciences, or any point or line of contact, as it were. Natural science will never reveal to us the inside of things, i.e., that which is not appearance but can nonetheless serve as the highest ground of explanation for the appearances; but it does not need this for its physical explanations; nay, if such were offered to it from elsewhere (e.g., the influence of immaterial beings), natural science should indeed reject it and ought by no means bring it into the progression of its explanations,

4: 353

---

[a] Final question mark added, with Vorländer.
[b] *Grenzen*
[c] *Schranken*

but should always base its explanations only on that which can belong to experience as an object of the senses and which can be brought into connection with our actual perceptions in accordance with laws of experience.

But metaphysics, in the dialectical endeavors of pure reason (which are not initiated arbitrarily or wantonly, but toward which the nature of reason itself drives), does lead us to the boundaries; and the transcendental ideas, just because they cannot be avoided and yet will never be realized, serve not only actually to show us the boundaries of reason's pure use, but also to show us the way to determine such boundaries; and that too is the end and use of this natural predisposition of our reason, which bore metaphysics as its favorite child, whose procreation (as with any other in the world) is to be ascribed not to chance accident but to an original seed that is wisely organized toward great ends. For metaphysics, perhaps more than any other science, is, as regards its fundamentals, placed in us by nature itself, and cannot at all be seen as the product of an arbitrary choice, or as an accidental extension from the progression of experiences (it wholly separates itself from those experiences).

Reason, through all of its concepts and laws of the understanding, which it finds to be adequate for empirical use, and so adequate within the sensible world, nonetheless does not thereby find satisfaction for itself; for, as a result of questions that keep recurring to infinity, it is denied all hope of completely answering those questions. The transcendental ideas, which have such completion as their aim, are such problems for reason. Now reason clearly sees: that the sensible world could not contain this completion, any more than could therefore all of the concepts that serve solely for understanding that world: space and time, and everything that we have put forward under the name of the pure concepts of the understanding. The sensible world is nothing but a chain of appearances connected in accordance with universal laws, which therefore has no existence for itself; it truly is not the thing in itself, and therefore it necessarily refers to that which contains the ground of those appearances, to beings that can be cognized not merely as appearances,[a] but as things in themselves. Only in the cognition of the latter can reason hope to see its desire for completeness in the progression from the conditioned to its conditions satisfied for once.

Above (§§33, 34) we noted limits of reason with respect to all cognition of mere beings of thought; now, since the transcendental ideas nevertheless make the progression up to these limits necessary for us, and have therefore led us,[b] as it were, up to the contiguity of the filled

4: 354

---

[a] Reading *Erscheinungen* for *Erscheinung* (here and just previously), with Vorländer.
[b] Reading *uns* for *nur*, with Vorländer.

space (of experience) with empty space (of which we can know nothing – the *noumena*), we can also determine the boundaries of pure reason; for in all boundaries there is something positive (e.g., a surface is the boundary of corporeal space, yet is nonetheless itself a space; a line is a space, which is the boundary of a surface; a point is the boundary of a line, yet is nonetheless a locus in space), whereas limits contain mere negations. The limits announced in the cited sections are still not enough after we have found that something lies beyond them (although we will never cognize what that something may be in itself). For the question now arises: How does our reason cope with this connection of that with which we are acquainted to that with which we are not acquainted, and never will be? Here is a real connection of the known to a wholly unknown (which will always remain so), and even if the unknown should not become the least bit better known – as is not in fact to be hoped – the concept of this connection must still be capable of being determined and brought to clarity.

We should, then, think for ourselves an immaterial being, an intelligible world, and a highest of all beings (all noumena), because only in these things, as things in themselves, does reason find completion and satisfaction, which it can never hope to find in the derivation of the appearances from the homogeneous grounds of those appearances; and we should think such things for ourselves because the appearances actually do relate to something distinct from them (and so entirely heterogeneous), in that appearances always presuppose a thing in itself,[a] and so provide notice of such a thing, whether or not it can be cognized more closely.

4: 355

Now since we can, however, never cognize these intelligible beings according to what they may be in themselves, i.e., determinately – though we must nonetheless assume such beings in relation to the sensible world, and connect them with it through reason – we can still at least think this connection by means of such concepts as express the relation of those beings to the sensible world. For, if we think an intelligible being through nothing but pure concepts of the understanding, we really think nothing determinate thereby, and so our concept is without significance; if we think it through properties borrowed from the sensible world, it is no longer an intelligible being: it is thought as one of the phenomena and belongs to the sensible world. We will take an example from the concept of the supreme being.

The *deistic* concept is a wholly pure concept of reason, which however represents merely a thing that contains every reality, without being able to determine a single one of them, since for that an example would have

[a] *Sache an sich selbst*

144

to be borrowed from the sensible world, in which case I would always have to do only with an object of the senses, and not with something completely heterogeneous which cannot be an object of the senses at all. For I would, for instance, attribute understanding to it; but I have no concept whatsoever of any understanding save one like my own, that is, one such that intuitions must be given to it through the senses, and that busies itself with bringing them under rules for the unity of consciousness. But then the elements of my concept would still lie within appearance; I was, however, forced by the inadequacy of the appearances to go beyond them, to the concept of a being that is in no way dependent on appearances nor bound up with them as conditions for its determination. If, however, I separate understanding from sensibility, in order to have a pure understanding, then nothing but the mere form of thinking, without intuition, is left; through which, by itself, I cannot cognize anything determinate, hence cannot cognize any object. To that end I would have to think to myself a different understanding, which intuits objects,[75] of which, however, I do not have the least concept, since the human understanding is discursive and can cognize only by means of universal concepts. The same thing happens to me if I attribute a will to the supreme being: For I possess this concept only by drawing it from my inner experience, where, however, my[a] dependence on satisfaction through objects whose existence we need, and so sensibility, is the basis – which completely contradicts the pure concept of a supreme being.

4: 356

Hume's objections to deism are weak and always concern the grounds of proof but never the thesis of the deistic assertion itself. But with respect to theism, which is supposed to arise through a closer determination of our (in deism, merely transcendent) concept of a supreme being, they are very strong, and, depending on how this concept has been framed, they are in certain cases (in fact, in all the usual ones) irrefutable. Hume always holds to this: that through the mere concept of a first being to which we attribute none but ontological predicates (eternity, omnipresence, omnipotence), we actually do not think anything determinate at all; rather, properties would have to be added that can yield a concept *in concreto*: it is not enough to say: this being is a cause, rather we need to say how its causality is constituted, e.g., by understanding and willing – and here begin Hume's attacks on the matter in question, namely on theism, whereas he had previously assaulted only the grounds of proof for deism, an assault that carries no special danger with it. His dangerous arguments relate wholly to anthropomorphism, of which he holds that it is inseparable from theism and makes theism

---

[a] Rejecting various emendations recorded by Vorländer.

self-contradictory, but that if it is eliminated, theism falls with it and nothing but deism remains – from which nothing can be made, which can be of no use to us, and can in no way serve as a foundation for religion and morals. If this unavoidability of anthropomorphism were certain, then the proofs for the existence of a supreme being might be what they will, and might all be granted, and still the concept of this being could never be determined by us without our becoming entangled in contradictions.

If we combine the injunction to avoid all transcendent judgments of pure reason with the apparently conflicting command to proceed to concepts that lie beyond the field of immanent (empirical) use, we become aware that both can subsist together, but only directly on the *boundary* of all permitted use of reason – for this boundary belongs just as much to the field of experience as to that of beings of thought – and we are thereby at the same time taught how those remarkable ideas serve solely for determining the boundary of human reason: that is, we are taught, on the one hand, not to extend cognition from experience without bound, so that nothing at all remains for us to cognize except merely the world, and, on the other, nevertheless not to go beyond the boundary of experience and to want to judge of things outside that boundary as things in themselves.

But we hold ourselves to this boundary if we limit our judgment merely to the relation that the world may have to a being whose concept itself lies outside all cognition that we can attain within the world. For we then do not attribute to the supreme being any of the properties *in themselves* by which we think the objects of experience, and we thereby avoid *dogmatic* anthropomorphism; but we attribute those properties, nonetheless, to the relation of this being to the world, and allow ourselves a *symbolic* anthropomorphism, which in fact concerns only language and not the object itself.

If I say that we are compelled to look upon the world *as if* it were the work of a supreme understanding and will, I actually say nothing more than: in the way that a watch, a ship, and a regiment are related to an artisan, a builder, and a commander, the sensible world (or everything that makes up the basis of this sum total of appearances) is related to the unknown – which I do not thereby cognize according to what it is in itself, but only according to what it is for me, that is, with respect to the world of which I am a part.

§58

This type of cognition is cognition *according to analogy*, which surely does not signify, as the word is usually taken, an imperfect similarity between

4: 357

two things, but rather a perfect similarity between two relations in wholly dissimilar things.* By means of this analogy there still remains a concept of the supreme being sufficiently determinate *for us*, though we have omitted everything that could have *determined* this concept uncondition-ally and *in itself*; for we determine the concept only with respect to the world and hence with respect to us, and we have no need of more. The attacks that *Hume* makes against those who want to determine this con-cept absolutely – since they borrow the materials for this determination from themselves and from the world – do not touch us; he also cannot reproach us that nothing whatsoever would remain for us if objective anthropomorphism were subtracted from the concept of the supreme being.

For if one only grants us, at the outset, the *deistic* concept of a first being as a necessary hypothesis (as does Hume in his *Dialogues* in the person of Philo as opposed to Cleanthes), which is a concept in which one thinks the first being by means of ontological predicates alone, of substance, cause, etc. (*something that one must do*, since reason, being driven in the sensible world solely by conditions that are always again conditioned, cannot have any satisfaction at all without this being done, and *something that one very well can do* without falling into that anthro-pomorphism which transfers predicates from the sensible world onto a being wholly distinct from the world, since the predicates listed here are mere categories, which cannot indeed provide any determinate concept of that being, but which, for that very reason, do not provide a concept of it that is limited to the conditions of sensibility) – then nothing can keep us from predicating of this being a *causality through reason* with re-spect to the world, and thus from crossing over to theism, but without our being compelled to attribute this reason to that being in itself, as a

---

* Such is an analogy between the legal relation of human actions and the me-chanical relation of moving forces: I can never do anything to another without giving him a right to do the same to me under the same conditions; just as a body cannot act on another body with its motive force without thereby caus-ing the other body to react just as much on it. Right and motive force are here completely dissimilar things, but in their relation there is nonetheless complete similarity. By means of such an analogy I can therefore provide a concept of a relation to things that are absolutely unknown to me. E.g., the promotion of the happiness of the children = a is to the love of the parents = b as the welfare of humankind = c is to the unknown in God = x, which we call love: not as if this unknown had the least similarity with any human inclination, but because we can posit the relation between God's love and the world to be similar to that which things in the world have to one another. But here the concept of the relation is a mere category, namely the concept of cause, which has nothing to do with sensibility.

147

4: 359

property inhering in it. For, concerning the *first point*,[a] the only possible way to compel the use of reason in the sensible world (with respect to all possible experience) into the most thoroughgoing harmony with itself is to assume, in turn, a supreme reason as a cause of all connections in the world; such a principle must be thoroughly advantageous to reason and can nowhere harm it in its use in nature. Regarding the *second point*,[b] however, reason is not thereby transposed as a property onto the first being in itself, but only *onto the relation* of that being to the sensible world, and therefore anthropomorphism is completely avoided. For here only the *cause* of the rational form found everywhere in the world is considered, and the supreme being, insofar as it contains the basis of this rational form of the world, is indeed ascribed reason, but only by analogy, i.e., insofar as this expression signifies only the relation that the highest cause (which is unknown to us) has to the world, in order to determine everything in it with the highest degree of conformity to reason. We thereby avoid using the property of reason in order to think God, but instead think the world through it in the manner necessary to have the greatest possible use of reason with respect to the world in accordance with a principle. We thereby admit that the supreme being, as to what it may be in itself, is for us wholly inscrutable and is even unthinkable by us *in a determinate manner*; and we are thereby prevented from making any transcendent use of[c] the concepts that we have of reason as an efficient cause (through willing) in order to determine the divine nature through properties that are in any case always borrowed only from human nature, and so from losing ourselves in crude or fanatical concepts, and, on the other hand, we are also prevented from swamping the contemplation of the world with hyperphysical modes of explanation according to concepts of human reason we have transposed onto God, and so from diverting this contemplation from its true vocation, according to which it is supposed to be a study of mere nature through reason, and not an audacious derivation of the appearances of nature from a supreme reason. The expression suitable to our weak concepts will be: that we think the world AS IF it derived from a supreme reason as regards its existence and inner determination; whereby we in part cognize the constitution belonging to it (the world) itself, without presuming to want to determine that of its cause in itself, and, on the other hand, we in part posit the basis of this constitution (the rational form of the world) *in the relation* of the highest cause to the world, not finding the world by itself sufficient thereto.*

4: 360

---

* I will say: the causality of the highest cause is that, with respect to the world, which human reason is with respect to its works of art. Thereby the nature of the highest cause itself remains unknown to me: I compare only its effect (the order of the world), which is known to me, and the conformity with reason of this effect, with the effects of human reason that are known to me, and in

In this way the difficulties that appear to oppose theism disappear, in that to *Hume's* principle, not to drive the use of reason dogmatically beyond the field of all possible experience, we conjoin another principle that Hume completely overlooked, namely: not to look upon the field of possible experience as something that bounds itself in the eyes of our reason. A critique of reason indicates the true middle way between the dogmatism that Hume fought and the skepticism he wanted to introduce instead – a middle way that, unlike other middle ways, which we are advised to determine for ourselves as it were mechanically (something from one side, and something from the other), and by which no one is taught any better, is[d] one, rather, that can be determined precisely, according to principles.[76]

§59

At the beginning of this note I made use of the metaphor of a *boundary* in order to fix the limits of reason with respect to its own appropriate use. The sensible world contains only appearances, which are still not things in themselves, which latter things (noumena) the understanding must therefore assume for the very reason that it cognizes the objects of experience as mere appearances. Both are considered together in our reason, and the question arises: how does reason proceed in setting boundaries for the understanding with respect to both fields? Experience, which contains everything that belongs to the sensible world, does not set a boundary for itself: From every conditioned it always arrives merely at another conditioned. That which is to set its boundary must lie completely outside it, and this is the field of pure intelligible beings. For us, however, as far as concerns the *determination* of the nature of these intelligible beings, this is an empty space, and to that extent, if dogmatically determined concepts are intended, we cannot go beyond the field of possible experience. But since a boundary is itself something positive, which belongs as much to what is within it as to the space lying outside a given totality, reason therefore, merely by expanding up to this boundary, partakes of a real, positive cognition, provided that it does not try to go out beyond the boundary, since there it finds an empty space before it, in which it can indeed think the

4: 361

consequence I call the highest cause a reason, without thereby ascribing to it as its property the same thing I understand by this expression in humans, or in anything else known to me.

[a] "something that one must do . . ."
[b] "something that one very well can do . . ."
[c] Reading *von* for *nach*, with Vorländer.
[d] Adding *ist* after *Mittelwege*, as suggested by Vorländer.

forms to things, but no things themselves. But *setting the boundary* to the field of experience through something that is otherwise unknown to it is indeed a cognition that is still left to reason from this standpoint, whereby reason is neither locked inside the sensible world nor adrift outside it, but, as befits knowledge of a boundary, restricts itself solely to the relation of what lies outside the boundary to what is contained within.

Natural theology is a concept of this kind, on the boundary of human reason, since reason finds itself compelled to look out toward the idea of a supreme being (and also, in relation to the practical, to the idea of an intelligible world), not in order to determine something with respect to this mere intelligible being (and hence outside the sensible world), but only in order to guide its own use within the sensible world in accordance with principles of the greatest possible unity (theoretical as well as practical), and to make use (for this purpose) of the relation of that world to a free-standing reason as the cause of all of these connections – not, however, in order thereby merely *to fabricate* a being, but, since beyond the sensible world there must necessarily be found something that is thought only by the pure understanding, in order, in this way, *to determine* this being,[a] though of course merely through analogy.

In this manner our previous proposition, which is the result of the entire *Critique*, remains: "that reason, through all its a priori principles, never teaches us about anything more than objects of possible experience alone, and of these, nothing more than what can be cognized in experience"; but this limitation does not prevent reason from carrying us up to the objective *boundary* of experience – namely, to the *relation* to something that cannot itself be an object of experience, but which must nonetheless be the highest ground of all experience – without, however, teaching us anything about this ground in itself, but only in relation to reason's own complete use in the field of possible experience, as directed to the highest ends. This is, however, all of the benefit that can reasonably even be wished for here, and there is cause to be satisfied with it.

4: 362

§60

We have thus fully exhibited metaphysics in accordance with its subjective possibility, as metaphysics is actually given *in the natural predisposition* of human reason, and with respect to that which forms the essential goal of its cultivation. But because we found that, if reason is not reined in and given limits by a discipline of reason, which is only possible through a scientific critique, this *wholly natural* use of this sort of predisposition of our reason entangles it in transcendent *dialectical* inferences, which are partly

---

[a] Omitting *nur* after *dieses*, with Vorländer.

specious, partly even in conflict among themselves; and, moreover, because we found that this sophistical metaphysics is superfluous, nay, even detrimental to the advancement of the cognition of nature, it therefore still remains a problem worthy of investigation, to discover the *natural purposes* toward which this predisposition of our[a] reason[b] to transcendent concepts may be aimed, since everything found in nature must originally be aimed at some beneficial purpose or other.

Such an investigation is in fact uncertain; I also admit that it is merely conjectural (as is everything I know to say concerning the original purposes of nature), something I may be permitted in this case only, since the question does not concern the objective validity of metaphysical judgments, but rather the natural predisposition to such judgments, and therefore lies outside the system of metaphysics, in anthropology.[77]

If I consider[c] all the transcendental ideas, which together constitute the real problem for natural pure reason – a problem that compels reason to forsake the mere contemplation of nature and go beyond all possible experience, and, in this endeavor, to bring into existence the thing called metaphysics (be it knowledge or sophistry) – then I believe I perceive that this natural predisposition is aimed at making our concept sufficiently free from the fetters of experience and the limits of the mere contemplation of nature that it at the least sees a field opening before it that contains only objects for the pure understanding which no sensibility can reach: not with the aim that we concern ourselves speculatively with these objects (for we find no ground on which we can gain footing), but rather with practical principles,[d] which, without finding such a space before them for their necessary expectations and hopes, could not extend themselves to the universality that reason ineluctably requires with respect to morals.

4: 363

Here I now find that the *psychological* idea, however little insight I may gain through it into the pure nature of the human soul elevated beyond all concepts of experience, at least reveals clearly enough the inadequacy of those concepts of experience, and thereby leads me away from materialism, as a psychological concept unsuited to any explanation of nature and one that, moreover, constricts reason with respect to the practical. Similarly, the *cosmological* ideas, through the manifest inadequacy of all possible cognition of nature to satisfy reason in its rightful demands,

---

[a] Reading *unserer* for *unsere*, with Ak.
[b] Reading *Vernunft*, with the original edition; Ak has *Natur* (a typographical error).
[c] Supplying *betrachte* as the verb, with Vorländer; Ak supplies *zusammennehme*.
[d] There is a generally acknowledged ellipsis at this point. I avoid adopting any of the lengthy interpolations recorded in Vorländer by extending the meaning of the previous verb, *zu beschäftigen*, beyond *sondern*, so as to provide a context for *practische Principien* (a solution that also would require some emendation of the German).

serve to deter us from naturalism, which would have it that nature is sufficient unto itself. Finally, since all natural necessity in the sensible world is always conditioned, in that it always presupposes the dependence of one thing on another, and since unconditioned necessity must be sought only in the unity of a cause distinct from the sensible world, although the causality of that cause, in turn, if it were merely nature, could never make comprehensible the existence of the contingent as its consequence, reason, therefore, by means of the *theological* idea, frees itself from fatalism – from blind natural necessity both in the connection of nature itself, without a first principle, and in the causality of this principle itself – and leads the way to the concept of a cause through freedom, and so to that of a highest intelligence. The transcendental ideas therefore serve, if not to instruct us positively, at least to negate the impudent assertions of *materialism*, *naturalism*, and *fatalism* which constrict the field of reason, and in this way they serve to provide moral ideas with space outside the field of speculation; and this would, I should think, to some extent explain the aforementioned natural predisposition.

The practical benefit that a purely speculative science may have lies outside the boundaries of this science; such benefit can therefore be seen simply as a scholium, and like all scholia does not form part of the science itself. Nonetheless, this relation at least lies within the boundaries of philosophy, and especially of that philosophy which draws from the wellsprings of pure reason, where the speculative use of reason in meta-physics must necessarily have unity with its practical use in morals. Hence the unavoidable dialectic of pure reason deserves, in a metaphysics considered as natural predisposition, not only to be explained as an illusion that needs to be resolved, but also (if one can) as a *natural institution* in accordance with its purpose – although this endeavor, as supererogatory, cannot rightly be required of metaphysics proper.

The solution to the questions that proceed in the *Critique* from pages 647 to 668 would have to be taken for a second scholium, more closely related to the content of metaphysics.[78] For there certain principles of reason are put forward that determine the order of nature *a priori*, or rather determine the understanding *a priori*, which is supposed to search for the laws of this order by means of experience. These principles seem to be constitutive and law-giving with respect to experience, though they spring from mere reason, which cannot, like the understanding, be regarded as a principle of possible experience. Now whether this agreement rests on the fact that, just as nature does not in itself inhere in the appearances or in their source, sensibility, but is found only in the relation of sensibility to the understanding, so too, a thoroughgoing unity in the use of this understanding, for the sake of a unified possible experience (in a system), can belong to the understanding only in relation to reason, hence experience, too, be indirectly subject to the legislation of reason – this may be further pondered by those who want to track the nature of reason even beyond its use in metaphysics, into the universal principles for making natural history generally systematic; for in the book itself I have indeed presented this problem as important, but have not attempted its solution.*

And thus I conclude the analytic[79] solution of the main question I myself have posed: How is metaphysics in general possible?, since I have ascended from the place where its use is actually given, at least in the consequences, to the grounds of its possibility.

4: 365

* It was my unremitting intention throughout the *Critique* not to neglect anything that could bring to completion the investigation of the nature of pure reason, however deeply hidden it might lie. Afterwards it is in each person's discretion, how far he will take his investigation, if he only has been apprised of what may still need to be done; for it can properly be expected, from one who has made it his business to survey this entire field, that afterward he leave future additions and optional divisions to others. Hereto belong both of the scholia, which, on account of their dryness, could hardly be recommended to amateurs, and have therefore been set out only for experts.

Solution
to the General Question
of the Prolegomena
How is metaphysics possible as science?

Metaphysics, as a natural predisposition of reason, is actual, but it is also of itself (as the analytical solution to the third main question proved) dialectical and deceitful. The desire to derive principles from it, and to follow the natural but nonetheless false illusion in their use, can therefore never bring forth science, but only vain dialectical art, in which one school can outdo another but none can ever gain legitimate and lasting approbation.

In order that metaphysics might, as science, be able to lay claim, not merely to deceitful persuasion, but to insight and conviction, a critique of reason itself must set forth the entire stock of *a priori* concepts, their division according to the different sources (sensibility, understanding, and reason), further, a complete table of those concepts, and the analysis of all of them along with everything that can be derived from that analysis; and then, especially, such a critique must set forth the possibility of synthetic cognition *a priori* through a deduction of these concepts, it must set forth the principles of their use, and finally also the boundaries of that use; and all of this in a complete system. Therefore a critique, and that alone, contains within itself the whole well-tested and verified plan by which metaphysics as science can be achieved, and even all the means for carrying it out; by any other ways or means it is impossible. Therefore the question that arises here is not so much how this enterprise is possible, but only how it is to be set in motion, and good minds stirred from the hitherto ill-directed and fruitless endeavor to one that will not deceive, and how such an alliance might best be turned toward the common end.

This much is certain: whosoever has once tasted of critique forever loathes all the dogmatic chatter which he previously had to put up with out of necessity, since his reason was in need of something and could not find anything better for its sustenance. Critique stands to the ordinary school metaphysics precisely as *chemistry* stands to *alchemy*, or *astronomy* to the fortune-teller's *astrology*. I'll guarantee that no one who has thought through and comprehended the principles of critique, even if only in these prolegomena, will ever again return to that old and sophistical pseudoscience; he will on the contrary look out with a certain delight upon a metaphysics that is now fully in his power, that needs no more preliminary discoveries, and that can for the first time provide reason with lasting satisfaction. For this is an advantage upon which metaphysics alone, among all the possible sciences, can rely with confidence, namely, that it can be completed and brought into a permanent state, since it cannot be further changed and is not susceptible to any augmentation through new discoveries – because here reason has the sources of its cognition not in objects and their intuition (through which reason cannot be taught one thing more), but in itself, and, if reason has presented the fundamental laws of its faculty fully and determinately (against all misinterpretation), nothing else remains that pure reason could cognize *a priori*, or even about which it could have cause to ask. The sure prospect of a knowledge so determinate and final has a certain attraction to it, even if all usefulness (of which I will say more hereafter) is set aside.

All false art, all empty wisdom lasts for its time; for it finally destroys itself, and the height of its cultivation is simultaneously the moment of its decline. That this time has now come as regards metaphysics is proven by the condition into which it has fallen among all learned peoples, amidst all the zeal with which sciences of all kinds are otherwise being developed. The old organization of university studies still preserves the shadow of metaphysics, a lone academy of sciences now and then, by offering prizes, moves someone or other to make an effort in it, but metaphysics is no longer reckoned among serious sciences, and each may judge for himself how a clever man, whom one wished to call a great metaphysician, would perhaps receive this encomium, which might be well meant but would hardly be envied by anyone.

But although the time for the collapse of all dogmatic metaphysics is undoubtedly here, much is still lacking in order to be able to say   4: 367 that, on the contrary, the time for its rebirth, through a thorough and completed critique of reason, has already appeared. All transitions from one inclination to its opposite pass through a state of indifference, and this moment is the most dangerous for an author, but nonetheless, it seems to me, the most favorable for the science. For if the partisan spirit has been extinguished through the complete severance of former ties, then minds are best disposed to[a] hear out, bit by bit, proposals for an alliance according to another plan.

If I say that I hope these *Prolegomena* will perhaps excite investigation in the field of critique, and provide the universal spirit of philosophy, which seems to want nourishment in its speculative part, with a new and

---

[a] Reading *um* for *nur*, with Ak.

quite promising object of sustenance, I can already imagine beforehand that everyone who[a] has been made weary and unwilling by the thorny paths on which I have led him in the *Critique* will ask me: On what do I base this hope? I answer: *On the irresistible law of necessity.*

That the human mind would someday entirely give up metaphysical investigations is just as little to be expected, as that we would someday gladly stop all breathing so as never to take in impure air. There will therefore be metaphysics in the world at every time, and what is more, in every human being, and especially the reflective ones; metaphysics that each, in the absence of a public standard of measure, will carve out for himself in his own manner. Now what has hitherto been called metaphysics can satisfy no inquiring mind, and yet it is also impossible to give up metaphysics completely; therefore, a critique of pure reason itself must finally be *attempted*, or, if one exists, it must be *examined* and put to a general test, since there are no other means to relieve this pressing need, which is something more than a mere thirst for knowledge.

Ever since I have known critique, I have been unable to keep myself from asking, upon finishing reading through a book with metaphysical content, which has entertained as well as cultivated me by the determination of its concepts and by variety and organization and by an easy
4: 368 presentation: *has this author advanced metaphysics even one step?* I ask forgiveness of the learned men whose writings have in other respects been useful to me and have always contributed to a cultivation of mental powers, because I confess that I have not been able to find, either in their attempts or in my own inferior ones (with self-love speaking in their favor), that the science has thereby been advanced in the least, and this for the wholly natural reason that the science did not yet exist, and also that it cannot be assembled bit by bit but rather its seed must be fully preformed beforehand in the critique. However, in order to avoid all misunderstanding, it must be recalled from the preceding that although the understanding certainly benefits very much from the analytical treatment of our concepts, the science (of metaphysics) is not advanced the least bit thereby, since these analyses of concepts are only materials, out of which the science must first be constructed. The concept of substance and accident may be analyzed and determined ever so nicely; that is quite good as preparation for some future use. But if I simply cannot prove that in all that exists the substance persists and only the accidents change, then through all this analysis the science has not been advanced in the least. Now metaphysics has not as yet been able to prove, as *a priori* valid, either this proposition or the principle of sufficient reason, still less any more composite proposition, such as, for instance, one belonging

---

[a] Reading *den* for *der*, with Ak.

156

to psychology or cosmology, nor, in general, any synthetic proposition whatsoever; hence, through all this analysis nothing has been achieved, nothing created and advanced, and, after so much bustle and clatter, the science is still right where it was in Aristotle's time, although the preparations for it incontestably have been much better laid than before, if only the guiding thread to synthetic cognition had first been found.

If anyone believes himself wronged in this, he can easily remove the above indictment if he will cite only a single synthetic proposition belonging to metaphysics that he offers to prove *a priori* in the dogmatic manner; for only when he accomplishes this will I grant to him that he has actually advanced the science (even if the proposition may otherwise have been sufficiently established through common experience). No challenge can be more moderate and more equitable, and in the (infallibly certain) event of nonfulfillment, no verdict more just, than this: 4: 369 that up to now metaphysics as science has never existed at all.

In case the challenge is accepted, I must forbid only two things: first, the plaything of *probability* and conjecture, which suits metaphysics just as poorly as it does geometry; second, decision by means of the divining rod of so-called *sound common sense,*[a] which does not bend for everyone, but is guided by personal qualities.

For, *as regards the first*, there can be nothing more absurd than to want to base one's judgments in metaphysics, a philosophy from pure reason, on probability and conjecture. Everything that is to be cognized *a priori* is for that very reason given out as apodictically certain and must therefore also be proven as such. One might just as well want to base a geometry or an arithmetic on conjectures; for as concerns the *calculus probabilium*[b] of arithmetic, it contains not probable but completely certain judgments about the degree of possibility of certain cases under given homogeneous conditions, judgments which, in the sum total of all possible cases, must be found to conform to the rule with complete infallibility, even though this rule is not sufficiently determinate with respect to any single case. Only in empirical natural science can conjectures (by means of induction and analogy) be tolerated, and even then, the possibility at least of what I am assuming must be fully certain.

Matters are, if possible, even worse with the *appeal to sound common sense,* if the discussion concerns[c] concepts and principles, not insofar as they are supposed to be valid with respect to experience, but rather insofar as they are to be taken as valid beyond the conditions of experience.

---

[a] *gesunden Menschenverstandes*
[b] "calculus of probability"
[c] Adding *die Rede ist,* with Ak.

For what is *sound common sense?*[a] It is the *ordinary understanding,*[b] insofar as it judges correctly. And what now is the ordinary understanding? It is the faculty of cognition and of the use of rules *in concreto*, as distinguished from the *speculative understanding*, which is a faculty of the cognition of rules *in abstracto*. The ordinary understanding will, then, hardly be able to understand the rule: that everything which happens is determined by its cause, and it will never be able to have insight into it in such a general way. It therefore demands an example from experience, and when it hears that this rule means nothing other than what it had always thought when a windowpane was broken or a household article had disappeared, it then understands the principle and grants it. Ordinary understanding, therefore, has a use no further than the extent to which it can see its rules confirmed in experience (although these rules are actually present in it *a priori*); consequently, to have insight into these rules *a priori* and independently of experience falls to the speculative understanding, and lies completely beyond the horizon of the ordinary understanding. But metaphysics is concerned indeed solely with this latter type of cognition, and it is certainly a poor sign of sound common sense to appeal to this guarantor, who has no judgment here, and whom we otherwise look down upon, except if we find ourselves in trouble, and without either advice or help in our speculation.

4: 370

It is a common excuse, habitually employed by these false friends of ordinary common sense (which they extol on occasion, but usually despise), to say: There must in the end be some propositions that are[c] immediately certain, and for which not only no proof, but indeed no account at all need be given, since otherwise there would never come an end to the grounds for one's judgments; but in proof of this right they can never cite anything else (other than the principle of contradiction, which is however inadequate for establishing the truth of synthetic judgments) that is undoubted and can be ascribed directly to ordinary common sense, except for mathematical propositions: e.g., that two times two makes four, that between two points there is only one straight line, and still others. These judgments are, however, worlds apart from those of metaphysics. For in mathematics, everything that I conceive through a concept as possible I can make for myself (construct) by means of my thought; to one two I successively add the other two, and myself make the number four, or I draw in thought all kinds of lines from one point to the other, and can draw only one that is self-similar in all its parts (equal as well as unequal).[80] But from the concept of a thing I cannot, with all my powers of thought, draw forth the concept of something else whose existence is

---

[a] *gesunde Verstand*
[b] *gemeine Verstand*
[c] Reading *seien* for *seyn*, with Vorländer.

necessarily connected with the first thing, but must consult experience; and, although my understanding provides me *a priori* (though always only in relation to possible experience) with the concept of a connection of this sort (causality), I nevertheless cannot exhibit this concept in intuition *a priori*, like the concepts of mathematics, and thus exhibit its possibility *a priori*; rather, this concept (together with principles of its application), if it is to be valid *a priori* – as is indeed required in metaphysics – always has need of a justification and deduction of its possibility, for otherwise one does not know the extent of its validity and whether it can be used only in experience or also outside it. Therefore in metaphysics, as a speculative science of pure reason, one can never appeal to ordinary common sense, but one can very well do so if one is forced to abandon metaphysics and to renounce all pure speculative cognition, which must always be knowledge,[a] hence to renounce metaphysics itself and its teaching (on certain matters), and if a reasonable belief[b] is alone deemed possible for us, as well as sufficient for our needs (perhaps more wholesome indeed than knowledge itself). For then the shape of things is completely altered. Metaphysics must be science, not only as a whole but also in all its parts; otherwise it is nothing at all, since, as speculation of pure reason, it has a hold on nothing else save universal insights. But outside metaphysics, probability and sound common sense can very well have their beneficial and legitimate use, though following principles entirely their own, whose importance always depends on a relation to the practical.

4: 371

That is what I consider myself entitled to require for the possibility of a metaphysics as science.

Appendix
On what can be done in order to make *metaphysics as science* actual

Since all paths hitherto taken have not attained this end, and it may never be reached without a preceding critique of pure reason, the demand that the attempt at such a critique which is now before the public be subjected to an exact and careful examination does not seem unreasonable – unless it is considered more advisable still to give up all claims to metaphysics entirely, in which case, if one only remains true to one's intention, there is nothing to be said against it. If the course of events is taken as it actually runs and not as it should run, then there are two kinds of judgments: a *judgment that precedes the investigation*, and in our case this is one in which the reader, from his own metaphysics, passes judgment on the *Critique of Pure Reason* (which is supposed first of all to investigate the possibility of

4: 372

[a] *ein Wissen*
[b] *vernünftiger Glaube*

that metaphysics); and then a different *judgment that comes after the investigation*, in which the reader is able to set aside for a while the consequences of the critical investigation, which might tell pretty strongly against the metaphysics he otherwise accepts, and first tests the grounds from which these consequences may have been derived. If what ordinary metaphysics presents were undeniably certain (like geometry, for instance), the first way of judging would be valid; for if the consequences of certain principles conflict with undeniable truths, then those principles are false and are to be rejected without any further investigation. But if it is not the case that metaphysics has a supply of incontestably certain (synthetic) propositions, and perhaps is the case that a good number of them, which are as plausible as the best among them, nevertheless are,[a] in their consequences, in conflict even among themselves, while there is not to be found overall in metaphysics any secure criterion whatsoever of the truth of properly metaphysical (synthetic) propositions: then the first way of judging cannot be allowed, but rather the investigation of the principles of the *Critique* must precede all judgment of its worth or unworth.

Specimen of a judgment about the *Critique* which precedes the investigation

This sort of judgment is to be found in the *Göttingische gelehrte Anzeigen*, the third part of the supplement, from January 19, 1782, pages 40 ff.[81]

If an author who is well acquainted with the object of his work, who has been assiduous throughout in putting reflection into its composition that is completely his own, falls into the hands of a reviewer who for his part is sufficiently clear-sighted to espy the moments upon which[b] the worth or unworth of the piece actually rests, who does not hang on words but follows the subject matter, and who examines and tests only[c] the principles from which the author has proceeded, then although the severity of the judgment may certainly displease the author, the public is, by contrast, indifferent to it, for it profits thereby; and the author himself can be content that he gets the opportunity to correct or to elucidate his essays, which have been examined early on by an expert, and, if he believes he is basically right, in this way to remove in good time a stumbling block that could eventually be detrimental to his work.

I find myself in a completely different situation with my reviewer. He appears not at all to see what really mattered in the investigation with which I have (fortunately or unfortunately) occupied myself, and,

4: 373

[a] Reading *sind* for *seyn*, with Ak.
[b] Reading *denen* for *die*, with Vorländer.
[c] Deleting *nicht* prior to *bloss*, with Vorländer.

whether it was impatience with thinking through a lengthy work, or ill-temper over the threatened reform of a science in which he believed he had long since put everything in order, or whether, as I reluctantly surmise, it was the fault of a truly limited conception, through which he could never think himself beyond his school metaphysics – in short, he impetuously runs through a long series of propositions, with which one can think nothing at all without knowing their premises, he disperses his rebukes to and fro, for which the reader no more sees any basis than he understands the propositions toward which they are supposedly directed, and therefore the reviewer can neither help to inform the public nor do me the least bit of harm in the judgment of experts; consequently, I would have passed over this review completely, if it did not provide me occasion for a few elucidations that in some cases might save the reader of these *Prolegomena* from misconception.

In order, however, that the reviewer might adopt a viewpoint from which he could, without having to trouble himself with any special investigation, most easily present the entire work in a manner disadvantageous to the author, he begins and also ends by saying: "this work is a system of transcendental[a] (or, as he construes it, higher)* idealism."[b]

At the sight of this line I quickly perceived what sort of review would issue thence – just about as if someone who had never seen or heard anything of geometry were to find a Euclid, and, being asked to pass judgment on it, were perhaps to say, after stumbling onto a good many figures by turning the pages: "the book is a systematic guide to drawing; the author makes use of a special language in order to provide obscure, unintelligible instructions, which in the end can achieve nothing more than what anyone can accomplish with a good natural eye, and so on."

4: 374

---

* On no account *higher*. High towers and the metaphysically-great men who resemble them, around both of which there is usually much wind, are not for me. My place is the fertile *bathos* of experience, and the word: transcendental – whose signification, which I indicated so many times, was not caught once by the reviewer (so hastily had he looked at everything) – does not signify something that surpasses all experience, but something that indeed precedes experience (*a priori*), but that, all the same, is destined to nothing more than solely to make cognition from experience possible. If these concepts cross beyond experience, their use is then called transcendent, which is distinguished from the immanent use (i.e., use limited to experience). All misinterpretations of this kind have been sufficiently forestalled in the work itself; but the reviewer found his advantage in misinterpretations.

[a] Reading *transcendentalen* for *transscendenten*, in accordance with Kant's wording in his footnote; the Garve–Feder review itself has the word *transscendentellen* here (p. 40), a spelling that Kant did not use.
[b] The parenthetical aside is Kant's insertion.

Let us, however, look at what sort of idealism it is that runs through my entire work, although it does not by far constitute the soul of the system.

The thesis of all genuine idealists, from the Eleatic School up to Bishop Berkeley,[82] is contained in this formula: "All cognition through the senses and experience is nothing but sheer illusion, and there is truth only in the ideas of pure understanding and reason."

The principle that governs and determines my idealism throughout is, on the contrary: "All cognition of things out of mere pure understanding or pure reason is nothing but sheer illusion, and there is truth only in experience."

But this is, of course, the direct opposite of the previous, genuine idealism; how then did I come to use this expression with a completely opposite intention, and how did the reviewer come to see genuine idealism everywhere?

4: 375

The solution to this difficulty rests upon something that could have been seen very easily from the context of the work, if one had wanted to. Space and time, together with everything contained in them, are not things (or properties of things) in themselves, but belong instead merely to the appearances of such things; thus far I am of one creed with the previous idealists. But these idealists, and among them especially Berkeley, viewed space as a merely empirical representation, a representation which, just like the appearances in space together with all of the determinations of space, would be known to us only by means of experience or perception; I show, on the contrary, first: that space (and time as well, to which Berkeley gave no attention), together with all its determinations, can be cognized by us a priori, since space (as well as time) inheres in us before all perception or experience as a pure form of our sensibility and makes possible all intuition from sensibility, and hence all appearances. From this it follows: that, since truth rests upon universal and necessary laws as its criteria, for *Berkeley* experience could have no criteria of truth, because its appearances (according to him) had nothing underlying them a priori; from which it then followed that experience is nothing but sheer illusion, whereas for us space and time (in combination with the pure concepts of the understanding) prescribe a priori their law to all possible experience, which law at the same time provides the sure criterion for distinguishing truth from illusion in experience.*

---

* Genuine idealism always has a visionary purpose and can have no other; but my idealism is solely for grasping the possibility of our a priori cognition of the objects of experience, which is a problem that has not been solved before now, nay, has not even once been posed. By that means all visionary idealism

My so-called (properly, critical) idealism is therefore of a wholly peculiar kind, namely such that it overturns ordinary idealism, and such that by means of it all cognition *a priori*, even that of geometry, first acquires objective reality, which, without my proven ideality of space and time, could not have been asserted by even the most zealous of realists. With matters standing so, I have wished that I could name this concept of mine something else, in order to*b* prevent all misunderstanding; but this concept cannot be completely changed. I may therefore be permitted in the future, as has already been stated above, to call it formal, or better, critical idealism, in order to distinguish it from the dogmatic idealism of *Berkeley* and the skeptical idealism of *Descartes*.

I find nothing else worthy of note in the review of this book. Its author judges *en gros*[c] throughout, a mode that is cleverly chosen, since it does not betray one's own knowledge or ignorance; a single comprehensive judgment *en détail*,[d] if, as is proper, it had considered the main question, would have perhaps exposed my error, perhaps also the degree of the reviewer's insight into investigations of this kind. It was no ill-considered trick, for removing early on the desire to read the book itself from readers who are used to forming a conception of books from newspaper articles only, to recite one after another a great many propositions, which, torn from the context of their arguments and explications (especially as antipodean as these propositions are in relation to all school metaphysics), must of necessity sound nonsensical; to assault the reader's patience to the point of disgust; and then, after having introduced me to the witty proposition that constant illusion is truth, to conclude with the harsh, though paternal, reprimand: To what end, then, the conflict with accepted*e* language, to what end, and whence, the idealistic distinction?[83] A judgment that ultimately renders everything peculiar to my book into merely verbal innovation (though previously the book was supposed to be metaphysically heretical), and that clearly proves that my would-be judge has not correctly understood

4: 376

---

collapses, which (as was already to be seen with Plato) always inferred, from our cognitions *a priori* (even those*a* of geometry), to another sort of intuition (namely, intellectual) than that of the senses, since it did not occur to anyone that the senses might also intuit *a priori*.

a Reading *denen* for *derer*, with Ak.
b Reading *um* for *nun*, with Ak.
c "in the large"
d "in detail"
e Omitting the antecedent addition of *gemein* or *gemeine* by Ak and Vorländer (respectively) as not required; Vorländer's emendation was based on the draft ms. (Ak 23:55).

the least bit of it, and, what's more, has not correctly understood himself.*

The reviewer, however, talks like a man who must be aware of important and exquisite insights, which, however, he still keeps secret; for nothing has become known to me of late regarding metaphysics that could justify such a tone. But he is doing a great wrong in withholding his discoveries from the world; for there are doubtless many others like me who, with all the fine things that have been written in this field for some time now, have still been unable to find that the science has thereby been advanced a finger's breadth. In other respects, we do indeed find definitions being sharpened, lame proofs provided with new crutches, the patchwork garment of metaphysics given new pieces, or an altered cut – but that is not what the world demands. The world is tired of metaphysical assertions; what's wanted[b] are the possibility of this science, the sources from which certainty could be derived in it, and sure criteria for distinguishing truth from the dialectical illusion of pure reason. The reviewer must possess the key to all this, otherwise he surely would never have spoken in so high a tone.

4: 377

But I come to suspect that this sort of need of the science perhaps may never have come into his head; for otherwise he would have directed his review toward this point, and in such an important matter even a failed attempt would have gained his respect. If that is so, then we are good friends again. He may think himself as deeply into his metaphysics as seems good to him, no one will stop him; only he is not permitted to judge of something that lies outside metaphysics, i.e., its source located in reason. But that my suspicion is not unfounded, I prove by the fact that he did not say a word about the possibility[c] of synthetic cognition *a priori*, which was the real problem, on the solution of which the fate

---

* The reviewer mostly fights his own shadow. When I oppose the truth of experience to dream, it never enters his head that the point of discussion is merely the notorious *somnio objective sumto[a]* of the Wolffian philosophy, which is merely formal, and whereby no regard at all is given to the difference between sleeping and waking, which also cannot be seen in transcendental philosophy.[84] Moreover, he calls my deduction of the categories and the table of principles of the understanding, "commonly known principles of logic and ontology, expressed in the manner of idealism."[85] The reader need only examine these *Prolegomena* on this subject to be convinced that a more deplorable, and even a more historically incorrect judgment could not be given.

---

[a] "dreams taken objectively"
[b] Not adopting Vorländer's additions, loosely based on the the draft ms. (Ak 23:58, 62), of *untersucht wissen* after *werden könne*, and *haben* after *Criterien*.
[c] Reading *Möglichkeit* for *Metaphysik*, with Ak, as confirmed by the draft ms. (Ak 23:62).

of metaphysics wholly rests, and to which my *Critique* (just as here my *Prolegomena*) was entirely directed. The idealism upon which he chanced, and to which he then held fast, was taken up into the system only as the sole means for solving this problem (although it then also received its[a] confirmation on yet other grounds); and so he would have had to show either that this problem does not have the importance that I attribute to it (as also now in the *Prolegomena*), or that it could not be solved at all by my concept of appearances, or could better be solved in another way; but I find not a word of this in the review. The reviewer therefore understood nothing of my work and perhaps also nothing of the spirit and nature of metaphysics itself, unless on the contrary, which I prefer to assume, a reviewer's haste, indignant at the difficulty of plowing his way through so many obstacles, cast an unfavorable shadow over the work lying before him and made it unrecognizable to him in its fundamentals.

There is still a great deal needed for a learned gazette, however well-chosen and carefully selected its contributors may be, to be able to uphold its otherwise well-deserved reputation in the field of metaphysics (just as elsewhere). Other sciences and areas of learning[b] have their standards. Mathematics has its standard within itself, history and theology in secular or sacred books, natural science and medicine in mathematics and experience, jurisprudence in law books, and even matters of taste in ancient paradigms. But in order to assess the thing called metaphysics, the standard must first be found (I have made an attempt to determine this standard as well as its use). Until it is ascertained, what is to be done when works of this kind must be judged? If they are of the dogmatic kind, one may do as one likes; no one will for long play the master over others in this without finding someone who repays him in kind. But if they are of the critical kind, and not indeed with regard to other writings but to reason itself, so that the standard of appraisal cannot be already assumed but must first be sought: then objection and censure are not to be forbidden, but they must be rooted in tolerance, since the need is common to us all, and the lack of the required insight makes an air of judicial decisiveness unsuitable.

But in order at the same time to tie this my defense to the interest of the philosophizing community, I propose a test, which is decisive as to the way in which all metaphysical investigations must be directed toward their common end. This is nothing else than what mathematicians have done before, in order to decide the merits of their methods in a contest – that is, a challenge to my reviewer to prove in his own way any single truly metaphysical (i.e., synthetic, and cognized *a priori*

4: 378

---

[a] Reading *seine* for *ihre*, with Ak.
[b] *Kenntnisse*

from concepts) proposition[a] he holds, and at best one of the most indispensable, such as the principle of the persistence of substance or of the necessary determination of the events in the world through their cause – but, as is fitting, to prove it on *a priori* grounds. If he can't do this (and silence is confession), then he must admit: that, since metaphysics is absolutely nothing without the apodictic certainty of propositions of this sort, their possibility or impossibility would first, before all else, have to be settled in a critique of pure reason, and hence he is obliged either to acknowledge that my principles of critique are correct or to prove their invalidity. Since, however, I already foresee that, as heedlessly as he has hitherto been relying on the certainty of his principles, still, now that it comes down to a rigorous test, he will not find a single principle in the whole compass of metaphysics with which he can dare come forward, I will therefore grant him the most favorable terms that can ever be expected in a competition; namely, I will take the *onus probandi*[b] from him and will have it put on me.

In particular, in these *Prolegomena* and in my *Critique*, pp. 426–61,[86] he will find eight propositions which are, pair by pair, always in conflict with one another, but each of which belongs necessarily to metaphysics, which must either accept it or refute it (although there is not a single one of them that has not in its day been accepted by some philosopher or other). He now has the freedom to pick any one of these eight propositions he likes, and to assume it without proof (which I concede to him), but only one (for wasting time will be no more useful to him than to me), and then he is to attack my proof of the antithesis. But if I can rescue it, and in this way show that the opposite of the proposition he adopted can be proven exactly as clearly, in accordance with principles that every dogmatic metaphysics must of necessity acknowledge, then by this means it is settled that there is an hereditary defect in metaphysics that cannot be explained, much less removed, without ascending to its birthplace, pure reason itself, and so my *Critique* must either be accepted or a better one put in its place, and therefore it must at least be studied; which is the only thing I ask for now. If, on the contrary, I cannot rescue my proof, then a synthetic *a priori* proposition is established from dogmatic principles on my opponent's side, my indictment of ordinary metaphysics was therefore unjust, and I offer to recognize his censure of my *Critique* as legitimate (although this is far from being the likely outcome). But hereto it would be necessary, I should think, *to emerge from being incognito*, since I do not otherwise see how to prevent my being honored or assailed with many problems from unknown and indeed unbidden opponents, instead of just one.[87]

4: 379

4: 380

[a] Adding *Satz*, with Vorländer.
[b] "burden of proof"

Proposal for an investigation of the *Critique*,
after which the judgment can follow

I am obliged to the learned public for the silence with which it has honored my *Critique* for so long a time; for this after all demonstrates a suspension of judgment, and thus some suspicion that, in a work that abandons all the usual paths and pursues a new one in which one cannot immediately find one's way, something might nonetheless perhaps be found through which an important but now moribund branch of human knowledge could receive new life and fertility, and so demonstrates a cautiousness, not to break off and destroy the still fresh graft through an overly hasty judgment. A specimen of a judgment that was delayed for such reasons has only just now come before me in the *Gothaische gelehrte Zeitung*,[88] a judgment whose well-foundedness every reader will perceive for himself (without taking into account my own suspect praise) from the clear and candid presentation of a portion of the first principles of my work.

And now I propose, since a large edifice cannot possibly be instantly judged as a whole through a quick once-over, that it be examined piece by piece from its foundation, and that in this the present *Prolegomena* be used as a general synopsis, with which the work itself could then be compared on occasion. This suggestion, if it were based on nothing more than the imagined importance that vanity customarily imparts to all one's own products, would be immodest and would deserve to be dismissed with indignation. But the endeavors of all speculative philosophy now stand at the point of total dissolution, although human reason clings to them with undying affection, an affection that now seeks, though vainly, to turn itself into indifference, only because it has been constantly betrayed.

In our thinking age it is not to be expected but that many meritorious men would use every good opportunity to work together toward the common interest of an ever more enlightened reason, if only there appears some hope of thereby attaining the goal. Mathematics, natural science, law, the arts, even morals (and so on) do not completely fill up the soul; there still remains a space in it that is marked off for mere pure and speculative reason, and its emptiness drives us to seek out, in grotesques and trivialities, or else in delusions, what seems to be occupation and amusement, but is at bottom only distraction to drown out the troublesome call of reason, which, as befits its vocation, demands something that satisfies it for itself and does not merely stir it to activity on behalf of other purposes or in the service of inclinations. Therefore, for everyone who has even tried to enlarge his conception in this way, contemplation that occupies itself only with this sphere of reason existing for itself has a great attraction, because exactly in this sphere all other areas of learning and even ends must, as I have reason to suppose, join

4: 381

together and unite in a whole – and, I dare say, it has a greater attraction than any other theoretical knowledge, for which one would not readily exchange it.

But I propose these *Prolegomena* as the plan and guide for the investigation, and not the work[a] itself, because, with respect to the latter, though I am even now quite satisfied as regards the content, order, and method, and the care that was taken to weigh and test each proposition accurately before setting it down (for it took years for me to be fully satisfied not only with the whole, but sometimes also with only a single proposition, as regards its sources), I am not fully satisfied with my presentation in some chapters of the Doctrine of Elements, e.g., the Deduction of the Concepts of the Understanding or the chapter on the Paralogisms of Pure Reason,[89] since in them a certain prolixity obstructs the clarity, and in their stead the examination can be based on what the *Prolegomena* here say with respect to these chapters.

The Germans are praised for being able to advance things further than other peoples in matters where persistence and unremitting industry are called for. If this opinion is well-founded, then an opportunity presents itself here to bring to completion an endeavor whose happy outcome is hardly to be doubted and in which all thinking persons share equal interest, but which has not succeeded before now – and to confirm that favorable opinion; especially since the science concerned is of such a peculiar kind that it can be brought all at once to its full completion, and into a *permanent state* such that it cannot be advanced the least bit further and can be neither augmented nor altered by later discovery (herein I do not include embellishment through enhanced clarity here and there, or through added utility in all sorts of respects): an advantage that no other science has or can have, since none is concerned with a cognitive faculty that is so fully isolated from, independent of, and unmingled with other faculties. The present moment does not seem unfavorable to this expectation of mine, since in Germany nowadays one hardly knows how he could keep himself otherwise still occupied outside the so-called useful sciences and have it be, not mere sport, but at the same time an endeavor through which an enduring goal is reached.

4: 382

I must leave it to others to contrive the means by which the efforts of the learned could be united toward such an end. In the meantime it is not my intention to expect of anyone a simple adherence to my theses, nor even to flatter myself with hope of that; rather, whether it should, as it happens, be attacks, revisions, and qualifications that bring it about, or confirmation, completion, and extension, if only the matter is investigated from the ground up, then it now can no longer fail that

[a] Reading *das Werk* for *des Werks*, with Ak.

a system would thereby come into being (even if it were not mine) that could become a legacy to posterity for which it would have reason to be thankful.

It would be too much to show here what sort of metaphysics could be expected to follow if one were first right about the principles of a critique, and how it would by no means have to appear paltry and cut down to just a small figure because its false feathers had been plucked, but could in other respects appear richly and respectably outfitted; but other large benefits that such a reform would bring with it are apparent at once. The ordinary metaphysics has indeed already produced benefits, because it searched for the elementary concepts of the pure understanding in order to render them clear through analysis and determinate through explication. It was thereby a cultivation of reason, wherever reason might subsequently think fit to direct itself. But that was all the good that it did. For it undid this merit again by promoting self-conceit through rash assertions, sophistry through subtle evasions and glosses, and shallowness through the facility with which it overcame the most difficult problems with a little school wisdom – a shallowness that is all the more enticing the more it has the option of, on the one hand, taking on something from the language of science, and, on the other, from popularity, and thereby is everything to everyone, but in fact is nothing at all. By contrast, through critique our judgment is afforded a standard by which knowledge can be distinguished with certainty from pseudo-knowledge; and, as a result of being brought fully into play in metaphysics, critique establishes a mode of thinking that subsequently extends its wholesome influence to every other use of reason, and for the first time excites the true philosophical spirit. Moreover, the service it renders to theology, by making it independent of the judgment of dogmatic speculation and in that way securing it against all attacks from such opponents, is certainly not to be underrated. For the ordinary metaphysics, although promising to assist theology greatly, was subsequently unable to fulfill this promise, and beyond this, in calling speculative dogmatism to its aid, had done nothing other than to arm enemies against itself. Fanaticism, which cannot make headway in an enlightened age except by hiding behind a school metaphysics, under the protection of which it can venture, as it were, to rave rationally, will be driven by critical philosophy from this its final hiding place; and beyond all this it cannot fail to be important to a teacher of metaphysics to be able, for once with universal assent, to say that what he propounds is now at last *science*, and that through it genuine benefit is rendered to the commonweal.

4: 383

Metaphysical foundations of natural science

Translator's introduction

The *Metaphysische Anfangsgründe der Naturwissenschaft* (hereinafter: *Metaphysical Foundations*) first appeared in 1786 (with second and third printings in 1787 and 1800 respectively). This work thus belongs to the most creative decade of Kant's so-called critical period: the decade of the first edition of the *Critique of Pure Reason* (1781), the *Prolegomena* (1783), the *Groundwork of the Metaphysics of Morals* (1785), the second edition of the *Critique of Pure Reason* (1787), the *Critique of Practical Reason* (1788), and finally the *Critique of Judgement* (1790). Until very recently, however, the *Metaphysical Foundations* has had by far the least impact of any of these works, and has accordingly attracted the least amount of scholarly attention. Both the content and the form of the work have contributed to this situation. For, on the one hand, the *Metaphysical Foundations* is concerned with relatively specialized questions belonging to natural philosophy and even to physics: questions about the character and behavior of attractive and repulsive forces, for example, or about impact and the communication of motion. And, on the other hand, it is written in an inhospitable and forbidding style – organized in quasi-mathematical fashion into definitions ("explications"), propositions, proofs, remarks, and so on. In both of these respects the *Metaphysical Foundations* is more akin to some of Kant's precritical writings on natural philosophy – especially the *Physical Monadology* (1756) – than to the great works of the critical period. It is tempting, then, to dismiss the *Metaphysical Foundations* as a more or less unaccountable regression into the outmoded preoccupations of the precritical period – thereby both explaining and justifying its traditional neglect. This, however, would be a serious mistake.

First of all, the close kinship between the *Metaphysical Foundations* and Kant's precritical writings on natural philosophy is of the greatest interest. For we thereby learn more than we can from any other work of the critical period about both the continuities and the discontinuities linking the concerns of the later period with those of the earlier one. In both the *Physical Monadology* and the *Metaphysical Foundations*, for example, Kant formulates a so-called "dynamical theory of matter," according to which attractive and repulsive forces constitute the very nature or essence of matter. In particular, the impenetrability of matter is grounded in a force of repulsion rather than being taken as a primitive and irreducible nondynamical property of hardness or solidity. Yet there is, nonetheless, a striking and fundamental difference between the two works in this regard. In the precritical *Physical Monadology*, Kant is still operating within the context of the Leibniz–Wolffian monadology. Matter consists of ultimate simple substances which determine, through the "sphere of activity" of their repulsive forces, elementary small volumes of space otherwise empty of intervening material. Matter is thus only *finitely* divisible into such elementary volumes. In the *Metaphysical Foundations*, by contrast, matter is explicitly taken to be continuous or infinitely divisible, and material *substance*, in particular, is now characterized precisely by the impossibility of elementary monadic simple elements. Accordingly, the problem posed by the infinite divisibility of space that the *Monadology* had solved by invoking finite "spheres of activity" is now solved by invoking the transcendental idealism articulated in the Antinomy of Pure Reason of the first *Critique* – and, specifically, the argument of the Second Antinomy. Matter is infinitely *divisible* but never, in experience, ever infinitely *divided*; hence, since matter is a mere appearance and is thus given only in the "progress of experience," it consists neither in ultimate simple elements nor in an actual or completed infinity of ever smaller spatial parts. Here, therefore, the deeply critical character of the *Metaphysical Foundations* becomes evident – and in a way, moreover, that illuminates both the relationship of the critical to the precritical period and, via application to a concrete example, such characteristically critical doctrines as the transcendental idealism of the Antinomies.

Indeed, there is an even more fundamental aspect of transcendental idealism that is centrally implicated here – the doctrine, namely, that space is not a property or relation of things in themselves but a pure form of our sensible intuition. In the precritical period of the *Physical Monadology*, space is viewed as a derivative "phenomenon" of the relations (of interaction) between the ultimate simple substances – substances that can be conceived purely intellectually independently of all spatial properties. The ultimate simple substances are not actually in space; rather, space itself is first constituted by their (interactive) relations. On the precritical view, therefore, space, on broadly Leibnizean grounds, just is a relation between "noumena" or things in themselves. In the critical period, however, Kant's transcendental idealism about space is explicitly intended as a middle ground between Leibnizean "relationalism" and the Newtonian doctrine of absolute space (cf. A 39–41/B 56–58), and the *Metaphysical Foundations* greatly illuminates the precise sense in which the critical position secures this middle ground. In particular, Kant here attempts to preserve the distinction between "true" and "apparent" motion required by Newtonian mathematical physics without being thereby committed to a metaphysically objectionable postulation of absolute space. Thus, by focusing from the outset on the problem of *motion* (on matter as "the movable in space"), the *Metaphysical Foundations* shows how transcendental idealism is intertwined with the profound conceptual problems about the proper dynamical characterization of space, time, and motion that divided the natural philosophies of Newton and Leibniz.

More generally, a continuous struggle aimed at integrating the Leibnizean and Newtonian natural philosophies is clearly visible throughout the precritical period: beginning with Kant's first published work, *Thoughts on the True Estimation of Living Forces* (1747), continuing through the *Universal Natural History and Theory of the Heavens* (1755) and *Physical Monadology*, and on into the *Attempt to Introduce the Concept of Negative Magnitude into Philosophy* (1763) and *Enquiry Concerning the Clarity of the Principles of Natural Theology and Ethics* (1764). In the latter two works the opposition between Leibniz–Wolffianism and Newtonianism is considered especially in its methodological aspect. For the Wolffian tradition had promulgated a deductive, quasimathematical method for philosophy, while simultaneously claiming that the actual results of mathematical natural science (i.e., Newtonian natural science) must yield pride of place to the more certain doctrines of metaphysics (i.e., Leibniz–Wolffian metaphysics). For the Newtonians, by contrast, metaphysics or philosophy – if it is now even possible at all – must rather receive its orientation from the more certain results of mathematical natural science: metaphysics is now possible at all, that is, only by following an inductive rather than a deductive method. Kant, in the methodological works of the early 1760s, is in explicit agreement with the Newtonians in this respect: metaphysics is possible only in the context of an "analytic" as opposed to a "synthetic" method – whereby, in particular, we inductively follow the secure results of mathematical natural science rather than attempting deductively to legislate for such science. And this "Newtonian" conception of metaphysical method finds clear echoes in the critical period as well – especially in the *Prolegomena*, where the question, "How is metaphysics in general possible?" is approached by way of the questions, "How is pure mathematics possible?" and "How is pure natural science possible?"

We have now arrived at the second point I wish to emphasize: namely, the central place of the *Metaphysical Foundations* within the critical period. For the answer to the question concerning pure natural science posed by the *Prolegomena* (which question, we should remember, corresponds to the Transcendental Analytic of the first *Critique*) is given its most explicit and developed answer in the *Metaphysical Foundations*. Indeed, the task of this work is to articulate in detail what Kant calls the "metaphysical part" of pure natural science – the "metaphysical foundations of the doctrine of body." Moreover, Kant's preoccupation, at precisely this time, with the metaphysical foundations of the doctrine of body is intimately bound up with his further articulation of the critical philosophy. As is well known, the first (1781) edition of the *Critique* received a hostile review from Garve and Feder in 1782, in which Kant was accused of presenting a system of subjective idealism of the Berkeleyan variety. The

175

Prolegomena of 1783 then explicitly replies to this review by emphasizing that Kantian "appearances" are bodies external to us in space and that the doctrine of space as an *a priori* form of intuition is quite incompatible with Berkeley's empiricist account of space. In this context, the metaphysical foundations of the doctrine of body serve precisely to emphasize that the objects whose possibility the critical philosophy is to explain – i.e., "appearances" – are spatiotemporal objects of natural scientific knowledge and, accordingly, that the point of the *Critique* is to secure the *a priori* foundations of this type of knowledge rather than to reduce the external physical world to a play of subjective mental states.

Indeed, the central importance of the *Metaphysical Foundations* in this regard is clearly visible in the second (1787) edition of the *Critique*. This is most evident in the General Remark to the System of the Principles that Kant added there (B 288–294), which claims, in particular, that "in order to understand the possibility of things in conformity with the categories, and thus to verify the *objective reality* of the latter, we require not merely intuitions, but always even *outer intuitions*," so that "in order to give something *permanent* in intuition corresponding to the concept of *substance* (and thereby to verify the objective reality of this concept) we require an intuition *in space* (of matter)" (B 291). This passage is closely related, in turn, to the Refutation of Idealism that Kant also added to the second edition (B 274–279), which claims, in particular, that "we have nothing permanent on which we could base the concept of substance, as intuition, except only *matter*" (B 278). Both passages make it as explicit as possible that the objects of cognition with which the transcendental idealism of the first *Critique* is concerned are, first and foremost, physical objects or bodies – the objects of natural science – and thus, along with other related additions and changes in the second edition, they thereby function to distance Kant's doctrine from the subjective idealism of Berkeley. And it is perhaps for this reason, above all, that Kant also emphasizes, in a passage from the Preface to the *Metaphysical Foundations* closely related to the above passage from the General Remark to the System of Principles, that "general metaphysics, in all instances where it requires examples (intuitions) in order to provide meaning for its pure concepts of the understanding, must always take them from the general doctrine of body," which thereby "does excellent and indispensable service for *general* metaphysics, in that the former furnishes examples (instances *in concreto*) in which to realize the concepts and propositions of the latter (properly speaking, transcendental philosophy), that is, to give a mere form of thought sense and meaning."

The third point I wish to emphasize is that Kant's concern with the foundations of natural science extends beyond the critical period as well. From approximately 1796 until his death in 1804, Kant was struggling with a work which he thought, at that time, was necessary to complete the system of the critical philosophy. This work was never successfully brought into publishable form, and has instead come down to us in a collection of drafts, fragments, and sketches bound together as the *Opus postumum*. Despite its fragmentary and unfinished character, however, the *Opus postumum* is of the greatest interest in indicating how Kant envisioned a radical transformation of the critical philosophy toward the end of his creative life. But what is of most importance, from our present point of view, is the title of the proposed work that Kant was attempting to draft: *Transition from the Metaphysical Foundations of Natural Science to Physics*. As this title suggests, the transformation of the critical philosophy with which Kant was struggling here took its impetus precisely from a fundamental reconsideration of the philosophy of natural science articulated in the *Metaphysical Foundations* of 1786. Thus, the *Metaphysical Foundations* is of central importance, not only, as emphasized above, for understanding both the relationship of the critical to the precritical period and the internal development of the critical period itself, but also for understanding the later trajectory and ultimate transformation of the critical philosophy in what we might call Kant's postcritical period. Indeed, from this point of view, the *Metaphysical Foundations* appears as the central work linking all three periods together. It is no wonder, then, that serious scholarly attention to this work – and to Kant's evolving philosophy of natural science more generally – has been markedly increasing in recent years (see the following bibliography).

There is one final issue worth considering here: namely, the forbidding quasi-mathematical form of the *Metaphysical Foundations* – its organization into definitions ("explications"), propositions, proofs, observations, and so on. This form is not merely an annoying hindrance to the reader, it also poses a fundamental philosophical problem. For one of the key doctrines of the *Critique of Pure Reason* is that there is an essential distinction between mathematical and philosophical reasoning – so that, in particular, it is entirely inappropriate for philosophy to attempt to "imitate" mathematics (see the Discipline of Pure Reason in its Dogmatic Employment: A 712–738/B 740–766). Indeed, as noted above, we find this doctrine already in the precritical methodological works of the early 1760s, where Kant advocates a Newtonian inductive or "analytic" style of metaphysics that is explicitly opposed to the deductive, quasi-mathematical or "synthetic" style of metaphysics of the Wolffian school. So why does Kant, at the height of the critical period, employ precisely such a quasi-mathematical style in the *Metaphysical Foundations*? I cannot attempt adequately to answer this question here, but I can offer some preliminary suggestions.

First, we should take this quasi-mathematical style, as stated above, as presenting us with a philosophical problem – a problem that is connected, in turn, with the content of the *Metaphysical Foundations*. In the

Preface, for example, Kant explains that pure natural science has two interdependent parts: a metaphysical part (the metaphysical foundations of the doctrine of body), but also a mathematical part. For, as perhaps the best-known sentence of the *Metaphysical Foundations* puts it, "in any special doctrine of nature there can be only as much *proper* science as there is *mathematics* therein." For this reason, in fact, even the metaphysical part of pure natural science must contain "principles for the *construction* of the concepts that belong to the possibility of matter in general." Indeed, at one point Kant even appears to say that pure natural science contains both "metaphysical and mathematical constructions" – thereby seeming explicitly to contradict the doctrine of the first *Critique*, noted above, that philosophy, as opposed to mathematics, *cannot* proceed by "construction."

Second, although a quasi-mathematical organization into definitions, propositions, proofs, and observations is quite rare in the critical period, it is not entirely absent from other critical works. It is used, for example, throughout §§1–8 of the *Critique of Practical Reason* (where we also find "corollaries" and "problems") and, which is of more relevance to our present concerns, in the Refutation of Idealism of the *Critique of Pure Reason*. Due to the close connection, noted above, between the content of the Refutation of Idealism and that of the *Metaphysical Foundations*, this correspondence in form as well is of particular interest.

Third, although the quasi-mathematical style of the *Metaphysical Foundations* exhibits the deductive form rejected in the methodological works of the 1760s, this is by no means in the service of a Wolffian devaluation of mathematical-physical content. Indeed, as Kant himself explains in the Preface, he uses a quasi-mathematical style here precisely to encourage a closer connection between metaphysics of nature and mathematical natural science:

In this treatise, although I have not followed the mathematical method with thoroughgoing rigor (which would have required more time than I had to spend thereon), I have nonetheless imitated that method – not in order to obtain a better reception for the treatise through an ostentatious display of exactitude, but rather because I believe that such a system is certainly capable of this rigor and also that such perfection can certainly be reached in time by a more adept hand if, stimulated by this sketch, mathematical natural scientists should find it not unimportant to treat the metaphysical part, which they cannot leave out in any case, as a special fundamental part in their general physics and to bring it into union with the mathematical doctrine of motion.

Accordingly, Kant's own attitude towards the relative claims of metaphysics and mathematical natural science is one of striking modesty:

Newton, in the preface to his *Mathematical First Principles of Natural Science*, says (after he had remarked that geometry requires only two of the mechanical operations that it postulates: namely, to describe a straight line and a circle): *Geometry is proud of the fact that with so little derived from without it is able to produce so much.* By contrast, one can say of metaphysics: *it is dismayed that with so much offered to it by pure mathematics it can still accomplish so little.* Nevertheless, this small amount is still something that even mathematics unavoidably requires in its application to natural science, and thus, since it must here necessarily borrow from metaphysics, need also not be ashamed to let itself be seen in community with the latter.

Kant's view of the relationship between metaphysics and mathematical natural science – and, in particular, the mathematical natural science of Newton's *Principia* – could not be more different from that of the Wolffian school.

In carrying out the translation I have consulted the two previous English renderings: those of E. Belfort Bax (London, 1883) and James Ellington (Indianapolis and New York, 1970). Although he revises the earlier translation in several significant respects, Ellington still follows Bax rather closely. I have chosen, however, to deviate quite fundamentally from both Ellington and Bax, and to begin again from scratch. First, I have attempted to be as scrupulous as possible about respecting the nuances of Kant's technical terminology and phraseology – so that, in particular, Kant's conceptual distinctions are reflected as faithfully as possible. Second, I have also attempted, as far as possible, to render Kant's sentences into readable English – so as not to create additional problems for the reader in grappling with an already forbidding text.

The translation is based on the text in volume 4 of the Akademie Edition of *Kant's gesammelte Schriften*, the page numbers of which appear in the margins. Where I have deviated from that text in favor of the original edition I have appended an explanatory note.

For help and advice on the translation I am indebted to Frederick Beiser, Robert Butts, Eckart Förster, Hannah Ginsborg, Paul Guyer, Peter McLaughlin, and Daniel Warren. For carefully reading and correcting the entire text I am indebted to Martin Carrier, Martin Schönfeld (who also helped with the notes and glossary), Henry Allison, and, especially, Peter Heath. I am of course solely responsible for any errors that remain.

I am grateful for a Fellowship from the National Endowment for the Humanities in support of this project during the academic year 1992–93.

BIBLIOGRAPHY

ADICKES, E. (1924). *Kant als Naturforscher*, Berlin.
BECK, L. , ed. (1974). *Kant's Theory of Knowledge*, Dordrecht.
BRITTAN, G. (1978). *Kant's Philosophy of Science*, Princeton.

BUCHDAHL, G. (1969). *Metaphysics and the Philosophy of Science*, Oxford.

BUSSE, F. (1828). *Metaphysische Anfangsgründe der Naturwissenschaft*, Dresden und Leipzig.

BUTTS, R. , ed. (1986). *Kant's Philosophy of Physical Science*, Dordrecht.

CRAMER, K. (1985). *Nicht-reine synthetische Urteile a priori*, Heidelberg.

DREWS, A. (1894). *Kants Naturphilosophie als Grundlage seines Systems*.

FRIEDMAN, M. (1992). *Kant and the Exact Sciences*, Cambridge, Mass.

FRIES, J. (1882). *Die mathematische Naturphilosophie nach philosophischer Methode bearbeitet*, Heidelberg.

GLOY, K. (1976). *Die Kantische Theorie der Naturwissenschaft*, Berlin.

HARMAN, P. (1982). *Metaphysics and Natural Philosophy*, Brighton.

HOPPE, H. (1969). *Kants Theorie der Physik*, Frankfurt.

MARTIN, G. (1951). *Immanuel Kant. Ontologie und Wissenschaftslehre*, Köln; translated as *Kant's Metaphysics and Theory of Science* (Manchester, 1955).

PLAASS, P. (1965). *Kants Theorie der Naturwissenschaft*, Göttingen; translated as *Kant's Theory of Natural Science* (Dordrecht, 1994).

SCHÄFER, L. (1966). *Kants Metaphysik der Natur*, Berlin.

STADLER, A. (1883). *Kants Theorie der Materie*, Leipzig.

STÖHR, A. (1884). *Analyse der reinen Naturwissenschaft Kants*, Wien.

TUSCHLING, B. (1971). *Metaphysische und transzendentale Dynamik in Kants Opus postumum*, Berlin.

VUILLEMIN, J. (1955). *Physique et Métaphysique Kantiennes*, Paris.

WAIDHAUS, D. (1985). *Kants System der Natur*, Frankfurt.

WOOD, A. , ed. (1984). *Self and Nature in Kant's Philosophy*, Ithaca.

Metaphysical foundations of natural science

Contents

If the word nature is taken simply in its *formal* meaning, where it means the first inner principle of all that belongs to the existence of a thing,* then there can be as many different natural sciences as there are specifically different things, each of which must contain its own peculiar inner principle of the determinations belonging to its existence. But nature is also taken otherwise in its *material* meaning, not as a constitution,[a] but as the sum total of all things, insofar as they can be *objects of our senses*, and thus also of experience. Nature, in this meaning, is therefore understood as the whole of all appearances, that is, the sensible world, excluding all nonsensible objects. Now nature, taken in this meaning of the word, has two principal parts, in accordance with the principal division of our senses, where the one contains the objects of the *outer* senses, the other the object of *inner* sense. In this meaning, therefore, a twofold doctrine of nature is possible, the *doctrine of body* and the *doctrine of the soul*, where the first considers *extended* nature, the second *thinking* nature.

Every doctrine that is supposed to be a system, that is, a whole of cognition ordered according to principles, is called a science. And, since such principles may be either principles of *empirical* or of *rational* connection of cognitions into a whole, then natural science, be it the doctrine of body or the doctrine of the soul, would have to be divided into *historical* 4: 468 or *rational* natural science, were it not that the word *nature* (since this signifies a derivation of the manifold belonging to the existence of things from their inner *principle*) makes necessary a cognition through reason of the interconnection of natural things, insofar as this cognition is to deserve the name of a science. Therefore, the doctrine of nature can be better divided into *historical doctrine of nature*, which contains nothing but systematically ordered facts about natural things (and would in turn consist of *natural description*, as a system of classification for natural things in accordance with their similarities, and *natural history*, as a systematic presentation of natural things at various times and places), and natural

---

* Essence is the first inner principle of all that belongs to the possibility of a thing. Therefore, one can attribute only an essence to geometrical figures, but not a nature (since in their concept nothing is thought that would express an existence).

[a] *Beschaffenheit*

science. Natural science would now be either *properly* or *improperly* so-called natural science, where the first treats its object wholly according to *a priori* principles, the second according to laws of experience.

What can be called *proper* science is only that whose certainty is apodictic; cognition that can contain mere empirical certainty is only *knowledge*[a] improperly so-called. Any whole of cognition that is systematic can, for this reason, already be called *science*, and, if the connection of cognition in this system is an interconnection of grounds and consequences, even *rational* science. If, however, the grounds or principles themselves are still in the end merely empirical, as in chemistry, for example, and the laws from which the given facts are explained through reason are mere laws of experience, then they carry with them no consciousness of their *necessity* (they are not apodictally certain), and thus the whole of cognition does not deserve the name of a science in the strict sense; chemistry should therefore be called a systematic art rather than a science.

A rational doctrine of nature thus deserves the name of a natural science, only in case the fundamental natural laws therein are cognized *a priori*, and are not mere laws of experience. One calls a cognition of nature of the first kind *pure*, but that of the second kind is called *applied* rational cognition. Since the word nature already carries with it the concept of laws, and the latter carries with it the concept of the *necessity* of all determinations of a thing belonging to its existence, one easily sees why natural science must derive the legitimacy of this title only from its pure part – namely, that which contains the *a priori* principles of all other natural explanations – and why only in virtue of this pure part is natural science to be proper science. Likewise, [one sees] that, in accordance with demands of reason, every doctrine of nature must finally lead to natural science and conclude there, because this necessity of laws is inseparably attached to the concept of nature, and therefore makes claim to be thoroughly comprehended. Hence, the most complete explanation of given appearances from chemical principles still always leaves behind a certain dissatisfaction, because one can adduce no *a priori* grounds for such principles, which, as contingent laws, have been learned merely from experience.

4: 469

All *proper* natural science therefore requires a *pure* part, on which the apodictic certainty that reason seeks therein can be based. And because this pure part is wholly different, in regard to its principles, from those that are merely empirical, it is also of the greatest utility to expound this part as far as possible in its entirety, separated and wholly unmixed with the other part; indeed, in accordance with the nature of the case it is an unavoidable duty with respect to method. This is necessary in

---

[a] *Wissen*. Cf. "science [*Wissenschaft*]" in the previous sentence.

order that one may precisely determine what reason can accomplish for itself, and where its power begins to require the assistance of principles of experience. Pure rational cognition from mere *concepts* is called pure philosophy or metaphysics; by contrast, that which grounds its cognition only on the *construction* of concepts, by means of the presentation of the object in an *a priori* intuition, is called mathematics.

Properly so-called natural science presupposes, in the first place, metaphysics of nature. For laws, that is, principles of the necessity of that which belongs to the *existence* of a thing, are concerned with a concept that cannot be constructed, since existence cannot be presented *a priori* in any intuition. Thus proper natural science presupposes metaphysics of nature. Now this latter must always contain solely principles that are not empirical (for precisely this reason it bears the name of a metaphysics), but it can still either: *first*, treat the laws that make possible the concept of a nature in general, even without relation to any determinate object of experience, and thus undetermined with respect to the nature of this or that thing in the sensible world, in which case it is the *transcendental* part of the metaphysics of nature; or *second*, concern itself with a particular nature of this or that kind of things, for which an empirical concept is given, but still in such a manner that, outside of what lies in this concept, no other empirical principle is used for its cognition (for example, it takes the empirical concept of matter or of a thinking being as its basis, and it seeks that sphere of cognition of which reason is capable *a priori* concerning these objects), and here such a science must still always be called a metaphysics of nature, namely, of corporeal or of thinking nature. However, [in this second case] it is then not a general, but a *special* metaphysical natural science (physics or psychology), in which the above transcendental principles are applied to the two species of objects of our senses.[1]

4: 470

I assert, however, that in any special doctrine of nature there can be only as much *proper* science as there is *mathematics* therein. For, according to the preceding, proper science, and above all proper natural science, requires a pure part lying at the basis of the empirical part, and resting on *a priori* cognition of natural things. Now to cognize something *a priori* means to cognize it from its mere possibility. But the possibility of determinate natural things cannot be cognized from their mere concepts; for from these the possibility of the thought (that it does not contradict itself) can certainly be cognized, but not the possibility of the object, as a natural thing that can be given outside the thought (as existing). Hence, in order to cognize the possibility of determinate natural things, and thus to cognize them *a priori*, it is still required that the *intuition* corresponding to the concept be given *a priori*, that is, that the concept be constructed. Now rational cognition through construction of concepts is mathematical. Hence, although a pure philosophy of nature in general, that is, that which investigates only what constitutes the concept of a nature in general, may indeed be possible even without mathematics, a pure doctrine of nature concerning *determinate* natural things (doctrine of body or doctrine of soul) is only possible by means of mathematics. And, since in any doctrine of nature there is only as much proper science as there is *a priori* knowledge therein, a doctrine of nature will contain only as much proper science as there is mathematics capable of application there.

4: 471 So long, therefore, as there is still for chemical actions of matters on one another no concept to be discovered that can be constructed, that is, no law of the approach or withdrawal of the parts of matter can be specified according to which, perhaps in proportion to their density or the like, their motions and all the consequences thereof can be made intuitive and presented *a priori* in space (a demand that will only with great difficulty ever be fulfilled), then chemistry can be nothing more than a systematic art or experimental doctrine, but never a proper science, because its principles are merely empirical, and allow of no *a priori* presentation in intuition. Consequently, they do not in the least make the principles of chemical appearances conceivable with respect to their possibility, for they are not receptive to the application of mathematics.

Yet the empirical doctrine of the soul must remain even further from the rank of a properly so-called natural science than chemistry. In the first place, because mathematics is not applicable to the phenomena of inner sense and their laws, the only option one would have would be to take the *law of continuity* in the flux of inner changes into account – which, however, would be an extension of cognition standing to that which mathematics provides for the doctrine of body approximately as the doctrine of the properties of the straight line stands to the whole of geometry. For the pure inner intuition in which the appearances of the soul are supposed to be constructed is *time*, which has only one dimension. [In the second place,] however, the empirical doctrine of the soul can also never approach chemistry even as a systematic art of analysis or experimental doctrine, for in it the manifold of inner observation can be separated only by mere division in thought, and cannot then be held separate and recombined at will (but still less does another thinking subject suffer himself to be experimented upon to suit our purpose), and even observation by itself already changes and displaces the state of the observed object. Therefore, the empirical doctrine of the soul can never become anything more than an historical doctrine of nature, and, as such, a natural doctrine of inner sense which is as systematic as possible, that is, a natural description of the soul, but never a science of the soul, nor even, indeed, an experimental psychological doctrine. This is also the reason for our having used, in accordance with common custom, the general title of natural science for this work, which actually contains the principles of the doctrine of body, for only to it does this title belong in the proper sense, and so no ambiguity is thereby produced.[2]

But in order to make possible the application of mathematics to the doctrine of body, which only through this can become natural science, principles for the *construction* of the concepts that belong to the possibility of matter in general must first be introduced. Therefore, a complete analysis of the concept of a matter in general will have to be taken as the basis, and this is a task for pure philosophy – which, for this purpose, makes use of no particular experiences, but only that which it finds in the isolated (although intrinsically empirical) concept itself, in relation to the pure intuitions in space and time, and in accordance with laws that already essentially attach to the concept of nature in general, and is therefore a genuine *metaphysics of corporeal nature*.

4: 472

Hence all natural philosophers who have wished to proceed mathematically in their occupation have always, and must have always, made use of metaphysical principles (albeit unconsciously), even if they themselves solemnly guarded against all claims of metaphysics upon their science. Undoubtedly they have understood by the latter the folly of contriving possibilities at will and playing with concepts, which can perhaps not be presented in intuition at all, and have no other certification of their objective reality than that they merely do not contradict themselves. All true metaphysics is drawn from the essence of the faculty of thinking itself, and is in no way fictitiously invented[a] on account of not being borrowed from experience. Rather, it contains the pure actions of thought, and thus *a priori* concepts and principles, which first bring the manifold of *empirical representations* into the law-governed connection through which it can become *empirical* **cognition**, that is, experience. Thus these mathematical physicists could in no way avoid metaphysical principles, and, among them, also not those that make the concept of their proper object, namely, matter, *a priori* suitable for application to outer experience, such as the concept of motion, the filling of space, inertia, and so on.[3] But they rightly held that to let merely empirical principles govern these concepts would in no way be appropriate to the apodictic certainty they wished their laws of nature to possess, so they preferred to postulate such [principles], without investigating them with regard to their *a priori* sources.

Yet it is of the greatest importance to separate heterogeneous principles from one another, for the advantage of the sciences, and to place each in a special system so that it constitutes a science of its own kind, in order to guard against the uncertainty arising from mixing things together, where one finds it difficult to distinguish to which of the two the limitations, and even mistakes, that might occur in their use may be assigned. For this purpose I have considered it necessary [to isolate] the former from the pure part of natural science (*physica generalis*), where

4: 473

---

[a] *erdichtet*

metaphysical and mathematical constructions customarily run together, and to present them, together with principles of the construction of these concepts (and thus principles of the possibility of a mathematical doctrine of nature itself), in a system.[4] Aside from the already mentioned advantage that it provides, this isolation has also a special charm arising from the unity of cognition, when one takes care that the boundaries of the sciences do not run together, but rather each takes in its own separated field.

The following can serve as still another ground for commending this procedure. In everything that is called metaphysics one can hope for the *absolute completeness* of the sciences, of such a kind one may expect in no other type of cognition. Therefore, just as in the metaphysics of nature in general, here also the completeness of the metaphysics of corporeal nature can confidently be expected. The reason is that in metaphysics the object is only considered in accordance with the general laws of thought, whereas in other sciences it must be represented in accordance with data of intuition (pure as well as empirical), where the former, because here the object has to be compared always with *all* the necessary laws of thought, must yield a determinate number of cognitions that may be completely exhausted, but the latter, because they offer an infinite manifold of intuitions (pure or empirical), and thus an infinite manifold of objects of thought, never attain absolute completeness, but can always be extended to infinity, as in pure mathematics and empirical doctrine of nature. I also take myself to have completely exhausted this metaphysical doctrine of body, so far as it may extend, but not to have thereby accomplished any great [piece of] work.

4: 474

But the schema for completeness of a metaphysical system, whether it be of nature in general, or of corporeal nature in particular, is the table of categories.* For there are no more pure concepts of the understanding which can be concerned with the nature of things. All determinations of

4: 475

the general concept of a matter in general must be able to be brought

---

* In the *Allgemeine Literatur Zeitung*, No. 295, in the review of *Institutiones Logicae et Metaphysicae* by Prof. *Ulrich*, I find doubts, which are not directed against this table of pure concepts of the understanding, but rather against the inferences drawn therefrom to the determination of the limits of the entire faculty of pure reason, and thus all metaphysics, [doubts] with respect to which the deeply delving reviewer declares himself to be in agreement with the no less penetrating author. And, in fact, since these doubts are supposed to concern precisely the principal basis of my system articulated in the *Critique*, they would be grounds for thinking that this system, with respect to its principal aim, does not come close to carrying that apodictic conviction that is required for eliciting an unqualified acceptance. This principal basis is said to be the *deduction* of the pure concepts of the understanding, which is expounded partly in the *Critique* and partly in the *Prolegomena*, and which, however, in the part of the

under the four classes of [pure concepts of the understanding], those of   4: 476
quantity, of *quality*, of *relation*, and finally of *modality* – and so, too, [must]
all that may be either thought *a priori* in this concept, or presented in

Critique that ought to be precisely the most clear, is rather the most obscure,
or even revolves in a circle, etc. I direct my reply to these objections only to
their principal point, namely, the claim that *without an entirely clear and sufficient
deduction of the categories* the system of the *Critique of Pure Reason* totters on its
foundation. I assert, on the contrary, that the system of the *Critique* must carry
apodictic certainty for whoever subscribes (as the reviewer does) to my propositions concerning the sensible character of all our intuition, and the adequacy
of the table of categories, as determinations of our consciousness derived from
the logical functions in judgments in general, because it is erected upon the
proposition *that the entire speculative use of our reason never reaches further than to
objects of possible experience.* For if we can prove **that** the categories which reason
must use in all its cognition can have no other use at all, except solely in relation to objects of possible experience (insofar as they simply make possible the
form of thought in such experience), then, although the answer to the question
how the categories make such experience possible is important enough for
completing the deduction where possible, with respect to the principal end of
the system, namely, the determination of the limits of pure reason, it is in no
way *compulsory*, but merely *meritorious*. For the deduction is already carried *far
enough* for this purpose if it shows that categories of thought are nothing but
mere forms of judgments insofar as they are applied to intuitions (which for us
are always sensible), and that they thereby first of all obtain objects and become
cognitions; because this already suffices to ground with complete certainty the
entire system of *Critique* properly speaking. Thus Newton's system of universal
gravitation stands firm, even though it involves the difficulty that one cannot
explain how attraction at a distance is possible; but *difficulties are not doubts.* That
the above fundamental basis stands firm, even without a complete deduction
of the categories, I now prove from the following granted propositions:

1. *Granted*: that the table of categories contains all pure concepts of the under-   4: 475
standing, just as it contains all formal actions of the understanding in judging,
from which the concepts of the understanding are derived, and from which
they differ only in that, through the concepts of the understanding, an object
is thought as *determined* with respect to one or another function of judgment.
(Thus, for example, in the categorical judgement *the stone is hard*, the *stone* is
used as subject, and *hard* as predicate, in such a way that the understanding
is still free to exchange the logical function of these concepts, and to say that
something hard is a stone. By contrast, if I represent it to myself as *determined
in the object* that the stone must be thought only as subject, but hardness only as
predicate, in any possible determination of an object (not of the mere concept),
then the very same logical functions now become *pure concepts of the understanding* of objects, namely, as *substance* and *accident*.)

2. *Granted*: that the understanding by its nature contains synthetic *a priori*
principles, through which it subjects all objects that may be given to it to
these categories, and, therefore, there must also be intuitions given *a priori*

mathematical construction, or given as a determinate object of experience. There is no more to be done, or to be discovered, or to be added

that contain the conditions required for the application of these pure concepts of the understanding, because *without intuition there can be no object*, with respect to which the logical function could be determined as category, and thus no cognition of any object whatsoever, and hence without pure intuition no principle that determines it *a priori* for this purpose.

3. *Granted*: that these pure intuitions can never be anything other than mere forms of the *appearances* of outer or of inner sense (space and time), and therefore of the *objects of possible experience* alone.

It then follows: that all use of pure reason can never extend to anything other than objects of experience, and, since nothing empirical can be the condition of *a priori* principles, the latter can be nothing more than principles of the *possibility of experience* in general. This alone is the true and sufficient basis for the determination of the limits of pure reason, but not the solution to the problem **how** experience is now possible by means of these categories, and only through these categories alone. The latter problem, although without it the structure still stands firm, has great importance nonetheless, and, as I now understand it, [it can be solved with] just as much ease, since it can almost be accomplished through a single inference from the precisely determined definition of a *judgment* in general (an action through which given representations first become cognitions of an object). The obscurity that attaches to my earlier discussions in this part of the deduction (and which I do not deny), is to be attributed to the common fortunes of the understanding in its investigations, in which the shortest way is commonly not the first way that it becomes aware of. Therefore, I shall take up the next opportunity to make up for this deficiency (which concerns only the manner of presentation, and not the ground of explanation, which is already stated correctly there), so that the perceptive reviewer may not be left with the necessity, certainly unwelcome even to himself, of taking refuge in a preestablished harmony to explain the surprising agreement of appearances with the laws of the understanding, despite their having entirely different sources from the former. This remedy would be much worse than the evil it is supposed to cure, and, on the contrary, actually cannot help at all. For the *objective necessity* that characterizes the pure concepts of the understanding (and the principles of their application to appearances), in the concept of cause in connection with the effect, for example, is still not forthcoming. Rather, it all remains only *subjectively necessary*, but objectively merely contingent, placing together, precisely as Hume has it when he calls this mere illusion from custom. No system in the world can derive this necessity from anywhere else than the principles lying *a priori* at the basis of the possibility of *thinking itself*, through which alone the cognition of objects whose appearance is given to us, that is, experience, becomes possible. Even if we suppose, therefore, that the explanation of **how** experience thereby becomes possible in the first place could never be sufficiently carried out, it still remains incontrovertibly certain **that** it is possible solely through these concepts, and, conversely, that these concepts are capable of meaning and use in no other relation than to objects of experience.

here, except, if need be, to improve it where it may lack in clarity or exactitude.[a]

The concept of matter had therefore to be carried through all four of the indicated functions of the concepts of the understanding (in four chapters), where in each a new determination of this concept was added. The basic determination of something that is to be an object of the outer senses had to be motion, because only thereby can these senses be affected. The understanding traces back all other predicates of matter belonging to its nature to this, and so natural science, therefore, is either a pure or applied *doctrine of motion*. The *metaphysical* foundations of natural science are therefore to be brought under *four* chapters. The *first* considers *motion* as a pure *quantum* in accordance with its composition, without any quality of the movable, and may be called **phoronomy**. The *second* takes into consideration motion as belonging to the *quality* of matter, under the name of an original moving force, and is therefore called **dynamics**. The *third* considers matter with this quality as in *relation* to another through its own inherent motion, and therefore appears under the name of **mechanics**. The *fourth* chapter, however, determines matter's motion or rest merely in relation to the mode of representation or *modality*, and thus as appearance of the outer senses, and is called **phenomenology**.

4: 477

Yet aside from the inner necessity to isolate the metaphysical foundations of the doctrine of body, not only from physics, which needs empirical principles, but even from the rational premises of physics that concern the use of mathematics therein, there is still an external, certainly only accidental, but nonetheless important reason for detaching its detailed treatment from the general system of metaphysics, and presenting it systematically as a special whole. For if it is permissible to draw the boundaries of a science, not simply according to the constitution of the object and its specific mode of cognition, but also according to the end that one has in mind for this science itself in uses elsewhere; and if one finds that metaphysics has busied so many heads until now, and will continue to do so, not in order thereby to extend natural knowledge (which takes place much more easily and surely through observation, experiment, and the application of mathematics to outer appearances), but rather so as to attain cognition of that which lies wholly beyond all boundaries of experience, of God, Freedom, and Immortality; then one gains in the advancement of this goal if one frees it[b] from an offshoot that certainly springs from its root, but nonetheless only hinders its regular growth, and one plants this offshoot specially, yet without failing to appreciate the origin of [this offshoot] from it,[c] and without

[a] *Gründlichkeit*
[b] *Sie*. The reference is most likely to "metaphysics" – or possibly to "this science."
[c] *Jener*. See the previous note.

omitting the mature plant from the system of general metaphysics. This does not impair the completeness of general metaphysics, and in fact facilitates the uniform progress of this science toward its end, if, in all instances where one requires the general doctrine of body, one may call only upon the isolated system, without swelling this greater system with the latter. It is also indeed very remarkable (but cannot be expounded in detail here)[5] that general metaphysics, in all instances where it requires examples (intuitions) in order to provide meaning for its pure concepts of the understanding, must always take them from the general doctrine of body, and thus from the form and principles of outer intuition; and, if these are not exhibited completely, it gropes uncertainly and unsteadily among mere meaningless concepts. This is the source of the well-known disputes, or at least obscurity, in the questions concerning the possibility of a conflict of realities, of intensive magnitude, and so on, in which the understanding is taught only by examples from corporeal nature what the conditions are under which such concepts can alone have objective reality, that is, meaning and truth. And so a separated metaphysics of corporeal nature does excellent and indispensable service for *general* metaphysics, in that the former furnishes examples (instances *in concreto*) in which to realize the concepts and propositions of the latter (properly speaking, transcendental philosophy), that is, to give a mere form of thought sense and meaning.

In this treatise, although I have not followed the mathematical method with thoroughgoing rigor (which would have required more time than I had to spend thereon), I have nonetheless imitated that method[6] – not in order to obtain a better reception for the treatise, through an ostentatious display of exactitude,[a] but rather because I believe that such a system is certainly capable of this rigor, and also that such perfection can certainly be reached in time by a more adept hand, if, stimulated by this sketch, mathematical natural scientists should find it not unimportant to treat the metaphysical part, which they cannot leave out in any case, as a special fundamental part in their general physics, and to bring it into union with the mathematical doctrine of motion.

Newton, in the preface to his *Mathematical First Principles of Natural Science*, says (after he had remarked that geometry requires only two of the mechanical operations that it postulates, namely, to describe a straight line and a circle): *Geometry is proud of the fact that with so little derived from without it is able to produce so much.*[*,7] By contrast, one can

4: 478

4: 479

---

* "It is the glory of geometry that from those few principles, brought from without, it is able to produce so many things." *Newton Princ. Phil. Nat. Math. praefat.*

[a] *Gründlichkeit*

192

say of metaphysics: *it is dismayed that with so much offered to it by pure mathematics it can still accomplish so little*. Nevertheless, this small amount is still something that even mathematics unavoidably requires in its application to natural science; and thus, since it must here necessarily borrow from metaphysics, need also not be ashamed to let itself be seen in community with the latter.

First Chapter
Metaphysical foundations of phoronomy

EXPLICATION[8] 1

Matter is the *movable* in space. That space which is itself movable is called material, or also *relative space*; that in which all *motion* must finally be thought (and which is therefore itself absolutely[a] immovable) is called pure, or also *absolute space*.

Remark 1

Since in phoronomy nothing is to be at issue except motion, no other property is here ascribed to the *subject* of motion, namely, matter, aside from *movability*. It can itself so far, therefore, also be considered as a point, and one abstracts in phoronomy from all inner constitution, and therefore also from the quantity of the movable, and concerns oneself only with motion and what can be considered as quantity in motion (speed and direction).[9] – If the expression "body" should nevertheless sometimes be used here, this is only to anticipate to some extent the application of the principles of phoronomy to the more determinate concepts of matter that are still to follow, so that the exposition may be less abstract and more comprehensible.

Remark 2

If I am to explicate the concept of matter, not through a predicate that belongs to it itself as object, but only by relation to that cognitive faculty in which the representation can first of all be given to me, then every *object of the outer senses* is matter, and this would be the merely metaphysical explication thereof. Space, however, would be merely the form of all outer sensible intuition (we here leave completely aside the question whether just this form also belongs *in itself* to the outer object we call matter, or remains only in the constitution of our sense). *Matter*, as opposed to *form*, would be that in the outer intuition which is an object of sensation, and thus the properly empirical element of sensible and outer

---

[a] *schlechterdings*

intuition, because it can in no way be given *a priori*. In all experience something must be sensed, and that is the real of sensible intuition, and therefore the space, in which we are to arrange our experience of motion, must also be sensible – that is, it must be designated[a] through what can be sensed – and this, as the totality of all objects of experience, and itself an object of experience, is called *empirical space*. But this, as material, is itself movable. But a movable space, if its motion is to be capable of being perceived, presupposes in turn an enlarged material space, in which it is movable; this latter presupposes in precisely the same way yet another; and so on to infinity.

Thus all motion that is an object of experience is merely relative; and the space in which it is perceived is a relative space, which itself moves in turn in an enlarged space, perhaps in the opposite direction, so that matter moved with respect to the first can be called at rest in relation to the second space, and these variations in the concept of motions progress to infinity along with the change of relative space. To assume an absolute space, that is, one such that, because it is not material, it can also not be an object of experience, as *given in itself*, is to assume something, which can be perceived neither in itself nor in its consequences (motion in absolute space), for the sake of the possibility of experience – which, however, must always be arranged without it. Absolute space is thus *in itself* nothing, and no object at all, but rather signifies[b] only any other relative space, which I can always think beyond the given space, and which I can only defer to infinity beyond any given space, so as to include it and suppose it to be moved. Since I have the enlarged, although still always material, space only in thought, and since nothing is known to me of the matter that designates it, I abstract from the latter, and it is therefore represented as a pure, nonempirical, and absolute space, with which I compare any empirical space, and in which I can represent the latter as movable (so that the enlarged space always counts as immovable). To make this into an actual thing is to transform the *logical universality* of any space with which I can compare any empirical space, as included therein, into a *physical universality* of actual extent, and to misunderstand reason in its idea.[10]

Finally, I further remark that, since the *movability* of an object in space cannot be cognized *a priori*, and without instruction through experience, I could not, for precisely this reason, enumerate it under the pure concepts of the understanding in the *Critique of Pure Reason*;[11] and that this concept, as empirical, could find a place only in a natural science, as applied metaphysics, which concerns itself with a concept given through experience, although in accordance with *a priori* principles.

4: 482

[a] *bezeichnet*
[b] *bedeutet*

EXPLICATION 2

Motion of a thing is the *change of its outer relations* to a given space.

Remark 1

I have so far placed the concept of motion at the basis of the concept of matter. For, since I wanted to determine this concept independently of the concept of extension, and could therefore consider matter also in a point, I could allow the common explication of *motion as change of place* to be used. Now, since the concept of a matter is to be explicated generally, and therefore as befitting also moving bodies, this definition is no longer sufficient. For the place of any body is a point. If one wants to determine the distance of the moon from the earth, one wants to know the distance between their places, and for this purpose one does not measure from an arbitrary point of the surface or interior of the earth to any arbitrary point of the moon, but chooses the shortest line from the central point of the one to the central point of the other, so that for each of these bodies there is only one point constituting its place. Now a body can move without changing its place, as in the case of the earth rotating around its axis. But its relation to external space still changes thereby; since it turns, for example, its different sides toward the moon in 24 hours, from which all kinds of varying effects then follow on the earth. Only of a movable, that is, physical, *point* can one say that motion is always change of place. One could object to this explication by pointing out that inner

4: 483   motion, fermentation, for example, is not included; but the thing one calls moving must to that extent be considered as a unity. For example, that matter, as a *cask of beer*, is moved, means something different from the *beer in the cask* being in motion. The motion of a thing is not the same as motion in this thing, but here we are concerned only with the former case. But the application of this concept to the second case is then easy.

Remark 2

Motions can be either *rotating* (without change of place) or progressive, and the latter can be either motions that enlarge the space, or are limited to a given space. Of the *first* kind are the rectilinear motions, and also the curvilinear motions that do *not return* on themselves. Of the *second* [kind] are the motions that *return* on themselves. The latter in turn are either *circulating* or *oscillating*, that is, either circular or oscillatory motions. The former always traverse precisely the same space in the same direction, the latter always alternately back in the opposite direction, as in the case of oscillating pendulums. Belonging to both is still *tremor* (*motus tremulus*), which is not the progressive motion of a body, but nonetheless a reciprocating motion of a matter, which does not thereby change its place as a whole, as in the vibrations of a struck bell, or the tremors of the air set in motion by the sound. I only make mention of these various kinds of motion in phoronomy, because one commonly uses the word *speed*, in the case of all nonprogressive [motions], in another meaning than in the case of the progressive ones, as the following remark shows.

Remark 3

In every motion direction and speed are the two moments for considering motion, if one abstracts from all other properties of the movable. I here presuppose the usual definitions of both, but that of direction still requires various qualifications. A body moving in a circle changes its direction continuously, in such a way that it follows all possible directions in a surface along its way back to the point from which it set off, and yet one says that it moves always in the same direction, for example, a planet from west to east.[a]

But what is here the *side* toward which the motion is directed? This has a kinship with the following question: On what rests the inner difference of snails, which are otherwise similar and even equal, but among which one species is wound rightward, the other leftward; or the winding of the kidney bean and the hop, where the first runs around its pole like a corkscrew, or, as sailors would express it, *against the sun*, whereas the second runs *with the sun?* This is a concept which can certainly be constructed, but, as a concept, can in no way be made clear in itself by means of universal characteristics and in the discursive mode of cognition, and can yield no thinkable difference in the inner consequences in the things themselves (for example, in the case of those unusual people where all parts on dissection were found in agreement physiologically with other humans, except that all organs were transposed leftward or rightward contrary to the usual order), but is nevertheless a genuine mathematical, and indeed inner difference, which is connected with, although not identical to, the difference between two circular motions that are otherwise equal in all parts, but differ in direction. I have shown elsewhere[12] that, since this difference can certainly be given in intuition, but can in no way be captured in clear concepts, and thus cannot be rationally explicated (*dari, non intelligi*), it supplies a good confirming ground of proof for the proposition that space in general does not belong to the properties or relations of *things in themselves*, which would necessarily have to be reducible to objective concepts,[b] but rather belongs merely to the subjective form of our sensible intuition of things or relations, which

4: 484

---

[a] *von Abend gegen Morgen*
[b] *die sich notwendig auf objective Begriffe müßten bringen lassen*

must remain completely unknown to us as to what they may be in themselves. Yet this is a digression from our present business, in which we must necessarily treat space as a *property* of the things under consideration, namely, corporeal beings, because these things are themselves only appearances of the outer senses, and only require to be explicated as such here. As far as the concept of speed is concerned, this expression sometimes acquires in use a deviant meaning. We say that the earth rotates faster around its axis than the sun, because it does this in a shorter time, although the motion of the latter is much faster. The circulation of the blood in a small bird is much faster than that in a human being, although its flowing motion in the first case has without any doubt less speed, and so also in the case of vibrations in elastic materials. The brevity of the time of return, whether it be circulating or oscillating motion, constitutes the basis for this usage, which, so long as one avoids misunderstanding, is also not incorrect. For this mere increase in the rapidity of the return, without increase in spatial speed, has its own very important effects in nature, concerning which, in the circulation of fluids in animals, perhaps not enough notice has yet been taken. In phoronomy we use the word "speed" purely in a spatial meaning $C = S/T$.[13]

EXPLICATION 3

Rest is perduring presence[a] (*praesentia perdurabilis*) at the same place; what is *perduring* is that which exists throughout a time, that is, endures.

Remark

A body in motion is at every point of the line that it traverses for a moment. The question is now whether it rests there or moves. Without a doubt one will say the latter; for it is present at this point only insofar as it moves. Assume, however, that the motion of the body is such:

$$A \qquad B \qquad a$$
$$\text{o}\text{———————}\text{o} \cdot \cdot \text{o'}$$

that the body travels along the line AB with uniform speed forwards and backwards from B to A, and that, since the moment when it is at B is common to both motions, the motion from A to B is traversed in 1/2 sec., that from B to A also in 1/2 sec., and both together in one whole second, so that not even the smallest part of the time pertains to the presence of the body at B; then, without the least increase of these motions, the latter, having taken place in the direction BA, can be transformed into that in

[a] *beharrliche Gegenwart*

the direction Ba, lying in a straight line with AB, in which case the body, when it is at B, must be viewed as not at rest there, but as moved. It would therefore have to be also viewed as moved at the point B in the first case of motion returning back on itself – which, however, is impossible; since according to what was assumed, this point comprises only a moment – belonging to the motion AB and simultaneously to the motion BA, which is opposite to AB and joined to AB in one and the same moment – of complete lack of motion. Therefore, if this constituted the concept of rest, then rest of the body would also have to be manifested in the uniform motion Aa at every point, for example, at B, which contradicts the above assertion. Suppose, however, that one imagines the line AB as erected above the point A, so that a body rising from A to B falls back again from B to A after it has lost its motion at B through gravity; I then ask whether the body at B can be viewed as moved or as at rest. Without a doubt one will say at rest; for all previous motion has been taken from it once it has reached this point, and after this an equivalent motion back is about to follow, and thus is not yet there; but the lack of motion, one will add, is rest. Yet in the first case of an assumed uniform motion, the motion BA could also not take place except through the fact that the motion AB had previously ceased, and that from B to A was not yet there, so that a lack of all motion at B had to be assumed, and, according to the usual explication, also rest – but one may not assume it, because no body at a point of its uniform motion at a given speed can be thought of as at rest. So on what is based the appropriateness of the concept of rest in the second case, where the rising and falling are likewise separated from one another only by a moment? The reason for this lies in the fact that the latter motion is not thought of as uniform at a given speed, but rather first as uniformly decelerated and thereafter as uniformly accelerated,[14] so that the speed at point B is not completely diminished, but only to a degree that is smaller than any given speed. With this [speed], therefore, the body, if it were to be viewed always as still rising, so that instead of falling back the line of its fall BA were to be erected in the direction Ba, would uniformly traverse, with a mere moment of speed (the resistance of gravity here being set aside), a space smaller than any given space in any given time, however large, and thus would in no way change its place (for any possible experience) in all eternity. It is therefore put into the state of an *enduring* presence at the same place, that is, a state of rest, even though, because of the continual influence of gravity, that is, the change of this state, it is immediately destroyed. To be in a *perduring state* and to *perdure in this state* (if nothing else displaces it) are two different, although not incompatible, concepts. Thus rest cannot be explicated as lack of motion, which, as = o, can in no way be constructed, but must rather be explicated as perduring presence at the same place, since this concept can also be constructed, through the representation of a motion

4: 486

199

with infinitely small speed throughout a finite time, and can therefore be used for the ensuing application of mathematics to natural science.

EXPLICATION 4

To **construct** the concept of a *composite motion* means to present a motion *a priori* in intuition, insofar as it arises from two or more given motions united in one movable.

Remark

It is required for the construction of concepts that the conditions of their presentation not be borrowed from experience, and thus not presuppose certain forces whose existence can only be derived from experience; or, in general, that the condition of the construction must not itself be a concept that can by no means be given *a priori* in intuition, such as, for example, the concept of cause and effect, action and resistance, etc. Now here it is above all to be noted that phoronomy has first to determine the construction of motions in general as *quantities*, and, since it has matter merely as *something movable* as its object, in which no attention at all is therefore paid to its quantity, [it has to determine] these motions *a priori* solely as quantities, with respect to both their speed and direction, and, indeed, with respect to their composition. For so much must be constituted wholly *a priori*, and indeed intuitively, on behalf of applied mathematics. For the rules for the connection of motions by means of physical causes, that is, forces, can never be rigorously expounded, until the principles of their composition in general have been previously laid down, purely mathematically, as basis.

4: 487

PRINCIPLE

Every motion, as object of a possible experience, can be viewed arbitrarily as motion of the body in a space at rest, or else as rest of the body, and, instead, as motion of the space in the opposite direction with the same speed.

Remark

To make the motion of a body into an experience, it is required that not only the body, but also the space in which it moves, be objects of outer experience, and thus material. Hence an absolute motion, that is, [one] in relation to a nonmaterial space, cannot be experienced at all, and thus is nothing for us (even if one wanted to grant that absolute space were something in itself). But in all relative motion the space itself, since it is assumed to be material, can in turn be represented as either at rest or as moved. The first occurs when, beyond the space in which I view the body as moved, no further enlarged space is given to me that includes it (as when I see a ball moving on the table in the cabin of a ship); the second occurs when, beyond the given space, another space that includes it is given (in the example mentioned, the bank of the river), since I can then, in relation to the latter, view the nearest space (the cabin) as moved, and the body itself as possibly at rest. Now because it is completely impossible to determine for an empirically given space, no matter how enlarged it may be, whether it may or may not be moved in turn, in relation to an inclusive space of still greater extent, it must then be completely the same for all experience, and every consequence of experience, whether I wish to view a body as moved, or as at rest, but the space as moved in the opposite direction with the same speed. Further, since absolute space is nothing for all possible experience, the concepts are also the same whether I say that a body moves in relation to this given space, in such and such direction with such and such speed, or I wish to think the body as at rest, and to ascribe all this, but in the opposite direction, to the space. For any concept is entirely the same as a concept whose differences from it have no possible example at all, being only different with respect to the connection we wish to give it in the understanding.

4: 488

We are also incapable, in any experience at all, of assigning a fixed point in relation to which it would be determined what motion and rest are to be absolutely; for everything given to us in this way is material, and thus movable, and (since we are acquainted with no outermost limit of possible experience in space) is perhaps also actually moved, without our being able to perceive this motion. – Of this motion of a body in empirical space, I can give a part of the given speed to the body, and the other to the space, but in the opposite direction, and the whole possible experience, with respect to the consequences of these two combined motions, is entirely the same as that experience in which I think the body as alone moved with the whole speed, or the body as at rest and the space as moved with the same speed in the opposite direction. *But here I assume all motions to be rectilinear.* For in regard to curvilinear motions, it is not in all respects the same whether I am authorized to view the body (the earth in its daily rotation, for example) as moved and the surrounding space (the starry heavens) as at rest, or the latter as moved and the former as at rest, which will be specially treated in what follows. Thus in phoronomy, where I consider the motion of a body only in relation to the space (which has no influence at all on the rest or motion of the body), it is completely undetermined and arbitrary how much speed, if any, I wish to ascribe to the one or to the other. Later, in mechanics, where a moving body is to be considered in active relation to other bodies in the space of its motion, this will no longer be entirely the same, as will be shown in the proper place.[15]

EXPLICATION 5

The *composition of motion* is the representation of the motion of a point as the same as two or more motions of [this point] combined together.

Remark

In phoronomy, since I am acquainted with matter through no other property but its movability, and may thus consider it only as a point, motion can only be considered as the *describing of a space* – in such a way, however, that I attend not solely, as in geometry, to the space described, but also to the time in which, and thus to the speed with which, a point describes the space. Phoronomy is thus the pure theory of quantity (*mathesis*) of motions. The determinate concept of a quantity is the concept of the generation of the representation of an object through the composition of the homogeneous.[16] Now since nothing is homogeneous with motion except motion in turn, phoronomy is a doctrine of the composition of the motions of one and the same point in accordance with its speed and direction, that is, the representation of a single motion as one that contains two or more motions at the same time, or two motions of precisely the same point at the same time, insofar as they constitute one motion *combined* – that is, [they] are the same as the latter, and do not, for example, produce it, as causes produce their effect. In order to find the motion arising from the composition of several motions, as many as one wishes, one need only, as in all generation of quantity, first seek for that motion which, under the given conditions, is composed from *two* motions; this is then combined with a third; and so on. Therefore, the doctrine of the composition of all motions can be reduced to that of two. But two motions of one and the same point, which are found there at the same time, can be distinguished in two ways, and, as such, can be combined there in three ways. First, they occur either in one and the *same line*, or in *different lines* at the same time; the latter are motions comprising an angle. Those occurring in one and the *same line* are now, with respect to direction, either *opposite* to one another or have the *same direction*. Because all these motions are considered as occurring at the same time, the ratio of speed results immediately from the ratio of the lines, that is, from the described spaces of the motion in the same time. There are therefore three cases: (1) The *two motions* (they may have equal or unequal speeds) are to constitute a composite motion combined in one body in the same

direction. (2) The *two motions* of the same point (of equal or unequal speed), combined in opposite directions, are to constitute, through their composition, a third motion in the same line. (3) The two motions of a point are considered as composed with equal or unequal speeds, but in different lines comprising an angle.

PROPOSITION

The composition of two motions of one and the same point can only be thought in such a way that one of them is represented in absolute space, and, instead of the other, a motion of the relative space with the same speed occurring in the opposite direction is represented as the same as the latter.

Proof

First case. Two motions in *one and the same line and direction* belong to one and the same point.

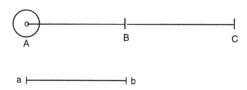

Two speeds AB and ab are to be represented as contained in one speed of motion. If one assumes these speeds to be equal for the moment, so that AB = ab, then I say that they cannot be represented at the same time in one and the same space (whether absolute or relative) in one and the same point. For, since the lines AB and ab designating the speeds are, properly speaking, the spaces they traverse in equal times, then the composition of these spaces AB and ab = BC, and hence the line AC as the sum of the spaces, would have to express the sum of the two speeds. But neither the part AB nor the part BC represents the speed = ab, for they are not traversed in the same time as ab. Therefore, the doubled line AC, traversed in the same time as the line ab, does not represent the twofold speed of the latter, which, however, was required. Therefore, the composition of two speeds in one direction cannot be represented intuitively *in the same space.*

By contrast, if the body A with speed AB is represented as moved in absolute space, and, moreover, I give to the relative space a speed ab = AB in the opposite direction ba = CB, then this is precisely the same as if I had imparted the latter speed to the body in the direction AB (Principle). The body then moves through the sum of the lines AB and BC = 2ab in the same time in which it would have traversed the line ab = AB alone, and its speed is thus represented as the sum of the two equal speeds AB and ab, which is what was required. 4: 491

Second case. Two motions are to be combined in *precisely opposite directions* in one and the same point.

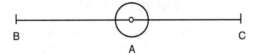

Let AB be one of these motions and AC the other in the opposite direction, whose speed we will assume here as equal to the first. Then even the thought of representing two such motions at the same time in exactly the same point within one and the same space would be impossible, and thus so would the case of such a composition of motions itself, which is contrary to the presupposition.

By contrast, think instead the motion AB in absolute space, but, instead of the motion AC in the same absolute space, the opposite motion CA of the relative space with exactly the same speed, which (according to the Principle) counts as entirely the same as the motion AC, and can therefore be posited wholly in place of the latter. Then two precisely opposite and equal motions of the same point at the same time can perfectly well be represented. Because the relative space now moves with the same speed CA = AB in the same direction as the point A, this point, or the body found there, does not change its place in relation to the relative space. That is, a body moved in two exactly opposite directions with the same speed is at rest, or, expressed in general: its motion is equal to the difference of the speeds in the direction of the greater (which can easily be concluded from what has been proved).

4: 492   *Third case.* Two motions of one and the same point are to be represented as combined in *directions comprising an angle.*

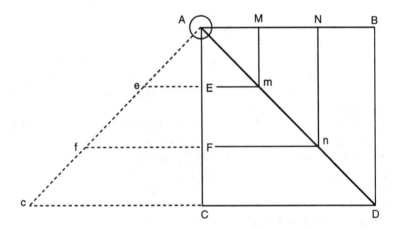

The two given motions are AB and AC, whose speeds and directions are expressed by these lines, but the angle comprised by these lines [is expressed] by BAC (it may, as here, be a right angle, but also any arbitrary oblique angle). Now if these two motions were to occur at the same time in the directions AB and AC, and in one and the same space, then they would still not be able to occur at the same time in these two *lines* AB and AC, but only in lines running parallel to these. It would therefore have to be assumed that one of these motions effected a change in the other (namely, directing it from the given path), if both directions were to remain the same. But this is contrary to the presupposition of the Proposition, which indicates by the word "composition" that the two given motions are to be *contained* in a third, and therefore are to be the same as the latter, and are not to produce a third, in that one *changes* the other.

By contrast, assume the motion AC as proceeding in absolute space, but, instead of the motion AB, the motion of the relative space in the opposite direction. Let the line AC be divided into three equal parts AE, EF, FC. While the body A traverses the line AE in absolute space, the relative space, together with the point E, traverses the space Ee = MA. While the body traverses the two parts together = AF, the relative space, together with the point F, describes the line Ff = NA. Finally, while the body traverses the whole line AC, the relative space, together with the point C, describes the line Cc = BA. But all of this is precisely the same as if the body A had traversed the lines Em, Fn, and CD = AM, AN, AB in these three parts of the time, and in the whole time, in which it traverses AC, the line CD = AB. It is thus in the last moment at the point D, and in this whole time successively at all points of the diagonal AD, which therefore expresses both the direction and speed of the composite motion. 4: 493

Remark 1

Geometrical *construction* requires that one quantity be the *same* as another or that two quantities in composition be the *same* as a third, not that they produce the third as causes, which would be mechanical construction. Complete similarity and equality, insofar as it can be cognized only in intuition, is *congruence*. All geometrical construction of complete identity rests on congruence. Now this congruence of two combined motions with a third (as with the *motus compositus* itself) can never take place if these two combined motions are represented in one and the same space, for example, in relative space. Therefore, all attempts to prove the above Proposition in its three cases were always only mechanical analyses – namely, where one allows moving causes to produce a third motion by combining one given motion with another[17] – but not proofs that the two motions are the same as the third, and can be represented as such *a priori* in pure intuition.

Remark 2

If, for example, a speed AC is called doubled, nothing else can be understood by this except that it consists of two simple and equal speeds AB and BC (see Figure 1). If, however, one explicates a doubled speed by saying that it is a motion through which a doubled space is traversed in the same time, then something is assumed here that is not obvious in itself – namely, that two equal speeds can be combined in precisely the same way as two equal spaces – and it is not clear in itself that a given speed consists of smaller speeds, and a rapidity of slownesses, in precisely the same way that a space consists of smaller spaces. For the parts of the speed are not external to one another like the parts of the space, and if the former is to be considered as a quantity, then the concept of its quantity, since this is *intensive*, must be constructed in a different way from that of the *extensive* quantity of space.[18] But this construction is possible in no other way than through the *mediate* composition of two equal motions, such that one is the motion of the body, and the other the motion of the relative space in the opposite direction, which, however, for precisely this reason, is entirely the same as a motion of the body in the original direction that is equal to it. For two equal speeds cannot be combined in the same body in the *same direction*, except through external moving causes, for example, a ship, which carries the body with one of these speeds, while another moving force combined immovably with the ship impresses on the body the second speed that is equal to the first. But here it must always be presupposed that the body conserves itself in *free* motion with the first speed, while the second is added – which, however, is a law of nature of moving forces that can in no way be at issue here, where the question is solely how the concept of speed as a quantity is to be *constructed*. So much, then, for the addition of speeds to one another. If, however, the subtraction of one from the other is at issue, then this can indeed easily be *thought*, as soon as the possibility of speed as a quantity through addition is granted, but this concept cannot so easily be *constructed*. For, to this end two opposite motions must be combined in one body; and how is this supposed to happen? It is impossible to think two equal motions in the same body in opposite directions immediately, that is, in relation to precisely the same space at rest. But the representation of the impossibility of these two motions in one body is not the concept of its *rest*, but rather of the *impossibility of constructing* this composition of opposite motions, which is nonetheless assumed as possible in the Proposition. This construction is possible in no other way, however, except through the combination of the motion of the body with the *motion of the space*, as was shown. Finally, with respect to the composition of two motions with directions comprising an angle, this cannot be thought in the body in reference to one and the same space either, unless we assume that one of them is effected through an *external* continually influencing *force* (for example, a vehicle carrying the body forward), while the other is conserved unchanged – or, in general, one must take as basis moving forces, and the generation of a third motion from two united *forces*, which is indeed the *mechanical* execution of what is contained in a concept, but not its *mathematical construction*, which should only make intuitive what the object (as quantum) *is to be*, not how it may be *produced* by nature or art by means of certain instruments and forces. – The composition of motions, in order to determine their ratio to others as quantity, must take place in accordance with the rules of congruence, which is only possible in all three cases by means of the motion of the space congruent to one of the two given motions, so that the two [together] are congruent to the composite [motion].

4: 495

Remark 3

Phoronomy, not as pure doctrine of motion, but merely as pure doctrine of the quantity of motion, in which matter is thought with respect to no other property than its mere movability, therefore contains no more than this single Proposition, carried out through the above three cases, of the composition of motion – and, indeed, of the possibility of *rectilinear motions* only, not curvilinear [ones]. For since in these latter the motion is continually changed (in direction), a cause of this change must be brought forward, which cannot now be the mere space. But that one normally understood, by the term *composite motion*, only the single case where the directions comprise an angle, did no harm to physics, but rather to the principle of classification of a pure philosophical science in general. For, with respect to the former, all three cases treated in the above Proposition can be sufficiently presented in the *third alone*. For if the angle comprised by the two given motions is thought as infinitely small, then it contains the first case; but if it is represented as different from a single straight line only by an infinitely small amount, then it contains the second case; so that all three cases named by us can certainly be given in the well-known proposition of composite motion in a general formula. But one could not, in this way, learn to comprehend the doctrine of the quantity of motion *a priori* with respect to its parts, which also has its uses for several purposes.

If anyone is interested in connecting the above three parts of the general phoronomic Proposition with the schema of classification of all pure concepts of the understanding – namely, here that of the concept of *quantity* – then he will note that, since the concept of quantity always contains that of the composition of the homogeneous, the doctrine of the composition of motion is, at the same time, the pure doctrine of the quantity of motion, and, indeed, in accordance with all three moments suggested by [the structure of] space: *unity* of line and direction, *plurality* of directions in one and the same line, and the *totality* of directions, as well as lines, in accordance with which the motion may occur, which contains the determination of all possible motion as a quantum, even though the quantity of motion (in a movable point) consists merely in the speed. This remark has its uses only in transcendental philosophy.

Second Chapter
Metaphysical foundations of dynamics

EXPLICATION 1

Matter is the *movable* insofar as it *fills* a *space*. To *fill* a space is to resist every movable that strives through its motion to penetrate into a certain space. A space that is not filled is an *empty space*.

Remark

This is now the dynamical explication of the concept of matter. It presupposes the phoronomical [explication], but adds a property relating as cause to an effect, namely, the power to resist a motion within a certain space; there could be no mention of this in the preceding science, not even when dealing with motions of one and the same point in opposite directions. This filling of space keeps a certain space free from the penetration of any other movable, when its motion is directed toward any place in this space. Now the basis for the resistance of matter exerted in all directions,[a] and what this resistance is, must still be investigated. But one already sees this much from the above explication: Matter is not here considered as it resists, *when it is driven out of its place*, and thus moved itself (this case will be considered later, as mechanical resistance), but rather when merely the *space* of its own extension is to be *diminished*. One uses the expression *to occupy a space*, that is, to be immediately present in all points of this space, in order to designate the *extension* of a thing in space. However, it is not determined in this concept what effect arises from this presence, or even whether there is any effect at all – whether to resist others that are striving to penetrate within; or whether it means merely a space without matter, in so far as it is a complex of several spaces, as one can say of any geometrical figure that it occupies a space by being extended; or even whether there is something in the space that compels another movable to penetrate deeper into it (by attracting others) – because, I say, all this is undetermined by the concept of occupying a space, *filling a space* is a more specific determination of the concept of *occupying* a space.

4: 497

---

[a] *nach allen Seiten gerichtete*

PROPOSITION 1

Matter fills a space, not through its mere *existence*, but through a *particular moving force*.

Proof

Penetration into a space (in the initial moment this is called a striving to penetrate) is a motion. Resistance to motion is the cause of its diminution, or even of the change of this motion into rest. Now nothing can be combined with a motion, which diminishes it or destroys it, except another motion of precisely the same movable in the opposite direction (Phoron. Prop.). Therefore, the resistance that a matter offers in the space that it fills to every penetration by other matters is a cause of the motion of the latter in the opposite direction. But the cause of a motion is called a moving force. Thus matter fills its space through a moving force, and not through its mere existence.

Remark

Lambert and others called the property of matter by which it fills a space *solidity* (a rather ambiguous expression), and claim that one must assume this in every thing *that exists* (substance), at least in the outer sensible world. According to their ideas[a] the presence of something *real* in space[19] must already, through its concept, and thus in accordance with the principle of noncontradiction, imply this resistance, and bring it about that nothing else can be simultaneously in the space where such a thing is present. But the principle of noncontradiction does not repel a matter advancing to penetrate into a space where another is found. Only when I ascribe to that which occupies a space a force to repel every external movable that approaches, do I understand how it contains a contradiction for yet another thing of the same kind to penetrate into the space occupied by a thing. Here the mathematician has assumed something, as a first datum for constructing the concept of a matter, which is itself incapable of further construction. Now he can indeed begin his construction of a concept from any chosen datum, without engaging in the explication of this datum in turn. But he is not therefore permitted to declare this to be something entirely incapable of any mathematical construction,[b] so as thereby to obstruct us from going back to first principles in natural science.

4: 498

---

[a] *Begriffen*
[b] *jenes für etwas aller mathematischen Construction ganz Unfähiges zu erklären*

EXPLICATION 2

Attractive force is that moving force by which a matter can be the cause of the approach of others to it (or, what is the same, by which it resists the removal of others from it).

Repulsive force is that by which a matter can be the cause of others removing themselves from it (or, what is the same, by which it resists the approach of others to it). The latter force will also sometimes be called *driving* force, the former *drawing* force.

Note

Only these two moving forces of matter can be thought. For all motion that one matter can impress on another, since in this regard each of them is considered only as a point, must always be viewed as imparted in the straight line between the two points. But in this straight line there are only two possible motions: the one through which the two points *remove* themselves from one another, the second through which they *approach* one another. But the force causing the first motion is called *repulsive force*,   4: 499 whereas the second is called *attractive force*. Therefore, only these two kinds of forces can be thought, as forces to which all moving forces in material nature must be reduced.

PROPOSITION 2

Matter fills its space through the repulsive forces of all of its parts, that is, through an expansive force of its own, having a determinate degree, such that smaller or larger degrees can be thought to infinity.

Proof

Matter fills a space only through moving force (Prop. 1), a force resisting the penetration (that is, the approach) of others. Now this is a repulsive force (Explication 2). Therefore, matter fills its space only through repulsive forces, and, indeed, through repulsive forces of all of its parts. For otherwise a part of its space (contrary to the presupposition) would not be filled, but only enclosed. But *the force of something extended in virtue of the repulsion of all of its parts* is an *expansive force*. So matter fills its space only through an expansive force of its own, *which was the first* [thing to be shown]. Now, beyond any given force a greater force must be thinkable, for that force beyond which no greater is possible would be one whereby an infinite space would be traversed in a finite time (which is impossible). Further, below any given force a smaller force must be thinkable (for the smallest force would be one whereby its infinite addition to itself throughout a given time could generate no finite speed, which, however, means the absence of all moving force). Thus, below any given degree of a moving force a smaller must always be capable of being given, *which is the second* [thing to be shown]. Consequently, the expansive force by which every matter fills its space has a degree, which is never the greatest or the smallest, but is such that beyond it both greater and smaller degrees can be found to infinity.

4: 500

Note 1

The expansive force of a matter is also called *elasticity*. Now, since it is the basis on which the filling of space rests, as an essential property of all matter, this elasticity must therefore be called *original*, because it can be derived from no other property of matter. All matter is therefore originally elastic.

Note 2

Beyond every expanding force a greater moving force can be found. But the latter can also act contrary to the former, whereby it would then decrease the space that the former strives to enlarge, in which case the latter would be called *compressing* force. Therefore, for every matter a compressing force must also be discoverable, which can drive it from the space it fills into a decreased space.

EXPLICATION 3

A matter *penetrates* another in its motion, when it completely destroys the space of the latter's extension through compression.

Remark

When, in the barrel of an air pump filled with air, the piston is driven closer and closer to the bottom, the air-matter is compressed. If this compression could now be driven so far that the piston completely touched the bottom (without the least amount of air escaping), then the air-matter would be penetrated. For the matters enclosing the air would leave no remaining space for it, and it would thus be found between the piston and the bottom without occupying a space. This penetrability of matter through external compressing forces, if someone wished to assume or even to think such a thing, could be called *mechanical* penetration. I have reason thus to distinguish this penetrability of matter from another kind, whose concept is perhaps just as impossible as the first, but of which I may yet have occasion to say something later on.[20]

PROPOSITION 3

4: 501

Matter can be *compressed* to infinity, but can *never* be *penetrated* by a matter, no matter how great the compressing force of the latter may be.

Proof

An original force, with which a matter strives to extend itself on all sides beyond a given space that it occupies, must be greater when enclosed in a smaller space, and infinite when compressed into an infinitely small space. Now, for a given expanding force of matter, a greater compressing force can be found, which forces the former into a smaller space, and so on to infinity, which was the first [thing to be shown]. But a compression of matter into an infinitely small space, and thus an infinite compressing force, would be required for its penetration, and this is impossible. Therefore, a matter cannot be penetrated by any other through compression, which is the second [thing to be shown].

Remark

In this proof I have assumed from the very beginning that an expanding force must counteract all the more strongly, the more it is driven into a smaller space. But this would not in fact hold for every kind of merely derivative elastic forces. However, it can be postulated in matter, insofar as essential elasticity belongs to it, as matter in general filling a space. For expansive force, exerted from every point, and in every direction, actually constitutes this concept. But the same quantum of extending forces, when brought into a smaller space, must repel all the more strongly at every point, the smaller the space in which this quantum diffuses its activity.

EXPLICATION 4

I call the *impenetrability* of matter that rests on resistance increasing in proportion to the degree of compression *relative* impenetrability. But that resting on the *presupposition* that matter as such is capable of no compression at all is called *absolute* impenetrability. The *filling of space* with absolute impenetrability can be called *mathematical* filling of space, whereas that with mere relative impenetrability can be called *dynamical* filling of space.[21]

4: 502

Remark 1

According to the purely mathematical concept of impenetrability (which presupposes no moving force as originally belonging to matter), matter is not capable of compression except insofar as it contains empty spaces within itself. Hence matter as matter resists all penetration utterly[a] and with absolute necessity. However, according to our discussion of this property, impenetrability rests on a physical basis. For expanding force first makes matter itself possible, as an extended thing filling its space. But this force has a degree that can be overpowered, and thus the space of its extension can be diminished, that is, penetrated up to a certain amount by a given compressing force, but only in such a way that complete penetration is impossible, because this would require an infinite compressing force; *therefore the filling of space must be viewed only as relative impenetrability.*

Remark 2

Absolute impenetrability is in fact nothing more nor less than an occult quality.[b] For one asks what the cause is for the inability of matters to penetrate one another in their motion, and one receives the answer: because they are impenetrable. The appeal to repulsive force is not subject to this reproach. For, although this force cannot be further explicated in regard to its possibility, and therefore must count as a fundamental force, it does yield a concept of an acting cause, together with its laws, whereby the action, namely, the resistance in the filled space, can be estimated in regard to its degrees.

EXPLICATION 5

4: 503

Material substance is that in space which is movable in itself, that is, in isolation from everything else existing external to it in space. The motion of a part of matter, whereby it ceases to be a part, is *separation*. The separation of the parts of a matter is *physical division*.

Remark

The concept of a substance means the ultimate subject of existence, that is, that which does not itself belong in turn to the existence of another merely as a predicate. Now matter is the subject of everything that may be counted in space as belonging to the existence of things. For, aside from matter, no other subject would be thinkable except space itself, which, however, is a concept that contains nothing existent at all, but merely the necessary conditions for the external relations of possible objects of the outer senses. Thus matter, as the movable in space, is the substance

[a] *schlechterdings*
[b] *qualitas occulta*

therein. But all parts of matter must likewise be called substances, and thus themselves matter in turn, insofar as one can say of them that they are themselves subjects, and not merely predicates of other matters. They are themselves subjects, however, if they are movable in themselves, and thus exist in space outside their connection with other neighboring parts. Therefore, the movability belonging to matter, or any part of it, is at the same time a proof that this movable thing, and any movable part thereof, is substance.

PROPOSITION 4

Matter is *divisible to infinity*, and, in fact, into parts such that each is matter in turn.

Proof

Matter is impenetrable, through its original expansive force (Prop. 3).[22] But this is only a consequence of the repulsive forces of each point in a space filled with matter. Now the space filled by matter is mathematically divisible to infinity, that is, its parts can be distinguished to infinity, although they cannot be moved, and thus cannot be divided (according to geometrical proofs). But in a space filled with matter, every part of it contains repulsive force, so as to counteract all the rest in all directions, and thus to repel them and to be repelled by them, that is, to be moved a distance from them. Hence, every part of a space filled with matter is in itself movable, and thus separable from the rest as material substance through physical division. Therefore, the possible physical division of the substance that fills space extends as far as the mathematical divisibility of the space filled by matter. But this mathematical divisibility extends to infinity, and thus so does the physical [divisibility] as well. That is, all matter is divisible to infinity, and, in fact, into parts such that each is itself material substance in turn.

4: 504

Remark 1

The proof of the infinite divisibility of space has not yet come close to proving the infinite divisibility of matter, if it has not previously been shown that there is material substance in every part of space, that is, that parts movable in themselves are to be found there. For suppose that a *monadist* wished to assume that matter consisted of physical points, each of which (for precisely this reason) had no movable parts, but nonetheless filled a space through mere repulsive force. Then he could grant that space would be divided, but not the substance that acts in space – that the sphere of activity of this substance [would be divided] by the division of space, but not the acting movable subject itself.[23] Thus he would assemble matter out of physically indivisible parts, and yet allow them to occupy a space in a *dynamical fashion*.

But this way out is completely taken away from the monadist by the above proof. For it is thereby clear that there can be no point in a filled space that does not exert repulsion in all directions, and is itself repelled, and thus would be movable in itself, as a reacting subject external to every other repelling point. Hence the hypothesis of a point that would fill a space through mere driving force, and not by means of other equally repelling forces, is completely impossible. In order to make this intuitive, and hence also the proof of the preceding Proposition, let us assume that A is the place of a monad in space, and ab is the diameter of the sphere of its repulsive force, so that aA is the radius of this sphere:

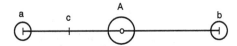

Then between a, where the penetration of an external monad into the space occupied by this sphere is resisted, and the center A, it is possible to specify a point c (according to the infinite divisibility of space). But if A resists that which strives to penetrate into a, then c must also resist the two points A and a. For, if this were not so, they would approach one another without hindrance, and thus A and a would meet at the point c, that is, the space would be penetrated. Therefore, there must be something at c that resists the penetration of A and a, and thus repels the monad A, the same as it is also repelled by A. But since *repelling* is a [kind of] moving, c is something movable in space, and thus matter, and the space between A and a could not be filled through the sphere of activity of a single monad, nor could the space between c and A, and so on to infinity.

When mathematicians represent the repulsive forces of the parts of elastic matters as increasing or decreasing, in accordance with a certain proportion of their distances from one another, at greater or lesser compression of these parts (for example, that the smallest parts of the air repel one another in inverse ratio to their distances from one another, because the elasticity of these parts stands in inverse ratio to the spaces in which they are compressed), then one completely misses their meaning, and misinterprets their language, if one ascribes that which necessarily belongs to the procedure of constructing a concept to the concept in the object itself. For by the latter [procedure], any contact can be represented as an infinitely small distance – which must also necessarily be so in those cases where a greater or smaller space is to be represented

4: 505

as completely filled by one and the same quantity of matter, that is, one and the same quantum of repulsive forces. So even in the case of something divisible to infinity, no actual distance of the parts may therefore be assumed – they always constitute a continuum, no matter how enlarged is the space, even though the possibility of such an enlargement can only be made intuitive under the idea of an infinitely small distance.

Remark 2

To be sure, mathematics in its internal use can be entirely indifferent with regard to the chicanery of a misguided metaphysics, and can persist in the secure possession of its evident claims as to the *infinite divisibility of space*, whatever objections may be put in its way by a sophistry splitting hairs on mere concepts. However, in the application of its propositions governing space to the substance that fills it, mathematics must nonetheless accede to an examination in accordance with mere concepts, and thus to metaphysics. The above Proposition is already a proof of this. For it does not necessarily follow that matter is physically divisible to infinity, even if it is so from a mathematical point of view, even if every part of space is a space in turn, and thus always contains [more] parts external to one another. For so far it cannot be proved that in each of the possible parts of this *filled* space there is also *substance*, which therefore also exists in separation from all else as movable in itself. Thus something without which this proof could not find secure application to natural science was until now still missing in the mathematical proof, and this deficiency is remedied in the above Proposition. Now, however, when it comes to the remaining metaphysical attacks on what will henceforth   4: 506
be the *physical Proposition* of the infinite divisibility of matter, the mathematician must leave them entirely to the philosopher, who in any case ventures, by means of these objections, into a labyrinth, from which it becomes difficult for him to extricate himself, even in those questions immediately pertaining to him. He therefore has quite enough to do for himself, without the mathematician being permitted to involve himself in this business. For if matter is divisible to infinity then (concludes the dogmatic metaphysician) *it consists of an infinite aggregate of parts*; for a whole must already contain in advance all of the parts in their entirety, into which it can be divided. And this last proposition is undoubtedly certain for every whole *as thing in itself*. But one cannot admit that matter, or even space, *consists of infinitely many parts* (because it is a contradiction to think an infinite aggregate, whose concept already implies that it can never be represented as completed, as entirely completed). One would therefore have to conclude either, in spite of the geometer, that *space is not divisible to infinity*, or, to the annoyance of the metaphysician, that

space is not a property of a thing in itself, and thus that matter is not a thing in itself, but merely an appearance of our outer senses in general, just as space is the essential form thereof.

But here the philosopher is caught between the horns of a dangerous dilemma. To deny the first proposition, that space is divisible to infinity, is an empty undertaking; for nothing can be argued away from mathematics by sophistical hairsplitting.[a] But viewing matter as a thing in itself, and thus space as a property of the thing in itself, amounts to the denial of this proposition. The philosopher therefore finds himself forced to deviate from this last proposition,[24] however common and congenial to the common understanding it may be. But he does this, of course, only provided that, after making matter and space into mere appearances (and thus the latter into the form of our outer sensible intuition, so that both [are made] not into things in themselves, but only into subjective modes of representation of objects unknown to us in themselves), he is thereby helped out of that difficulty due to the *infinite divisibility* of matter, whereby it still does *not* consist of *infinitely many parts*. Now this latter can perfectly well be thought through reason, even though it cannot be made intuitive and constructed. For what is only actual by being given in the representation also has no *more* given of it than what is met with in the representation – no more, that is, than the progress of representations reaches. Therefore, one can only say of appearances, whose division proceeds to infinity, that there are just so many parts in the appearance as we may provide, that is, so far as we may divide. For the parts, as belonging to the existence of an appearance, exist only in thought, namely, in the division itself. Now, the division does of course proceed to infinity, but it is still never given as infinite. Thus it does not follow, from the fact that its division proceeds to infinity, that the divisible contains an infinite aggregate of parts *in itself*, and outside of our representation. For it is not the thing, but only this representation of it, whose division, although it can indeed be continued to infinity, and there is also a ground for this in the object (which is unknown in itself), can nonetheless never be completed, and thus be completely given; and this also proves no actual infinite aggregate in the object (which would be an explicit contradiction).[25] A great man,[26] who has contributed perhaps more than anyone else to preserving the reputation of mathematics in Germany, has frequently rejected the presumptuous metaphysical claims to overturn the theorems of geometry concerning the infinite divisibility of space by the well-founded reminder *that space belongs only to the appearance of outer things*. But he has not been understood. This proposition was taken to be asserting that space appears to us, though it is otherwise a thing, or relation of things, in itself, but that the mathematician considers

4: 507

[a] *dem Mathematik läßt sich nichts wegvernünfteln*

it only as it appears. Instead, it should have been understood as saying that space is in no way a property that attaches in itself to any thing at all outside our senses. It is, rather, only the subjective form of our sensibility, under which objects of the outer senses, with whose constitution in itself we are not acquainted, appear to us, and we then call this appearance matter. Through this misunderstanding one went on thinking of space as a property also attaching to things outside our faculty of representation, but such that the mathematician thinks it only in accordance with common concepts,[a] that is, confusedly (for it is thus that one commonly explicates appearance). And one thus attributed the mathematical theorem of the infinite divisibility of matter, a proposition presupposing the highest [degree of] clarity in the concept of space, to a confused representation of space taken as basis by the geometer – whereby the metaphysician was then free to compose space out of points, and matter out of simple parts, and thus (in his opinion) to bring clarity into this concept. The ground for this aberration lies in a poorly understood *monadology*, [a theory] which has nothing at all to do with the explanation of natural appearances, but is rather an intrinsically correct *platonic* concept of the world devised by *Leibniz*, insofar as it is considered, not at all as object of the senses, but as thing in itself, and is merely an object of the understanding, which, however, does indeed underlie the appearances of the senses. Now the *composite of things in themselves* must certainly consist of the simple, for the parts must here be given prior to all composition. But the *composite in the appearance* does not consist of the simple, because in the appearance, which can never be given otherwise than as composed (extended), the parts can only be given through division, and thus not prior to the composite, but only in it. Therefore, Leibniz's idea,[b] so far as I comprehend it, was not to explicate space through the order of simple beings next to one another, but was rather to set this order alongside space as corresponding to it, but as belonging to a merely intelligible world (unknown to us). Thus he asserts nothing but what has been shown elsewhere: namely, that space, together with the matter of which it is the form, does not contain the world of things in themselves, but only their appearance, and is itself only the form of our outer sensible intuition.

4: 508

PROPOSITION 5

The possibility of matter requires an *attractive force* as the second essential fundamental force of matter.

---

[a] *gemeinen Begriffen*
[b] *Meinung*

Proof

Impenetrability, as the fundamental property of matter, whereby it first manifests itself to our outer senses, as something real in space, is nothing but the expansive power of matter (Proposition 2). Now an essential moving force, whereby the parts of matter flee from one another, cannot, *in the first place*, be limited by itself, for matter is thereby striving instead continuously to enlarge the space that it fills; *in the second place*, [such a force] can also not be determined by space alone to a certain limit of extension, for the latter, although it can certainly contain the ground for the expansive force becoming weaker in inverse proportion to the increase of volume of an expanding matter, can never contain the ground for this force ceasing anywhere, because smaller degrees are possible to infinity for any moving force. Hence matter, by its repulsive force (containing the ground of impenetrability), would, [through itself] alone and if no other moving force counteracted it, be confined within no limit of extension; that is, it would disperse itself to infinity, and no specified quantity of matter would be found in any specified space. Therefore, with merely repulsive forces of matter, all spaces would be empty, and thus, properly speaking, no matter would exist at all. So all matter requires for its existence forces that are opposed to the expansive forces, that is, compressing forces. But these, in turn, cannot originally be sought in the contrary striving*a* of another matter, for this latter itself requires a compressive force in order to be matter. Hence there must somewhere be assumed an original force of matter acting in the opposite direction to the repulsive force, and thus to produce approach, that is, an attractive force. Yet since this attractive force belongs to the possibility of a matter as matter in general, and thus precedes all differences of matter, it may not be ascribed merely to a particular species of matter, but must rather be ascribed to all matter originally and as such. Therefore, an original attraction is attributed to all matter, as a fundamental force belonging to its essence.

4: 509

Remark

In this transition from one property of matter to another, specifically different from it, and belonging equally to the concept of matter, *even though not contained in it*, the procedure of our understanding must be considered more closely. If attractive force is originally required even for the possibility of matter, why do we not use it, just as much as impenetrability, as the first distinguishing mark of a matter? Why is the latter immediately given with the concept of a matter, whereas the former is

---

a *Entgegenstrebung*

not thought in the concept, but only adjoined to it through inferences? That our senses do not allow us to perceive this attraction so immediately as the repulsion and resistance of impenetrability cannot yet provide a sufficient answer to the difficulty. For even if we had such a capacity, it is still easy to see that our understanding would nonetheless choose the filling of space in order to designate substance in space, that is, matter, and how precisely this *filling*, or, as one otherwise calls it, *solidity*, is then posited to be characteristic of matter, as a thing different from space. Attraction, even if we sensed it equally well, would still never disclose to us a matter of determinate *volume* and *figure*, but only the striving of our organ to approach a point outside us (the center of the attracting body). For the attractive force of all parts of the earth can affect us no more, and in no other way, than as if it were wholly united in the earth's center, and this alone influenced our sense, and the same holds for the attraction of a mountain, or any stone, etc.[27] But we thereby obtain no determinate concept of any object in space, since neither figure, nor quantity, nor even the place where it would be found can strike our senses. (The mere direction of attraction would be perceivable, as in the case of weight: the attracting point would be unknown, and I do not even see how it could be ascertained through inferences, without perception of matter insofar as it fills space). It is therefore clear that the first application of our concepts of *quantity* to matter, through which it first becomes possible for us to transform our outer perceptions into the empirical concept of a matter, as object in general, is grounded only on that property whereby it fills a space – which, by means of the sense of feeling,[a] provides us with the quantity and figure of something extended, and thus with the concept of a determinate object in space, which forms the basis of everything else one can say about this thing. Precisely this circumstance is undoubtedly the reason, despite the clearest proofs from elsewhere that attraction must belong to the fundamental forces of matter, just as much as repulsion, that one nevertheless struggles so much against the former, and will admit no other moving forces at all except those through impact and pressure (both mediated by impenetrability). For that whereby space is filled is substance, one says, and this is also perfectly correct. But this substance discloses its existence to us in no other way than through that sense whereby we perceive its impenetrability, namely, feeling, and thus only in relation to contact, whose onset (in the approach of one matter to another) is called impact, and whose persistence is called pressure. It therefore seems as if every immediate action of one matter on the other could never be anything but pressure or impact, the only two influences we can sense immediately. Attraction, on the other hand, can give us in itself either no sensation at all, or at least no determinate object of

4: 510

---

[a] *Gefühl*

sensation, and is therefore difficult for us to understand as a fundamental force.

PROPOSITION 6

No matter is possible through mere attractive force without repulsion.

Proof

4: 511

Attractive force is that moving force of matter whereby it impels another to approach it; consequently, if it is found between all parts of matter, matter thereby strives to diminish the distance of its parts from one another, and thus the space that they occupy together. But nothing can hinder the action of a moving force except another moving force opposed to it, and that which opposes attraction is repulsive force. Hence, without repulsive forces, through mere convergence,[a] all parts of matter would approach one another unhindered, and would diminish the space that they occupy. But since, in the case assumed, there is no distance of the parts at which a greater approach due to attraction would be made impossible by a repulsive force, they would move toward one another so far, until no distance at all would be found between them; that is, they would coalesce into a mathematical point, and space would be empty, and thus without any matter. Therefore, matter is impossible through mere attractive forces without repulsive forces.

Note

A property on which the inner possibility of a thing rests, as a condition, is an essential element thereof. Hence repulsive force belongs to the essence of matter just as much as attractive force, and neither can be separated from the other in the concept of matter.

Remark

Since only two moving forces can be thought everywhere in space,[b] repulsion and attraction, it was previously necessary, in order to prove *a priori* the uniting of the two in the concept of a matter in general, that each be considered on its own, so as to see what either in isolation could achieve for the presentation of a matter. It is now manifest that, whether one takes neither as basis, or assumes merely one of them, space would always remain empty, and no matter would be found therein.

[a] *Annäherung*
[b] *Weil überall nur zwei bewegende Kräfte im Raum gedacht werden können*

EXPLICATION 6

Contact in the physical sense is the immediate action and reaction of *impenetrability*. The action of one matter on another in the absence of contact is *action at a distance* (*actio in distans*). This action at a distance, which is possible even without the mediation of matter lying in between, is called immediate action at a distance, or the *action* of matters on one another *through empty space*.

4: 512

Remark

Contact in the mathematical sense is the common boundary of two spaces, which is therefore within neither the one nor the other space. Thus two straight lines cannot be in contact with one another; rather, if they have a point in common, it belongs as much to one of these lines as to the other when they are produced,[a] that is, they intersect. But a circle and a straight line, or two circles, are in contact at a point, surfaces at a line, and bodies at surfaces. Mathematical contact is the basis for physical contact, but does not yet constitute the latter by itself, since for the one to arise from the other a dynamical relation must also be added in thought – and, indeed, not of attractive, but of repulsive forces, that is, of impenetrability. Physical contact is the interaction of repulsive forces at the common boundary of two matters.

PROPOSITION 7

The *attraction essential to all matter* is an immediate action of matter on other matter through empty space.

Proof

The original attractive force contains the very ground of the possibility of matter, as that thing which fills a space to a determinate degree, and so contains even [the ground] of the possibility of a physical contact thereof. It must therefore precede the latter, and its action must thus be independent of the condition of contact. But the action of a moving force that is independent of all contact is also independent of the filling of space between the moving and the moved [matters]; that is, it must also take place without the space between the two being filled, and thus as action through empty space. Hence the original attraction essential to all matter is an immediate action of matter on other matter through empty space.

[a] *fortgezogen*

Remark 1

That the possibility of the fundamental forces should be made conceivable is a completely impossible demand; for they are called fundamental forces precisely because they cannot be derived from any other, that is, they can in no way be conceived. But the original attractive force is in no way *more inconceivable* than the original repulsion. It simply does not present itself so immediately to the senses as impenetrability, so as to furnish us with concepts of determinate objects in space. Thus, because it is not felt, but is only to be inferred,[a] it has so far the appearance of a derived force, exactly as if it were only a hidden play of moving forces through repulsion. On closer consideration we see that it can in no way be further derived from anywhere else, least of all from the moving force of matters through their impenetrability, since its action is precisely the reverse of the latter. The most common objection to immediate action at a distance is that a matter cannot act immediately *where it is not*. When the earth immediately impels the moon to approach it, the earth acts on a thing that is many thousands of miles away from it, and yet immediately; the space between it and the moon may well be viewed as completely empty. For even though matter may lie between the two bodies, it still contributes nothing to this attraction. It therefore acts immediately at a place where it is not, which is apparently contradictory. In truth, however, it is so far from being contradictory that one may rather say that every thing in space acts on another only at a place where the acting thing is not. For if it should act at the same place where it itself is, then the thing on which it acts would not be *outside it* at all; for this *outsideness* means presence at a place where the other is not. If earth and moon were to be in contact with one another, the point of contact would still be a place where neither the earth nor the moon is, for the two are distanced from one another by the sum of their radii. Moreover, no part of either the earth or the moon would be found at the point of contact, for this point lies at the boundary of the two filled spaces, which constitutes no part of either the one or the other. Hence to say that matters cannot act immediately on one another at a distance, would amount to saying that they cannot act immediately on one another except through the forces of impenetrability. But this would be as much as to say that repulsive forces are the only ones whereby matters can be active, or that they are at least the necessary conditions under which alone matters can act on one another, which would declare attractive force to be either completely impossible or always dependent on the action of repulsive forces. But these are both groundless assertions. The confusion of mathematical contact

of spaces and physical contact through repulsive forces constitutes the

---

[a] *Weil sie also nicht gefühlt, sondern nur geschlossen werden will*

ground of misunderstanding here. To attract one another immediately in the absence of contact means to approach one another in accordance with an invariable law, without a force of repulsion containing the condition for this. And this must be just as thinkable as an immediate repulsion of one another, that is, to flee from one another in accordance with an invariable law, without the force of attraction having any part therein. For the two moving forces are of completely different kinds, and there is not the slightest ground for making one of them dependent on the other, and contesting its possibility unmediated by the other.

Remark 2

No motion at all can arise from attraction in contact; for contact is interaction of impenetrability, which therefore prevents all motion. Hence, some sort of immediate attraction must be found in the absence of contact, and thus at a distance. For otherwise even the forces of pressure and impact, which are supposed to bring about the striving to approach by acting in the opposite direction to that of the repulsive force of matter, would have no cause, or at least none lying originally in the nature of matter. We may call that attraction which takes place without mediation of the repulsive forces *true* attraction, whereas that which takes place merely in that way is *apparent* attraction. For, properly speaking, the body which another is striving to approach, merely because the latter has been driven toward it from elsewhere by impact, exerts no attractive force at all on this body. But even these apparent attractions must in the end have a true one as their ground. For matter whose pressure or impact is supposed to serve instead of attraction would not even be matter without attractive forces (Prop. 5), and so the mode of explaining all phenomena of approach by *merely apparent* attraction revolves in a circle. It is commonly supposed that Newton did not at all find it necessary for his system to assume an immediate attraction of matter, but, with the most rigorous abstinence of pure mathematics, allowed the physicists full freedom to explain the possibility of attraction as they might see fit, without mixing his propositions with their play of hypotheses. But how could he ground the proposition that the universal attraction of bodies, which they exert at equal distances around them, is proportional to the quantity of their matter, if he did not assume that all matter, merely as matter, therefore, and through its essential property, exerts this moving force? For although between two bodies, when one attracts the other, whether their matter be similar or not, the mutual approach (in accordance with the law of equality of interaction) must always occur in inverse ratio to the quantity of matter, this law still constitutes only a principle of mechanics, but not of dynamics. That is, it is a law of the *motions* that follow from attracting forces, not of the proportion of the *attractive forces*

4: 515

themselves, and it holds for all moving forces in general.[28] Thus, if a magnet is at one time attracted by another equal magnet, and at another by the same magnet enclosed in a wooden box of double the weight, the latter will impart more relative motion to the former in the second case than in the first, even though the wood, which increases the quantity of matter of this second magnet, adds nothing at all to its attractive force, and manifests[a] no magnetic attraction of the box. Newton says (Cor. 2, Prop. 6, Book III, *Principia*): "if the aether or any other body were without weight, it could, since it differs from every other matter only in its form, be transformed successively by gradual change of this form into a matter of the same kind as those which on earth have the most weight; and so the latter, conversely, by gradual change of their form, could lose all their weight, which is contrary to experience, etc."[29] Thus he did not himself exclude the aether (much less other matters) from the law of attraction. So what other kind of matter could he then have left, by whose impact the approach of bodies to one another might be viewed as mere apparent attraction? Thus, one cannot adduce this great founder of the theory of attraction as one's predecessor, if one takes the liberty of substituting an apparent attraction for the true attraction he did assert, and assumes the *necessity* of an impulsion through *impact* to explain the phenomenon of approach. He rightly abstracted from all hypotheses purporting to answer the question as to the cause of the universal attraction of matter, for this question is physical or metaphysical, but not mathematical. And, even though he says in the advertisement to the second edition of his *Optics*, "to show that I do not take *gravity* for an *essential* property of bodies, I have added one question concerning its cause,"[30] it is clear that the offense taken by his contemporaries, and perhaps even by Newton himself, at the concept of an original attraction set him at variance with himself. For he could by no means say that the attractive forces of two planets, those of Jupiter and Saturn for example, manifested at equal distances from their satellites (whose mass is unknown), are proportional to the quantity of matter of these heavenly bodies,[31] if he did not assume that they attracted other matter merely as matter, and thus according to a universal property of matter.

4: 516

EXPLICATION 7

I call a moving force whereby matters can act immediately on one another only at the common surface of contact, a *surface force*. But that whereby a matter can act immediately on the parts of others, even beyond the surface of contact, I call a *penetrating force*.

[a] *beweiset*

Note

The repulsive force whereby matter fills a space is a mere surface force, for the parts in contact mutually limit their spaces of action. Repulsive force cannot move a part at a distance without the mediation of those lying in between, and an immediate action, passing straight through the latter, of one matter on another by expansive forces, is impossible. By contrast, no intervening matter sets limits to the action of an attractive force, whereby matter occupies a space *without filling it*, so that it thereby acts on other distant matter *through empty space*. Now the original attraction, which makes matter itself possible, must be thought in this way, and it is therefore a penetrating force, and for this reason alone is always proportional to the quantity of matter.

PROPOSITION 8

The original attractive force, on which the very possibility of matter as such rests, extends immediately to infinity throughout the universe, from every part of matter to every other part.

Proof

Because the original attractive force belongs to the essence of matter, it also pertains to every part of matter to act immediately at a distance as well. But suppose there were a distance beyond which it did not extend. Then this *limiting* of the sphere of its activity would rest either on the 4: 517 *matter* lying within this sphere, or merely on the magnitude of the *space* in which it diffuses this influence. The first [case] does not hold; for this attraction is a penetrating force and acts *immediately* at a distance through that space, as an empty space, regardless of any matter lying in between. The second [case] likewise does not hold; for, since every attraction is a moving force having a degree, below which ever smaller degrees can always be thought to infinity, a greater distance would indeed be a reason for the degree of attraction to diminish in inverse ratio, in accordance with the measure of the diffusion of this force, but never for it to cease altogether. Thus, since there is nothing that has anywhere limited the sphere of activity of the original attraction of every part of matter, it extends beyond all specified limits to every other matter, and thus throughout the universe to infinity.

Note 1

From this original attractive force, as a penetrating force exerted by all matter, and hence in proportion to its quantity, and extending its action to all matter at all possible distances, it should now be possible, in combination with the force counteracting it, namely, repulsive force, to derive the limitation of the latter, and thus the possibility of a space filled to a determinate degree. And thus the dynamical concept of matter, as that of the movable filling its space (to a determinate degree), would be constructed. But for this one needs a law of the ratio of both original attraction and repulsion at various distances of matter and its parts from one another, which, since it now rests simply on the difference in direction of these two forces (where a point is driven either to approach others or to move away from them), and on the magnitude of the space into which each of these forces diffuses at various distances, is a purely mathematical task, which no longer belongs to metaphysics – nor is metaphysics responsible if the attempt to construct the concept of matter in this way should perhaps not succeed. For it is responsible only for the correctness of the elements of the construction granted to our rational cognition, not for the insufficiency and limits of our reason in carrying it out.

4: 518

Note 2

Since every given matter must fill its space with a determinate degree of repulsive force, in order to constitute a determinate material thing, only an original attraction in conflict with the original repulsion can make possible a determinate degree of the filling of space, and thus matter. Now it may be that the former flows from the individual attraction of the parts of the compressed matter among one another, or from the uniting of this attraction with that of all matter in the universe.[a]

The original attraction is proportional to the quantity of matter and extends to infinity. Therefore, the determinate filling, in accordance with its measure, of a space by matter,[b] can in the end be effected only by the attraction of matter extending to infinity, and imparted to each matter in accordance with the measure of its repulsive force.

The *action* of the universal attraction immediately exerted by each matter on all matters, and at all distances, is called *gravitation*; the tendency to move in the direction of greater gravitation is *weight*. The action of the general[c] repulsive force of the parts of every given matter is called its *original elasticity*. Hence this property and weight constitute the sole universal characteristics of matter, which are comprehensible *a priori*, the former internally, and the latter in external relations. For the possibility of matter itself rests on these two properties. *Cohesion*, if this is explicated as the mutual attraction of matter limited solely to the

---

[a] *aller Weltmaterie*
[b] *die dem Maße nach bestimmte Erfüllung eines Raumes durch Materie*
[c] *durchgängig*

condition of contact, does not belong to the possibility of matter in general, and cannot therefore be cognized *a priori* as bound up with this. This property would therefore not be metaphysical but rather physical, and so would not belong to our present considerations.

Remark 1

Yet I cannot forbear adding a small preliminary suggestion on behalf of the attempt at such a perhaps possible construction.

(1) Of any force that acts immediately at various distances, and is limited, as to the degree with which it exerts moving force on any given point at a certain distance, only by the magnitude of the space into which it must diffuse so as to act on this point, one can say that in all the spaces, large or small, into which it diffuses, it always constitutes an equal quantum, but [also] that the degree of its action on that point in this space is always in inverse ratio to the space, into which it has had to diffuse, so that it could act on this point. Thus light, for example, diffuses from an illuminating point in all directions on spherical surfaces, which constantly increase with the squares of the distance, and the quantum of illumination on all of these spherical surfaces, which become greater to infinity, is always the same in total. But it follows from this that a given equal part of one of these spherical surfaces must become ever less illuminated with respect to its degree, as the surface of diffusion of precisely the same light quantum becomes greater. And so, too, with all other forces, and the laws whereby they must diffuse, either on surfaces or in volumes,[a] so as to act on distant objects in accordance with their nature. It is better to represent the diffusion of a moving force at all distances from a point in this way, rather than as is customary, for example, in optics, by means of rays diverging from one another radially from a central point. For since, as an unavoidable consequence of their divergence, lines drawn in this way can never fill the space through which they spread, nor the surfaces on which they fall, no matter how many are drawn or plotted, they give rise only to troublesome inferences, and these in turn to hypotheses, which might well be avoided by merely taking into consideration the magnitude of the whole spherical surface – which is to be *uniformly* illuminated by the same quantity of light; and the degree of its illumination at every place is then naturally taken in inverse ratio of its magnitude to the whole, and similarly for any other diffusion of a force through spaces of different magnitudes.

(2) If the force is an immediate attraction at a distance, then it is even more necessary to represent the directed lines of attraction, not as if they

4: 519

---

[a] *körperlichen Raum*

diverged like rays from the attracting point, but rather as converging from every point of the surrounding spherical surface (whose radius is the given distance) toward it. For the very directed line of motion toward the point, which is the cause and goal of this motion, already yields the *terminus a quo* from which the lines must begin, namely, from every point of the surface from which they take their direction toward the attracting central point, and not conversely. For this magnitude of the surface alone determines the aggregate of lines; the central point leaves this undetermined.*

4: 520   (3) If the force is an immediate repulsion, by which a point (in the merely mathematical presentation) fills a space *dynamically*, and the question is by what law of infinitely small distances (which here count as equivalent to contacts) an original repulsive force (whose limitation thus rests simply on the space in which it is diffused) acts at various distances, then it is even less possible to make this force representable by diverging rays of repulsion from the assumed repelling point, even though the direction of motion has this point as its *terminus a quo*. For the space into

---

4: 520   * It is impossible by lines radiating from a point to represent surfaces at given distances as completely filled with their action, whether of illumination or attraction. Thus, in the case of such diverging light rays, the lesser illumination of a distant surface would rest merely on the circumstance that between the illuminated places remain unilluminated ones, and the more distant the surface the larger they are. Euler's hypothesis avoids this impropriety, but has all the more difficulty in making the rectilinear motion of light conceivable. Yet this difficulty flows from an easily avoidable mathematical representation of light matter as an agglomeration of little spheres, which would certainly yield a lateral motion of light in accordance with their varying obliquity to the direction of impact. Instead of this, however, there is no obstacle to thinking the matter in question as an original fluid, and, indeed, as fluid throughout, without being divided into rigid particles. If the mathematician wants to make intuitive the decrease of light at increasing distances, he uses rays diverging radially to represent the magnitude of the space on the spherical surface of its diffusion, wherein the same quantity of light is supposed to be uniformly diffused between these rays, and thus to represent the decrease of the degree of illumination. But he does not want one to view these rays as the only sources of illumination, as if places empty of light, which would be greater at greater distances, were always to be found between them. If one wants to imagine each such surface as illuminated throughout, then the same quantity of illumination as covers the smaller surfaces must be thought as uniformly [spread] over the larger surfaces; so, in order to indicate the rectilinear direction, straight lines from the surface, and all of its points, must be drawn toward the illuminating point. The action and its quantity must be thought of beforehand, and the cause thereupon specified. Precisely the same holds for rays of attraction, if one wants to call them that, and indeed, for all directions of forces that are supposed to fill a space, and even a volume, proceeding from a point.

which the force must be diffused in order to act at a distance is a volume, which is supposed to be thought as filled. (The manner in which a point could do this by moving force, that is, dynamically fill a volume, is certainly not capable of further mathematical presentation.) And diverging rays from a point cannot possibly make representable the repulsive force of a filled volume. Rather, one would simply estimate the repulsion, at various infinitely small distances of these mutually impelling points, as merely in inverse ratio to the volumes that each of them fills dynami- 4: 521 cally, and thus to the cube of their distances, without being able to construct it.

(4) Thus the original attraction of matter would act in inverse ratio to the squares of the distance at all distances, the original repulsion in inverse ratio to the cubes of the infinitely small distances, and, through such an action and reaction of the two fundamental forces, matter filling its space to a determinate degree would be possible. For since repulsion increases with the approach of the parts to a greater extent than attraction, the limit of approach, beyond which no greater is possible by the given attraction, is thereby determined, and so is that degree of compression which constitutes the measure of the intensive filling of space.

Remark 2

I am well aware of the difficulty in this mode of explaining the possibility of a matter in general. It consists in this, that if a point cannot immediately propel another by repulsive force, without at the same time filling the entire volume up to the given distance with its force, then it appears to follow that this volume would have to contain several impelling points, which contradicts the presupposition, and was refuted above (Proposition 4) under the name of a sphere of repulsion of the simple [elements] in space. But there is a difference between the concept of an actual space, which can be given, and the mere idea of a space, which is thought simply for determining the ratio of given spaces, but is not in fact a space. In the case put forward, of a supposed physical monadology, there were supposed to be actual spaces filled dynamically by a point, namely, through repulsion;[32] for they would exist as points prior to any possible generation of matter therefrom, and would determine, through their own spheres of activity, that part of the space to be filled which could belong to them. So on this hypothesis, matter cannot be viewed as divisible to infinity, and as *quantum continuum*. For the parts that immediately repel one another have a determinate distance from one another (the sum of the radii of the spheres of their repulsion). By contrast, if, as is actually the case, we think matter as a continuous quantity, there is then no distance at all between the points immediately repelling one another, and thus no increasing or decreasing sphere of their activity. But matters can expand or be compressed (like air), and here one does represent to oneself a distance of their adjacent parts, which can increase and decrease. Yet since the adjacent parts of a *continuous* matter are in contact with one another, whether it is further expanded or compressed, one then thinks these distances as *infinitely small*, and this infinitely small space as filled by its repulsive force to a greater or lesser degree. But the infinitely small intervening space is not at all different from contact. Hence it is only the idea of a space, which serves to make intuitive the enlargement of a matter as a continuous quantity, although it cannot, in fact, be actually conceived in this way. If it is said, therefore, that the repulsive forces of the parts of matter that immediately impel one another stand in inverse ratio to the cubes of their distances, this means only that they stand in inverse ratio to the volumes one imagines between parts that are nevertheless in immediate contact, and whose distance must for precisely this reason be called *infinitely small*, so as to be distinguished from every actual distance. Hence one must not object to a concept itself because of difficulties in constructing it, or, rather, because of a misunderstanding of this construction. For otherwise it would apply to the mathematical presentation of the proportion in accordance with which attraction takes place at various distances, no less than to that whereby every point in an expanding or contracting whole of matter immediately repels the others. The universal law of dynamics would in both cases be this: the action of the moving force, exerted by a point on every other point external to it, stands in inverse ratio to the space into which the same quantum of moving force would need to have diffused, in order to act immediately on this point at the determinate distance.

4: 522

From the law of the parts of matter repelling one another originally in inverse cubic ratio to their infinitely small distances, a law of expansion and contraction of matter completely different from Mariotte's law for the air must therefore necessarily follow; for the latter proves fleeing forces of its adjacent parts standing in inverse ratio to their distances, as Newton demonstrates (*Principia*, Book II, Prop. 23, Schol.).[33] But we may also view the expansive force of air, not as the action of *originally* repelling forces, but as resting rather on *heat*, which compels the proper parts of air (to which, moreover, actual distances from one another are attributable) to flee one another, not merely as a matter penetrating it, but rather, to all appearances, through its vibrations. But that these tremors must impart a fleeing force to the adjacent parts, standing in inverse ratio to their distances, can doubtless be made conceivable in accordance with the laws of communication of motion through the oscillation of elastic matters.

I declare, furthermore, that I do not want the present exposition of the law of an original repulsion to be viewed as necessarily belonging to the goals of my metaphysical treatment of matter. Nor do I want this latter (for which it is enough to have presented the filling of space as a dynamical property of matter) to be mixed up with the conflicts and doubts that could afflict the former.

4: 523

GENERAL NOTE TO DYNAMICS

If we look back over all our discussions of the subject, we will notice that we have therein considered the following: *first*, the *real* in space (otherwise called the solid), in the filling of space through *repulsive force*; *second*, that which in relation to the first, as the proper object of our outer perception, is *negative*, namely, *attractive force*, whereby, for its own part, all space would be penetrated, and thus the solid would be completely destroyed; *third*, the *limitation* of the first force by the second, and the determination of the *degree of filling* of a space that rests on this. Hence, the *quality* of matter, under the headings of *reality*, *negation*, and *limitation*, has been treated completely, so far as pertains to a metaphysical dynamics.

GENERAL REMARK TO DYNAMICS

The general principle of the dynamics of material nature is that everything real in the objects of the outer senses, which is not merely a determination of space (place, extension, and figure), must be viewed as moving force. So by this principle the so-called solid or absolute impenetrability is banished from natural science, as an empty concept, and repulsive force is posited in its stead. But the true and immediate attraction, by contrast, is thereby defended against all sophistries of a metaphysics that misunderstands itself, and, as a fundamental force, is declared necessary for the very possibility of the concept of matter. Now from this it follows that space, if it should be necessary, can be assumed to be completely *filled*, and in different degrees, even *without dispersing empty interstices* within matter.[34] For, in accordance with the originally different degree of the repulsive forces, on which rests the first property of matter, namely, that of filling a space, their relation to the original attraction (whether of any [piece of] matter separately, or to the united attraction of all matter in the universe) can be thought of as infinitely various. This is because attraction rests on the aggregate of matter in a given space, whereas its expansive force, by contrast, rests on the degree of filling of this space, which can be very different specifically (as the same quantity of air, say, in the same volume, manifests more or less elasticity in accordance with its greater or lesser heating). The general ground for this is that through true attraction *all parts* of a matter act immediately *on every part* of another, whereas through expansive force only those *at the surface of contact* act, so that it is all the same whether

4: 524

much or little of this matter is found behind that surface. Now a great advantage for natural science already arises here, since it is thereby relieved of the burden of fabricating a world from the full and the empty in accordance with mere fantasy. On the contrary, all spaces can be thought of as full, and yet as filled in different measures, whereby empty space at least loses its *necessity*, and is demoted to the value of an hypothesis. For it could otherwise usurp the title of a principle, under the pretense of being a necessary condition for explaining the different degrees of the filling of space.

In all this the advantage of a metaphysics that is here used methodically, to get rid of principles that are equally metaphysical, but have not been brought to the test of criticism, is apparently only *negative*. Nevertheless, the field of the natural scientist is thereby indirectly enlarged. For the conditions by which he formerly limited himself, and through which all original moving forces were philosophized away, now lose their validity. But one should guard against going beyond that which makes possible the general concept of a matter as such, and wishing to explain *a priori* its particular, or even specific, determination and variety. The concept of matter is reduced to nothing but moving forces, and one could not expect anything else, since no activity or change can be thought in space except mere motion. But who pretends to comprehend the possibility of the fundamental forces? They can be assumed only if they unavoidably belong to a concept that is demonstrably fundamental and not further derivable from any other (like that of the filling of space), and these, in general, are repulsive forces and the attractive forces that counteract them. We can indeed certainly judge *a priori* about the connection and consequences of these forces, whatever relations among them one can think without contradiction, but cannot yet presume to suppose one of them as actual. For to be authorized in erecting an hypothesis, it is unavoidably required that the *possibility* of what we suppose be completely *certain*, but with fundamental forces their possibility can never be comprehended. And here the mathematical-mechanical mode of explanation 4: 525 has an advantage over the metaphysical-dynamical [mode], which cannot be wrested from it, namely, that of generating from a thoroughly homogeneous material a great specific variety of matters, which vary in both density and (if foreign forces are added) mode of action, through the varying shape of the parts and the empty interstices interspersed among them. For the possibility of both the shapes and the empty interstices can be verified with mathematical evidence. By contrast, if the material itself is transformed into fundamental forces (whose laws we cannot determine *a priori*, and are even less capable of enumerating reliably a manifold of such forces sufficient for explaining the specific variety of matter), we lack all means for *constructing* this concept of matter, and presenting what we thought universally as possible in intuition. Conversely, however, a merely mathematical physics pays doubly for this advantage on the other side. First, it must take an empty concept (of absolute impenetrability) as basis; and second, it must give up all forces *inherent* in matter; and beyond this, further, with its original configurations of the fundamental material and its interspersing of empty spaces, as the need for explanation requires them, such a physics must allow more freedom, and indeed rightful claims, to the imagination in the field of philosophy than is truly consistent with the caution of the latter.

Instead of a sufficient explanation for the possibility of matter and its specific variety from these fundamental forces, which I cannot provide, I will present completely, so I hope, the moments to which its specific variety must collectively be reducible (albeit not conceivable in regard to its possibility). The remarks inserted between the definitions*a* will explain their application.

1. A **body**, in the physical sense, is *a matter between determinate boundaries* (which therefore has a figure). *The space between these boundaries, considered in accordance with its magnitude*, is the **volume** [of the body].*b* The degree of the filling of a space with determinate content*c* is called **density**. (Otherwise the term *dense* is also used absolutely for what is *not hollow*, that is, vesicular or porous.) In this sense, there is an absolute density in the system of absolute impenetrability, that is, when a matter contains no empty interstices at all. In accordance with this concept of the filling of space we make comparisons, and call one matter denser than another when it contains less emptiness, until finally that in which no part of the space is empty is called perfectly dense. One can only make use of the latter expression in connection with the merely mathematical concept of matter, but in the dynamical system of a merely relative impenetrability there is no maximum or minimum of density, and yet every matter, however rarefied, can still be called completely dense, if it fills its space entirely without containing empty interstices, and is thus a *continuum*, not an *interruptum*. In comparison with another matter, however, it is less dense, in the dynamical sense, if it fills its space entirely, but not to the same degree. But in this system, too, it is inappropriate to think of matters as related with respect to their density, if we do not imagine them as specifically of the same kind, so that one can be generated from the other by mere compression. Now since the latter [condition] by no means appears to be necessary to the nature of all matter in itself, no comparison with regard to their density can properly take place between matters of different kinds, between water and mercury, for example, even though it is customary.

4: 526

---

a *Definitionen*
b **Raumesinhalt** (*volumen*)
c *Der Grad der Erfüllung eines Raumes von bestimmtem Inhalt*

2. *Attraction, insofar as it is thought merely as active in contact*, is called **cohesion**. (To be sure, it is confirmed by very good experiments that the same force, which in contact is called cohesion, is also found to be active at a very small distance. But attraction is still called cohesion, only *insofar* as I think it merely in contact, in accordance with common experience, where it is hardly ever observed at small distances. Cohesion is commonly taken for an entirely general property of matter, not because one is already led to it by the concept of a matter, but because experience shows it everywhere. But this generality must not be understood *collectively*, as if every matter acted, through this kind of attraction, on every other matter in the universe *at once*, like gravitation; it must rather be understood merely *disjunctively*, as acting, that is, on one matter or another with which it comes into contact, of whatever kind it may be. For this reason, and since such attraction, as various grounds of proof can show, is not a penetrating, but only a surface force; since it is not even determined everywhere in accordance with density; since for full strength of cohesion a prior state of fluidity of the matters and their subsequent rigidification is required, whereby the closest possible contact of broken solid matters at precisely the same surfaces where they previously cohered so strongly, in a cracked mirror, for example, is still very far from permitting any longer that degree of attraction it had gained on rigidification from a fluid state; I therefore take this attraction in contact to be no fundamental force of matter, but only a derivative one; of which more below.) *A matter whose parts, however strong their mutual cohesion, can nonetheless be mutually displaced by every moving force, however small, is* **fluid**. *But parts of a matter are so* **displaced**, *when they are merely compelled, without reducing the*

4: 527

quantum of contact, to interchange such contact. Parts, and thus also matters, are **separated**, *when the contact is not merely exchanged with others, but destroyed or reduced in quantity.* A **solid** – or better a **rigid** – body (*corpus rigidum*) *is one whose parts cannot be so displaced by every force* – and therefore resist displacement with a certain degree of force. – *The resistance to such mutual displacement of matters is* **friction**. The resistance *to separation* of matters in contact is cohesion. Fluid matters therefore undergo no friction when divided; where it occurs, the matters, at least in their smallest parts, are taken to be rigid, in greater or lesser degree, where the latter is called viscosity.[a] *A rigid body is* **brittle**, *when its parts cannot be mutually displaced without breaking apart*, and thus when their cohesion cannot be changed without at the same time being destroyed. (It is quite wrong to locate the difference between fluid and solid matters in the different degree of cohesion of their parts. For to call a matter fluid does not depend on the degree of resistance it opposes to the breaking up of its parts, but only on its opposition to their mutual displacement. The former can be

---

[a] *Klebrigkeit (viscositas)*

as large as one wishes, but in a fluid matter the latter is still always $= 0$. Consider a drop of water. If a particle within it is drawn to one side by an attraction, however great, of the neighboring parts that are in contact with it, it is still drawn just as much to the opposite side as well; and since the attractions mutually cancel their effects, the particle is just as easily movable as if it were in empty space. That is, the force that is to move it has no cohesion to overcome, but only the so-called inertia, which it would have to overcome in all matter, even if the latter did not cohere with anything. Thus a small microscopic organism will move just as easily within the drop as if there were no cohesion at all to separate. For it actually has no cohesion of the water to destroy, nor any internal contact thereof to diminish – it needs only to change this contact. But if you imagine that this same small organism wants to work its way out through the external surface of the drop, then it should first be noticed that the mutual attraction of the parts of this water droplet causes them to keep moving until they have attained the greatest contact with one another, and thus the smallest contact with empty space, that is, until they have formed a spherical shape. Now if the insect in question is striving to work its way out beyond the surface of the drop, it must change the spherical shape, and thus create more contact between the water and empty space, and hence less contact of its parts with one another, that is, [it must] diminish the cohesion of these parts. And here the water   4: 528
resists it primarily through its cohesion, but not within the drop, where the mutual contact of the parts is not diminished at all, but only changed into contact with other parts, so that they are not in the least separated, but only displaced. One can also apply to the microscopic organism, and indeed on similar grounds, what Newton says of the light ray: that it is repulsed, not by dense matter, but only by empty space.[35] It is clear, therefore, that the increase in cohesion of the parts of a matter does not impair its fluidity in the least. Water coheres far more strongly in its parts than is commonly believed, when one relies on the experiment of a metal plate pulled off the surface of the water; this settles nothing, because here the water is not torn loose over the whole surface of first contact, but on a much smaller one, which, in fact, it has finally arrived at through the displacement of its parts, as a stick of soft wax, say, can be first drawn out thinner by a hanging weight, and must then rupture at a much smaller surface than was originally assumed. But what is entirely decisive in regard to our concept of fluidity is this: that *fluid* matters can also be defined[a] as those, *in which every point endeavors to move in all directions with precisely the same force with which it is pressed toward any one of them*, a property on which rests the first law of hydrodynamics, although it can never be attributed to an agglomeration of smooth and yet solid

[a] *erklärt*

corpuscles, as can be shown by a very easy calculation of its pressure in accordance with the laws of composite motion, thereby proving the original character of the property of fluidity. If the fluid matter were to suffer the least resistance to displacement, and thus even the smallest amount of friction, then the latter would increase with the strength of the pressure by which its parts are pressed against one another, and a pressure would finally obtain at which its parts could not be displaced along one another by any small force. Consider, for example, a bent tube with two arms, one of which may be arbitrarily wide, and the other arbitrarily narrow, so long as it is not a capillary tube;[36] if one imagines both arms several hundred feet high, then, according to the laws of hydrostatics, the fluid matter in the narrow arm would stand precisely as high as in the wide one. But since the pressure on the bases of the tubes, and hence also on the part that joins them in common, can be thought as increasing to infinity in proportion to the heights, it follows that if the least amount of friction occurred between the parts of the fluid, a height for the tubes could be found, at which a small quantity of water, poured into the narrower tube, did not disturb that in the wider one from its place. So the water column in the former would come to

4: 529   stand higher than that in the latter, because the lower parts, at such great pressure against one another, could no longer be displaced by so small a moving force as that of the added weight of water. But this is contrary to experience, and even to the concept of a fluid. The same holds if, instead of pressure by weight, one posits cohesion of the parts, however great one cares to make it. The cited second definition of fluidity, on which rests the fundamental law of hydrostatics – namely, that it is that property of a matter whereby any part of it strives to move in all directions with precisely the same force by which it is pushed in any given direction – follows from the first definition, if one combines it with the principle of general dynamics that all matter is originally elastic. For this matter must then be striving to expand in all directions of the space in which it is compressed, with the same force by which the pressure occurs in any direction, whatever it may be, that is, if the parts of a matter can be displaced along one another by any force, without resistance, as is actually the case with fluids, it must be striving to move in all directions. Hence friction, properly speaking, is attributable only to rigid matters (whose possibility requires yet another ground of explanation besides the cohesion of the parts), and friction already presupposes the property of rigidity. But why certain matters, even though they may have no greater, and perhaps even a lesser force of cohesion than other matters that are fluid, nevertheless resist the displacement of their parts so strongly, and hence can be separated in no other way than by destroying the cohesion of all parts in a given surface at once, which then yields the semblance of a superior cohesion – how, that is, rigid bodies are possible – is still an unsolved problem, no matter how easily the common doctrine of nature presumes to have settled it.

3. **Elasticity** (spring-force) is the capacity of a matter, *when its magnitude or figure are changed by another moving force, to reassume them again when this latter is diminished*. It is either *expansive* or *attractive* elasticity: one to regain a previously greater volume after compression, the other a previously smaller volume after expansion. (Attractive elasticity is obviously derivative, as the term already shows. An iron wire, stretched by a hanging weight, springs back into its volume when the band is cut. In virtue of the same attraction that is the cause of its cohesion, or, in the case of fluid matters, if heat were suddenly to be extracted from mercury, the matter would quickly reassume the previously smaller volume. The elasticity that consists only in regeneration of the previous figure is always attractive, as in the case of a bent sword-blade, where the parts, stretched away from one another on the convex surface, strive to reassume their previous proximity, and so a small drop of mercury can likewise be called elastic. Expansive elasticity, however, can be either original or derivative. Thus air has a derivative elasticity in virtue of the matter of heat, which is most intimately united with it, and whose own elasticity is perhaps original. By contrast, the fundamental material of the fluid we call air must nonetheless, as matter in general, already have original elasticity in itself. It is not possible to decide with certainty to which type an observed elasticity belongs in any given case.)

4: 530

4. *The action of moved bodies on one another by communication of their motion is called* **mechanical**; *but the action of matters is called* **chemical**, *insofar as they mutually change, even at rest, the combination of their parts through their inherent forces*. This chemical influence is called **dissolution**, insofar as it *has the separation of the parts of a matter as its effect*. (Mechanical separation, by means of a wedge driven between the parts of a matter, for example, is therefore entirely different from chemical separation, because the wedge does not act by means of inherent force.) But that chemical influence whose effect is to isolate two matters dissolved in one another is **decomposition**. A dissolution of specifically different matters by one another, in which no part of the one is found that would not be united with a specifically different part of the other, in the same proportion as the whole, is *absolute dissolution*, which can also be called *chemical penetration*. Whether the dissolving forces that are actually to be found in nature are capable of effecting a complete dissolution may remain undecided. Here it is only a question of whether such a dissolution can be thought. Now it is obvious that, so long as the parts of a dissolved matter remain small clots (*moleculae*), a dissolution of them is no less possible than that of the larger parts. Indeed, if dissolving force remains, such a dissolution must actually proceed until there is no longer any part that is not made up of the solvent and the solute, in the same proportion in

which the two are found in the whole. Thus, because in such a case there can be no part of the volume of the solution that would not contain a part of the solvent, the latter must fill this volume completely as a continuum. In precisely the same way, because there can be no part of this same volume of the solution that would not contain a proportional part of the solute, the latter must also fill the whole space constituting the volume of the mixture, as a continuum. But if two matters fill one and the same space, and each of them does this completely, they *penetrate* one another. Hence a complete chemical dissolution would be a penetration of matters, which would nonetheless be entirely different from mechanical penetration. For in the latter case it is thought that, as the moved matters approach one another more closely, the repulsive force of the one can completely surpass that of the other, so that one or both can

4: 531 have their extension shrink to nothing. Here, by contrast, the extension remains, and it is only that the matters together occupy a space, which accords with the sum of their densities, not outside, but inside one another, that is, through intussusception[37] (as it is customarily called). It is not easy to make any objection to the possibility of this complete dissolution, and thus chemical penetration, even though it contains a *completed* division to infinity, which, in this case, still involves no contradiction, because the dissolution takes place continuously throughout a time, and thus equally through an infinite series of moments with acceleration. By the division, moreover, the sum of the surfaces of the matters yet to be divided increases, and, since the dissolving force acts continuously, the entire dissolution can be completed in a *specifiable* time. The inconceivability of such a chemical penetration of two matters is to be attributed to the inconceivability of dividing any such continuum in general to infinity. If one recoils from this complete dissolution, then one must assume that it proceeds only up to certain small clots of the solute, which swim in the solvent at given distances from one another, without being able to offer the slightest reason why these clots are not equally dissolved, since they are still always divisible matter. It may always be true in nature, so far as experience reaches, that the solvent acts no further; but all that is at issue here is the possibility of a dissolving force that also dissolves this clot, as well as anything left over from that, until solution is completed. The volume occupied by the solution may be equal to, smaller than, or even greater than the sum of the spaces occupied by the mutually dissolving matters before mixing, depending on the ratio of the attracting forces to the repulsions. In the solution, each matter by itself, and both united, constitute *an elastic medium*, and this, *on its own*, can supply a sufficient reason why the solute does not again separate from the solvent through its weight. For the attraction of the latter, since it takes place equally strongly in all directions, itself destroys the resistance of the solute; and to assume a certain viscosity in the fluid by no means accords with the great force that such dissolved matters, acids diluted with water, for example, exert on metallic bodies. They do not merely lie on them, as would have to happen if they were merely afloat in their medium; rather, they split them up with great attractive force, and spread throughout the entire space of the vehicle. Moreover, even if we supposed that art had no such dissolving forces at its disposal as to effect a complete dissolution, nature, in its vegetable or animal operations, could still perhaps manifest them, and thereby generate matters that, although certainly mixed, can be separated again by no art.[38] This chemical penetration could also be found even where one of two matters is not in fact separated by and literally dissolved in the other, as caloric, for example, penetrates bodies; for if it merely dispersed into their empty interstices, the solid substance would itself remain cold, since it could not absorb anything from it. We might even imagine, in this way, an apparently free passage of certain matters through others, for example, of magnetic matter, without preparing, for this purpose, open passages and empty interstices in all matters, even the most dense. Yet here is not the place to uncover hypotheses for particular phenomena, but only the principle in accordance with which they are all to be judged. Everything that relieves us of the need to resort to empty spaces is a real gain for natural science, for they give the imagination far too much freedom to make up by fabrication[a] for the lack of any inner knowledge of nature. In the doctrine of nature, the absolutely empty and the absolutely dense are approximately what blind accident and blind fate are in metaphysical science, namely, an obstacle to the governance of reason, whereby it is either supplanted by fabrication or lulled to rest on the pillow of occult qualities.

4: 532

But now as to the procedure of natural science with respect to the most important of all its tasks – namely, that of explaining a potentially infinite *specific variety of matters* – one can take only two paths in this connection: the *mechanical*, by combination of the absolutely full with the absolutely empty, and an opposing *dynamical* path, by mere variety in combining the original forces of repulsion and attraction to explain all differences of matters. The first has as materials for its derivation *atoms* and the *void*. An atom is a small part of matter that is physically indivisible. A matter is physically *indivisible* when its parts cohere with a force that cannot be overpowered by any moving force in nature. An atom, insofar as it is specifically distinguished from others by its figure, is called a *primary particle*. A body (or particle) whose moving force depends on its figure is called a *machine*. The mode of explaining the specific variety of matters by the constitution and composition of their smallest parts, as machines, is the *mechanical natural philosophy*. But that

---

[a] *Erdichtung*

which derives this specific variety from matters, not as machines, that is, mere instruments of external moving forces, but from the moving forces of attraction and repulsion originally inherent in them, can be called the *dynamical natural philosophy*. The mechanical mode of explanation, since it is the most tractable for mathematics, has, under the name of *atomism* or the *corpuscular philosophy*, always retained its authority and influence on the principles of natural science, with few changes from Democritus of old, up to Descartes, and even to our time. What is essential therein is the presupposition of the *absolute impenetrability* of the primitive matter, the *absolute homogeneity* of this material, leaving only differences in the shape, and the *absolute insurmountability* of the cohesion of matter in these fundamental particles themselves. These were the *materials* for generating specifically different matters, so as not only to have at hand an invariable, and, at the same time, variously shaped fundamental material for explaining the invariability of species and kinds, but also to explain *mechanically*, from the shapes of these primary parts, as machines (where nothing further is lacking but an external impressed force), the manifold workings of nature. But the first and foremost authentication for this system rests on the apparently unavoidable *necessity* for using *empty spaces on behalf of the specific difference in the density* of matters. These spaces were taken to be distributed within the matters, and between these particles, in any proportion found necessary, so great, indeed, for the sake of some phenomena, that the filled part of the volume of even the densest matter is virtually negligible relative to the empty part. – In order now to introduce a dynamical mode of explanation (which is much more appropriate and conducive to experimental philosophy, in that it leads us directly to the discovery of matter's inherent moving forces and their laws, while restricting our freedom to assume empty interstices and fundamental particles of determinate shapes, neither of which are determinable or discoverable by any experiment), it is not at all necessary to frame new hypotheses. It is only necessary to refute the postulate of the merely mechanical mode of explanation – namely, *that it is impossible to think a specific difference in the density of matters without interposition of empty spaces* – by simply advancing a mode of explanation in which this can be thought without contradiction. For once the postulate in question, on which the merely mechanical mode of explanation rests, is shown to be invalid as a principle, then it obviously does not have to be adopted as an hypothesis in natural science, so long as a possibility remains for thinking the specific difference in densities even without any empty interstices. But this necessity[39] rests on the circumstance that matter does not fill its space (as merely mechanical natural scientists assume) by absolute impenetrability, but rather by repulsive force, which has a degree that can be different in different matters; and, since in itself it has nothing in common with the attractive force, which

depends on the quantity of matter, it may be *originally different* in degree   4: 534
in different matters whose attractive force is the same. Thus the degree
of expansion of these matters, when the quantity is the same, and, conversely, the quantity of matter at the same volume, that is, its density,
originally admit of very large specific differences. In this way, one would
not find it impossible to think a matter (as one imagines the aether, for
example) that completely filled its space without any emptiness, and yet
with an incomparably smaller quantity of matter, at the same volume,
than any bodies we can subject to our experiments. In the aether, the
repulsive force must be thought as incomparably larger in proportion to
its inherent attractive force than in any other matters known to us. And
this, then, is the one and only assumption that we make, simply *because
it can be thought*, but only to controvert an hypothesis (of empty spaces),
which rests solely on the pretension that such a thing *cannot be thought*
without empty spaces. For, aside from this, no law of either attractive or
repulsive force may be risked on *a priori* conjectures. Rather, everything,
even universal attraction as the cause of weight, must be inferred, together with its laws, from data of experience. Still less may such laws be
attempted for chemical affinities otherwise than by way of experiments.
For it lies altogether beyond the horizon of our reason to comprehend
original forces *a priori* with respect to their possibility; all natural philosophy consists, rather, in the reduction of given, apparently different
forces to a smaller number of forces and powers that explain the actions
of the former, although this reduction proceeds only up to fundamental
forces, beyond which our reason cannot go. And so metaphysical investigation behind that which lies at the basis of the empirical concept of
matter is useful only for the purpose of guiding natural philosophy, so
far as this is ever possible, to explore dynamical grounds of explanation.
For these alone permit the hope of determinate laws, and thus a true
rational coherence of explanations.

   This is now all that metaphysics can ever achieve toward the construction of the concept of matter, and thus to promote the application of
mathematics to natural science, with respect to those properties whereby
matter fills a space in a determinate measure – namely, to view these properties as dynamical, and not as unconditioned original positings,*a* as a
merely mathematical treatment might postulate them.

   The well-known question as to the admissibility of empty spaces in
the world may serve as our conclusion. The *possibility* of such spaces cannot be disputed. For space is required for all forces of matter, and, since
it also contains the conditions of the laws of diffusion of these forces,
it is necessarily presupposed prior to all matter. Thus attractive force is   4: 535
attributed to matter insofar as it *occupies* a space around itself, through

a *Positionen*

attraction, without at the same time *filling* this space. Thus this space can be thought as empty, even where matter is active, because matter is not active there by repulsive forces, and hence does not fill this space. But no experience, or inference therefrom, or necessary hypothesis for their explanation, can justify us in assuming empty spaces as *actual*. For all experience yields only comparatively empty spaces for our cognition, which can be completely explained, to any arbitrary degree, by the matter's property of filling its space with greater or infinitely diminishing expansive force, without requiring empty spaces.

Third Chapter
Metaphysical foundations of mechanics

EXPLICATION 1

Matter is the movable insofar as it, as such a thing, has moving force.

Remark

This is now the third definition of matter. The merely dynamical concept could consider matter also as at rest; for the moving force there dealt with had merely to do with the filling of a certain space, without the matter filling it needing to be seen as itself moved.[a] Repulsion was therefore an originally-moving force for *imparting* motion. In mechanics, by contrast, the force of a matter set in motion is considered as *communicating* this motion to another. It is clear, however, that the movable would have no moving force *by means of its motion*, if it did not possess originally-moving forces, by which it is active in every place where it is found, prior to any inherent motion of its own.[b] No matter would impress proportionate motion on another matter lying straight *ahead* and in the way of its motion, if both did not possess original laws of repulsion; nor could a matter, by its motion, compel another *to follow* straight *behind* it (to drag it along behind), if both did not possess attractive forces. Thus all mechanical laws presuppose dynamical laws, and a matter, as moved, can have no moving force except by means of its repulsion or attraction, on which, and with which, it acts immediately in its motion, and thereby communicates its own inherent motion to another. I will be forgiven if I do not here further discuss the communication of motion by attraction (for example, if a comet, perhaps, with stronger attractive power than the earth, were to drag the latter in its wake in passing ahead of it), but only that by means of repulsive forces, and thus by pressure (as by means of tensed springs), or through impact. For, in any event, the application of the laws of the one case to those of the other differs only in regard to the line of direction, but is otherwise the same in both cases.

---

[a] *ohne daß die Materie, die ihn erfüllte, selbst als bewegt angesehen werden durfte*
[b] *vor aller eigener Bewegung*

EXPLICATION 2

The *quantity of matter* is the aggregate of the movable in a determinate space. Insofar as all its parts are considered as acting (moving) together in their motion, it is called *mass*, and one says that a matter *acts in mass*, when all its parts, moved in the same direction, *together* exert their moving force externally. A mass of determinate shape is called a *body* (in the mechanical meaning). The *quantity of motion* (estimated mechanically) is that which is estimated by the quantity of the moved matter and its speed together; *phoronomically* it consists merely in the degree of speed.

PROPOSITION 1

The quantity of matter, in comparison with *every* other matter, can be estimated only by the quantity of motion at a given speed.

Proof

Matter is infinitely divisible. So its quantity cannot be immediately determined *by an aggregate* of its parts. For even if this occurs in comparing the given matter with another of the same kind, in which case the quantity of matter is proportional to the size of the volume, it is still contrary to the requirement of the proposition, that it is to be estimated in comparison with every other (including the specifically different). Hence matter cannot be validly estimated, either immediately or mediately, in comparison with every *other*, so long as we abstract from its own inherent motion; no other generally valid measure remains, therefore, except the quantity of its motion. But here the difference of motion, resting on the differing quantity of matters, can be given only when the speed of the compared matters is assumed to be the same; hence, etc.

4: 538

Note

The quantity of motion of bodies is in compound ratio to that of the quantity of their matter and their speed, that is, it is one and the same whether I make the quantity of matter in a body twice as large, and retain the same speed, or double the speed, and retain precisely this mass. For the determinate concept of a quantity is possible only through the construction of the quantum. But in regard to the concept of quantity, this is nothing but the *composition* of the equivalent; so construction of the quantity of a motion is the composition of many motions equivalent to one another. Now according to the phoronomical propositions, it is one and the same whether I impart to a single movable a certain degree of speed, or to each of many movables all smaller degrees of speed,

246

resulting from the given speed divided by the aggregate of movables. From this first arises a seemingly phoronomical concept of the quantity of a motion, as composed of many motions of movable points, external to one another yet united in a whole. If these points are now thought as something that has moving force *through its motion*, then there arises from this the mechanical concept of the quantity of motion. In phoronomy, however, it is not appropriate to represent a motion as composed of many motions *external to one another*, since the movable, as it is here represented as devoid of moving force, yields no other difference in the quantity of motion, in any composition with several of its kind, than that which consists merely in speed. As the quantity of motion in a body relates to that of another, so also does the magnitude of their action, but this is to be understood as the *entire* action. Those who merely took the quantity of a space filled with resistance as the measure of the entire action (for example, the height to which a body with a certain speed can rise against gravity, or the depth to which it can penetrate into soft matters) came out with another law of moving forces for *actual* motions – namely, that of the compound ratio of the quantity of matters and the squares of their speeds. But they overlooked the magnitude of action in the given time, during which the body traverses its space at a lower speed; and yet this alone can be the measure of a motion that is exhausted by a given uniform resistance. Hence there can be no difference, either, between living and dead forces, if the moving forces are considered mechanically, that is, as those which bodies have insofar as they themselves are moved, whether the speed of their motion be finite or infinitely small (mere striving toward motion). Rather, it would be much more appropriate to call dead forces those, such as the original moving forces of dynamics, whereby matter acts on another, even when we abstract completely from its own inherent motion, and also even from its striving to move; by contrast, one could call living forces all mechanical moving forces, that is, those moving by inherent motion, without attending to the difference of speed, whose degree may even be infinitely small – if in fact these terms for dead and living forces still deserve to be retained.[40]

4: 539

Remark

In order to avoid prolixity we will merge the explanation of the previous three statements into one remark.

That the quantity of matter can only be thought as the aggregate of movables (external to one another), as the definition expresses it, is a remarkable and fundamental proposition of general mechanics. For it is thereby indicated that matter has no other magnitude than that consisting in the *aggregate* of manifold [elements] *external to one another*, and hence has no *degree* of moving force at a given speed that would be independent of this aggregate, and could be considered merely as intensive magnitude – which would be the case, however, if matter consisted of monads, whose reality in every relation must have a degree that can be larger or smaller, without depending on an aggregate of parts external to one another. As to the concept of mass in this same explication, one cannot take it in the customary way to be the same as that of quantity [of matter]. Fluid matters can act by their own inherent motion in a mass,[a] but they can also act as a fluid.[b] In the so-called water hammer, the impulsive water acts in a mass, that is, with all its parts together.[41] The same thing happens when water enclosed in a vessel presses down with its weight on the scale on which it stands. By contrast, the water of a millstream does not act on the paddle of an undershot waterwheel in a mass, that is, with all its parts impinging on this paddle together, but only one after the other.[42] Thus, if the quantity of matter, which is moved with a certain speed, and has moving force, is to be determined here, one must first look for the *water body*, that is, that quantity of matter which, if it acts in a mass with a certain speed (with its weight), can bring about the same effect. So we also customarily understand by the word *mass* the quantity of matter in a *solid body* (the vessel in which a fluid is contained can also stand proxy for its solidity). Finally, there is something peculiar in the Proposition together with its appended Note. According to the former the quantity of matter must be estimated by the quantity of motion at a given speed, but according to the latter the quantity of motion (of a body, for that of a point consists merely in the degree of speed) must, at the same speed, in turn be estimated by the quantity of the matter moved. And this seems to revolve in a circle, and to promise no determinate concept from either the one or the other. This alleged circle would be an actual one, if it were a reciprocal derivation of two identical concepts from one another. But it contains only the explication of a concept, on the one hand, and that of its application to experience, on the other. The quantity of the movable in space is the quantity of matter; but this quantity of matter (the aggregate of the movable) *manifests itself*[c] in experience only by the quantity of motion at equal speed (for example, by equilibrium).[d]

It is to be noted, further, that the quantity of matter is the *quantity of substance* in the movable, and thus not the magnitude of a certain quality of the movable (the repulsion or attraction that are cited in dynamics), and that the quantum of substance here means nothing else but the mere aggregate of the movable that constitutes matter. For only this aggregate

[a] *in Masse*
[b] *im Flusse*
[c] *beweiset sich*
[d] *Gleichgewicht*

of the moved can yield, at the same speed, a difference in the quantity of motion. But that the moving force a matter has *in its own inherent* motion alone manifests[a] the quantity of *substance*, rests on the concept of the latter as the ultimate *subject* in space (which is in turn no predicate of another) – which, for precisely this reason, can have no other magnitude than that of the aggregate of homogeneous [elements] external to one another. Now since the *inherent motion* of matter is a predicate that determines its subject (the movable), and indicates in a matter, as an aggregate of movables, a plurality of the subjects moved (at the same speed and in the same way), which is not the case for dynamical properties, whose magnitude can also be that of the action of a single subject (where an air particle, for example, can have more or less elasticity); it therefore becomes clear how the quantity of substance in a matter has to be estimated mechanically only, that is, by the quantity of its own inherent motion, and not dynamically, by that of the original moving forces.[43] Nevertheless, *original attraction*, as the cause of universal gravitation, can still yield a measure of the quantity of matter, and of its substance (as actually happens in the comparison of matters by weighing), even though a dynamical measure – namely, attractive force – seems here to be the basis, rather than the attracting matter's own inherent motion.[44] But since, in the case of this force, the action of a matter with all its parts is exerted immediately on all parts of another, and hence (at equal distances) is obviously proportional to the aggregate of the parts, the attracting body also thereby imparts to itself a speed of its own inherent motion (by the resistance of the attracted body), which, in like external circumstances, is exactly proportional to the aggregate of its parts; so the estimation here is still in fact mechanical, although only indirectly so.

4: 541

PROPOSITION 2

First Law of Mechanics. In all changes of corporeal nature the total quantity of matter remains the same, neither increased nor diminished.

Proof

(From general metaphysics we take as basis the proposition that in all changes of nature no substance either arises or perishes, and here it is only shown what substance shall be in matter.)[45] In every matter the movable in space is the ultimate subject of all accidents inhering in matter, and the aggregate of these movables, external to one another, is the quantity of substance. Hence the quantity of matter, with respect to its substance, is

4: 542

[a] *beweise*

nothing else but the aggregate of substances of which it consists. Therefore, the quantity of matter cannot be increased or diminished except in
such a way that new substance thereof arises or perishes. Now substance
never arises or perishes in any change of matter; so the quantity of matter
is also neither increased nor diminished thereby, but remains always the
same, and, indeed, as a whole – in such a way, that is, that somewhere
in the world it persists in the same quantity, although this or that matter can be increased or diminished, through addition or separation of
parts.

Remark

What is essential in this proof to the characterization of the *substance*
that is possible only in space, and in accordance with its condition, and
thus possible only as object of the *outer* senses, is that its quantity cannot
be increased or diminished without substance arising or perishing. For,
since all quantity of an object possible merely in space must consist of
parts external to one another, these, if they are real (something movable),
must therefore necessarily be substances. By contrast, that which is considered as object of inner sense can have a magnitude, as substance, which
does not consist of parts external to one another; and its parts, therefore, are
not substances; and hence their arising or perishing need not be the
arising or perishing of a substance; and their augmentation or diminution, then, is possible without violating the principle of the persistence
of substance. So *consciousness*, and thus the clarity of representations in
my soul, and therefore the faculty of consciousness, apperception, and
even, along with this, the very substance of the soul, have a *degree*, which
can be greater or smaller, without any substance at all needing to arise
or perish for this purpose. But since, from its gradual diminution, the
complete disappearance of the faculty of apperception would finally have
to result, the very substance of the soul would still be subject to a gradual
perishing, even if it were of a simple nature; for this disappearance of its
fundamental force could result, not by division (separation of substance
from a composite), but rather, as it were, by expiration[a] – and this, too,
not in a moment, but by a gradual waning of its degree, whatever the
cause of this might be.[46] The *I*, the general correlate of apperception,
and itself merely a thought, designates, as a mere prefix, a thing of undetermined meaning – namely, the subject of all predicates – without any
condition at all that would distinguish this representation of the subject
from that of a something in general: a substance, therefore, of which,
by this term, one has no concept of what it may be. By contrast, the
concept of a matter as substance is the concept of the movable *in space*.

4: 543

[a] *Erlöschen*

It is therefore no wonder if the persistence of substance can be proved of the latter, but not of the former, since, in the case of matter, it already results from its *concept* – namely, that it is the movable, which is possible only in space – that what has quantity therein contains a plurality of the real *external to one another*, and thus a plurality of substances; and hence the quantity of matter can be diminished only by division, which is not disappearance – and the latter would also be impossible in matter according to the law of constancy.*a* The thought *I*, by contrast, is *no concept* at all, but only inner perception, and so nothing at all can be inferred from it (except for the total distinctness of an object of inner sense from that which is thought merely as object of the outer senses) – including, in particular, the persistence of the soul as substance.

PROPOSITION 3

Second Law of Mechanics. Every change in matter has an external cause. (Every body persists in its state of rest or motion, in the same direction, and with the same speed, if it is not compelled by an external cause to leave this state.)

Proof

(From general metaphysics we take as basis the proposition that every change has a *cause*, and here it is only to be proved of matter that its change must always have an *external cause*.)[47] Matter, as mere object of the outer senses, has no other determinations except those of external relations in space, and therefore undergoes no change except by motion. With respect to the latter, as change of one motion into another, or of a motion into rest, or conversely, a cause must be found (by the principle of metaphysics). But this cause cannot be internal, for matter has no essentially internal determinations or grounds of determination. Hence every change in a matter is based on external causes (that is, a body persists, etc.).

Remark

4: 544

This mechanical law must alone be called the law of *inertia* (*lex inertiae*); the law of an equal and opposite reaction for every action cannot bear this name. For the latter says what matter does, but the former only what it does not do, which is more appropriate to the term *inertia*. The inertia of matter is, and means, nothing else than its *lifelessness*, as matter in itself. *Life* is the faculty of a *substance* to determine itself to act from an

a *nach dem Gesetze der Stetigkeit*

internal principle, of a *finite substance* to change, and of a *material substance* [to determine itself] to motion or rest, as change of its state. Now we know no other internal principle in a substance for changing its state except *desiring*, and no other internal activity at all except *thinking*, together with that which depends on it, the *feeling* of pleasure or displeasure, and *desire* or willing. But these actions and grounds of determination in no way belong to representations of the outer senses, and so neither [do they belong] to the determinations of matter as matter. Hence all matter, as such, is *lifeless*. The principle of inertia says this, and nothing more. If we seek the cause of any change of matter in life, we will have to seek it forthwith in another substance, different from matter, yet combined with it. For in natural knowledge we first have to be acquainted with the laws of matter, as such a thing, and to purge them from the admixture of all other active causes, before we connect them with these latter, in order properly to distinguish how, and in what manner, each of them acts in itself alone. The possibility of a proper natural science rests entirely and completely on the law of inertia (along with that of the persistence of substance). The opposite of this, and thus also the death of all natural philosophy, would be *hylozoism*. From this very same concept of inertia, as mere *lifelessness*, it follows at once that it does not mean a *positive striving* to conserve its state. Only living beings are called inert in this latter sense, because they have a representation of another state, which they abhor, and against which they exert their power.

PROPOSITION 4

Third mechanical law. In all communication of motion, action and reaction are always equal to one another.

Proof

(From general metaphysics we must borrow the proposition that all external action in the world is *interaction*. Here, in order to stay within the bounds of mechanics, it is only to be shown that this interaction (*actio mutua*) is at the same time *reaction* (*reactio*); but here I cannot wholly leave aside this metaphysical law of community, without detracting from the completeness of the insight.)[48] All *active* relations of matters *in space*, and all changes of these relations, insofar as they may be *causes* of certain actions or effects,[a] must always be represented as mutual; that is, because all change of matter is motion, we cannot think any motion of a body in relation to another *absolutely at rest* that is thereby also to be set in motion. Rather, the latter must be represented as only *relatively at rest*

4: 545

---

[a] *Wirkungen* [actions or effects]

with respect to the space that we relate it to, but as moved, together with this space, in the opposite direction, with precisely the same quantity of motion in absolute space as the moved body there has toward it. For the change of relation (and thus the motion) between the two is completely mutual; as much as the one body approaches every part of the other, by so much does the other approach every part of the first. And, since it is here a question, not of the empirical space surrounding the two bodies, but only of the line lying between them (in that they are considered simply in relation to one another, in accordance with the influence that the motion of the one can have on the change of state of the other, abstracting from all relation to the empirical space), their motion is therefore considered as determinable merely in absolute space, in which each of the two must have an equal share in the motion that is ascribed to one of them in relative space, in that there is no reason to ascribe more of this motion to one than to the other. On this basis,[a] the motion of a body A with respect to another body B at rest, in regard to which it can thereby be moving, is reduced to absolute space; that is, as a relation of acting causes merely related to one another, this motion is so considered that both have an equal share in the motion which, in the appearance, is ascribed to body A alone. And the only way this can happen is that the speed ascribed in relative space to body A alone is apportioned between A and B in inverse ratio to their masses – to A alone its speed in absolute space, and to B, *together with the relative space* in which it is at rest, its speed in the opposite direction. The same appearance of motion is thereby perfectly maintained, but the action in the community of the two bodies is constructed as follows.

4: 546

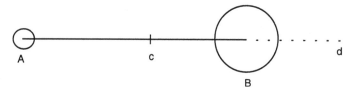

Let a body A be approaching the body B, with a speed = AB with respect to the relative space in which B is *at rest*. One divides the speed AB into two parts, Ac and Bc, which relate to one another inversely as the masses B and A, and imagines that A is moved with speed Ac in absolute space, while B is moved with speed Bc in the opposite direction, *together with the relative space*; thus the two motions are equal and opposite to one another, and, since they mutually cancel one another, the two bodies place themselves relative to one another, that is, in absolute space, at rest.[49] But now B was in motion, *together with the relative space*, with

---

[a] *Auf diesem Fuß*

speed Bc, in the direction BA exactly opposite to that of body A, namely, AB. Hence, if the motion of body B is canceled through the impact, the motion of the relative space is not thereby canceled as well. Therefore, *the relative space* moves after the impact, with respect to the two bodies A and B (now at rest in absolute space), in the direction BA with speed Bc, or, equivalently, both bodies move after the impact, with equal speed Bd = Bc, in the direction of the impacting body AB. But now, according to the preceding, the quantity of motion of body B in the direction and with the speed Bc, and hence also that in the direction Bd with the same speed, is equal to the quantity of motion of body A, with the speed and in the direction Ac. Therefore, the action or effect, that is, the motion Bd in relative space that body B receives through the impact, and thus also the action of body A with speed Ac, is always equal to the reaction Bc. Precisely the same law (as mathematical mechanics teaches) holds without modification, if, instead of an impact on a body at rest, one assumes an impact of the same body on one similarly moved. Moreover, the communication of motion through *impact* differs from that through *traction* only in the direction in which the matters resist one another in their motions. It follows, then, that *in all communication of motion* action and reaction are always equal to one another (that every impact can communicate the motion of one body to another only by means of an equal counter-impact, every pressure by means of an equal counter-pressure, and every traction only through an equal counter-traction).*

4: 547

4: 547

* In phoronomy, where the motion of a body was considered merely with respect to space, as change of relation *in space*, it was all the same whether I wanted to grant motion to the body in space, or an equal but opposite motion to the relative space instead; the two yielded entirely the same appearance. The quantity of motion of the space was merely the speed, and hence that of the body was likewise nothing but its speed (for which reason it could be considered as a mere movable point). But in mechanics, where a body is considered in motion relative to another, with regard to which, through its motion, it has a *causal relation* – namely, that of moving the body itself – in that it enters into community with [the body] either in its approach through the force of impenetrability or in its withdrawal through that of attraction, it is no longer the same whether I wish to ascribe a motion to one of these bodies, or an opposite motion to the space. For another concept of the quantity of motion now comes into play, namely, not that which is thought merely with respect to space, and consists only in the speed, but rather that whereby the quantity of substance (as moving cause) must be brought into the calculation at the same time; and here it is no longer arbitrary, but rather *necessary*, to assume each of the two bodies as moved, and, indeed, with equal quantity of motion in the opposite direction – but if one is relatively at rest with respect to the space, to ascribe the required motion to it, *together with the space*. For one body cannot act on the other through its own inherent motion, except either in approach by means of repulsive force, or in withdrawal by means of attraction. Now

Note 1

From this there follows a law of nature that is not unimportant for general mechanics: any body, however great its mass, must be *movable* by the impact of any other body, however small its mass or speed. For to the motion of A in the direction AB there necessarily corresponds an opposite and equal motion of B in the direction BA. The two motions cancel one another through their impact in absolute space. But the two bodies thereby acquire a speed Bd = Bc in the direction of the impacting body; hence body B is movable by any force of impact, however small.

Note 2

This, then, is the *mechanical law* of the equality of action and reaction, which rests on the fact that no *communication* of motion takes place, except insofar as we presuppose a *community* of these motions, and thus on the fact that no body impacts another that is at rest *relative to it*; rather, the second body is at rest relative to space, only insofar as it moves, *together with this space*, in the same amount, but in the opposite direction, with that motion which then falls to the first as its relative share, and together would originally yield the quantity of motion that we would ascribe to the first in absolute space. For no *motion* that is to be *moving* with respect to another body, can be *absolute*; but if it is relative with respect to the latter, then there is no relation in space that would not be mutual and equal. – There is, however, another law of the equality of action and reaction among matters – namely, a *dynamical law* – not insofar as one matter *communicates* its motion to another, but rather as it *imparts* this motion originally to it, and, at the same time, produces the same in itself through the latter's resistance. This can easily be shown in a similar way. For, if matter A exerts traction on[a] matter B, then it *compels* the latter to *approach* it, or, equivalently, it *resists* the force with which the latter might

since both forces always act mutually and equally in opposite directions, no body can act by means of them on another body through its motion, without just as much reaction from the other with the same quantity of motion. Hence no body can impart motion to an *absolutely resting* body through its motion; rather, the latter must be moved precisely with the same quantity of motion (together with the space) in the opposite direction as that which it is supposed to receive through the motion, and in the direction, of the first. – The reader will easily become aware that, despite the somewhat unaccustomed character of this mode of representing the communication of motion, it can nonetheless be set in the clearest light, if one does not shy away from the prolixity of the explanation.

[a] *zieht*

strive to *remove* itself. But since it is all the same whether B removes itself from A, or A from B, this resistance is, at the same time, a resistance exerted by body B against A, insofar as the latter may be striving to remove itself from the former; and so traction and counter-traction are equal to one another. In just the same way, if A repels matter B, then A resists the *approach* of B. But, since it is all the same whether B approaches A, or A approaches B, B also resists the approach of A to precisely the same extent; so pressure and counter-pressure are also always equal to one another.

4: 549

Remark 1

Such, then, is the construction of the communication of motion, which at the same time brings with it, as its necessary condition, the law of the equality of action and reaction. *Newton* by no means dared to prove this law *a priori*, and therefore appealed rather to *experience*. Others, for its sake, introduced into natural science a special force of matter, under the name, first introduced by *Kepler*, of a *force of inertia* (*vis inertiae*),[50] and thus they, too, derived it in principle from experience. Finally, still others posited in the concept a mere communication of motion, which they viewed as a gradual transfer of the motion of the one body into the other, whereby the mover would have to lose precisely as much motion as it imparts to the moved, until it impresses no more on the latter (that is, until it has already arrived at equality of speed with the latter in the same direction).* In this way, they eliminated in principle all reaction, that is, all actual reacting force of the impacted body on

---

* The equality of action with the (in this case falsely so-called) reaction comes out equally well, if, on the hypothesis of *transfusion* of motion from one body into another, one allows the moved body A to deliver its entire motion in an instant to the body at rest, so that it is itself at rest after the impact – this case was inevitable as soon as one thought both bodies as *absolutely hard* (which property must be distinguished from elasticity). But since this law of motion would agree neither with experience, nor with itself in application, no other remedy was known but to deny the existence of absolutely hard bodies, which amounted to admitting the contingency of this law, in that it was supposed to rest on a particular quality of matters that move one another. In our presentation of this law, by contrast, it is all the same whether one wishes to think the colliding bodies as absolutely hard or not. It is completely inconceivable to me, however, how the *transfusionists* of motion would explain, in their fashion, the motion of *elastic* bodies through impact. For here it is clear that the resting body does not, merely as resting, acquire motion lost by the impacting body, but that, in the collision, it exerts actual force on the latter in the opposite direction, so as to compress, as it were, a *spring* between the two, which requires just as much actual motion on its part (but in the opposite direction) as the moving body itself has need of for this purpose.

4: 549

the impacting one (which would be capable, for example, of tensing a spring). Moreover, they do not demonstrate what is properly meant in the law in question, and did not at all explain the *communication* of motion itself with regard to its possibility. For the term *transfer* of motion from one body to another explains nothing, and, if it is not meant to be taken literally (in violation of the principle that accidents do not wander from one substance to another),[51] as if motion were poured from one body into another like water from one glass into another, then we here have precisely the problem of how to make this possibility conceivable – where the explanation thereof in fact rests on precisely the same ground as that from which the law of the equality of action and reaction is derived. One cannot think at all how the motion of a body A must be necessarily combined with the motion of another body B, except by thinking forces in both that pertain to them (dynamically) prior to all motion (for example, repulsion), and now being able to demonstrate that the motion of body A, in its approach toward B, is necessarily combined with the approach of B toward A (and, if B is viewed as at rest, with its motion, *together with its space*, toward A), insofar as the bodies, with their (original) moving forces, are considered to be in motion merely relative to one another. This latter can be comprehended completely *a priori*, once it is seen that, whether body B is at rest or moved relative to the empirically knowable space, it still must be viewed, relative to body A, as necessarily moved, and, indeed, in the opposite direction. For otherwise no influence of B on the repulsive force of the two bodies would occur, and without this no mechanical action of the matters on one another – that is, no communication of motion by impact – is possible at all.

Remark 2

Regardless of the famous name of its creator, the terminology of inertial force (*vis inertiae*) must therefore be entirely banished from natural science, not only because it carries with it a contradiction in terms, nor even because the law of inertia (lifelessness) might thereby easily be confused with the law of reaction in every communicated motion, but primarily because the mistaken idea of those who are not properly acquainted with the mechanical laws is thereby maintained and even strengthened – according to which the reaction of bodies discussed under the name of inertial force would amount to a draining off, diminution, or eradication of the motion in the world; but the mere communication of motion would not be effected thereby, because the moving body would have to apply a part of its motion solely in overcoming the inertia of the one at rest (which would then be a pure loss), and could set the latter in motion only with the remaining part; but if none were left over, it would completely fail to move the latter by its impact, because of its great mass. But nothing can resist a motion except the opposite motion of another body, and certainly not its state of rest. Thus here the inertia of matter, that is, the mere incapacity for self-movement, is not the cause of a resistance. A special, entirely peculiar force merely to resist, without being able to move a body, under the name of an inertial force, would be a word without any meaning. The three laws of general mechanics could therefore more appropriately be named the laws of *self subsistence, inertia*, and *reaction of matters (lex subsistentiae, inertiae, et antagonismi) in all of their changes*. That these laws, and thus all Propositions of the present science, precisely answer to the categories of *substance, causality*, and *community*, insofar as these concepts are applied to matter, needs no further discussion.

GENERAL REMARK TO MECHANICS

The communication of motion occurs only by means of such moving forces as also inhere in a matter at rest (impenetrability and attraction). The action of a moving force on a body in an instant is its *solicitation*; the speed effected in the latter through solicitation, insofar as it can increase in equal proportion to the time, is the *moment* of acceleration.[a] (The moment of acceleration must therefore contain only an infinitely small speed, because otherwise the body would thereby attain an infinite speed in a given time, which is impossible; moreover, the possibility of *acceleration*[b] in general, by means of a continued moment thereof, rests on the law of inertia.) The solicitation of matter by expansive force (of compressed air bearing a weight, for example) occurs always with a finite speed, but the speed thereby impressed on (or extracted from) another body can only be infinitely small; for expansion is only a surface force, or, what is the same, the motion of an infinitely small quantum of matter, which therefore must occur with finite speed, in order to be equal to the motion of a body with finite mass and infinitely small speed (a weight). By contrast, attraction is a penetrating force, and with such a force a finite quantum of matter exerts moving force on another similarly finite quantum. The solicitation of attraction must therefore be

4: 552 infinitely small, because it is equal to the moment of acceleration (which must always be infinitely small) – which is not the case with repulsion, since an infinitely small part of matter is to impress a moment on a finite one. No attraction can be thought with a finite speed, without the matter having to *penetrate* itself by its own force of attraction. For the attraction that a finite quantity of matter exerts on a finite one, with a finite speed, must at all points of the compression be greater than any finite speed whereby the matter reacts through its impenetrability, but with only an

---

[a] *Moment der Acceleration*
[b] *Beschleunigung*

infinitely small part of the quantity of its matter. If the attraction is only a surface force, as we think cohesion to be, then the opposite of this would result. But it is impossible to think cohesion in this way if it is to be true attraction (and not mere external compression).

An absolutely hard body would be one whose parts attracted[a] one another so strongly that they could neither be separated, nor changed *in their situation* relative to one another, by any weight. Now since the parts of the matter of such a body would have to attract[b] one another with a moment of acceleration that would be infinite with respect to that of gravity, but finite with respect to that of the mass that is to be driven thereby, the resistance by means of impenetrability, as expansive force, since it always occurs with an infinitely small quantity of matter, would then have to take place with a more than finite speed of solicitation, that is, the matter would strive to expand with infinite speed, which is impossible. Hence an absolutely hard body, that is, one that would, on impact, *instantaneously* oppose a body moved at finite speed, with a resistance equal to the total force of that body, is impossible.[52] Consequently, by means of its impenetrability or cohesion, a matter attains instantaneously only an infinitely small resistance to the force of a body in finite motion. And from this there now follows the mechanical law of continuity (*lex continui mechanica*): namely, that in no body is the state of rest or motion, or the speed or direction of the latter, changed by impact instantaneously, but only in a certain time, through an infinite series of intermediate states, whose difference from one another is less than that between the first state and the last. A moved body that impacts on a matter is thus not brought into a state of rest by the latter's resistance all at once, but only through a continuous retardation; and one that was at rest is put into motion only through a continuous acceleration;[c] and it is changed from one degree of speed to another only in accordance with the same rule. In the same way, the direction of its motion is changed into one that makes an angle with it no otherwise than by means of all possible intermediate directions, that is, by means of motion in a curved line. (And, on similar grounds, this law can be extended also to the change of state of a body by attraction). This *lex continui* is based on the law of the inertia of matter, whereas the *metaphysical* law of continuity would have to be extended to all changes in general (inner as well as outer), and thus would have to be based on the mere *concept of a change in general*, as quantity, and on the generation thereof (which would necessarily proceed continuously in a certain time, as does time itself). This metaphysical law can therefore find no place here.[53]

4: 553

---

[a] *zögen*
[b] *ziehen*
[c] *Acceleration*

Fourth Chapter
Metaphysical foundations of phenomenology

EXPLICATION

Matter is the movable insofar as it, as such a thing, can be an object of experience.

Remark

Motion, like everything that is represented through the senses, is given only as appearance. For its representation to become experience, we require, too, that something be thought through the understanding – namely, besides the mode in which the representation inheres in the *subject*, also the determination of an *object* thereby. Hence the movable, as such a thing, becomes an object of experience, when a certain *object* (here a material thing) is thought as *determined* with respect to the *predicate* of motion. But motion is change of relation in space. There are thus always two correlates here, such that either, *first*, the change can be attributed in the appearance to one just as well as to the other, and either the *one* or the *other* can be said to be moved, because the two cases are equivalent;[a] or, *second*, one must be thought in experience as moved to the exclusion of the other; or, *third*, both must be necessarily represented through reason as equally moved. In the appearance, which contains nothing but the relation in the motion (with respect to its change), none of these determinations are contained. But if the movable, *as such a thing*, namely, with respect to its motion, is to be thought of as determined for the sake of a possible experience, it is necessary to indicate the conditions under which the object (matter) must be determined in one way or another by the predicate of motion. At issue here is not the transformation of semblance[b] into truth, but of appearance into experience; for, in the case of semblance, the understanding with its object-determining judgments is always in play, although it is in danger of taking the subjective for objective; in the appearance, however, no judgment of the understanding is to be met with at all[54] – which needs to be noted, not merely here, but in the whole of philosophy, because otherwise, when appearances are in

[a] *weil beides gleichgültig ist*
[b] *Schein*

question, and this term is taken to have the same meaning as semblance, one is always poorly understood.

PROPOSITION 1

The rectilinear motion of a matter with respect to an empirical space, as distinct from the opposite motion of the space, is a merely *possible* predicate. The same when thought in no relation at all to a matter external to it, that is, *as absolute motion*, is *impossible*.

Proof

Whether a body is said to be moved in a relative space, and the latter at rest, or whether, conversely, the latter shall be said to be moved, with the same speed in the opposite direction, with the former at rest, is not a dispute about what pertains to the object, but only about its relation to the subject, and belongs therefore to appearance and not to experience. For if the observer locates himself in that space as at rest, the body counts as moved for him; if he locates himself (at least in thought) in another space comprehending the first, relative to which the body is likewise at rest, then that relative space counts as moved. Thus in experience (a cognition that determines the object validly for all appearances) there is no difference at all between the motion of the body in the relative space, and the body being at rest in absolute space, together with an equal and opposite motion of the relative space. Now the representation of an object through one of two predicates, which are equally valid with respect to the object, and differ from one another only in regard to the subject and its mode of representation, is not a determination in accordance with a *disjunctive judgement*, but merely a choice in accordance with an *alternative judgement*. (In the former, of two *objectively* opposed predicates, one is assumed to the exclusion of the other for the determination of the object; in the latter, of two judgments objectively equivalent, yet subjectively opposed to one another, one is assumed for the determination of the object without excluding its opposite – and thus by mere choice.)* This means that through the concept of motion, as object of experience, it is in itself undetermined, and therefore equivalent, whether a body be represented as moved in the relative space, or the latter with respect to the former. Now that which is in itself undetermined with respect to two opposed predicates is to that extent *merely possible*. Hence the rectilinear motion of a matter in empirical space, as distinct from the equal opposite motion of the space, is a

4: 556

---

* More will be said about this distinction between disjunctive and alternative opposition in the General Remark to this Chapter.

merely possible predicate in experience – which was the first [thing to be proved].

Since, moreover, a relation, and thus also a change thereof, that is, motion, can be an object of experience only insofar as both correlates are objects of experience, whereas the pure space that is also called absolute space, in contrast to relative (empirical) space, is no object of experience, and in general[a] is nothing, a rectilinear motion without reference to anything empirical, that is, absolute motion, is completely impossible – which was the second [thing to be proved].

Remark

This Proposition determines the modality of motion with respect to *phoronomy*.

PROPOSITION 2

4: 557

The circular motion of a matter, as distinct from the opposite motion of the space, is an *actual* predicate of this matter; by contrast, the opposite motion of a relative space, assumed instead of the motion of the body, is no actual motion of the latter, but, if taken to be such, is mere semblance.

Proof

Circular motion (like all curvilinear motion) is a continuous change of rectilinear motion, and, since the latter is itself a continuous change of relation with respect to the external space, circular motion is a change of a change in these external relations in space, and is thus a continuous arising of new motions. Now since, according to the law of inertia, a motion, insofar as it arises, must have an external cause, while the body, at every point on this circle (according to precisely the same law), is striving, for its own part, to proceed in the straight line tangent to the circle, which motion acts in opposition to this external cause, it follows that every body in circular motion manifests,[b] by its motion, a moving force. But the motion of the space, as distinct from that of the body, is merely *phoronomic*, and has no moving force. Thus the judgment that here either the body is moved, or the space is moved in the opposite direction, is a *disjunctive* judgment, whereby, if one of the terms (namely, the motion of the body) is posited, the other, (namely, that of the space) is excluded. Thus the circular motion of a body, as distinct from that of

[a] *überall*
[b] *beweiset*

262

the space, is an *actual* motion, so that the latter, even though it agrees with the former according to the appearance, nevertheless contradicts it in the context of all appearances, that is, of a possible experience, and so is nothing but mere semblance.

Remark

This Proposition determines the modality of motion with respect to *dynamics*; for a motion that cannot take place without the influence of a continuously acting external moving force manifests,[a] directly or indirectly, originally moving forces of matter, whether of attraction or repulsion. – Moreover, *Newton's* Scholium to the Definitions he has prefixed to his *Principia* may be consulted on this subject, toward the end, where it becomes clear that the circular motion of two bodies around a common central point (and thus also the axial rotation of the earth) can still be known by experience even in empty space, and thus without any empirically possible comparison *with an external space*;[55] so that a motion, therefore, which is a change of external relations in space, can be empirically given, even though this space is not itself empirically given, and is no object of experience. This is a paradox that deserves to be solved.

4: 558

PROPOSITION 3

In every motion of a body, whereby it is moving relative to another, an opposite and equal motion of the latter is *necessary*.

Proof

According to the Third Law of Mechanics (Proposition 4), the communication of motion of bodies is possible only by the community of their original moving forces, and the latter only by mutually opposite and equal motion. The motion of both is therefore actual. But since the actuality of this motion does not rest (as in the second Proposition) on the influence of external forces, but follows immediately and unavoidably from the concept of the relation of the *moved* in space to anything else *movable* thereby, the motion of the latter is *necessary*.

Remark

This Proposition determines the modality of motion with respect to mechanics. – Moreover, it is obvious that these three Propositions

---

[a] *beweiset*

determine the motion of matter with respect to its *possibility*, *actuality*, and *necessity*, and thus with respect to all three categories of *modality*.

GENERAL REMARK TO PHENOMENOLOGY

Thus here appear three concepts, whose use in general natural science is unavoidable, and whose precise determination is therefore necessary, although not that easy or comprehensible – namely, [first,] the concept

4: 559 of *motion in relative* (movable) *space*, second, that of *motion in absolute* (immovable) *space*, and third, that of *relative motion* in general, as distinct from absolute motion. The concept of absolute space is the basis for all of them. But how do we arrive at this peculiar concept, and what underlies the necessity of its use?

It cannot be an object of experience, for space without matter is no object of perception, and yet it is a necessary concept of reason, and thus nothing more than a mere *idea*. For in order that motion may be given, even merely as appearance, an empirical representation of space is required, with respect to which the movable is to change its relation; but the space that is to be perceived must be material, and thus itself movable, in accordance with the concept of a matter in general. Now, to think of it as moved, one may think it only as contained in a space of greater extent, and take the latter to be at rest. But the same can be done with the latter, with respect to a still further extended space, and so on to infinity, without ever arriving by experience at an immovable (immaterial) space, with respect to which either motion or rest might absolutely[a] be attributed to any matter. Rather, the concept of these relational determinations will have to be continually revised, according to the way that we will consider the movable in relation to one or another of these spaces. Now since the condition for regarding something as at rest or moved is always conditioned in turn, *ad infinitum*, in relative space, it becomes clear, *first*, that all motion or rest can be relative only and never absolute, that is, that matter can be thought as moved or at rest solely in relation to matter, and never with respect to mere space without matter, so that absolute motion, thought without any relation of one matter to another, is completely impossible; and *second*, for precisely this reason, that no concept of motion or rest valid *for all appearance* is possible in relative space. Rather, one must think a space in which the latter can itself be thought as moved, but which depends for its determination on no further empirical space, and thus is not conditioned in turn – that is, an absolute space to which all relative motions can be referred, in which everything empirical is movable, precisely so that in it all motion

[a] *schlechthin*

264

of material things^a may count as merely relative with respect to one another, as alternatively-mutual,* but none as absolute motion or rest (where, while one is said to be moved, the other, in relation to which it is moved, is nonetheless represented as absolutely^b at rest). Absolute space is therefore necessary, not as a concept of an actual object, but rather as an idea, which is to serve as a rule for considering all motion therein merely as relative; and all motion and rest must be reduced to absolute space, if the appearance thereof is to be transformed into a determinate concept of experience (which unites all appearances).

4: 560

Thus the rectilinear motion of a body in relative space is reduced to absolute space, when I think the body as in itself at rest, but this space as moved in the opposite direction in absolute space (which is not apprehended by the senses), and when I think this representation as that which yields precisely the same appearance, whereby all possible appearances of rectilinear motions that a body may have at the same time are reduced to the concept of experience which unites them all, namely, that of merely relative motion and rest.

Because *circular motion*, according to the second Proposition, can be given as actual motion in experience, even without reference to the external empirically given space, it indeed seems to be absolute motion. For relative motion with respect to the external space (for example, the axial rotation of the earth relative to the stars of the heavens) is an *appearance*,

---

* In logic the *either-or* always signifies a *disjunctive* judgment, where, if the one is true, the other must be false. For example, a body is *either* moved *or* not moved, that is, at rest. For here [in logic] one speaks solely of the relation of the cognition to the object. In the doctrine of appearance, where it is a matter of the relation to the subject, so as to determine the relation to the object therefrom, the situation is different. For here the proposition that the body is either moved and the space at rest, or conversely, is not a disjunctive proposition in an objective relation, but only in a subjective one, and the two judgments contained therein are valid *alternatively*. In precisely the same phenomenology, where the motion is considered, not merely phoronomically, but rather dynamically, the disjunctive proposition is instead to be taken in an *objective* meaning; that is, I cannot assume, in place of the rotation of a body, a state of rest of the latter and the opposite motion of the space instead. But wherever the motion is considered *mechanically* (as when a body approaches another seemingly at rest), then the formally disjunctive judgment must be used *distributively* with respect to the object, so that the motion must not be attributed *either* to one *or* to the other, but rather an equal share of it to each. This distinction among *alternative*, *disjunctive*, and *distributive* determinations of a concept with respect to opposing predicates has its importance, but cannot be further discussed here.

4: 559

4: 560

---

^{a} *Materiellen*
^{b} *schlechthin*

in place of which the opposite motion of this space (of the heavens) in the same time can be supposed as completely equivalent to the former; but, according to the Proposition in question, it certainly may not be so substituted in experience. Hence, that rotation is not to be represented as externally relative, which sounds as if this kind of motion is to be taken as absolute.

But it should be noted that it is here a question of true (actual) *motion*, which does not, however, *appear* as such, so that, if one wished to evaluate it merely in accordance with empirical relations to space, it could be taken for *rest*; it is a question, that is, of *true motion* as distinct from *semblance*, but not of absolute motion in contrast to relative. Thus, circular motion, although it in fact exhibits no change of place in the appearance, that is, no phoronomic change in the relations of the moved body *to* (empirical) *space*, exhibits nonetheless a continuous dynamical change, demonstrable through experience, in the relations of matter *within its space*, for example, a continual diminution of attraction in virtue of a striving to escape, as an action or effect[a] of the circular motion, and thereby assuredly indicates its difference from semblance. For example, one may represent to oneself the earth as rotating on its axis in infinite empty space, and also verify this motion by experience, even though neither the relation of the earth's parts among one another, nor to the space outside it, is changed phoronomically, that is, in the appearance. For, with respect to the first, as empirical space, nothing changes its position in or on the earth; and, as regards the second, which is completely empty, no externally changed relation, and thus no appearance of a motion, can take place anywhere. But if I represent to myself a deep hole descending to the center of the earth, and I let a stone fall into it, I find, however, that the falling stone deviates from its perpendicular direction continuously, and, in fact, from west to east, even though gravity, at all distances from the center of the earth, is always directed toward it, and I conclude, therefore, that the earth is rotating on its axis from west to east.[b] Or, if I also remove the stone further out from the surface of the earth, and it does not remain over the same point of the surface, but moves away from it from east to west,[56] then I will infer to the very same previously mentioned axial rotation of the earth, and both observations will be sufficient to prove the actuality of this motion. The change of relation to the external space (the starry heavens) does not suffice for this, since it is mere appearance, which may proceed from two in fact opposing grounds, and is not a cognition derived from the explanatory ground of all appearances of this change, that is, experience. But that this motion, even though it is no change of relation to the empirical space, is nevertheless not absolute

[a] *Wirkung* [action or effect]
[b] *von Abend gegen Morgen*

motion, but rather a continuous change in the relations of matters to one another, which, although represented in absolute space, is thus actually only relative, and, for just that reason, is true motion – this rests on the representation of the mutual and continuous *withdrawal* of any part of the earth (outside the axis) from any other part lying diametrically opposite to it at the same distance from the center. For this motion is actual in absolute space, in that the reduction of the distance in question, which gravity by itself would induce in the body, is thereby continuously made up, and, in fact, without any dynamical repulsive cause (as may be seen from the example chosen by Newton in the *Principia*, page 10 of the 1714 edition);* hence it is made up through actual motion, which relates, however, to the space inside of the moved matter (namely, its center), and not to that outside it.[57]

4: 562

In the case of the *third Proposition*, to show the truth of the mutually opposed and equal motions of the two bodies, even without reference to the empirical space, we do not even need the active dynamical influences, given through experience, that are required in the second case (gravity or a tensed cord). Rather, the mere dynamical possibility of such an influence, as a property of matter (repulsion or attraction), leads by itself, and from mere concepts of a relative motion, from the motion of one body to the simultaneous equal and opposite motion of the other, when the latter is considered in absolute space, that is, in accordance with truth. Hence like everything sufficiently provable from mere concepts, this is a law of an absolutely necessary counter-motion.

There is thus no absolute motion, even when a body in empty space is thought as moved with respect to another; their motion here is not considered relative to the space surrounding them, but only to the space between them, which, considered as absolute space, alone determines their external relations to one another, and is in turn only relative. Absolute motion would thus be only that which pertained to a body without relation to any other matter. Only the rectilinear motion of the *cosmos*,[a] that is, the system of all matter, would be such a motion. For if, outside

---

* There he says: "It is indeed a matter of great difficulty to discover, and effectually to distinguish, the true motions of particular bodies from the apparent; because the parts of that immovable space, in which these motions are performed, do by no means come under the observation of our senses. Yet the thing is not altogether desperate." He then lets two spheres connected by a cord revolve around their common center of gravity in empty space, and shows how the actuality of their motion, together with its direction, can nonetheless be discovered by means of experience. I have attempted to show this also in the case of the earth moved around its axis, in somewhat altered circumstances.

[a] *Weltganzen*

a matter, there were any other at all, even separated from it by empty space, then the motion would already be relative. For this reason, any proof of a law of motion, which amounts to showing that its opposite would have to result in a rectilinear motion of the entire cosmic system,[a] is an apodictic proof of its truth, simply because absolute motion would then follow, which is utterly impossible. Such is the law of *antagonism* in all community of matter through motion. For any deviation from it would shift the common center of gravity of all matter, and thus the entire cosmic system, from its place – which would not happen, however, if one wanted to imagine this system as rotating on its axis. Hence it is always possible to think such a motion, although to suppose it would, so far as one can see, be entirely without any conceivable use.

To the various concepts of motion and moving forces there also correspond the various concepts of *empty space*. Empty space in the *phoronomical* sense, which is also called absolute space, should not properly be called an empty space; for it is only the idea of a space, in which I abstract from all particular matter that makes it an object of experience, in order to think therein the material space, or any other empirical space, as movable, and thereby to think of motion, not merely in a one-sided fashion as absolute, but always mutually, as a merely relative predicate. It is therefore nothing at all that belongs to the existence of things, but merely to the determination of concepts, and to this extent no empty space *exists*. Empty space in the *dynamical* sense is that which is not filled, that is, in which no other movable resists the penetration of a movable, and thus no repulsive force acts; it can either be empty space *within* the world (*vacuum mundanum*) or, if the latter is represented as bounded, empty space *outside* the world (*vacuum extramundanum*). The former, too, can be represented either as dispersed (*vacuum disseminatum*, which constitutes only a part of the volume of matter), or as accumulated empty space (*vacuum coacervatum*, which separates bodies, for example, the heavenly bodies, from one another). This latter distinction is certainly not an essential one, since it rests only on a difference in the locations assigned to empty space within the world, but is still employed for various purposes: the first, to derive specific differences in density, and the second, to derive the possibility of a motion in the universe free from all external resistance. That it is not *necessary* to assume empty space for the *first purpose* has already been shown in the General Remark to Dynamics; but that it is *impossible* can in no way be proved from its concept alone, in accordance with the principle of noncontradiction. Nevertheless, even if no merely logical reason for rejecting this kind of empty space were to be found here, there could still be a more general

---

[a] *Weltgebäude*

physical reason for expelling it from the doctrine of nature – that of the possibility of the composition of a matter in general, if only this were better understood. For if the *attraction* assumed in order to explain the cohesion of matter should be only apparent, not true attraction, and were merely the effect, say, of a *compression* by external matter (the aether) distributed everywhere in the universe, which is itself brought to this pressure only through a universal and original attraction, namely, gravitation (a view that is supported by several reasons), then empty space within matter, although not logically impossible, would still be so dynamically, and thus physically, since any matter would expand of itself into the empty spaces assumed within it (since nothing resists its expansive force here), and would always keep them filled. An empty space *outside the world*, understood as the totality of preeminently attractive matters (the large heavenly bodies), would be impossible for precisely the same reasons, since in accordance with their mass, as the distance from them increases, the attractive force on the aether (which encloses all these bodies, and, driven by that force, conserves them in their density by compression) decreases in inverse proportion, so that the latter would itself only decrease indefinitely in density, but nowhere leave space completely empty. It should not surprise anyone, however, that this refutation of empty space proceeds entirely hypothetically, for the assertion of empty space fares no better. Those who venture to settle this disputed question dogmatically, whether for or against, rely in the end on plainly metaphysical presuppositions, as can be seen from the Dynamics – and here it was necessary at least to show that these can do nothing at all to resolve the problem. As for empty space in the third, or *mechanical sense*, it is the emptiness accumulated within the cosmos to provide the heavenly bodies with free motion. It is easy to see that the possibility or impossibility of this does not rest on metaphysical grounds, but on the mystery of nature, difficult to unravel, as to how matter sets limits to its own expansive force. Nevertheless, if one grants what was said in the General Remark to Dynamics concerning the possibility of an ever-increasing expansion of specifically different materials, at the same quantity of matter (in accordance with their weight), it may well be unnecessary to suppose an empty space for the free and enduring motion of the heavenly bodies; since even in spaces completely filled, the resistance can still be thought as small as one likes.

4: 564

And so ends the metaphysical doctrine of body with the *empty*, and therefore the inconceivable, wherein it shares the same fate as all other attempts of reason, when it strives after the first grounds of things in a retreat to principles – where, since its very nature entails that it can never conceive anything, except insofar as it is determined under given conditions, and since it can therefore neither come to a halt at the conditioned, nor make the unconditioned comprehensible, nothing is left to it, when thirst for knowledge invites it to comprehend the absolute totality of all conditions, but to turn away from the objects to itself, so as to explore and determine, not the ultimate limits of things, but rather the ultimate limits of its own unaided powers.

On a discovery whereby any new critique
of pure reason is to be made superfluous
by an older one

Translator's introduction

Kant's short treatise, *Über eine Entdeckung, nach der alle neue Kritik der reinen Vernunft durch eine ältere entbehrlich gemacht werden soll* (*On a Discovery whereby Any New Critique of Pure Reason Is to Be Made Superfluous by an Older One*, henceforth to be referred to as *On a Discovery*) appeared in April, 1790, simultaneously with the *Critique of Judgment*, to which it alludes in its closing pages. It is a polemical piece, containing Kant's response to the critique of his philosophy launched by the Wolffian philosopher and professor at Halle, Johann August Eberhard (1739–1809).

Eberhard's opposition to Kant's philosophy dates back to the first appearance of the *Critique of Pure Reason* (1781), and he continually criticized it in his lectures. With the publication of the second edition in 1787, however, he evidently felt the need to make his opposition known to a wider public. Thus, together with other Wolffians, most notably J. G. Mass and J. E. Schwab, he founded in 1788 a journal, the *Philosophisches Magazin*, the general purpose of which was to provide an organ for a full-scale attack on the Kantian philosophy from the standpoint of the rationalism of Leibniz and Wolff. More specifically, its intent was to counter the *Allgemeine Literatur-Zeitung*, a journal which had been founded in Jena in 1785 by Kant's friend and ally J. G. Schultz for the purpose of defending and promulgating the critical philosophy. In order to gain a wider public, however, Eberhard's journal did not concern itself exclusively with Kant and his defenders, but devoted at least some space in each issue to other topics, including some of a nonphilosophical nature.

The first volume of the *Philosophisches Magazin* appeared in four issues in 1788 and 1789. It unabashedly affirmed the superiority of the Leibnizian over the Kantian philosophy, claiming that whatever is true in Kant is already found in Leibniz, and that wherever Kant differs from Leibniz, he is wrong. This was immediately rebutted in the *Allgemeine Literatur-Zeitung*, with reviews by August Wilhelm Rehberg and Karl Leonard Reinhold, the latter making use of material provided by Kant. Eberhard and his collaborators responded to these reviews and raised some fresh objections in the second volume of the *Philosophisches Magazin*, which appeared in 1790. This was followed by two more volumes of the journal in 1791 and 1792, which were addressed largely to the continuing defense of the critical philosophy issuing from the Kantian camp, and include a response by Eberhard to the objections raised by Kant in his essay. Although there are some interesting further criticisms of Kant's philosophy of mathematics, especially as interpreted by Schultz, much of the discussion consists of a rehash of previous arguments. Finally, the *Philosophisches Magazin* was succeeded by the *Philosophisches Archiv*, which appeared in two volumes in 1793 and 1794. Here Eberhard and his followers continued their attack on Kant, engaged in a counterattack on Schultz, who mounted an extended critique of the Eberhardian position in the second part of his *Prüfung der Kantischen Critik der reinen Vernunft* (*Examination of the Kantian Critique of Pure Reason*) (1792), and gradually turned their attention to Reinhold, who by that time had set out on a path of his own.

It appears that Kant was first informed of Eberhard's activities against him by his correspondent Ludwig Heinrich Jakob. Writing from Halle, Eberhard's home base, on July 17, 1786, Jakob tells Kant of his own efforts to clarify and popularize the critical philosophy, and as evidence of the need for this he cites Eberhard's claim that the *Critique of Pure Reason* is incomprehensible and his consequent effort to discourage his students from reading it (Ak 10:459). This news was confirmed by Kant's friend Johann Christoph Berens, who, writing from Berlin on December 5, 1787, reports to Kant on the reception of the *Critique* in the various parts of Germany he has visited, and notes that "Professor Eberhard fears the moral consequences of your teaching, and feels that you should have followed the old views" (Ak 10:507–8).

Kant next learned of Eberhard's activities against him in another letter from Jakob. Writing again from Halle, on February 28, 1789, he tells Kant that he has just received the third issue of the first volume of the *Philosophisches Magazin*, and notes that "Eberhard speaks therein almost entirely alone, and the entire issue is directed against the *Critique*." But he then goes on to add: "The reasoning therein is for the most part correct, and the bulk of the propositions which it affirms are true and may be justified. The strangest thing, however, is the assertion that the *Critique* maintains the opposite" (Ak 11:5).

A more realistic assessment of the situation was provided shortly afterward by Reinhold, who, writing on April 9, 1789, notifies Kant of the disastrous effect on public opinion already created by Eberhard's misrepresentations of the critical philosophy. He asserts that this misrepresentation must not be allowed to go unanswered, but requests that Kant not waste his precious time and energy by entering personally into the controversy. Instead, he recommends that Kant make a simple and direct statement to the effect that Eberhard and his followers have not correctly interpreted the teachings of the *Critique*, and thus that their criticisms are beside the point. He also asks Kant to note briefly some of the principal areas of misunderstanding in his next letter, so that he can make use of them in a published rebuttal (Ak 11:17–18).

Kant did not reply to Reinhold until May 12 (Ak 11:33–40), excusing his delay on the grounds that he had to go to the public library to find the first three issues of Eberhard's journal. It thus seems clear that until then Kant did not have any firsthand knowledge of Eberhard's criticisms, but was relying entirely on information provided by his correspondents. But after actually having read Eberhard's criticisms for the first time, he remarks bitterly to Reinhold: "*That Mr. Eberhard, like many others, has not understood me, is the least one can say* (for that could be partly my fault); but, as I shall show you in the following remarks, he actually sets out to misunderstand me and to make me incomprehensible" (Ak 11:33). Kant then proceeds to discuss certain specific passages from Eberhard, largely dealing with the latter's formulation and interpretation of the analytic–synthetic distinction. This discussion later became the basis for the second part of *On a Discovery*, which is concerned precisely with this distinction.

This is followed one week later by a second letter to Reinhold (Ak 11: 40–8), in which Kant develops in some detail the criticisms suggested in the first letter, reiterates his convictions concerning Eberhard's lack of honesty, and gives Reinhold leave to use these remarks in whatever manner he sees fit. But pleading the "infirmities of age" and his labors on the *Critique of Judgment*, he still declines to engage personally in the controversy.

Following Kant's instructions, Reinhold replied on June 14 that he planned to include the material supplied to him by Kant in a review of the third issue of Eberhard's journal. He also expresses an intention, however, initially to make use only of the material from Kant's first letter, and to "keep the rest in reserve," in anticipation of the inevitable counterattack by the Eberhardian forces (Ak 11:59–63).

It was apparently at about this time that Kant changed his mind concerning the decision not to enter directly into the controversy. Thus, in his letter of September 21, he informs Reinhold that he is in fact preparing a short essay against Eberhard, which he expects to finish that Michaelmas. At the same time, he also asks Reinhold to make sure that a copy of the first issue of the second volume of the *Philosophisches Magazin*, which had already appeared but, as usual, was not yet available in Königsberg, be sent to him from Berlin (Ak 11:88–9).

Once again, however, Kant changed his mind. Thus, we find him writing to Reinhold on December 1, reporting favorably on his initial reading of the latter's new work, *Versuch einer neuen Theorie des menschlichen Vorstellungsvermögens* (*Essay towards a new Theory of the Human Faculty of Representation*); again lamenting the difficulties of old age, which he now offers as an excuse for not giving Reinhold's work more careful attention; and notifying him that he is preparing a substantial work on Eberhard, which he expects to send him by Easter, together with the long-awaited

Critique of Judgment (Ak 11:111–12). This work turned out to be *On a Discovery*; so it seems that in the space of less than three months, the initially projected brief essay had assumed the proportions of a small book. Moreover, for once Kant's estimation of the time required to complete a project turned out to be accurate, since the work was published, along with the *Critique of Judgment*, on April 20, 1790.

Because of its polemical intent, *On a Discovery* basically follows the order of argumentation used by Eberhard in the first issue of the *Philosophisches Magazin*. Thus, the work is divided into two main parts, corresponding to the "two acts" of which Kant believed the Eberhardian "play" was composed. The work concludes, however, with a brief and somewhat ironical discussion of Leibniz, the intent of which is to suggest that, properly construed, the Leibnizian philosophy is really in essential agreement with the *Critique*. It is in this spirit that Kant suggests at the end of the work that "the *Critique of Pure Reason* might well be the true apology for Leibniz" (Ak 8:250).

The first part deals with the alleged objective reality of those concepts to which no corresponding sensory intuition can be given, that is, with "ideas of reason," in Kant's terminology. It features analyses of the principle of sufficient reason and the concept of the simple. As a defender of the rationalism of Leibniz and Wolff against the *Critique*'s insistence on the limitation of knowledge to objects of possible experience, Eberhard had claimed, following Baumgarten, to have demonstrated the "transcendental validity" of the principle of sufficient reason. Similarly, he claimed to have established the validity, that is, the objective reality, of simple, nonsensible beings (Leibnizian monads), which supposedly underlie phenomena. In both cases his aim was to show that, contrary to the doctrine of the *Critique*, it is possible to attain demonstrative knowledge of a reality that transcends sensible experience.

Kant responds by accusing Eberhard of a combination of misunderstanding the basic teachings of the *Critique*, fallacious reasoning, and deliberate obfuscation. Since Eberhard's purported demonstration of the principle of sufficient reason involves the attempt to derive it from the principle of contradiction, Kant claims that Eberhard is in effect treating it merely as a logical principle governing propositions, even though his intent is to establish it as a real (i.e., metaphysical) principle governing the relation between things. Moreover, he suggests that Eberhard attempts to hide this from the reader by deliberately choosing vague formulations, which lie ambiguously between the two quite different senses of the principle.

Eberhard's attempt to demonstrate the reality of simple, nonsensible beings as the ultimate grounds or constituents of phenomena is treated in a similar fashion. Basically, Kant accuses Eberhard of trading on an ambiguity in the concept of the nonsensible, which reflects his systematic misrepresentation of the Kantian theory of sensibility in its distinction from the Leibnizian theory. For Kant, human sensibility contains positive, *a priori* forms (space and time) through which everything given in intuition and, therefore, everything cognizable by the human intellect is conditioned. According to this position, then, the "nonsensible" refers to something merely thought (a purely intelligible entity or noumenon), which, since it cannot be intuited, can never become an object of cognition. Consequently, for Kant, the difference between the sensible and the nonsensible is one of kind or, as he also terms it, "transcendental." For Leibniz, by contrast, sensibility is thought of primarily as the source of the obscurity of our representations. Thus, the difference between the sensible and the nonsensible is a matter of degree (the senses providing obscure or confused representations of what the intellect grasps clearly and distinctly). But, Kant argues, in his attempt to demonstrate the reality of simple, nonsensible beings, Eberhard glosses over the distinction between these two accounts of sensibility, first using the Leibnizian theory to infer the nonsensible from the sensible, and then claiming to have provided a demonstration that satisfies the requirement of the Kantian theory. And, once again, Kant treats this as a deliberate obfuscation on Eberhard's part.

As already noted, the second part of *On a Discovery* is devoted essentially to the discussion and defense of the analytic–synthetic distinction. Consequently, it is the portion of the text that holds the greatest interest for the contemporary reader. In his essay "On the Distinction of Judgments into Analytic and Synthetic," which caught Kant's attention more than perhaps anything else in the *Philosophisches Magazin*, Eberhard challenged the clarity, originality, and significance of this famous Kantian distinction. In his attack, Eberhard focuses on the formulation in the Introduction to the *Critique*, where Kant distinguishes between merely explicative (analytic) judgments, which "add nothing through the predicate to the concept of the subject," and genuinely ampliative (synthetic) judgments, which "add to the concept of the subject a predicate which has not been in any wise thought in it" (A 7/B 10–11). Interpreting this in terms of the Leibnizian theory of predication (according to which the predicate in every true proposition is contained in the concept of the subject, either explicitly or implicitly), Eberhard suggests, by way of clarification, that the predicate in what Kant terms an analytic judgment must be either the essence of the subject or one of its essential parts. Correlatively, Kantian synthetic judgments on Eberhard's reformulation turn out to be those in which the predicate is either an attribute of the subject (a property that is not part of the essence but is grounded therein according to the principle of sufficient reason), an accident, or a relation. The former constitute the class of synthetic *a priori* judgments, while the latter two are synthetic *a posteriori*. Having thus "clarified" the Kantian distinction, Eberhard has no difficulty denying its originality, since (on his reading) it amounts to nothing more than the distinction between identical and nonidentical judgments, which had already been clearly formulated by Wolff and Baumgarten. And since, so construed, the distinction does not entail any restriction of synthetic *a priori* judgments to objects of possible experience, Eberhard is able to deny its significance for metaphysics as well.

Although Kant's response to this multifaceted line of objection does not contain anything radically new, it does provide important clarifications and amplifications of the familiar formulations of the distinction in the Introduction to the *Critique* and the *Prolegomena*. Of particular interest in this regard is Kant's emphasis on the fact that, in spite of the impression created by these familiar formulations, the distinction is not (as Eberhard took it to be) a purely logical one having to do merely with the relation between subject and predicate concepts in a judgment. It concerns instead the epistemic grounds for their connection, that is, the basis for the predication of a concept of an object in a judgment. Either the basis is purely logical (the principle of noncontradiction), in which case the judgment is analytic, regardless of whether the predicate is part of the essence or an attribute of the subject; or it is something extra-logical or "real," that is, a sensory intuition, in which case the judgment is synthetic. This way of formulating the distinction has the virtue of bringing out the connection between synthetic judgments and intuition and between synthetic judgments *a priori* and pure intuition, which is a central theme for Kant. In addition, it helps to underscore both the originality of the distinction and its relevance to metaphysics.

Beyond its clarification of the analytic–synthetic distinction, *On a Discovery* is perhaps most valuable for the light it sheds on Kant's understanding of the relationship between his critical philosophy and the philosophy of Leibniz. Kant's motivation was no doubt largely to underscore Eberhard's misunderstanding and misrepresentation of the Leibnizian philosophy as well as of his own; but the result is a more balanced and appreciative account of his relationship to his great predecessor than is to be found in his earlier discussions of the topic, including that in the *Critique*.

The present translation is a complete revision of my original translation in *The Kant–Eberhard Controversy*, which was the first English version of *On a Discovery*. In my revision, I was greatly assisted by my coeditor, Peter Heath, who saved me from any number of errors, and whose sage advice on stylistic and grammatical points I have almost always followed. As in the original version, I have also consulted the French translation by Roger Kempf (*Réponse à Eberhard*, Paris: Librairie Philosophique J. Vrin, 1959). The translation is based on the text in volume 8 of the Akademie Edition of *Kants gesammelte Schriften*, and the page numbers from that edition are given in the margins.

BIBLIOGRAPHY

ALLISON, HENRY E. *The Kant–Eberhard Controversy*, Baltimore and London: The Johns Hopkins University Press, 1973.
"The Originality of Kant's Distinction between Analytic and Synthetic Judgments," in *The Philosophy of Immanuel Kant*, ed. Richard Kennington, Washington, D.C.: The Catholic University of America Press, 1985, pp. 15–38.

BECK, LEWIS WHITE. "Kant's Theory of Definition," in his *Studies in the Philosophy of Kant*, Indianapolis and New York: Bobbs-Merrill, 1965, pp. 61–73.
"Can Kant's Synthetic Judgments Be Made Analytic?" *Studies in the Philosophy of Kant*, pp. 74–91.

BEISER, FREDERICK C. *The Fate of Reason: German Philosophy from Kant to Fichte*, Cambridge, Mass.: Harvard University Press, 1987, pp. 217–25.

DAVAL, ROGER. *La métaphysique de Kant*, Paris: Presses Universitaires de France, 1951.

EBERHARD, JOHANN AUGUST, ed. *Philosophisches Magazin*, 4 vols., Halle: Johann Jacob Gebauer, 1789–92. Reprinted in the series *Aetas Kantiana*, Culture et Civilisation, Brussels, 1968.
Philosophisches Archiv, 2 vols., Berlin: Carl Matzdorf, 1793–4. Reprinted in *Aetas Kantiana*, 1968.

EBERSTEIN, WILHELM L. G. VON. *Versuch einer Geschichte der Logik und Metaphysik bey den Deutschen von Leibniz bis auf gegenwärtige Zeit*, vol. 2, Halle: Joh. Gottf. Ruff, 1794, pp. 165–291. Reprinted in *Aetas Kantiana*, 1970.

FERBER, EDUARD O. *Der philosophische Streit zwischen I. Kant und Johann Aug. Eberhard*, dissertation, Giessen, 1894.

GAWLINA, MANFRED. *Das Medusanhaupt der Kritik, Die Kontroverse zwischen Immanuel Kant und Johann August Eberhard*, Berlin and New York: Walter de Gruyter, 1996.

KEMPF, ROGER. *Réponse à Eberhard, Traduction, Introduction et Notes*, Paris: Librairie Philosophique J. Vrin, 1959.

SCHULTZ, JOHANN [spelled Schulze]. *Prüfung der Kantischen Critik der reinen Vernunft*, second part, Königsberg: Friedrich Nicolovius, 1792. Reprinted in *Aetas Kantiana*, 1968.

VLEESCHAUWER, H. J. DE. *La Déduction Transcendentale dans l'Oeuvre de Kant*, vol. 3, Paris: Leroux, 1937, pp. 370–443.

On a discovery whereby any new critique
of pure reason is to be made superfluous
by an older one

Mr. Eberhard has made the discovery that, as his *Philosophisches Magazin*   8: 187
(vol. I, p. 289) proclaims, "the Leibnizian philosophy contains just as
much of a critique of reason as the more recent one, whereby it nevertheless introduces a dogmatism grounded in a careful analysis of the
cognitive faculties, therefore containing everything that is true in the
latter, but still more besides in a grounded extension of the domain of
the understanding." How it came to pass that these things were not long
ago already seen in the great man's philosophy and in its daughter, the
Wolffian, he does not, to be sure, explain; yet how many discoveries regarded as new are not now seen with complete clarity in the ancients by
skilled interpreters, once they have been shown what they should look
for!

One could let pass the failure of a claim to originality, did not the
older critique contain in its results the exact opposite of the new one;
for in that case, the *argumentum ad verecundiam* (as Locke called it),[1]
which Mr. Eberhard, fearing that his own might not suffice, craftily uses
(sometimes, as on p. 298, with distortion of meaning), would be a great
obstacle to the acceptance of the latter. Yet it is a dubious enterprise to
refute propositions of pure reason by means of *books* (which can themselves have been based on no sources other than those to which we are
just as near as their author). Perspicacious as Mr. Eberhard generally is,
he has perhaps not seen clearly this time. Besides, he sometimes speaks
as if he will not vouch for Leibniz (e.g., p. 381 and p. 393 note).[2] It is
therefore best to leave the great man out of the picture and to consider
the propositions which Mr. Eberhard ascribes to his name and uses as
weapons against the *Critique*, as his own assertions; for otherwise we
would find ourselves in the nasty situation, that in justifiably parrying
the blows which he administers to us in the other's name, we might hit
a great man, thereby drawing upon ourselves the odium of those who
admire him.

According to the example of the jurists in the conduct of a trial,   8: 188
the first item that we have to consider in this quarrel is the form.
Mr. Eberhard explains his position here as follows (p. 255): "According
to the arrangement of the journal, it is perfectly permissible to break off
or continue our journeys at will, *we can proceed forwards and backwards* and
turn in all directions." – Now, one can readily grant that a magazine[3]
may contain entirely different things in its different sections and divisions (as in this one, a treatise on *logical truth* is followed immediately
by a contribution to the history of *beards*, and this by a *poem*); but Mr.
Eberhard will hardly be able to justify by means of this characteristic
of a magazine (which would then become a junk-closet) that completely
heterogeneous things should be mixed with one another in the same section, or that the hindmost be brought to the fore and the lowest to the
top, especially if, as is here the case, the concern is with the comparison

of two philosophical systems; and, in fact, he is far from judging in this way.

This seemingly artless arrangement of themes is actually very carefully contrived, in order to entice the reader into accepting in advance, before the touchstone of truth has been determined and while he therefore still has none, propositions that require a close examination, and afterwards to prove the validity of the touchstone, which is only selected subsequently, not, as it should be, on the basis of its own nature, but by means of those very propositions that it puts to the test (not those that put the test to it). It is a clever *hysteron proteron*,[4] designed to avoid gracefully the search for the elements of our *a priori* cognition and the ground of their validity with regard to objects prior to all experience, and therefore the deduction of their objective reality (as lengthy and difficult labors), and, where possible, to refute the *Critique* with a stroke of the pen, while at the same time making room for an unlimited dogmatism of pure reason. For as everyone knows, the critique of pure understanding begins with this inquiry, which has as its goal the solution of the general question: how are synthetic propositions possible *a priori*? And only after a laborious consideration of all of the conditions requisite for this can it arrive at the decisive conclusion: that to no concept can its objective reality be secured, save insofar as it can be presented in a corresponding intuition (which for us is always sensory), so that beyond the bounds of sensibility and thus of possible experience, there can be no cognition whatever, that is, no concepts of which one is sure that they are not empty. – The magazine begins with the refutation of this proposition by means of the demonstration of the opposite: namely, that there is indeed an extension of cognition beyond objects of the senses, and ends with the investigation of how this is possible *a priori* through synthetic propositions.

8: 189

So the plot of the first volume of the Eberhardian magazine is really made up of two acts. In the *first* the objective reality of our concepts of the nonsensible is to be established, in the *other* the problem of how synthetic propositions are possible *a priori* is to be solved. For so far as concerns the principle of sufficient reason, which he expounds on pp. 163–66, it is there in order to establish the reality of the concept of ground in this synthetic principle; but by the author's own account on p. 316, it also belongs to the number of those synthetic and analytic judgments, where something is first of all to be decided concerning the possibility of synthetic principles. All of the remainder, that is mentioned here and there beforehand, or in between, consists of allusions to future proofs, appeals to earlier proofs, citations from Leibniz and other assertions, as well as attacks on expressions, usually with distortion of their sense, and the like; exactly according to the advice that Quintilian gives to the orator about his arguments, in order to deceive his audience: *Si non possunt valere, quia magna sunt, valebunt quia multa sunt. – Singula levia sunt et communia, universa tamen nocent; etiamsi non ut fulmine, tamen ut grandine;*[5] all of which only deserves to be taken up in a postscript. It is bad enough to have to deal with an author who knows no order, but it is even worse to deal with one who affects disorder in order to let shallow or false propositions slip through unnoticed.

Section One
Concerning the objective reality of those concepts to which no corresponding sensory intuition can be given, according to Mr. Eberhard

Mr. Eberhard devotes himself (pp. 157–58) to this undertaking with a solemnity appropriate to the importance of the subject: he speaks of his long, unprejudiced efforts on behalf of a science (metaphysics), which he regards as a realm from which, if need be, a considerable portion could be abandoned, and yet an even more considerable area would remain; he speaks of flowers and fruits promised by the *undisputedly* fertile fields of ontology,* and even in regard to the contested fields of cosmology, he exhorts us not to stop working; for, he says, "We can always continue to work for its expansion, we can always seek to enrich it with new truths, *without having first to concern ourselves with the transcendental validity of these truths*" (which is here equivalent to the objective reality of its concepts), and he adds: "In this way have the mathematicians themselves completed the delineation of entire sciences, *without saying a single word about the reality of their object.*" Meanwhile, desiring that the reader should be fully attentive to this point, he says: "This may be illustrated by a notable example, by an *example* that is too pertinent and *instructive* for me not to be allowed to cite it here." Yes, quite instructive; for never has a more ex-

cellent example been given as a warning not to appeal to arguments from sciences that one does not understand, not even on the assurance of other famous men who merely report on the matter; since it is to be expected that one will not understand this either. For Mr. Eberhard could not have more forcefully refuted himself and his announced project than by the judgment repeated from Borelli [6] concerning the *Conica* of *Apollonius.* [7]

---

* But these are precisely the fields whose concepts and principles, *as claims to a cognition of things in general*, have been challenged, and have been limited to the much narrower field of objects of possible experience. This endeavor to refuse in advance to be concerned with the question of the *titulum possessionis* reveals right away an artifice to keep the actual point of the dispute out of sight of the judge.

Apollonius first constructs the concept of a cone, that is, he exhibits it *a priori* in intuition (this is the first action whereby the geometer verifies in advance the objective reality of his concept). He cuts it according to a determinate rule, e.g., parallel to a side of the triangle which intersects the base of the cone (*conus rectus*) at right angles through its vertex, and proves *a priori* in intuition the attributes of the curved line produced by this cut on the surface of the cone, and he thus extracts a concept of the ratio in which its ordinates stand to the parameter, which concept, namely (in this case), the parabola, is thereby given *a priori* in intuition; consequently, its objective reality, that is, the possibility that a thing with these properties can be given, is proven in no other way *than by providing the corresponding intuition.* – Mr. Eberhard wanted to prove that one can very well extend one's cognition and enrich it with new truths, without first considering whether one is proceeding with a concept which is entirely empty and can have no object (an assertion which is in plain contradiction with common sense), and he turned to the mathematicians for confirmation of his opinion. He could not, however, have hit upon a more unfortunate source. – But the misfortune stemmed from the fact that he was not acquainted with *Apollonius* himself and did not understand *Borelli*,[8] who is reflecting on the procedure of the ancient geometers. The latter speaks of the mechanical *construction* of concepts of conic sections (with the exception of the circle), and notes that mathematicians teach the properties of the conic sections without mentioning the mechanical construction; certainly a true, albeit a very insignificant remark; for instruction *to draw* a parabola according to the prescription of the theory is addressed to the artist only, not to the geometer.* Mr. Eberhard could have learned this from the passage from the remark

8: 192

---

* The following may serve to secure against misuse the expression '*construction of concepts*' of which the *Critique of Pure Reason* speaks several times, and has thereby first made an accurate distinction between the procedure of reason in mathematics and in philosophy. In a general sense one may call construction all *exhibition* of a concept through the (spontaneous) production of a corresponding intuition. If it occurs through mere imagination in accordance with an *a priori* concept, it is called *pure* construction (such as must underlie all the demonstrations of the mathematician; hence he can demonstrate by means of a circle which he draws with his stick in the sand, no matter how irregular it may turn out to be, the properties of a circle in general, as perfectly as if it had been etched in copperplate by the greatest artist). If it is carried out on some kind of material, however, it could be called *empirical* construction. The first can also be called *schematic*, the second *technical* construction. Now the latter construction, which is really improperly so-called, (because it belongs not to science but to art and is done by means of instruments) is either the *geometrical*, by compass and ruler, or the *mechanical*, for which other instruments are necessary, as for example, the drawing of the other conic sections besides the circle.

of Borelli which he himself cites and has even underscored. It says there: *Subjectum enim definitum assumi potest, ut affectiones variae de eo demonstrentur, licet praemissa non sit ars subjectum ipsum efformandum delineandi.*[9] It would be highly absurd, however, to construe this as claiming that the geometer was first expecting proof, from this mechanical construction, of the possibility of such a line, and hence of the objective reality of his concept. One could rather address to the modern geometers a reproach of the following nature: not that they derive the properties of a curved line from its definition without first being assured of the possibility of its object (for in doing so they are fully aware at the same time of the *pure*, merely schematic construction, and they also carry out the *mechanical* construction afterwards if it is necessary), but that they arbitrarily conceive such a line (e.g., the parabola through the formula $ax = y^2$), and do not, according to the example of the ancient geometers, first bring it forth as given in the conic section, which would be more in keeping with the elegance of geometry, for the sake of which we have often been advised not to neglect so completely the synthetic method of the ancients in favor of the analytic method which is so rich in inventions.

Mr. Eberhard therefore sets to work as follows, not according to the example of the mathematicians, but, rather, in the manner of that clever fellow who could weave a rope out of grains of sand.

8: 193

In the first part of his magazine, he had already distinguished the principles of the *form* of cognition, which are supposed to be the principles of contradiction and sufficient reason, from those of its *matter* (according to him, representation and extension), whose principle he locates in the simple of which they are composed; and since nobody denies him the transcendental validity of the principle of contradiction, he now seeks in the first place to establish that of the *principle of sufficient reason*, and therewith the objective reality of the latter concept, and secondly, the reality of the concept of a simple being, without, as the *Critique* demands, requiring them to be validated by a corresponding intuition. For of what is true, we do not first have to ask if it is possible, and to that extent logic has the principle *ab esse ad posse valet consequentia*[10] in common with metaphysics, or rather lends it to the latter. – We shall likewise now proceed in our examination in accordance with this division.

A. Demonstration of the objective reality of the concept of sufficient reason according to Mr. Eberhard

It is first of all worthy of note that Mr. Eberhard wishes to have the principle of sufficient reason listed merely among the *formal* principles of cognition, though he nevertheless views it (p. 160) as a question occasioned by the *Critique*: "*whether it also has transcendental validity*" (is in general a transcendental principle). Now, either Mr. Eberhard must have no conception whatever of the difference between a *logical* (formal) and a *transcendental* (material) principle of cognition or, as is more likely, this is one of his artful maneuvers to substitute for the question at issue another which no one is asking about.

That *every proposition must have a reason*[a] is the logical (formal) principle of cognition, which is subordinated to, and not set beside, the principle of contradiction.* That *every thing must have its ground*[a] is the transcendental (material) principle, which no one has ever proven or will prove by means of the principle of contradiction (and in general from mere concepts without relation to sensory intuition). It is clear enough, and has been stated countless times in the *Critique*, that a transcendental principle must determine something *a priori* in regard to objects and their possibility; consequently, it does not, like the logical principles (which abstract completely from everything concerning the possibility of the object), merely concern itself with the formal conditions of judgment. Mr. Eberhard, however, wished (p. 163) to gain acceptance for his principle under the formula: *all* has a reason, and since (as may be seen from the example he has there given), he desired to smuggle in the actually material principle of causality by means of the principle of contradiction, he uses the word '*all*,' and is careful not to say '*every thing*,' because it would then become only too obvious that it is not a formal and logical, but a material and transcendental principle of cognition, which can already have its place in logic (as can any principle which rests on the principle of contradiction).

---

* The *Critique* has noted the distinction between problematic and assertoric judgments. An assertoric judgment is a *proposition*. The logicians are by no means correct in defining a proposition as a judgment expressed *in words*; for we must also, in thought, use words in judgments which we do not regard as propositions. In the conditional proposition: *if a body is simple, then it is unalterable*, there is a relation of two judgments, neither of which is a proposition; only the consequence of the latter (the *consequens*) from the former (*antecedens*) constitutes the proposition. The judgment: *some bodies are simple*, may, indeed, be contradictory; it can nevertheless still be affirmed in order to see what follows from it, if it were to be stated as an assertion, i.e., a proposition. The assertoric judgment: *every body is divisible*, says more than the merely problematic (let us suppose that every body is divisible etc.) and stands under the universal logical principle of propositions, namely, that each proposition must be *grounded* (not be a merely possible judgment), which follows from the principle of contradiction, because otherwise there would be no proposition.

8: 194

[a] The term '*Grund*' may be rendered by either 'reason' or 'ground,' depending on whether it is taken logically to refer to the basis (logical ground) of the truth of a proposition or metaphysically to refer to the cause (real ground) of a state of affairs. Kant's point in the following is that Eberhard systematically conflates these senses in his treatment of the concept or principle of sufficient reason. – Tr.

It is, however, not without mature consideration, and with a purpose which he would gladly conceal from the reader, that he endeavors to demonstrate this transcendental principle on the basis of the principle of contradiction. He wishes to validate this concept of a ground (and with it, unnoticed, the concept of causality) for all things in general, that is, to prove its objective reality, without restricting it merely to objects of the senses, thereby evading the condition added by the *Critique*, namely, the need for an intuition by means of which this reality is first demonstrable. Now, it is clear that the principle of contradiction is a principle that is valid for all that we can possibly think, whether or not it is a sensible object with a possible intuition attached; because it is valid for thought in general, without regard to any object. Thus, whatever conflicts with this principle is obviously nothing (not even a thought). If he therefore wished to establish the objective reality of the concept of *a ground*, without letting himself be bound by its restriction to objects of sensory intuition, he had to make use for that purpose of the principle that is valid for thought as such, the concept of a reason; but also to present it in such a way that, although it is in fact of merely logical significance, it should still seem to include under itself the concept of a real ground (and, consequently, that of causality). He has, however, accorded to the reader more naive trust than he has a right to assume, even in those with the most mediocre judgment.

But, as is apt to happen with stratagems, Mr. Eberhard has entangled himself in his own. Initially, he had hung the whole of metaphysics on *two* hinges: the principle of contradiction and that of sufficient reason; and he stands by this claim of his when he holds, following Leibniz (at least in the way he interprets him), that for the purpose of metaphysics the first needs to be supplemented by the second. Now, however, he says (p. 163): "The universal truth of the principle of sufficient reason can be *demonstrated* only from this (the principle of contradiction)," which he then boldly sets to work doing. So in that case the whole of metaphysics again hangs upon only *one* hinge, whereas previously there were supposed to have been two; for the mere conclusion from a principle, taken in its entire universality, and without the addition of at least a new condition of its application, is certainly not a new principle, which would compensate for the deficiences of the previous one!

However, before Mr. Eberhard presents this demonstration of the principle of sufficient reason (together with the objective reality of the concept of a cause, but without requiring anything more than the principle of contradiction), he raises the expectations of the reader by means of a certain pomp in the division of his work (pp. 161–62), and this by a further comparison, as unfortunate as the first, of his method with that of the mathematicians. *Euclid* himself is supposed to "have among his axioms propositions which certainly are in need of demonstration, but

8: 195

8: 196

290

are nevertheless presented without proof." Now, speaking of the mathematician, he adds: "As soon as you deny him one of his *axioms*, all of the theorems which depend upon it fall as well. But this is *such a rare occurrence* that he does not believe it necessary to sacrifice the simple elegance of his *exposition* and the *beautiful proportions* of his system. Philosophy must be more obliging." So there is now a *licentia geometrica*, just as there has long been a *licentia poetica*. If only this *obliging philosophy* (in proofs, as is added at once) had also been obliging enough to produce an example from *Euclid*, where he presents a proposition which is *mathematically* demonstrable as an axiom; for of what can be demonstrated merely philosophically (from concepts), e.g., the whole is greater than its parts, the proof does not belong to mathematics, if its method is stated in a fully rigorous way.

Now follows the promised *demonstration*. It is good that it is not lengthy; for its cogency is all the more striking. We shall therefore state it in full: "Either everything has a reason or not everything has a reason. In the latter case, something could be possible and conceivable, the reason for which would be nothing. – But if, of two opposite things, one could be without a sufficient reason, so likewise could the other be without a sufficient reason. For example, if a mass of air could move eastward and thus the wind blow towards the east, without the air in the east becoming warmer and more rarified, then this mass of air would *equally well* be able to move westward as eastward; the same air would therefore be able to move *at the same time* in two opposite directions, east and west, and consequently, eastward and not eastward, that is to say, it could *at the same time* be and not be, which is contradictory and impossible."

This demonstration, whereby the philosopher should, with respect to thoroughness, be even more obliging than the mathematician, has all the attributes that a demonstration must have in order to serve in logic as an example of how a demonstration should not be conducted. – *First of all*, the proposition to be demonstrated is ambiguously expressed, so that one can make either a logical or a transcendental principle out of it, since the word '*all*' can signify either every *judgment*, which we take as a proposition about something or other, or every *thing*. If it is taken in the first sense (so that it would have to read: 'every proposition has its reason'), it is then not only universally true, but is even inferred immediately from the *principle of contradiction*; however, if by '*all*' every *thing* were to be understood, then an entirely different mode of demonstration would be required. 8: 197

Second, the demonstration lacks unity. It actually consists of two demonstrations. The first is the well-known proof of Baumgarten,[11] to which nobody is likely to appeal any more; except for the missing conclusion ("which is self-contradictory"), which each must add for himself, it is completed where I have inserted the dash. This is followed immediately by another demonstration, which by means of the word '*but*' is presented as a mere step in the chain of reasoning leading to the conclusion of the first, though if one omits the word '*but*' it constitutes a self-sufficient demonstration; since in order to find a contradiction in the proposition that there is something without a reason more is needed than in the first, which found it immediately in this proposition itself; and since, in order to conjure up a contradiction, the present demonstration must add the proposition that the opposite of the thing would also be without a reason, it is therefore conducted quite differently from the Baumgartian proof, of which it was still supposed to form a part.

Third, the *new direction*, which Mr. Eberhard has sought to give to his demonstration (p. 164), is very unfortunate; for the inference by which it proceeds has four terms. – Put in syllogistic form, it runs as follows:

> A wind that blows east without reason, might just as well (*instead of this*) blow west.
>
> Now (as the opponent of the principle of sufficient reason asserts) the wind blows east without reason.
>
> Consequently, it can *simultaneously* blow east and west (which is a contradiction).

It is clear that I am fully justified in inserting the phrase '*instead of this*' in the major premise; for without such a restriction in meaning no one could accept it. If someone wagers a certain sum on a lucky toss and wins, someone wishing to dissuade him from playing might very well say that he could just as well have had a miss, and thus lost a good deal; but only *instead* of a hit, not hit and miss *together* on the same toss. Similarly, the artist who has carved a god out of a piece of wood might just as well (instead of this) have made a bench out of it; but it does not follow from this that he could have made both from it *at the same time*.

Fourth, the proposition itself, in the unlimited universality in which it there stands, is, if it is to be valid of things, obviously false; for according to it there would be absolutely nothing unconditioned; but to seek to avoid this embarrassing consequence, by saying of the supreme being that it does, indeed, also have a ground of its existence, but that this lies within it, leads to a contradiction; for the ground of the existence of a thing, as real ground, must always be distinguished from this thing and this must then necessarily be thought as dependent upon another. Of a proposition I can very well say that it has the reason (the logical reason) for its truth in itself; since the concept of the subject is something other than that of the predicate, and can contain the reason thereof; but if I allow no other ground for the existence of a thing to be accepted save this thing itself, I mean by this that it has no further real ground.

Mr. Eberhard has thus accomplished nothing of what he intended to achieve in regard to the concept of causality, namely, to establish the validity of this category, and presumably that of the others with it, for things

8: 198

in general, without restricting its use and validity for the *cognition* of things to objects of experience, and he has vainly employed the sovereign principle of contradiction for this purpose. The teaching of the *Critique* therefore stands firm: that no category can contain or bring forth the least cognition, if it cannot be given a corresponding intuition, which for us human beings is always sensory, so that the use of it in regard to the theoretical cognition of things can never extend beyond the limits of all possible experience.

B. Proof of the objective reality of the concept of the simple with regard to objects of experience according to Mr. Eberhard

Mr. Eberhard had previously spoken of a concept of the understanding (that of causality) which can indeed be applied to objects of the senses, but which also, without being restricted to objects of the senses, may be   8: 199
valid of things in general, and he has thus presumed to have proven the objective reality of at least *one* category, namely, causality, independently of the conditions of intuition. On pp. 169–73 he now goes a step further and even wishes to secure the objective reality of a concept of that which admittedly cannot be an object of the senses at all, namely, that of a *simple being*; thereby opening the way to his vaunted fertile fields of rational psychology and theology, from which the Medusa head of the *Critique* endeavored to deter him. His proof (pp. 169–70) proceeds as follows:

"Concrete time,* or the time which we sense (it should rather say: in   8: 200
which we sense something) is nothing other than the succession of our

---

* The expression '*abstract* time,' (p. 170) in contrast to the here occurring '*concrete* time' is entirely incorrect, and should never be accepted, especially when it is a question of the greatest logical precision, even though this misuse has been authorized by modern logicians. One does not abstract a *concept* as a common mark, rather one abstracts in the *use* of a concept from the diversity of that which is contained under it. Chemists are only able to abstract something when they remove a liquid from other matter in order to isolate it; the philosopher abstracts *from* that which he does not wish to take into consideration in a certain use of the concept. Whoever wishes to formulate rules for education can do so by basing them either merely on the concept of a child *in abstracto* or on a child in civil society (*in concreto*), without mentioning the difference between the abstract and the concrete child. The distinction between abstract and concrete concerns only the use of concepts, not the concepts themselves. The neglect of this scholastic precision often falsifies the judgment concerning an object. If I say: abstract time or space have such and such properties, this suggests that time and space were first given in the objects of the senses, like the red of a rose or cinnabar, and are only extracted therefrom by a logical operation. If I say, however, that in time and space considered *in abstracto*, i.e., prior to all empirical conditions, such and such properties are to be noted, I at least

293

representations; for even the succession in motion may be reduced to the succession of representations. Concrete time is therefore something composite, its simple elements being representations. Since all finite things are in a continual flux (how does he know *a priori* that this applies to all *finite* things and not merely to appearances?), these elements can never be *sensed*, the inner sense can never sense them separately; they are always sensed together with something that precedes and follows. Furthermore, since the flux of the alterations of all finite things is a *continuous* (this word is underlined by him), uninterrupted flux, no *sensible* part of time is the smallest or a completely simple part. The simple elements of concrete time therefore lie *completely* outside the sphere of sensibility. – But now the understanding raises itself above this sphere of sensibility by discovering the *unimageable*[a] simple, without which the image of sensibility, even with respect to time, is not possible. It therefore recognizes first of all that something objective pertains to the image of time, namely these indivisible elementary representations, which together with the subjective grounds that lie in the limits of the finite mind, give to sensibility the image of concrete time. For because of these limits such representations cannot be simultaneous, and because of the very same limits they cannot be distinguished in the image." On page 171, he says of space: "The many-sided similarity of the other form of intuition, space, to that of time saves us from the trouble of repeating in its analysis all that it has in common with the analysis of time, – the first elements of the composite with which space is simultaneously present are, no less than the elements of time, simple and beyond the field of sensibility; they are objects of understanding,[b] unimageable, they cannot be intuited under any sensory form; but they are nonetheless true objects, all of which they have in common with the elements of time."

8: 201 Mr. Eberhard has chosen his demonstrations, if not with a particularly happy degree of logical cogency, at least with due deliberation and an adroitness suitable to his purpose; and although, for easily discernible

---

leave it open to me to regard this as also knowable independently of experience (*a priori*), which I am not free to do if I regard time as a concept merely abstracted from experience. In the first case, I can judge, or at least endeavor to judge, by means of *a priori* principles about pure, in contrast to empirically determined, time and space in that I abstract from everything empirical, whereas in the second case, I am prevented from doing so if (as is claimed) I have only abstracted those concepts from experience (as in the above example of the red color). – Thus, those who with their semblance of knowledge endeavor to avoid a careful examination must hide behind expressions which will conceal their subterfuge.

[a] *unbildliche*
[b] *Verstandeswesen*

reasons, he does not actually disclose this purpose, it is nevertheless not difficult, and for its proper evaluation not irrelevant, to bring the plan of it to light. He wishes to demonstrate the objective reality of the concept of a simple being as pure object of understanding, and he seeks it in the *elements* of a sensible object, a stratagem which might appear to be ill-considered and contrary to his purpose. Nevertheless, he had good reasons for it. If he had wanted to prove generally from mere concepts, as the proposition is commonly demonstrated, that the ultimate grounds of the composite must necessarily be sought in the simple, one would have granted him that, but not without adding that this, indeed, holds of our Ideas, if we wish to think of things-in-themselves, of which we cannot obtain the least knowledge; but that it does not hold of objects of the senses (appearances), which are the only objects we can know; so the objective reality of the concept is by no means demonstrated. He had therefore, contrary to his intent, to seek that object of the understanding in objects of the senses. How was this to be accomplished? By means of a shift, which he does not let the reader properly note, he had to give another meaning to the concept of the nonsensible than the one which not only the *Critique*, but everyone, is wont to attach to it. At times it is said to be that in the sensory representation which is no longer consciously apprehended, but whose existence is still recognized by the understanding, such as that of the small particles of bodies, or even of the determinations of our faculty of representation, which cannot be represented clearly in isolation. At other times, however (especially when the point is that these small parts are to be thought of, precisely, as simple), the nonsensible is said to be the unimageable, of which no image is possible, and which cannot be represented in any sensory form (namely, in an image) (p. 171). – If ever an author has been justly reproached for the deliberate falsification of a concept (not confusion, which can also be inadvertent), it is in this case. The *Critique* always understands by the nonsensible only that which cannot at all, not even the least part, be contained in a sensory intuition, and it is a deliberate deception of the inexperienced reader to foist upon him in place of that something in the sensible object, because no image of it (meaning thereby an intuition containing a manifold in certain relations, and thus a form) can be given. 8: 202 Should this (not very subtle) deception succeed, he believes that the genuinely simple, which the understanding conceives in things that are met with only in Idea, will have been shown to the reader (without his noticing the contradiction) in objects of the senses, and that the objective reality of the concept will thereby have been exhibited in an intuition.

We now want to examine this demonstration in detail. It is based on two assertions: *first*, that concrete time and space consist of simple elements, and *second*, that these elements are nevertheless nothing sensible, but rather objects of understanding. These assertions are both equally erroneous, the first because it contradicts mathematics, the second because it contradicts itself.

We can be quite brief with regard to the first of these errors. Although Mr. Eberhard (despite his frequent allusions to them) seems to have no special acquaintance with mathematicians, he will surely find intelligible the demonstration, given by Keil in his *Introductio in veram physicam*,[12] from the mere division of a straight line by infinitely many others, and would see from this that there can be no simple elements of such a line by the mere principle of geometry that not more than one straight line can pass through two given points. This mode of proof can be varied in many ways, and can also yield a demonstration of the impossibility of supposing simple parts of time, if one bases it on the movement of a point along a line. – Now one cannot here prevaricate by claiming that concrete time and space are not subject to that which mathematics demonstrates of its abstract space (and time) as a being of the imagination.[a] For not only in this way would physics, in very many cases (e.g., in the laws of falling bodies), have to be concerned about lapsing into error, if it follows exactly the apodictic doctrines of geometry, but it can also be just as apodictically demonstrated that each thing in space, each alteration in time, as soon as it occupies a portion of space or time, can be divided into just as many things or alterations as are the space or time which it occupies. In order to avoid the paradox that is felt in this connection (in that reason, which ultimately requires the simple as the foundation of all composites, contradicts what mathematics demonstrates with regard to sensory intuition), one can and must admit that space and time are merely things of thought[b] and beings of the imagination, which have not been invented by the latter, but must underlie all of its combinations and inventions because they are the essential form of our sensibility and the receptivity of our intuitions, whereby in general objects are given to us, and whose universal conditions are necessarily at the same time *a priori* conditions of the possibility of all objects of the senses, as appearances, and so must accord with them. The simple in temporal succession, as in space, is therefore absolutely impossible, and if Leibniz has occasionally so expressed himself that one might sometimes interpret his doctrine of simple being, as if he wanted to understand matter as a composite thereof, it is fairer, so long as it is reconcilable with his express words, to understand him to mean by the simple not a *part* of matter, but the ground of the appearance, transcending everything sensible and completely unknowable by us, which we call matter (which may itself indeed be a simple being, even if the matter which constitutes the appearance is a composite), or, if no such reconciliation is possible, then we must reject

8: 203

[a] *Wesen der Einbildungskraft*
[b] *Gedankendinge*

even Leibniz's claims. For he is not the first great man, and will also not be the last, who will have to concede this freedom of inquiry to others.

The second error concerns such an obvious contradiction that Mr. Eberhard must necessarily have noticed it, but has plastered and whitewashed it as best he could, in order to make it imperceptible: namely, that the whole of an empirical intuition lies inside the sphere of sensibility, but the simple elements of the same intuition lie completely outside it. That is to say, he does not wish to have the simple *subtilized into^a* the *ground* for the intuitions in space and time (in which case he would have come too close to the *Critique*), but rather that it be met with in the elementary representations of sensory intuition itself (albeit without clear consciousness); and he insists that the composite of these elements must be a sensible being,^b but its parts objects of understanding^c rather than objects of the senses. "The elements of concrete time (as well as of concrete space) do not lack this intuitive quality,"^d he says (p. 170); nevertheless "they cannot be intuited under any sensory form" (p. 171).

First of all, what led Mr. Eberhard to such a strange and manifestly absurd confusion? He saw himself that, unless a concept is given a corresponding intuition, its objective reality would be totally unsubstantiated. But he wished to secure the latter [objective reality] for certain rational concepts, such as here the concept of a simple being, and yet to do so in such a way that the latter would not become an object, of which (as the *Critique* claims) no further cognition whatsoever is possible; for in that case that intuition, for whose possibility that super-sensible object was thought, would have had to count as mere appearance, which he likewise did not want to grant to the *Critique*; he thus had to compose the sensory intuition out of parts that are not sensible, which is an obvious contradiction.*

8: 204

* It should certainly be noted here that he now does not wish to have sensibility consist merely in the confusedness of representations, but also in the fact that an *object* is given to the senses (p. 299), exactly as if he had thereby achieved something to his advantage. On p. 170 he had attributed the representation of time to sensibility, because, due to the limitations of the finite mind, its simple parts cannot be distinguished (so the representation is therefore confused). Later on (p. 299), wanting to make this concept somewhat narrower, so that he may avoid the sound objections to this view, he adds to it precisely that condition which is the most disadvantageous to him, because he wanted to demonstrate that simple beings are objects of the understanding, and so brings a contradiction into his own assertion.

^a *hinzu vernünftele*
^b *Sinneswesen*
^c *Verstandeswesen*
^d *Anschauende*

But how does Mr. Eberhard extricate himself from this difficulty? He does so by means of a mere play with words, which through their ambiguity, are supposed to delay us for a moment. A *nonsensible*[a] part is completely outside the sphere of sensibility; but the nonsensible is that which can never be sensed *separately*, and this is the simple in things as well as in our representations. The second word, which is intended to make objects of the understanding out of the parts of a sensory representation or its object, is the *unimageable* simple. He seems to like this expression best, for he uses it most frequently in the sequel. To be nonsensible and yet to constitute a part of the sensible, seemed even to him to be too obviously contradictory to enable him to insinuate the concept of the nonsensible into sensory intuition.

8: 205

A *nonsensible* part here means a part of an empirical intuition of whose representation one is *not conscious*. Mr. Eberhard will not say this straight out, for were he to have given the latter explanation of it, he would have admitted that for him sensibility means nothing more than a state of confused representations in a manifold of intuition, and he wants to avoid any such rebuke from the *Critique*. If, on the other hand, the word 'sensible' is used in its proper meaning, it is obvious that, if no simple part of an object of the senses is sensible, then this latter as a whole cannot be sensed either, and conversely, that if something is an object of the senses and of sensation, all of its simple parts would have to be so as well, even though clarity of representation may be lacking in them; but that this obscurity of the partial representations of a whole, so long as the understanding does but realize that they must nevertheless be contained in this whole and its intuition, cannot raise them above the sphere of sensibility and convert them into objects of the understanding. No microscope has yet been able to detect Newton's *lamellae*,[13] of which the colored particles of bodies consist, but the understanding recognizes (or assumes) not only their existence, but also that they really are represented, albeit without consciousness, in our empirical intuition. It has not, however, occurred to any of his followers to declare them on that account to be entirely nonsensible and moreover to be objects of understanding; but now between such small parts and completely simple parts there is no difference other than in the degree of diminution. If the whole is to be an object of the senses, all of its parts would necessarily have to be so as well.

But the fact that there is no *image* of a simple part, even though it is itself a part of an image, that is, of a sensory intuition, cannot raise it into the sphere of the super-sensible. Simple beings raised above the bounds of the sensible must indeed (as the *Critique* shows) be thought, and to their concept no corresponding image, that is, no intuition at all can be given; but then they cannot also be counted as parts of the sensible. But if

[a] *nicht-empfindbar*

298

(contrary to all the demonstrations of mathematics), they are counted as such, it does not at all follow from the fact that no image corresponds to them that their representation is something super-sensible; for it is simple sensation, and thus an element of sensibility, and the understanding has thereby no more raised itself above sensibility, than if it were to have conceived them as composite. For the latter concept, of which the former is merely the negation, is just as much a concept of the understanding. He would only have raised himself above sensibility, if he had completely 8: 206 banished the simple from sensory intuition and its objects, and with the infinite divisibility of matter (as enjoined by mathematics) opened up for himself the vista of a microcosm;[a] but precisely because of the inadequacy of an inner explanatory ground of the sensibly composite (whose division lacks completeness because of the total lack of the simple), he could then have inferred such a simple *outside* the whole field of sensory intuition, which would therefore be thought not as a part therein, but as the to us unknown ground for it, present merely in the Idea; though in doing so, to be sure, the admission, which Mr. Eberhard is so loath to make, that we cannot have the least cognition of this super-sensible simple, would then have been unavoidable.

In fact, to avoid acknowledging this, his alleged demonstration is governed by a curious equivocation. The passage where it says "The flux of the alterations *of all finite things is* a continuous, uninterrupted flux . . . no *sensible* part is the smallest or completely simple," sounds as if it had been dictated by the mathematician. But immediately thereafter there are simple parts in the very same alterations, though they are recognized only by the understanding, since they are not sensible. But once they are in these this *lex continui* of the flux of alterations is false, and they occur discontinuously,[b] and the fact that they are not, as Mr. Eberhard falsely puts it, sensed, that is, consciously *perceived*, in no way abolishes their specific nature as parts belonging to a merely empirical, sensory intuition. Does Mr. Eberhard then have a determinate concept of *continuity*?

In a word: the *Critique* had asserted that the objective reality of a concept is never established, without giving the intuition corresponding to it. Mr. Eberhard wanted to demonstrate the opposite, and he subscribes to something that is notoriously false, namely that the understanding cognizes the simple in things as objects of intuition in space and time, a view which we will nevertheless concede to him. But in that case, he has, in his own way, fulfilled, rather than refuted, the demand of the *Critique*. For the latter demanded nothing more than that the objective reality should be demonstrated in intuition; but by this a corresponding intu- 8: 207 ition is given to the concept, which is precisely what the *Critique* required and he wanted to refute.

[a] *eine Welt im Kleinen*
[b] *ruckweise* [literally, jerkily or by fits and starts]

I would not dwell so long on so clear an issue, if it did not furnish an incontrovertible proof of how completely Mr. Eberhard has failed to grasp the intent of the *Critique* in distinguishing between the sensible and the nonsensible in objects, or, if he prefers, that he has misunderstood it.

C. The method of ascending from the sensible to the nonsensible according to Mr. Eberhard

The conclusion that Mr. Eberhard draws from the above demonstrations, especially the latter (p. 262), is this: "Thus, the truth that space and time have both subjective and objective grounds . . . has been proven fully apodictically. It was demonstrated that their *ultimate objective grounds* are things-in-themselves." Now any reader of the *Critique* will admit that these are exactly my own assertions; thus with his apodictic demonstrations (to what extent they are such can be seen from the foregoing analysis) Mr. Eberhard has asserted *nothing against the Critique*. But that these objective grounds, namely, the things-in-themselves, are not to be sought in space and time, but, rather, in what the *Critique* calls their extra or super-sensible substrate (noumenon) – that was the claim of mine, of which Mr. Eberhard wanted to prove the opposite, although never, not even here in his conclusion, will he state it in so many words.

Mr. Eberhard says (p. 258, nos. 3 and 4): "Besides the subjective, space and time also have *objective grounds*, and these objective grounds are not appearances, but true, cognizable things" (p. 259); "their *ultimate grounds* are things-in-themselves," all of which the *Critique* likewise literally and repeatedly asserts. How, then, did it come about that Mr. Eberhard, who otherwise looks keenly enough to his advantage, on this occasion did not see what tells against him? We are dealing with a clever man who does not see something because he does not want it to be seen. He actually did not want the reader to see that his objective *grounds*, which are not to be appearances but things-in-themselves, are merely *parts* (simple) of appearances; for the unsuitability of such a manner of explanation would then have been noticed immediately. He therefore makes use of the word '*grounds*,' because parts, after all, are also grounds of the possibility of a composite, and there he is at one with the *Critique* in speaking of ultimate grounds which are not appearances. But had he spoken candidly of parts of appearances, which are nevertheless not themselves appearances, of a sensible, whose parts, however, are nonsensible, the absurdity would have been readily apparent (even if one were to grant the presupposition of simple parts). But the word 'ground' masks all of this; for the unwary reader, believing himself to understand thereby something which is entirely different from these intuitions, as does the *Critique*, is persuaded that proof has been given of a capacity for cognition of the super-sensible by the understanding, even in objects of the senses.

8: 208

300

The most important thing in the evaluation of this deception, is that the reader keep well in mind what we have said about the Eberhardian deduction of space and time, and hence also of sensory cognition in general. According to him, something is sensory cognition and the object thereof appearance, only so long as the representation of the object contains parts which are not, as he puts it, *sensible*, that is, perceived in intuition with consciousness. It immediately ceases to be sensory, and its object is no longer recognized as appearance, but as thing-in-itself, in a word, it is henceforth noumenon, as soon as the understanding discerns and discovers the first *grounds* of the appearance, which he takes to be the latter's own parts. So between a thing as phenomenon and the representation of the noumenon underlying it there is no more difference than there is between a group of men which I see a long way off and the same group when I am close enough to count the individuals; except that he claims that *we could never come that close to it*, which makes no difference in the thing, but only in the degree of our perceptual capacity, which thereby remains of the same kind throughout. If this were really the distinction which the *Critique* so elaborately draws in its *Aesthetic* between the cognition of things as appearances and the conception of them according to what they are as things-in-themselves, then this distinction would have been mere child's play, and even a thorough refutation of it would deserve no better name. But now the *Critique* (to cite only one 8: 209 example out of many) shows that in the corporeal world, as the totality of all objects of outer sense, there are, indeed, everywhere composite things, but that the simple is not to be found *in it* at all. At the same time, however, it demonstrates that if reason thinks a composite of substances as thing-in-itself (without relating it to the special character of our senses), it must absolutely conceive it as composed of simple substances. In virtue of what is necessarily involved in the intuition of objects in space, reason cannot and should not conceive any simple *that would be in them*, from which it follows that even if our senses were infinitely sharpened, it would still have to remain completely impossible for them even to get closer to the simple, still less finally to reach it, since it is not to be found in such objects at all. So no recourse remains but to admit that bodies are not things-in-themselves at all, and that their sensory representation, which we denominate corporeal things, is nothing but the appearance of something, which as thing-in-itself can alone contain the simple,* but which for us remains entirely unknowable, because the

* The representation of an object as simple is a merely negative concept, which reason cannot avoid, because it alone contains the unconditioned for every composite (as a thing, not as mere form), the possibility of which is always conditioned. This concept does not, therefore, serve to extend our cognition, but merely designates a something, so far as it needs to be distinguished from

intuition under which it is alone given to us, provides us not with the properties which pertain to it as it is in itself, but only with the subjective conditions of our sensibility under which alone we can receive an intuitive representation of it. – Thus, according to the *Critique*, everything in an appearance is itself still appearance, however far the understanding may resolve it into its parts and demonstrate the actuality of parts which are no longer clearly perceptible to the senses; according to Mr. Eberhard, however, they then immediately cease to be appearances and are the thing itself.[a]

8: 210

Since it might perhaps seem unbelievable to the reader that Mr. Eberhard should have willfully perpetrated such an obvious misrepresentation of the concept of the sensible given by the *Critique* which he was endeavoring to refute, or himself have installed such an insipid and metaphysically quite pointless concept of the difference between objects of sense and objects of the understanding as is the mere logical form of the mode of representation, we shall let him explain for himself what he means.

After expending (pp. 271–72) much unnecessary labor in proving what no one ever doubted, and having furthermore marvelled, as was natural, that critical idealism could have overlooked such a thing, namely that the objective reality of a concept, which in detail can be demonstrated only of objects of experience, can nevertheless unquestionably be proved in general as well, that is, of things as such, and that such a concept is not without any sort of objective reality (although it is false to conclude that this reality can thereby also be demonstrated for concepts of things which cannot be objects of experience), he continues: "I must here employ an example, of whose appropriateness we can only later become

objects of the senses (which all contain a composite). If I now say: that which *grounds* the possibility of the composite, and therefore alone can be conceived as not composite, is the noumenon (for it is not to be found in the sensible), I am not saying thereby: that an aggregate of *so many simple beings*, as pure objects of understanding, grounds body as appearance; but rather that nobody can have the least knowledge of whether the super-sensible which underlies that appearance as substrate is, as thing-in-itself, either composite or simple, and it is a completely erroneous view of the theory of sensible objects as mere appearances, which must be underlaid by something nonsensible, if we imagine or try to get others to imagine, that what is meant thereby is that the super-sensible substrate of matter will be divided into its monads, just as I divide matter itself; for then the *monas* (which is only the *Idea* of a not-further-conditioned condition of the composite) would be placed in space, whereupon it ceases to be a noumenon, and again becomes itself composite.

[a] *die Sache selbst*

persuaded. The senses and imagination of man *in his present condition* are incapable of forming an exact image of a chiliagon, that is, an image whereby it could, for example, be distinguished from a figure with nine hundred and ninety-nine sides. Nevertheless, as soon as I know that a figure is a chiliagon, my understanding can attribute various predicates to it, etc. So how can it be demonstrated that the understanding can neither affirm nor deny anything at all of a *thing-in-itself*, on the grounds that the imagination can form no image of it, or because we do not know all of the determinations pertaining to its individuality?" Subsequently (pp. 291–92), he explains himself as follows, concerning the distinction made by the *Critique* between sensibility in its logical and in its transcendental meaning: "The objects of understanding are *unimageable*, those of sensibility, on the other hand, are *imageable*," and he now cites from Leibniz* the example of eternity, of which we can form no image, but may still frame an intellectual conception.[a] At the same time, however, he also cites that of the aforementioned chiliagon, of which he says: "The senses and the imagination of man *in his present condition* can form no exact image by which to distinguish it from a polygon with nine hundred and ninety-nine sides."

8: 211

One could not ask for a clearer demonstration than Mr. Eberhard here gives, I will not say of a deliberate misinterpretation of the *Critique*, for it is far from being sufficiently plausible to deceive in that respect, but of a complete incomprehension of the question at issue. A pentagon, according to him, is still an object of sense, but a chiliagon is already a mere object of the understanding, something nonsensible (or, as he terms it, unimageable). I suspect that a nonagon would already lie more than halfway out from the sensible to the super-sensible; for if one does not count the sides with one's fingers, one can hardly determine the number by mere inspection. The question was whether we can hope to acquire a cognition of that to which no corresponding intuition can be given. This was *denied* by the *Critique* in regard to that which cannot be an object of the senses, because for the objective reality of the concept we always have need of an intuition, but ours, even

---

* The reader will do well not to ascribe immediately to Leibniz everything that Mr. Eberhard infers from his teachings. Leibniz wanted to refute the empiricism of Locke. For this purpose examples taken from mathematics were well suited to prove that such cognitions reach much further than empirically acquired concepts could do, and thereby to defend the *a priori* origin of the former against Locke's attacks. But it could not have occurred to him at all to affirm that the objects thereby cease to be mere objects of sensory intuition and presuppose another species of being as their underlying ground.

[a] *Verstandesidee*

8: 212 that given in mathematics, is only sensory. Mr. Eberhard, by contrast, responds *affirmatively* to the question and unhappily cites the mathematician, who always demonstrates everything in intuition, as if the latter could perfectly well attribute various predicates to the object of his concept through the understanding, without giving to this concept an *exactly* corresponding intuition in the imagination, and could thereby *cognize* the object even without that condition. Now when *Archimedes* described a *polygon of ninety-six sides* around a circle, and a similar figure within it, in order to determine that, and by how much, the circle is smaller than the first and greater than the second, did he or did he not ground his concept of the above-mentioned regular polygon on an intuition? He inevitably did so, not in that he actually drew it (which would be an unnecessary and absurd demand), but rather, in that he knew the rule for the construction of his concept, and hence that he could determine its magnitude as closely to that of the object itself as he wished, and could give it in intuition in accordance with the concept, and thereby demonstrated the reality of the rule itself, and likewise that of this concept for the use of the imagination. If he had been asked to find out how a totality could be composed of monads, then knowing that he was not required to look for such beings of reason*a* in space, he would have acknowledged that nothing whatever can be said about them because they are super-sensible entities, which can be found only in thought, but never, as such, in intuition. – Mr. Eberhard, however, either insofar as they are too small for the degree of sharpness of our senses or because the number of them in a given intuitive representation is too large for the present degree of our imagination and its power of comprehension,*b* would have them be regarded as *nonsensible* objects, about which we should be able to know a great deal through the understanding; at which point we shall take leave of him, for such a concept of the nonsensible has nothing in common with that of the *Critique*, and since it already contains a verbal contradiction, will hardly have any followers.

It can be clearly seen from the above that Mr. Eberhard seeks the matter for all cognition in the senses, and he is not at fault for doing so. But he also wishes to employ this matter for the cognition of the supersensible. As a bridge to make that transition, he uses the principle of sufficient reason, which he not only assumes in its unlimited universality (where he requires, however, a quite different manner of distinguishing the sensible from the intellectual than he is probably willing to allow), but also, by his formula, prudently distinguishes from the principle of

8: 213

a *Vernunftwesen*
b *Fassungsvermögen*

causality, because otherwise he would be obstructing his own purposes.*
This bridge is not sufficient, however, for one cannot build on the far
shore with any materials of sensory representation. To be sure, he uses
these materials only because (like all other men) he lacks any others;
but this simple, which earlier on he believes himself to have found as a
part of sensory representation, he washes and cleanses of this stain by
boasting of having *demonstrated* it *into* matter, since it would never be
found in the sensory representation through mere perception. But now
once it is in matter as object of the senses, this partial representation
(the simple) is said by him to be real; and despite the demonstration,
there remains in that always the one small difficulty as to how one is to
secure the reality of a concept, which one has demonstrated only of a
sensible object, when it is supposed to signify something that cannot be
an object of the senses at all (not even a homogeneous part of one). For
it is at once uncertain whether, when one takes away from the simple
all the properties whereby it can be a part of matter, there is anything
at all remaining which could be called a possible thing. Consequently,
by means of that demonstration he would have proved the objective
reality of the simple as part of matter, and thus as an object belonging
solely to sensory intuition and *an intrinsically possible* experience, but by   8: 214
no means for any object, including the super-sensible beyond it, which
was, however, precisely the question at issue.

   In all that now follows (pp. 263–306) and is intended to serve as a
confirmation of the above, there is, as one can easily foresee, nothing
else to be found save distortion of the propositions of the *Critique*, and
more particularly misrepresentation and confusion of logical propositions, which concern merely the form of thinking (without taking any

---

* The proposition, 'All things have their ground,' or in other words, everything exists only as a consequence, that is, depends for its determination upon
  something else, holds without exception of all things as appearances in space and
  time, but in no way of things-in-themselves, for the sake of which Mr. Eberhard
  has actually attributed such generality to the proposition. It would have been
  even less suitable to his plans, however, to express it in universal form as the
  principle of causality: 'Everything that exists has a cause,' that is, exists only
  as effect; because his intent was to demonstrate the reality of the concept of a
  supreme being, which is not dependent on any further cause. It therefore becomes necessary to hide behind expressions which can be twisted at will; as he
  then (p. 259) uses the word 'ground' in such a way that one is led to believe that
  he has in mind something distinct from sensations, when on this occasion he
  merely means the part-sensations,[a] which, from a logical point of view, we are
  equally accustomed to call grounds of the possibility of a whole.

[a] *Theilempfindungen*

object into consideration) with transcendental propositions (which are concerned with how the understanding applies this, quite purely and without needing any source other than itself, to the *a priori* cognition of things). To the first belongs, among many other things, the translation of the inferences of the *Critique* into syllogistic form. He says (p. 270) that I would reason as follows: "All representations that are not appearances are *devoid* of forms of sensory intuition (an improper expression, which nowhere occurs in the *Critique*, but may be allowed to stand). – All representations of things-in-themselves are representations that are not appearances (this too is formulated contrary to the usage of the *Critique*, where it says that they are representations *of things* that are not appearances). – Therefore, they are absolutely empty." Here there are four terms, and he says that I ought to have concluded: "Therefore, these representations are devoid of the forms of sensory intuition."

Now the latter is really the only conclusion that can be drawn from the *Critique*, and the preceding one has only been read into it by Mr. Eberhard. But according to the *Critique* the following episyllogisms now follow from it, whereby that conclusion does eventually emerge: viz., representations that are devoid of the forms of sensory intuition are devoid of all intuition (for all our intuition is sensory). – Now the representations of things-in-themselves are devoid of, etc. – Therefore, they are devoid of all intuition. And finally: representations that are devoid of all intuition (to which, as concepts, no corresponding intuition can be given) are absolutely empty (without cognition of their object). – Now representations of things that are not appearances are devoid of all intuition. – Therefore, they are (as to cognition) absolutely empty.

What is to be doubted here, the understanding or the sincerity of Mr. Eberhard?

8: 215 Of his complete misunderstanding of the *Critique*, and of the groundlessness of what he purports to be able to put in its place in behalf of a better system, only a few examples can here be given; for even the most resolute comrade of Mr. Eberhard would grow weary of the labor of bringing the elements of his objections and counter-assertions into a self-consistent unity.

Having raised the question (p. 275): "Who (what) gives sensibility its matter, namely sensations?" he believes himself to have pronounced against the *Critique* when he says (p. 276): "We may choose what we will – we nevertheless arrive at *things-in-themselves*." Now that, of course, is the constant contention of the *Critique*; save that it posits this ground of the matter of sensory representations not once again in things, as objects of the senses, but in something super-sensible, which *grounds* the latter, and of which we can have no cognition. It says that the objects as things-in-themselves *give* the matter to empirical intuitions (they contain the ground by which to determine the faculty of representation in accordance with its sensibility), but they *are* not the matter thereof.

Immediately after this it is asked how the understanding works upon this matter (however it may be given). The *Critique* demonstrated in the *Transcendental Logic* that this occurs through subsumption of the sensory (pure or empirical) intuitions under the categories which, as concepts of things in general, must be wholly grounded *a priori* in the pure understanding. Mr. Eberhard, on the other hand, lays bare his own system when he says (pp. 276–79): "We cannot have any general concepts that we have not *derived* from the things that we have perceived through the senses, or from those of which we are conscious in our own soul," which separation from the particular he then precisely delineates in the same paragraph. This is the first act of the understanding. The second consists (p. 279) in this, that it again puts concepts together out of this sublimated matter. By means of *abstraction*, the understanding has therefore arrived (from sensory representations) at the categories, and now it ascends from these, and from the essential components of things to their attributes. Thus he says (p. 278): "So the understanding with the help of reason therefore obtains new composite concepts, just as it *ascends* for its own part, by means of abstraction, to ever more general and simple concepts, up to the concepts of the *possible* and the *grounded*," etc.

8: 216

This ascent (if that can be called an ascent which is only an abstraction from the empirical in the use of the understanding in experience, since that still leaves the intellectual, namely the category, which we ourselves, in accordance with the nature of our understanding, have installed *a priori* beforehand) is only *logical*, an ascent, that is, to more general rules, whose use, however, always remains merely within the scope of possible experience, because these rules are simply abstracted from the use of the understanding therein, where the categories are given a corresponding sensory intuition. – For the true *real* ascent, namely to another species of being that can in no way be given to the senses, not even to the most perfect, another mode of intuition would be needed, which we have named intellectual (because whatever belongs to cognition, and is not sensible, can have no other name and meaning); but with this we would not only have no further need for the categories, they would be of absolutely no use to an understanding of that nature. But who could provide us with such an intuitive understanding, or can acquaint us with it, if it somehow lies hidden within us?

Mr. Eberhard, however, can also tell us about that. For according to pp. 280–81, "there are also *intuitions which are not sensory* (but also not intuitions of the understanding) – another intuition than the sensory in space and time." – "The first elements of concrete time and the first elements of concrete space are no longer appearances (objects of sensory intuition)." They are therefore the true things, the *things-in-themselves*. He distinguishes (p. 299) this nonsensory intuition from the sensory on the grounds that it is that in which something "is represented *indistinctly* or confusedly through the *senses*," and he wishes (p. 295) to have the understanding defined as the "faculty of distinct cognition." – So the difference between his sensory and nonsensory intuition consists in the fact that the simple parts in concrete space and time are represented confusedly in sensory and distinctly in nonsensory intuition. In this way, of course, the demand of the *Critique* is fulfilled with respect to the objective reality of the concept of simple beings, as a corresponding intuition (albeit not a sensory one) is given to it.

8: 217   Now that was an *ascent* only to fall deeper. For once those simple beings were insinuated into the intuition itself, then their representations were established as parts contained in the empirical intuition, and with them too, the intuition remained what it was in regard to the whole, namely sensory. The consciousness of a representation makes no difference in the specific nature of the latter; for it can be conjoined with all representations. The consciousness of an empirical intuition is called perception. So the fact that these alleged simple parts are not *perceived* does not make the least difference in their nature as sensory intuitions, such that, if our senses were sharpened, the imaginative power, to grasp the manifold of their intuition with consciousness, would at the same

8: 218   time be so much enlarged as to perceive in them something nonsensible, by virtue of the distinctness* of this representation. – At this point, it may

---

* For there is also a *distinctness* in the intuition, and hence also in the representation of the individual, not merely of things in general (p. 295), which may be called *aesthetic* and is quite different from *logical* distinctness through concepts (supposing an Australian aborigine, for example, were to see a house for the first time, and was near enough to distinguish all its parts, though without having the least concept of it), though it cannot, of course, be contained in a logic textbook; and because of this it is also quite impermissible to adopt for this purpose, as he demands, the definition of the understanding as the faculty of *distinct* cognition, instead of that of the *Critique*, where it is said to be the *faculty of cognition through concepts*.[14] In particular, the latter definition is alone satisfactory because the understanding is thereby also characterized as a transcendental faculty of concepts (the categories) which originally spring only from it alone, whereas the former, by contrast, refers merely to the logical capacity to produce distinctness and universality, even in sensory representations, merely by clear representation and separation of their marks. It is, however, of great import to Mr. Eberhard to provide his definitions with ambiguous marks, so that he can evade the most important critical investigations. This also includes the expression (p. 295 and elsewhere): a cognition of *universal things*; a thoroughly reprehensible scholastic expression, which can reawaken the conflict between nominalists and realists, and which, although found, to be

---

perhaps occur to the reader to ask why, when Mr. Eberhard is elevated above the sphere of sensibility (p. 169), he still continues to use the expression 'nonsensible,' rather than '*super-sensible*.' Yet this happens with full forethought. For with the latter it would have been all too apparent that he could not extract it from sensory intuition, just because it is sensory. 'Nonsensible,' however, indicates a mere deficiency (e.g., in the consciousness of something in the representation of an object of the senses), and the reader will not immediately discern that a representation of real objects of another kind is to be foisted upon him. It is the same with the expression 'universal things' (instead of 'universal predicates of things'), of which we shall speak later, whereby the reader believes that he must understand a particular species of being, or with the expression '*nonidentical*' (instead of 'synthetic') judgments. It requires much skill in the choice of indefinite terms to sell puerilities to the reader as significant things.

If, therefore, Mr. Eberhard has correctly expounded the Leibniz–Wolff conception of the sensibility of intuition: that it consists merely in the confusedness of the manifold of the representations therein, but that they nevertheless still represent things-in-themselves, whose distinct cognition must depend on the understanding (which recognizes the simple parts in that intuition), then the *Critique* has not falsely imputed or ascribed anything to that philosophy, and it only remains to determine whether it is correct in saying that this standpoint, which the latter has assumed in order to characterize sensibility (as a special faculty of receptivity), is mistaken.* He confirms the correctness of that meaning of the conception of sensibility, which was attributed to the Leibnizian philosophy in the *Critique*, in that he posits (p. 303) the subjective ground of appearances, as confused representations, in the *incapacity* to distinguish

8: 219

---

sure, in many metaphysical compendia, still belongs merely to logic and certainly not to transcendental philosophy, since it does not designate any difference in the nature of things, but only in the use of concepts, whether they are applied universally or to particulars. Nevertheless, this expression, as well as that of the unimageable, serves to suggest to the reader for a moment that a special class of objects, e.g., the simple elements, might be intended thereby.

* Mr. Eberhard huffs and puffs in a comical fashion (p. 298) over the audacity of such a rebuke (in addition to incorrectly rewording it). If it ever occurred to anyone to rebuke Cicero because he did not write good Latin, then some Scioppius[15] (a grammarian reputed for his zeal) would put him pretty firmly, though properly, in his place; for *what constitutes good Latin* we can learn only from Cicero (and his contemporaries). But if anyone believed himself to have found an error in Plato's or Leibniz's philosophy, indignation that there should even be something to criticize in Leibniz would be ridiculous. For *what is philosophically correct* neither can nor should be learned from Leibniz; rather the touchstone, which lies equally to hand for one man as for another, is common human reason, and there are no *classical authors* in philosophy.

all the marks (partial representations of sensory intuition), and when rebuking the *Critique* for not having conceded this (p. 377), he says that it resides in the limitations of the subject. That besides these subjective grounds of the logical form of intuition, the appearances also have *objective* grounds is claimed by the *Critique* itself, and in this it does not contradict Leibniz. But that if these objective grounds (the simple elements) lie as parts in the appearances themselves and owing merely to their confusedness cannot be perceived as such, but only demonstrated into them, they ought to be called sensory and yet not merely sensory, but also, for the latter reason, intellectual *intuitions* as well, is an obvious contradiction, and Leibniz's conception of sensibility and appearances cannot be so interpreted, and either Mr. Eberhard has given an utterly erroneous account of that view, or it must be rejected without hesitation. One of the two: either the intuition is entirely intellectual with regard to the object, that is, we intuit things as they are in-themselves, and then sensibility consists merely in the confusedness that is inseparable from such a multifaceted intuition; or it is not intellectual, and we understand by it only the mode in which we are affected by an object, which in-itself is entirely unknown to us; and then sensibility is so far from consisting in confusedness that, on the contrary, its intuition might even have the highest degree of distinctness, and so far as there are simple parts in it, its clear distinction could extend to these as well, though it would still not in the least contain anything more than mere appearance. Both cannot be thought together in one and the same conception of sensibility. Consequently, sensibility, as Mr. Eberhard attributes the concept of it to Leibniz, differs from intellectual cognition[a] either merely in its logical form (confusedness), while as to its content it contains pure intellectual representations of things-in-themselves, or it differs from the latter transcendentally as well, that is, in origin and content, in that it contains nothing at all of the nature of the object in-itself, but merely the mode in which the subject is affected, however distinct it might otherwise choose to be. In the latter case we have the contention of the *Critique*, to which one cannot oppose the first opinion without positing sensibility merely in the confusedness of the representation that the given intuition contains.

8: 220

For a statement of the infinite difference between the theory of sensibility as a special kind of intuition, which has its form determinable *a priori* by universal principles, and that which takes this intuition to be merely empirical apprehension of things-in-themselves, which (as sensory intuition) differs from an intellectual intuition only by the indistinctness of the representation, one can do no better than Mr. Eberhard

[a] *Verstandeserkenntniss*

310

does it, against his will. From the *incapacity*, the *weakness*, and the *limits* of the faculty of representation (the very terms employed by Mr. Eberhard himself) one can derive no extensions of cognition, no positive determinations of objects. The given principle must itself be something positive, which forms the substrate for such propositions, albeit no more than subjectively, and with validity for objects only insofar as they are taken merely as appearances. If we grant to Mr. Eberhard his simple parts of the objects of sensory intuition, and allow that he explains their combination to the best of his ability by his principle of sufficient reason, how and through what arguments will he derive from his conceptions of monads and their connection by forces the representation of space: that as a whole it has three dimensions, and likewise that, of its triple boundaries, two are themselves still spaces, while the third, namely the point, is the boundary of all boundaries? Or, with regard to the objects of inner sense, how will he tease out their underlying conditions, time, as a magnitude, but of only *one* dimension, and (as space is also) a continuous magnitude, from simple parts, which in his opinion are perceived by sense, though not separately, yet are apprehended in thought by the understanding? And how will he derive from limits, indistinctness, and therefore from mere deficiencies, such a positive cognition, which contains the conditions of those sciences (geometry and universal physics), which extend themselves *a priori* the most of all? He must take all these properties as false and merely tacked on (since they directly contradict those simple parts that he accepts), or he must seek their objective reality not in things-in-themselves, but in things as appearances, that is, by seeking the form of their representation (as objects of sensory intuition) in the subject and in its receptive quality of being susceptible to an immediate representation of given objects, which form now makes conceivable *a priori* (even before the objects are given) the possibility of a manifold cognition of the conditions under which alone objects can appear to the senses. Now compare this with what Mr. Eberhard says (p. 377): "What the subjective ground of appearances may be, Mr. K. has not determined. – It is the limits of the subject" (that is now his determination). Read and judge.

Mr. Eberhard is (p. 391) uncertain whether I "understand by the form of sensory intuition the limits of the cognitive power, by which the manifold becomes the *image* of time and space, or these images in general themselves." – "He who conceives them as *themselves original*, not *implanted in their grounds*, conceives a *qualitas occulta*. If, however, he accepts one of the two preceding explanations, then his theory is either wholly or partially contained in the Leibnizian theory." He demands (p. 378) instruction as to this *form* of *appearance*; "whether it be gentle," he says, "or harsh." It has pleased him in this section to adopt mainly

8: 221

the latter tone. I shall adhere to the former, as is proper for one with superior reasons on his side.

The *Critique* admits absolutely no implanted[a] or innate[b] *representations*. One and all, whether they belong to intuition or to concepts of the understanding, it considers them as *acquired*. But there is also an original acquisition (as the teachers of natural right call it), and thus of that which previously did not yet exist at all, and so did not belong to anything prior to this act. According to the *Critique*, these are, *in the first place*, the form of things in space and time, *second*, the synthetic unity of the manifold in concepts; for neither of these does our cognitive faculty get from objects as given therein in-themselves, rather it brings them about, *a priori*, out of itself. There must indeed be a ground for it in the subject, however, which makes it possible that these representations can arise in this and no other manner, and be related to objects which are not yet given, and this ground at least is *innate*. (Since Mr. Eberhard himself notes that in order to be entitled to the use of the term '*implanted*,' the existence of God would have to be presupposed as proven, why does he then use it rather than the old term 'innate' in a critique which deals with the first foundations of all cognition?) Mr. Eberhard says (p. 390): "the grounds of the general, still undetermined images of space and time, and with them the soul is created," but on the following page he is again doubtful whether by the form of intuition (it should be: the ground of all forms of intuition) I mean the *limits* of the cognitive power or those *images* themselves. How he has been able to conjecture the former, even in a doubtful manner, is beyond comprehension, since he must be aware that his aim was to vindicate that method of explaining sensibility in op-position to the *Critique*; the second option, however, namely that he is doubtful whether I do not mean the indeterminate images of space and time themselves, may be explained but not excused. For where have I ever called the intuitions of space and time, in which images are first of all possible, themselves images[16] (which always presuppose a concept of which they are the *presentation*, e.g., the indeterminate image for the concept of a triangle, wherein neither the ratios of the sides nor those of the angles are given)? He has become so inured to the deceptive rit-ual of using the term '*image*' instead of '*sensible*' that it accompanies him everywhere. The ground of the possibility of sensory intuition is nei-ther of the two, neither *limit* of the cognitive faculty nor *image*; it is the mere *receptivity* peculiar to the mind, when it is affected by something (in sensation), to receive a representation in accordance with its subjec-tive constitution. Only this first formal ground, e.g., of the possibility of an intuition of space, is innate, not the spatial representation itself. For

8: 222

[a] *anerschaffene*
[b] *angeborne*

impressions would always be required in order to determine the cognitive faculty to the representation of an object (which is always a specific act) in the first place. Thus arises the formal *intuition* called space,[17] as an originally acquired representation (the form of outer objects in general), the ground of which (as mere receptivity) is nevertheless innate, and whose acquisition long precedes the determinate *concepts* of things that are in accordance with this form; the acquisition of the latter is an *acquisitio derivativa*, in that it already presupposes universal transcenden-   8: 223
tal concepts of the understanding, which are likewise acquired and not innate,* though their *acquisitio*, like that of space, is no less *originaria* and presupposes nothing innate save the subjective conditions of the spontaneity of thought (in conformity with the unity of apperception). No one can be in doubt as to this meaning of the ground of the possibility of a pure sensory intuition, save someone who may be leafing through the *Critique* with the help of a dictionary, but has not thought it through.

How little Mr. Eberhard understands the *Critique* in its clearest propositions, or even how he deliberately misunderstands it, may be illustrated by the following.

It was said in the *Critique* that the mere category of substance (like any other) contains absolutely nothing more than the logical function, in regard to which an object is thought as determined, and that by this alone no cognition whatsoever of the object is produced, not even by the least (synthetic) predicate, *save insofar as we provide it with an underlying sensory intuition*; from which it was then justly inferred that, since we cannot judge of things at all without categories, absolutely no cognition of the *super-sensible* (always taken here in the theoretical sense) is possible. Mr. Eberhard purports (pp. 384–5) to be able to provide this cognition of the pure category of substance, even without the help of sensory intuition: "It is the *force* which engenders the accidents." But now force itself is again nothing other than a category (or the predicable thereof), namely that of *causality*, of which I have likewise declared that without an underlying sensory intuition its objective validity can no more be demonstrated than that of the concept of a substance. Now he does in fact base this demonstration (p. 385) on the presentation of accidents, and of force too as their ground, in sensory (inner) intuition. For he actually relates the concept of cause to a series of states of the mind in time, of successive representations or degrees thereof, whose ground is contained "in the thing, fully determined by all its present, past and future alterations," "and hence," he says, "this thing is a force; hence it is a substance." But the *Critique* itself requires no more than   8: 224

---

* In what sense Leibniz takes the word 'innate,' when he uses it of certain elements of knowledge will thereby be assessable. An article by Hissmann in the *Teutsche Merkur* (October, 1777) can facilitate this assessment.[18]

the *presentation* in inner sensory intuition of the concept of force (which, we note in passing, is entirely different from that to which he wanted to secure reality, namely substance,)* and the objective reality of a substance as sensible being is thereby secured. The issue, however, was whether such reality could be demonstrated of the concept of force as a pure category, i.e., even apart from its application to objects of sensory intuition, and hence as valid also of super-sensible objects, that is, mere objects of understanding; for then all consciousness that rests on temporal conditions, and hence too every sequence of past, present, and future, together with the whole law of the continuity of altered states of the mind would have to go, and thus nothing would remain by which the accidents could be *given* and which could serve as *evidence* for the concept of force. So if, as is required, Mr. Eberhard were to remove the concept of man (in which the concept of a body is already contained), as well as that of representations whose existence is determinable in time, and thus everything that contains conditions of outer as well as inner intuition (for that he must do if he wants to secure the reality of the concepts of substance and cause as pure categories, i.e., as concepts which can serve, if need be, for cognition of the super-sensible), then he is left with nothing else of the concept of substance but the notion of a something whose existence must be thought only as that of a subject, and not as a mere predicate of something else; of the concept of cause, however, he is left only with the concept of a relation of something to something else in existence, whereby if I posit the first, the other is also determined and necessarily posited. Now from these two concepts he can extract absolutely no cognition of the thing so constituted, not even whether such a constitution is possible, i.e., whether there can be anything in which it is found. The question ought not to be raised at present, whether, *in relation to practical principles a priori*, the categories of substance and cause would

8: 225

---

* The proposition: 'the thing (the substance) *is* a force,' instead of the perfectly natural 'substance *has* a force,' is in conflict with all ontological concepts and, in its consequences, very prejudicial to metaphysics. For the concept of substance, that is, of inherence in a subject, is thereby basically entirely lost, and instead of it that of dependence on a cause is posited; just as Spinoza wanted to have it, since he affirmed the universal dependence of all things in the world on an original being, as their common cause, while making this universal active force itself into a substance, and in so doing converted that dependence of theirs into inherence in the latter. In addition to its relation as *subject* to accidents (and their inherence), a substance certainly also has the relation to them of *cause* to effects; but the former is not identical with the latter. Force is not that which contains the ground of the existence of accidents (for substance contains that); it is rather the concept of the mere relation of substance to the latter, *insofar* as it contains their ground, and this relation is completely different from that of inherence.

not obtain objective reality in regard to the pure practical determination of reason, if the concept of a thing (as noumenon) underlies them. For the possibility of a thing that can exist merely as subject and never in turn as predicate of another thing, or of the property in regard to the existence of another of having the relation of ground but not, conversely, that of consequent to the same, must, for the purpose of a theoretical cognition, certainly be made evident by an intuition corresponding to these concepts, because without this no objective reality is attached to them, and thus no cognition of such an object would be attained; but if those concepts should yield, not constitutive, but merely regulative principles of the use of reason (as is always the case with the Idea of a noumenon), they can also, as merely logical functions for the concepts of things whose possibility is unprovable, have a use for reason that is indispensable to it from a practical viewpoint, because they would then be valid, not as objective grounds of the possibility of noumena, but as subjective principles (of the theoretical or practical use of reason) in regard to phenomena. – But here, as has been said, we are still talking merely of the constitutive principles of the cognition of things, and whether it be possible to acquire cognition of any object by merely speaking of it through categories, without vindicating the latter through intuition (which for us is always sensory), as Mr. Eberhard believes, though for all his boasts as to the fecundity of the arid ontological wasteland, is not able to effect.

Section Two
The solution of the problem, How are synthetic judgments possible a priori? according to Mr. Eberhard

8: 226   This problem, considered in its generality, is the stumbling block on which all metaphysical dogmatists must inevitably founder, and which they circumvent as much as possible; so that I have yet to find a single opponent of the *Critique* who has endeavored to provide a solution to this problem that would be valid for all cases. Armed with his principles of contradiction and sufficient reason (which he nevertheless only presents as an analytic principle), Mr. Eberhard ventures on this task; with what success we shall soon see.

     Mr. Eberhard has, it would seem, no distinct concept of what the *Critique* terms dogmatism. Thus, he speaks (p. 262) of apodictic demonstrations, which he claims to have furnished, and adds; "If he is a dogmatist who accepts things-in-themselves with certainty, then, no matter what the cost, we must submit ourselves to the indignity of being called dogmatists," and then he says (p. 289), "that the Leibnizian philosophy contains just as much of a critique of reason as the Kantian; for it grounds its dogmatism on a precise analysis of the cognitive faculties, what is possible for each one." Now if it really does this, then it does not contain a dogmatism in the sense in which our *Critique* always uses this term.

     By *dogmatism* in metaphysics the *Critique* understands this: the general trust in its principles, *without* a previous *critique* of the faculty of reason itself, merely because of its success; *by skepticism*, however, the general mistrust in pure reason, without a previous critique, merely because of the failure of its assertions.* The *criticism* of the procedure concerning

---

* Success in the use of principles *a priori* lies in their constant confirmation in application to experience; for then one almost concedes to the dogmatist his demonstration *a priori*. But failure in their use, which gives rise to skepticism, occurs solely in cases where demonstrations *a priori* can alone be required, because experience can neither affirm nor deny anything regarding them, and consists in the fact that demonstrations *a priori* of equal strength, which establish precisely the opposite, are contained in the common human reason. The former are also mere principles of the possibility of experience and are

everything pertaining to metaphysics (the doubt of deferment) is, on the other hand, the maxim of a general mistrust of all its synthetic propositions, until a universal ground of their possibility has been discerned in the essential conditions of our cognitive faculty.

8: 227

One does not therefore escape from the justified reproach of dogmatism by appealing, as on p. 262, to so-called apodictic demonstrations of one's metaphysical assertions; for even when no obvious error is to be found therein (which is certainly not the case above), they are so commonly a failure, and demonstrations of the opposite so often oppose them with no less clarity, that the skeptic, though he should have nothing at all to bring against the argument, is still fully justified in placing his *non liquet*[a] against it. Only if the demonstration is conducted by a route whereon a mature critique has safely pointed in advance to the possibility of *cognition a priori* and its universal conditions, can the metaphysician clear himself of the charge of dogmatism, which, failing that, is still always blind in all demonstrations, and the critique's canon for this kind of assessment is contained in the general solution of the problem: *how is a synthetic cognition possible a priori?* If this problem has not previously been solved, then all metaphysicians until now have not been free of the charge of blind dogmatism or skepticism, no matter how great a name they may justly possess for their achievements elsewhere.

8: 228

Mr. Eberhard would have it otherwise. He proceeds as if such a cautionary call, which is warranted by so many examples in the *Transcendental Dialectic*, were not addressed to the dogmatist at all, and long before any critique of our capacity to judge synthetically *a priori*, he takes for granted a synthetic proposition that has long been in much dispute, namely that time and space and the things in them consist of simple elements, without undertaking even the slightest prior critical investigation as to the very possibility of such a determination of the sensible by Ideas of the

contained in the *Analytic*. But since, if the *Critique* has not previously secured them as such, they can easily be taken for principles that apply more widely than merely to objects of experience, a dogmatism arises in regard to the supersensible. The latter refer to objects, not like the former through concepts of the understanding, but rather through Ideas, which can never be given in experience. Now, since in that case the demonstrations, for which the principles have been thought merely for objects of experience, would necessarily have to contradict each other, it follows that if one ignores the *Critique*, which can alone determine the boundary line, not only must a skepticism arise in regard to all that is thought through mere Ideas of reason, but ultimately a suspicion against all knowledge *a priori*, which then leads in the end to the doctrine of universal doubt concerning metaphysics.

[a] An expression from Roman law, used by a jury when it declines to pronounce a verdict of either guilt or innocence.

super-sensible, which should nonetheless have been forced on him by the contradiction of this proposition with mathematics, and gives, in his own procedure, the best example of what the *Critique* calls dogmatism, which must forever remain banished from all transcendental philosophy, and the meaning of which will now, I hope, be clearer to him from his own example.

Now before proceeding to the solution of this principal problem, it is of course absolutely necessary to have a distinct and determinate concept, *first*, of what the *Critique* understands in general by synthetic as distinguished from analytic judgments, and *second*, of what it means by characterizing such judgments as judgments *a priori*, as distinct from empirical. – The first point has been stated by the *Critique* as clearly and repeatedly as can be required. They are judgments through whose predicate I attribute *more* to the subject of the judgment than I think in that concept of which I assert the predicate; the latter therefore extends my cognition beyond what that concept contained; this does not occur through analytic judgments, which do nothing more than represent *clearly* and assert as belonging to it, what was already really thought and contained in the given concept. – The second point, namely, what is *a judgment a priori* as distinct from an empirical one, here causes no difficulty; for it is a distinction long known and named in logic, and does not like the first at least (as Mr. Eberhard would have it) appear under a *new name*. Still, for the benefit of Mr. Eberhard, it is not superfluous to note here that a predicate, which is attributed to a subject by an *a priori* proposition, is for that very reason asserted to belong to it *necessarily* (be inseparable from the concept thereof). The latter are also called predicates that belong to the essence or inner possibility of the concept (*ad essentiam* pertinentia*), so that all propositions which are valid *a priori* must contain them; the others, namely those that are separable from the concept (without detriment to it) are called extra-essential marks (*extraessentialia*). Now the first belong to the essence, either as constituents thereof (*ut constitutiva*), or as consequences of it, adequately grounded therein (*ut rationata*). They are called essential parts (*essentialia*), which therefore contain no predicate that might be derived from others contained in the same concept, and their totality constitutes the logical essence (*essentia*); the second are called properties (*attributa*). The extra-essential marks are either inner (*modi*) or relational marks (*relationes*), and cannot serve as predicates in propositions *a priori*, because they are separable from the concept of the subject, and therefore not necessarily connected with it. – Now it is clear that if one has not already given some prior

8: 229

---

* In order to avoid even the least appearance of a *circular explanation* with these words, one may use instead of the expression *ad essentiam* what is here the equivalent expression *ad internam possibilitatem pertinentia*.

criterion for a synthetic proposition *a priori*, to say that its predicate is an attribute would in no way illuminate its distinction from an analytic proposition. For by calling it an attribute nothing more is said than that it may be derived as a necessary consequence from the essence: whether analytically, by the principle of contradiction, or synthetically, by some other principle, remains thereby completely undetermined. Thus, in the proposition 'every body is divisible,' the predicate is an attribute, because it can be derived as a necessary consequence from an essential part of the concept of the subject, namely extension. But it is an attribute which is represented as belonging to the concept of body by the principle of contradiction; therefore the proposition itself, even though it asserts an attribute of the subject, is nevertheless analytic. Permanence, on the other hand, is also an attribute of substance; for it is an absolutely necessary predicate thereof, but it is not contained in the concept of substance itself, and so cannot be derived from it by any analysis (by the principle of contradiction), and thus the proposition 'every substance is permanent' is a synthetic proposition. If it is therefore said of a proposition that it has for its predicate an attribute of the subject, nobody yet knows if it is analytic or synthetic; one must therefore add: it contains a synthetic attribute, i.e., a necessary (albeit derived), and thus *a priori* knowable predicate in a synthetic judgment. So according to Mr. Eberhard, the explanation of synthetic judgments *a priori* is that they are judgments which assert synthetic attributes of things. Mr. Eberhard plunges into this tautology in order, where possible, not only to say something better and more determinate about the character of synthetic judgments *a priori*, but also with the definition of them to indicate at the same time their general principle, whereby their possibility can be judged, a task which the *Critique* was able to accomplish only after much difficult labor. According to him (p. 315): "analytic judgments are those whose predicates assert the essence or some of the essential parts of the subject; synthetic judgments, however (p. 316), if they are necessary truths, have attributes for their predicates." Through the word 'attribute' he characterized synthetic judgments as judgments *a priori* (owing to the necessity of their predicates), but at the same time as those which assert the *rationata* of the essence, not the essence itself or some of its parts; he is thus alluding to the principle of sufficient reason, by means of which alone they can be predicated of the subject, and was relying on it not being noticed that here this ground *should* only be a logical ground, namely one which says no more than that the predicate is being derived from the concept of the subject, only mediately, to be sure, but still always in accordance with the principle of contradiction; whence, even though it asserts an attribute, it can then still be analytic, and so does not bear the hallmark of a synthetic proposition. He was very careful to avoid saying openly that it would have to be a synthetic attribute in order for the proposition

8: 230

319

to which it serves as predicate to be assignable to the latter class; though it must surely have occurred to him that this limitation is necessary; for otherwise the tautology would have been all too plainly apparent, and so he came out with something which to the inexperienced seems to be new and substantive, but in fact is merely a haze that is easily seen through.

We now also see what is signified by his principle of sufficient reason, which he propounded above in such a way that we were led to believe (to judge primarily by the example there cited) that he understood by it a real ground, since ground and consequence are distinct from one another *realiter* and the proposition which combines them is in this way a synthetic proposition. By no means! Already at that point he was shrewdly looking ahead to future instances of its use, and had stated it in so indeterminate a manner that he could give it whatever meaning the occasion required, and so might also use it now and then as the principle of analytic judgments without the reader noticing it. Is the proposition 'every body is divisible' any the less analytic because its predicate is first of all derivable by analysis from that which pertains immediately to the concept (to the essential part), namely extension? If, from a predicate which is directly cognized in a concept by the principle of contradiction, another is inferred, which is likewise derived therefrom by the principle of contradiction, is it any the less derived from that concept by the principle of contradiction than the first one?

It is therefore apparent: first, that the hope of explaining synthetic propositions *a priori* through propositions which have attributes of their subject as predicates is destroyed, unless one is willing to add to this that *they are synthetic*, and so perpetrate an obvious tautology; second, that limits are set to the principle of sufficient reason, if it is to yield a special principle, viz., that it will never be admitted as such into transcendental philosophy save insofar as it legitimizes a synthetic connection of concepts. We may now compare with this the joyous proclamation of our author (p. 317): "So we would thus have already derived the distinction of judgments into analytic and synthetic, and indeed *with the most accurate demarcation of their boundaries* (that the first pertains merely to the essentials,[a] the second to attributes), from the most fruitful and illuminating principle of division (an allusion to his previously vaunted fertile fields of ontology), and *with the fullest certainty* that the division completely *exhausts* its principle of division."

Yet in this triumphant cry of victory Mr. Eberhard does not seem to be so wholly assured. For on p. 318, after taking it as fully established that Wolff and Baumgarten would have long known and expressly characterized, albeit in different terms, what the *Critique* merely puts forward under a different name, he becomes at once uncertain which predicates

8: 231

8: 232

[a] *Essentialien*

in synthetic judgments I may well have in mind; and now he raises such a dust cloud of distinctions and classifications of the predicates that can occur in judgments, that the topic in hand can no longer be seen for it; all in order to demonstrate that I *should have defined* synthetic judgments, especially the *a priori* variety, as distinct from the analytic, in *some other way* than I have done. Nor is there anything said here of my manner of solving the problem of how such judgments are possible, but only of what I *understand* thereby, and that, if I accept one kind of predicate in them (p. 319), my concept is too *wide*, but that if I understand them to be of another kind (p. 320), it is too *narrow*. Yet it is clear that if a concept first proceeds from the definition, it is impossible for it to be too narrow or too wide, for it then signifies nothing more, and also nothing less, than what the definition says of it. The only thing that might still be objected to in it would be that it contains something inherently incomprehensible, which is thus of no value to the explanation. But the greatest master in the obfuscation of what is clear can bring nothing against the definition the *Critique* gives of *synthetic* propositions: they are propositions whose predicate contains more in it than is really thought in the concept of the subject; in other words, through whose predicate something is added to the thought of the subject, which was not contained therein; *analytic* are those whose predicate merely contains the same as what was thought in the concept of the subject of these judgments. Now the predicate of the first kind of propositions may, if they are *a priori* propositions, be an attribute (of the subject of the judgment) or who knows what else, but this determination neither can nor ought to enter into the definition, even were it to be demonstrated of the subject in a manner as instructive as that employed by Mr. Eberhard; that belongs to the deduction of the possibility of the cognition of things through judgments of that kind, which must first appear *after* the definition. But now he finds the definition incomprehensible, too wide or too narrow, because it does not accord with his own allegedly more precise determination of the predicate of such judgments.

In order to bring a perfectly clear and simple matter into as much confusion as possible, Mr. Eberhard employs a variety of expedients, though the effect they have is entirely contrary to his purpose.

"The whole of metaphysics," he claims (p. 308), "according to Mr. Kant, *contains nothing but analytic judgments*," and in support of this allegation he cites a passage from the *Prolegomena* (p. 33).[19] He states this as if I were saying it of metaphysics *in general*, when at that point my sole concern is with *previous* metaphysics *insofar as its propositions are based on valid demonstrations*. For of metaphysics in itself the *Prolegomena* asserts (p. 36): "*Properly metaphysical* judgments are one and all synthetic."[20] But even as to previous metaphysics, it is said in the *Prolegomena*, immediately after the passage cited, "that it also presents synthetic propositions, 8: 233

which are readily granted to it, though it has never demonstrated them *a priori.*" So what is affirmed in the passage in question is not that previous metaphysics contains no synthetic propositions (for it has more than enough of them), and among them some that are perfectly true (namely those that are principles of a possible experience), but only that it has not demonstrated any of them on *a priori* grounds; and to refute this assertion of mine, Mr. Eberhard would have needed to provide only one such apodictically demonstrated proposition; for the principle of sufficient reason with its demonstration (pp. 163–64 of his Magazine) will certainly not refute my assertion. Equally fictitious is the claim (p. 314) "that I assert that mathematics is the only science that contains synthetic judgments *a priori.*" He has not cited the place where this was supposedly said by me; but the second part of the main transcendental question, how pure natural science is possible (*Prolegomena*, pp. 71–124),²¹ should have made it perfectly obvious to him that I expressly maintain the opposite, had he not been bent on seeing the very contrary of this. On p. 318 he ascribes to me the claim that, "apart from the judgments of mathematics, only the judgments of experience are synthetic," even though the *Critique* (First Edition, pp. 158–235) presents the idea of a complete system of metaphysical, and indeed *synthetic* principles, and establishes them through *a priori* demonstrations. My assertion was that these principles are nevertheless only principles of the *possibility of experience*; he takes this to mean "that they are only *empirical judgments*," thereby making what I term a ground of experience into a consequence of it. Thus everything that comes into his hands from the *Critique* is first marred and distorted in order to let it appear for a moment in a false light.

8: 234   Yet another stratagem, so as to avoid being tied down to his counterassertions, is that he presents them in completely general terms and as abstractly as possible, and takes care not to give any example, from which it might be known with certainty what he wants to claim. Thus, on p. 318 he divides the attributes into those that are cognized either *a priori* or *a posteriori*, and says that *it seems to him* that I understand by my synthetic judgments "merely the not absolutely necessary truths, and of the absolutely necessary, the latter kind of judgments, whose necessary predicates can be cognized only *a posteriori* by the human understanding." It seems to me, however, that something else should have been said by these words than he actually did say; for as they stand, they contain an obvious contradiction. Predicates that are cognized only *a posteriori* but yet as *necessary*, and likewise attributes of such a nature that, according to p. 321, they "cannot be derived from the essence of the subject" are by the explanation which Mr. Eberhard himself gave above of the latter, completely inconceivable things. But if something is nevertheless thought thereby, and if an answer is to be given to the objection that Mr. Eberhard raises, by his barely intelligible distinction, to the usefulness of the definition of synthetic judgments given in the *Critique*, then he should have offered an example of this strange species of attribute; for I cannot refute an objection to which I am unable to attach any meaning. He avoids, as much as he can, introducing examples from metaphysics, but restricts himself, as long as possible, to those from mathematics, whereby he also proceeds entirely in accordance with his best interests. For he wishes to escape from the severe rebuke that *previous* metaphysics has been absolutely unable to demonstrate its synthetic propositions *a priori* (because it wishes to demonstrate them from their concepts as valid of things-in-themselves), and he therefore always chooses examples from mathematics, whose propositions are grounded in rigorous proofs because they are based upon *a priori* intuition; though certainly he cannot let this rank as an essential condition of the possibility of *all* synthetic propositions *a priori*, without at the same time giving up all hope of extending his cognition to the super-sensible, to which no intuition possible for us corresponds, and thus leaving uncultivated his potentially fertile fields of psychology and theology. So if we cannot particularly applaud either his insight or his willingness to shed light on a controversial subject, we must at least do justice to his prudence in neglecting no advantage, were it only a seeming one.

But when it happens that Mr. Eberhard stumbles, as if by chance, upon an example from metaphysics, he always comes to grief with it, in that it proves the very opposite of what he thereby sought to confirm. He had earlier wished to prove that there must be another principle of the possibility of things besides the principle of contradiction, and says, indeed, that it would have to be deduced from the principle of contradiction, as he then in fact also attempts to derive it. He now says p. 319: "The proposition: everything necessary is eternal, all necessary truths are eternal truths, is *obviously a synthetic* proposition, and yet it can be cognized *a priori*." It is, however, *obviously analytic*, and one can sufficiently see from this example what a distorted conception Mr. Eberhard continues to have of this distinction among propositions, with which he claims to be so thoroughly conversant. For he will not, of course, want to regard truth as a particular thing existing in time, whose existence is either eternal or only persists for a certain time. That all bodies are extended is necessarily and eternally true, whether they exist now or not, and whether that existence is brief or lengthy, or goes on throughout all time, i.e., eternally. The proposition says only: these truths do not depend upon experience (which must occur at one time or another), and are therefore not limited by any temporal conditions, i.e., they are cognizable as truths *a priori*, which is completely identical with the proposition: they are cognizable as necessary truths.

The same applies to the example introduced on p. 325, which must also be noted as an example of his punctiliousness in referring to

8: 235

propositions of the *Critique*, in that he says: "I do not see how one can wish to deprive metaphysics of all synthetic judgments." Now far from doing this, the *Critique* (as has already been noted) has, on the contrary, presented an entire and, in fact, complete system of such judgments as true principles; though it has at the same time shown that they collectively express only the synthetic unity of the manifold of intuition (as condition of the possibility of experience), and are therefore applicable to objects only insofar as they can be given in intuition. The metaphysical example which he now offers of *synthetic* propositions *a priori*, though with the cautious qualification: if metaphysics demonstrates such a proposition,[22] viz., all finite things are mutable, and the infinite thing is immutable, is in both parts *analytic*. For *realiter*, i.e., *as to existence*, the mutable is that whose determinations can follow one another in time; so only that is mutable which cannot exist other than in time. This condition is not, however, necessarily connected with the concept of a finite thing as such (which does not have all reality), but only with a thing as object of sensory intuition. Now since Mr. Eberhard wishes to affirm his *a priori* propositions as independent of this latter condition, his proposition that everything finite is, as such, mutable (i.e., as to its mere concept, and thus even as noumenon) is false. So the proposition: everything finite is, as such, mutable, would have to be understood only from the determination of its concept, and thus *logically*, since in that case by 'mutable' would be meant that which is not thoroughly determined through its concept, and thus what can be determined in many opposing ways. But in that case the proposition that *finite* things, i.e., all save the most real being, are logically mutable (in regard to the concept which one can form of them) would be an analytic proposition; for it is completely identical to say: I think a thing finite in that it *does not possess all* reality, and to say: through the concept thereof it is not determined what, or *how much* reality I should accord to it, i.e., I can attribute now this, now that to it, and *change* its determination in many ways without affecting the concept of its finitude. It is in just the same way, namely logically, that the infinite being is immutable; for if by it is understood that being which, in virtue of its concept, can have nothing save reality as its predicate and hence is already thoroughly determined thereby (with regard, that is, to predicates of which we are uncertain[a] whether or not they are truly real), then

8: 236 (margin)

---

[a] The Akademie-*Ausgabe*, as well as other standard editions, all have *gewiss* [certain]. But, as Manfred Gawlina has suggested in correspondence, Kant must have meant *ungewiss*. Kant's concern here is to contrast the logical with the real, and his point is that, though we know that an infinite being is immutable in virtue of its concept (logically), since it is the concept of a being that is thoroughly determined, we do not know whether the predicates we attribute to such a being on this basis are objectively real. If we did we would have synthetic *a priori* knowledge of its nature, which is just what Kant denies.

no single predicate of it can be replaced by another without prejudice to its concept; but at the same time this shows it to be a merely analytic proposition, namely one that attributes no other predicate to its subject than can be derived from it through the principle of contradiction.* If we play with mere concepts, without considering their objective reality, then we can very easily produce many such illusory extensions of science without needing intuition; but it is quite another matter when the aim is to extend our cognition of the object. Another such extension, though a merely apparent one, is to be found in the proposition: the infinite being (taken in the above metaphysical sense) is itself not mutable *realiter*, i.e., its inner determinations do not follow one another in time (since its existence as mere noumenon cannot without contradiction be thought in time), which is likewise a merely analytic proposition, if we presuppose the synthetic principles of space and time to be formal intuitions of things as phenomena. For it is then identical with the proposition of the *Critique: the concept of the most real being is not the concept of a phenomenon*, and so far from expanding our cognition of the infinite being as a synthetic proposition, it precludes that concept from any expansion by denying it intuition. – Still, it should be noted that in enunciating the above-mentioned proposition, Mr. Eberhard cautiously adds, "if metaphysics can demonstrate it." I have immediately indicated the premise whereby it tends to deceive, as though it entailed a synthetic proposition, and which is also the only possible means whereby determinations (such as that of the immutable), which have a certain sense

8: 237

8: 238

---

* Among the propositions that belong merely to logic, but by the ambiguity of their expression are palmed off as metaphysical, and thus, in spite of being analytic, are taken to be synthetic, belongs also the proposition: *the essences of things are immutable*, i.e., one cannot alter anything in what essentially belongs to their concept without simultaneously abolishing the concept itself. This proposition, which occurs in Baumgarten's *Metaphysics §132²³* and indeed in the Chapter on the mutable and immutable, where *alteration* is (quite properly) explained by the existence of a thing's determinations one after another (their succession), and thus by their sequence in time, sounds as if thereby a law of nature were being promulgated, which *expanded* our concepts of the objects of the senses (especially since the topic is existence in time). So even novices believe they have learned something considerable by this, and by declaring that the essences of things are immutable make short work, for example, of the opinion of some mineralogists, that silica might be gradually transformed into alumina. But this metaphysical adage is a poor identical proposition that has nothing whatever to do with the existence of things, and their possible or impossible alterations; it belongs entirely to logic, and enjoins something that nobody can think of denying anyway, namely that if I want to retain the concept of one and the same object, I must not alter anything in it, i.e., must not predicate of it the opposite of what I think thereby.

in relation to the logical essence (of the concept), are subsequently employed in a completely different sense, in relation to the real essence (the nature of the object). So the reader need not let himself be put off with dilatory answers (which in the end will still come from dear Baumgarten, who also takes concept for thing), but can judge for himself on the spot.

One sees from the entire discussion here that Mr. Eberhard either has no concept whatever of synthetic judgments *a priori*, or, more probably, that he deliberately seeks to confuse it so that the reader will grow doubtful of what is well within reach. The only two metaphysical examples he would dearly like to slip through as synthetic, though when carefully considered they are analytic, are: all necessary truths are *eternal* (here he could just as well have used the word *immutable*), and: the necessary being is immutable. The paucity of examples, when the *Critique* offers him a number of them that are genuinely synthetic, is quite easy to explain. He was concerned to have such predicates for his judgments as he could demonstrate to be attributes of the subject from the mere concept thereof. Now since this will not do if the predicate is synthetic, he had to seek out one that has already been commonly played with in metaphysics, in that it has sometimes been considered in its merely logical relation to the concept of the subject, and sometimes in its real relation to the object, while yet a single meaning was thought to be found therein, namely the concept of the mutable and immutable; which predicate, if the existence of its subject is posited in time, certainly yields an attribute of this subject and a synthetic judgment, but then also presupposes sensory intuition and the thing itself, although only as phenomenon, which it by no means suited him to assume, however, as a condition of synthetic judgments. Now instead of taking the predicate *immutable* as valid of things (in their existence), he employs it of concepts of things, since then, indeed, immutability becomes an attribute of all predicates, insofar as they necessarily belong to a certain concept; now this concept may itself have some object corresponding to it, or it may also be an empty concept. – He had already played the same game before with the principle of sufficient reason.[a] We were supposed to think that he was presenting a metaphysical proposition, which determines something of things *a priori*, and it is a merely logical one, which says nothing more than that for a judgment to be a proposition, it must be represented not merely as possible (problematic) but at the same time as grounded (no matter whether it be analytic or synthetic). The metaphysical principle of *causality* was very dear to him; but he took care not to touch it (for the example which he gives of it does not accord with the universality of that supposedly supreme principle of all synthetic judgments). The

8: 239

[a] *Satz des Grundes*

reason was that he wanted to slip through a logical rule, which is wholly analytic and abstracts from every particularity of things, as a principle of nature, which is solely the business of metaphysics.

Mr. Eberhard must have feared that the reader might eventually see through this deception, and to put it once and for all out of sight he therefore says at the conclusion of this issue (p. 331) that "the dispute as to whether a proposition be analytic or synthetic is of little moment in regard to its logical truth." But in vain. Plain common sense must seize hold of this question once it is clearly posed to it. That I can extend my cognition beyond a given concept is taught me by the daily increase of my knowledge through an ever-enlarging experience. But if it is said that I can increase it beyond the given concepts even without experience, i.e., can judge synthetically *a priori*, and to this it is added that something more is necessarily required for this purpose than to have these concepts, that a *ground* is also needed whereby I can truthfully add more than I already think in them, then I would laugh at anyone who told me that this proposition, that I must also have some ground beyond my concept, in order to say more than lies within it, is that very principle, which already suffices for this extension, in that I only need represent to myself this addition, which I think *a priori* as pertaining to the concept of a thing, though not contained in it, as an *attribute*. For I want to know what sort of ground it may be, which, besides what is essentially proper to my concept and what I already knew, acquaints me with more, and does so necessarily, as an attribute belonging to a thing, albeit not contained in its concept. Now I found that the extension of my cognition through experience rests upon empirical (sensory) intuition, in which I encoun- 8: 240 tered much that corresponded to my concept, but could also learn more than was yet thought in this concept, as connected thereto. Now once it is pointed out to me, I can easily see that, if an extension of cognition beyond my concept is to take place *a priori*, then, just as an empirical intuition was needed there, so a pure intuition *a priori* will be needed for the latter purpose; I am merely at a loss where to find it and how I am to explain its possibility. But now I am instructed by the *Critique* to omit all that is empirical or sensibly real in space and time, and thus to abolish all things in their empirical representation, and I then find that space and time remain over, like single beings, whose intuition precedes all concepts of them and of the things in them; and that given such a constitution for these originary modes of representation, I am nevermore to think of them as anything but merely subjective (though positive) forms of my sensibility (not merely as a lack of clarity in the representations obtained through them), not as forms of *things-in-themselves*, but only as forms of the objects of all sensory intuition, and hence of mere appearances. From this it now becomes clear to me, not only how synthetic cognitions *a priori* may be possible in both mathematics and natural science, in that these *a priori* intuitions make this extension possible, and the synthetic unity which the understanding must in each case give to the manifold in order to think an object thereof makes it actual; but I must also realize that, since the understanding for its part cannot intuit, these synthetic propositions *a priori* cannot be extended beyond the limits of sensory intuition: because all concepts going beyond this sphere are empty and must be without a corresponding object; for in order to attain such cognitions, I would either have to omit from the means I employ for cognition of objects of the senses, something which in such cognition can never be omitted, or else combine the remainder as it can never be combined therein, and so venture to form concepts about which, though they do not contain a contradiction, I still can never know whether or not in general an object corresponds to them, and which therefore remain completely empty for me.

By comparing what is said here with what Mr. Eberhard proclaims from p. 316 on in his exposition of synthetic judgments, the reader may now judge for himself *which* one of us offers for public consumption empty verbiage rather than solid knowledge.

On p. 316, too, the characterization is, "that in *eternal truths* they have as their predicates attributes of the subject; in *temporal truths*, contingent properties or relations," and he now compares what p. 317 calls this "*most fruitful* and illuminating" principle of division, with the concept the *Critique* gives of them, namely that synthetic judgments are those whose principle is not the principle of contradiction! "But what is it then?," Mr. Eberhard asks indignantly, and thereupon designates his discovery (allegedly drawn from Leibniz's writings), namely the principle of sufficient reason, which along with the principle of contradiction, on which *analytic* judgments turn, is thus the second hinge on which the human understanding moves, namely in its *synthetic* judgments.

From what I have just set forth as a summary of the analytic portion of the critique of the understanding, we now see that the latter expounds with all necessary detail the principle of synthetic judgments in general, which follows necessarily from their definition: *that they are not possible save under the condition of an intuition underlying the concept of their subject*, which, if they are judgments of experience, is empirical, and if they are synthetic judgments *a priori*, is pure intuition *a priori*. Any reader must easily discern what consequences this proposition may have, not only for determining the limits of the use of human reason, but even for insight into the true nature of our sensibility (for it can be demonstrated independently of the derivation of the representations of space and time, and thus serve to demonstrate their ideality, even before we have inferred it from their inner nature).

Compare with this the alleged principle which the Eberhardian determination of the nature of synthetic propositions *a priori* involves. "They

are those which assert of the concept of a subject the attributes thereof,"
i.e., those which belong to it necessarily but only as consequences, and
because, when so regarded, they must be related to some ground, their
possibility is conceivable through the principle of [sufficient] reason.[a]
But now one justifiably asks whether this ground of its predicate is to
be sought in the subject according to the principle of contradiction (in
which case the judgment, in spite of the principle of [sufficient] reason,
would always be merely analytic), or cannot be derived by that principle
from the concept of the subject, in which case alone is the attribute
synthetic. Therefore neither the name 'attribute' nor the principle of
sufficient reason distinguishes synthetic from analytic judgments; but
if by the former are meant judgments *a priori*, then nothing more can
be intended by this designation than that their predicate is necessarily *grounded* in some way in the essence of the concept of the subject,
and is thus an attribute, but not merely in consequence of the principle
of contradiction. But now how, as synthetic attribute, it can come into
connection with the concept of the subject, when it cannot be extracted
therefrom by an analysis of the latter, is not to be learned from the concept of an attribute and the proposition that it has some ground; and
Mr. Eberhard's definition is thus completely empty. The *Critique*, however, clearly points to this ground of the possibility: namely that it will
have to be the pure intuition underlying the concept of the subject
whereby it is possible, indeed alone possible, to link a synthetic predicate
a priori with a concept.

What is decisive here is that logic can give absolutely no information
concerning the question of how synthetic propositions are possible *a
priori*. Were it to say: derive from what constitutes the essence of your
concept the synthetic predicates sufficiently determined thereby (which
are then called attributes), then we are no further along than before.
How am I to set about going with my concept beyond this concept itself,
affirming more of it than is thought therein? The problem will never
be solved if, as logic does, one takes into consideration the conditions
of cognition merely from the side of the understanding. Sensibility, and
that as a faculty of *a priori* intuition, must also be taken into account, and
whoever hopes to find consolation in the classifications which logic
makes of concepts (in that it abstracts, as it must, from all objects thereof)
will lose his trouble and toil. Mr. Eberhard does however, judge logic
in this way and from the indications he derives from the concept of attributes (and that principle of synthetic judgments *a priori* which solely
belongs to them, the principle of sufficient reason), perceives it as so
pregnant and promising for the solution of dark questions in transcendental philosophy that he even sketches (p. 322) a new table of the

8: 242

8: 243

[a] *Princip des Grundes*

division of judgments for logic (in which, however, the author of the *Critique* declines to occupy the place assigned to him), to which *Jacob Bernoulli* has prompted him, by an allegedly new division of these judgments, cited on p. 320.[24] One might well say of such innovations in logic what was once said in a learned journal: "Alas! someone has once again invented a new thermometer." For as long as one must be satisfied with the two fixed points of division, the freezing and boiling points of water, without being able to determine how the temperature at either point is related to absolute temperature, it matters little whether the interval is divided into eighty or one hundred degrees, etc. Thus, so long as we have not yet been instructed in general how the attributes (synthetic, of course), which cannot be derived from the concept of the subject itself, arrive nevertheless at being necessary predicates of it (p. 322, I, 2), or even can be received as such by the subject, all that systematic division intended to explain the possibility of judgments, which it can seldom ever do anyway, is a totally useless burden on the memory and would hardly find a place in any new system of logic, just as the bare idea of synthetic judgments *a priori* (which Mr. Eberhard very absurdly calls *nonessential*) does not belong to logic at all.

Finally, a word about the claim advanced by Mr. Eberhard and others that the distinction between analytic and synthetic judgments is not new, but has long been known (and presumably also neglected because of its insignificance). To someone concerned with truth, especially if he uses a distinction of a type at least *unattempted* till now, it can matter little if it has already been made by someone else; and it is, of course, the common fate of everything new in the sciences that, if nothing can be said against it, it is at least found to have been long known by our elders. But if, from an observation presented as new, strikingly important consequences at once meet the eye, that could not possibly have been overlooked if it had already been made elsewhere, then a suspicion would still have to arise as to the correctness or importance of that very division, which might stand in the way of its use. But now if the latter is put beyond doubt, and there is likewise no mistaking the necessity with which these consequences obtrude, then one may assume with the utmost probability that it had not yet been made.

8: 244

Now the question of how *cognition a priori* is possible has long been raised and discussed, especially since the time of Locke; what would then be more natural than that, as soon as the distinction between the analytic and synthetic had been clearly noted therein, this general question would have been restricted to the particular one: how are *synthetic* judgments possible *a priori*? For as soon as this has been raised, it becomes apparent to everyone that the success or failure of metaphysics depends entirely upon how the latter problem might come to be resolved; all dogmatic dealings with that subject would assuredly have been suspended until sufficient information had been received concerning this single problem; a critique of pure reason would have become the watchword before which even the loudest trumpeting of its dogmatic claims could not have prevailed. But now, since this has not happened, one can only conclude that the aforesaid distinction among judgments has never been properly discerned. This was also inevitable, if it was regarded in the manner of Mr. Eberhard, who extracts from the predicates of judgments a mere distinction of attributes from the essence and essential parts of the subject, and was thus assigned to logic; for the latter has nothing to do with the possibility of cognition in regard to its content, but merely with its form insofar as it is a *discursive* cognition, whereas investigation of the origin of *a priori* cognition of objects must be left exclusively to transcendental philosophy. Nor could this insight and positive usefulness have been achieved by the said division, when it exchanged, for the terms analytic and synthetic, expressions so badly chosen as those of *identical* and *nonidentical* judgments. For the latter provide not the slightest indication of a particular manner of possibility for any such unification of representations *a priori*; whereas the term *synthetic* judgment (as opposed to analytic) immediately carries with it an allusion to an *a priori synthesis* in general, and must naturally prompt the investigation, which is no longer logical but already transcendental, as to whether there are not concepts (categories) which affirm nothing else but the pure *synthetic* unity of a manifold (in some intuition) with regard to the concept of an object in general, and which lie *a priori* at the basis of all cognition thereof; and since these [concepts] concern merely the thought of an object in general, whether the manner in which it would have to be given, namely a form of its intuition, must not likewise be presupposed *a priori* for any such synthetic cognition; since then the attention directed to this point would inevitably have transformed that logical distinction, which otherwise can be of no use, into a transcendental problem.

8: 245

It was therefore no mere verbal affectation, but a step in the advance of knowledge, when the *Critique* made knowable *for the first time* the distinction between judgments which rest entirely on the principle of identity or contradiction, and those which require another principle, by naming them analytic as opposed to synthetic judgments. For by the term synthesis it is clearly indicated that something outside of the given concept must be added as a substrate, which makes it possible to go beyond the concept with my predicates; so that the investigation is directed to the possibility of a synthesis of representations with regard to cognition in general, which soon had to lead to a recognition of *intuition* as its indispensable condition, but of *pure intuition* for *a priori* cognition; a direction that could not be expected through the characterization of synthetic judgments as *nonidentical*, and has never in fact resulted from it. In order to be satisfied of this, we have only to examine the examples hitherto cited to prove that the distinction in question is already known and fully developed in philosophy, albeit under other names. The first one (pointed out by myself, though only as somewhat like it) is from *Locke*,[25] who assigns what he calls knowledge of coexistence to judgments of experience, and knowledge of relation to moral judgments; but he does not give a name to the synthetic aspect of judgments in general; nor, by this distinction from propositions of identity, has he extracted the most trifling of general rules for pure *a priori* cognition as such. The example from *Reusch*[26] belongs entirely to logic, and merely shows the two different ways of clarifying given concepts, without concern for any expansion of cognition, especially *a priori*, with regard to objects. The third, from *Crusius*,[27] alludes only to metaphysical propositions that are not demonstrable through the principle of contradiction. No one has therefore grasped this distinction in its universality, for the purpose of a critique of reason in general; for otherwise mathematics, with its great abundance of synthetic *a priori* cognition, would have had to be cited as a prime example, though its prominence in comparison with pure philosophy, and the latter's poverty with respect to such propositions (though it is rich enough in the analytic variety), would inevitably have been bound to occasion an investigation into the possibility of the former. Meanwhile, it may be left to anyone to judge whether or not he is conscious of having already had this distinction in general before his eyes, or of having found it in other authors; just so long as he does not on that account neglect the said inquiry as superfluous and its goal as long since attained.

8: 246

* *

*

May we be finished now and forever with this discussion of what is supposedly a mere reinstatement of an older critique of pure reason, which gives metaphysics the right to extensive claims. It has emerged with sufficient clarity that, if there ever was such a critique, it was at least not granted to Mr. Eberhard to see it, to understand it, or at any point to satisfy this need of philosophy, even at second hand. – The other brave men, who till now have endeavored by their objections to keep the critical enterprise on course, will not interpret this single exception to my resolve (not to involve myself in any formal controversy), as implying that their arguments and philosophical standing have struck me as of lesser importance; it has happened this once, only in order to call attention to a certain mode of conduct that has something typical about it, and seems characteristic of Mr. Eberhard and to be worthy of note. For the rest, may the *Critique of Pure Reason* continue to stand firm, if it can, through its intrinsic solidity. Once it has gained currency, it will not disappear without at least having engendered a sounder system of pure philosophy than was previously to be had. But if one tries to envisage such an event, the current course of things affords ample evidence that the seeming concord, which now reigns among opponents of the *Critique*, is really a covert discord, since they are poles apart as to the principle they propose to set in its place. It would therefore provide us with an exhibition, as amusing as it is instructive, if they would for a time set aside their conflict with their common enemy in order to try to reach an accord on the principles they wish to maintain against it; but they would be no more likely ever to finish with that than the man who tried to construct a bridge the length of the stream rather than across it. 8: 247

Given the anarchy which inevitably prevails among philosophizing folk, since it is only an invisible thing, namely reason, that they recognize as their sole sovereign, it has always been a saving remedy to gather this turbulent crew around some great man as a rallying point. But for those with no understanding of their own, or no desire to use it, or who, though not deficient in either, still behaved as if they had them only on loan from someone else, to *understand* such a man was a difficulty, which has hitherto prevented the formation of a durable constitution, and will at least greatly impede the latter for a long time to come.

Leibniz's metaphysics contained primarily three peculiarities: (1) the principle of sufficient reason, and that so far as it was merely meant to indicate the insufficiency of the principle of contradiction for the knowledge of necessary truths; (2) the doctrine of monads; (3) the doctrine of the pre-established harmony. On account of these three principles, he has been plagued by many opponents who did not understand him; but he has also (as a great connoisseur, and worthy eulogist of his, remarks on a certain occasion) been mistreated by his would-be *followers* and interpreters;[28] as also happened to other philosophers in antiquity, who might well have said: God protect us only from our friends; our enemies, we can take care of for ourselves.

I. Is it really credible that Leibniz wished to have his principle of sufficient reason construed objectively (as a natural law), when he attributed great importance to it as an addition to previous philosophy? It is, of course, so generally acknowledged and (within suitable limits) so manifestly clear, that not even the weakest mind can believe itself to have made therein a new discovery; and it has also been greeted with much ridicule by opponents who have misunderstood it. But this principle was for him a merely subjective one, having reference only to a critique of reason. For what does it mean to say that there must be other principles besides the principle of contradiction? It is to say, in effect, that by the principle of contradiction can be known only what already lies in the concept of the object; if something more is to be said of it [the object], then something else must be added beyond this concept, and to show how this 8: 248

is possible we have to look for a special principle, distinct from that of contradiction, i.e., it will have to have its special ground. Since the latter kind of propositions are (now at least) called synthetic, Leibniz wanted to say only that beyond the principle of contradiction (as the principle of analytic judgments), still another principle, namely that of synthetic judgments, must be added. This was certainly a new and noteworthy pointer to investigations that were yet to be instituted in metaphysics (and in fact have only lately begun there). Now if his disciple proclaims this pointer to a separate principle, which at that time was still sought, to be the (already found) principle (of synthetic cognition) itself, and if Leibniz has been thought thereby to have made a new discovery, is this follower not exposing him to ridicule, just when he thought that he was singing his praises?

II. Is it really believable that Leibniz, such a great mathematician! wanted to compose bodies out of monads (and hence space out of simple parts)? He did not mean the physical world, but rather its substrate, unknowable by us, the intelligible world, which lies merely in the Idea of reason and in which we really do have to represent everything we think therein as composite substance to be composed of simple substances. He also seems, with Plato, to attribute to the human mind an original, though by now dim, intellectual intuition of these super-sensible beings, though from this he inferred nothing concerning sensible beings, which he would wish to be taken for things related to a special mode of intuition, of which we are capable solely with regard to cognitions that are possible for us, in the strictest sense as mere appearances, tied to (specific, particular) forms of intuition; we should not therefore let ourselves be disturbed by his account of sensibility as a confused mode of representation, but must rather replace it by another, more suited to his purpose; for otherwise his system will be inconsistent. Now to accept this error as a deliberate and wise precaution on his part (as imitators, to be just like their original, also copy his gestures and faults of speech) can scarcely be credited to them as a service to their master's honor. The innateness of certain concepts, as an expression for a *fundamental faculty* with respect to *a priori* principles of our cognition, which he uses merely against Locke, who recognizes only an empirical origin, is likewise incorrectly understood if it is taken literally.

III. Is it possible to believe that, by his pre-established harmony between soul and body, Leibniz should have understood the accord of two entities that are by nature completely independent of each other, and cannot be brought into community through any powers of their own? That would be precisely to proclaim idealism; for why should we accept bodies at all, if it is possible to view everything that happens in the soul as an effect of its own powers, which it would also exercise that way in complete isolation? Soul and that substrate of *appearances*,

8: 249

wholly unknown to us, which we call body, are, to be sure, entirely different entities, but these *appearances* themselves, as mere forms of its intuition, resting on the constitution of the subject (soul), are merely representations, and there the community between understanding and sensibility in the same subject can well be conceived under certain *a priori* laws, along with the necessary natural dependence of the latter [sensibility] upon external things, without surrendering these things to idealism. As for this harmony between understanding and sensibility, insofar as it makes possible cognitions of universal laws of nature *a priori*, the *Critique* has definitively shown that without it no experience is possible, and that the objects (since they partly, as to their intuition, accord with the formal conditions of our sensibility, and partly, as to the connection of the manifold, accord with the principles of its ordering in one consciousness, as a condition of the possibility of cognition thereof) would never be taken up by us into the unity of consciousness and enter into experience, and would therefore be nothing for us. But we could still provide no reason why we have precisely such a mode of sensibility and an understanding of such a nature, that by their combination experience becomes possible; nor yet, why, as otherwise fully heterogeneous sources of cognition, they always conform so well to the possibility of empirical cognition in general, but especially (as the *Critique of Judgment* will intimate) for the possibility of an experience of nature under its manifold *particular* and merely empirical laws, of which the understanding teaches us nothing *a priori*, as if nature were deliberately ordered for our comprehension; this we could not further explain (and neither can anyone else). Leibniz termed the ground of this agreement, especially in regard to the cognition of body, and thereunder primarily our own, as the middle ground of this relation, a *pre-established harmony*, by which he had obviously not explained this agreement, nor was seeking to do so, but was merely indicating that we would have to suppose thereby a certain purposiveness in the dispositions of the supreme cause, of ourselves as well as of all things outside us; and this indeed as something already lodged in creation (predetermined), albeit a predetermination, not of things existing in separation, but only of the mental powers in us, sensibility and understanding, each in its own way for the other, just as the *Critique* teaches that for the *a priori* cognition of things they must stand in a reciprocal relationship to one another in the mind. That this was his true, though not clearly developed opinion, may be surmised from the fact that he extends that pre-established harmony much further than to the agreement of soul and body, namely to that between the *Kingdoms* of *Nature* and of *Grace* (the Kingdom of Ends in relation to the final end, i.e., mankind under moral laws), where a harmony has to be thought between the consequences of our concepts of nature and those of our concept of freedom, a union, therefore, of two totally

8: 250

different faculties, under wholly dissimilar principles *in us*, and not that of a pair of different things, existing in harmony *outside each other* (as morality actually requires); though, as the *Critique* teaches, it can by no means be conceived from the constitution of the world, but rather as an agreement that for us at least is contingent, and comprehensible only through an intelligent world-cause.

In this way, then, the *Critique of Pure Reason* might well be the true apology for Leibniz, even against those of his disciples who heap praises upon him that do him no honor; as it may also be for sundry older philosophers, whom many an historian of philosophy – for all the praise he bestows on them – still has talking utter nonsense; whose intention he does not divine, in that he neglects the key to all accounts of what pure reason produces from mere concepts, the critique of reason itself (as the common source of all them), and in examining the words they spoke, cannot see what they had wanted to say.

8: 251

*What real progress has metaphysics
made in Germany since the time
of Leibniz and Wolff?*

Editor's introduction

HENRY ALLISON

Welches sind die wirklichen Fortschritte, die die Metaphysik seit Leibnitzens und Wolf's Zeiten in Deutschland gemacht hat? (*What Real Progress Has Metaphysics Made in Germany since the Time of Leibniz and Wolff?*, henceforth to be referred to as *Progress*) constitutes Kant's projected, but never submitted or even completed, contribution to the prize essay contest on that topic announced by the Académie Royal des Sciences et des Belles-Lettres in Berlin. Unfortunately, Kant's original manuscript has been lost, and the text that we have is a compilation of three different manuscripts by Kant's friend and dinner companion Friedrich Theodor Rink. Kant apparently gave the material to Rink sometime between 1800 and 1802, and Rink published it in April, 1804, two months after Kant's death.

The proposed topic for the essay contest was first announced within the Academy itself on January 24, 1788, with the expectation that the public announcement would be made the following year. For some reason, however, the Academy failed to announce the contest until 1790, at which time it set a deadline for contributions of January 1, 1792. But having by then received only one submission, that of the Wolffian Johann Christof Schwab (a collaborator with Eberhard on the anti-Kantian *Philosophisches Magazin* – see the introduction to *On a Discovery*), the Academy extended the submission date to June 1, 1795, and doubled the prize. By the latter date it had received over thirty submissions, and first prize was awarded to Schwab and second prizes to Karl Leonard Reinhold and Johann Heinrich Abicht, each of whom advocated a basically Kantian position, though they were primarily concerned to defend their own ideas. Honorable mention was also awarded to Christian F. Jenisch, another Kantian. The three prize-winning essays were then published by the Academy in the following year.

Because of the paucity of references to it in his extant correspondence, very little is known about Kant's attitude toward the prize essay competition. Nevertheless, it seems clear that the topic itself must have been of the utmost interest to him, since it pointedly addresses the question of the historical significance of the critical philosophy and calls to mind the bitter polemic in which he had been recently engaged with

Eberhard and his colleagues concerning this very question. In spite of this, however, it does not seem that Kant decided to enter the competition when it was first publicly announced. In fact, the earliest concrete evidence we have of Kant's intentions in this regard are two "jottings" (*Lose Blätter*) dated 1793, that is, after the reannouncement of the competition with the June, 1795, deadline. These deal in outline form with topics taken up in the manuscripts (*Reflexion* 6342, Ak 18:640–44; and *Lose Blatt* D14; Ak 20:335–7).[1] But for reasons that remain unknown, Kant must have abandoned the project sometime before the latter date, since, as noted above, his essay remained incomplete and was never submitted to the Academy for consideration.[2]

In addition to constituting something less than a complete text, the materials published by Rink contain a good deal of overlap. Kant's general plan envisaged a division of metaphysics, both systematic and historical, into three stages. The first of the three manuscripts (Ak 20:259–86) contains Kant's Preface and discussion of the first stage. The second manuscript (Ak 20:286–311) contains his accounts of the second and third stages and an overview of the whole. The third manuscript (Ak 20:315–32) is basically an Appendix, and is composed of what Rink describes as a more polished version of the opening discussion (Appendix I in the present translation, Ak 20:315–26), a new version of the discussion of the second stage of metaphysics, corresponding to the last part of the first manuscript (Appendix II, Ak 20:326–29), and a collection of marginal notes to the second manuscript (Appendix III, Ak 20:329–32).[3] In addition, the translation includes a set of "jottings" that relate to *Progress*, but were not included in the material published by Rink and, therefore, presumably not in the material given to him by Kant (Ak 20:335–51). They have been included here because they were published in the Academy edition in connection with the text by its editor, Gerhard Lehmann.

It should be further noted that Rink's editorial skills and procedures have been severely criticized. In fact, this criticism extends beyond the present work to his handling of the materials contained in the lectures on *Physical Geography* and *Pedagogy*, both of which were edited and published by him on the basis of manuscripts provided by Kant.[4] With regard to *Progress*, the basic complaints echoed by Lehmann and H. J. de Vleeschauwer, the Kant scholar who has devoted the most attention to this work, are that he did not provide a more detailed account of the material that Kant gave him and, specifically, that he failed to indicate the original locations in the text of the marginal notes which he included in the third manuscript.[5] Beyond this, questions have been raised about his use of asterisks to mark lacunae in the text in places where he takes Kant's argument to be incomplete (see Ak 20:276, 277, 280, 290, and 292).

Unfortunately, the imperfect state of the text as it has been bequeathed to us by Rink creates many interpretive difficulties and puzzles, which presumably would not have arisen if we had been dealing with a completed work by Kant. Particularly noteworthy among these is a certain vacillation on Kant's part with regard to two competing conceptions of the "stages" or "advances" of metaphysics: one supposedly historical and the other systematic. It is not that these two conceptions are incompatible, but rather that Kant's tendency to move from one to the other, combined with somewhat misleading similarities between them (e.g., each is triadic and assigns a pivotal role to the Antinomies), sometimes makes the course of the argument difficult to follow.

The first conception, announced in the Preface, sees the history of metaphysics as commencing with dogmatism, moving quickly to skepticism, and then vacillating between these two poles until put on the right path by the critical philosophy (Ak 20:263–4). It thus traces the advance from what for Kant is illusory metaphysics to the true metaphysics established by the *Critique*. Kant also states, without any explanation, that this temporal sequence is based on the nature of our cognitive faculties (Ak 20:264). Although the roots of dogmatism, understood as the attempt to attain by pure reason a knowledge of super-sensible reality without a prior critical analysis of the capacity of human reason for such a task, are traced to pre-Platonic thought, its culmination is not surprisingly seen to lie in the philosophy of Leibniz and Wolff. And by skepticism, according to this scheme, Kant pointedly understands neither of the familiar Cartesian and Humean varieties that are directed against our knowledge of the sensible world, but rather a skepticism regarding the super-sensible, that is, metaphysical, use of reason. This is, of course, the kind of skepticism that arises from the discovery of the antinomies, and Kant likewise assigns it an ancient lineage.

The second conception involves an immanent development within genuine metaphysics, which Kant also terms "the stages of pure reason" (Ak 20:273). Here the triad consists of a theoretico-dogmatic stage called "doctrine of science," where there is a sure advance, a "doctrine of doubt," which serves as a halting point, and a practico-dogmatic stage called "doctrine of wisdom," which is the culmination of metaphysics (20:273). Moreover, even within the latter scheme, which is the one Kant emphasizes, there are significant discrepancies between various formulations, which seem to reflect an uncertainty on Kant's part about whether to base the divisions on the familiar distinctions within traditional metaphysics (i.e., general metaphysics or ontology and special metaphysics and its subdivisions – rational psychology, rational cosmology, and rational theology) or on the divisions of the critical philosophy (which partly coincide with these). For example, the first stage, that of the doctrine of science, is correlated with both ontology and transcendental philosophy;

but ontology is sometimes identified with the Wolffian analysis of concepts (Ak 20:260–61) and sometimes with the subject matter of the Transcendental Aesthetic and Transcendental Analytic of the first *Critique*, and even with the results of the *Metaphysical Foundations* (Ak 20:266–76). In short, ontology is sometimes viewed as an essentially sterile domain of analytic knowledge, which has scarcely advanced a step since the days of Aristotle (Ak 20:260), and sometimes as the sum total of synthetic *a priori* knowledge regarding objects of possible experience, which was first put on a firm footing by the *Critique*. Similarly, the second stage, that of the doctrine of doubt, is sometimes viewed as encompassing the dialectical disciplines of rational psychology and cosmology, and sometimes as containing simply the doctrine of the antinomies. And, finally, the third stage, containing the doctrine of wisdom, is sometimes equated with rational theology and sometimes with moral theology, which consists of Kant's own morally practical metaphysics based on the postulates of God, freedom, and immortality.[6]

But these difficulties notwithstanding, *Progress* remains an important text for students of Kant for a number of reasons. To begin with, it provides a concise synoptic overview of the critical philosophy in its entirety, as Kant saw it near the end of his career, after writing all three *Critiques*. Moreover, this overview makes it clear that Kant saw his philosophy as embodying and, indeed, completing metaphysics, understood as the transition from the sensible to the super-sensible, rather than as merely providing a propaedeutic or prolegomenon to such a metaphysics, as is suggested by the more familiar accounts in the first *Critique* and the *Prolegomena*.

Furthermore, one should not be misled by the fact that Kant characterizes the third stage of genuine metaphysics as "practico-dogmatic" into assuming that it marks some kind of reversion to a long-discarded form of dogmatism. For "dogmatic," as Kant here uses it, does not involve dogmatism. Instead, it has the sense given to it in the Transcendental Doctrine of Method in the first *Critique*, where Kant divides all synthetic *a priori* propositions into *dogmata* and *mathemata*: the former including all those derived directly from concepts (i.e., all those pertaining to philosophy) and the latter those derived from the construction of concepts (which pertain to mathematics) (A 736/B 764). Thus, the propositions of this metaphysics, which are based upon the requirements of practical reason, namely the necessity of postulating God, freedom, and immortality as conditions of the realizability of the highest good, are dogmata but not dogmatic. Kant also uses the term in this sense in connection with the first stage of genuine metaphysics (the doctrine of science), which is termed "theoretico-dogmatic." The difference between these two stages is that the synthetic *a priori* propositions of the latter refer merely to appearances or objects of possible experience, while those of the former concern the super-sensible, which remains for Kant the real object of metaphysics.

As a direct result of this reorientation toward the super-sensible, the basic concerns of the Transcendental Analytic of the first *Critique* assume merely subordinate significance. Given the limitation of the synthetic *a priori* knowledge gained through the understanding to objects of possible experience, the central question becomes how a genuine transition to the super-sensible is possible, as opposed to the illusory transition made by the Leibnizian philosophy and other forms of dogmatism. As already indicated, Kant's answer is by way of practical reason; but this poses a problem for him, and his attempt to deal with it (though cryptic and incomplete) is in my judgment one of the most noteworthy features of the work. The problem stems from the question of the Academy as Kant understood it. He assumed (undoubtedly correctly) that the framers of the question understood by metaphysics theoretical rather than practical knowledge, that is, metaphysics of nature rather than metaphysics of morals in his terms. But given the limitation of the scope of the former kind of metaphysics to objects of possible experience, together with the relegation of claims about the super-sensible to the domain of the morally-practical, the suspicion naturally arises that, rather than answering the question posed by the Academy, Kant is merely changing the subject.

As the text makes clear, Kant was keenly aware of the problem (see Ak 20:293). Moreover, his attempt to deal with it, though extremely cryptic and hardly intelligible unless viewed in light of the discussion in the *Critique of Judgment*, underscores the systematic significance he attributed to the latter work, which is also centrally concerned with the problem of a transition from the sensible to the super-sensible (from nature to freedom).

The key to the solution lies in an appeal to the concept of the purposiveness (*Zweckmässigkeit*) of nature, the central concept of the third *Critique*, which he now interprets in strictly teleological terms (Ak 20:293–4). The significance of this concept stems from the fact that it has a foot, as it were, in both the sensible and the super-sensible, which uniquely qualifies it to serve as a mediator between the two domains. On the one hand, it is a concept of nature, since it applies to a set of objects given in experience (living organisms). On the other hand, since it requires us to think about such objects as if they were products of an intelligent cause acting in light of an end rather than of the mere mechanism of nature, it points to something beyond nature. By linking them with reflective rather than determinative judgment in the third *Critique*, however, Kant makes it clear that such appeals to purposiveness reflect merely how we are constrained to think about organisms (given the discursive nature of our intellect), and, therefore, do not yield knowledge of their actual genesis. Now he makes the same point by denying that the use of the concept of purposiveness can be dogmatic (in the sense indicated above).

But for this very reason, though the concept of the purposiveness of nature points to the super-sensible, it is not of itself sufficient to take us there. The actual transition, as Kant conceives it, occurs through the connection of this concept with the concept of freedom, the conceivability of which in the face of natural causality was preserved in the first *Critique* through the resolution of the third antinomy. This connection is grounded in the fact that the latter concept provides what the former cannot, namely the idea of an unconditioned or ultimate purpose (*Endzweck*). This is the idea of the highest good possible in the world (the perfect union of virtue and happiness). Since this good is regarded as an end to be realized in the world, it involves the thought of nature (particularly human nature) as amenable to it. But since it is an end that cannot be thought as attainable through nature alone, it necessarily brings with it the thought of a super-sensible ground of nature (God), as well as the other conditions required for its attainment (freedom and immortality). In Kant's pithy formula, it leads to the super-sensible "in us" (freedom), "above us" (God), and "after us" (immortality) (Ak 20:294).

Moreover, even though Kant continues to maintain (as he had in all three *Critiques*) that the grounding of these super-sensibles holds only from the morally practical point of view, and therefore yields merely a rational belief (*Glaube*) rather than knowledge, he also insists that they are themselves theoretical principles. Indeed, they are the very principles that have been the concern of metaphysics since its dogmatic inception. Consequently, Kant now feels entitled to claim that with the critical philosophy metaphysics has finally attained not simply its true foundation (in a critique of our cognitive capacities), but its actual completion.

The second major theme running throughout the work as a whole is a critique of the metaphysical pretensions of the Leibnizian philosophy and its Wolffian offshoot. In this respect it is very much a continuation of the polemical engagement with the proponents of that philosophy begun in *On a Discovery*, in response to Eberhard's attack on both the validity and originality of the critical philosophy. It is, however, a continuation with a significant difference, at least in tone, if not in substance. For whereas in the early work, Kant, at least partly for strategic reasons, tended to be highly conciliatory to the philosophy of Leibniz, he now has no qualms about spelling out what he takes to be the underlying fallacies and confusions in his predecessor's thought.

The centerpiece of this attack is a systematic critique of the four cardinal principles of Leibnizian metaphysics; viz., the identity of indiscernibles, the principle of sufficient reason, the preestablished harmony, and the monadology (Ak 20:282–5). But beyond this, there are critical discussions of the Leibniz–Wolff rational or transcendent theology (Ak 20:301–4), its moral theology (Ak 20:307), and its rational psychology (Ak 20:308–10). In fact, from the point of view of the Academy's question the latter are crucial, since these concern the three central ideas of metaphysics as Kant conceives it (God, freedom, and immortality). Thus, by criticizing these doctrines Kant is at the same time revealing the merely illusory nature of the "progress" in metaphysics supposedly made by the Leibniz–Wolff philosophy. Admittedly, as in *On a Discovery*, there is nothing in this that is radically new, and a good deal of what Kant says here closely parallels the discussion in the Amphiboly chapter of the first *Critique*. Nevertheless, these works taken together provide us with an invaluable overview of Kant's conception of the relation of the critical philosophy to the Leibnizian, an overview which we probably would not have had Kant not been provoked by the attack of Eberhard and his associates.

In addition to these general themes, there are a number of specifics in *Progress* that are worthy of note, of which I shall mention three. The first is Kant's introduction of the concept of the "composite, as such" (*die Zusammengesetzte, als eines solchen*). As in the *Critique*, Kant emphasizes that human knowledge rests on both sensible intuition through which objects are given and concepts of the understanding through which they are thought. And more explicitly than in the *Critique*, he insists that synthetic *a priori* knowledge requires both pure intuitions (space and time) and pure concepts (the categories), each of which is a contribution of the mind. But in characterizing the specific contribution of the understanding (in contrast to sensibility), Kant now suggests that it can be fully defined in terms of this concept of the composite, as such. This is because of all the representations required for experience, it is the only one that cannot be attributed to sensibility, but must rather be assigned to the spontaneity of the understanding (Ak 20:275–6). Thus, in a sense, this concept is granted a conceptual priority over the twelve categories, which are now seen as the specific forms in which this compositeness or composition is thought. In introducing this concept, Kant may have been influenced by the philosopher J. S. Beck, with whom he had been corresponding at this time; though it can also be viewed as the development of a line of thought that is already in place in the second edition version of the Transcendental Deduction in the *Critique*.[7]

A second noteworthy feature is Kant's clarification of his conception of an analytic judgment through its distinction from an identical judgment or tautology. Though his discussions of the analytic–synthetic distinction in *Progress* are not as detailed as in *On a Discovery*, on this point he goes beyond the latter work, as well as the *Critique*. For in his initial formulation of the analytic–synthetic distinction in the *Critique*, Kant had characterized (affirmative) analytic judgments as those in which "the connection of the predicate with the subject is thought through identity" (A 7/B 10); and this has led many to assume that by analytic judgments Kant meant identical ones, that is, tautologies fitting the schema a = a. Furthermore, since it is clear that most of our knowledge, including the unquestioned *a priori* knowledge contained in mathematics, does not fit this schema, it was easy for Eberhard and his associates to point to this formulation in support of their charge that Kant's distinction provides nothing really new and that the relevant distinction between two kinds of *a priori* knowledge had already been drawn by Leibniz. Thus, it was probably with this in mind that in Appendix I (the second version of the first stage of metaphysics) Kant explicitly distinguishes between analytic and identical judgments, stating that the former "are indeed *founded* upon identity, and can be resolved into it, but they *are* not identical, for they need to be dissected and thereby serve to elucidate the concept; whereas by identical judgments...nothing whatever would be elucidated" (Ak 20:322).

The third and final point to be noted concerns Kant's discussion of freedom. Kant is notorious for using this term in a wide variety of senses, and this has been the source of considerable confusion for his commentators.[8] One particularly puzzling feature of his account, however, is that freedom seems to be treated in two quite different ways and to receive different justifications in the *Critique of Practical Reason*. On the one hand, it is claimed to be the "*ratio essendi* of the moral law" (Ak 5:4n) and its reality is said to be deduced from the moral law, after the latter is certified through the "fact of reason" (Ak 5:48). On the other hand, it is treated, together with God and immortality, as a postulate of practical reason (Ak 5:132). Now this makes sense only if something different is understood by "freedom" in these two places. Moreover, though Kant does not make this explicit in the second *Critique*, he does in the present work. This is accomplished by making it clear that the kind of freedom that is postulated as a condition of the highest good is that of *autocracy* rather than the more familiar *autonomy*, that is, the actual power or strength of will to do what is required of us with respect to the highest good in spite of the hindrances which nature exerts on us as sensory beings (Ak 20:295). And since our contribution to the highest good is virtue, this means that freedom in the sense of autocracy is equivalent to virtue, and its attainability, like the existence of God and immortality, is a matter of faith.[9] Thus, it seems that in addition to providing an invaluable overview of the critical philosophy in its completion, a systematic critique of Leibnizian metaphysics, and important clarifications of essential points in the theoretical philosophy, *Progress* makes a significant contribution to our understanding of Kant's practical philosophy as well.

BIBLIOGRAPHY

ALLISON, HENRY E. *The Kant-Eberhard Controversy*, Baltimore and London: The Johns Hopkins University Press, 1973.

GUILLERMIT, LOUIS, trans. *Les Progrès de la métaphysique en Allemagne depuis le temps de Leibniz et de Wolf*, Paris: Librarie Philosophique J. Vrin, 1973.

GAWLINA, MANFRED. *Das Medusanhaupt der Kritik, Die Kontroverse zwischen Immanuel Kant und Johann August Eberhard*, Berlin and New York: Walter de Gruyter, 1996.

HUMPHREY, TED, ed. and trans. *What Real Progress Has Metaphysics Made in Germany since the Time of Leibniz and Wolff?*, New York: Abaris Books, 1983.

VLEESCHAUWER, H. J. DE. "La Cinderella dans l'oeuvre Kantienne," *Kant-Studien, Akten des 4. Internationalen Kant-Kongress, Mainz 6–10 April 1974*, Teil I, pp. 304–6.

La Déduction transcendentale dans l'Oeuvre de Kant, vol. iii, Paris: Leroux, 1937, pp. 444–90.

The Development of Kantian Thought, trans. A. R. C. Duncan, London: Thomas Nelson and Sons, 1962.

Translator's note

The text of this translation has been taken from volume 20 of the *Akademie Ausgabe*, which reprints that of the posthumous edition of 1804, in which F. T. Rink presented his arrangement of the prize essay material consigned to him by Kant. It also includes the related matter from Kant's unpublished notes, which the *Akademie* editors appended to Rink's text. The critical apparatus to that section has, however, been omitted, since the detailed description of handwritten documents in one language cannot usefully be carried over to another. Some other problems of translation have been settled by resort to the French version by Louis Guillermit (*Les Progrès de la Métaphysique* [Paris, Librairie Philosophique J. Vrin, 1973]). The example of this work has also been followed in compiling a Table of Contents from the section headings, some of which, at least, are presumably Kant's own, though others are due to Rink. The single-f spelling of 'Wolf' has been retained, as a period touch, despite a modern editorial preference for 'Wolff'. Neither form seems to be any more correct than the other, and works of reference often give both.

My thanks are due to Eusebia Estes, for her accurate typing of my own longhand, and to my coeditor Henry Allison, not only for valuable comments on the translation, but for generously undertaking the Introduction. Kant's polemic against Eberhard, and his *Progress* papers, are cognate works of the same period, so it is a great advantage to have both of them presented by the same experienced hand.

P.H.

What real progress has metaphysics made in Germany since the time of Leibniz and Wolff?

Table of Contents

What real progress has metaphysics made in Germany?

The Royal Academy of Sciences calls for a survey of the advances in one part of philosophy, in one part of academic Europe, and also during one part of the present century.

That seems to be a readily performable task, for it only has to do with history, and since the advances in astronomy and chemistry, qua empirical sciences, have already found their historians, while those in mathematical analysis or pure mechanics, achieved in the same country and period, will soon find theirs, too, if wanted, there seems to be equally little difficulty with the science here in question.

But this science is metaphysics, and that completely alters the situation. This is a shoreless sea, in which progress leaves no trace behind, and whose horizon contains no visible goal by which one might perceive how nearly it has been approached. In regard to this science, which itself has almost always existed in idea only, the prescribed task is very difficult, the very possibility of resolving it a thing to be almost despaired of, and even should it succeed, the condition laid down, of presenting in brief compass the advances it has achieved, makes the difficulty greater still. For metaphysics is by nature and intention a completed whole; either nothing or everything. So what is required for its final purpose cannot be dealt with in a fragmentary way, as in mathematics or empirical natural science, where progress is constant and unending. But we shall attempt the task nonetheless.

The first and most necessary question is doubtless this: What does reason actually want with metaphysics? What purpose does it have in view in treating of the subject? For that end is the great, perhaps the greatest, indeed the one and only purpose which reason can ever look to in its speculation, since all men are more or less engaged in it, and since there is no understanding why, given the ever-apparent futility of their efforts in this field, it would still be in vain to tell them that they should at last give up rolling this stone of Sisyphus,[1] were not the interest that   20: 260
reason takes in the subject the most ardent that can be entertained.

This ultimate purpose, to which the whole of metaphysics is directed, is easy to discover, and can in this respect found a definition of the subject: "It is the science of progressing by reason from knowledge of the sensible to that of the super-sensible."

But within the sensible[2] we include that whose representation is considered in relation, not merely to the senses, but also to the understanding, so long as the pure concepts of the latter are thought in their application to objects of the senses, and thus for purposes of a possible *experience*; thus the nonsensory, such as the concept of cause, which has its seat and origin in the understanding, can still, as regards knowledge of an object by means of it, be said to belong to the field of the sensory, that is, to objects of the senses.

Ontology[3] is that science (as part of metaphysics) which consists in a system of all concepts of the understanding, and principles, but only so far as they refer to objects that can be given to the senses, and thus confirmed by experience. It makes no allusion to the super-sensible, which is nevertheless the final aim of metaphysics, and thus belongs to the latter only as a propaedeutic, as the hallway or vestibule of metaphysics proper, and is called transcendental philosophy, because it contains the conditions and first elements of all our *knowledge a priori*.

In this field there has not been much progress since the days of Aristotle. For as grammar is the resolution of a speech-form into its elementary rules, and logic a resolution of the form of thought, so ontology is a resolution of knowledge into the concepts that lie *a priori* in the understanding, and have their use in experience; a system whose troublesome elaboration we may very well be spared, if only we bear in mind the rules for the right use of these concepts and principles, for purposes of empirical knowledge; for experience always confirms or corrects it, which does not happen if our design is to progress from the sensible to the super-sensible, for which purpose an assessment of the powers of understanding and its principles must indeed be carried out with thoroughness and care, in order to know from whence, and with what props and crutches, reason can venture upon its transition from the objects of experience to those that are not of this kind.

20: 261

Now the celebrated Wolf has rendered an incontestable service to ontology, by his clarity and precision in analysing these powers; but not by any addition to our knowledge in that area, since the subject matter was exhausted.

However, the above definition, which merely indicates what is *wanted of* metaphysics, not what there needs to be done *in it*, would simply mark it out from other doctrines as a discipline belonging to philosophy in the specific meaning of the term, i.e., to the doctrine of wisdom,[4] and prescribe its principles to the absolutely necessary practical use of reason; though that has only an indirect relation to metaphysics considered as a scholastic science and system of certain theoretical cognitions *a priori*, which are made the immediate topic of concern. Hence the explanation of metaphysics according to the notion of the schools will be that it is the system of all principles of purely theoretical rational knowledge through concepts; or in brief, that it is the system of pure theoretical philosophy.

It therefore contains no practical doctrines of pure reason, though it does contain the theoretical doctrines which underlie their possibility. It contains no mathematical propositions, i.e., such as produce rational knowledge through the construction of concepts, but does contain the principles of the possibility of a mathematics as such. By reason in this definition we are, moreover, to understand only the capacity for knowledge *a priori*, i.e., knowledge which is not empirical.

Now to have a yardstick for what has *lately* been happening in metaphysics, we must compare it to what has been done in the subject *of old*, and both to what ought to have been done there. But we shall be able to reckon in as a part of the progress, i.e., as a negative advance, the conscious and deliberate recurrence to maxims of the mode of thought, since even if it were only the removal of a deep-seated error, spreading far and wide in its consequences, something can still be done thereby for the benefit of metaphysics; just as a person who has strayed from the right path, and returns to his starting point in order to pick up his compass, is at least commended because he did not go on wandering up the wrong road, or come to a halt, but reverted to his point of departure in order to orient himself.

The first and oldest steps in metaphysics were not ventured merely as risky attempts, say, but were made, rather, with complete confidence, though without having first initiated any careful inquiries as to the possibility of *a priori* cognitions. What was the cause of this trust that reason had in itself? Its imagined *success*. For in mathematics reason succeeded in knowing *a priori* the constitution of things, well beyond all expectation of the philosophers; why should there not be just as much success in philosophy?[5] As to the possibility of knowledge *a priori*, it did not strike the metaphysicians as a radical difference, to be treated as an important problem, that mathematics proceeds on the terrain of the sensory, since reason itself can construct concepts for it, i.e., present them *a priori* in intuition, and thus know the objects *a priori*, whereas philosophy undertakes an extension of reason's knowledge by mere concepts, where its objects cannot, as in the other case, be set before us, since they hover, as it were, ahead of us in the air. It was enough to extend *a priori* knowledge, even outside mathematics, by mere concepts, and that this extension contains truth is evidenced by the agreement of such judgments and principles *with experience*.

Now although the super-sensible, to which the aim of reason is directed in metaphysics, actually provides no basis whatever for theoretical knowledge, the metaphysicians still sallied confidently forth under the guidance of their ontological principles, which are admittedly *a priori* in origin, but valid only for objects of experience; and although the imagined yield of transcendent insights upon the road could be confirmed by no experience, it could also, precisely because it relates to the

20: 262

super-sensible, be refuted by no experience either; it was necessary only to beware of letting any self-contradiction intrude into one's judgments, which can perfectly well be done, even though these judgments, and the concepts underlying them, may otherwise be completely empty.

This path of the dogmatists, which dates back to an age still earlier than that of Plato and Aristotle, and reaches forward to include even that of a Leibniz and Wolf, is, if assuredly not the right path, at least the most natural one to the goal of reason, and to the delusive conviction that everything which reason undertakes on the analogy of its procedure when successful, must equally be bound to succeed.

20: 263 The second and almost equally ancient move made by metaphysics was, on the other hand, a regression, which would have been wise and profitable to the subject, if only it had extended back to the starting point of the venture, though not to halt there with the resolve of attempting no further advance, but rather with that of resuming it in a new direction.

This regression, putting an end to all further initiatives, was based on the total *failure* of all attempts in metaphysics. But how could this failure, and the shipwreck of its grand enterprises, be recognized? Is it experience, perchance, that refuted them? By no means. For what reason proclaims to be the extension *a priori* of its knowledge of the objects of possible experience, in mathematics and ontology alike, are real steps, proceeding in a forward direction, and by which it assuredly gains ground. No, it is with intended and imagined conquests in the field of the super-sensible, where it is a question of the absolute totality of Nature, which no sense apprehends, and likewise of God, Freedom and Immortality; it is there, and chiefly in connection with the latter three objects, in which reason takes a practical interest, that all attempts at extension now miscarry; a thing seen, however, not because a deeper knowledge of the super-sensible, a higher metaphysics, teaches us the opposite of those earlier opinions; for we cannot compare the one with the other, since as transcendent objects they are unknown to us. It is because there are principles in our reason whereby, to every proposition that would extend our knowledge of such objects, a seemingly no less authentic counter-proposition is opposed, so that reason itself destroys its own attempts.[6]

This path of the skeptic is naturally of somewhat later origin, though still old enough, and it continues at the same time to persist in very good minds everywhere, albeit that another interest than that of pure reason constrains many to conceal the impotence of reason in this matter. The extension of skepticism even to the principles of knowledge of the sensible, and to experience itself, cannot properly be considered a serious view that has been current in any period of philosophy, but has perhaps been a challenge to the dogmatists, to demonstrate those *a priori* principles on which the very possibility of experience depends; and since they could not do this, a way of presenting those principles to them as doubtful too.

The third and most recent step that metaphysics has taken, by which its fate must be decided, is the critique of pure reason itself, in regard to its power of effecting an *a priori* extension of human knowledge generally, whether it be concerned with the sensible or the super-sensible. If this critique has performed what it promises, namely to determine the scope, the content, and the bounds of such knowledge – if it has done this in Germany, and done it since the days of Leibniz and Wolf – then the problem of the Royal Academy of Sciences will have been resolved.

There are therefore three stages which philosophy had to traverse in its approach to metaphysics. The first was the stage of dogmatism; the second that of skepticism; and the third that of the criticism of pure reason.[7]

This temporal sequence is founded in the nature of man's cognitive capacity. Once the first two stages have been passed, the state of metaphysics can continue to vacillate for many centuries, leaping from an unlimited self-confidence of reason to boundless mistrust, and back again. But a critique of its own powers would put it into a condition of stability, both external and internal, in which it would need neither increase nor decrease, nor even be capable of this.

20: 264

20:265   The solution of the problem in hand can be divided into two sections, of which one deals with the *formal* in reason's procedure for creating metaphysics as a theoretical science, while the other derives from that procedure the *material* – the final aim that reason has in view with metaphysics, whether that aim be achieved or not.

The *first* part will therefore present merely the steps towards metaphysics that have lately been taken; the *second*, the advances of metaphysics itself in the field of pure reason. The first contains the current state of transcendental philosophy, the second that of metaphysics proper.

FIRST SECTION
History of Transcendental Philosophy
among Us in Recent Times

The *first step* to have been undertaken in this investigation of reason is the distinction of analytic from synthetic judgments generally.[8] Had this been clearly recognized in the days of Leibniz or Wolf, we should somewhere find such a distinction not only touched upon, in a Logic or Metaphysics that has since appeared, but also emphasized as important. For the first type of judgment is invariably *a priori*, and coupled with the consciousness of its necessity. The second can be empirical, and logic is unable to furnish the condition under which a synthetic *a priori* judgment would occur.

20: 266   The *second step* is simply to have posed the question: How are synthetic *a priori* judgments possible? For that there are such judgments is proved by numerous examples from the general theory of Nature, but especially from pure mathematics. Hume has already performed a service in pointing out a case, namely that of the law of causality, whereby he put all metaphysicians into a quandary.[9] What would have happened if he, or someone else, had propounded the question in general! The whole of metaphysics would have had to remain in abeyance until it had been resolved.

The *third step* is the problem: "How is an *a priori* knowledge possible from synthetic judgments?" Knowledge is a judgment from which proceeds a concept that has objective reality, i.e., to which a corresponding object can be given in experience. But all experience consists in the intuition of an object, i.e., an immediate and individual representation, through which the object is given as to knowledge, and a concept, i.e., a mediate representation through a characteristic common to many objects, whereby it is therefore thought. Neither of the two types of representation constitutes knowledge on its own, and if there are to be synthetic *a priori* cognitions, there must also be *a priori* intuitions as well as concepts, whose possibility must therefore first be discussed, and then their objective reality proved through the necessary use of them, in virtue of the possibility of experience.

An intuition that is to be possible *a priori* can only relate to the form under which the object is intuited, for that means to represent something *a priori* to oneself, to make a representation of it to oneself prior to perception, i.e., prior to and independent of empirical consciousness. But the empirical in perception, the sensation or impression (*impressio*), is the matter of intuition, in which therefore the intuition would not be an *a priori* representation. Such an intuition, therefore, as relates merely to form, is called pure intuition, which if it is to be possible must be independent of experience.[10]

But it is not the form of the object, as it is in itself, which makes intuition *a priori* possible, but rather that of the subject, namely the form of sense, of that kind of representation which he, the subject, is capable of. For if this form were to be taken from the object itself, we would first have to perceive this, and could become aware of its nature only in this perception. But that would then be an empirical intuition *a priori*. But whether it be the latter or not is something of which we can persuade ourselves, as soon as we attend to whether the judgment which attributes this form to the object carries necessity with it, or not; for in the latter case it is merely empirical.

20: 267

The form of the object, as it can alone be represented in an intuition *a priori*, is therefore based, not upon the constitution of this object in itself, but on the natural constitution of the subject who is capable of an intuitive representation of the object; and this subjective in the formal constitution of sense, as receptivity for the intuition of an object, is the only thing which makes possible *a priori*, i.e., in advance of all perception, an *a priori* intuition; and now both this, and the possibility of synthetic *a priori* judgments from the standpoint of intuition, can be quite well understood.

For one can know *a priori* how and in what form the objects of sense will be intuited, namely as is entailed by the subjective form of sensibility, i.e., the receptivity of the subject for the intuition of those objects; and strictly speaking, one should really not say that the form of the object is represented by us in pure intuition, but rather that it is a merely formal and subjective condition of sensibility, under which we intuit given objects *a priori*.

This, therefore, is the peculiar constitution of our (human) intuition, so far as the representation of objects is possible to us merely as sensory beings. We might certainly imagine for ourselves an immediate (direct) way of representing an object, which does not intuit objects according to conditions of sensibility, and so does it by way of the understanding. But we have no tenable concept of such an intuition, though we need to think of it, in order not to subject all beings that have powers of cognition to our own form of intuition. For it may be that some beings in the world might intuit the same objects under another form; and even if this form should be just the same, and necessarily so, in all such beings, we still have no more insight into this necessity than we do into the possibility of a supreme understanding, free, in his knowledge, from all sensibility, and at the same time from the need to know by concepts, who knows objects perfectly in mere (intellectual) intuition.[11]

20: 268

Now the critique of pure reason proves, of the representations of space and time, that they are pure intuitions such as we have just insisted that they must be, in order to lie *a priori* at the basis of all our knowledge of things, and I can confidently appeal to that proof, without having to trouble about objections.

I would only note further, that in regard to inner sense, the doubled self in consciousness of myself, namely that of inner sensory intuition, and that of the thinking subject, seems to many to presuppose two subjects in one person.

This, then, is the theory, that space and time are nothing but subjective forms of our sensory intuition, and in no way determinations appertaining to objects in themselves; but that precisely for this reason we are able to determine these intuitions of ours *a priori*, with consciousness of the necessity of the judgments in which we determine them, as in geometry, for example. But to determine is to judge synthetically.

This theory can be called the doctrine of the ideality of space and time,[12] since the latter come to be represented as something in no way dependent on things in themselves; a doctrine that is not just a mere hypothesis, so as to be able to explain the possibility of synthetic *a priori* knowledge, but a demonstrated truth, since it is absolutely impossible to extend one's knowledge beyond the given concept without founding it on some intuition, and if this extension is to be a *a priori*, on an *a priori* intuition; and an *a priori* intuition is likewise impossible without seeking it in the formal constitution of the subject, not in that of the object; because on the former assumption all objects of sense are presented in intuition according to that formal constitution, and thus must be known *a priori* and as necessary according to it; whereas if the latter assumption were to be made, synthetic *a priori* judgments would be empirical and contingent, which is a contradiction.

This ideality of space and time is nevertheless, at the same time, a doctrine of their perfect reality in regard to objects of the senses (outer and inner) qua *appearances*, i.e., as intuitions so far as their *form* depends on the subjective constitution of the senses; the knowledge of which, since it is founded on *a priori* principles of pure intuition, permits a certain and demonstrable science; whereas those subjective factors which concern the constitution of sense-intuition in regard to its matter, namely sensation, e.g., of bodies in light as color, in sound as tones, or in taste as sour, etc., remain merely subjective, and can provide no knowledge of the object, and thus no generally valid representation in empirical intuition; nor can they yield any example of such, in that they do not, like space and time, contain data for *a priori* cognitions, and cannot even be counted as knowledge of objects at all.

20: 269

It should further be noted that appearance, taken in the transcendental sense, where we say of things that they *are* appearances (*phaenomena*), is a concept quite different in meaning from that whereby I say that this thing appears to me this way or that, which is meant to indicate the physical appearance, and can be called *apparency*, or seeming.[13] For in the language of experience these are objects of the senses, because I can compare them only with other sensible objects; for example, the heaven with all its stars, though it actually be mere appearance, can be considered as a thing-in-itself; and if it is said of this that it has the look of a vault, the semblance here signifies the subjective in the presentation of a thing, which may result in falsely taking it in a judgment for objective.

And thus the proposition that all presentations of the senses acquaint us only with objects as appearances is in no way equivalent to the judgment that they contain only the *semblance* of objects, as the idealist would maintain.[14]

But in the theory of all objects of sense as mere appearances, there is nothing that creates a stranger impression than that I, regarded as the object of inner sense, i.e., as soul, can be known to myself as appearance merely, not according to that which I am as thing-in-itself; and yet the representation of time, as mere formal inner intuition *a priori*, which underlies all knowledge of myself, permits no other way of explaining the possibility of acknowledging that form as condition of self-consciousness.

The *subjective* in the form of sensibility, which is the *a priori* basis of all intuition of objects, made it possible for us to have a knowledge *a priori* of objects as they *appear* to us. We shall now define this term more accurately, in that we declare this subjective to be the mode of representation whereby our senses are affected by objects, from without or within (i.e., from ourselves), so as to be able to say that we know these objects only as appearances.

20: 270   That I am conscious of myself is a thought that already contains a twofold self, the self as subject and the self as object. How it should be possible that I, who think, can be an object (of intuition) to myself, and thus distinguish myself *from* myself, is absolutely impossible to explain, although it is an undoubted fact; it demonstrates, however, a power so far superior to all sensory intuition, that as ground of the possibility of an understanding it has as its consequence a total separation from the beasts, to whom we have no reason to attribute the power to say 'I' to oneself, and looks out upon an infinity of self-made representations and concepts. We are not, however, referring thereby to a dual personality; only the self that thinks and intuits is the person, whereas the self of the object that is intuited by me is, like other objects outside me, the thing.

    Of the self in the first sense (the subject of apperception), the logical self as *a priori* representation, it is absolutely impossible to know anything further as to what sort of being it is, or what its natural constitution may be; it is like the substantial, which remains behind after I have taken away all the accidents that inhere in it, but absolutely cannot be known any further at all, since the accidents were precisely that whereby I was able to know its nature.

    But the self in the second sense (as subject of perception), the psychological self as empirical consciousness, is capable of being known in many ways, among which time, the form of inner intuition, is that which underlies *a priori* all perceptions and their combination whose apprehension (*apprehensio*) conforms to the manner in which the subject is thereby affected, i.e., to the condition of time, in that the sensory self is determined by the intellectual to take up this condition into consciousness.[15]

    That this is so, every inner psychological observation that we undertake can serve us as proof and example; since for this we are required to affect the inner sense, in part also doubtless to the point of fatigue, by means of attention (for thoughts, as factual determinations of the power of representation, also belong to the empirical representation of our state), in order to have first of all in the intuition of ourself a knowledge of what inner sense is presenting to us; which then merely makes us aware of ourself as we appear to ourselves; whereas the logical self does
20: 271   indeed point to the subject as it is in itself, in pure consciousness, not as receptivity but as pure spontaneity, but beyond that is also incapable of knowing anything of its nature.

Of *a priori* Concepts

Once the subjective form of sensibility is applied, as it must be if its objects are to be taken as appearances, to objects as the forms thereof, it brings about in its determination a representation inseparable from this, namely that of the composite.[16] For we can represent a determinate space to ourselves no otherwise than by drawing it, i.e., by adding one space to the other, and so also with time.

Now the representation of a composite, as such, is not a mere intuition, but requires the concept of a compounding, so far as it is applied to the intuition in space and time. So this concept (along with that of its opposite, the simple) is one that is not abstracted from intuitions, as a part-representation contained in them, but is a basic concept, and *a priori* at that – in the end the sole basic concept *a priori*, which is the original foundation in the understanding for all concepts of sensible objects.

There will thus be as many *a priori* concepts resident in the understanding, to which objects given to the senses must be subordinated, as there are types of compounding (*synthesis*) with consciousness, i.e., as there are types of synthetic unity of apperception of the manifold given in intuition.

Now these concepts are the pure concepts of the understanding for all objects that might be presented to our senses; set forth by Aristotle under the name of categories, albeit mingled with alien concepts, and by the Scholastics under that of predicaments, with exactly the same errors, these concepts could well have been drawn up into a systematically ordered table, if what logic has to teach concerning the formal diversity of judgments had previously been put into the framework of a system.

The understanding shows its power solely in judgments, which are nothing else but the unity of consciousness in relation to concepts as such, regardless of whether that unity is analytic or synthetic. Now the pure concepts of understanding, of objects as such that are given in intuition, 20: 272 are the very same logical functions, but only insofar as they present *a priori* the synthetic unity of the apperception of the manifold that is given in an intuition as such; thus the table of categories, parallel to that of the logical functions, could be outlined completely, though this had not been done prior to the publication of the *Critique of Pure Reason*.[17]

It should be noted, however, that these categories, or predicaments (as they are otherwise called), presuppose no particular kind of intuition which (like that which alone is possible to us men) is sensory as space and time are; they are merely thought-forms for the concept of an object of intuition as such, of whatever kind that may be, and even if it were a supersensible intuition, of which we are unable to frame any specific concept. For we must always frame to ourselves through pure understanding a concept of an object of which we wish to judge something *a priori*, even though we subsequently find it to be transcendent, and such that no objective reality can be procured for it; so that the category per se does not depend upon the forms of sensibility, space and time, but may also be based upon other forms quite unthinkable to us, so long as they relate only to the subjective which is antecedent *a priori* to all knowledge, and makes synthetic *a priori* judgments possible.

Among the categories, as original concepts of the understanding, are included also the predicables, as *a priori* concepts either of pure understanding, or sensorily conditioned, which arise from such compounding, and are thus derivative; the first of them yields existence considered as magnitude, i.e., duration, or change, as existence with opposite determinations; the second, the concept of motion, as change of position in space – examples which could likewise be completely enumerated and systematically presented in a table.

20: 273

Transcendental philosophy, i.e., the doctrine of the possibility of all *a priori* knowledge as such, which is that critique of pure reason whose elements have now been completely set forth, has as its purpose the founding of a metaphysic, whose purpose in turn envisages as an aim of pure reason the extension of the latter from the limits of the sensible to the field of the super-sensible; a transit which, if it is not to be a dangerous leap,[18] seeing that it is not, after all, a continuous progression in the same order of principles, makes necessary a scrupulous attention to the bounds of both domains, which obstructs progress.

From thence follows the division of the stages of pure reason, into doctrine of science, as a sure advance; doctrine of doubt, as a halting-point; and doctrine of wisdom, as a transition to the ultimate purpose of metaphysics: so that the first will contain a theoretico-dogmatic doctrine, the second a skeptical discipline, and the third a practico-dogmatic creed.

FIRST SECTION
Of the Scope of the Theoretico-Dogmatic Use of Pure Reason

The content of this section is the proposition: The scope of the theoretical knowledge of pure reason extends no further than to objects of the senses.

In this proposition, as an exponible judgment, two others are contained:

(1) that reason, as a power of knowing things *a priori*, extends to objects of the senses;
(2) that in its theoretical use it can certainly produce the concepts, but never a theoretical knowledge, of that which cannot be an object of the senses.

For proof of the first proposition it is also proper to consider how an *a priori* knowledge of sensible objects may be possible, since without that we would not be quite sure whether judgments about those objects were also in fact cognitions; but as to their nature, in being *a priori* judgments, it is automatically evinced through the consciousness of their necessity.

For a representation to be a cognition (though here I mean always a theoretical one), we need to have concept and intuition of an object combined in the same representation, so that the former is represented as containing the latter under itself. Now if a concept is one drawn from 20: 274 the sensory representation, i.e., an empirical concept, it contains as a characteristic, i.e., as a part-representation, something that was already apprehended in the sensory intuition, and differs from the latter in logical form only, viz., in respect of its generality, e.g., the concept of a four-footed animal in the representation of a horse.

But if the concept is a category, a pure concept of the understanding, it lies entirely outside all intuition, and yet an intuition must be subsumed under it if it is to be used for knowledge; and if this knowledge is to be an *a priori* cognition, a pure intuition must be underlaid, and one which conforms to the synthetic unity of apperception of the manifold in the intuition which is being thought through the category; i.e., the power of representation must interpose beneath the pure concept of the understanding an *a priori* schema,[19] without which it could have no object at all, and thus serve for no cognition.

Now since all the knowledge of which man is capable is sensory, and the *a priori* intuition of it space and time, and since both present objects only as objects of the senses, not as things proper, our theoretical knowledge as such, even if it be knowledge *a priori*, is still confined to objects of the senses, and within these confines can certainly proceed dogmatically, by laws that it prescribes *a priori* to Nature, as the collective body of sense objects; but can never get out beyond this circle, in order to extend itself, still theoretically, by means of its concepts.

The knowledge of sense objects as such, i.e., through empirical representations of which we are conscious (through combined perceptions), is experience.[20] Hence our theoretical knowledge never transcends the field of experience. Now since all theoretical knowledge must accord with experience, this will be possible only in one of two ways, in that either experience is the ground of our knowledge, or knowledge the ground of experience. So if there is a synthetic knowledge *a priori*, then the only way out is that it must contain conditions *a priori* of the possibility of experience as such. But in that case it also contains the conditions of the possibility of the objects of experience as such, since only through experience can they be knowable objects for us. But the *a priori* principles 20: 275

by which alone experience is possible are the forms of the objects, space and time, and the categories, which contain *a priori* the synthetic unity of consciousness, so far as empirical representations can be subsumed under it.

The supreme problem of transcendental philosophy is therefore: How is experience possible?

The basic principle, that all knowledge begins solely from experience, involves a *quaestio facti,*[a] and is thus not at issue here, since the fact is unreservedly granted. But whether it is also to be derived solely from experience, as the supreme ground of knowledge, is a *quaestio juris*, an affirmative answer to which would inaugurate the empiricism of transcendental philosophy, and a negative one the rationalism of the same.

The first is a self-contradiction; for if all knowledge is of empirical origin, then regardless of what may be grounded *a priori* in the understanding, and can ever be admitted, by the law of contradiction, to reflection and its logical principle, the synthetic in knowledge, which constitutes the essence of experience, is still purely empirical, and possible only as knowledge *a posteriori*; and transcendental philosophy is itself an absurdity.

But since, however, of those propositions which prescribe *a priori* the rule to possible experience, such as, e.g., *All change has its cause*, it cannot be denied that they are strictly universal and necessary, and yet are nevertheless synthetic, it follows that empiricism, which declares all this synthetic unity of our representations in cognition to be a mere matter of custom,[21] is totally untenable, and there is a transcendental philosophy firmly grounded in our reason, even though, if one wished to represent it as destructive of itself, another and absolutely insoluble problem would arise. Whence do sensible objects acquire the connection and regularity of their coexistence, so that it is possible for the understanding to bring them under general laws and discover their unity according to principles? – for which the law of contradiction alone does not suffice,[22] since in that case rationalism would inevitably have to be called in.

If we therefore find ourselves compelled to seek out an *a priori* principle of the possibility of experience itself, the question is, what sort of principle is there? All representations which constitute an experience can be assigned to sensibility, with one solitary exception, namely that of the composite, as such.

Since compounding cannot fall under the senses, but has to be performed by ourselves, it belongs, not to the receptive nature of sensibility, but to the spontaneity of the understanding, as an *a priori* concept.

Space and time, subjectively regarded, are forms of sensibility, but in order to frame a concept of them, as objects of pure intuition (without

20: 276

---

[a] question of fact . . . question of law

which we could say nothing at all about them), we require *a priori* the concept of a composite, and thus of the compounding (synthesis) of the manifold, and thus synthetic unity of apperception in combining this manifold; which unity of consciousness, in virtue of the diversity of intuitable representations of objects in space and time, requires different functions to combine them; these are called categories, and are *a priori* concepts of the understanding, which do not in themselves yet found any *knowledge* of an object as such, but do however found it of that which is given in empirical intuition, which would thereupon constitute experience. The empirical, however, i.e., that whereby an object is represented as given in respect of its existence, is called *sensation* (*sensatio, impressio*), which constitutes the matter of experience, and, conjoined with consciousness, is called perception, to which must be appended the form, i.e., the synthetic unity of apperception thereof in the understanding, whereby the *a priori* is thought, in order to produce experience as empirical knowledge; since space and time themselves, wherein we must assign by concepts a place to every object of perception, are not immediately perceived by us, *a priori* principles according to mere concepts of the understanding are necessary for this purpose, which prove their reality through sensory intuition, and, in combination with the latter, in accordance with its *a priori* given form, make possible *experience*, which is a quite certain knowledge *a posteriori*.

* *

*

But so far as outer experience is concerned, there arises against this certainty an important doubt, not as to whether knowledge of objects by means of it might possibly be uncertain, but as to whether the object that we posit outside us could not perhaps be always within us, so that it may well be quite impossible to recognize anything outside us to be so with certainty. If this question were to be left quite undecided, metaphysics would thereby forfeit nothing of its advances, since there the perceptions and the form of the intuition in them, from which we generate experience according to principles through the categories, may yet always be within us, and whether anything outside us also corresponds to them or not makes no change in the extension of knowledge, in that we cannot therefore hold to the objects in any case, but only to our perception, which is always within us.   20: 277

* *

*

From thence follows the principle for the division of the whole of metaphysics: So far as the speculative power of reason is concerned, no knowledge of the super-sensible is possible (*Noumenorum non datur scientia*).[a],[23]

* *

*

So much has transpired of late in transcendental philosophy, and had to transpire, before reason could make a step into metaphysics proper, or even one towards it; inasmuch as the Leibniz–Wolfian philosophy was always confidently pursuing its course in Germany on another tack, in the belief that, in addition to the old Aristotelian principle of contradiction, it had handed the philosophers a new compass to guide them, namely the principle of sufficient reason for the existence of things,[24] in contrast to their mere possibility according to concepts, and likewise that of the distinction between obscure, clear but still confused, and distinct representations, to mark the difference between intuition and knowledge according to concepts; though with all this elaboration it unknowingly continued always to remain in the field of logic, merely, and had achieved not a step towards metaphysics, let alone one within it, and thereby demonstrated that it had no clear acquaintance at all with the distinction between synthetic and analytic judgments.[25]

The proposition "Everything has its ground," which is allied to "Everything is a consequence," can to that extent belong only to logic, and mark the distinction between judgments which are thought problematically and those that are meant to hold assertorically, and is purely analytic, since if it were to be valid of things, and say that every thing should be viewed only as a consequence of the existence of some other thing, the sufficient reason whereby it was so viewed would be nowhere at all to be found; against which absurdity refuge would then be sought in the proposition that a thing (*ens a se*)[b] does indeed always have a ground of its existence, but in itself, i.e., exists as a consequence of itself; where, if the absurdity is not to be obvious, the proposition could hold, not of things at all, but only of judgments, and of mere analytic judgments at that. For example, the proposition "Every body is divisible"[26] does admittedly have a ground, and that within itself, i.e., it can be viewed as inferring the predicate from the concept of the subject according to the law of contradiction, and thus by the principle of analytic judgments; whence it is grounded merely upon an *a priori* principle of logic, and advances not a step in the field of metaphysics, where it is a matter of extending knowledge *a priori*, to which analytic judgments contribute nothing. But if the supposed metaphysician wished, in

20: 278

[a] There is no knowledge of noumena.
[b] thing by itself

addition to the law of contradiction, to introduce the equally logical grounding law, he would not yet have given a complete enumeration of the modality of judgments; for he would then have to append the law of excluded middle between two judgments contradictorily opposed to one another, since only so would he have propounded the logical principles of the possibility, the truth or logical reality, and the necessity of judgments, in problematic, assertoric, and apodictic judgments, insofar as they all stand under a single principle, namely that of the analytic judgment. This omission proves that, so far as completeness of classification is concerned, the metaphysician himself was not even clear about logic.

But as to Leibniz's principle of the logical difference between the indistinctness and distinctness of representations, when he claims that the former, that mode of presentation which we were calling mere intuition, is actually only the confused concept of its object, so that intuition differs from concepts of things, not in kind, but only according to the degree of consciousness, and thus the intuition, for example, of a body in thoroughgoing consciousness of all the presentations contained in it would yield the concept of it as an aggregate of monads – to this the critical philosopher will reply that in that way the proposition "Bodies consist of monads" could arise from experience, merely by analysis of perception, if only we could see sharply enough (with appropriate awareness of part-representations). But since the coexistence of these monads is represented as possible only in space, this metaphysician of the old school will have to explain space to us as a merely empirical and confused representation of the juxtaposition of elements of the manifold outside each other.

But how, in that case, is he in a position to claim the proposition that space has three dimensions as an apodictic proposition *a priori*, seeing that by even the clearest consciousness of all part-representations of a $\qquad$ 20: 279 body he would not have been able to demonstrate that this must be so, but at most, only, that as perception tells him, it is so. But if he assumes space, with its property of three dimensions, to be necessary and lying *a priori* at the basis of all representations of body, how is he going to explain this necessity, which he cannot, after all, quibble away? For this mode of representation, on his own showing, is still of merely empirical origin, which yields no necessity. But if he is equally willing to shrug off this demand, and accept space, with this property it has, whatever may be the nature of that supposedly confused representation, then geometry, and thus reason, demonstrates to him, not by notions that hover in the air, but by the construction of concepts, that space, and also that which occupies it, namely body, absolutely does not consist of simple parts; albeit that if we wanted to make the possibility of body comprehensible to ourselves by mere ideas, we would certainly have to make the simple fundamental, by starting from the parts and thus proceeding from them to the composite; whereby one is then finally compelled to admit that intuition (such as is the representation of space) and concept are modes of representation utterly different in kind, and that the former cannot be transformed into the latter by merely resolving the confusedness of the representation. Precisely the same is also true of the representation of time.

How to Confer Objective Reality on the Pure Concepts of Understanding and Reason

To represent a pure concept of the understanding as thinkable in an object of possible experience is to confer objective reality upon it, and in general to present it. Where we are unable to achieve this, the concept is empty, i.e., it suffices for no knowledge. If objective reality is accorded to the concept directly (*directe*) through the intuition that corresponds to it, i.e., if the concept is immediately presented, this act is called schematism; but if it cannot be presented immediately, but only in its consequences (*indirecte*), it may be called the symbolization of the concept. The first occurs with concepts of the sensible, the second is an expedient for concepts of the super-sensible which are therefore not truly presented, and can be given in no possible experience, though they still necessarily appertain to a cognition, even if it were possible merely as a practical one.

20: 280

The symbol of an Idea (or a concept of reason) is a representation of the object by analogy, i.e., by the same relationship to certain consequences as that which is attributed to the object in respect of its own consequences, even though the objects themselves are of entirely different kinds; for example, if I conceive of certain products of Nature, such as organized things, animals or plants, in a relation to their cause like that of a clock to man, as its maker, viz., in a relationship of causality as such, *qua* category, which is the same in both cases, albeit that the subject of this relation remains unknown to me in its inner nature, so that only the one can be presented, and the other not at all.

In this way I can indeed have no theoretical knowledge of the super-sensible, e.g., of God, but can yet have a knowledge by analogy, and such as it is necessary for reason to think; it is founded upon the categories, because they necessarily pertain to the form of thinking, whether it be directed to the sensible or the super-sensible, even though these categories constitute no knowledge, and this precisely because they do not by themselves yet determine any object.

On the Delusiveness of Attempts to Ascribe Objective Reality, even without Sensibility, to Concepts of the Understanding

It is a contradiction to think, by mere concepts of the understanding, of two things as external to one another, though in regard to all inner determinations (of quantity and quality) they would nevertheless be entirely of a kind; it is always merely one and the same thing thought twice over (numerically one).

This is Leibniz's law of indiscernibility,[27] to which he attaches no small importance, though it is violently in conflict with reason, since there is no understanding why a drop of water at one place should prevent an identical drop from being encountered at another. But this collision proves at once that, in order to be known, things in space must be represented, not merely through concepts of the understanding, as things-in-themselves, but also in accordance with their sensory intuition as appearances; and that space is not a property or relation of things-in-themselves, as Leibniz supposed; and that pure concepts of the understanding yield no knowledge on their own.

SECOND SECTION
Of What has been Accomplished, since the Age of Leibniz and Wolf, in regard to the Object of Metaphysics, i.e., its Final Goal.

The progress of metaphysics during this period can be divided into *three stages*: *First* into that of theoretico-dogmatic *advance*, *second* into that of skeptical *stasis*, and *third* into that of the practico-dogmatic *completion* of its course, and the arrival of metaphysics at its final goal.* The first proceeds solely within the bounds of ontology, the second within those of transcendental or pure cosmology, which also, as a doctrine of Nature, i.e., applied cosmology, considers the metaphysic of bodily and that of thinking Nature; the former as object of the outer senses, the latter as object of inner sense (*physica et psychologia rationalis*),[a] according to what is knowable *a priori* in them. The third stage is that of theology, with all the cognitions *a priori* that lead to it and make it necessary. An empirical psychology which by academic custom has been episodically interpolated into metaphysics, is legitimately disregarded here.

First Stage of Metaphysics in the Period and Region under Review

So far as concerns the classification of the pure concepts of the understanding, and of the *a priori* principles employed for experiential knowledge, as that in which ontology consists, we cannot deny to the two philosophers in question, and especially to the celebrated Wolf, the great merit of having displayed more clarity, precision, and urge to demonstrative thoroughness than has ever been shown previously, or outside Germany, in the domain of metaphysics. But even without censuring the lack of completeness, since no critique had yet established a table of categories according to a fixed principle, the want of all intuition *a priori*,

20: 282 which was simply not known as a principle, and which Leibniz in fact intellectualized, i.e., transformed into mere confused concepts, was his reason for considering impossible what he could not make intelligible through mere concepts of the understanding, and thus for setting up principles which do violence even to the common understanding, and have no tenability. Examples of the erroneous course pursued on such principles are contained in what follows.

(1) The principle of the identity of indiscernibles (*principium identitatis indiscernibilium*), that if we form of A and B, which are completely

---

* See above, p. 20: 273.

[a] rational physics and psychology

alike in regard to all their inner determinations (of quality and quantity), a concept of their being two things, we are mistaken, and must take them to be one and the same thing (*numero eadem*).[a] That we can still distinguish them by position in space, because quite similar and equal spaces can be represented outside each other, without our therefore having to say that they are one and the same space (since in that way we could bring the whole of infinite space into a cubic inch, and even less), was something he could not grant, since he admitted only a distinction by concepts, and would not recognize a mode of representation specifically different from these, namely intuition, and *a priori* intuition at that; the latter, rather, he thought he had to resolve into mere concepts of coexistence or succession, and thus he offended against common sense, which will never let itself be persuaded that if a drop of water is at one place, this prevents an absolutely similar and equal drop from existing at another.

(2) His principle of sufficient reason, since he did not feel obliged to found it on any intuition *a priori*, but traced the idea of it to mere *a priori* concepts, produced the consequence that all things, metaphysically considered, would be compounded of reality and negation, of being and nonbeing, as in Democritus everything in the universe is made up of atoms and void; and the ground of a negation can only be that there is no reason why something should be posited, i.e., no reality present; and thus out of all so-called metaphysical evil, in combination with good of that kind, he created a world of mere light and shadows, without considering that, in order to put a space in shadow, a body must be present, and hence something real that prevents the light from penetrating into the space. According to him, pain would be grounded merely on lack of pleasure, vice merely on the want of virtuous motives, and the rest of a moving body merely on the absence of moving force, since by mere concepts reality = a can be contrasted, not to reality = b, but only to privation = o – there being no consideration of the fact that in intuition, e.g., of the outer, *a priori*, namely in space, an opposition of the real (the moving force) to another real, namely a moving force in the opposite direction, can be combined in one subject, and that by analogy, in inner intuition, mutually opposed real motives can likewise be so combined, and that the *a priori* knowable result of this conflict of realities might be negation. But for this purpose he would assuredly have had to assume mutually opposing directions, which can be represented only in intuition and not in mere concepts; and thence arose the principle, at variance both with common sense and even with morality, that all evil as ground = o, i.e., mere limitation, or, as the metaphysicians say, is the formal in things. Thus his principle of sufficient reason, since he located it in mere concepts, was also not of the slightest help to him in getting beyond the

20: 283

[a] in number the same

principle of analytic judgments, the law of contradiction, and extending himself in synthetic *a priori* fashion by reason.

(3) His system of pre-established harmony, though the aim of it was really to explain the association of mind and body, had therefore to be first directed, in general, to explaining the possibility of communion among different substances, whereby they constitute a whole; and there was really no way to avoid dealing with this, since substances, by their very concept, if nothing else is added to this, must be represented as perfectly isolated. For since in any one of them, by virtue of its subsistence, no accident may inhere that is grounded upon another substance, it being the case, rather, that if other substances exist, it may not depend upon them in any respect, even if they were all to depend upon a third (the primal being) as effects of its cause, there is therefore no reason at all why the accidents of any one substance should have to be grounded upon another equally external in respect of this its state. So if they are nevertheless to stand in communion as world-substances, this must only be an ideal influence and cannot be a real (physical) one, since the latter assumes the possibility of interaction, as though it were to be intelligible in virtue of their mere existence (which is not in fact the case); we must, that is, presume the author of existence to be an artist, who either so modifies on occasion these intrinsically quite isolated substances, or has already so fashioned them at the creation, that they harmonize together, as though they were really influencing one another, in accordance with the relation of cause and effect. So because the system of occasional causes does not appear so suitable as the other for explaining everything upon a single principle, the *systema harmoniae praestabilitae,*[a] the strangest figment ever to be excogitated by philosophy, was therefore bound to arise, simply because everything had to be explained and made intelligible by concepts.

If, on the other hand, we take the pure intuition of space, as it underlies *a priori* all outer relations, and comprises but one space, all substances are thereby bound together in relationships which make physical influence possible, and constitute a whole, so that all entities, as things in space, together make up only one world, and cannot be a number of worlds external to each other; which principle of world-unity, if it is to be pursued by mere concepts, without resting it upon such an intuition, is absolutely incapable of proof.

(4) His monadology. By mere concepts, all substances in the world are either simple, or composed of simples. For composition is merely a relationship, without which they would equally have to maintain their existence as substances; but what remains over, if I do away with all composition, is the simple. So all bodies, if they are conceived merely through the understanding, as aggregates of substances, consist of simple

20: 284

[a] system of pre-established harmony

substances. But all substances, apart from their relationships to one another, and the forces whereby they may have influence upon one another, must still have certain real determinations inwardly inherent in them, i.e., it is not enough to credit them with accidents which consist merely in external relationships; one must also accord them internal ones, relating purely to the subject. But we know of no internal real determinations which could be attributed to a simple, except for representations, and what depends on them; but these, since they cannot be attributed to the bodies, must be attributed, rather, to their simple parts, if we are not to presume the latter, as substances, to be internally quite empty. But simple substances, that have in themselves the capacity for representations, are what Leibniz has called monads. So bodies consist of monads, as mirrors of the universe, i.e., as endowed with powers of representation which differ from those of thinking substances only through lack of consciousness, and are therefore called sleeping monads, of which we know not whether fate might not one day awaken them, and may perhaps already have awoken infinitely many of them, one by one, and let them fall back to sleep again, in order for them one day to awake once more, and as animal souls to struggle up gradually into human souls, and thence onward to higher stages; a sort of enchanted world, which that celebrated author can only have been led to postulate in that he took sense-representations, *qua* appearances, not, as he should have done, for a mode of representation entirely different from all concepts, namely intuition, but for a knowledge, albeit a confused one, through concepts, which reside in the understanding and not in sensibility.

20: 285

The principle of *the identity of indiscernibles*, the principle of *sufficient reason*, the system of *pre-established harmony*, and lastly the *monadology*, together make up the new element which Leibniz, and after him Wolf (whose metaphysical contribution was far greater in practical philosophy), have attempted to introduce into the metaphysics of theoretical philosophy. Whether these attempts deserve to be called progress in the subject, though there is no denying that they may certainly have prepared for this, may at the end of this stage be left to the discretion of those who do not let themselves be led astray by great reputations.

The theoretico-dogmatic part of metaphysics also includes the general rational theory of Nature, i.e., pure philosophy as to objects of the senses, those of outer sense, i.e., the rational doctrine of bodies, and those of inner sense, i.e., the rational doctrine of the soul, whereby the principles of the possibility of an experience in general are applied to two kinds of perceptions, without otherwise employing anything empirical as foundation, save that two such objects do exist. In both there

20: 286   can be science only insofar as mathematics, i.e., the construction of concepts, can be applied therein, and hence the spatiality of objects can do more *a priori* for physics, than the form of time which underlies intuition through inner sense, since the latter has only one dimension.

The concepts of full and empty space, of motion and moving forces, can and must be brought in rational physics to their *a priori* principles, whereas in rational psychology nothing else but the concept of the immateriality of a thinking substance, that of its change, and that of the identity of the person amidst these changes, alone represent *a priori* principles; but all else is empirical psychology, or rather mere anthropology, since it can be shown that it is impossible for us to know whether and what the life-principle in man (the soul) is able to do in thinking without the body, and everything here amounts only to empirical knowledge, i.e., to a knowledge that we can acquire in life, and hence in a combination of soul with body, and is thus unsuited to the final goal of metaphysics, of attempting to pass over from the sensible to the super-sensible. The latter is to be met with in the second stage of pure reason's attempts in philosophy, which we now proceed to explain.

Metaphysics: Second Stage

The first stage of metaphysics can be called that of ontology, since it does not teach us to investigate the essence of our concepts of things by a resolution into their elements, which is the business of logic; it tells us, rather, what concepts of things we frame to ourselves *a priori*, and how, in order to subsume thereunder whatever may be given to us in intuition generally; which in turn could not happen save insofar as the form of *a priori* intuition in space and time makes these objects knowable to us merely as appearances, not as things-in-themselves. In this stage, reason sees itself obliged, in a series of conditions, subordinated one to another and each in turn conditioned without end, to progress incessantly towards the unconditioned,[28] since every space and every time can never

20: 287   be represented as anything but part of a still larger given space or time, in which the conditions for what is given to us in each intuition must still be sought, in order to attain to the unconditioned.

The second great advance that is now expected of metaphysics is that of getting from the conditioned in objects of possible experience to the unconditioned, and of extending its knowledge to the completion of this series by means of reason (for what has hitherto transpired took place through understanding and judgment); the stage which it now has to traverse will therefore be describable as that of transcendental cosmology, since space and time have now to be considered in their total magnitude, as the sum of all conditions, and represented as the containers of all connected real things; and the totality of the latter, so far as they occupy the former, has now to be made intelligible under the concept of a world.

Here, and indeed in the totality of the ascending series in which they are subordinated to one another, the synthetic conditions (*principia*) of the possibility of things, i.e., their grounds of determination (*principia essendi*), are sought for the conditioned (the *principiata*), in order to attain to the unconditioned (*principium quod non est principiatum*).[a] Reason demands this, in order to satisfy itself. With the descending series from the condition to the conditioned it has no trouble, since for this it requires no absolute totality, and the latter as consequence may always remain incomplete, since the consequences follow automatically, if only we are given the supreme ground that they depend upon.

Now it turns out that in space and time everything is conditioned, and that the unconditioned in the ascending series of conditions is absolutely unattainable. To think the concept of an absolute whole of the merely conditioned as unconditioned, involves a contradiction; the unconditioned can thus be considered only as a term of the series, which delimits the latter as ground, and is itself no consequence of another ground; and the inability to reach a ground, which runs through all classes of the categories, insofar as they are applied to the relationship of consequences to their grounds, is that which embroils reason with itself in a conflict never to be settled, so long as objects in space and time are taken for things-in-themselves, and not for mere appearances; which before the epoch of the critique of pure reason was unavoidable, so that thesis and antithesis were forever engaged in mutual destruction of one another, and were bound to plunge reason into the most hopeless skepticism; and this could not but turn out badly for metaphysics, since if it cannot even satisfy its demand for the unconditioned in regard to objects of the senses, there could be no thought whatever of a transition to the super-sensible, which is nevertheless its final goal.*

Now if, in the ascending series from the conditioned to the conditions, we advance to a world-totality, in order to arrive at the unconditioned, we find, in the theoretico-dogmatic cognition of a given world-totality, the following true or merely seeming contradictions of reason with itself. *First*, by mathematical ideas of the composition or division of the

---

* The proposition that the totality of all conditioning in time and space is unconditioned, is false. For if everything in space and time is conditioned (internally), no totality thereof is possible. So those who assume an absolute totality of mere conditioned conditions contradict themselves, whether they take it to be bounded (finite) or unbounded (infinite); and yet space must be regarded as such a totality, and so must elapsed time.

[a] principle not subject to a condition

similar; *second*, by dynamical ideas of the grounding of the existence of the conditioned upon unconditioned existence.

[I. In regard to the *extensive magnitude* of the world in measuring it, i.e., the repeated adding of the similar and equal unit, as the measure, in order to obtain a definite concept of it, (a) as to its spatial magnitude, and (b) as to its temporal extent, insofar as both are given – so that the latter is to measure the elapsed time of its duration – reason declares of both with equal justification that they are infinite, and yet that they are not infinite, and thus are finite. Yet the proof of each – remarkably enough – cannot be obtained directly, but only apagogically, i.e., by refutation of the opposite. Thus

(a) *Thesis*: The world is of infinite magnitude in space, for if it were finite it would be bounded by empty space, which itself is infinite, yet nothing existent in itself, though it would presuppose the existence of something as the object of a possible perception, namely that of a space which contains nothing real, and yet would have a content as the boundary of the real, i.e., as the observable last condition of what is mutually bounded in space; which is a contradiction. For empty space can neither be perceived nor carry with it a (detectable) existence.

(b) *Antithesis*: The world is also infinite in respect of elapsed time.

20: 289 For if it had a beginning, an empty time would have preceded it, which would likewise have made the origin of the world, and hence the nothing that preceded it, into an object of possible experience; which is a contradiction.

II. In regard to *intensive magnitude*, i.e., the degree to which this magnitude occupies space or time, the following antinomy[29] emerges.

(a) *Thesis*: Corporeal things in space consist of simple parts; for if we suppose the opposite, the parts would indeed be substances; yet if all their composition were taken away as mere relation, then nothing would be left but mere space, as the simple subject of all relations. So bodies would not consist of substances, which contradicts the thesis.

(b) *Antithesis*: Bodies do not consist of simple parts.]

Whether the first [type of] antinomy arises from the fact that in the concept of magnitude of things in the world, in both space and time, we can ascend from the thoroughly conditioned, given parts to the unconditioned whole in the composition, or descend by division from the given whole to the parts considered as unconditioned – whether we assume, that is, in regard thereto, that the world is infinite as to space and elapsed time, or that it is finite, we are inevitably embroiled in self-contradiction. For if the world, like the space and elapsed time it occupies, is given as infinite magnitude, it is then a given magnitude that can never be wholly given, which is a contradiction. If every body, or every time in the change of state of things, consists of simple parts, then since both space and time are infinitely divisible (as mathematics demonstrates), an infinite multitude must be given, which yet by its concept can never be wholly given; which is likewise a contradiction.

With the second class of Ideas, of the dynamically unconditioned, the situation is the same. For on the one hand it is argued: There is no freedom – on the contrary, everything in the world occurs by natural necessity. For the series of effects in relation to their causes is governed throughout by natural mechanism, namely that every change is predetermined by the preceding state. This is countered, on the other hand, by the following general claim of the antithesis: Some events must be thought of as possible through freedom, and they cannot all stand under the law of natural necessity, since otherwise everything would occur merely as conditioned, and thus nothing unconditioned would be encountered in the series of causes; but to suppose a totality of conditions in a series of the merely conditioned is a contradiction.

20: 290

Finally, the thesis pertaining to the dynamic class, which is otherwise sufficiently clear, namely that in the series of causes not everything can be contingent, since there must, rather, be some being existing with absolute necessity, is subject to the antithesis, that no being we can ever think of is conceivable as absolutely necessary cause of other world-beings; a well-founded rebuttal, since in that case it would belong with the things in the world, as a term in the ascending series of effects and causes, in which no causality is unconditioned, though here it would have to be assumed as unconditioned, which is a contradiction.

Remark. If the proposition: The world is in itself infinite, is intended to mean that it is larger than any number (in comparison with a given measure), then that proposition is false, for an infinite number is a contradiction. If the statement be that it is not infinite, then this is doubtless true, but then we do not know what that number may be. If I say it is finite, then that too is false, since its boundary is not the object of a possible experience. I affirm then, in regard to both given space and elapsed time, that it is required only for purposes of opposition. Each statement is then false, since possible experience has neither a boundary, nor can it be infinite, and the world as appearance is merely the object of possible experience.

* *

*

The following observations now arise on this point:

First, the proposition that for all that is conditioned an absolutely unconditioned must be given, holds as a principle of all things inasmuch as their connection is conceived by pure reason, i.e., as a connection among things-in-themselves. If we now find in practice that it cannot be applied without contradiction to objects in space and time, then there is no possible escape from this contradiction, unless we assume that objects in space and time, as objects of possible experience, are not to be regarded as things-in-themselves, but merely as appearances, whose form depends on the subjective constitution of our mode of intuiting them.

20: 291   Thus the antinomy of pure reason leads inevitably back to that limiting of our knowledge, and what was previously proved in the Analytic, in dogmatic *a priori* fashion, is here likewise incontestably confirmed in the Dialectic, by an experiment of reason, which it performs on its own powers. In space and time the unconditioned is not to be met with, though reason has need of it, and there is nothing left for the latter to hope for, but an everlasting progression to conditions, which never reaches completion.

Second, the conflict between these propositions of reason is not merely a logical conflict of analytical opposition (*contradictorie oppositorum*), i.e., a mere contradiction, for in that case, if one of them is true, the other would have to be false, and conversely. E.g., *the world is infinite in space*, compared to the antithesis, *it is not infinite in space*. It is, rather, a transcendental conflict of synthetic opposition (*contrarie oppositorum*), e.g., *the world is finite in space*, a proposition which says more than is required for logical opposition; for it does not say merely that in the progression to conditions the unconditioned will not be met with, but furthermore that this series of conditions, in which one is subordinated to the other, is nevertheless *in toto* an absolute whole; so that these two propositions can both of them be false – like two judgments in logic that are contrarily opposed to one another (*contrarie opposita*) – and that is what they actually are, since they are talking of appearances as if they were things-in-themselves.

Third, the thesis and antithesis may also contain less than is needed for logical opposition, and may both be true – like two judgments in logic that are opposed to one another merely by difference in their subjects (*judicia subcontraria)[a]* – as is actually the case in the antinomy of the dynamical principles; if, that is, the subject of the opposing judgments is taken in a different meaning in each; for example, the concept of cause, as *causa phenomenon* in the thesis: *All causality of phenomena in the world of sense is subject to the mechanism of Nature*, seems to stand in contradiction to the antithesis: *Some causality of these phenomena is not subject to this law*; but such contradiction is not necessarily to be met with there, since in the antithesis the subject can be taken in a different sense from that in the thesis – the same subject, that is, can be conceived as *causa noumenon*, and then both propositions may be true, and the same subject, *qua* thing-in-itself, be free from determination by natural necessity, which 20: 292   *qua* appearance, with respect to the same action, is not free. And so too with the concept of a necessary being.

[a] subcontrary judgments

Fourth, this antinomy of pure reason, which seems necessarily to bring it to a skeptical standstill, eventually leads by way of criticism to dogmatic advances of reason, if it turns out, that is, that such a noumenon, *qua* thing-in-itself, is really and even by its own laws knowable, at least from a practical viewpoint, even though it is super-sensible.

Freedom of choice is this super-sensible, which by moral laws is not only given as real in the subject, but is also determinant from a practical viewpoint with regard to the object, though theoretically it would be quite unknowable, albeit that it is the true objective of metaphysics.

The possibility of such an advance of reason by way of dynamical ideas is based on the fact that in them the synthesis of the true connection of the effect with its cause, or of the contingent with the necessary, does not have to be a combination of the similar, as in mathematical synthesis; it is possible, rather, for ground and consequent, the condition and the conditioned, to be different in kind, and hence in the advance from the conditioned to the condition, from the sensible to the super-sensible as supreme condition, a transition according to principles can occur.

* *

*

Like two particular propositions, for example, the two dynamical anti-nomies say less than is required for opposition. So both can be true.

In the dynamical antinomies, something dissimilar can be assumed as condition. By the same token, we there have something whereby the super-sensible (God, who is truly the end in view) can be known, because a law of freedom as super-sensible is given.

The ultimate purpose is directed to the super-sensible in the world (the spiritual nature of the soul), and outside it (God), and thus to im-mortality and theology.

Metaphysics: Third Stage
Practico-Dogmatic Transition to the Super-sensible

20: 293

It must certainly be borne in mind from the outset, that throughout this whole treatise, in accordance with the problem posed by the Academy, metaphysics is intended merely as a theoretical science, or, as it can also be called, a *metaphysic of Nature*; which means that its transition to the super-sensible must not be understood as a step into a quite dif-ferent rational science, the morally-practical, which can be called *meta-physic of morals*. For this would be to stray into a wholly different field (μετάβασις εἰς ἄλλο γένος), even though the latter also has as its object something super-sensible, namely freedom, albeit not in respect of what it is by nature, but rather in virtue of what it grounds for practical principles, in regard to action and omission.

Now by all the inquiries pursued in the second stage, the unconditioned is absolutely not to be met with in Nature, i.e., in the world of the senses, though it necessarily has to be assumed. But of the super-sensible there is no theoretico-dogmatic knowledge (*noumenorum non datur scientia*). So a practico-dogmatic transition to the metaphysic of Nature seems to contradict itself, and this third stage of it to be impossible.

But among the concepts pertaining to knowledge of Nature, whatever they may be, we still find one having the special feature, that by means of it we can grasp, not what is in the object, but rather what we can make intelligible to ourselves by the mere fact of imputing it to the object; which is therefore actually no constituent of knowledge of the object, but still a means or ground of knowledge given by reason, and this of theoretical, but yet not to that extent dogmatic knowledge. And this is the concept of a *purposiveness* of Nature, which can also be an object of experience, and is thus, not a transcendent, but an immanent concept, like that of the structure of eyes and ears; though of this, so far as experience is concerned, there is no further knowledge than what Epicurus granted it, namely that after Nature had formed eyes and ears, we use them for seeing and hearing, though that does not prove that the cause producing them must itself have had the intention of forming this structure in accordance with the purpose in question; for this we cannot perceive, but can only introduce by reasoning, in order merely to recognize a purposiveness in such objects.

We thus have the concept of a teleology[30] in Nature, and this *a priori*, since we would otherwise have no right to introduce it into our representation of Nature's objects, but could only extract it therefrom, as empirical intuition; and the *a priori* possibility of such a mode of representation, which is still no knowledge, is based on the fact that we perceive within ourselves a power of connecting according to purposes (*nexus finalis*).[a]

So although the physico-teleological doctrines (of purposes in Nature) can therefore never be dogmatic, and still less are able to suggest the concept of an ultimate purpose, i.e., the unconditioned in the series of purposes, nevertheless the concept of freedom, as it occurs, even in cosmology, *qua* sensorily-unconditioned causality, remains indeed skeptically assailed, but still unrefuted, and with it also the concept of an ultimate purpose; from a morally-practical viewpoint such a concept is actually unavoidable, although as with all purposiveness of given or imagined objects generally, its objective reality cannot be assured from a theoretico-dogmatic point of view.

20: 294

---

[a] linkage to ends

This ultimate purpose of pure practical reason is the highest good, so far as it is possible in the world, though it is to be sought not merely in what Nature can furnish, namely happiness (the greatest amount of pleasure); it lies, rather, in what is also the supreme requirement, or condition, under which alone reason can accord happiness to the rational world-being, namely that the latter's behavior should simultaneously conform to the utmost with the moral law.

This object of reason is super-sensible; to progress toward it, as ultimate purpose, is duty; that there has to be a stage of metaphysics for this transition, and for progress therein, is therefore indubitable. Yet without any theory this is still impossible, for the ultimate purpose is not wholly within our power, and hence we must frame to ourselves a theoretical concept of the source from which it can spring. Such a theory cannot, however, be framed by what we cognize in objects, but at most by what we impute to them, since the object is super-sensible. Hence this theory will be framed only from a practico-dogmatic viewpoint, and will be able to assure to the idea of the ultimate purpose an objective reality sufficient only from this point of view.

As to the concept of purpose, it is framed always by ourselves, and that of the ultimate purpose must be framed *a priori* through reason.　20: 295

If set forth analytically, these fabricated concepts, or rather, from a theoretical viewpoint, transcendent Ideas, are three in number, namely the super-sensible *in* us, *above* us, and *after* us:[31]

(1) *Freedom*, from which we have to start, since only from this super-sensible in the world's constitution do we know, under the name of moral laws, the laws whereby the ultimate purpose is alone possible; and know them *a priori*, which is to say dogmatically, although only in a practical respect. So according to these laws, the *autonomy* of pure practical reason is simultaneously taken to be *autocracy*,[32] i.e., as the power, in regard to its formal condition, namely morality, to attain this final purpose here in our earthly life, albeit as simultaneously intelligible beings, despite all the hindrances which the influence of Nature may exert upon us as sensory beings. This is the *belief in virtue*, as the principle *in us*, for attaining to the highest good.

(2) *God*, the all-sufficing principle of the highest good *above us*, who as moral world-creator makes up for our incapacity even in regard to the material condition of this final purpose, that of a happiness in the world commensurate to morality.

(3) *Immortality*, i.e., the continuance of our existence *after us*, as mortals, with those infinitely continuing moral and physical consequences which are commensurate to the moral behavior of such beings.

When set forth according to a synthetic method, these same stages in the practico-dogmatic knowledge of the super-sensible begin from the unrestricted possessor of the highest original good, go on to what is derived (through freedom) in the world of sense, and end with the consequences of this objective final purpose of man in an intelligible future world; and so here they stand systematically connected in the sequence: God, Freedom, and Immortality.

As to the fitness of human reason in determining these concepts to a real knowledge, it requires no proof, and metaphysics, which has become a necessary inquiry, precisely in order to achieve such knowledge, needs no justification for its unceasing endeavors to that end. But has it, since the days of Leibniz and Wolf, discovered anything, and how much has it discovered, and what can it discover in general, in regard to that supersensible whose knowledge is its final goal? That is the question which has to be answered, if it is addressed to the fulfilment of that ultimate purpose for which metaphysics in general is supposed to exist.

20: 296

Resolution of the Problem Posed
by the Academy

I

What Sort of Progress can Metaphysics achieve in regard to the Super-sensible?

It has been sufficiently demonstrated by the critique of pure reason that there can be absolutely no theoretical knowledge beyond the objects of the senses, nor any theoretico-dogmatic knowledge, since in that case everything would have to be known *a priori* through concepts; and this for the simple reason, that all concepts must be capable of resting upon an intuition of some sort, to provide them with objective reality; but all our intuition is sensuous. That means, in other words, that we can know nothing whatever of the nature of super-sensible objects, of God, of our own capacity for freedom, or of our soul (in separation from the body); nor anything as to this inner principle of all that pertains to the existence of these things, their consequences and effects, whereby their appearances could be even in the slightest degree explicable to us, and their principle, the object itself, be possible for us to know.

Thus the only question now still at issue is whether, in spite of that, there could not be a practico-dogmatic knowledge of these super-sensible objects, which would then constitute the third stage of metaphysics, and that which fulfilled its entire purpose.

In this case we would have to investigate the super-sensible thing, not in respect of what it is in itself, but only with regard to how we have to think it, and assume its nature to be, in order for it to be apposite, for ourselves, to the practico-dogmatic object of the pure moral principle, namely the final end, which is the highest good. We should not, then, be instituting inquiries as to the nature of the things which we frame to ourselves, and this merely for necessary practical purposes, and which perhaps have no existence at all outside our idea and maybe could not exist (though this otherwise involves no contradiction), since in doing so 20: 297 we might merely be lapsing into extravagance; we simply want to know what sort of moral principles of action are incumbent on us, in accordance with that idea which reason necessarily and inevitably frames for us; and here would ensue a practico-dogmatic knowledge and acquaintance with the nature of the object, along with complete renunciation of any theoretical knowledge (*suspensio judicii*);[a] and as to the first it is almost solely a matter of the name we confer upon this modality of our assent, so that it should not contain too little for such a purpose (as in mere opining), yet also not too much (as in taking to be probable), and thus concede victory to the skeptic.

Persuasion,[33] however, which is a form of assent of which we cannot make out on our own whether it rests on merely subjective, or on objective grounds, as distinct from merely felt conviction, in which the subject thinks himself to be conscious of those objective grounds, and of their sufficiency, though he cannot name them or get clear as to their connection with the object, can neither of them be reckoned among the modalities of assent in dogmatic knowledge, whether it be theoretical or practical, since the latter is meant to be a knowledge from principles, and must therefore also be capable of a clear, intelligible and communicable representation.

The meaning of this form of assent, distinct from the opinion and knowledge that are founded on judgment in the theoretical sense, can now be expressed in the term *belief*, whereby we understand an assumption, presupposition or hypothesis, which is necessary only because it is necessarily implied by an objective practical rule of conduct, as to which we do not, indeed, theoretically discern the possibility of its performance, or of the resultant object in itself, but yet subjectively recognize in that possibility the only way for them to accord with the final end.

Such a belief is the assent to a theoretical proposition, e.g., *there is a God*, by practical reason, considered here as pure practical reason, where, in that the final end, the accordance of our striving to the highest good, stands under an absolutely necessary practical rule, namely a moral rule, whose effect, however, we can conceive to be possible no otherwise than by presupposing the existence of an original highest good, we are necessitated *a priori* to assume this from a practical point of view.

20: 298 Thus for that section of the public which has nothing to do with the corn trade, the prospect of a bad harvest is a mere *opinion*, once the drought has persisted for the entire spring, and after that a piece of *knowledge*; but for the merchant, whose purpose and occupation is to profit by this trade, it is a *belief* that the harvest will turn out badly, and that he must therefore husband his supplies, because he must resolve to do something about it, in that it bears upon his occupation and business; save only that the necessity of this decision, taken by rules of prudence, is merely conditioned, whereas one that presupposes a moral maxim rests on a principle that is absolutely necessary.

Hence belief, in a morally-practical context, also has a moral value on its own account, since it contains a free affirmation. The *Credo* in

[a] suspension of judgment

the three articles of confession of pure practical reason: I believe in one God, as the original source of all good in the world, that being its final end; – I believe in the possibility of conforming to this final end, to the highest good in the world, so far as it is in man's power; – I believe in a future eternal life, as the condition for an everlasting approximation of the world to the highest good possible therein; – this *Credo*, I say, is a *free* affirmation, without which it would also have no moral value. It permits of no imperative, therefore (no *crede*),[a] and the argument for its correctness is no proof of the truth of these propositions, considered as theoretical, and thus no objective teaching as to the reality of their objects, for in regard to the super-sensible this is impossible; instead, it is merely an injunction, subjectively and indeed practically valid, and in this respect sufficient, so to act, as though we knew that these objects were real. Nor must this mode of representation be regarded here either as necessary in a technico-practical sense, as a prudential doctrine (better to profess too much than too little); because in that case the belief would not be sincere. It is necessary only in a moral sense, in order to add a supplement of the theory of the possibility of that to which we are already *ipso facto* constrained, namely to strive for promotion of the highest good in the world; and to add this by mere ideas of reason, in that we simply frame these objects, God, freedom in its practical aspect, and immortality, in consequence of the demand of the moral law within us, and voluntarily grant them objective reality, since we are assured that no contradiction can be found in these ideas, and since the effect of assuming them, upon the subjective principles of morality and their reinforcement, and thus upon action and omission themselves, is again by intention of a moral kind.

20: 299

But should there not also be theoretical proofs of the truth of these articles of faith, of which it might be said that in virtue of them it is *probable* that a God exists, that a moral order will be met with in the world, conforming to His will and appropriate to the idea of the highest good, and that for every human being there is a future life? The answer is that in this application the expression of probability is altogether absurd. For the probable (*probabile*) is that which has a reason for assenting to it which is greater than half of the sufficient reason, and is thus a mathematical determination of the modality of the assent, where the elements thereof must be assumed to be similar, so that an approximation to certainty is possible; whereas the ground of the more or less likely (*verosimile*) can also consist of dissimilar reasons, which is precisely why its relation to the sufficient reason cannot be known at all.

But now the super-sensible differs in its very species (*toto genere*) from the sensuously knowable, since it lies beyond all knowledge that is

---

[a] I believe ... thou shalt believe

possible to us. Hence there is no way at all of reaching it by those very same steps whereby we may hope to arrive at certainty in the field of the sensible; thus there is no approximation to it either, and therefore no assent whose logical value could be called probability.

From a theoretical viewpoint, the most strenuous efforts of reason do not bring us nearer in the least to conviction of the existence of God, the existence of the highest good, or the prospect of a future life, since we have no insight whatever into the nature of super-sensible objects. But in a practical point of view, we frame these objects to ourselves, inasmuch as we judge the idea of them to be helpful to the final end of our pure reason; which final end, since it is morally necessary, can then 20: 300 admittedly produce the illusion of believing that what has reality in a subjective context, namely for the use of man's freedom, is also, since it has been presented to experience in actions that conform to this its law, a knowledge of the existence of the object corresponding to this form.

By this time we can now describe the third stage of metaphysics in the progression of pure reason to its final goal. It takes the form of a circle, whose boundary line returns into itself, and thus includes a totality of knowledge of the super-sensible, outside which there is nothing more of this kind, and yet which also comprises everything that can suffice for the needs of this reason. For once it has freed itself from everything empirical, wherein it was still always embroiled in the first two stages, and from the conditions of sensory intuition, whereby it was presented with objects only in appearance, and has stationed itself at the standpoint of Ideas, whence it considers its objects in terms of what they are in themselves, then reason describes their horizon; setting out theoretico-dogmatically, from freedom as a super-sensible capacity, though one that can be known through the canon of morality, it returns there also in a practico-dogmatically oriented direction, i.e., one addressed to the final end, namely the highest good to be promoted in the world, whose possibility is reinforced by the ideas of God and immortality, and the confidence, dictated by morality itself, of achieving this purpose, and thus confers upon this concept an objective but practical reality.

The propositions: there is a God; there exists in the nature of the world an original, though incomprehensible, propensity to conform with moral purposiveness; there exists, finally, in the human soul a disposition which renders it capable of a neverending progression towards this; – to wish to prove these propositions in a theoretico-dogmatic sense would amount to a plunge into transcendence, though so far as the second of them is concerned, the elucidation of it by way of the physical purposiveness to be met with in the world can do much to fortify the assumption of this moral purposiveness. The same is true of the modality of assent, the imagined knowing and acquaintance wherein we forget that these Ideas have been arbitrarily framed by ourselves, and are not derived from the objects, and thus entitle us to nothing more than *assumption* in a theoretical sense, though they also allow us to maintain the rationality of such an assumption from a practical point of view.   20: 301

Now from this there follows also the notable consequence that in its third stage, in the field of theology, and precisely because it is directed to the final goal, the progress of metaphysics is the easiest of all, and although it is concerned here with the super-sensible, does not become transcendent, but is just as intelligible to ordinary human reason as to the philosophers, and this to such a point that the latter are obliged to orient themselves by the former, lest they lapse into transcendency. Philosophy as doctrine of wisdom enjoys this advantage over philosophy as speculative science by virtue of arising from nothing else but pure practical rationality, i.e., morality, so far as it has been derived from the concept of freedom, as a principle super-sensible, indeed, but practically knowable *a priori*.

The fruitlessness of all attempts of metaphysics to extend itself theoretico-dogmatically in that which concerns its final purpose, namely the super-sensible – *first* in regard to knowledge of the divine nature, as the highest original good; *second* in regard to knowledge of the nature of a world, in which and through which the highest derived good is supposed to be possible; and *third* in regard to knowledge of human nature, insofar as it is endowed with the natural constitution requisite to a progression appropriate to this final goal; – the fruitlessness, I say, of all attempts made therein up to the close of the Leibniz–Wolf epoch, and likewise the inevitable miscarriage of all that are yet to be instituted in future, should now demonstrate that metaphysics has no hope of arriving at its final goal by the theoretico-dogmatic route, and that all supposed knowledge in this field is transcendent, and thus altogether empty.

Transcendent Theology[34]

Reason, in metaphysics, seeks to create for itself a concept of the origin of all things, the primal being (*ens originarium*) and its inner constitution, and begins subjectively from the primal concept (*conceptus originarius*) of thinghood as such (*realitas*), i.e., of that whose concept intrinsically represents a being, rather than a nonbeing; albeit that in order to also conceive objectively the unconditioned in this primal being, it represents the latter as containing the all (*omnitudo*) of reality (*ens realissimum*), and thus thoroughly determines the concept of it, as that of the highest being;   20: 302 which no other concept can do, and which, so far as the possibility of such a being is concerned, creates – as Leibniz adds – no difficulty in proving it, since realities, as positive affirmations, cannot contradict one another, and what is thinkable because its concept does not contradict itself, i.e., everything whose concept is possible, is also a possible thing; at which reason, however, guided by critique, ought certainly to shake its head.

And so too should metaphysics, if here it is not just taking concept for thing, but also thing, or rather the name of it, for concept, and thus ratiocinating itself totally into the void.

It is true that if we wish to frame to ourselves a concept of a thing as such, and thus ontologically, we always lay down in thought, as primal concept, the notion of a most real being of all; for a negation, as determination of a thing, is always a merely derived representation, since one cannot think of it as a removal (*remotio*), without having first thought of the reality opposed to it as something that is posited (*positio seu reale*);[a] and hence, if we make this subjective condition of thinking into an objective condition of the possibility of things themselves, all negations have to be regarded merely as limitations of the conceptual sum-total of realities, and everything else but this one concept of their possibility as merely derived from this.

This One which metaphysics – we wonder how – has now conjured up for itself, is the highest metaphysical good. It contains the wherewithal for the creation of all other possible things, as the marble quarry does for statues of infinite diversity, which are all of them possible only through limitation (separation of a certain part of the whole from the rest, and hence solely through negation); and so evil differs from good in the world merely as the formal side of things, like shadows in the sunlight that irradiates the whole universe; and things of this world are evil only because they are mere parts, and do not constitute the whole, being partly real and partly negative; in which carpentering of a world this *metaphysical God* (the *realissimum*) likewise falls very much under the suspicion (despite all protestations against Spinozism),[35] that as a universally existing being He is identical with the universe.

But, waiving all these objections, let us now examine the supposed proofs of the existence of such a being, which may for this reason be called ontological.

Here there are only two arguments, nor can there be any others. Either we infer from the concept of the most real being to its existence, or from the necessary existence of something to a determinate concept that we have to frame of it.

The first argument proceeds as follows: A metaphysically most perfect of all beings must necessarily exist, since if it did not exist it would be lacking in a perfection, namely existence.

[a] postulated or real

20: 303

The second argues conversely: A being that exists as a necessary being must have all perfection, since if it did not have all perfection (reality) in itself, it would not be thoroughly determined as *a priori* by its concept, and so could not be thought of as a necessary being.

The deficiency in the first proof, in which existence is conceived as a special determination, superadded to the concept of a thing, whereas it is merely the positing of the thing with all its determinations, by which this concept is not therefore enlarged at all – this deficiency, I say, is so evident that there is no occasion to dwell upon this proof, which already seems, in any case, to have been abandoned by the metaphysicians as untenable.

The argument of the second is more plausible, in that it does not attempt to enlarge knowledge *a priori* by mere concepts, but relies upon experience, albeit only the experience, in general, that something exists; and now concludes from this that, because all existence must be either necessary or contingent, though the latter always presupposes a cause that can have its complete ground only in a noncontingent and thus necessary being, there exists a being, therefore, of the latter kind.

Now since we can know the necessity of a thing's existing, like any other necessity, only so far as we derive its existence *a priori* from concepts, while the concept of something existing is a concept of a thing that is thoroughly determinate, the concept of a necessary being will be one which contains at the same time the thoroughgoing determinacy of this thing. But we have only one such concept, namely that of the most real being of all. Hence the necessary being is a being that contains all reality, whether as ground or as totality.

This is an advance of metaphysics through the back door. It wishes to demonstrate *a priori*, and yet relies upon an empirical datum, which it uses to apply its lever, as Archimedes[36] did with his fixed point outside the earth (though here it is on the earth), and so attempts to raise knowledge up to the super-sensible.

20: 304

But if, granting the proposition that something absolutely necessary exists, it is likewise equally certain that we can frame absolutely no concept of anything existing in this fashion, and hence are utterly unable to determine it as such according to its nature (for the analytical predicates, i.e., those that are merely identical with the concept of necessity, such as the immutability, eternity, and even the simplicity of the substance, are not determinations, so that even the unity of such a being cannot be proved at all) – if, I say, the attempt to frame a concept of it fares so badly, then the concept of this metaphysical God remains always an empty one.

It is absolutely impossible, moreover, to define exactly the concept of a being, of such a nature that a contradiction would arise if I were to abolish it in thought, even supposing that I assume it to be the whole of reality. For a contradiction occurs in a judgment only if I abolish a predicate therein, and yet retain in the concept of the subject a predicate identical with this – never, though, if I abolish the thing along with all of its predicates, and say, for example, that there is no most real being of all.

Hence we can frame no concept whatever of an absolutely necessary thing as such (the reason being that it is a mere concept of modality, which contains no relation to the object as a property of the thing, and pertains to it merely by linking the representation of it to the faculty of cognition). So from its presupposed existence we cannot infer in the least to determinations which extend our knowledge of it beyond the idea of its necessary existence, and might thus form the basis of a kind of theology.

Hence the proof which some call the cosmological, though it is actually transcendental (since it does in fact assume an existent world), and which might equally well be assigned to ontology (since it does not profess to have inferred anything from the nature of a world, but only from presupposing the concept of a necessary being, i.e., from a pure rational concept *a priori*), sinks, like its predecessor, back into its own nothingness.

20: 305

Transition of Metaphysics to the Super-sensible since the Epoch of Leibniz and Wolf

The first stage in the transition of metaphysics to that super-sensible which underlies Nature, in that it is the supreme condition of everything conditioned therein, and is thus made fundamental to theory, is the transition to theology; to a knowledge, that is, of God, albeit only by an analogy of the concept thereof to that of an intelligent being, as a primal ground of all things, essentially distinct from the world. Such a theory does not itself proceed from reason in its theoretical aspect, but only in a practico-dogmatic and thus subjectively moral sense. It is brought in, that is, not to ground morality as to its laws, or even its final purpose, for here these are postulated, rather, as subsisting for themselves; it is to confer reality on this idea of the highest good possible in a world (a good which, objectively and theoretically regarded, lies beyond our power) with reference to this good, and thus in a practical point of view; for which purpose the mere possibility of conceiving such a being becomes sufficient, and at the same time a transition to this super-sensible, a knowledge of it, becomes possible, but only in a practico-dogmatic sense.

This, then, is an argument to prove God's existence as a moral being, sufficiently for human reason so far as the latter is morally practical, i.e., sufficiently for assuming that existence; and an argument to ground a theory of the super-sensible, but only as a practico-dogmatic transition thereto; and thus really not a proof of God's existence absolutely (*simpliciter*), but only in a certain respect (*secundum quid*), namely in relation to the final end which the moral man has and should have, and thus with reference merely to the rationality of *assuming* such a being; whereby man is then enabled to accord influence upon his decisions to an idea which he frames for himself, on moral principles, exactly as if he had drawn this idea from a given object.

Theology of such a kind is admittedly not *theosophy*,[37] i.e., knowledge of the divine nature, which is unattainable; it is a knowledge, rather, of the inscrutable determining ground of our willing, which we find, in ourselves alone, to be inadequate to its final ends, and therefore assume it in another, the supreme being above us, in order, through the idea of a super-sensible Nature, to furnish this willing with the supplement, as yet lacking to theory, whereby it may conform to what practical reason prescribes for it.

20: 306

The moral argument would thus be describable as an *argumentum* κατ᾽ ἄνθρωπον,[38] valid for men as rational creatures generally, and not merely for the contingently adopted thought-habit of this man or that; and would have to be distinguished from the theoretico-dogmatic κατ᾽ ἀλήθειον, which claims more to be certain than man can possibly know.

II
Supposed Theoretico-Dogmatic Advances in Moral Theology, during the Epoch of Leibniz and Wolf

For this stage in the progress of metaphysics the philosophy in question admittedly made no special provision, but attached it, rather, to theology, in the chapter on the final end of creation; but it is included, nevertheless, in the explanation given thereof, namely that this final purpose is the *glory of God*,[39] which can mean nothing else but that in the real world there is a combination of purposes such as to contain, on the whole, the highest good possible in a world, and thus the *teleologically* supreme condition for its existence, and to be worthy of a God as its moral creator.

But if not the whole, at least the supreme condition of the world's perfection consists in the morality of rational beings, which in turn depends on the concept of freedom; of which, as unconditioned self-activity, these beings must again themselves be conscious, if they are to be capable of being morally good. But on such a presupposition it is utterly impossible to view them theoretically, in accordance with this their purposiveness, as beings that have arisen by creation, and thus by the will of another; as one may certainly ascribe this, in nonrational creatures, to a cause distinct from the world, and can therefore conceive them as endowed to an infinitely varied extent with physico-teleological perfection; whereas morally-teleological perfection, which must have its original ground in the man himself, cannot be the effect, nor therefore the purpose either, which another might take it upon himself to bring about.

Now man, from a theoretico-dogmatic viewpoint, is quite unable to comprehend the possibility of the final purpose which he is required to strive for, though without having it fully within his power; for if he bases its furtherance upon the physical aspect of such a teleology, he abolishes the morality which is nevertheless its principal component; while if he founds the end wholly on a moral basis, he is deprived of that which compensates his inability to delineate such an end, in the coupling with the physical, which equally cannot be separated from the concept of the highest good, as his final purpose. Yet there remains to him, nevertheless, a practico-dogmatic principle of transition to this ideal of world-perfection, namely – and despite the obstacles placed in the path of such progress by the course of the world-as-appearance – to assume therein, as object-in-itself, a morally teleological connection, such that, by an ordering of Nature beyond his comprehension, it tends to the final purpose, as super-sensible goal of his practical reason, namely the highest good.

That the world as a whole is constantly improving, no theory entitles him to assume; but he is so entitled by practical reason, which dogmatically bids him to act on such a hypothesis, and so by this principle he fashions a theory, to which he cannot, indeed, ascribe more than thinkability in this respect; from a theoretical viewpoint, that is by no means sufficient to prove the objective reality of this ideal, though it is quite satisfactory to reason from a morally-practical point of view.

So what is impossible in a theoretical respect, namely the progress of reason to the super-sensible of the world we live in (*mundus noumenon*),[a] i.e., to the highest derived good, is actual in a practical respect, viz., to present the course of man's life here upon earth as if it were a life in heaven. On the analogy, that is, with the physical teleology which Nature allows us to perceive, we can and should assume *a priori* (even independent of this perception), that the world is destined to coincide with the object of moral teleology, namely the final purpose of all things according to laws of freedom; and this in order to strive toward the Idea of the highest good, which, as a moral product, demands man himself as originator (so far as it is in his power), and whose possibility, either by creation based upon an external author, or by insight into the capacity of human nature to be adapted to such a purpose, is not, theoretically speaking, a tenable concept, as the Leibniz–Wolfian philosophy supposes, but rather a transcendent one; though from a practico-dogmatic viewpoint, it is, however, a real concept and sanctioned by practical reason for our duty.

20: 307

20: 308

[a] original of the world

III
Supposed Theoretico-Dogmatic Advance
of Metaphysics in Psychology, in the Epoch
of Leibniz and Wolf

Psychology,[40] for human understanding, is nothing more, and can become nothing more, than anthropology, i.e., than a knowledge of man, albeit restricted to the condition: So far as he is acquainted with himself as object of inner sense. He is, however, also conscious of himself as object of his outer senses, i.e., he has a body linked with that object of inner sense which is called the soul of man.

That he is not wholly and solely a body can (if this appearance be considered as thing-in-itself) be rigorously proved, since the unity of consciousness, which must necessarily be met with in every cognition (and so likewise in that of himself), makes it impossible that representations distributed among many subjects should constitute unity of thought; hence materialism can never be employed as a principle for explaining the nature of our soul.

If, however, we consider both body and soul as phenomena, merely, which is not impossible, since both are objects of sense, and bear in mind that the noumenon which underlies this appearance, i.e., the outer object, as thing-in-itself, may perhaps be a simple being. . . .[a]

But disregarding this difficulty, i.e., if both soul and body are assumed to be two specifically different substances, whose association constitutes man, it remains impossible for all philosophy, and especially for metaphysics, to make out what and how much the soul, and what or how much the body itself may contribute to the representations of inner sense; or whether, indeed, if one of these substances were split off from the other, the soul, perhaps, would not absolutely forfeit every kind of representation (intuition, sensation, and thinking).

Hence it is absolutely impossible to know whether, after a man's death, when his material part is dispersed, the soul, even if its substance remains over, is able to go on living, i.e., to continue to think and will; whether, that is, it be a spirit[41] or not (for by this term we understand a being which, even without a body, can be conscious of itself and its representations).

20: 309

The metaphysics of Leibniz and Wolf has, indeed, given us much in the way of theoretico-dogmatic demonstration on this subject, i.e., has professed to prove, not only the future life of the soul, but even the impossibility of losing it by human death, i.e., its immortality; but has been able to convince nobody. On the contrary, it can be seen *a priori* that such a proof is quite impossible, because it is inner experience alone whereby we know ourselves, and all experience can be engaged in only in

---

[a] [There is a blank left in the manuscript at this point (Rink).]

life, i.e., if soul and body are still linked together; hence we are absolutely unacquainted with what we shall be, and be capable of, after death, and so cannot know the separated nature of the soul at all. We would therefore have to rely, say, on making trial of translating the soul out of the body while still alive, which would be not unlike the experiment which the man attempted by closing his eyes in front of the mirror, and when asked his purpose in doing so replied: I just wanted to know how I look when I'm asleep.

From a moral point of view, however, we do have sufficient reason to assume a life for man after death (the end of his earthly life) and even for eternity, and hence the immortality[42] of the soul; and this doctrine is a practico-dogmatic transition to the super-sensible, i.e., to that which is a mere Idea, and can be no object of experience, yet possesses objective reality, albeit valid only in a practical sense. The onward striving to the highest good, as ultimate purpose, compels the assumption of a duration proportionate to so endless a task, and covertly supplies the want of any theoretical proof, so that the metaphysician does not feel the insufficiency of his theory, because in secret the moral influence allows him not to perceive the deficiency of the knowledge he has supposedly drawn from the nature of things, which in this case is impossible.

20: 310 These, then, are the three stages in the transition of metaphysics to the super-sensible, in which its true final end consists. It was a vain labor that it traditionally gave itself, to reach the super-sensible by way of speculation and theoretical knowledge, and thus that science became the leaking sieve of the Danaids.[43] It was not until the moral laws unveiled the super-sensible in man, namely freedom (whose possibility no reason can explain, though it can prove the reality thereof in those practico-dogmatic teachings), that reason made proper claim to knowledge of the super-sensible, though only when confined to its use in the latter capacity; for then there appears a certain organization of pure practical reason, in which *first* the subject of universal law-giving, as world-creator, *second* the object of the creatures' willing, as their appropriate final purpose, and *third* the state of the latter in which alone they are capable of reaching it, are self-created Ideas in a practical sense, though they must not, of course, be asserted in a theoretical one; because if so they turn theology into theosophy, moral teleology into mysticism, and psychology into a pneumatics, whereby things of which we might make some use for knowledge in a practical respect are misplaced into the realm of transcendence, where they are, and remain, quite inaccessible to our reason.

Metaphysics, on this showing, is itself only the Idea of a science, as a system which, after completion of the critique of pure reason, can and should be constructed, and for which, indeed, the building materials and specifications are to hand: a whole which, like pure logic, neither needs nor is capable of any enlargement, and must likewise be constantly occupied and kept in structural repair, if spiders and satyrs, who will never be backward in seeking accommodation here, are not to settle in and make it uninhabitable for reason.

Nor is this structure extensive, but for the sake of elegance, which consists essentially in its precision, not to say clarity, it will have need of the combined efforts and judgment of a variety of artists, in order to render it eternal and immutable; and thus the project of the Royal Academy, not merely to enumerate the advances of metaphysics, but also to measure out the stage it has traversed, would be fully accomplished in the modern critical age.

Supplement in Review of the Whole 20: 311

If a system is so constructed that *firstly*, any principle in it is demonstrable for itself, and that *secondly*, if one were to be anxious about its correctness, it still also leads unavoidably, as a mere hypothesis, to all its other principles as consequences, then nothing more whatever can be demanded in order to acknowledge its truth.

Now that is actually the case with metaphysics, if the critique of reason pays careful attention to all its steps, and takes account of where they ultimately lead to. For there are two hinges on which it turns: *First*, the doctrine of the ideality of space and time, which in regard to theoretical principles merely points toward the super-sensible, but for us unknowable, in that on its way to this goal, where it is concerned with the knowledge *a priori* of objects of sense, it is theoretico-dogmatic; *second*, the doctrine of the reality of the concept of freedom, as that of a knowable super-sensible, in which metaphysics is still only practico-dogmatic. But both hinges are sunk, as it were, into the doorpost of the rational concept of the unconditioned in the totality of all mutually subordinated conditions, where there is need to remove that illusion which creates an antinomy of pure reason, by confusion of appearances with things-in-themselves, and which contains, in this very dialectic, an invitation to make the passage from the sensible to the super-sensible.

Appendices

No. I
Beginning of this Work
according to
the Third Manuscript

INTRODUCTION

The task proposed by the Royal Academy of Sciences tacitly contains two questions within it:

I. Whether metaphysics, from time immemorial until immediately after the days of Leibniz and Wolf, has taken even a single step in what constitutes its true purpose and the ground of its existence; for only if this has occurred, can we ask about the further advances that it might have made subsequent to a certain point in time.

II. The second question is: Whether the supposed advances of metaphysics are *real*.

What is called metaphysics (for I refrain, as yet, from a specific definition of it) must certainly, at any given time after a name had been found for it, have had some sort of domain. But only that domain which it was *intended* to gain possession of by working at it, and which thus constitutes its aim – not the stock of means collected for that purpose – is that of which an accounting is now demanded, when the Academy asks whether this science has made real advances.

In one of its parts (ontology), metaphysics contains elements of human knowledge *a priori*, both in concepts and principles, and must by intent contain them; by far the greatest part of them, however, finds application in the objects of possible experience, e.g., the concept of a cause, 20: 316 and the principle that all change is related thereto. But for purposes of knowing such experiential objects, a metaphysics has never yet been undertaken in which those principles were carefully sifted out, and they have often, indeed, been so unhappily demonstrated on *a priori* grounds, that if the unavoidable procedure of the understanding in accordance with those principles, whenever we engage in experience, and their continuous confirmation thereby, had not done their best, there would have been but poor prospects of convincing anyone of such a principle by rational demonstration. In physics (if we take this, in its most general meaning, to signify the science of the rational knowledge of all objects of possible experience), these principles have at all times been employed as though they belonged within its sphere (the physical), without separating them off on the ground that they are *a priori* principles, or creating a special science for them; because, after all, the purpose they were used for extended only to objects of experience, in which connection, also, they could alone be made intelligible to us, though this was not the true purpose of metaphysics. So in regard to this use of reason there would never have been any thought of metaphysics, as a separate science, if reason had not found within itself a higher interest in the enterprise, for which the unearthing and systematic combination of all elementary concepts and principles that are the *a priori* foundation of our knowledge of the objects of experience, was merely a preparation.

The old name of this science, μετὰ τὰ φυσικά, already gives a pointer to the kind of knowledge at which its aim was directed. The purpose is to proceed by means of it beyond all objects of possible experience (*trans physicam*), in order, where possible, to know that which absolutely cannot be an object thereof, and hence the definition of metaphysics, which contains the reason for advocating such a science, would be: It is a science of progressing from knowledge of the sensible to that of the super-sensible (by the sensible here I mean nothing more than that which can be an object of experience. That everything sensible is mere appearance, and not the object-of-representation in itself, will be proved later on). Now because this cannot occur by way of empirical grounds of knowledge, metaphysics will contain *a priori* principles, and although mathematics likewise has them, albeit always only such as refer to objects of possible *sensory* intuition, with which one cannot, however, get out to the super-sensible, metaphysics will nevertheless differ therefrom by being marked out as a philosophical science, which is a totality of rational knowledge *a priori, from concepts* (without constructing them). Because, in the end, to extend knowledge *beyond* the bounds of the sensible, there is first of all need for a complete acquaintance with all *a priori* principles, which are also applied to the sensible, metaphysics, if it is to be explained not so much by its purpose, but rather by the means of attaining to a knowledge of any sort by *a priori* principles, i.e., by the mere form of its procedure, must be defined as the system of all pure rational knowledge of things through concepts. 20: 317

Now it can be stated with the utmost certainty, that up to the time of Leibniz and Wolf, and including both of them, metaphysics, in regard to this its essential purpose, had yielded not the slightest return, not even that of the mere concept of any super-sensible object, such that it could simultaneously have proved in theory the reality of this concept, which would have constituted the smallest possible progression to the super-sensible; where *knowledge* of this object posited beyond all possible experience would still have continued to be lacking, and where even if transcendental philosophy had obtained some enlargement, here or there, in regard to its *a priori* concepts which are valid for objects of experience, this would not yet have been that envisaged by metaphysics; whence it can justly be maintained that, up to that point in time, this science had still made no progress whatever to its own destination.

We know, therefore, what advances of metaphysics are being asked about, and what it actually has to make, and can distinguish the *a priori* knowledge whose consideration serves only as a means, and which does not constitute the aim of this science – namely that which, though grounded *a priori*, can nonetheless find the objects for its concepts in experience – from the knowledge which does constitute the aim, in that its object lies beyond all bounds of experience, and which metaphysics, beginning from the former, does not so much *step up to*, as rather wish to *step over to*, since it is separated therefrom by an immeasurable chasm. Aristotle, with his categories, adhered almost solely to the first kind of knowledge, while Plato, with his Ideas, was striving for the second. But after this preliminary assessment of the matter with which metaphysics is concerned, we must also give consideration to the form in which it is supposed to proceed.

20: 318   For the second demand that is tacitly contained in the task prescribed by the Royal Academy would require it to be proved that the advances which metaphysics may boast of having made are *real*. A severe demand, which alone must plunge the numerous supposed conquerors in this field into embarrassment, if they wish to grasp and take it to heart.

As for the reality of those elementary concepts of all *a priori* knowledge which can find their objects in experience, and likewise the principles whereby these objects are subsumed under those concepts, experience itself can serve to demonstrate their reality, even though we do not see how it is possible for them, being underived from experience, and hence *a priori*, to have their origin in the pure understanding; e.g., the concept of a substance, and the principle that in all changes substance persists, and only the accidents arise or pass away. That this step of metaphysics is real, and not just imagined, the physicist assumes without hesitation; for he employs it with great success in all researches into Nature that proceed by way of experience, confident of never being refuted by a single instance, not because an experience has never yet refuted it, though he also cannot prove the principle, exactly as it is to be met with *a priori* in the understanding, but rather because it is an indispensable guideline to the latter, in order to engage in such experience.

But as to that which is the true business of metaphysics, namely to find, for the concept of what lies beyond the realm of possible experience, and for the extension of knowledge by means of such a concept, a touchstone for whether they are indeed real, that is something the

bold metaphysician might well-nigh despair of, if he does but understand the demand that is made upon him. For if he advances beyond his
concept, whereby he can only think objects, but cannot confirm them
by any possible experience, and if that thought is but possible, which he
arrives at by so framing it that he does not contradict himself therein;
then whatever the objects he may please to think up, he is sure that
he cannot run into any experience that refutes him, since he will have
thought up an object, e.g., a spirit, of precisely such a description that it
absolutely cannot be an object of experience. For that not a single experience confirms this idea of his, cannot injure him in the least, since he
wanted to think a thing according to determinations that put it beyond
all bounds of experience. Thus such concepts can be quite empty, and
the propositions assuming objects thereof to be real can therefore be
utterly erroneous, and yet there is no touchstone available to discover
this error.

    20: 319

    Of the very concept of the super-sensible, in which reason takes so
much interest, that that is why metaphysics, at least as an enterprise,
exists at all, has always existed, and will continue to exist hereafter –
of this concept, for the same reason, it cannot be directly determined,
on theoretical lines, by any touchstone, whether it possesses objective
reality, or is mere fabrication. For though contradiction is not to be
found therein, there is no direct proof or refutation by any test that we
might apply to it, whether everything that is and can be might not also
be object of possible experience, and whether the concept of the super-
sensible as such might not therefore be wholly empty, and the supposed
progression from the sensible to the super-sensible far removed, in that
case, from deserving to be considered real.

    But before metaphysics had yet reached the point of making this
distinction, it had intermingled Ideas, which can only have the super-
sensible as their object, with *a priori* concepts, to which objects of experience are appropriate, in that it simply never occurred to it that the
origin of these Ideas could be different from that of other pure *a priori*
concepts; whence it has then come about – a thing particularly notable
in the history of the aberrations of human reason – that since the latter feels itself capable of acquiring a large range of cognitions *a priori*
concerning things of Nature, and in general concerning that which can
be object of possible experience (not merely in natural science, but also
in mathematics), and has demonstrated the reality of these advances in
practice, it is quite unable to foresee why it cannot progress still further
with its *a priori* concepts, namely to penetrate successfully to things or
properties thereof which do not belong to objects of experience. It was
necessarily bound to take the concepts from both fields for concepts of
the same kind, because in their origin they are to this extent really alike,
that both are grounded *a priori* in our faculty of cognition, are not created

from experience, and thus seem to be entitled to an equal expectation of a real domain and extension thereof.

However, another strange phenomenon was bound eventually to startle reason, as it slumbered on the pillow of its supposed knowledge, extended by Ideas beyond all bounds of possible experience, and that is 20: 320 the discovery that although the *a priori* propositions confined to such experience are not only in good agreement, but even form a system of *a priori* knowledge of Nature, those, on the other hand, which overstep the bounds of experience, though they do appear to be of similar origin, come into conflict and mutual attrition, partly among themselves, and partly with those that refer to natural knowledge; whereby they seem, however, to rob reason, in the theoretical field, of all confidence, and to promote an unmitigated skepticism.

Now for this misfortune there is no remedy save that of subjecting pure reason itself, i.e., the faculty of knowing anything at all *a priori*, to an exact and thorough critique; and this in such a way as to assume the possibility of a real extension of knowledge thereby in regard to the sensible, and the same for the super-sensible, or if this should not be possible here, to look into a restriction of reason in that respect; and so far as the super-sensible is concerned, as the purpose of metaphysics, to assure to the latter the domain that it is capable of, not by direct proofs, which have so often been found deceptive, but by deduction of the title of reason to determinations *a priori*. Mathematics and natural science, so far as they contain pure rational knowledge, require no critique of human reason as such. For the touchstone of the truth of their propositions lies in themselves, since their concepts go only so far as the objects corresponding thereto can be given; whereas in metaphysics they are put to a use which is supposed to overstep these limits and to extend to objects which cannot be given at all, or at least not in the degree that the intended use of the concept calls for, i.e., that which is appropriate to it.

Treatise

Metaphysics is quite especially distinguished among all other sciences, in that it is the only one that can be set forth in full completeness; so that nothing remains for posterity to add, or enlarge upon in regard to its content – indeed if the absolute whole does not systematically emerge at once from the idea of it, the concept of it may be deemed incorrectly framed. The cause of this is that its possibility presupposes a critique of the entire faculty of pure reason, where what the latter can achieve *a priori* in regard to objects of possible experience, or what comes to the same (as will be shown in the sequel), what it can achieve in regard to the *a priori* principles of the possibility of an experience as such, and thus for knowledge of the sensible, can be completely exhausted; though what that critique, impelled merely by the nature of pure reason, perhaps only asks, but perhaps may also know, in regard to the super-sensible, can and should be exactly stated by the very constitution and unity of this pure faculty of knowledge. From this, and from the fact that through the idea of a metaphysic it is at once determined *a priori* what can and should be open to encounter within it, and what constitutes its whole possible content, it now becomes possible to judge how the knowledge employed in it is related to the whole, and how the real possession at one time, or in one nation, is related to that in every other, and likewise to the want of the knowledge that is sought therein; and since, in regard to the requirement of pure reason, there can be no national difference, we may judge by a sure yardstick from the example of what has occurred, miscarried, or succeeded in one people, at the same time the defectiveness or progress of the science as such at every time and in every people; so that the problem assigned can be resolved as a question about human reason in general.

It is therefore simply the poverty of this science, and the narrowness of the limits that enclose it, which make it possible to set it forth completely in a short outline, and yet sufficiently to judge every true possession therein. But on the other hand, the comparatively large variety of consequences, from few principles, that the critique of pure reason leads to, does make very much harder the attempt to set it forth completely, nonetheless, in so small a compass as the Royal Academy requires; for by inquiry conducted in piecemeal fashion nothing therein is sorted out – the agreement of every proposition to the whole of the pure employment of reason is the only thing which can provide a guarantee of the reality of its advances. A brevity that is fruitful, but yet does not degenerate into obscurity, will therefore demand almost more attentive care in the discussion to follow, than the difficulty of doing justice to the task that is now to be discharged.

First Section
On the General Task of the Reason that subjects itself to a Critique

This is contained in the question: How are synthetic *a priori* judgments possible?[44]

Judgments are *analytic*, we may say, if their predicate merely presents clearly (*explicite*) what was thought, albeit obscurely (*implicite*), in the concept of the subject; e.g., any body is extended. If we wanted to call such judgments identical, we should merely cause confusion; for judgments of that sort contribute nothing to the clarity of the concept which all judging must yet aim at, and are therefore called empty; e.g., any body is a bodily (or in other words a material) entity. Analytical judgments are indeed *founded* upon identity, and can be resolved into it, but they *are* not identical, for they need to be dissected and thereby serve to elucidate the concept; whereas by identical judgments, on the other hand, *idem per idem*,[a] nothing whatever would be elucidated.

Synthetic judgments are those which by means of their predicate go beyond the concept of the subject, in that the former contains something that was not thought at all in the concept of the latter, e.g., all bodies are heavy. Now here we are by no means asking whether the predicate is always *connected* with the concept of the subject or not; we say merely that *in* this concept it is not concurrently thought whether the predicate must necessarily be appended to it. Thus, for example, the proposition: Any three-sided figure has three angles (*figura trilatera est triangula*), is a synthetic proposition. For although, if I think three straight lines as enclosing a space, it is impossible that three angles should not simultaneously be formed thereby, I still, in this concept of the three-sided, by no means think the inclination of these sides to one another, i.e., the concept of the angle is not truly thought *in* it.

All analytical judgments are judgments *a priori*, and hence are valid with strict universality and absolute necessity, because they are founded entirely upon the principle of contradiction. But synthetic judgments can also be judgments of experience, which do indeed tell us how certain things are constituted, but never that they necessarily must be so, and cannot be constituted otherwise: e.g., all bodies are heavy; for in this case their universality is merely comparative: All bodies, so far as we know of them, are heavy, which universality we might call the empirical, as distinct from the rational, which as known *a priori*, is a *strict* universality. Now if there were to be synthetic propositions *a priori*, they would not rest upon the principle of contradiction, and in regard to them there would thus arise the aforementioned question, never before proposed in its universality, let alone resolved: How are synthetic *a priori* propositions

20: 323

---

[a] the same by the same

possible? But that there actually are such propositions, and that reason does not serve merely to enlarge analytically on concepts already acquired (a very necessary enterprise, if it is first to get a good understanding of itself), but rather is actually capable of synthetically extending its stock *a priori*, and that metaphysics, indeed, as to the means it employs, relies on the former, but in respect of its aim rests entirely on the latter – all this will be amply shown as the present discussion proceeds. But since the advances which metaphysics professes to have made might still be doubted, as to whether they are real or not, pure mathematics still stands, like a colossus, to prove the reality of knowledge extended solely by pure reason, despite the attacks of the boldest doubter; and though itself in no need whatever of any critique of the pure faculty of reason, in order to confirm the rectitude of its claims, being warranted, rather, by the very fact of itself, it provides, nonetheless, a firm example to demonstrate at least the reality of the problem so exceedingly necessary for metaphysics: How are synthetic *a priori* propositions possible?

It was proof more than anything else of the philosophical spirit of Plato,[45] an accomplished mathematician, that he could be thrown into such astonishment at the greatness of pure reason, in touching the understanding with so many grand and unexpected principles in geometry, that it swept him off into the wild idea of considering all these findings, not as new acquisitions in our earthly life, but as a mere reawakening of much earlier Ideas, which could be based upon nothing less than community with the divine understanding. A mere mathematician might well have been rejoiced by these products of his reason to the point, perhaps, of sacrificing a hecatomb, but their possibility would not have thrown him into astonishment, because he was brooding merely upon his object, and had no occasion to consider and marvel also at the subject, so far as it is capable of such deep knowledge thereof. A mere philosopher like Aristotle, on the other hand, would have paid too little heed to the vast difference between the *pure* faculty of reason, so far as it extends itself from within, and that which, guided by empirical principles, progresses to the more general by inference; and hence would also not have felt such an astonishment, but, in that he regarded metaphysics merely as a physics ascending to higher levels, would have found nothing strange or incomprehensible in its pretensions, extending even to the super-sensible, for which the key should be even so hard to find as in fact it is.

20: 324

Second Section
Definition of the Task in hand, with regard to the Cognitive Faculties which constitute Pure Reason in Ourselves.

The foregoing task can be resolved in no other way but this: that we consider it first in relation to the faculties in man, whereby he is capable

20: 325

of extending his knowledge *a priori*, and which constitute that in *him* which can be called specifically *his* pure reason. For if, by a pure reason of a being in general, we understand the power of knowing things independently of experience, and thus of sense-representations, we have thereby determined not at all in what way generally such a knowledge may be possible in him (e.g., in God, or another higher spirit), and the problem is thus undefined.

As to man, however, such a knowledge in him consists of concept and intuition. Each of these two is representation, indeed, but not yet knowledge. To entertain something through concepts, i.e., in general, is to *think*, and the power to think, understanding. The immediate representation of the individual is intuition. Knowledge through *concepts* is called *discursive*, that in *intuition, intuitive*; for a cognition we in fact require both combined together, but it is called after that to which I particularly attend on each occasion, as the determining ground thereof. That both can be either empirical or pure modes of representation pertains to the specific constitution of the human faculty of cognition, which we shall soon examine more closely. By the intuition that accords with a concept the object is *given*; without that it is merely *thought*. By this mere intuition without concept the object is given, indeed, but not thought; by the concept without corresponding intuition it is thought but not given; thus in both cases it is not known. If, to a concept, the corresponding intuition can be supplied *a priori*, we say that this concept is *constructed*; if it is merely an empirical intuition, it is called simply an instance of the concept; the act of appending the intuition to the concept is called in both cases presentation (*exhibitio*) of the object, without which (whether it occurs mediately or immediately) there can be no knowledge whatever.

The possibility[46] of a thought or concept rests on the principle of contradiction, e.g., that of a thinking immaterial being (a spirit). The thing of which even the mere thought is impossible (i.e. the concept is self-contradictory), is itself impossible. But the thing of which the concept is possible is not on that account a possible thing. The first possibility may be called logical, the second, real possibility; the proof of the latter is the proof of the objective reality of the concept, which we are entitled to demand at any time. But it can never be furnished otherwise than by presentation of the object corresponding to the concept; for otherwise

20: 326

it always remains a mere thought, of which, until it is displayed in an example, it always remains uncertain whether any object corresponds to it, or whether it be empty, i.e., whether it may serve in any way for knowledge.

A certain author wishes to rebut this requirement by a case which in fact is the only one of its kind, namely the concept of a necessary being, of whose existence we might be certain, since the ultimate cause, at least, must be an absolutely necessary being, and hence the objective reality of this concept can be proved without having to provide an intuition corresponding to it in any example. But the concept of a necessary being is still by no means the concept of a thing in any way determined. For existence is not a determination of any thing, and which inner predicates attach to a thing, on the ground that we assume it to be a thing independent in its existence, can absolutely not be known from its mere existence, whether it be assumed as necessary or as not necessary.

No. II
The Second Stage of Metaphysics
Its Standstill in the Skepticism of Pure Reason

Although a standstill cannot be called an advance, or really a stage accomplished either, still, if progress in a certain direction unavoidably results in an equally large regression, the outcome of this is just the same as if we had not stirred from the spot.

Space and time contain relationships of the conditioned to its conditions, e.g., the particular size of a space is only possible under a condition, namely, that another space encloses it; likewise a particular time, in that it is represented as part of a still larger time, and that is the situation with all given things, as appearances. But reason demands to know the unconditioned, and therewith the totality of all conditions, for otherwise it does not cease to question, just as if nothing had yet been answered.

Now this by itself would not yet leave reason bewildered, for how often do we not ask in vain about the why in the theory of Nature, and yet have found the excuse of ignorance a valid one, since at least it is better than error. But reason becomes bewildered with itself, in that, guided by the surest principles, it believes that it has found the unconditioned on one side, and yet on other, equally assured principles, brings itself to believe at the same time that it must be sought on the opposite side. 20: 327

This antinomy[47] of reason not only throws it into an uncertainty of mistrust towards the one as much as the other of these its claims, which would still leave open the hope of a judgment deciding this way or that, but casts it into a despair of reason in itself, to abandon all claim to certainty, which we may call the state of dogmatic skepticism.

But such a struggle of reason with itself has this peculiarity, that reason thinks of the conflict as a duel in which, if it takes the attack, it is certain of defeating the opponent, but so far as it has to defend itself, is equally certain of being defeated. In other words, it cannot so much depend on proving its claim as on refuting that of the opponent – a thing by no means certain, in that both might well be judging falsely, or even both might well be right, if only they had first reached agreement about the meaning of the question.

This antinomy divides the contestants into two classes, of which one seeks the unconditioned in the compounding of what is similar, the other in the manifold thereof, which may also be dissimiliar. The former is mathematical, and proceeds from the parts of a similar quantity, by addition, to the absolute whole, or from the whole to the parts, of which none is in turn a whole. The latter is dynamical and proceeds from the consequences to the supreme synthetic ground, which is thus something different, *realiter*, from the succession, either the supreme determining ground of the causality of a thing, or that of the existence of this thing itself.

Now the opposites of the first class are, as said, of a double kind. The one which proceeds thus from the parts to the whole: *The world has a beginning*, and the one that says: *It has no beginning*, are both equally false; and those which go from the consequences to the grounds, and then synthetically back again, though opposed to one another, can still both be true, since a sequence can have several grounds, which yet are transcendentally different, in that the ground is an object either of sensibility or of pure reason, whose representation cannot be given in empirical representation; e.g., everything is natural necessity, and hence there is no freedom, to which there stands opposed the antithesis: there is freedom and not everything is natural necessity, where a skeptical position thus enters, which produces a standstill of reason.

For so far as the first are concerned, just as in logic two contrarily opposed judgments can both be false, since the one says more than is required for opposition, so the same can be true in metaphysics. Thus the propositions that the world has no beginning, and that the world has a beginning, contain neither more nor less than is required for opposition, and one of the two would have to be true, the other false. But if I say that it has no beginning, but has existed from all eternity, I am saying more than is required for opposition. For in addition to what the world is not, I go on to say what it is. Now the world, considered as an absolute whole, is thought as a noumenon, and yet by its beginning or infinite duration as phenomenon. If I now assert this intellectual totality of the world, or if I ascribe limits to it *qua* noumenon, both statements are false. For with the absolute totality of conditions in a sensory world, i.e., in time, I contradict myself, whether I may fancy it given to me in a possible intuition as infinite, or as having limits.

On the other hand, just as in logic subcontrary judgments opposed to one another can both be true, since each says less than is required for opposition, so in metaphysics two synthetic judgments, which refer to objects of sense, but concern only the relationship of consequence to grounds, can both be true, since the series of conditions is regarded in one of two different ways, namely as object of sensibility or object of mere reason. For the conditioned consequences are given in time, but the grounds or conditions are added in thought, and can be various. So if I say: All events in the world of sense come about through natural causes, I am imputing conditions to them in the shape of phenomena. If the opponent says: Not everything occurs from purely natural causes (*causa phaenomenon*), the first statement would have to be false. But if I say: Not everything occurs from purely natural causes, for it may also occur at the same time from super-sensible grounds (*causa noumenon*), I am then saying less than is required to form an antithesis to the totality of conditions in the world of sense, for I am assuming a cause that is confined, not to conditions of that kind, but to those of sensory representation, and so am not contradicting conditions of the latter type; for I am thinking merely of the intelligible, whose thought is already present in the concept of a *mundus phaenomenon* in which everything is conditioned, so that reason is not here contesting the totality of conditions.

20: 329

This skeptical standstill, which contains no skepticism, i.e., no renunciation of certainty in the extension of our rational knowledge beyond the limits of possible experience, is now very beneficial; for without it we should have either had to abandon man's greatest concern, which metaphysics treats as its ultimate goal, and confine our use of reason merely to the sensible, or been compelled, as has happened for so long, to fob off the enquirer with untenable pretensions to insight: had there been no intervention from the critique of pure reason, which by dividing the legislature of metaphysics into two chambers has redressed both the despotism of empiricism and the anarchical mischief of unbridled philodoxy.

No. III
Marginal Notes

The unconditioned possibility of a thing, and the impossibility of its nonexistence, are alike transcendent notions, which cannot be thought at all, since without any condition we have grounds neither to posit anything, nor to abolish it. So the proposition that a thing exists with absolute contingency, or absolute necessity, has in both cases never any ground at all. The disjunctive proposition therefore has no object. It's as if I said: Any given thing is either X or non-X, and knew nothing at all of this X.

All the world has some sort of metaphysic as the aim of reason, and along with morality, this is what philosophy proper consists of.

The concepts of necessity and contingency do not seem to refer to substance. Nor do we ask about the cause of the existence of a substance, since it is that which always was and must remain, and on which, as a substrate, the mutable grounds its relationships. At the concept of a substance, the concept of cause leaves off. It is itself cause, but not effect. And how should anything be cause of a substance outside it, so that the former also continued its power through the latter? For then the consequences of the latter would merely be effects of the former, and the latter would thus itself be no ultimate subject.

The proposition: Everything contingent has a cause, should run thus: Everything, that can exist only in conditioned fashion, has a cause.

Likewise the necessity of the *ens originarium*[a] is nothing but the notion of its unconditioned existence. – But necessity means more, namely that we may also know, and from its very concept, that it exists.

The need of reason, to ascend from the conditioned to the unconditioned, also pertains to the concepts themselves. For all things contain reality, and indeed a degree thereof. This is always regarded as only conditionally possible, namely insofar as I presuppose a concept of the *realissimum*, of which the latter contains only the limitation: Everything conditioned is contingent, and conversely.

The primal being, as the highest being (*realissimum*), can or [must] be thought as a being that contains all reality as a determination in itself. This is not actual for us, since we do not know all reality in a pure sense, or at least cannot perceive that with all its diversity it may be encountered in one being alone. We shall thus assume it to be *ens realissimum* as ground, and by this it can be represented as a being that is wholly unknowable to us in regard to what it contains.

There is a particular illusion in this, that since in transcendental theology we demand to know the unconditionally existing object, since that alone can be necessary, we first of all lay down the unconditioned concept of an object, consisting in the fact that all concepts of limited objects are derived as such, i.e., by attached negations or *defectus*, and only the concept of the *realissimum*, that is, of the being in which all predicates are real, is *conceptus logice originarius*[b] (unconditioned). This is taken for a proof that only an *ens realissimum* can be necessary, or conversely, that the absolutely necessary is the *ens realissimum*.

We want to avoid the proof that [an] *ens realissimum* necessarily exists, and would sooner prove that if such a being exists, it would have to be a *realissimum*. (So one would now have to prove that one among all that exists, exists with absolute necessity, and that can certainly be done.) But the proof says no more than that we have no concept whatever of

---

[a] primal being
[b] logically prime concept

what pertains to a necessary being, as such, in the way of properties, save that it exists unconditionally in respect of its existence. But what that involves, we know not. Among our concepts of things is the logically unconditioned but yet thoroughly determined notion of the *ens realissimum*. So if we could also assume for this concept an object that corresponded to it, it would be the *ens realissimum*. But we are not entitled to assume for our mere concept an object of this kind.

On the hypothesis that something exists, it follows also that something necessarily exists, but yet absolutely and without any condition it cannot be known that something necessarily exists, be the concept of a thing, in respect of its inner predicates, assumed as it may, and it can be proved that this is utterly impossible. I have thus concluded to the concept of a being, of whose possibility nobody can form a concept.

But why do I conclude to the unconditioned? Because this is supposed to contain the supreme ground of the conditioned. The conclusion is therefore: (1) If something exists, there is also something unconditioned. (2) What exists unconditionally, exists as absolutely necessary being. The latter is no necessary inference, for the unconditioned can be necessary for a series, though itself, and the series, may always be contingent. This latter is not a predicate of things (as, for example, whether they are conditioned or unconditioned), but pertains to the existence of things, with all their predicates, whether they are in fact necessary in themselves or not. It is thus a mere relationship of the object to our concept.

Any existential proposition is synthetic, and so too is the proposition that God exists. Were it to be analytic, the existence of God would have to be deducible from the mere concept of such a possible being. Now this has been attempted in two ways: (1) In the concept of the most real being of all, its existence is implied, for such existence is reality. (2) In the concept of a necessarily existing being is implied the concept of the highest reality, as the sole way in which the absolute necessity of a thing (which must be assumed, if anything exists), can be thought. Now should a necessary being already include in its concept the highest reality, but the latter (as No. 1 says) not include the concept of an absolute necessity, so that the concepts cannot be reciprocated, then the concept of the *realissimum* would be *conceptus latior*[a] than the concept of *necessarium*, i.e. other things besides the *realissimum* could be *entia necessaria*[b] But now this proof is effected precisely through the supposition that the *ens necessarium* can only be thought in a single way, etc.

The πρῶτον ψεῦδος[c] actually lies in this, that the *necessarium* contains in its concept the existence, consequently of a thing, as *omnimoda*

20: 332

---

[a] wider concept
[b] necessary beings
[c] cart before the horse

411

determinatio,[a] so that this *omnimoda determinatio* can be derived (not merely inferred) from its concept, which is false, since it is proved only that if it is to be derivable from a concept, this must be the concept of the *realissimum* (which alone is a concept that contains thoroughgoing determinacy).

So the position is, that if we were to be able to perceive the existence of a *necessarium*, as such, we would have to be able to derive the existence of a thing from some concept, i.e., the *omnimoda determinatio*. But this is the concept of a *realissimum*. So we would have to be able to derive the existence of a *necessarium* from the concept of the *realissimum*, which is false. We cannot say that a being has those properties, without which I would not know its existence, as necessary, from concepts, even if those properties are assumed, not as constitutive products of the first concept, but merely as *conditio sine qua non*.[b]

It pertains to the principle of the knowledge that is *a priori* synthetic, that compounding is the only *a priori* which, if it occurs according to space and time at all, must be done by us. For experience, however, knowledge contains the schematism, either the real schematism (transcendental), or the schematism by analogy (symbolic). The objective reality of the categories is theoretical, that of the Idea is only practical. – Nature and freedom.

[a] thoroughgoing determinacy.
[b] indispensable condition.

Prize Question

1. What did the ancients want with metaphysics? – To know the supersensible. 2. This distinction is as old as philosophy. 3. By *noumena* they conceived of all objects, so far as they could be known *a priori*, and Plato included in that the properties of figures, and came upon the controversy over innate ideas. 4. God, freedom and immortality. 5. On the 1st and 3rd they readily agreed, but not about the second. 6. Origin of the critical philosophy is morality, in regard to accountability for actions. 7. On this, unceasing controversy. 8. All philosophies are essentially not at variance, until the critical. 9. What is the essence of pure philosophy, in the manner of treating its objects.

In regard to theoretical problems of every kind, there is no need for any *analytic* and metaphysic at all, if the concept of freedom is but transformed into that of mechanical necessity. Whether objects of outer, or even of inner sense present themselves to us as they are in themselves, or merely as they appear: Whether the concepts whereby this manifold is brought to experience in a general connection are given *a priori* in advance of experience, or *a posteriori* in experience, is a matter of indifference to the theoretical inquirer, for ... since all that we could know and even the ... which set forth to an unconditioned which in the world of sense ... would have no further effect than that of self-limitation merely to objects of sense (*Quae supra nos nihil ad nos*).[a] The concept of God and immortality ... are always present as hypotheses, albeit anthropomorphistically ... comes the moral law which freedom preaches and ... concept with all the theoretical philosophy of *reality* ... is irreconcilable, so that the doctrine of freedom and with it morality is ... which { } reason to metaphysics and abolishes the whole mechanism of nature.[*]   20: 336

Every intrinsically contingent (and thus synthetic) consequence of events in the world must have a cause. Contingency is thought in purposiveness.

---

[*] The lacunae indicated in the above passage are due to a large inkblot on the manuscript.

[a] what is above us is nothing to us.

Now the harmony of happiness in the world with the worthiness to be happy (if such a harmony is constantly to occur) is a contingent consequence of events in the world.

So this harmony, if it exists or is postulated must also have a cause (and one different from all causes in the world).

This cause must lie in the world and in the beings that reside there, for the law of causality applies only to sensory beings. But because this harmony, in comparison with its principle of perfection, cannot be known by us to be appropriate for all eternity, or even for the whole world, it is a matter of belief. Or rather the knowledge of its possibility belongs to the intelligible ground, namely of the existence both of rational and of free beings, whose causes of existence by the *catego*...

The good will must arise from itself, but is no phenomenon, since it relates to maxims and not to actions which take place in the world. The conjunction of the two is an occurrence. One may say of it that God is the originator of the highest sum of morality, and so far as it is not perfect, of the greatest harmony with happiness.

Harmony can be possible in that God might be the cause of morality and also of happiness in proportion, but that is not thinkable since it would be mechanism and not freedom: Man is himself regarded as cause of his actions that take place in the world, but why he has acted thus rather than otherwise, and this from freedom, is incomprehensible to himself, since it is freedom. Of the good or bad will as the world of maxims we say only *secundum analogiam* that God gives it and that he improves or hardens the heart. We know only the actions and also the phenomenon of their adoption into our maxims; the intelligible character on which they are founded, we are unable to examine.

20: 337   The reality of the concept of this harmony has its ground in pure practical reason, to work towards a supreme good, and thus also to think it in an idea as possible through our powers.

The subjective of intuition must determine this constitution it has, since otherwise it could not be *a priori* and necessary. So too with the subjective of concepts, i.e. of the method of framing a concept thereof in general. Without that there would also be no necessity.

To construct concepts, i.e. to give them *a priori* in intuition, space and time are required; for experience, in addition to *a priori* concepts, we also need that of existence (*realitas*) for perception (the empirical). But to construct always requires, for time, the describing of a line whose parts are nevertheless simultaneous, and for the line a time whose parts are successive.

No more than it is possible to infer from the concept of a being to its necessity, is it possible to infer from its necessity to the concept that one has to frame of it; for modality and content of a thing have nothing in common with each other.

The first of these three stages contains the advances in metaphysics in two of its divisions, theory of being and general theory of Nature. Ontology and rational physics. In the latter, objects are regarded as given in experience, save that what must be thought of them *a priori* as objects either of outer or inner sense represents the general theory of body and soul together, as general theory of Nature. *Physica rationalis* and *Psychologia rationalis*. General physics belongs to ontology as totality of the *a priori* conditions under which objective reality can be given to its concepts of the latter: yet in such a way that no experiential theory of bodily and thinking Nature, *physica and psychologia empirica*, must appear therein.

20: 338

To this formal theory of Nature there also belongs discussion of (1) whether the principle of the ideality of space goes so far that one may also do wholly without the existence of outer objects of the senses, and (2) whether that of the ideality of time goes so far that the inner sense, distinct from consciousness, and thus the empirical self, might be abolished. The rational self gives no knowledge, but only the synthesis of the manifold of intuition as such, for the possibility of a cognition.

Whether there is an outer sense that is distinct from the consciousness of our representations. Whether there is an inner sense that is distinct from the consciousness of inner representations.

If the first were not so, the object (my mere representation) would be simply in myself. Now since I must be able to become aware of my entire state, I would locate everything external simply in time. Space as something whose parts are successive. If I knew myself as I am, not as I appear to myself, my change would create a contradiction in me. I would never be the same person. The identity of the self would be abolished.

The logical *subject* is not an object of knowledge for itself, but the physical self certainly is, to *itself*, and that by the categories, as modes of compounding of the manifold of inner (empirical) intuition, so far as it (the compounding) is possible *a priori*.

Hoc est vivere bis, vita posse priori frui.[a] Martial (Epigrams, Bk. 5, no. 23, 7–8)

---

[a] This is to live twice, that the life of our ancestors can be enjoyed.

415

The upshot of the first stage is that the human power of theoretical cognition could not extend beyond the objects of the senses or the bounds of possible experience, and these objects are not things in themselves, but merely their appearances.

1. Distinction of analytic from synthetic judgments.
2. Of synthetic *a priori* and synthetic empirical judgments.
3. How they are both possible – through the intuitions, *a priori* or empirical, that underlie concepts.
4. How is intuition *a priori* possible
5. How concepts *a priori*
6. How is general logic possible, and what does it contain
7. How is transcendental logic possible
8. What is the logic of immanent and transcendent judgments which yield no knowledge, – and of the whole of logic.

That all concepts which I do not borrow from the subjective form of intuition must be empirical, and can bring no necessity with them, since they are drawn from the perception of objects.

Intuition [=] Immediate Representation

(1) How are synthetic propositions possible as such? In that over and above my concept I take something as a mark from the intuition underlying it, and combine it with this concept.

Empirical//synthetic judgments are those in which the subject is a concept to which an empirical intuition corresponds; *a priori*//synthetic those to whose subject *a priori* intuition corresponds. Hence there are no synthetic propositions (though metaphysics is full of them) without there being pure intuitions *a priori*.

(2) What are pure intuitions? Forms of sensibility of the outer and inner sense, space and time, which precede everything empirical.

(3) How is it possible that we can know synthetically *a priori* the properties of things in space and time? No otherwise than by our thinking this form, not as pertaining to objects, but as attaching subjectively to the representing being; for then there can be *a priori* determination, not of what attaches as such to objects that depend on the conditions of space and time, but of how they must necessarily appear to the subject.

(4) By mere concepts we can produce no synthetic *a priori* propositions. For supposing space and time were confusedly represented features of things, then perception of their properties would have only empirical validity, and necessity would depart from them, since these properties would be derived synthetically, and indeed *a posteriori*, i.e. empirically, from the objects by perception.

(5) Are mere intuitions, pure or empirical, adequate for synthetic knowledge without concepts *a priori*? No, without *synthesis a priori*, and the concept of compounding from the manifold of this intuition, no judgment *a priori* would be possible. For the unity of consciousness that is required for every judgment, and indeed the unity of consciousness in a *synthesis a priori*, becomes required for such a judgment, and these concepts are the *categories*, which first give knowledge with intuitions and not without them, and hence do not give it as mere categories.

(6) How far can these *a priori* principles extend? Merely to objects in appearance, and thus only to objects of the senses, and that only as they appear to us.

(7) How is it possible that a subject should be conscious of itself as mere appearance, and in an immediate way, and yet at the same time be aware of itself as thing-in-itself? The first by empirical apperception, the second by pure apperception.

Of a Philosophizing History of Philosophy

All historical knowledge is empirical, and hence knowledge of things as they are; not that they necessarily have to be that way. Rational knowledge presents them according to their necessity. Thus a historical presentation of philosophy recounts how philosophizing has been done hitherto, and in what order. But philosophizing is a gradual development of human reason, and this cannot have set forth, or even have begun, upon the empirical path, and that by mere concepts. There must have been a need of reason (theoretical or practical) which obliged it to ascend from its judgments about things to the grounds thereof, up to the first, initially through common reason, e.g., from the world-bodies and their motion. But purposes were also encountered: and finally, since it was noticed that rational grounds can be sought concerning all things, a start was made with enumerating the concepts of reason (or those of the understanding) beforehand, and with analyzing thinking in general, without any object. The former was done by Aristotle, the latter even earlier by the logicians.

20: 341

A philosophical history of philosophy is itself possible, not historically or empirically, but rationally, i.e., *a priori*. For although it establishes facts of reason, it does not borrow them from historical narrative, but draws them from the nature of human reason, as philosophical archaeology. What have the thinkers among men been able to reason out concerning the origin, the goal, and the end of things in the world? Was it the purposiveness in the world, or merely the chain of causes and effects, or was it the purpose of mankind from which they began?

On the Incapacity of Men to Communicate Completely
with One Another

In things that can be presented, this goes on well; far less so in feelings; and least of all in those sensations which follow upon ideas. Aristippus counted purely on the latter as the absolutely real. But communication is doubtful – deficiencies of language – morality contains the highest communicability of feelings, but then it is most successful when it is most abstract, and ultimately has as its determining ground only the mere feeling of our receptivity to morality.

The Ideas of God and a future state do not acquire objective theoretical reality on moral grounds, but only the practical reality, so to act as though there were another world.

Idealism. Time can be determinately thought only in the apprehension of space (and in comprehension for simultaneity). Now should nothing as outwardly given underlie the intuition of space, then the representation of something external would be merely a thought, and so really given to the mind by nothing external. Thus it would at least be possible to think of one's inner representations as in space, which is contradictory.

20: 342

Whether a *history* of philosophy might be written mathematically; how dogmatism must have arisen, and from it skepticism, and from both together criticism. But how is it possible to bring a history into a system of reason, which requires the contingent to be derived, and partitioned, from a principle?

Of the first intellectual [Idea] that yet has objective practical reality in morality, namely Freedom.
Of determination of the concept of God, not as sum-total, but as ground of all reality – otherwise it is anthropomorphism.
That there is no probability in regard to the super-sensible, but a transition into a quite different kind of assent by reason, an assent that is universally valid, and yet is thought in relation to the subject, namely to accept something as true in relation to the *maxims* of the will, which are necessary, and yet which would otherwise be an *empty* will without object.

Whether a schema could be drawn up *a priori* for the history of philosophy, with which, from the extant information, the epochs and opinions of the philosophers so coincide, that it is as though they had had this very schema themselves before their eyes, and had progressed by way of it in knowledge of the subject.

Yes! if, that is, the idea of a metaphysic inevitably presents itself to human reason, and the latter feels a need to develop it, though this science lies wholly prefigured in the soul, albeit only in embryo.

One cannot write a history of the thing that has not happened, and for which nothing has ever been provided as preparation and raw materials.

20: 343

Whether the history of *philosophy* might itself be a part of philosophy, or would have to be part of the history of learning as such.

Whatever advances *philosophy* may have made, the history thereof is nevertheless distinct from philosophy itself, or the latter must be a mere ideal of a source, lying in human reason, of the philosophy of pure reason, whose development also has its rule in human nature. *Fülleborn*.[48]

A history of philosophy is of such a special kind, that nothing can be told therein of what has happened, without knowing beforehand what should have happened, and also what can happen. Whether this has been investigated beforehand or whether it has been reasoned out haphazardly. For it is the history, not of the opinions which have chanced to arise here or there, but of reason developing itself from concepts. We do not want to know what has been reasoned out, but what has been surveyed by reasoning through mere concepts. Philosophy is to be viewed here as a sort of rational genius, from which we demand to know what it should have taught, and whether it has furnished this. To get to the bottom of this, we have to inquire what and why one interest, and one so great, has hitherto been taken in metaphysics. We shall find that it is not the analysis of concepts and judgments such as can be applied to objects of the senses, but the super-sensible, especially insofar as practical Ideas are founded upon it.

Task of the Academy

(A) Prolegomena

1. What sort of knowledge should the thing subsequently called metaphysics have been from the earliest times until now: a science of the objects of reason, or a science of reason itself, and of its power to arrive at knowledge of those objects?

2. What has metaphysics been from the earliest times, up to and including Leibniz and Wolf, especially in Germany?

20: 344

3. What is it now: has it lately made advances in Germany?

4. If so, what will be its fate hereafter, a further progress, or a regression, or the status of a depot which, without being capable of increase or diminution, must be preserved for the use of reason (the negative use)?

The answers to the first two questions serve as *Prolegomena* to introduce the problem; that to the third alone as a discussion designed to solve it; the answer to the fourth is a supplement or scholium to the discussion.

    1. Concept of metaphysics, what we mean by it, without yet defining completely what it ought to be.

For all science from concepts *a priori* we have a metaphysics. It does not cover all knowledge of things by reason, for it does not include mathematics, though it judges concerning the possibility of the latter.

    1. Critique.   2. System.   3. Comparison with that at the time of Leibniz and Wolf in Germany.

It is a matter of whether we have cognitions *a priori*, and these not merely elucidatory, but also enlarging upon the given concept. The latter contain concepts *a priori* of objects.

    a. If any concept of the super-sensible should be accepted, it is a question of what we should found its reality upon. Not on a knowledge given thereby, for that is not possible of the super-sensible; so only through the practical, and that as a ground thereof which must be determinant, not according to laws of nature, but actually against them.

20: 345

    It seems difficult to present so great a diversity as that embraced by metaphysics, within a small compass, and yet with completeness in respect of its sources; but in fact it is made easy by the organic combination of all powers of knowledge under the supreme government of reason, since one may start from many points and yet complete the whole circle according to a principle, so that the only difficulty is to choose where we want to set out from. It seems to me most advisable to begin with what first engendered interest in founding a metaphysics (freedom, so far as it is made known through moral laws), since the solution of the difficulty associated with that occasions a complete anatomy of our cognitive faculty, and thus one might run through the whole circle, for here there is given a concept of the super-sensible with its reality (albeit merely of the practical kind).

    All authors have labored to realize the three super-sensible entities. To which morality partly moved them, and partly could alone provide a determinate concept.

    That man (has αὐτεξουσίαν – self-command),[49] is superior to all obstacles in the way of his good will, cannot be immediately maintained with certainty. The moral law ordains this conquest, so it must be possible. *Predeterminism*. Since physical necessity here pertains to time, the *causality* of the free will must not be tied to the temporal condition, although man as a being of Nature is tied thereto. From this it follows that man distinguishes himself as appearance from himself as *noumenon*.

In all our knowledge, what we call an *a priori* cognition is not only the noblest, because – independent of restrictive conditions of experience – it extends over more objects than the empirical cognition; as a necessary cognition it itself also confers upon the empirical judgments whose possibility it underlies that validity which is independent of subjective conditions, viz., that these judgments are truly valid of the object, and are cognitions. But these cognitions *a priori* contain at the same time a secret which a critique of pure reason has as a necessary preliminary task, prior to metaphysics, namely to render intelligible also the possibility of *a priori* knowledge. If there are *a priori* concepts, a *deduction* of them and their validity (not their production), and whether there are *a priori* propositions . . .

20: 346

Knowledge *a priori* is independent of experience, yet the representations therein can be empirical, although the judgment is analytic. If it is synthetic, however, the concept under which something empirical, e.g., some event, is subsumed, must be an *a priori* concept; for empirical and diverse concepts can be synthetically bound no otherwise than by experience. *A priori* knowledge is even the ground of the possibility of experience, or at least of that which constitutes the objective unity in judgments. For cognitions the requisite elements thereof are concepts and intuition, the latter either as likewise empirical or as pure intuition. Thinking and intuiting: without the latter there is no object, and without the former we do not think and do not know the object.

That opposition,[50] considered according to pure rational concepts, i.e., principles of freedom, is a conflict of the internally determining grounds of man's choice, to take up into his maxims either the moral or the pathological motive of actions; which (if it is allowable to personify the mere capacity of man allegorically) can be represented as the conflict of the good spirit with a bad one. For natural drives are in themselves innocent, and between them and the moral law there is really no conflict: but to make it one's maxim to follow the law, independent of these drives, and even against them, is an act of freedom in conflict with these drives, to whose reality experience attests in human actions, though its possibility cannot be grasped; which is why the phenomenon is then allegorized on the analogy of two independent principles dwelling in man, that are at war with one another. But to distinguish the two of them, everyone has the criterion at hand: If the representation of the law precedes the feeling of pleasure or displeasure in an action, the latter is moral; if the other way round, it is pathological. But to adopt the latter unconditionally into one's maxims is a principle of evil.

20: 347

If, in the maxim, the representation of the law precedes, and the feeling (of pleasure or displeasure at the object of choice) immediately follows it, then this feeling is morally intellectual and the good principle rules in man. If it is the other way round, and the feeling of pleasure or displeasure at the object precedes the law, then the feeling is pathological (sensuous), and the bad principle rules in man, for to subordinate the maxim unconditionally (in respect of the law) to the motives of sensibility (of the flesh) is always bad. Sensibility (of the flesh) is not, indeed, what the good principle has to combat, for it is innocent; rather, the bad principle in us is the propensity, which is free, to take one's maxim according to these urges of sensibility. Yet the flesh is named as the enemy which wars against the spirit, because it does mediately produce actions contrary to law, if and in that man adopts it into his maxim. But to explain the possibility of such maxims, and in general how actions arise from free choice, belongs among the problems which utterly transcend human insight.

If we compare this with the metaphysics of Leibniz and Wolf, the latter, since it was wholly theoretico-dogmatic and devoid of any critique of pure reason, has no merit whatever in regard to this stage; unless it were to consist in this, that it was able, far more methodically than heretofore, to give a veneer of speculative insight to what the moral principles of reason of the common understanding of mankind had already long since been recommending men to believe and accept, and to secure a hearing for it as to form (system) through the seeming connection in a scientific whole; whereby the workers in this field were at least constrained to thoroughness in their explanations, proofs, and arrangement.

A necessary being is one from whose concept his existence can be derived (which by No. 1 is not feasible). So if I still have no concept of such a being, I cannot know his existence *a priori* either: for existence, even though it is thought with absolute necessity, is mere modality and gives no concept of the thing that exists. However, then, I might wish to fashion any concept whatsoever of a thing, I can still always abolish it without contradiction. That is the . . .

To conclude from the contingency of the world, that is inferred from change, to a necessary *cause that is distinct from the world*, will not do, because its contingency is not thereby demonstrated. Only purposiveness is allowable, for that is contingent; though it is not a property of things, but one which we put into our concept of things in order to explain their possibility to ourselves.

physico-theological argument

Of the unity of God, and that he is nameless, since his *quality* and *quantity* are simply unique

Of the aggregate of *realities*, whence *anthropomorphism*.   20: 349
Of the representation of God by analogy.

In the transcendental concepts of reality, by a *vitium subreptionis*[a] of thought, a concept is taken for a thing, the subjective of thinking for the objective of what is thought, which latter cannot be met with in thinking, but only in intuition, and here in an empirical intuition, since it is the object of sensation in general which has to be given as example of the concept, i.e., as object of the empirical intuition, which in regard to the super-sensible is impossible. That whose concept contains a being, in contrast to that whose concept contains a nonbeing, are modalities of positing and abolishing to which we can give no objective meaning, since they contain merely the subjective of thinking, namely the *copula* of the predicate in relation to the subject, that is, the power of representation in general. The transcendental *vitium subreptionis*. Leibniz's completion of Anselm's argument:[51]

1. A most real being of all must exist (is a necessary being). For if it did not exist, it would lack a reality, namely existence.

2. Conversely (through the back door), a necessary being, i.e., one completely determined by its concept, must contain all reality. For if it did not contain this, it would not be completely determined by its concept, and so would not be necessary.

Now a necessary being exists, etc. This latter proposition is tautological, not an extension of knowledge. If the concept of a necessary being were possible in virtue of its objective reality, i.e., in virtue of the determination of the object thereof, then it would be just as if one were to say: A necessary being exists necessarily. The necessity of presupposing something in order to make an object comprehensible to oneself, e.g., matter, because without it even space would not be an object of perception, is taken for objective necessity, and here is *realitas phaenomenon*.

To take the concept for the thing, and the name of a thing for the   20: 350
concept.

The concept of a thing whose nonbeing is in itself contradictory, is false – for nonbeing never contradicts itself (so if I call a thing necessary in itself, I merely want to say: I have no concept of its nonbeing).

If I say: If something exists, then there also exists something else that is absolutely necessary – since if nothing necessary existed, everything would be contingent, and thus have another thing for its cause – the first question that arises is whether this proposition is analytic or synthetic. In

[a] vice of pilfering

the first case the existence is contained in the concept, in the second it is appended to the concept as a determination thereof. But both are false, it being equally untrue that an existence is contained in the concept, and that existence is something which is appended as determination of a thing, over and above the concept thereof. For the concept *of the thing* is not thereby extended – the thing itself is merely posited. So this question contains merely a relation of things to thinking, and not to one another: whether my thinking (positing or abolishing) is necessary or contingent. So here concept is taken for thing, or rather the appearance of that which...

A solid proof is valid only for the theoretico-dogmatic judgment, but an argument can also hold for the practico-dogmatic. It then justifies a free assent, not to be extorted by demonstration, but nonetheless assured to this extent, that he who so considers it is sure in a practical sense of not losing faith in it. Such an argument occurs in regard to those three types of the super-sensible. In regard to these Ideas he may be in doubt from a theoretical viewpoint, but cannot do without them, like beacons to lighten his path.

20: 351

Of anthropomorphism in the representation of the *realissimum* as aggregate. I then have no need to attribute to him understanding (albeit unlike our own) and will; he is the ground, rather, of all that we cannot think possible otherwise than through understanding, and so, too, of the will.

If the feeling of pleasure precedes the law, it is sensuous; if the reverse, it is intellectual, i.e. a moral feeling.

Of feeling that precedes the law, in comparison with that which follows upon the representation thereof.

It is not the opposition of practical reason and sensibility, but of the appearances of the former.

Of the representation of the sensible on the analogy with practical reason.

*On a recently prominent tone of
superiority in philosophy*

Translator's introduction

Von einem neuerdings erhobenen vornehmen Ton in der Philosophie was first published in May, 1796, in the *Berlinische Monatsschrift* 27, 387–426. It was the opening shot in a controversy that later drew in a number of other writers, and to which Kant was to contribute a second essay: *Verkündigung des nahen Abschlusses eines Traktats zum ewigen Frieden in der Philosophie*, which appeared in December of that year (*BM* 28, 485–504). In the meantime, a side-dispute had also broken out with the mathematician J. A. H. Reimarus, over an allusion to Pythagorean triangles in the first essay; it led Kant to pen a brief explanation: *Ausgleichung eines auf Missverstand beruhenden mathematischen Streits*, which was printed in the August, 1796, number of the same journal. It had nothing to do with the main issues in contention, and in some editions of Kant's works has become detached from its context, to lead a separate existence of its own. It has here been inserted in its proper place.

Kant's attack on fine airs in philosophy, and the "proclamation of peace" that succeeded it, are primarily directed at the writings of Johann Georg Schlosser, a retired administrator and gentleman-amateur in philosophy, who happened also to be Goethe's brother-in-law. Having published, in 1795, a translation of Plato's letters, Schlosser had joined forces with another amateur Platonist, translator, and poetical light of the Göttinger Dichterbund, Count Friedrich Leopold zu Stolberg (1750–1819). Around them they had gathered a coterie of sympathizers, for whom the mystical elements in Platonism, as they understood it, supplied a convenient cover for their own brand of reactionary Christian élitism. The pair knew little, if anything, of philosophy in the academic sense. Oblivious to the message of the Copernican revolution, they preached a vague gospel of illumination by intuition and feeling, accessible only to the favored few, and aired their views in a high-flown, condescending style which Kant, for one, found sufficiently offensive to deserve a satirical rebuke.

Schlosser – unwisely – replied to (and reprinted) Kant's attack, in his *Schreiben an einen jungen Mann, der die Kantische Philosophie studieren wollte* of 1796. His advice to the studious young man was, of course, don't. But his attempt to explain Kantianism to his pupil was so riddled with absurd misunderstandings,[†] that it brought down a second salvo, the above-mentioned *Proclamation of Perpetual Peace*, in which Schlosser was this time identified by name, and again put in his place. He did not subside, however, and went on to produce a second letter, more foolish than the first, which was thereupon ridiculed and abused in print by such notables as Friedrich Schlegel, the critic, the poet Schiller, and the twenty-two-year-old Schelling, and repudiated in private by Goethe himself.

With such a phalanx having arisen in his defense, Kant saw no need to return to the fray, and later spoke kindly enough of the ailing Schlosser (who died in 1799). He even met and conversed amicably with Count Stolberg when the latter visited his publisher, Nicolovius, in Königsberg, though he declined an invitation to dinner. As is evident from the jocular tone of his two papers, Kant had never taken his opponents very seriously, being well aware that they were lightweights, unworthy of his powder and shot. It was only what they stood for, and their manner of expressing it, that were sufficiently obnoxious to the cause of enlightenment to lead him to make an example of them. New arguments he did not need. The dangers of dogmatism and *Schwärmerei* are a perennial theme in all of Kant's major writings, and had been fully set forth, for example, in the Discipline of Pure Reason section of the first *Critique*. The Schlosser affair was no more than a particularly blatant instance of why such discipline was needed, to prevent quackery, and to curb those excesses of idle speculation to which Kant's countrymen have always been somewhat prone.

With the waning of the controversy, interest in these two short papers seems largely to have lapsed, for all but a few hardy specialists. In English-speaking bibliographies, the habit of mistranslating the word *vornehm* as 'gentle', 'noble', 'elevated', or 'dignified' has obscured the fact that Kant, so far from commending such a tone, is in actuality deriding and condemning it. The point is fortunately not lost on Peter Fenves, the only recent translator, though his general title, *Raising the Tone of Philosophy* (Baltimore: Johns Hopkins University Press, 1993), might suggest otherwise. In this work, the Kantian originals are prefixed to a version of Jacques Derrida's latter-day pastiche: *On a Newly Arisen Apocalyptic Tone in Philosophy* (1980). The historical notes appended to these pieces are the best (indeed only) source of information in English for the details of this curious dispute.

[†] For example, that Kant's principle of "universalizing the maxim" of an action meant that anyone of lustful or homicidal tendencies would thereby be authorized to fornicate or murder as he pleased (cf. 8: 421).

On a recently prominent tone of
superiority in philosophy

Once it had lost its first meaning, as a scientific *wisdom of life*, the name 8: 389
of philosophy very soon came into demand as a decorative title for the
understanding possessed by uncommon thinkers, for whom it now represented a sort of unveiling of a mystery. To the *ascetics* in the Makarian
desert,[1] their *monkishness* was said to be philosophy. The *alchemist* called
himself *philosophus per ignem.*[a] The *lodges* of old and later times are adepts
of a mystery handed down to them, of which they jealously *refuse* to tell
us anything (*philosophus per initiationem*). And finally, the most recent
possessors of it are those who have it *within them*, but are unfortunately
incapable of uttering and disseminating it generally, by means of language (*philosophus per inspirationem*). Now if there were a knowledge of
the super-sensible (alone a true mystery, from the theoretical viewpoint),
which the human mind can nevertheless unravel from a practical point
of view, it would still, as a power of knowledge *through concepts*, be far
inferior to that which, as a power of *intuition*, might be perceived directly
through the understanding. For by means of the former the discursive
understanding must employ much labor on resolving and again compounding its concepts according to principles, and toil up many steps
to make advances in knowledge, whereas an *intellectual intuition* would
grasp and present the object immediately, and all at once. So whoever
may consider himself to be in possession of the latter will look down on
the former with disdain; and conversely, the comfort of such a use of
reason is a strong inducement to the bold postulation of such a power
of intuition, and likewise to the high commendation of a philosophy
founded upon it. The same can also be readily explained by the naturally
self-seeking tendency in man, which reason tacitly indulges.

For it is due not only to natural indolence, but also to the vanity of 8: 390
man (as to a misunderstood freedom), that those who *have enough to
live on*, whether in affluence or penury, consider themselves *superior* in
comparison with those who must work in order to live. The *Arab* or
Mongolian despises the townsman, and thinks himself superior by comparison, because wandering about in the desert with his horses and sheep
is more pastime than work. The *forest Tungus* intends to hurl a curse at
his brother's head when he says: "May you raise your cattle yourself, as
the *Burat*[2] does!" The latter passes on the compliment, and says: "May
you till the soil, as the *Russian* does!" The latter will likely say, according to his own way of thinking: "May you sit at the weaving-stool, like
a *German*!" All, in a word, consider themselves superior to the extent
that they believe they do not have to work. And in accordance with this
principle, things have lately gone so far that an alleged philosophy is
openly proclaimed to the public, in which one does not have to *work*,
but need only hearken and attend to the oracle within, in order to gain

---

[a] philosopher by fire

complete possession of all the wisdom to which philosophy aspires. And this, moreover, in a tone which shows that the proponents of this philosophy are not at all inclined to align themselves with those who – *like schoolmen* – consider themselves obliged to proceed slowly and circumspectly from the critique of their cognitive powers to dogmatic knowledge, but are able, rather – *like men of genius* – to accomplish by a single piercing glance within them everything that industry can ever hope to achieve, and a good deal more besides. In sciences that require work, such as mathematics, natural science, ancient history, linguistics, etc., and even in philosophy, so far as it is obliged to confine itself to a methodical development and systematic arranging of concepts, many a person can certainly perform *with pride*, in the pedantic style; but to none save the philosopher of *intuition*, who makes his demonstration, not by the Herculean labor of self-knowledge from below upwards, but soaring above this, by an apotheosis (which costs him nothing) from above downwards, can it be given to perform *with superiority*; since he is there speaking from his own observation, and is not obliged to be answerable to anyone else.

And now to the matter in hand!

8: 391

Plato, no less a mathematician than he was a philosopher, admired among the properties of certain geometrical figures, e.g., the circle, a sort of *purposiveness*, i.e., fitness to resolve a multiplicity of problems, or multiplicity in resolving one and the same problem (as in the theory of geometrical loci), from a principle, just as if the requirements for constructing certain quantitative concepts were laid down in them *on purpose*, although they can be grasped and demonstrated as necessary *a priori*. But purposiveness is thinkable only through relation of the object to an understanding, as its cause.

But now since with our understanding, as a faculty of cognition *through concepts*, we are unable to extend our *a priori* knowledge beyond our concept (though this does actually happen in mathematics), Plato was obliged to assume that we men possess *intuitions a priori*, which would, however, have their first *origin*, not in *our* understanding (for the latter is not a faculty of intuition, but only a discursive or thinking faculty), but rather in one that was simultaneously the ultimate ground of all things, i.e., the divine understanding, whose intuitions *direct* would then deserve to be called archetypes (Ideas).

But our intuiting of these divine Ideas (for we should still have to have an intuition *a priori*, if we wished to make intelligible to ourselves the capacity for synthetic *a priori* propositions in pure mathematics), would to us have been given only *indirectly*, at our birth, as an intuiting of copies (*ectypa*), as it were shadow-images of all things, which we know synthetically *a priori*; though that birth has simultaneously brought with it a darkening of these Ideas, through forgetfulness of their origin, as a

432

consequence of the fact that our mind (now called soul) has been thrust into a body, from whose fetters it would now have to be the noble task of philosophy to release us.*

But nor must we forget Pythagoras, of whom, indeed, we now know too little to make out anything certain about the metaphysical principle of his philosophy. As with Plato the wonders of shapes (in geometry), so with Pythagoras the wonders of numbers (in arithmetic), i.e., the appearance of a certain purposiveness, and a fitness seemingly imparted deliberately into their constitution for the solution of many rational tasks of mathematics, where intuition *a priori* (space and time), and not merely a discursive thinking, must be presupposed, awoke his attention as if to a sort of *magic*, simply in order to make intelligible the possibility, not only of the enlargement of our concepts of quantity as such, but also of their special and seemingly mysterious properties. History records that discovery of the numerical relation among the tones, and of the law by which they alone produce a music, led him to the idea that since, in this play of sensations, mathematics (as a science of numbers) contains the principle of its form as well (and even, it appears, *a priori*, in virtue of its necessity), we are therefore imbued with the admittedly only dim intuition of a nature which has been ordered according to numerical equations by an understanding that rules over it; which idea, when applied to the heavenly bodies, also brought forth the doctrine of the harmony of the spheres. Now nothing is more animating to the senses than music; but the animating principle in man is the *soul*; and since music, according to Pythagoras, rests entirely on perceived

8: 392

---

* In all these inferences, Plato at least proceeds consistently. Before him there undoubtedly hovered, albeit obscurely, the question that has only lately achieved clear expression: "How are synthetic propositions possible *a priori*?" Could he have guessed at that time, what has only been discovered since, that there are indeed intuitions *a priori*, but not of the human understanding, since (under the name of space and time) they are actually *sensuous*; that all objects of sense are therefore perceived by us merely as appearances, and that even their forms, which we are able to determine *a priori* in mathematics, are not those of things-in-themselves, but only (subjective) forms of our sensibility, which are therefore valid for all objects of possible experience, but not a step beyond that; he would not then have looked for pure intuition (which he needed, to make synthetic *a priori* knowledge intelligible to himself) in the divine understanding and its archetypes of all things, as independent objects; or thereby have put the torch to enthusiasm. For this he certainly perceived, that if, in the intuition that underlies geometry, he wished to claim that he could intuit *empirically* the object in itself, then the geometrical judgment and the whole of mathematics would be a merely empirical science, which contradicts the *necessity* which (besides intuitability) is precisely what assures to mathematics so high a rank among all the sciences.

8: 393

numerical relationships, and since (as we need to mark well) this animating principle in man, the soul, is at the same time a free, self-determining entity, his definition of it: *anima est numerus se ipsum movens*[a] can perhaps be made intelligible, and to some extent justified, if it be assumed that by this power of self-movement he wished to point out its difference from matter, as the intrinsically lifeless that is movable only through something external, and thus to allude to freedom.

Hence it was *mathematics* upon which both Pythagoras and Plato *were philosophizing*, when they assigned all *a priori* knowledge (whether it might contain intuition or concept) to the intellectual sphere, and by this philosophy fancied they had stumbled upon a *mystery*, where no mystery exists: not because reason can answer all the questions submitted to it, but because its oracle falls silent, once the question has been elevated so high that it now no longer has any meaning. If, for example, geometry proposes some *already* named properties of the circle (as may be found in Montucla),[3] and the question is now asked: whence does it possess these properties, which seem to contain a sort of extended utility and purposiveness? – no other answer can be given to this but: *Quaerit delirus, quod non respondet Homerus.*[b] Anyone who wishes to solve a mathematical problem philosophically, thereby contradicts himself; for example, why is it that the *ratio* of the three sides of a right-angled triangle can only be that of the numbers 3, 4, and 5?[4] But he who *philosophizes* upon a mathematical problem believes that here he has stumbled upon a mystery, and for that reason is seeing something transcendently great, where he is not seeing anything, and finds, in the very fact that he is brooding inwardly upon an idea, which he can neither make intelligible to himself, nor communicate to others, the true philosophy (*philosophia arcani*),[c] where the poetic talent then finds food for itself in feeling, and the pleasures of speculation: which is certainly far more inviting and splendid than the law of reason, to earn oneself a possession by work; but in which both poverty and arrogance create the ridiculous appearance of hearing philosophy speak in a *superior* tone.

The philosophy of Aristotle, on the other hand, is work. But (like the two preceding) I consider him here only as a metaphysician, that is, a dismemberer of all knowledge *a priori* into its elements, only, as a craftsman of reason, to put it all together again out of those elements (the categories); whose treatment, so far as it goes, has retained its utility, albeit that in *progressing* it failed to extend those principles which he ranks as sensuous (without his noticing the dangerous leap that he had to make here), to the super-sensible as well, whither his categories were unable

---

[a] The soul is number moving itself.
[b] The madman asks what Homer cannot answer.
[c] philosophy of the hidden

to carry him: at which point it was necessary beforehand to analyze and   8: 394
measure the organ of thinking in itself, namely reason, according to the
two fields thereof, the theoretical and the practical; though this labor
was reserved for a later age.

But now let us listen to and evaluate the new tone in philosophizing
(whereby philosophy may be dispensed with).

That *superior* persons philosophize, should it even be up to the peaks of
metaphysics, must be regarded as greatly to their credit, and they deserve
indulgence in their (scarcely avoidable) clash with the school, since they
do, after all, condescend to the latter on a footing of civil equality.*

But that would-be philosophers *behave in a superior fashion* can by no
means be indulged in them, since they elevate themselves above their
guild-brothers, and violate the inalienable right of the latter to freedom
and equality in matters of mere reason.

The principle of wishing to philosophize by influence of a higher   8: 395
feeling is the most suitable of all for the tone of superiority; for who will
dispute my feeling with me? And if I can now but make it credible that this
feeling is not merely subjective in *myself*, but can be demanded of anyone,
and thus also ranks as objective, and a piece of knowledge, not merely
in being excogitated as a concept, but as an intuition (apprehension of
the object itself): then I have a great advantage over all who must first

---

* There is, however, a difference between philosophizing and making philosophers. The latter happens in the tone of superiority, if despotism over the reason
of the people (and even over one's own reason), by fettering it to a blind belief,
is given out as philosophy. To this, for example, belongs "belief in the thunder-
legion in the days of Marcus Aurelius,"[5] likewise "in the fire that miraculously
broke out under the ruins of Jerusalem, to hinder Julian the Apostate";[6] which
was given out as the genuinely true philosophy, and the opposite of it called
"colliers' unbelief" (just as if the charcoal-burners, deep in their woods, were
renowned for being very incredulous in regard to the tales that were brought
to them): to which may be added the assurance that philosophy has already
come to an end two thousand years ago, because "the Stagirite[7] has conquered
so much for science, that he has left little of importance any more for his suc-
cessors to spy out." Thus the levelers of the political order are not only those
who desire, with Rousseau, that the citizenry should be collectively equal to
one another, because any one is *all*; there are also those who wish all to be equal
to one another, because but for One they would collectively be *nothing*, and
are monarchists out of necessity: elevating now Plato, and now Aristotle to the
throne, so that, being conscious of their own incapacity for personal thought,
they do not have to endure the hateful comparison with others still living. And
thus (principally by the latter judgment) the superior person creates philosophers, in that by obscuration he puts an end to any further philosophizing. The
phenomenon cannot be better represented in its proper light than by the fable
of Voss (*Berliner Monatsschrift*, November 1795, last page), a tale that is worth
a hecatomb,[8] all by itself.

resort to justification in order to plume themselves on the truth of their claims. I can therefore speak in the tone of a commander, who is exempt from the onus of proving his title to possession (*beati possidentes*).[a] So long live the philosophy of feeling, which leads us directly to the heart of the matter! Away with ratiocination from concepts, which attempts the task only by the roundabout method of general attributes, and which, before it yet has a matter which it can grasp immediately, first demands specific forms to which it may subject this matter! And given also that reason can offer no further explanation whatever about the legitimacy of the outcome of these its high insights, there remains nevertheless a fact: "Philosophy has its secrets that *can be felt*."[*]

* A celebrated possessor thereof expresses himself thus on the subject: "As long as reason, *qua* law-giver of willing, must say to the phenomena (which here, of course, are the free actions of men): *you please me – you please me not*, for so long must it regard the phenomena as effects of realities"; from which he then concludes that the law-giving of reason has need, not merely of a *form*, but of a *matter* (material purpose) as determining ground of willing, i.e., a *feeling of pleasure* (or displeasure) at an object *must precede*, if reason is to be practical. This error, which, if it is allowed to creep in, would destroy all morality and leave nothing behind but the maxim of happiness, which can have no objective principle whatever (since it varies with difference in the subject) – this error, I say, can be confidently brought to light only through the following *touchstone of feeling*. That *pleasure* (or displeasure) which must necessarily *precede the law*, if the act is to take place, is *pathological*; but that which the *law* must necessarily *precede*, for this to happen, is *moral*. The former is based on empirical principles (the matter of choice); the latter on a pure principle *a priori* (in which the only concern is with the form of determination of the will). With this it is likewise easy to discover the fallacy (*fallacia causae non causae*),[b] when the eudaemonist announces that the pleasure (*satisfaction*) that a righteous man has in view, in order to feel it one day in the consciousness of his well-conducted course of life (and thus the prospect of his future felicity), is in fact the true *motive* for conducting his affairs well (in accordance with the law). For since I must assume him beforehand to be righteous and obedient to the law, i.e., to be one in whom *the law precedes the pleasure*, in order for him subsequently to feel a pleasure of the soul in the consciousness of his well-conducted course of life, it is an empty circle in the reasoning to make the pleasure, which is a *consequence*, into the *cause* of that course of life.

Yet as for the plain *syncretism* of certain moralists, whereby though not wholly, yet *in part*, they make *eudaemonia* into the objective principle of morality (it being granted that it also has, unawares, a concurrent subjective influence on determining the human will in accordance with duty), that is the direct way, of course, to having no principle at all. For the mixed motives borrowed from

[a] happy the possessors
[b] fallacy of 'false cause'

With this alleged feelability of an object, which can nevertheless be   8: 396
met with only in pure reason, the situation is now as follows. Hitherto we
had heard only of three stages of apprehension, down to its disappearance in total ignorance: knowledge, belief, and opinion.*

---

felicity, even if they tend to exactly the same *actions* as those that flow from pure
moral laws, still contaminate and weaken at the same time the moral disposition
itself, whose value and high rank consist precisely in this, that regardless of
these motives, and prevailing, even, over all their solicitations, it demonstrates
obedience to nothing else but the law.

* The central term is also used, on occasion, in the theoretical sense, as a syn-
onym for holding something to be *probable*; and here it must indeed be noted,
that of that which lies beyond all bounds of possible experience, we can say
neither that it is *probable*, nor that it is *improbable*, so that in regard to such
an object, even the word 'belief' does not occur at all in a *theoretical sense*.
By the statement that this or that is *probable*, we understand an intermediate
(in apprehension) between opining and knowing; and here it turns out as with
all other intermediates, namely that we can make of them *what we want*. But
if somebody says, for example: It is at least *probable* that the soul lives on after
death, he does not know *what he is wanting*. For we call probable that which,
when apprehended, has more than half the certainty (the sufficient reason)
on its side. The reasons must therefore collectively contain a partial cognition, a part of the *knowledge* of the object on which we are passing judgment.
Now if the object is in no way the object of a knowledge possible to us (such
as is the nature of the soul, qua living substance, in the absence of any connection with a body, i.e., as a spirit), then about its possibility we can judge
neither the probability nor the improbability, since we cannot judge at all.
For the alleged grounds of knowledge are in a series which comes nowhere
near to the sufficient reason, and thus to knowledge itself, since they relate
to something super-sensible of which, as such, no theoretical knowledge is
possible.

The position is just the same with belief in the *witness* of another, that
allegedly has reference to something super-sensible. The authenticity of a report is always an empirical matter; and the person in whose testimony I am to
believe must be the object of an experience. But if he is taken to be a super-
sensible being, then I can be taught by no experience (since that would be
self-contradictory), as to his very existence, nor as to the fact that it is such
a being who testifies this to me; nor can I even infer this from the subjective
impossibility of being able to explain to myself the appearance of an inner
summons vouchsafed to me, as due to anything else but supernatural influence
(in view of what has just been said of the judgment according to probability).
Hence there is no theoretical belief in the super-sensible.

In a practical (morally-practical) sense, however, a belief in the super-
sensible is not only possible, but is actually inseparably bound up with that
point of view. For the sum of morality in myself, although super-sensible, and
thus not empirical, is nevertheless given with unmistakable truth and authority

8: 397

Now a new one is introduced, which has nothing whatever in common with logic, and is to be no advance of the understanding, but rather a premonition (*praevisio sensitiva*) of that which is not an object of the senses at all, viz., an *intimation* of the super-sensible.

8: 398

Now here we self-evidently encounter a certain mystical touch, an overleap (*salto mortale*)[9] from concepts to the unthinkable, a power of seizing upon that which no concept attains to, an expectation of mysteries, or rather a dangling of them before us, which is actually a turning of heads towards enthusiasm. For intimation is obscure expectation, and contains the hope of a solution, though in matters of reason this is possible only through concepts; if these are transcendent, therefore, and can lead to no true *knowledge* of the object, they must necessarily promise a surrogate thereof, supernatural information (mystical illumination): which is then the death of all philosophy.

Plato the academic, therefore, though through no fault of his own (for he used his intellectual intuitions only backwards, to *explain* the possibility of a synthetic knowledge *a priori*, not forwards, to extend it through those Ideas that were legible in the divine understanding), became the father of all enthusiasm *by way of philosophy*. But I would not wish to confuse him with *Plato the letter-writer* (lately translated into German).[10] The latter, to "the four *things* pertaining to knowledge, the *name* of the object, the *description*, the *presentation* and the *science*" would add "yet a *fifth*" (wheel to the coach);[11] "namely the very object itself and *its true being*."

(through a categorical imperative), albeit that the latter prescribes a purpose (the highest good), which, theoretically regarded, cannot be achieved through my powers alone, without the contributory might of a world-governor. But to *believe* in this, from a moral and practical viewpoint, does not mean to apprehend its reality beforehand in a theoretical sense, so that to understand this prescribed purpose one would obtain enlightenment, and to effect it, motives; for the law of reason is already in itself objectively adequate to this. It means, rather, to act according to the ideal of this purpose, as though such a world-government were real. For this imperative (which prescribes, not belief, but action), contains, on the side of man, obedience and subjection of his [*arbitrary*] *choice* under the law; but at the same time, on the side of the *will* that prescribes a purpose to him, a capacity (which is not the human one) adapted to that purpose, on whose behalf the reason of man can indeed prescribe actions, but not their outcome (the fulfilment of the purpose), since that is not always or wholly within human power. So in the categorical imperative of the materially practical reason, which tells man: I will that your actions be concordant with the final purpose of all things, there is therefore already simultaneously thought the presupposition of a law-giving will, which contains all power (of the divine), and has no need of being specially imposed.

"This unalterable essence, which can be intuited only in and through the soul, but as if by a leaping spark of fire, spontaneously kindles a light therein," he claims (as an exalted philosopher) "to have grasped; though it cannot be spoken of, to the people at least, since one would at once become convinced of one's ignorance; for every attempt of this kind would already be dangerous, partly because these high truths might be exposed to a coarse contempt, partly" (which is the only sensible point to be made here) "because the soul might become prey to empty hopes and the vain delusion of knowing greatsecrets."

Who can fail to see here the mystagogue, who not only raves on his own behalf, but is simultaneously the founder of a club, and in speaking to his adepts, rather than to the people (meaning all the uninitiated), plays the *superior* with his alleged philosophy! I take leave to adduce some more recent examples of the same thing.

8: 399

In the latest mystico-Platonic idiom we are told:[12] "All human philosophy can show only the dawn: the sun must be divined." But nobody, after all, can divine a sun, if he has not otherwise already seen one; for it might well be that on our globe day regularly followed night (as in the Mosaic account of creation), without anyone ever getting to see a sun, owing to the constantly overcast sky, and yet that all affairs would equally take their appropriate course according to this alternation (of day and season). Yet in such a state of things a true philosopher would not indeed *divine* a sun (for that is not his business), but could still perhaps *guess* at it, in order, by assuming the hypothesis of such a heavenly body, to explain that phenomenon; and might also in that way hit upon the truth. To look *into* the sun (the super-sensible) without being blinded is not possible; but to see it adequately in reflection (of the reason that morally enlightens the soul), and even from a practical viewpoint, as the older Plato did, is perfectly feasible. By contrast, the new Platonists "certainly give us only a stage sun," because they wish to deceive us by feelings (intimations), i.e., merely the subjective, which gives us no concept of the object, in order to buoy us up with the delusion of a knowledge of the objective, which borders on extravagance. Now the platonizing philosopher of feeling is inexhaustible in such pictorial utterances, which are supposed to make this divination intelligible; e.g., "to approach the goddess of wisdom so closely that one may hear the *rustle* of her robes"; and likewise in belauding the art of the *pseudo–Plato*, who "though unable to lift the veil of Isis,[13] can yet make it so thin that one may *divine* the goddess beneath it." How thin, we are not told; but presumably it is still thick enough for us to make what we please of the apparition, for otherwise it would be a seeing, which is certainly to be avoided.

To the very same end, in the absence of precise proofs, we are now offered by way of arguments, "analogies, probabilities" (already just

8: 400   alluded to) "and the danger of emasculating a reason become so high-strung through metaphysical*sublimation, that it will hardly be able to hold its own in the struggle against evil"; albeit that in these very principles *a priori* the practical reason correctly feels a strength that was

---

* What the new Platonist has said so far is, as to the treatment of his theme, pure *metaphysics*, and can therefore refer only to the formal principles of reason. But it also covertly interpolates a *hyperphysics*, i.e., not just principles of practical reason, but a theory of the *nature* of the super-sensible (of God and the human mind), and purports to know this in "not so very fine-spun" a fashion. But the *absolute nullity* of a philosophy, which here relates to the matter (the object) of pure rational concepts, if it has not (as in transcendental theology) been carefully detached from all empirical ties, may be illustrated by the following example.

   The transcendental concept of God, as the *ens realissimum,*[a] cannot be circumvented in philosophy, however abstract such a concept may be; for it pertains to the union, and at the same time the elucidation, of everything concrete that may subsequently enter into applied theology and theory of religion. The question now arises: am I to think of God as the *sum total (complexus, aggregatum)* of all realities, or as the supreme *ground* of them? If I do the first, I must produce examples of this material from which I put together the highest being, so that the concept thereof should not be altogether empty and without meaning. I shall therefore attribute to him *understanding,* or even a *will* and so on, as realities. But now all the understanding that I know of is a capacity to *think,* i.e., a discursive power of presentation, or one that is possible through a feature common to a number of things (from whose differences I must therefore abstract in thought), and is thus impossible without a *limitation* of the subject. Hence a divine understanding cannot be taken for a power to think. But of any other understanding, which might, say, be a faculty of intuition, I have not the slightest conception; hence the concept of an understanding which I posit in the supreme being is totally devoid of meaning. Again, if I posit in him another reality, a *will,* through which he is the cause of all things outside himself, I must presume one in which his satisfaction (*acquiescentia*) in no way depends on the existence of things outside him: for that would be limitation (*negatio*). Now again I have not the slightest notion, nor can I give any example, of a will in which the subject would not base his satisfaction on the *success* of his willing, and which would thus not *depend* upon the existence of the outside object. Thus, as in the previous case, the concept of a will in the supreme being, as a reality inherent to him, is either an empty one, or (what is even worse), an anthropomorphic concept, which if – as is unavoidable – it is extended into the practical, corrupts all religion and transforms it into idolatry. But if I frame to myself the concept of the *ens realissimum* as the *ground* of all reality, I am saying that God is the being who contains the ground of everything in the world *for which we men have need to suppose an understanding* (e.g., everything purposive therein); he is the being from whom the existence of all worldly being originates, not out of the

---

[a] most real being

otherwise never guessed at, and is actually emasculated and lamed far more by the substitution of empirical elements (which precisely for that reason are unsuitable for giving universal laws).   8: 401

The summons of the latest German wisdom, *to philosophize through feeling* (and not, like that of a few years ago, *to employ philosophy to put* the moral *feeling* into *force* and motion), is ultimately exposed to a test at which it is necessarily bound to fail. Its challenge runs: "The surest mark of authenticity in human philosophy is not that it should make us more certain, but that it should make us better." Of this test it cannot   8: 402 be demanded that the betterment of man (effected by the feeling of mystery) should be certified by an assay-master of his morality, trying

necessity of his *nature* (*per emanationem*), but according to a circumstance for which *we men* are obliged to suppose *a free will*, in order to make the possibility thereof intelligible to us. Now here what the *nature* of the supreme being may be (objectively) can be posited as wholly inscrutable to us, and quite beyond the sphere of any theoretical knowledge possible to us, and yet reality still be (subjectively) left to these concepts *in a practical respect* (with regard to the course of life); in relation to which, also, an *analogy* of the divine understanding and will to that of man and his practical reason can alone be assumed, notwithstanding that in a theoretical sense there is absolutely no analogy between them. From the moral law which our own reason authoritatively prescribes to us, and not from any theory of the nature of things-in-themselves, there now proceeds the concept of God which practical pure reason constrains us to *make for ourselves*.

If, therefore, it is said by one of those men of might, who have lately been proclaiming with ardor a wisdom that costs them no trouble, since they profess to have caught this goddess by the hem of her garment and seized hold of her, that "he despises anyone who thinks *to make his own God*," this is but one of the singularities of that tribe whose tone (as especially favored persons) is *superior*. For in itself it is evident that a concept which has to proceed from our reason will have to be made by ourselves. Had we sought to take it from any appearance (any object of experience), the ground of our knowledge would be empirical, and unable to yield validity for everybody, or the apodictic practical certainty which a universally binding law must possess. We should be compelled, rather, to first hold a wisdom that appeared to us in personal form up against that self-made concept of ours, as the archetype, in order to see whether this person also corresponded to the character of that self-made archetype; and even supposing that we encounter nothing therein that contradicts it, it is still utterly impossible to know of its appropriateness to such an archetype except by super-sensory experience (since the object is super-sensible): which is a self-contradiction. Thus *theophany* creates from the Platonic Idea an *idol*, which cannot be revered in anything but a superstitious fashion: whereas *theology*, proceeding from concepts of our own reason, sets up an *ideal* that compels our worship, since it has itself arisen from the holiest duties, which are independent of theology.

it in a cupel; anyone, to be sure, can easily weigh the coinage of good actions, but as to how much sterling metal they contain at heart, who can offer a *publicly valid* testimony to this? And yet such it would have to be, if it is thereby to be demonstrated that this feeling, as such, makes better men, whereas scientific theory is unfruitful and ineffective in this respect. No experience, therefore, can provide the touchstone for this; it must be sought solely in practical reason, as given *a priori*. Inner experience and feeling (which in itself is empirical and thus contingent) are aroused only by the voice of reason (*dictamen rationis*), which speaks clearly to everyone and is capable of being scientifically known; but not a particular practical rule for reason, introduced, say, by feeling, which is impossible; for in that case it could never be universally valid. We must therefore be able to perceive *a priori* which principle might make better men, and will do so, if only it is brought clearly and unceasingly to their souls, and they pay heed to the powerful impression that it makes upon them.

Now every man finds in his reason the idea of duty, and trembles on hearing its brazen voice, when inclinations arise in him, which tempt him to disobedience towards it. He is persuaded that, even though the latter all collectively conspire against it, the majesty of the law, which his own reason prescribes to him, must yet unhesitatingly outweigh them all, and that his will is therefore also capable of this. All this can and must be presented to man, clearly if not scientifically, if he is to be made aware both of the authority of his reason, which commands him, and also of its actual commandments; and is to that extent theory. Now I put it to man, as he puts it to himself: What is it in me which brings it about that I can sacrifice the innermost allurements of my instincts, and all wishes that proceed from my nature, to a law which promises me no compensating advantage, and threatens no loss on its violation; a law, indeed, which I respect the more intimately, the more strictly it ordains, and the less it offers for doing so? By astonishment at the magnitude and sublimity of the inward disposition in mankind, and at the same 8: 403 time the impenetrability of the mystery that veils it (for the answer, it is *freedom*, would be tautological, since that is precisely what constitutes the mystery), this question arouses the whole soul. We can never weary of giving attention to it, and admiring in itself a power that yields to no power in Nature; and this admiration is simply the feeling produced by Ideas, and if, besides the teaching of morality in school and pulpit, the presentation of this mystery were made a special and oft-repeated topic of instruction, this feeling would penetrate deep into the soul, nor would it fail to make men morally *better*.

Here, then, is that which Archimedes had need of, but did not find: a fixed point to which reason can apply its lever, in order by its principle to move the human will, even when the whole of Nature resists it; and this without resting it either upon the present or a future world, but merely upon its inner Idea of freedom, which lies there as a sure foundation through the unshakable moral law. This, then, is the secret which can become *possible to feel* only after slow development of the concepts of the understanding, and of carefully tested principles and thus only through work. It is given, not empirically (proposed to reason for solution), but *a priori* (as real insight within the bounds of our reason), and even extends the knowledge of reason up to the super-sensible, but only in a practical respect: not, say, by a *feeling*, which purports to be the basis of knowledge (the mystical), but by a clear *cognition* which acts upon feeling (the moral). The tone of one who considers himself possessed of this true secret cannot be superior: for only dogmatic or historical cognition is puffed up. The cognition of the former, chastened by critique of his own reason, inevitably obliges him to moderation in his claims (unpretentiousness); but the arrogance of the latter cognition, the erudition in Plato and the classics which pertains only to the cultivation of taste, cannot justify the wish to play the philosopher with it.

To censure such a claim did not strike me as superfluous at the present time, when adornment with the title of philosophy has become a matter of fashion, and the philosopher of *vision* (if we allow such a person) might – seeing how easy it is, by an audacious stroke, to attain without trouble to the summit of insight – be able unawares (since audacity is catching) to assemble a large following about him: which the police in the kingdom of the sciences cannot permit.

8: 404

The dismissive habit of crying down the *formal* in our knowledge (which is yet the preeminent business of philosophy) as a pedantry, under the name of "a pattern-factory," confirms this suspicion, namely that there is a secret intention, under the guise of philosophy to actually outlaw all philosophy, and as victor to play the superior over it (*pedibus subjecta vicissim obteritur, nos exaequat victoria coelo* – Lucretius).[a] But how little this attempt can succeed, under the illumination of an ever-vigilant critique, may be seen from the following example.

In form resides the essence of the matter (*forma dat esse rei*, as the schoolmen said), so far as this is to be known by reason. If this matter be an object of the senses, then it is the form of things in intuition (as appearances), and even pure mathematics is nothing else but a form-theory of pure *intuition*; just as metaphysics, *qua* pure philosophy, founds its knowledge at the highest level on *forms of thought*, under which every object (matter of knowledge) may thereafter be subsumed. Upon these forms depends the possibility of all synthetic knowledge *a priori*, which we cannot, of course, deny that we possess. But the transition to the super-sensible, to which reason irresistibly drives us, and which it can

---

[a] With it trampled underfoot in turn, victory exalts us to the skies [*De rerum natura* 1: 78–9].

accomplish only in a moral and practical respect, it can also effect solely through those (practical) laws which make as their principle, not the matter of free actions (their purpose), but only their form, the appropriateness of their maxims to the universality of a legislation as such. In both fields (theoretical and practical) it is not an arbitrary *form-giving* undertaken *by design*, or even *machine-made* (on behalf of the state), but above all a *piece of handwork*, dealing with the given object, and indeed with no thought of taking up and evaluating the preceding industrious and careful work of the subject, his own faculty (of reason); by contrast, the gentleman who opens up an oracle for the vision of the super-sensible will be unable to deny having contrived it by a mechanical manipulation of men's brains, and attached the name of philosophy to it for honorific purposes alone.

8: 405 But now why all this quarrelling between two parties, who at bottom have one and the same good intention, namely to make men wise and honest? It is much ado about nothing, disunion through misunderstanding, needing no reconciliation, but only explanation on either side, in order to conclude a treaty which makes concord henceforth more intimate than ever.

The veiled goddess, before whom we both bow the knee, is the moral law within us in its inviolable majesty. We hearken to her voice, indeed, and also understand her command well enough; but on listening are in doubt whether it comes from man himself, out of the absolute authority of his own reason, or whether it proceeds from another being, whose nature is unknown to him, and which speaks to man through this his own reason. At bottom we should perhaps do better to desist from this inquiry altogether, since it is merely speculative, and since what we are (objectively) obliged to do remains always the same, whether we base it on the one principle or the other; were it not that the didactic method, of bringing the moral law within us to clear concepts by logical instruction, is in truth the only *philosophical* method, whereas that of personifying this law and making out of morally commanding reason a veiled Isis (though we attribute to her no other properties than can be found by that method), is an *aesthetic* way of presenting exactly the same object; of which one can indeed subsequently make use, once the principles have been clarified by the first method, in order to vivify those ideas by sensory, albeit merely analogical presentation – though always with some danger of lapsing into visionary enthusiasm, which is the death of all philosophy.

To be able to *discern* this goddess would thus be to say no more than that one is guided by moral *feeling* to concepts of duty, before having yet been able to make *clear* to oneself the principles on which this feeling depends; which discernment of a law, as soon as it emerges into clear insight by logical treatment, is the true business of philosophy, without which that pronouncement of reason would be the voice of an *oracle*,* exposed to every kind of interpretation.

At any rate, without taking this proposal into comparison, "if," as Fontenelle said on another occasion, "Monsieur N. is still quite determined to believe in the oracle, nobody can prevent him."[14]

8: 406

---

* This mystery-mongering is of a quite peculiar sort. Its adepts make no secret of the fact that they have kindled their light from Plato; and this alleged Plato freely confesses that if asked what it is, then (which is thereby illuminated), he is not able to say. But all the better! For then it is self-evident that he, another Prometheus, has snatched the spark for it directly from heaven. So well may one talk in the superior tone, if one is of the old nobility, and can say: "In these advanced times of ours it will soon be the custom for everything that is said or done from feeling to be considered enthusiasm. Poor Plato, if you did not have the seal of antiquity upon you, and if one could make any claim to scholarship without having read you, who would still want to read you in this *prosaic* age, in which the highest wisdom is to see nothing but what lies at one's feet, and to accept nothing but what can be grasped with hands?" – But this conclusion is unfortunately not *justly drawn*; it proves too much. For Aristotle, an exceedingly prosaic philosopher, still certainly has the seal of antiquity upon him too, and by that principle, a claim to be read! At bottom, indeed, all philosophy is prosaic; and a proposal to now begin philosophizing poetically again might well be received as one would a suggestion that the merchant should henceforth write his catalogues, not in prose, but in verse.

Settlement of a mathematical dispute founded on misunderstanding

<hr>

In an essay in the *Berliner Monatsschrift* (May 1796, pp. 395–96), 8: 409 among other examples of the fanaticism that may be induced by attempts to philosophize about mathematical objects, I also attributed to the Pythagorean number-mystic the question: "Why is it that the ratio of the three sides of a right-angled triangle can only be that of the numbers 3, 4, and 5?" I had thus taken this proposition to be true; but Professor Reimarus refutes it, and shows (*Berliner Monatsschrift*, August, no. 6) that many numbers, other than those mentioned, can stand in the ratio in question.

So nothing seems clearer than that we find ourselves embroiled in a truly mathematical dispute (of a kind that is, in general, almost unheard of). But this quarrel amounts only to a misunderstanding. Each party takes the expression in a different sense; so soon as a mutual understanding is reached, the dispute vanishes, and both sides are correct. Now proposition and counter-proposition are related as follows:

R. says (or at least thinks his proposition thus): "In the infinite *multitude of all possible numbers* (considered *at large*) there exist, in regard to the sides of the right-angled triangle, more ratios than that of the numbers 3, 4, and 5."

K. says (or at least thinks his counter-proposition thus): "In the infinite *series of all numbers progressing in the natural order* (from o onwards, by the continuous addition of 1) there exists, among those that *immediately follow each other* (and are thus taken to be *connected*), no ratio of these sides save that of the numbers 3, 4, and 5."

Both propositions have strict proofs; and neither of the two (supposed) disputants has the honor of being the first discoverer of these proofs.

So it is merely a matter of deciding who is to blame for this *misunderstanding*. If the issue were purely mathematical, K. would have to bear it; for the *proposition* expresses in *general* the aforementioned property 8: 410 of numbers (without reference to any serial order among them). But here it was only meant to serve as an *example* of the nonsense that the Pythagorean number-mysticism makes of mathematics, when *seeking to philosophize* about its propositions; and there it might well have been assumed that the said *counter-proposition* would be taken in the sense in which a mystic might think himself to have found something *strange* and aesthetically remarkable among the properties of numbers; such as is a connection restricted to three immediately adjacent numbers in the infinite sequence thereof; even though mathematics encounters nothing to be surprised at here.

If Herr Reimarus should thus have been needlessly troubled with proving a proposition which nobody, to my knowledge, has yet doubted, he will not, I trust, hold me to blame for this.

Proclamation of the imminent conclusion
of a treaty of perpetual peace in philosophy

Section One
Happy Outlook for Imminent Perpetual Peace
From the Lowest Level of Man's Living Nature
to his Highest, that of Philosophy

Chrysippus says, in his pithy Stoic way:[1] "Nature has given the pig a *soul*, instead of *salt*, so that he should not become rotten." Now this is the lowest level of man's nature, prior to all cultivation, namely that of mere animal instinct. But it seems as if here the philosopher has thrown a prophetic glance into the physiological systems of our own day; save only that now, instead of the word 'soul', we have taken to using that of *living force* (and rightly so, since from an effect we can certainly infer to the *force* that produces it, but not forthwith to a *substance* specially adapted to this type of effect); we locate *life*, therefore, in the *action* of animating forces (life-impulse) and the ability to *react* to them (living-capacity), and call that man *healthy* in whom a proportionate stimulus produces neither an excessive nor an altogether too small effect: while conversely, the *animalic* operation of nature will pass over into a *chemical* one, which has decay as its consequence, so that it is not (as used to be thought) decay that must follow from and after death, but death that must follow from the preceding decay. Now here *nature* is presented in man even prior to his humanity, and thus in its generality, just as it acts in the beast, merely in order to evolve forces which can subsequently turn man to laws of freedom; though this activity and its arousal are not practical, but still merely mechanical.

A
On the Physical Causes of Man's Philosophy

In *addition* to the property of *self-consciousness*, by which man is to be distinguished above all other animals, and in virtue of which he is a *rational* animal (to whom also, owing to the unity of consciousness, only *one* soul can be attributed), there is also the *itch* to use this power for *trifling*, and thereafter to trifle methodically and even by concepts alone, i.e., to *philosophize*; and then also to grate polemically upon others with one's philosophy, i.e., to *dispute*, and since this does not readily happen without emotion, to *squabble* on behalf of one's philosophy, and finally, united in masses against one another (school against school, as contending armies) to *wage* open *warfare*; this itch, I say, or rather *drive*, will have to be viewed as one of the beneficent and wise arrangements of Nature, whereby she seeks to protect man from the great misfortune of decaying in the living flesh.

On the Physical Effect of Philosophy

It is the *health* (*status salubritatis*) *of reason*, as effect of philosophy. But since human health (by the above) is an incessant sickening and recovery, the mere *dietary* of practical reason (a sort of gymnastics thereof) is not yet sufficient to preserve the equilibrium which we call health, and which is poised upon a knife-edge; philosophy must also act (therapeutically) as a *medicine* (*materia medica*), for the use of which we need dispensaries and doctors (though the latter are alone entitled to *prescribe* such use); in which connection the authorities must be vigilant to see that it is qualified physicians who profess to *advise what philosophy should be studied,*[2] and not mere amateurs, who thereby practice quackery in an art of which they know not the first elements.

An example of the power of philosophy as a medication was given by the Stoic philosopher Posidonius,[3] through an experiment conducted on his own person in the presence of Pompey the Great (Cicero: *Tusculan Disputations*, Bk. 2, sec. 61), in that by contending vehemently against the Epicurean school he overcame a violent attack of gout, demonstrated it down into his feet, did not allow it to reach heart or head, and thus gave proof of the immediate *physical effect* of philosophy, which nature intends thereby (physical health), in that he declaimed upon the proposition *that pain is nothing bad.**

8: 415

On the Seeming Incompatibility of Philosophy with a Permanent State of Peace in the Subject

Dogmatism (e.g., that of the Wolfian school) is a pillow to fall asleep on, and an end to all vitality, which latter is precisely the benefit conferred

---

* The ambiguity in the terms *evil* (*malum*) and *bad* (*pravum*) is more easily prevented in Latin than in Greek. In regard to well-being and *evil* (of pain), man, like all sensuous beings, is subject to the law of *nature*, and is merely passive; in regard to *bad* (and good) he is under the law of *freedom*. The former contains what man *suffers*, the latter what he freely *does*. In regard to *fate*, the *difference* between right and left (*fato vel dextro vel sinistro*) is a mere difference in man's relations. But in regard to his freedom, and the relationship of the law to his inclinations, it is a difference within him. In the first case the *straight* is contrasted to the *slanting* (*rectum obliquo*); in the second, the straight to the *crooked* or maimed (*rectum pravo, sive varo, obtorto*).

That the Romans placed an unlucky event on the left side may well be because one is not so well able to ward off an attack with the left hand as with the right. But when, in auguries, the auspex, having turned his face southward to the so-called temple, declared happy the lightning-flash that occurred on the left, the reason seems to have been that the thunder-god, who was imagined facing the auspex, would then carry his bolt in the right hand.

by philosophy. *Skepticism*, which when fully set out represents the exact counterpart of this, has nothing with which it can exert influence upon a nimble reason, since it lays everything aside unused. *Moderatism*, which proceeds from halfway, and thinks to find the philosopher's stone in subjective *probability*, and by piling up a mass of isolated reasons (none in themselves probative) purports to supply the want of sufficient reason, is no philosophy at all; and with this medicine (of *doxology*) it is much as with plague-drops or Venetian theriac,[4] that owing to the all-too-*many good things* that are flung into them, right and left, they *are good for nothing*.

On the Real Compatibility of the Critical Philosophy with a Permanent State of Peace in the Subject

8: 416

Critical philosophy is that which sets out to conquer, not by *attempts* to build or overthrow systems, or even (like moderatism) to put up a roof, but no house, on stilts, for temporary accommodation, but rather by investigating the *power* of human reason (for whatever purpose), and so does not engage in vacuous hair-splitting on the subject of philosophemes that can have no basis in any possible experience. But now there actually is something in human reason, which can be known to us by no experience, and yet proves its reality and truth in effects that are presentable in experience, and thus can also (by an *a priori* principle, indeed) be absolutely commanded. This is the concept of *freedom*, and of the law that derives from this, of the categorical, i.e., absolutely commanding, imperative. Through this we acquire *Ideas* that would be utterly empty for merely speculative reason, though the latter inevitably points us towards them as cognitive grounds of our ultimate purpose – an admittedly only moral and practical reality: namely, so to *conduct* ourselves as if we were given the objects of these Ideas (God and immortality), which may therefore be postulated in this (practical) respect.

This philosophy, which is an outlook ever-armed (against those who perversely confound appearances with things-in-themselves), and precisely because of this unceasingly accompanies the activity of reason, offers the prospect of an eternal peace among philosophers, through the impotence, on the one hand, of *theoretical* proofs to the contrary, and through the strength of the *practical* grounds for accepting its principles on the other; a peace having the further advantage of constantly activating the powers of the subject, who is seemingly in danger of attack, and thus of also promoting, by philosophy, nature's intention of continuously revitalizing him, and preventing the sleep of death.

From this point of view, the utterance of a man eminent not only in his own (mathematical) field, but also in many others, and crowned

8: 417 with a productive and still vigorous old age, must be interpreted, not as words of ill-omen, but as a *felicitation*, when he utterly denies to the philosophers a peace resting comfortably on supposititious laurels;* in that a peace of that sort would indeed merely enfeeble the powers and defeat nature's purpose with regard to philosophy, as a continuing restorative to the ultimate purpose of mankind; whereas the disposition to contend is still no war, but rather can and should restrain the latter, and so assure peace, by a decisive preponderance of the practical grounds over those on the other side.

Hyperphysical Basis of Man's Life, for Purposes of a Philosophy thereof

By means of reason, the soul of man is endowed with a *spirit* (*mens*, νοῦσ), so that he may lead a life adapted, not merely to the mechanism of *nature* and its technico-practical laws, but also to the spontaneity of *freedom* and its morally-practical laws. This life-principle is not founded on concepts of the *sensible*, which collectively begin by presupposing *science*, i.e., theoretical knowledge (prior to any practical use of reason); it proceeds initially and at once from an Idea of the *super-sensible*, namely *freedom*, and from the morally categorical imperative of which the latter first informs us; and thereby forms the basis of a philosophy whose teaching is not, say (like mathematics), a good instrument (or tool for arbitrary purposes), and thus a mere means, but a doctrine which it *is in itself a duty* to make into a principle.

What is Philosophy, as the Doctrine which, of all Sciences, Constitutes Man's Greatest Need?

8: 418 It is that which its name already indicates: the *Pursuit of Wisdom*. But wisdom is the concordance of the will to the *ultimate purpose* (the highest good); and since this, so far as it is attainable, is also a duty, and conversely, if it is a duty, must also be attainable, and since such a law of actions is called moral, it follows that wisdom for man will be nothing else but the inner principle of *willing* to obey moral laws, of whatever kind the *object* of this willing may be; but that object will on every occasion be *super-sensible*, because a will determined by an empirical object can certainly be the basis for a technico-practical obedience to a rule, but not for a *duty* (which is a nonphysical relationship).

* "Henceforth forever wars shall cease
 By acting as the sage avers;
 And then will all men live in peace
 Except for the philosophers."   A. Kästner[5]

456

On the Super-sensible Objects of Our Knowledge

They are *God*, *Freedom*, and *Immortality*. 1. *God*, as the being to whom all duties are owed; 2. *Freedom*, as man's power to uphold the pursuit of his duties (as if they were divine commands) against all the might of nature; 3. *Immortality*, as a state in which man's weal or woe is to be allotted to him in proportion to his moral worth. We see that together they stand linked, as it were, like the three propositions of a *rational argument* to be worked out; and since, precisely because they are Ideas of the super-sensible, no objective reality can be attached to them in a theoretical respect, it will be possible, if such a reality has nevertheless to be imputed to them, to grant it to them only in a practical respect, as *postulates** of morally-practical reason.

So because its existence is contained in the categorical imperative, which admits of no doubt, the middle of these three Ideas, namely that of *freedom*, brings in the other two in its wake; in that as the supreme principle of *wisdom*, and thus presupposing also the ultimate purpose of the most perfect will (the highest blessedness in accordance with morality), 8: 419 it contains merely the conditions under which alone this purpose can be fulfilled. For the being who is alone able to carry out this proportionate distribution is God; and the state in which this consummation can alone be assigned to rational creatures, in full accordance with that purpose, is the assumption of a continuance of life already founded in their nature, i.e., *immortality*. For if the continuance of life were not so founded, it would signify merely the *hope* of a future life, and not one necessarily to be presupposed by reason (in consequence of the moral imperative).

Result

It is thus a mere misunderstanding, or a confusion of the morally-practical principles of ethics with those of theory – of which only the former can provide *knowledge* as to the super-sensible – if a quarrel is still raised about what philosophy affirms, as a doctrine of wisdom; and from this, since nothing else of any consequence will or can be objected to it, we may with good reason

> predict the imminent conclusion of a treaty of perpetual peace in philosophy.

---

* A *postulate* is a practical imperative, given *a priori*, which admits of no explanation of its possibility (and hence of no proof). Thus we postulate, not things, or in general the *existence* of any object, but only a maxim (or rule) of the action of a subject. Now if it is a duty to work toward a certain purpose (the highest good), I must also be entitled to assume that the conditions are present under which alone this performance of duty is possible, notwithstanding that they are super-sensible, and that we are incapable of obtaining any knowledge of them (in a theoretical respect).

Section Two
Dubious Outlook for Imminent Perpetual
Peace in Philosophy

To find respite, in a yet-not-inactive leisure, from the duty of administering the law at the behest of authority, Herr Schlosser, a man of great literary talent and (as we have reason to believe) a mind attuned to promotion of the good, has made an unexpected sally on to the battlefield of *metaphysics*, where there is far more traffic in bitterness than in the arena he had just left. The critical philosophy, which he believes himself to know, though he has only looked at the final results proceeding from it, and which – since he had not progressed with careful diligence through the steps that lead thither – he was necessarily bound to misunderstand, filled him with disgust; and so, without having first gone to school himself, he forthwith became the teacher "of a young man who (he says) wanted to study the critical philosophy," in order to advise him against

8: 420   doing so.

His only concern is to thrust aside the critique of pure reason wherever possible. His counsel is like the assurance of those good friends who proposed to the sheep that, if only the latter would get rid of the dogs, they might all live like brothers in continual peace. The pupil is a plaything in the hands of the master if he listens to this advice: "to fortify his taste (as the latter says) with the authors of antiquity (in the art of persuasion, on subjective grounds of approval, rather than the method of securing conviction on objective grounds)." He is then sure that the pupil will embrace *semblance of truth* (*verisimilitudo*) for *likelihood of truth* (*probabilitas*), and probability for certainty, in judgments that can absolutely proceed only *a priori* from reason. "The raw *barbaric* language of the critical philosophy" will then have no appeal to him; though in actual fact an *aestheticist* idiom, imported into elementary philosophy, must itself be regarded as barbaric there. He laments that "all intimations, vistas of the super-sensible, every genius of the poetic are to have their wings clipped" (if philosophy has anything to do with it)!

Philosophy, in that part (the theoretical) which contains the *theory of knowledge*, and which though largely directed to limiting pretensions in theoretical knowledge, can on no account be neglected, sees itself equally obliged, in its practical part, to revert to a *metaphysic* (of morals), as a set of merely *formal* principles of the concept of freedom, before there is yet any question of the purpose of actions (the matter of willing). Our anticritical philosopher skips this stage, or rather mistakes it so completely that he quite misunderstands the principle which may serve as the touchstone of all *legitimacy*: *Act on a maxim of which you can simultaneously will that it become a universal law*, and gives it a meaning which limits

458

it to empirical conditions, thereby making it unfit to be a canon of pure morally-practical reason (though such a canon there must be); whereby he projects himself into a field quite different from that to which this canon directs him, and draws venturesome conclusions from this.

It is obvious, however, that we are not talking here of a principle of *means* to be used for a certain *purpose* (for in that case it would be a prag- 8: 421 matic, not a moral principle); that it is not when the maxim of my willing, made into a universal law, is in contradiction to *someone else's* maxim of willing, that this is an infallible indication of the moral impossibility of the action, but rather when it contradicts *itself* (a thing I can judge by the principle of contradiction from the mere concept, *a priori*, without any empirical reference, e.g., "whether common ownership or private property is to be adopted into my maxim"). Mere ignorance, and perhaps also a rather mischievous propensity for quibbling, may have been the source of this attack, which cannot, however, do any damage to the *Proclamation of Perpetual Peace in Philosophy*.

For a peace-treaty so constituted that, if only the parties understand one another, it is at once concluded (without capitulation), can also be declared settled, or at least near to settlement.

Even though philosophy be presented solely as a *doctrine of wisdom* (which is also its true meaning), it cannot be passed over, either, as a doctrine of *knowledge*, insofar as this (theoretical) knowledge contains the elementary concepts employed by pure reason, albeit that it does so only to make the latter aware of its own limitations. Now it can hardly be a question, of philosophy in its first meaning, whether there should be free and open *confession* of what and whence we actually know in fact of its objects (sensible and super-sensible), and what we merely presuppose in a practical respect (since the assumption of such objects is required for the final purpose of reason).

It may be that not everything is *true* which a man takes to be so (for he may err); but in everything he says he must be *truthful* (he must not *deceive*), whether his profession be merely internal (before God), or also an external one. The violation of this duty of truthfulness is called a lie; whence there can be not only external lies, but also an internal one, so that both may occur united together, or also in contradiction to one another.

But a lie, whether internal or external, is of two kinds: 1. when someone gives out as *true*, what he nevertheless knows to be untrue; and 2. 8: 422 when he gives out as *certain*, what he nevertheless knows himself to be subjectively uncertain of.

The *lie* ("from the father of lies, whence all evil in the world hath come")[6] is the truly vile spot in human nature, however much the *tone of truthfulness* is at the same time the customary one, especially in what has to do with the super-sensible (after the example of many Chinese merchants, who write over their shops in golden letters: "No cheating here"). The commandment: *Thou shalt not lie* (were it even with the most pious intentions), if most sincerely adopted into philosophy, as a doctrine of wisdom, would alone be able, not only to procure eternal peace therein, but also to assure it for all time to come.

Editorial notes

1   For a discussion of some of the main changes that Kant made in the second
    edition of the *Critique*, see the General Introduction to their translation by
    Paul Guyer and Allen Wood, *Critique of Pure Reason*, in The Cambridge
    Edition of the Works of Immanuel Kant (Cambridge University Press, 1998),
    pp. 66–73.

2   Ak 10:269. For a challenge to the dating of this letter, see Gary Hatfield's
    introduction to his translation of the *Prolegomena*.

3   See, for example, the letters to Herz of June 7, 1771, and Feb. 21, 1772 (Ak
    10:123 and 129–33).

4   For a discussion of this and other issues related to the development of
    Kant's moral theory, see Allen Wood's General Introduction to *Practical Phi-
    losophy*, in The Cambridge Edition of the Works of Immanuel Kant, trans.
    and ed. Mary J. Gregor (Cambridge University Press, 1996), pp. xiii–xxxiii.

5   The other kind of intuition to which Kant here alludes is nonsensible
    or "intellectual intuition," which supposedly characterizes God's way of
    knowing.

6   Passages in the *Critique of Pure Reason* in which Kant identifies things
    considered as they are in themselves with these things as thought by a
    pure understanding (or its equivalent), that is, one not constrained by
    sensible conditions, include: A 28/B 44, A 35/B 51–52, A 206/B 251–52,
    A 249–50/B 307, A 252/B 310, A 259/B 315, A 264/B 320, A 279/B 335,
    A 284/B 340–41, A 500/B 528, and A 525/B 553. In the *Prolegomena* similar
    locutions are to be found at 4:286 and 354–5. For my views on this issue, see
    Allison, *Idealism and Freedom: Essays on Kant's Theoretical and Practical Philoso-
    phy* (Cambridge University Press, 1996), pp. 3–26.

7   The fact that Kant recognized a legitimate as well as an illegitimate ver-
    sion of rational psychology in the first *Critique* was noted by some of Kant's
    contemporaries. For reference to the relevant literature, see Gary Hatfield,
    "Empirical, Rational, and Transcendental Psychology: Psychology as Science
    and as Philosophy," in *The Cambridge Companion to Kant*, ed. Paul Guyer
    (Cambridge University Press, 1992), p. 227, note 18.

8   In this letter, Kant lists Herz himself and Tetens, together with Mendels-
    sohn, as the three on whom he had counted the most to explain his theory
    to the world (Ak 10:270). He makes a similar claim in a letter to Christian
    Garve of August 7, 1783, this time, however, listing Garve rather than Herz
    as one of those on whom he was relying (Ak 10:341).

9   As Guyer and Wood note in the General Introduction to their translation
    of the first *Critique*, there were two early and positive, but inconsequential,
    reviews (*Critique of Pure Reason*, p. 67). For a discussion of some of the early

reactions of which Kant may have been aware, see Hatfield's introduction to his translation of the *Prolegomena*.

10 For a discussion of this review, including an account of Feder's trans-formation of Garve's original version, see Frederick C. Beiser, *The Fate of Reason: German Philosophy from Kant to Fichte* (Cambridge, Mass.: Harvard University Press, 1987), pp. 172–77.

11 It is important to emphasize, however, that this is a clarification rather than a radical revision of this idealism from that which is to be found in the initial edition of the *Critique*. The latter is suggested by Beiser, who remarks that the redefinition of appearances as *of* things in themselves (rather than as being contrasted with such things) "is not even implied in the first edition of the *Kritik*" (*The Fate of Reason*, p. 175). For my own view of Kant's idealism, as contained in the first edition of the *Critique* and elsewhere, see *Kant's Transcendental Idealism* (New Haven: Yale University Press, 1983), and *Idealism and Freedom*, pp. 3–26.

12 In the first edition of the Transcendental Aesthetic, Kant does remark that the apodictic certainty of geometrical principles and the possibility of their *a priori* construction are grounded in the *a priori* necessity that was claimed to characterize space (A 24); and he similarly appeals to transcen-dental idealism to explain how apodeictic mathematical knowledge is pos-sible (A 38–41, 46–49). Nevertheless, a separate Transcendental Exposition was added only in the second edition in accordance with the reconfigura-tion of the transcendental problem effected in the *Prolegomena*. For further discussion of this point, see Hatfield's introduction to his translation of the *Prolegomena*.

13 For a discussion of the change in Kant's conception of his transcenden-tal project as enunciated in the *Prolegomena* and its connection with the revisions in the second edition of the *Critique* and Kant's understanding of transcendental philosophy in his later writings, see Tillman Pindar, "Kants Begriff der transzendental Erkenntnis," *Kant-Studien* 77 (1986), pp. 1–40.

14 Kant's understanding of Hume's views on mathematics is obviously based solely on the first *Enquiry*, where both arithmetic and geometry are characterized as concerned with the relation between ideas. Thus, he was ignorant of Hume's earlier discussion of geometry in the *Treatise*, where it is treated as essentially an empirical science, lacking in genuine demonstrative force. See the *Treatise*, Bk. I, part II, sect. IV.

15 See Hatfield's introduction to his translation of the *Prolegomena* for a discussion of Kant's blurring of the line between the analytic and synthetic methods in the second edition of the *Critique*. As previously noted, the new turn given to the critical philosophy by the *Prolegomena* has been emphasized by Tillman Pindar (see note 13).

16 See P. F. Strawson, *The Bounds of Sense, An Essay on Kant's Critique of Pure Reason* (London: Methuen & Co., 1966), p. 32.

17 See the *Jäsche Logic*, §40, Ak 9:114.

18 This compatibility is defended by Béatrice Longuenesse, *Kant and the Capacity to Judge* (Princeton: Princeton University Press, 1998), pp. 180–88.

19 Hume's famous renunciation of the *Treatise* in favor of the first *Enquiry* is contained in an advertisement that appeared in the posthumous 1777 edition

of the latter and is included in many modern editions. Admittedly, Kant's procedure in the *Prolegomena* is not strictly comparable to Hume's, since he never renounced the *Critique* as a whole. Nevertheless, given the importance attached to the Transcendental Deduction, there is a noteworthy similarity.

20 For further details on the relation between the *Metaphysical Foundations of Natural Science* and the projected but never delivered metaphysics of nature, see Hatfield's introduction to his translation of the *Prolegomena*, particularly note 14.

21 In the *Prolegomena* (§15), Kant cites two principles that supposedly belong to a "strictly universal" pure natural science: "that *substance remains* and persists" and "that *everything that happens* is always previously *determined by a cause* according to constant laws" (Ak 4:295). In affirming the strict universality of these principles, Kant is claiming that they apply to minds as well as to corporeal nature, which means that *a priori* knowledge is possible in the psychological domain. By adding the "u. s. w." ("and so on") to these two principles, which correspond to the First and Second Analogies in the *Critique*, Kant also implies that there are further propositions with this universality (presumably including the Third Analogy).

Unfortunately, he explains neither what he means here nor how the First (not to mention the Third) Analogy might apply to mental phenomena. Moreover, this does seem to be incompatible with the position that Kant adopts in the *Metaphysical Foundations*. For a discussion of some of the issues involved here, see Hatfield, "Empirical, Rational, and Transcendental Psychology," pp. 217–19.

22 Kant's negative assessment of the possibility of a genuinely scientific empirical psychology is discussed critically by Hatfield. See his "Empirical, Rational, and Transcendental Psychology," pp. 220–4.

23 See Friedman's introduction to his translation of the *Metaphysical Foundations* for a discussion of the relation of this theory of matter to Kant's precritical views.

24 On the latter point, see Friedman, *Kant and the Exact Sciences* (Cambridge, Mass.: Harvard University Press, 1992), pp. 44–7.

25 This ranking reflects the traditional contrast between ontology, or "first philosophy" for Aristotle, also characterized as "general metaphysics," and "special metaphysics," which includes the doctrines of God, freedom, and immortality. Although these are sharply distinguished in the *Critique*, Kant confuses matters in the *Metaphysical Foundations* by including both within general metaphysics, which is then contrasted with the special metaphysics of body.

26 For more on Ulrich and his work, see Hatfield's introduction to his translation of the *Prolegomena*.

27 I am here following the account of Frederick Beiser, *The Fate of Reason*, pp. 204–8.

28 See Reinhold's letter to Kant of October 12, 1787, Ak 10:500.

29 For my interpretation of the structure of the B Deduction in light of this "almost," see *Idealism and Freedom*, pp. 27–40, esp. pp. 35–37.

30 For a discussion of this see Eckart Förster, "Is There a Gap in Kant's Critical System?," *Journal of the History of Philosophy* 25 (1987), pp. 533–55;

"Kant's *Selbstsetzungslehre*," in *Kant's Transcendental Deductions*, ed. Eckart Förster (Stanford: Stanford University Press, 1989), pp. 217–38; and Friedman, *Kant and the Exact Sciences*, pp. 213–341.

31 For a discussion of this "reversal," which remains controversial, see Karl Ameriks, "Kant's Deduction of Freedom and Morality," *Journal of the History of Philosophy* 19 (1981), pp. 53–79, and *Kant's Theory of Mind*, (Oxford: Clarendon Press, 1982), pp. 189–233; and Allison, *Kant's Theory of Freedom* (Cambridge University Press, 1990), pp. 214–49.

32 These are two of the three famous questions in which Kant claims that all the interests of reason (speculative and practical) are united. The third, actually the first on Kant's list, is **"What can I know?"** (A 805 / B 833). Elsewhere he adds a fourth question, "What is man?," which he claims pertains to anthropology and encompasses the first three. (See *Jäsche Logic*, Ak 9:25.)

33 There is a special problem with freedom, which Kant characterizes in the second *Critique* as both a direct consequence of the moral law as the "fact of reason" and as a postulate of practical reason. The basic explanation is that these refer to two distinct conceptions of freedom. For a discussion of this issue, see the Introduction to *Progress*.

34 This connection with speculative reason stems from the fact that they are initially presented in the Transcendental Dialectic of the first *Critique* as modes of thinking the unconditioned for conditioned appearances. Strictly speaking, this pertains to the idea of the soul rather than to that of immortality. But since the goal traditionally underlying metaphysical speculation about the soul is to demonstrate its immortality, Kant tends to lump these ideas together.

35 See the *Critique of Practical Reason*, "On the Primacy of Practical Reason in Its Association with Speculative Reason" (Ak 5:119–21) and "How Is It Possible to Conceive of Extending Pure Reason in a Practical Respect without Thereby Extending Its Knowledge as Speculative?" (Ak 5:134–41).

36 Considered with respect to its logical function, Kant understands judgment as the faculty of subsuming under rules and argues that it must look elsewhere (namely to the understanding) for the rules under which it subsumes given particulars. In the *Critique of Pure Reason*, he does assign a transcendental function to judgment, but this consists in providing schemata for the pure concepts of the understanding (A 132/B 171 – A 136/B 175). Thus, from the standpoint of the first *Critique*, judgment may be said to lack autonomy, that is, an *a priori* principle unique to itself. This is changed in the third *Critique* with the introduction of the conception of a merely reflective judgment.

37 Eberhard, *Philosophisches Magazin* I: 289.

38 Schlosser and his associates were archconservatives and opponents of the French Revolution. For a discussion of the political context of the controversy, see Peter Fenves (ed. and transl.), *Raising the Tone of Philosophy: Late Essays by Immanuel Kant, Transformative Critique by Jacques Derrida* (Baltimore and London: Johns Hopkins University Press, 1993), pp. 79–80.

39 See also A 853–4 / B 881–2; and the *Jäsche Logic*, Ak 9:29–30.

40 Although Kant does not refer to the doctrine of recollection by name, this is clearly what he has in mind in his account of the Platonic teachings.

41   Admittedly, Kant does not express himself quite so explicitly in the present essay. But see the *Critique of Judgment*, Ak 5:362–3, where there is a parallel account in which Plato is likewise discussed.

42   Schlosser's response was a work with the revealing title, "Letter to a Young Man Who Wanted to Study the Critical Philosophy" (*Schreiben an einen jungen Mann, der die Kritische Philosophie studieren wollte*). Needless to say, his advice was not to bother. For more information, see Heath's introduction to his translation of *Proclamation*.

43   I am indebted for this point to Peter Fenves, who suggests it in a note to his translation of the essay. See *Raising the Tone of Philosophy*, p. 98, note 4.

Translator's introduction to the *Prolegomena*

1   The *Prolegomena* is cited by the pagination of the Akademie edition (Ak), Kant's *Gesammelte Schriften*, vol. 4, also shown in the margin of the translation. Citations to Kant's letters in Ak also appear in the text. The *Critique of Pure Reason* is cited by original pagination of the first and second editions, using A for the 1781 edition and B for the 1787 edition. All translations are my own.

2   Lewis White Beck propagated the view that Kant was saving mathematics and natural science from Humean skepticism, an endeavor that would be undercut by taking those sciences as given: see Beck, Editor's Introduction to *Prolegomena* (Indianapolis: Bobbs-Merrill, 1950), p. xiii. Norman Kemp Smith, *Commentary to Kant's "Critique of Pure Reason,"* 2d ed. (New York: Macmillan, 1929), pp. 44–9, 600–601, has Kant countering Hume's skepticism by starting from universally acknowledged facts about ordinary experience or self-consciousness, something the synthetic arguments of the *Critique* might do, but not the analytic method of the *Prolegomena*. See also Robert Paul Wolff, *Kant's Theory of Mental Activity* (Cambridge, Mass.: Harvard University Press, 1963), pp. 22–32, 44–56, and Beck, "Once More into the Breach: Kant's Answer to Hume, Again," *Ratio* 9 (1967), 33–7.

3   Manfred Kuehn, "Kant's Conception of Hume's Problem," *Journal of the History of Philosophy* 21 (1983), 175–194; Kuehn, "Kant's Transcendental Deduction: A Limited Defense of Hume," in *New Essays on Kant*, ed. Bernard den Ouden and Marcia Moen (New York: Peter Lang, 1987), pp. 47–72; Gary Hatfield, *The Natural and the Normative: Theories of Spatial Perception from Kant to Helmholtz* (Cambridge, Mass.: MIT Press/Bradford Books, 1990), pp. 59–60, 63–5; and Hatfield, "The Workings of the Intellect: Mind and Psychology," in *Logic and the Workings of the Mind: The Logic of Ideas and Faculty Psychology in Early Modern Philosophy*, ed. Patricia Easton (Atascadero, Calif.: Ridgeview Publishing Co., 1997), pp. 21–45.

4   Benno Erdmann dates the Preface to April (Ak 4:587); Hamann reports the bound copy to J. F. Kleuker, Hamann's *Briefwechsel*, ed. Arthur Henkel, 7 vols. (Wiesbaden: Insel, 1955–79), 4:312.

5   Late in 1765, Lambert and Kant exchanged letters about Kant's abortive intention, prematurely announced by his bookseller (J. J. Kanter), to publish a work on the method of metaphysics (Lambert to Kant, November 13,

1765; Kant to Lambert, December 31, 1765 [Ak 10:51, 55–6]). Kant was concerned with the method of metaphysics early; see his *New Elucidations* (1755) and subsequent works in Kant's *Theoretical Philosophy, 1755–1780*, trans. and ed. David Walford and Ralph Meerbote (Cambridge University Press, 1992). Work on the *Critique* began near the time of his February 21, 1772, letter to Marcus Herz (Ak 10:130), a former student who served as respondent to Kant's *Inaugural Dissertation* in 1770. Many of the letters from Ak cited herein are translated in Immanuel Kant, *Correspondence*, trans. and ed. Arnulf Zweig (Cambridge University Press, 1999).

6 Hamann to Hartknoch, April 8, 1781; to Johann Georg Herder, April 20, 1781 (Hamann, *Briefwechsel*, 4:278, 280, 285). See also Hamann to Herder, May 10, 1781 (*Briefwechsel*, 4:293–4). On Hamann's arrangements for the proofs, Hamann to Hartknoch, December 16, 1780, February 25 and April 8, 1781 (*Briefwechsel*, 4:249, 269, 278). Hamann wrote a sardonic review of the *Critique* dated July 1, 1781 (*Sämtliche Werke*, ed. Josef Nadler, 6 vols. [Vienna: Herder, 1949–57], 3:275–80), which he suppressed to spare Kant's feelings (Hamann to Herder, August 5; to Hartknoch, August 11, 1781, *Briefwechsel*, 4:317, 321). Hamann's opinions on the *Critique* fluctuated as he read; he liked the "transcendental theology" and by late summer was suspending judgment (to Hartknoch, May 7, August 11, November 23, 1781, *Briefwechsel*, 4:289, 321, 344).

7 Kant to Herz, May 1, 1781 (Ak 10:266–7); Kant to Herz, letter 166, fragment of a draft (see Ak 13:100), dated "after 11 May 1781" (Ak 10:269–70). The dating of letter 166 is too early. It apparently takes Kant's letter of May 11 to Carl Spener, Hartknoch's agent in Berlin, as the *terminus post quem*, since Kant tells Spener that Herz is arranging the presentation and dedicatory copies (Ak 10:268), and letter 166 presupposes that Herz has completed the task. On June 8, 1781, Kant wrote to Zedlitz's secretary, Johann Erich Biester, in Berlin, asking whether Herz had carried out his commission (Ak 10:273), which means that he had not yet received Herz's missing letter. On June 19 Hamann wrote to Hartknoch (*Briefwechsel*, 4:308) that eight days earlier (so, on June 11) Kant was still concerned with the dedicatory copy (to Zedlitz) and had written to Berlin about it (presumably the letter of June 8 to Biester). Since in letter 166 Kant responded to news from Herz about Mendelssohn's reaction to the work, before Kant could write that letter Herz would have needed time to have Spener order copies from the printer, F. A. Grunert in Halle, have them bound, deliver one to Mendelssohn, and learn that Mendelssohn had put it aside. The firm *terminus ante quem* for Herz's completed mission is September 14, 1781, when Hamann wrote Hartknoch that "the Kantian exemplars have been distributed" (*Briefwechsel*, 4:331). This statement would cover the dedicatory copy, though it most likely referred to the five copies sent to Königsberg (per Kant's request to Spener on May 11), one of which went to Hamann on July 22 and one to Johann Schultz on August 3 (Kant to Schultz, Ak 10:274). Presumably, Herz (in Berlin with Spener) received his copies before Kant did, and Kant knew Zedlitz had his copy before giving a bound copy to Hamann. In any event, Herz's letter had not arrived by June 8 (or 11, trusting Hamann), and more likely is from July, which puts Kant's draft

response near in time to his letter of August 18 to Hartknoch (discussed below).

8 Kant's prediction was accurate for a time. On December 31, 1781, Herder reported that "Danov in Jena had said in lecture that the book takes a year to read" – but Herder thought in his case it might take two or three (in Hamann's *Briefwechsel*, 4:361). Mendelssohn never warmed to the *Critique*, and on January 5, 1784, he wrote to Elise Reimarus confessing that he did not understand it and professing pleasure that her brother believed he was not "missing much" (*Gesammelte Schriften* [Stuttgart: Frommann, 1971–], 3:169). Johann Schultz, whose exposition Kant later extolled (Ak 12:367), wrote in the preface of his *Erläuterungen über des Herrn Professor Kant, Critik der reinen Vernunft* (Königsberg: Dingle, 1784) that nearly everyone complained about the work's "insuperable obscurity and unintelligibility," and added that "for the greater part of the learned public, it is as if it consisted solely of hieroglyphs" (pp. 5, 7); the 1791 edition of Schultz's work has been translated by James C. Morrison, *Exposition of Kant's Critique of Pure Reason* (Ottawa: University of Ottawa Press, 1995).

9 Kant to Herz, draft written after June 8, 1781, Ak 10:269. While working on the first *Critique*, Kant had mused on the requirements for popularity in philosophy (Kant to Herz, January, 1779, Ak 10:247). In the Jäsche *Logic* (first published in 1800), Kant suggested that the analytic method is appropriate for "the aim of popularity" (§117, Ak 9:154); earlier (§115, Ak 9:148), he had distinguished the "popular method" (which starts from the "customary" and "interesting" and "aims at entertainment") from popularity in exposition (to which his remark on analytic method referred).

10 Hamann to Herder, August 12, 1781; to Hartknoch, August 11, September 14, October 23, November 23, December 9, 1781 (*Briefwechsel*, 4:319, 323, 331–3, 344, 350).

11 Hamann to Hartknoch, January 11, February 8, 1782; to J. G. and Caroline Herder, April 22, 1782 (*Briefwechsel*, 4:364, 366, 376). The Göttingen review, written by Christian Garve and heavily edited by J. G. H. Feder, is reprinted in Vorländer (ed.), *Prolegomena* and in Albert Landau (ed.), *Rezensionen zur Kantischen Philosophie, 1781–87* (Bebra: Landau, 1991), pp. 10–17. It and Garve's unedited review (*Allgemeine deutsche Bibliothek*, 1783) are translated in Morrison's edition of Schultz's *Exposition*.

12 Hamann to Herder, August 25, 1782, mentions a fair copy and suggests that the title might have changed (see also Hamann to J. F. Reichardt, 27 August); Hamann to Hartknoch, September 16, 1782, reports that Kant was pleased with the Gotha review and asks for the "true title" and whether the work will appear by Michaelmas (September 29; the book fair would follow that date); Hamann to Hartknoch, October 8, November 5, and December 8 say that he "painfully" or "impatiently" awaits Kant's "prolegomena"; Hamann to Hartknoch, January 31, 1983, reports that Hamann and Kant both await the work; March 3, that Kant has received his copy; April 18, that Hamann knows of Kant's challenge to the Göttingen reviewer in the Appendix (*Briefwechsel*, 4:418, 424, 425–6, 428, 443, 465; 5:14, 33, 36). On April 15, 1783, Friedrich Plessing mentions to Kant that "Haman" told

him the *Prolegomena* had appeared (Ak 10:310–11). On the tardy printing, see Hartknoch to Kant, October 8, 1785 (Ak 10:411).

13 Earlier, in 1773, Kant had expressed his intention to Herz to "go on to metaphysics" when he had finished his critique of pure reason. He said that metaphysics "has only two parts: the metaphysics of nature and the metaphysics of morals," and that he planned to publish the latter work first (Ak 10:145). In 1781 the *Gothaische gelehrte Zeitungen* 59 (July 25, 1781), p. 488, presumably responding to the A Preface, announced that "the public can soon expect a *Metaphysics of Nature* from our excellent Prof. *Cant.*"

14 Christian Gottfried Schütz to Kant, July 10, 1784, eagerly asks after the "Metaphysics of Nature" (Ak 10:393); Kant to Schütz, September 13, 1785, explains that in order to provide concrete examples before offering the "pure science" of the metaphysics of nature he wrote the *Metaphysical Foundations*, which would now appear after Easter because his right hand was injured (Ak 10:406). On April 7, 1786, Kant reported to Johann Bering that it would be another two years before his "Metaphysics" appeared (Ak 10:441).

15 Christian Gottfried Schütz, *Allgemeine Literatur-Zeitung* (1785), 3:42.

16 Benno Erdmann (ed.), Kant's *Prolegomena* (Leipzig: Voss, 1878), Introduction, pp. ix–xx; Erdmann, *Historische Untersuchungen über Kants Prolegomena* (Halle: Niemeyer, 1904), chaps. 3–4. Erdmann (*Historische Untersuchungen*, p. 29) dated the original plan from May, using the erroneous dating of Kant's draft letter to Herz (Ak letter 166, discussed above).

17 Erdmann, 1878 Introduction, pp. xvii–xix, xcviii; *Historische Untersuchungen*, chaps. 5, 7.

18 Erdmann believed that the following portions of the *Prolegomena* were "additions" to the original draft: the entire Preface (4:255–64); in the Preamble, all of §3 (4:270), and a single full paragraph from §2, which appeared in §4 in the original edition and in Ak (4:272–3); in the General Questions, the penultimate paragraph of §4 (4:274–5), the second paragraph of §5 up to "Expressed with," the footnote to the third paragraph (4:276), and the fifth and sixth paragraphs (4:277–8); in the First Part, Notes I–III (4:287–94); in the Second Part, the footnote to §22 (4:305), §§27–31 on "Hume's doubt" (4:310–15), the note to §34 (4:316), and all of §39 (4:322–6); in the Third Part, the note to §48 (4:335–6), two sentences from §49, from "In this way" to "Cartesian idealism" (4:337), the note to §52b (4:341), and the Conclusion (4:350–65); and all of the Solution and the Appendix (4:365–83).

19 From late April through October, 1781, Hamann frequently expressed his opinions that Kant was indebted to Hume (to Herder, April 27/29, *Briefwechsel*, pp. 282, 285), that he might be called a "Prussian Hume" (to Herder, May 10; to Hartknoch, May 31; to Herder, June 3; to Hartknoch, October 23; *Briefwechsel*, pp. 293–4, 298, 305, 343), and that the two authors' views complement one another and should be studied together (to Kleuker, July 22; to Hartknoch, August 11; *Briefwechsel*, pp. 312, 322).

20 Erdmann, 1878 Introduction, pp. cvi–cviii.

21 Arnoldt, "Kants Prolegomena nicht doppelt redigiert" (originally published 1879), in his *Gesammelte Schriften*, ed. Otto Schörffer (Berlin: Bruno Cassirer, 1906–11), 3:1–101.

22 Vaihinger, "Die Erdmann–Arnoldtsche Kontroverse über Kants Prolegomena," *Philosophische Monatshefte* 16 (1880), 44–71.

23 Of course, Kant did not rest content with the *Prolegomena* versions, but rewrote the Deduction and the Paralogisms for the B *Critique*.

24 In the margin to a draft of his Appendix to the *Prolegomena*, Kant wrote: "My work has large faults, not however with respect to the content but solely in the presentation, and indeed faults some of which one would easily excuse for anyone at the beginning of a difficult investigation," and some of which are peculiar to him, concerning which he writes: "I perhaps indeed have the talent to determine my concepts precisely, but not to give ease to my presentation. Only others can do that." (Ak 23:60; Vorländer, p. 166)

25 Hermann Andreas Pistorius, review of *Prolegomena*, in *Allgemeine deutsche Bibliothek* 59 (1784), 322–56, on p. 322; reprinted, showing original pagination, in Landau (ed.), *Rezensionen*. For additional material on Kant's conclusion that the critique of reason could not achieve popularity, see Erdmann, *Historische Untersuchungen*, chap. 3.

26 The distinction between analytic and synthetic methods, sometimes described as the methods of regression (or resolution) and composition, is ancient. Pappus of Alexandria surveyed the distinction in mathematics, *Book 7 of the Collection*, ed. A. Jones (New York: Springer, 1986), pp. 82–4; see Jaako Hintikka and Unto Remes, *The Method of Analysis: Its Geometrical Origin and Its General Significance* (Dordrecht: Reidel, 1974). Aristotle's medieval followers described his method as that of resolution and composition: see John Losee, *A Historical Introduction to the Philosophy of Science*, 3d ed. (Oxford: Oxford University Press, 1993). This methodological distinction was widely discussed from the Renaissance onward; see John H. Randall, *The School of Padua and the Emergence of Modern Science* (Padua: Antenore, 1961). In mathematics the method of analysis was known as a method of discovery. If one wanted to prove something, one first proceeded as if it were already known, and worked backwards to discover the grounds of proof; one could then proceed synthetically from grounds to consequent. Within natural science, analysis (or resolution) was sometimes described as a method of discovery, sometimes as a method of explanation or exposition, and sometimes as a laboratory procedure. Descartes applied the distinction between analysis and synthesis to metaphysics in the Objections and Replies to the *Meditations*, treating analysis as a method of discovery and exposition and synthesis as the method of strict proof (*Philosophical Writings*, trans. John Cottingham, Robert Stoothoff, and Dugald Murdoch, 2 vols. [Cambridge University Press, 1984–85], 2:110–13). Antoine Arnauld and Pierre Nicole contrasted the methods in their *Logic or the Art of Thinking*, trans. Jill Vance Buroker (Cambridge University Press, 1996), pt. 4, chaps. 2–3. See also Ephraim Chambers, *Cyclopedia, or, An Universal Dictionary of Arts and Sciences*, 2 vols. (London: Knapton, 1728), "Method," 2:544–5.

27 Peter Gray Lucas (ed.), *Prolegomena* (Manchester: Manchester University Press, 1953), "Aids to Study," claims that Kant abandoned the analytic method in the Third Part because he was "not examining actually existing sciences, but criticising an existing pseudo-science, metaphysics" (p. xvi). Lucas overlooks Kant's suggestion that "Metaphysics is subjectively

actual (and necessarily so)," which permits us to ask "How is it (objectively) possible?" (4:327, note). Presumably the objective possibility pertains to the subjectively actual urge toward metaphysics, induced by the ideas of pure reason. The analytic solution of the Third Part extends the opening sentence of the A Preface: "Human reason has the peculiar fate in one genus of its cognition: that it is troubled by questions that it cannot refuse; for these questions are put to it by the nature of reason itself, which cannot answer them, for they surpass all power of human reason" (A vii).

28 Max Apel, *Kommentar zu Kants Prolegomena: Eine Einführung in die Kritische Philosophie*, 2d ed. (Leipzig: Felix Meiner, 1923); Erdmann, *Historische Untersuchungen*; Smith, *Commentary to Kant's "Critique of Pure Reason"*; Wolff, *Kant's Theory of Mental Activity*, chap. 3; and Beatrice Longuenesse, *Kant and the Capacity to Judge: Sensibility and Discursivity in the Transcendental Analytic of the Critique of Pure Reason*, trans. Charles T. Wolfe (Princeton: Princeton University Press, 1998), chap. 7.

29 Erdmann, *Historische Untersuchungen*, p. 4, claimed the A *Critique* contained no prototype for the assumed actuality of geometrical and natural scientific cognition. Although Kant does not in A explicitly ask how the actual synthetic *a priori* cognition we have is possible, he does argue from the certainty of geometry to the *a priori* necessity and hence ideality of space, as cited above. The *Prolegomena* asserts that mathematics and natural science had no need of a deduction for their own sakes (4:327).

30 See Longuenesse, *Kant and the Capacity to Judge*, chap. 7.

31 On Kant's knowledge of Hume, see Manfred Kuehn, "Kant's Conception of Hume's Problem," *Journal of the History of Philosophy* 21 (1983), 175–93.

32 Hamann (*Sämtliche Werke*, 4:364–7) translates David Hume, *Treatise of Human Nature* (London: Noon, 1739–40), Bk. 1, pt. 4, sec. 7, pp. 263–9 (about half of sec. 7). James Beattie, *Versuch über die Natur und Unveränderlichkeit der Wahrheit; im Gegensatze der Klügeley und der Zweifelsucht* (Copenhagen and Leipzig: Heineck und Faber, 1772), on which see Robert Paul Wolff, "Kant's Debt to Hume via Beattie," *Journal of the History of Ideas* 21 (1960), 117–23 (Wolff was unaware of Hamann's 1771 translation).

33 Hamann's abbreviated translation, produced between July 21 and August 7, 1780, filled eighteen folios with ninety-six handwritten pages. Kant had seen it by September 13 (Hamann to Hartknoch, *Briefwechsel*, 4:223). Hamann held up publication due to rumors of another version (Hamann to Herder, October 25, 1780, *Briefwechsel*, 4:229). On December 16 he told Hartknoch that Kant had requested and read the work a second time (*Briefwechsel*, 4:249). Hamann's translation was first published in the twentieth century (*Sämtliche Werke*, 3:245–74). Hamann's son sold the fair copy after his father's death in 1788, and it is lost; the printed version relies on a draft (Josef Nadler, *Die Hamannausgabe* [Halle: Niemeyer, 1930], pp. 55, 80). Erdmann (*Historische Untersuchungen*, p. 114) was aware that Hamann had translated Hume and shown it to Kant, but neither the translation nor evidence of Kant's second reading were available to him in print.

34 David Hume, *Dialogues Concerning Natural Religion* (London, 1779); *Gespräche über die natürliche Religion*, trans. Karl Gottfried Schreiter, annotated by Ernst Platner (Leipzig: Weygand, 1781). Hamann reported Kant's

acquisition to Herder, December 17, 1781 (*Briefwechsel*, 4:359). Kant owned a copy at his death, Arthur Warda, *Immanuel Kants Bücher* (Berlin: Breslauer, 1922), p. 50.

35 Elsewhere in A, Kant took a more reserved attitude toward skepticism. Opposing skepticism to the skeptical method that he used in the Antinomies, he described the former as "a principle of artful and scientific ignorance that undermines the foundations of all cognition in order, where possible, to leave no reliability or certainty of cognition overall" (A 424/B 451); it would seem that he considered Hume to be a fellow practitioner of the skeptical method (A 856/B 884). In the A Preface he compared skeptics to nomads who periodically disrupt the reign of dogmatic metaphysics (A ix), though the context suggests he had ancient (or at least pre-Lockean) skeptics in mind.

36 Schultz, *Erlauterungen*, p. 6. In a review of Schultz's work, Karl Adolph Cäsar, *Denkwürdigkeiten aus der philosophischen Welt* (1785), pp. 242–7 (reprinted in Landau [ed.], *Rezensionen*) suggested that it would be useful only for those already familiar with the *Critique* itself (p. 247).

37 Lossius, review of *Prolegomena*, in the *Uebersicht der neuesten Philosophischen Litteratur* (1784), 1:51–70, quotation from p. 66; reprinted in Landau (ed.), *Rezensionen*.

38 Pistorius, review of *Prolegomena*, p. 323.

39 Pistorius, review of *Prolegomena*, pp. 326–7, 331, 335, 340–1.

40 J. A. H. Ulrich, *Institutiones logicae et metaphysicae* (Jena: Cröker, 1785), pp. iv–vi.

41 Ulrich, *Institutiones*, §§4–6, 9–10, 12, 16–17, 106, 119, 176–8 (pp. 5–7, 8–9, 10, 12–14, 107–8, 126–8, 182–7).

42 On causation, Ulrich, *Institutiones*, §§309–12 (pp. 322–33); on substance, §§322–25 (pp. 351–5).

43 Tiedemann, "Ueber die Natur der Metaphysik; zur Prüfung von Hrn Professor Kants Grundsätzen," *Hessische Beiträge zur Gelehrsamkeit und Kunst* 1 (1785), 113–130, 233–48, 464–74.

44 Schultz's 1784 book drew on the *Prolegomena*, as in his summary of Note I (*Erläuterungen*, pp. 24–5). Ulrich, *Institutiones*, cited it in metaphysics (§§114, 275, pp. 120–1, 284). Carl Christian Erhard Schmid, *Critik der reinen Vernunft im Grundrisse zu Vorlesungen: nebst einem Wörterbuche zum leichtern Gebrauch der Kantischen Schriften* (Jena: Cröker, 1786) cited the *Prolegomena* in §§9 14, 36, 40, etc. (pp. 4, 7, 15, 18, etc.), and frequently in the appended dictionary (the *Grundrisse* and *Wörterbuch* were subsequently issued separately, each reaching a third edition by 1794–95). Samuel Heinicke, *Wörterbuch zur Kritik der reinen Vernunft* (Presburg: Mahler, 1788), used the *Prolegomena*. Joseph Weber, *Versuch, die harten Urtheile über die kantische Philosophie zu mildern* (Wirzburg: n. p., 1793), says the *Prolegomena* drew attention to Kant's philosophy (p. 78).

45 Hans Vaihinger, "Eine Blattversetzung in Kants *Prolegomena*," *Philosophische Monatshefte* 15 (1879), 321–32, 513–32; Sitzler, "Zur Blattversetzung in Kants Prolegomena," *Kant-Studien* 9 (1904), 538–9, followed by Vaihinger, "Nachwort," 539–44. The order of B 14–22 supports the Vaihinger-Sitzler thesis, although 4:272–3 is found with material summarizing §§4–5, rather than material corresponding to §2.

46 These dictionaries have been useful in translating Kant's archaic German: Joachim Heinrich Campe, *Wörterbuch der deutschen Sprache*, 6 vols. (Braunschweig, 1807–13; reprint, Hildesheim: Olms, 1969–70); Nathan Bailey, *Englisch-deutsches und deutsches-englisches Wörterbuch*, 2 vols. (Leipzig and Jena: Frommann, 1810); and U. U. W. Meissner, *Vollständiges englischdeutsches und deutsches-englisches Wörterbuch*, 2 vols. (Leipzig: Liebeskind, 1847).

Prolegomena to any future metaphysics that will be able to come forward as science

1 In the first half of the A Preface (A vii–xiv), metaphysics was portrayed as the scene of endless controversy, the question of the possibility of metaphysics was raised, and the general interest of human reason in the questions of metaphysics was acknowledged.

2 John Locke (1632–1704), *An Essay Concerning Human Understanding* (London: printed by Eliz. Holt, for Thomas Bassett, 1690). When Kant wrote the *Prolegomena*, Locke's *Essay* was available in Latin, French, and German translations: *De intellectu humano*, trans. Ezekiel Burridge (London: Churchill, 1701), *De intellectu humano*, 2 vols., trans. Gotthelf Heinrich Thiele (Leipzig: George, 1742); *Essai philosophique concernant l'entendement humain*, trans. Pierre Coste (Amsterdam: Schelte, 1700); *Versuch vom menschlichen Verstande*, trans. Heinrich Engelhard Poley (Altenburg: Richter, 1757).

3 Gottfried Wilhelm Leibniz (1646–1716), *Nouveaux essais sur l'entendement humain*, which first appeared in (and nearly filled) *Oeuvres philosophiques latines & francoises de feu Mr. de Leibnitz: Tirées de ses manuscrits qui se conservent dans la bibliotheque royale à Hanovre*, ed. Rudolf Erich Raspe (Amsterdam and Leipzig: Jean Schreuder, 1765). Kant surely consulted the French version soon after its appearance. A German translation was published as he was writing the first *Critique*, *Neue Versuche über den menschlichen Verstand*, in Leibniz, *Philosophische Werke nach Raspens Sammlung*, 2 vols., ed. and trans. Johann Heinrich Friderich Ulrich (Halle: Johann Christian Hendel, 1778–80).

4 David Hume (1711–1776), *A Treatise of Human Nature: Being an Attempt to Introduce the Experimental Method of Reasoning into Moral Subjects*, 3 vols. (London: Printed for John Noon, 1739–40), not fully translated into German until 1790–91, by Ludwig Heinrich Jakob; *Philosophical Essays Concerning Human Understanding* (London: Printed for A. Millar, 1748), retitled in the 1760 edition as *An Enquiry Concerning Human Understanding*; translated into German as *Philosophische Versuche über die menschliche Erkenntniss von David Hume; Als dessen vermischter Schriften zweyter Theil*, ed. Johann Georg Sulzer (Hamburg and Leipzig: G. C. Grund and A. H. Holle, 1755). Four volumes of Hume's *Vermischter Schriften* were published, 1754–56, and Kant owned them all (Warda X. 56, p. 50). When Kant wrote the *Prolegomena* he would not have been directly acquainted with the whole of Hume's *Treatise* itself, though he presumably had seen German translations of portions of it (see the Translator's Introduction).

5 Kant added a similar description of Hume's account of the origin of our causal concept to the B Introduction (B 5).

6 Kant here cites David Hume, *Moralische und politische Versuche, als dessen vermischter Schriften, vierter und letzter Theil* (Hamburg and Leipzig: G. C. Grund und A. H. Holle, 1756). His quotation of Hume contains an ellipsis (of the German translation) that somewhat distorts Hume's statement, which in the original English reads in full: "Monarchies, receiving their chief Stability from a superstitious Reverence to Priests and Princes, have abridged the Liberty of Reasoning, with Regard to Religion and Politics, and consequently Metaphysics and Morals. All these form the most considerable Branches of Science. Mathematics and natural Philosophy, which are the only ones that remain, are not half so valuable" (Essay 5, "Of the Rise and Progress of the Arts and Sciences," in *Essays, Moral and Political*, 2 vols. [Edinburgh: Kincaid, 1741–2], vol. 2, p. 79).

7 Thomas Reid (1710–1796), *An Inquiry into the Human Mind, on the Principles of Common Sense* (Dublin: A. Ewing, and Edinburgh: printed for A. Millar, London, and A. Kincaid & J. Bell, 1764); *Recherches sur l'entendement humain d'après des principes du sens commun*, 2 vols. (Amsterdam: Jean Meyer, 1768); *Untersuchung über den menschlichen Verstand, nach den Grundsätzen des gemeinen Menschenverstandes* (Leipzig: 1782). James Oswald (d. 1793), *An Appeal to Common Sense in Behalf of Religion* (Edinburgh: A. Kincaid and J. Bell, 1766); *Appelation an den gemeinen Menschenverstand zum Vortheil der Religion*, 2 vols., trans. F. E. Wilmsen (Leipzig: 1774). James Beattie (1735–1803), *An Essay on the Nature and Immutability of Truth, in Opposition to Sophistry and Scepticism* (Edinburgh: printed for A. Kincaid & J. Bell, et al., 1770); *Versuch über die Natur und Unveränderlichkeit der Wahrheit; im Gegensatz der Klügeley und Zweifelsucht* (Copenhagen and Leipzig: Heineck and Faber, 1772). Joseph Priestley (1733–1804), *An Examination of Dr. Reid's Inquiry into the Human Mind, on the Principles of Common Sense, Dr. Beattie's Essay on the Nature and Immutability of Truth, and Dr. Oswald's Appeal to Common Sense in Behalf of Religion* (London: printed for J. Johnson, 1774); not translated, but reviewed in the *Göttingische Anzeigen* (1775, no. 92, 17 August), 777–83. On Kant's knowledge of the first three Scottish philosophers, see Manfred Kuehn, *Scottish Common Sense in Germany, 1768–1800: A Contribution to the History of Critical Philosophy* (Kingston and Montreal: McGill–Queen's University Press, 1987), chap. 9.

8 The word translated as "plain" is *schlichten*; the variant form *schlechten Menschenverstande* (with the sense of "plain") occurred in a review of the 1774 translation of Oswald's *Appeal* by Hermann Andreas Pistorius, *Allgemeine deutsche Bibliothek* 28 (1776), pp. 157–9, on p. 157.

9 Compare Hume's essay, "The Natural History of Religion," in his *Four Dissertations* (London, 1757): "Since, therefore, the mind of man appears of so loose and unsteady a contexture, that, even at present, when so many persons find an interest in continually employing on it the chissel and the hammer, yet are they not able to engrave theological tenets with any lasting impression" (p. 84). This work did not appear in German during Kant's lifetime, but there was a French translation, *Histoire naturelle de la religion, avec un examen critique et philosophique de cet ouvrage*, trans. Johann Bernhard Merian

(Amsterdam: J. H. Schneider, 1759), in which the corresponding passage appears on p. 97.

10 In the introduction to the 1755 translation of Hume's first *Enquiry*, Sulzer expressed hope that this work would have such an effect on German philosophers: "Ich Hoffe, dass die Bekanntmachung dieses Werks sie aus ihrer müssigen Ruhe ein wenig aufwecken, und ihnen eine neue Thätigkeit geben werde" (p. [vi]).

11 The parallel between this passage and Hume's reference, in the *Treatise*, Bk. 1, pt. 4, sec. 7, to being shipwrecked and wanting to stay on his rock rather than venture again to sea, led to conjectures that Kant had read Hume's *Treatise* in English, despite evidence that he could not read English. But the passage in question was available to Kant in Hamann's 1771 translation of about half of sec. 7; see the Translator's Introduction and Kuehn, "Kant's Conception of Hume's Problem."

12 Moses Mendelssohn (1729–1786) was an acclaimed and prolific writer. His *Abhandlung über die Evidenz in metaphysischen Wissenschaften* (Berlin: Haude and Spener, 1764) won the prize competition set by the Royal Academy of Sciences in Berlin for 1763; Kant took second place with his *Inquiry Concerning the Distinctness of the Principles of Natural Theology and Morality*, which was published along with Mendelssohn's essay. Sulzer praised Hume's style of presentation and commended it to German philosophers in his 1755 introduction (pp. [vi–xxi]).

13 The terms "analytic" and "synthetic" as used here should not be confused with Kant's later distinction between analytic and synthetic propositions or judgments (in the Preamble). On the analytic and synthetic methods, see Kant's note in §5 and the Translator's Introduction.

14 The page reference is to the A edition (reprinted as B 740 and following), the Transcendental Doctrine of Method, chap. 1, sec. 1, in which Kant drew a distinction between philosophical cognition as "cognition through reason from concepts" and mathematical cognition as "cognition through reason from the construction of concepts" in intuition.

15 The material in §1 corresponds to the first paragraphs of the A and B Introductions (A 1–2, B 1–3, which themselves differ).

16 §2a closely follows a paragraph from the A Introduction (A 6–7/B 10–11).

17 §2b summarizes part of the Analytic of Principles (A 150–53/B 189–93), though the example of *a priori* cognition through the empirical concept of gold is new.

18 Johann Andreas Segner (1704–1777), *Anfangsgründe der Arithmetic, Geometrie und der Geometrischen Berechnungen: Aus dem Lateinischen übersetzt*, 2nd ed. (Halle: Renger, 1773). Kant had referred to the example of five points in the A *Critique* without naming Segner (A 140/B 179). He then introduced this sentence (and much of §2c2) verbatim into the B Introduction (B 15).

19 The reference is again to the Transcendental Doctrine of Method, chap. 1, sec. 1 (A 713/B 741).

20 The material from 4:268 to this point was introduced into B 14–18, with an addition as noted below. §2c to this point summarizes briefly points found in the Analytic of Principles (A 154/B 193, A 159–60/B 198–9, A

164–4/B 204–5). Further, §2c1 summarizs A 7–8/B 11–12, §2c2 draws from A 47–8/B 64–5, and §2c3 takes up a hint from A 10.

21 In fact, in the *Treatise* Hume had raised objections to the notions of equality and congruence (among others) in geometry, which objections appealed to experience (*Treatise*, Bk. 1, pt. 2, sec. 4, pp. 42–53), thereby subjecting mathematics to experience, and he also rejected the conception that mathematics considers its objects independently of their existence in nature; but presumably Kant was unaware of that fact. In the *Enquiry* Hume said that the objects of "Geometry, Algebra, and Arithmetic" are known through relations of ideas (translated in Sulzer as *Beziehungen der Begriffe*, 2:64), that is, through propositions that "are discoverable by the mere operation of thought, without dependence on what is any where existent in the universe" (sec. 4, pt. 1).

22 The preceding paragraph was introduced at B 19–20, whereas the material before and after it covers B 14–18. Within those pages, a paragraph on natural science (B 17–18) occurs prior to the discussion of metaphysics, with the heading: "Natural science (*physica*) contains within itself synthetic judgments *a priori*"; as examples of such judgments, it gives the conservation of the quantity of matter in the world, and the equality of action and reaction.

23 Compare Friedrich Christian Baumeister (1709–1785), *Philosophia definitiva, hoc est, definitiones philosophicae ex systemate lib. bar. a Wolf in unum collectae*, new ed. (Vienna: Trattner, 1775; first published in Wittenberg, 1733).

24 Christian Wolff (1679–1754) was the most influential German philosopher of the mid eighteenth century, publishing many works in philosophy, mathematics, and the sciences. Kant knew many of these works and taught from Wolff's mathematics textbooks (Ak 2:35). It is not clear that Wolff actually intended to ground the principle of sufficent reason on the principle of contradiction; see his *Vernünfftige Gedancken von Gott, der Welt, und der Seele des Menschen*, new ed. (Halle: Renger, 1751; originally published 1719), §§30–32, and *Philosophia prima, sive ontologia*, new ed. (Frankfurt am Main and Leipzig: Renger, 1736), pt. 1, sec. 1, chap. 2. Alexander Gottlieb Baumgarten (1714–1762) was an important follower of Wolff. Kant used his *Metaphysica*, 4th ed. (Halle: Hemmerde, 1757), as the textbook for his own lectures on metaphysics, which are available in Kant, *Lectures on Metaphysics*, trans. and ed. Karl Ameriks and Steve Naragon (Cambridge: Cambridge University Press, 1997). Baumgarten did seek to derive sufficient reason from contradiction, *Metaphysica*, §§7, 10, 20–2 (Ak 17:24, 31).

25 Locke, *Essay*, Bk. III, chap. iii, §9, spoke of the "Agreement, or Disagreement of our Ideas in Co-existence" and gave the ideas of flame and gold as examples. In §10 he allows that "the simple Ideas whereof our complex Ideas of Substances are made up, are, for the most part such, as carry with them, in their own Nature, no visible necessary connexion, or inconsistency with any other simple Ideas, whose co-existence with them we would inform our selves about." Poley rendered the phrase from §9 as *Uebereinstimmung oder Unübereinstimmung unserer Begriffe, im Absehen auf das zugleiche Daseyn* (pp. 581–2); Coste rendered it as *la convenance ou disconvenance de nos idées par rapport à leur coëxistence* (1700, p. 691) and Burridge as *idearum nempe nostrarum convenientiam aut repugnantiam quoad coexistentiam* (1701, p. 241).

26 In the *Critique*, Kant allowed that Hume may have had a glimmering of the distinction: "Hume perhaps had it in mind, although he never fully developed it, that in judgments of a certain kind we go beyond our concept of the object. I have called this sort of judgment *synthetic*" (A 764/B 792). Presumably, Kant was here referring to the distinction between "Relations of Ideas" and "Matters of Fact" in sec. 4, pt. 1, of Hume's first *Enquiry*, rendered in Sulzer's edition as a distinction between *Beziehungen der Begriffe* and *geschehene Dinge* (Sulzer, 2:64–5). Hume's term "idea" was regularly rendered as *Begriff* in the Sulzer edition.

27 Kant introduced a similar point into the B Introduction (B 22–3).

28 The material from here to the end of §5 was summarized in the B Introduction (B 19–22), including the assertion of the actuality of synthetic *a priori* cognition in mathematics and natural science, but without mention of the analytic method.

29 As in §1 and §2c2, the reference is to the Transcendental Doctrine of Method, chap. 1, sec. 1. There Kant explained: "mathematical cognition is cognition through reason from the *construction* of concepts. *To construct* a concept means, however: to exhibit *a priori* the intuition corresponding to it. For the construction of a concept, then, a *nonempirical* intuition is required, which therefore, as intuition, is an *individual* object, but which, as the construction of a concept (a universal representation), must nonetheless express (in the representation) universal validity for all possible intuitions belonging under that same concept" (A 713/B 741).

30 Kant developed his analysis of motion and time in the *Metaphysical Foundations of Natural Science*.

31 In Euclid's *Elements*, points are said to be the extremities or boundaries of lines and lines of planes (Bk. 1, defs. 3, 6, 13); planes are boundaries of spaces (Bk. 11, def. 2).

32 On the infinity or unboundedness of the space of intuition, see the Transcendental Aesthetic, On Space, para. 5 (A 25), retained as para. 4 (B 39–40). In the First Part thus far, §§8–12 generally repeat or extend points made at A 24 (para. 3) and A 46–9 / B 63–6. The point about congruence is new. The example of three dimensions had been used in the *Inaugural Dissertation* (Ak 2:402) and in the first *Critique* (A 24, para. 3; A 239/B 299); new instances were added in B (B 41, 154).

33 In the *Critique*, A 87–8 / B 119–20, Kant said that in the Aesthetic he had "by means of a transcendental deduction, pursued the concepts of space and time to their sources, and explained and determined their *a priori* objective validity."

34 A spherical triangle is one inscribed on the surface of a sphere. During Kant's time, such triangles were discussed in beginning mathematics texts under the rubric "spherical trigonometry," which was needed for astronomy and geography; see Christian Wolff, "Anfangs-Gründe der sphärischen Trigonometrie," in his *Anfangs-Gründe aller mathematischen Wissenschaften, Dritter Theil*, new ed. (Halle: Renger, 1750), a book that Kant owned at his death (Warda, VII. 28, p. 40) and from which he presumably taught (Ak 2:35). Spherical triangles are instances of incongruent counterparts; Kant provided examples from nature in the succeeding paragraph.

Incongruent counterparts were not discussed in the first *Critique*, but Kant had previously used them in arguing for absolute over relational space ("Directions in Space," Ak 2:381–3), and for the claim that space must be known through intuition (*Inaugural Dissertation*, Ak 2:402–3).

35 The word "phantasy" (*Phantasie*) refers to the faculty of imagination.

36 Kant had long been intent on supporting the applicability of geometry to both physical space and bodies, and on reconciling geometrical description with "philosophical" or "metaphysical" conceptions of body. The claim that geometrical descriptions would not apply to bodies composed of indivisibles had been raised by ancient skeptics (Sextus Empiricus, *Against the Physicists*, I. 281–4, II. 142–8). Kant was exposed to such arguments in John Keill's *Introductio ad veram physicam* (Oxford: Thomas Bennet, 1702), Lecture 3, in which Keill repeated a standard argument for the infinite divisibility of extension (considered as common to space and bodies) in opposition to those who argued that matter would not be divisible to infinity (Keill cited Jean Baptiste du Hamel). Kant repeated Keill's argument in his *The Employment in Natural Philosophy of Metaphysics Combined with Geometry, of which Sample I Contains the PHYSICAL MONADOLOGY* (1756) to support the infinite divisibility of matter. The topic of indivisible simples in relation to infinitely divisible absolute space was widely discussed in Prussia during the mid 1740s in response to the Berlin Academy's first prize contest in philosophy, announced in 1745 for decision in 1747, on whether the theory of monads could be sustained. Leonard Euler published an anonymous pamphlet against the metaphysical monadists and for the geometer's infinite divisibility, entitled *Gedancken von den Elementen der Körper* (1746; in Euler's *Opera omnia* [Leipzig: Teubner, 1911–], III. 2:347–66); in *Reflexions sur la space et tems* (*Opera omnia*, III.2:376–83), Euler supported absolute space and time against the "metaphysicians'" (monadists') position that space and time are "imaginary." Kant certainly knew the latter work (Ak 2:168, 379). Moreover, his *Physical Monadology* responded to the Berlin controversy by attempting to show how the Leibnizean or Wolffian commitment to metaphysical simples could be rendered consistent with the infinite divisibility of physical space. Kant argued that physical space (his term) "is the appearance of the external relations of unitary monads" (Ak 1:479), that is, of simple substances that fill an (infinitely divisible) space through their force of repulsion. In his *Inquiry Concerning the Principles of Natural Theology and Morality*, he used the infinite divisiblity of space and the composition of bodies from simples to exemplify positions that might be supported (respectively) by mathematical and philosophical argumentation (Ak 2:279). In the first *Critique* he framed the dispute between the mathematicians and metaphysicians as the Second Antinomy (A 434–5/B 462–3), and identified the "monadists" as denying the infinite divisibility of matter and as therefore treating mathematical concepts as "arbitrary concepts which could not be related to real things" (A 439/B 467). In the Aesthetic he argued that those who hold a relational view of space must treat the application of geometry to real things as something admitting of only *a posteriori* support, thereby depriving mathematics as applied to real things of its apodictic certainty. His handwritten notes in A make clear that he had Leibniz in mind, for at A 40 he writes: "Leibnitzens

System über Raum und Zeit war, beyde in intellectuelle, aber verworrene Begriffe zu verwandeln. Aus diesen aber lässt sich nicht die Möglichkeit der Erkenntniss *a priori* begreifen, denn da [müssen] beide vorhergehen" (Benno Erdmann, *Nachträge zu Kants Kritik der reinen Vernunft* [Kiel: Lipsius and Tischer, 1881], note XXX, p. 21; Ak 23:24). For a thorough examination of Kant's relations to monad theory through the first *Critique*, see Karl Vogel, *Kant und die Paradoxien der Vielheit*, 2d ed. (Frankfurt am Main: Hain, 1986). See also Irving Polonoff, *Force, Cosmos, Monads and Other Themes of Kant's Early Thought* (Bonn: Bouvier, 1973), pp. 77–92, 147–53.

37 Kant here gives the tenor of the Garve–Feder review of the first *Critique*, to which he explicitly responds at 4:373–5. The review sums up Kant's transcendental idealism as "an idealism that encompasses spirit and matter in the same way, that transforms the world and ourselves into representations, that has all objects arising from appearances as a result of the understanding connecting the appearances into *one* sequence of experience, and of reason necessarily, though vainly, trying to expand and unify them into *one* whole and complete world system" (*Göttingische gelehrte Anzeigen*, supplement, 3d part [January 19, 1782], pp. 40–8, on p. 40), and assimilates Kant's idealism to Berkeley's (p. 41).

38 Kant again gives the tenor of the Garve–Feder review, which charged that, according to the *Critique*, "space and time are nothing real outside us, are neither relations nor abstracted concepts, but subjective laws of our faculty of representation, forms of sensations, subjective conditions of sensory intuition" (review, p. 41). The review went on to suggest that, on Kant's position, there is no basis for distinguishing reality from fantasy, illusion, or dream (pp. 42–3). Kant responds to these charges at length in the present note, and again in the Appendix (4:376, note).

39 In the *Critique* Kant reproached Leibniz for having rendered sensation as confused intellectual representation (A 275–6/B 332–3), and he emphasized the importance of his own classification of sensory and intellectual representations as different in kind (A 22/B 36, A 50–2/B 74–6, A 67–8/B 92–3, A 258/B 313–14, etc.).

40 The German word *schwärmerisch*, and the related *Schwärmerei*, can also be translated as "enthusiastical" and "enthusiasm," in the sense of religious enthusiasm. The sense of "visionary" used here alludes to the belief that through the intellect human beings can achieve a vision of another reality than that available through the senses (see Kant's note in the Appendix, 4:375). The German words might also be translated as "fanatical" and "fanaticism," or as "delusive" and "delusions," which forms have been used in certain contexts below; they have the connotation of someone's being guided by imagination and feeling, perhaps to a pathological extreme.

41 René Descartes (1596–1650) raised a skeptical challenge concerning the existence of bodies in the first of his *Meditations* (original Latin edition, Paris: Michel Soly, 1641), but he in fact claimed to remove that doubt in the sixth. George Berkeley (1685–1753) presented his idealism, which granted existence only to immaterial beings and their ideas, in the *Treatise Concerning the Principles of Human Knowledge* (Dublin: A. Rhames for J. Pepyat, 1710) and *Three Dialogues between Hylas and Philonous* (London: G. James for H.

Clements, 1713). Berkeley's *Dialogues* were published in German in Johann Christian Eschenbach (ed. and trans.), *Samlung der vornehmsten Schriftsteller die die Wurklichkeit ihres Eignenkorpers und der ganzen Korperwelt Laugnen; Enthaltend des Berkeleys Gesprache zwischen Hylas und Philonous, und des Colliers Allgemeinen Schlussel* (Rostock: A. F. Röse, 1756), which contained Eschenbach's annotations and refutation. A collection of his works later appeared, *Philosophische Werke* (Leipzig: Schwickert, 1781). It is generally believed that Kant did not take much notice of Berkeley prior to 1782, that is, prior to the time of the Garve–Feder review.

42 Kant here echoes the charge from the Garve–Feder review that the idealism of the *Critique* "transforms the world and ourselves into representations" (review, p. 40). The reviewers' charge may well itself have been echoing Berkeley's own summary of his immaterialist position at the end of his *Three Dialogues*, where Philonous conjoins two phrases he attributes respectively to "the vulgar" and to philosophers: "that those things they immediately perceive are the real things," and "that the things immediately perceived are ideas which exist only in the mind" – which is in effect to equate things with (mere) ideas or representations.

43 In §§2 and 7 above Kant contrasts the *intuitive* judgments of mathematics with the *discursive* judgments of philosophy. In the first *Critique*, A 712–738/B 740–766, he discusses more generally his doctrine that philosophical method involves the analysis of concepts, whereas mathematics proceeds by "constructing" concepts in intuition.

44 In the phrase "universal physics," the word "physics" is used to mean the science of nature in general. As such, it draws on an understanding of that word that harks back to Aristotle and to seventeenth-century usages, according to which physics as the science of nature in general includes the study of living things and of the mind (psychology). During the eighteenth century the term generally came to be restricted ever more to the study of bodies, which might still include what was later to be called biology, but typically excluded psychology. See, for example, Wolff's so-called *Deutsche Physik*, entitled *Vernünfftige Gedancken von den Würckungen der Natur* (Halle: Renger, 1723).

45 *Materialiter* is Latin for "materially." In Kant's usage (ultimately derived from scholastic Aristotelianism), "matter" and "material" need not refer specifically to the physical matter of which objects are composed. Here he uses the term to refer to the totality of objects of experience (see also §36), by contrast with the general laws governing those objects (as discussed in §§15, 17).

46 Wormwood (*Wermut*) is a bitter-tasting herb used in making absinthe and vermouth.

47 Kant here mentions the insufficiency of judgment based upon mere comparison of perceptions (or intuitions) for the third time in §20 (see also §21a). In the *Jaesche Logic* he observes that comparison is part of concept formation (Ak 9:94). Here he is saying that a judgment that merely compared perceptions would not be sufficient to achieve the intersubjective validity of experience. As to those who, in Kant's view, have "commonly thought" that comparison of "intuitions" (or, earlier in the section, "perceptions") might generally be sufficient for judgment, recall that Locke founded judgment

upon the comparison of ideas (*Essay*, Bk. II, chap. xi, §2). Indeed, Johann Nicholas Tetens reported that "der grösste Theil der Vernunftlehrer sieht auch die *Urtheile* für nichts anders an, als für Vergleichungen und für ein Gewahrnehmen der Einerleyheit und Verschiedenheit" (*Philosophische Versuche* [Leipzig: Weidmann, 1777], p. 361), and he treated judgment as resting upon comparison (pp. 361–72).

48   Kant's point is that a collection of singular judgments that covers all individuals in a domain neither explicitly refers to the collected totality of such individuals (as a totality), nor explicitly denies the universality of its extension (a denial that would be suggested by calling such judgments "particular"); it refers to a plurality, that is, to more than one individual, but it leaves undetermined whether or not it covers all individuals in the domain (even if the judgment should in fact singly mention every individual in the domain, and thus have "proceeded to totality," albeit unawares).

49   The reference is to the Transcendental Doctrine of Judgment (or Analytic of Principles), chap. 1, On the Schematism of the Pure Concepts of the Understanding (A 137ff./B 176ff.).

50   In reading the next three sections, the obscurity will be reduced by keeping in mind that Kant is discussing the tables in §21. Here in §24 he relates the first two entries in the Physiological Table (Axioms and Anticipations) to the category of magnitude (respectively, extensive magnitude, and intensive magnitude or degree). In the A *Critique*, the two corresponding propositions read: Axiom, "All appearances are, as regards their intuition, extensive magnitudes" (A 162); and Anticipation, "In all appearances the sensation, and the *real* that corresponds to it in the object (*realitas phaenomenon*), has an intensive magnitude, i.e., a degree" (A 166).

51   The application of mathematics to natural science here envisioned by Kant is to the "real" in appearances, which is signified by sensations. At the same time, his argument asserts that sensations themselves have degree, which means that the understanding can anticipate that they will have intensive magnitude. Kant thus here allows application of mathematics to inner sense (and so to the object of empirical psychology), which stands in at least apparent tension with his declaration in the Preface to the *Metaphysical Foundations of Natural Science*, 4:470–71, that psychology cannot be a science because mathematics is not applicable to inner sense.

52   Here Kant first relates the third entry in the Physiological Table to the categories of Relation: Substance, Cause, and Community (a discussion that corresponds to that of the three Analogies of Experience in the *Critique*, A 176–218/B 218–65). In the following paragraph, he relates the fourth entry to the categories of Modality (a discussion that corresponds to that of the three Postulates of Empirical Thinking in the *Critique*, A 218–35 /B 265–74, 279–87). The distinction between "mathematical" and "dynamical" mentioned here is further elaborated in §§52c, 53.

53   The early philosophers mentioned here presumably include Plato, together with the Eleatics, whom Kant cites in this regard in the Appendix (4:374).

54   "Aesthetic" is to be taken here as meaning things pertaining to, and limited to, the senses by comparison to the intellect, as the word is used in labeling the Transcendental Aesthetic in the *Critique of Pure Reason*. At Ak 4:618 a

question is raised of whether *Analytik* should be read for *Aesthetik* in the above passage. But given Kant's desire, expressed at Ak 4:362–3 and in the *Critique*, B xxiv–xxv, to prevent the extension of the principles of sensibility to things in themselves (thus to noumena), the original text makes sense as it stands.

55 On the Schematism of the Pure Concepts of the Understanding (A 137ff./B 176ff.); On the Basis of the Distinction of All Objects in General into *Phaenomena* and *Noumena* (A 235ff./B 294ff.).

56 In the *Critique of Pure Reason*, the Transcendental Logic is the second part of the Transcendental Doctrine of Elements, coordinate with the Transcendental Aesthetic (mentioned in the previous paragraph), though much larger.

57 Christian August Crusius (1715–1775), an important opponent of the Wolffian philosophy; in his *Weg zur Gewissheit und Zuverlässigkeit der menschlichen Erkenntniss* (Leipzig: Gleditsch, 1747), he maintains that the divine understanding is the source of all truth and certainty in the human understanding, and that reflection on skepticism will bring one to see this (§§424–32). If Kant believed that only Crusius had proposed that a nonerring, nondeceiving deity might be responsible for our *a priori* knowledge of the laws of nature, then we must conclude that his knowledge of Descartes' philosophy was limited indeed.

58 Kant specifies below that each line is a chord, i.e., a line segment having both end points on the circumference of the circle.

59 A rhapsody was a portion of an ancient Greek poem recited on a single occasion, and might carry the connotation of rote repetition of an earlier epic work; etymologically, the word means "stitched together verse."

60 In the *Critique*, in Bk. 1, chap. 1 of the Dialectic, On the Paralogisms of Pure Reason, Kant presented the doctrines of rational psychology concerning the immaterial soul in a fourfold division corresponding to the categories of Substance, Unity, and Possibility, and to the "Quality" (second division of the Table) of simplicity (A 344/B 402). In Bk. 2, chap. 2, the Antinomy of Pure Reason, he presented the cosmological ideas in a fourfold table (A 415/B 442).

61 In the *Critique*, in the Amphiboly (the appendix to chap. 3 of the Analytic of Principles, on Phenomena and Noumena), Kant provides a fourfold division of the concept of nothing (A 292/B 348).

62 Ontology was the first major division of Baumgarten's *Metaphysica*. Baumgarten listed a great many predicates of being.

63 In letters to Johann Schultz of 26 August 1783 and 17 February 1784, Kant discusses the relations of the first and second to the third categories (as listed under the various headings in the Transcendental Table of Concepts of the Understanding), and he mentions the possibility of someone such as Schultz using the categories as the basis for an *ars characteristica combinatoria*.

64 In the Amphiboly of the Concepts of Reflection, Kant provides (A 260–68/B 316–28) a fourfold division of concepts pertaining to judgment itself (identity/difference, agreement/opposition, inner/outer, and determinable/determinate or matter/form), which he relates to the cognition of phenomena and noumena.

65 The word "philosophy" is here used broadly (as was normal in Kant's time) to include natural science or "natural philosophy" as one of its branches (other branches included ethics, logic, and metaphysics). Earlier, Kant drew attention to the intuitive basis of mathematics by contrast with the discursive basis of philosophy (§§1, 2, 7; also *Critique*, A 712–17/B 740–45).

66 Examples of "maxims of reason" or "maxims of speculative reason" are given in the *Critique* in the regulative use of the ideas of pure reason, and include "principles" of homogeneity or aggregation, of variety or division into species, and of affinity or continuity of forms (A 658/B 686, A 666–8/B 694–6). (And so with Vorländer, among others, I reject Hartenstein's emendation of this passage, which would read *Maximen der Verstandeserkenntnis* for *Maximen des Vernunfterkenntnisses*.) Kant says that the ideas of reason are regulative with respect to the use of the understanding in experience, and he gives the name "maxims" to the so-called principles that guide such use. In mentioning another respect in which it will be necessary to use the ideas of reason, we may suppose that Kant is speaking of their use in practical or moral reasoning.

67 Kant refers to the Transcendental Analytic in the *Critique*.

68 Compare Kant's discussion of the relation between reason and the understanding in the *Critique*, A 642–3/B 670–1.

69 *Critique*, A 341–405, Of the Paralogisms of Pure Reason; largely replaced by B 399–432.

70 *Critique*, A 182–9/B 224–32.

71 *Critique*, A 405–567/B 432–595, The Antinomy of Pure Reason.

72 *Critique*, A 571/B 599, On the Transcendental Ideal.

73 Ernst Platner (1744–1818), *Philosophische Aphorismen*, 2 vols. (Leipzig: Schwickert, 1776–82), 1:229. Kant omits the qualifier *menschliche* from Platner's first use of *Vernunft*; hence, a translation of Platner's text would begin: "If human reason . . .".

74 David Hume, *Dialogues Concerning Natural Religion* (London, 1779); *Gespräche über die natürliche Religion*, trans. Karl Gottfried Schreiter (Leipzig: Weygand, 1781). A French translation appeared in Amsterdam in 1779, but there is no evidence that Kant was aware of it. For Kant's acquaintance (in 1780) with Hamann's unpublished abbreviated translation, see the Translator's Introduction.

75 Kant elaborated the notion of an intuitive understanding in the second edition of the *Critique*, B 135, B 138–9, B 145.

76 In the final paragraph of the Garve–Feder review (pp. 47–8), the reviewers chastise Kant for not selecting the "right middle way" between skepticism and dogmatism, which according to them involves giving equal weight, in a commonsensical way, to both inner and outer sensation.

77 In Kant's time, anthropology (*Anthropologie*), or the science of man, included topics on the human mind such as were also discussed in empirical psychology. The topic here concerns the psychological tendencies of the human mind and the presumed purpose served by those tendencies. Kant lectured on anthropology for more than twenty years, from 1772 until his retirement from teaching in 1796, after which he edited his lectures and published them in 1798.

78 Kant here refers to part of the section in the *Critique* entitled On the Regulative Use of the Ideas of Pure Reason (A 647–68/B 675–96).

79 "Analytic" here refers to the analytic method; see General Question (§§ 4, 5) and the Translator's Introduction.

80 Kant here refers to the definition of a straight line. Euclid, *Elements*, Bk. 1, def. 4, defines a straight line as "lying evenly with the points on itself." Kant's definition is closer to that given by Wolff, as a line "of which the part is similar to the whole" (*Anfangsgründe aller mathematischen Wissenschaften*, new ed. [Frankfurt, Leipzig, and Halle: Renger, 1750–7], pt. 1, p. 119); Wolff refers to Plato's definition, to the effect that a straight line is one in which "the middle covers the ends" (when viewed end-on). Kant taught mathematics from a textbook by Wolff (Ak 2:35).

81 The review was written by Christian Garve (1742–1798), and heavily edited for publication by J. G. Feder (1740–1821); it is reprinted, with indication of the original pagination (pp. 40–8), in Albert Landau (ed.), *Rezensionen zur Kantischen Philosophie* (Bebra: Landau, 1991), pp. 10–17 (and also in Vorländer, but without the original pagination), and a translation may be found in J. Morrison's edition of Schultz's *Exposition*.

82 Traditionally, the Eleatic School is identified with the view that "all is one," and that change and plurality are unreal (strictly, the Eleatics were Parmenides and Zeno of Elea). On Berkeley, see Note III of the First Part.

83 Kant paraphrases the concluding sentences of the review (p. 48).

84 The Garve–Feder review briefly discusses Kant's theory that experience arises when the understanding properly applies concepts to sensory intuitions, and then asks how one can discern proper from improper use of the understanding. It then suggests that a *mark* would be needed in sensation (*Empfindung*) in order to allow experience to be distinguished from "mere phantasies and dreams" (p. 42). In the A *Critique*, Kant had on several occasions contrasted empirical truth and experience with mere dreaming and imagination (A 202/B 247; A 451/B 479; A 492/B 520–1; see also above, 4:336–7). On each of those occasions he relied on the connectibility of representations in accordance with laws of nature (mediated by the causal concept) to establish empirical truth, but he did not offer this as a criterion for distinguishing waking from sleeping, nor allude to a mark within sensation which could do that. Kant's claim that he was here alluding to the Wolffian doctrine of dreams taken objectively is credible. Wolff observed that in characterizing dreams as disordered, one must rely on a distinction between, on the one hand, the sequence of the "subjective" states of mind in dreams – the states of the mind themselves, which surely do follow one another in regular fashion – and, on the other, the disorder found in dream content, that is, in "dreams taken objectively" (a usage that draws on the Scholastic and Cartesian terminology of "objective" or "representational reality" to distinguish the content of a mental state from its status as simply a modification of mind). See Wolff, *Psychologia rationalis*, new ed. (Frankfurt and Leipzig: Renger, 1740), §§246–53, especially §249, where, having contrasted the ordered waking perception with the unordered perceptions of dream, Wolff qualifies: "Nimirum perceptiones hic materialiter seu objective consideramus, quatenus sunt rerum ab anima

diversarum imagines; non vero subjective, quatenus sunt actus animae & ad ejus modificationes pertinent." See also Wolff, *Psychologia empirica*, new ed. (Frankfurt and Leipzig: Renger, 1738), §§119–137, especially §§128, 136.

85 Kant paraphrases the review (p. 42).

86 *Critique*, A 426–61/B 454–89, The Antinomies of Pure Reason.

87 This challenge became known to Garve within months of its appearance, and he wrote to Kant on 13 July 1783 revealing his part in writing the original review but maintaining that Feder's revisions had distorted it (Ak 10:328–9). He made arrangements for a copy of his unadulterated review to be sent to Kant (Ak 10:331), and it later appeared in the *Allgemeine deutsche Bibliothek*, supplement, second part (1783), pp. 838–62 (reprinted in Landau, *Rezensionen*, pp. 34–55). On 7 August 1783 Kant allowed that responsibility for the review could not be assigned publicly, and he effectively dropped his challenge (Ak 10:342–43).

88 *Gothaische gelehrte Zeitung*, 24 August 1782, pp. 560–63 (reprinted in Landau, *Rezensionen*, pp. 17–23). Kant had seen the new review by mid-September (on which, see the Translator's Introduction).

89 In the B edition of the *Critique* the second section of the chapter on the Deduction replaced the second and third sections of the Deduction in A, and the chapter on the Paralogisms was completely rewritten, except for the first eight pages.

Metaphysical foundations of natural science

1 See the discussion in the Architectonic of Pure Reason in the first *Critique*: "Metaphysics in the narrower sense consists of *transcendental philosophy* and the *physiology* of pure reason. The former considers only the *understanding* and reason itself in a system of concepts and principles that relate to objects in general, without assuming objects that may be *given* (*Ontologia*). The latter considers *nature* – i.e., the totality of *given* objects . . . and is therefore *physiology* (although only *rationalis*)" (A 845/B 873). After explaining that the latter doctrine (rational physiology) consists in turn of "metaphysics of corporeal nature" or "rational physics," and "metaphysics of thinking nature" or "rational psychology" (A 846/B 874), Kant then continues as follows: "how can I expect an *a priori* cognition, and thus a metaphysics, of objects insofar as they are given to our senses, and therefore given *a posteriori*? . . . The answer is: we take no more from experience than what is necessary to *give* us an object – of either outer or inner sense. The former takes place through the mere concept of matter (impenetrable, lifeless extension), the latter through the concept of a thinking being (in the empirical inner representation: I think)" (A 847–8/B 875–6).

2 See A 381: "When we compare the *doctrine of the soul*, as the physiology of inner sense, with the *doctrine of body*, as a physiology of the objects of the outer senses, we find that, aside from the circumstance that much that is empirical can be cognized in both, there is still this remarkable difference: In the latter science much that is *a priori* can be synthetically cognized from the mere concept of an extended, impenetrable being, but in the former science nothing at all that is *a priori* can be synthetically cognized from

the concept of a thinking being." And compare the discussion of empirical psychology at A 848–9/B 876–7.

3 Compare the definition of matter cited in note 1 above ("impenetrable, lifeless extension") and the parallel discussion in §15 of the *Prolegomena* – which gives the relevant list of concepts as "the concept of *motion*, of *impenetrability* (on which the empirical concept of matter rests), of *inertia*, and others" (Ak 4:295). (Note that in the Remark to Proposition 3 of the Mechanics, "inertia" is equated with "lifelessness" [4:544].)

4 "Um deswillen habe ich für nöthig gehalten, von dem reinen Theile der Naturwissenschaft (*physica generalis*), wo metaphysische und mathematische Constructionen durch einander zu laufen pflegen, die erstere und mit ihnen zugleich die Prinzipien der Construction dieser Begriffe, also der Möglichkeit einer mathematischen Naturlehre selbst, in einem System darzustellen." This difficult sentence has led to considerable controversy. Plaass (1965) and Schäfer (1966) have made the notion of "metaphysical construction" central to their interpretations, whereas Hoppe (1969) and Gloy (1976) have suggested that "concepts" or "principles" should follow "metaphysical" in the sentence. Here, in any case, one should compare the section on the Discipline of Pure Reason in Its Dogmatic Employment from the Doctrine of Method of the first *Critique* (A 712–38/B 740–66) – which certainly suggests that the construction of concepts is precisely what *distinguishes* mathematics from philosophy.

5 See the General Remark to the System of Principles in the second edition of the *Critique*: "But it is even more remarkable that, in order to understand the possibility of things in conformity with the categories, and thus to verify the *objective reality* of the latter, we require not merely intuitions, but always even *outer intuitions*" (B 291).

6 Again, one should compare A 726/B 754 from the section of the first *Critique* cited in note 4 above, where Kant explicitly says that philosophy *cannot* imitate mathematics [*Meßkunst*]. See also A 735/B 763.

7 Kant quotes from the Latin: *Gloriatur Geometria, quod tam paucis principiis aliunde petitis tam multa praestet.* The quotation in the text is from I. Newton, *Mathematical Principles of Natural Philosophy* (1686), trans. A. Motte (1729), revised F. Cajori (Berkeley: University of California Press, 1934), p. xvii.

8 *Erklärung.* For the distinction between mathematical *definitions* [**Definitionen**] and philosophical *explications* [**Erklärungen**] see A 727–32/B 755–60).

9 *Geschwindigkeit und Richtung.* Since Kant thus explicitly distinguishes these two elements, it is clear that by *Geschwindigkeit* he means what we now refer to as the scalar quantity speed as opposed to the vector quantity velocity.

10 The notion of absolute space is further discussed in the General Remark to Phenomenology, where, in particular, it is characterized as a "necessary concept of reason" or "mere idea" (4:559)

11 Compare A 41/B 58; see also, from the second edition, B 155n.

12 See *Prolegomena to Any Future Metaphysics*, §13 (Ak 4:285–6).

13 That is, *Celeritas est Spatium per Temporum* [speed equals distance over time].

14 According to Galileo's law of free fall, an object thrown upward is uniformly decelerated on its upward trajectory and uniformly accelerated on its downward trajectory. In both cases, then, we have $v = gt$, where g

is the constant of gravity. Therefore, v continuously decreases to zero and then continuously increases from zero.

15 See, in particular, the footnote to the Proof of Proposition 4 of the Mechanics chapter (4:547).

16 Compare the first paragraph of the Axioms of Intuition in the second edition: "[Appearances] can be apprehended in no other way ... except through the synthesis of the manifold whereby the representation of a determinate space or time is generated, i.e., through the composition of the homogeneous and the consciousness of the synthetic unity of this (homogeneous) manifold. Now the consciousness of the manifold [of] homogeneous [elements] in intuition in general, in so far as the representation of an object first becomes possible, is the concept of quantity (*quanti*)" (B 202–3).

17 This, for example, is how Newton proceeds when he derives the law of the parallelogram of velocities using his First and Second Laws of Motion in Corollary I to the Laws of Motion in *Principia* (Motte-Cajori, p. 14).

18 See A 162/B 203: "I call an extensive quantity that in which the representation of the parts makes possible the representation of the whole (and thus necessarily precedes the latter)" For the contrasting concept of *intensive* quantity see A 167–70/B 209–12.

19 For the concept of "the *real* in space" compare A 173/B 215.

20 See, in particular, the discussion of *chemical* penetration under #4 of the General Remark to Dynamics (4:530–2).

21 Compare the General Remark to Dynamics for the contrast between the "mathematical" and "dynamical" natural philosophies (4: 532–5).

22 It appears that "Prop. 2" is meant.

23 In the *Physical Monadology* of 1756 Kant argues that a monad can fill a space in virtue of the "sphere of activity [*sphaera activitatis*]" of its repulsive force without detriment to the absolute simplicity and indivisibility of the substantial monad itself: Propositions IV – VII (Ak. 1: 479–82).

24 That is, the proposition that matter is a thing in itself.

25 See the discussion of the Second Antinomy in the first *Critique:* A 434–43/B 462–71, A 523–7/B 551–5.

26 Various possibilities have been suggested here, the most plausible of which are Leibniz, Euler, and Lambert. In view of the rest of the passage, Leibniz seems to be the most probable.

27 Proposition VIII of Book III of Newton's *Principia* states that the gravitational attraction of a sphere whose mass is distributed symmetrically about its center acts as if all the mass were concentrated there (Motte-Cajori, pp. 415–16). This does not hold, however, for arbitrary mass distributions.

28 In modern terms, the distinction here is between *inertial mass*, which governs the interaction of any forces at all in accordance with Newton's Second and Third Laws of Motion, and specifically *gravitational mass*, which plays a crucial role (both "active" and "passive") in the law of universal gravitation. Thus, the equality subsisting between inertial mass and (passive) gravitational mass implies that the acceleration of a gravitationally attracted body is independent of its particular constitution (all bodies fall alike in a gravitational field). This is certainly not true of electric

and magnetic forces, for example, where the corresponding acceleration depends explicitly on the mass/charge ratio of the body in question.

29 Kant's rendering deviates from Newton's text, which, in the translation of Motte-Cajori, reads instead as follows: "If the ether, or any other body, were either altogether void of gravity, or were to gravitate less in proportion to its quantity of matter, then, because (according to *Aristotle, Descartes,* and others) there is no difference between that and other bodies but in *mere* form of matter, by a successive change from form to form, it might be changed at last into a body of the same condition with those which gravitate most in proportion to their quantity of matter; and, on the other hand, the heaviest bodies, acquiring the first form of that body, might by degrees quite lose their gravity. And therefore the weights would depend upon the forms of bodies, and be changed: contrary to what was proved in the preceding Corollary." (Motte-Cajori, pp. 413–14)

30 Kant quotes from the second Latin edition: *ne quis gravitatem inter essentiales corporum proprietates me habere existimet, quaestionem unam de eus causa investiganda subieci.*

31 In Corollaries I and II of Proposition VIII of Book III of *Principia* Newton determines first the (relative) weights and then the (relative) masses of Jupiter and Saturn from the distances and periodic times of their satellites. This argument depends on the previous Proposition VII which shows that the force of gravity exerted by a body is proportional to the mass of that body (Motte-Cajori, pp. 414–16). In the terminology of note 28, then, what is here crucial is the proportionality of gravitational force to (active) gravitational mass and the equality of the latter to inertial mass.

32 In the *Physical Monadology* of 1756 Kant formulates the law of repulsion as in inverse ratio to the cube of the (*finite*) distance rather than as in inverse ratio to the cube of the *infinitely small* distance. See the Scholium to Proposition X (Ak. 1:484–485). (So "actual space" means *finite space* in the *Metaphysical Foundations*.) Compare also note 23 above.

33 At issue is what is now known as Boyle's Law: $PV = $ constant. Newton proves in Proposition XXIII of Book II that in a fluid composed of particles repelling one another, the force will be inversely as the distance if the density (that is, mass over volume) is as the compression, and conversely. The Scholium then generalizes this to show that if the force is as the nth power of the distance, then the cube of the compression will be as the $n+2^{nd}$ power of the density (Motte-Cajori, pp. 300–2).

34 See the discussion of this point in the Anticipations of Perception: A 173–5/B 215–16. (And the same point is discussed further below [4: 533–5].)

35 The reference appears to be to Proposition VIII of Part III of Book II of the *Optics*.

36 That is, a tube so narrow that adhesion to the sides, combined with cohesion and surface tension, can result in a liquid rising in the tube (a kind of "apparent attraction").

37 From the Latin *intus* (inside) and *suscipio* (to take up). The term is commonly used for organic processes of nourishment and growth; and it is so used by Kant at A 833/B 861, where he compares the system of pure reason to

an animal body that can grow "from inside (*per intus susceptionem*)" but not "from outside (*per appositionem*)."

38 "Gesetzt auch, daβ die Kunst keine chemische Auflösungskräfte dieser Art, die eine vollständige Auflösung bewirkten, in ihrer Gewalt hätte, so könnte doch vielleicht die Natur sie in ihren vegetabilischen und animalischen Operationen beweisen und dadurch vielleicht Materien erzeugen, die, ob sie zwar gemischt sind, doch keine Kunst wiederum scheiden kann." A traditional term for chemistry is *Scheidekunst*.

39 It would appear, rather, that "possibility" is intended here.

40 At issue here is the *vis viva* controversy concerning whether mv or mv^2 is the proper measure of moving force – a controversy Kant attempts to mediate in his first published work, *Thoughts on the True Estimation of Living Forces* (1747). By "actual motion" Kant refers to finite speed v as opposed to infinitesimal or "infinitely small" speed dv, and the terms "dead force" and "living force" are Leibnizian terms for mdv and mv^2 respectively. If one integrates mdv/dt with respect to space, one obtains what is now called mechanical work or kinetic energy, 1/2 mv^2. But if one integrates mdv/dt with respect to time, one obtains momentum, mv. So Kant is here siding unequivocally with mv as the proper measure of (mechanical) moving force.

41 The water hammer consists of a liquid (usually water) hermetically sealed in a glass tube from which all the air has been removed (commonly, by boiling the liquid so that the resulting steam forces the air out, and then sealing the tube). If such a tube is inverted, the liquid, due to the lack of intervening air, then rushes immediately to the other end and strikes it quite forcefully – resulting in a loud noise and sometimes the breaking of the tube.

42 An undershot waterwheel (*unterschlägiger Wasserrad*) is rotated by water flowing underneath – and thus independently of the action of gravity. Experiments by John Smeaton in 1759 suggested that overshot wheels (acted on by weight as well as by driving force) operate, on average, at double the efficiency of undershot wheels.

43 See the Remark to Explication 5 of the Dynamics (4:503).

44 Here we are concerned with *gravitational* mass in the sense of notes 28 and 31 above. The procedure of *weighing* (in a balance, say) depends on the equality of inertial mass with *passive* gravitational mass. Measuring the mass of the planets by the gravitational attraction on their satellites, by contrast, depends on the equality of inertial mass with *active* gravitational mass.

45 In the second edition of the *Critique*, Kant changed the statement of the First Analogy to read: "In all change of the appearances substance persists [*beharrt*], and the quantum of substance in nature is neither increased nor diminished" (B 224).

46 Compare the "Refutation of Mendelssohn's Proof of the Permanence of the Soul" in the second edition Paralogisms (B 413–15).

47 Compare §V of the Introduction to the *Critique of Judgment*: "A transcendental principle is that through which is represented *a priori* the universal cognition under which alone things can be objects of our cognition in general. By contrast, a principle is called metaphysical if it represents *a priori* the condition under which alone objects, whose concept must be empirically given, can be further determined *a priori*. Thus, the principle

of the cognition of bodies as substances and as changeble substances is transcendental, if it is thereby asserted that their changes must have a cause; it is metaphysical, however, if it is thereby asserted that their changes must have an *external* cause" (Ak 5:181).

48 In the second edition of the *Critique*, Kant changed the title of the Third Analogy to the "principle of simultaneity (*Zugleichsein*) in accordance with the law of interaction or community" and changed its statement to read: "All substances, insofar as they can be perceived as simultaneous (*zugleich*) in space, are in thoroughgoing interaction."

49 This is the ideal case of *perfectly inelastic* impact. In the contrary ideal case of *perfectly elastic* impact the two bodies are reflected on impact. According to the Leibnizian principle of the conservation of *vis viva* (cf. note 40 above), only perfectly elastic impact is possible. Kant's view, by contrast, appears to be that perfectly inelastic impact is the "natural case," which one can describe *a priori* by *abstracting* from all elasticity. See especially Kant's footnote to the following Remark 1 (4:549), where he claims, in particular, that absolutely hard bodies (since they are by hypothesis perfectly inelastic) could not obey the law of perfectly elastic impact. Compare also the precritical *Neuer Lehrbegriff der Bewegung und Ruhe* (1758), and R. 42 (around 1773) at Ak 14, pp. 202–3 (together with Adickes's notes thereto).

50 For Kepler, the force of inertia is exerted by a body to preserve its natural state of *rest*, whereas for Newton, of course, inertia maintains a body in its natural state of uniform rectilinear motion (which can also be zero). Newton's discussion of *vis inertiae* or *vis insita* is in Definition III of the *Principia* (Motte-Cajori, p. 2).

51 Kant gives the principle in Latin: *accidentia non migrant e substantiis in substantias.*

52 Compare note 49 above.

53 See A 206–11/B 252–6; and compare A 171–2/B 212–13.

54 Compare the discussion in Note III to the First Part of the *Prolegomena* (Ak 4:291 to the end of the paragraph).

55 Compare Kant's second footnote to the General Remark to Phenomenology (4:562), and see note 57 below.

56 In the original edition: *von Osten nach Westen.* The Akademie edition substitutes *von Westen nach Osten* here, on the grounds that the experiment of *throwing* a stone outward from the surface of the earth so as to observe its deviation from east to west is much more difficult than the experiment of *dropping* a stone from a tower so as to observe its deviation from west to east. In any case, however, what Kant is describing here – just as in the case of dropping a stone into a deep hole directed toward the earth's center – is the action of the *Coriolis force* of the earth's rotation.

57 "Denn diese Bewegung ist im absoluten Raume wirklich, indem dadurch der Abgang der gedachten Entfernung, den die Schwere für sich allein dem Körper zuziehen würde, und zwar ohne alle dynamische zurücktreibende Ursache (wie man aus dem von Newton *Prin. Ph. N. pag. 10 Edit. 1714** gewählten Beispiele ersehen kann), mithin durch wirkliche, aber auf den innerhalb der bewegten Materie (nämlich das Centrum derselben) beschlossenen, nicht aber auf den äußeren Raum bezogene Bewegung continuirlich

ersetzt wird." (Here the date of the second edition of *Principia* should rather be 1713.) In the footnote Kant quotes from the Latin: *Motus quidem veros corporum singulorum cognoscere et ab apparentibus actu discriminare difficillimum est: propterea, quod partes spatii illius immobilis, in quo corpora vere moventur, non incurrunt in sensus. Causa tamen non est prorsus desperata.* The quotation in the text is from the Motte-Cajori translation (Motte-Cajori, p. 12).

On a discovery whereby any new critique of pure reason is to be made superfluous by an older one

These notes are based largely on the factual explanations of Heinrich Maier, who edited the essay for the Academy Edition (8:495–7), and the notes of Roger Kempf in his French translation and edition (*Réponse à Eberhard*, Paris: Librairie Philosophique J. Vrin, 1959, pp. 111–24).

1 John Locke, *An Essay Concerning Human Understanding*, Bk. IV, chap. XVII, sec. 19. Locke coined the Latin expression to characterize an argument that appeals to authority in an effort to intimidate anyone who might attempt to challenge the claim at issue.

2 In both the places to which Kant refers, Eberhard reminds the reader that he is speaking for Leibniz rather than in his own voice.

3 Kant here appears to be playing on the two senses of the term '*Magazin*', namely a warehouse or storehouse and a periodical or journal.

4 A Greek expression referring to an argument that begs the question by assuming in advance what is to be proven.

5 Quintilian, *Institutio Oratio*, Bk. V, chap. XII, 1.522. "If they cannot prevail by their weight, they will do so because of their number. One by one they are flimsy and commonplace, but together they do damage, not like a thunderbolt, indeed, but rather as a hailstorm." Kant's rendering differs in minor ways from the Latin text, suggesting that he was quoting from memory.

6 J. A. Borelli (1608–1679), Italian physician, physicist, and mathematician; he edited Books V–VII of the *Conica* of Apollonius.

7 Apollonius Pergaeus, *Conica*, Bk. VIII.

8 As Eberhard later admits (*Philosophisches Magazin* III, 205–7), he was in error in initially attributing the account to Borelli, since it was taken from the 1665 edition of Books I–IV of the *Conica* of Apollonius by Claudius Ricardus rather than from Borelli's 1661 edition of Books V–VII. This was called to my attention by Michael Friedman.

9 "For the subject may be assumed definite, so that various properties may be proved from it, even though the manner of drawing the subject to be formed has not been stated beforehand." From Borelli's *Admonitio* to his edition of Apollonius, sec. XXII (cited by Eberhard, *Philosophisches Magazin* I, p. 159).

10 The inference from what is actual to what is possible is valid.

11 Kant is referring to Alexander Gottlob Baumgarten's *Metaphysica*, §20. In the fourth edition, which, according to Adickes, is the one Kant used and

which is reprinted in Volume 17 of the Academy Edition, the argument is as follows: "Everything possible either has a ground or it does not. If it has a ground, then something is its ground. If it has no ground, then its ground is nothing. Therefore the ground of whatever is possible is either something or nothing. If nothing were the ground of something possible, then it would be cognizable from nothing why it was possible. Consequently nothing would itself be representable and be something, and something impossible would be possible. Therefore everything possible has something as its ground, and everything possible is grounded, that is, *nothing is without a ground*, but, rather, as soon as something is posited, something is posited as its ground." [*Omne possibile aut habet rationem, aut minus. Si habet rationem, aliquid est eius ratio. Si non habet, nihil est eius ratio. Ergo omnis possibilis ratio aut nihil est, aut aliquid. Si nihil foret ratio alicunius possibilis, foret ex nihilo cognoscibile, cur illud sit, hinc ipsum nihilum representabile et aliquid, nihil aliquid. Hinc quoddam possibile impossibile. Ergo omnis possibilis aliquid est ratio, s. omne possibile est rationatum, s. nihil est sine rationem, seu, posito aliquo, ponitur aliquid eius ratio.*] (17; 31) In response (*Philosophisches Magazin* III, 188–9), Eberhard denies Kant's charge that he had simply taken over Baumgarten's proof and incorporated it into his own. Although he acknowledges that his proof begins in the same manner as Baumgarten's, he insists (with some justification) that his is quite distinct. This is because, according to Baumgarten's version, the denial of the principle of sufficient reason implies that nothing is representable, i.e., regarded as something, while his formulation turns on the point that the denial of the principle entails that something could exist at the same time as its opposite.

12 John Keill, *Introductio ad veram physicam, seu lectiones physicae* [*Introduction to true physics, or lectures on physics*], Lecture III, 2nd ed., London, 1705.

13 I. Newton, *Optics*, Bk. II, pt. III.

14 *Critique of Pure Reason*, A 68/B 93.

15 Kant is here referring to the philologist Kaspar Schoppe (1576–1649).

16 In the Schematism chapter of the *Critique of Pure Reason*, Kant does state that "The pure image [*Bild*] of all magnitudes (*quantorum*) for outer sense is space; that for all objects of the senses in general is time" (A 142/B 182).

17 In an important note to the second edition version of the Transcendental Deduction, Kant distinguishes between space as *form of intuition* and as *formal intuition* (B 160–1). See also A 429/B 457.

18 Michael Hissmann, "Bemerkungen für die Geschichtschreiber der philos. Systeme; über Dutens Untersuchungen; und über die angeborenen Begriffe des Plato, Descartes and Leibniz" [Observations for the Historian of Philosophical Systems; on the Investigations of Dutens; and on Innate Concepts in Plato, Descartes and Leibniz], *Teutsche Merkur* 1777, 4. Viertel, pp. 22–52.

19 *Prolegomena* 4:271.

20 *Prolegomena* 4:273.

21 *Prolegomena* 4:294–326.

22 The actual qualification Eberhard makes is "if the propositions...may be demonstrated *a priori*" (*Philosophisches Magazin*, I, p. 325).

23 The proposition in Baumgarten states: "The essences of things are...
absolutely and internally immutable." [*Essentiae rerum...sunt absolute et
interne immutabiles.*]

24 According to Maier, Eberhard is here referring to Jacob Bernoulli the elder
(1654–1705), who was professor of mathematics at Basle. As Maier notes,
however, Eberhard does not cite a specific reference.

25 In the *Prolegomena* (4:270) Kant claims to have found a "hint" [*Wink*] of
the analytic-synthetic distinction in Locke. The reference is to the *Essay
Concerning Human Understanding*, Bk. IV, chap. III, sec. 9, where Locke distinguishes between knowledge of the identity and diversity of our ideas and
of their coexistence in a subject. The former, Kant suggests, corresponds
roughly to his analytic judgments and the latter to his synthetic judgments.

26 The reference is to Johann Peter Reusch (1691–1758), a Wolffian logician
who authored the *Systema logicum* (1734) and the *Systema metaphysicum*
(1734).

27 The reference is to the anti-Wolffian philosopher and theologian Christian
August Crusius (1715–1775), *Weg zur Gewissheit und Zuverlässigkeit der
menschlichen Erkenntniss* [Path to the Attainment of Certainty and Reliability
in Human Knowledge] (Leipzig, 1747), §260. Eberhard (*Philosophisches
Magazin* I, p. 311) refers to a follower and commentator of Kant, who
claims that Kant's entire distinction is contained in this text of Crusius.
The latter is identified by Maier as Carl Christian Erhard Schmid, in his
Wörterbuch zum leichtern Gebrauch der Kantischen Schriften [Dictionary for
the Easier Use of the Kantian Writings] (first edition, Jena, 1786). In his
entry "*Synthetischer Satz*" [synthetic proposition], Schmid wrote: "We find
already in Crusius, among others, a trace of the division of judgments into
analytic and synthetic, which has, however, been little followed. What this
great man in his *Path to the Attainment of Certainty and Reliability in Human
Knowledge* terms hypothetical consequences from assumed concepts may
be compared with Kant's analytic, and what he terms real propositions
with the latter's synthetic cognitions." [Von der Einteilung der Urteile in
analytische und synthetische findet man unter andern schon bei Crusius
einige Spur, der man aber wenig gefolgt ist. Was dieser grosse Mann in
seinem *Weg zur Gewissheit und Zuverlässigkeit der menschlichen Erkenntniss*
(Leipzig 1746) §260. hypothetische Folgern aus angenommenen Begriffen
nennt, lässt sich mit Kants analytischen, und was bei ihm Realsätze heissen,
mit den synthetischen Erkenntnissen des letzteren Philosophen vergle-
ichen.] For recent discussions of Crusius's anticipation of, or influence on,
Kant's analytic–synthetic distinction see Lewis White Beck, "Analytic and
Synthetic Judgments before Kant," *Essays on Kant and Hume* (New Haven
and London: Yale University Press, 1978), pp. 92–4, and Henry E. Allison,
"The Originality of Kant's Distinction between Analytic and Synthetic
Judgments," *The Philosophy of Immanuel Kant*, ed. Richard Kennington,
(Washington, D.C.: The Catholic University of America Press, 1985),
pp. 15–17.

28 According to Maier, Kant is here referring to Michael Hissmann, *Versuch
über das Leben der Freih. von Leibnitz* [Essay on the Life of Baron von
Leibnitz] (Münster, 1783), pp. 58–60, 60f.

Editor's introduction to *What real progress has metaphysics made in Germany since the time of Leibniz and Wolff?*

1 On this point, see H. J. de Vleeschauwer, *La Déduction transcendentale dans l'oeuvre de Kant*, vol. III, (Paris: Librairie Ernest Leroux, 1937), p. 447, and Ted Humphrey, in the Introduction to his translation and edition of this work, *What Real Progress Has Metaphysics Made in Germany since the Time of Leibniz and Wolff?* (New York: Abaris Books, 1983), p. 13.

2 For interesting speculation about these possible reasons, see de Vleeschauwer, "La Cinderella dans l'oeuvre Kantienne," *Kant-Studien, Akten des 4. Internationalen Kant-Kongress, Mainz 6–10 April 1974*, Teil I, pp. 304–6. After noting and dismissing a number of prima facie plausible reasons such as age, engagement with other projects, and fear of retaliation by the conservative political powers and clergy in Berlin, de Vleeschauwer cites as possible reasons Kant's fear that doing justice to the project might involve producing a work of the scope of the first *Critique* (the explanation offered by Karl Vorländer) and that if he entered the contest, he might not win, an outcome which de Vleeschauwer suggests is quite conceivable.

3 Rink's Preface, where he describes the structure of the text, is printed in the Academy Edition, 20:257–8.

4 These criticisms were made by Traugott Weisskopf, *Immanuel Kant und die Pädagogic* (Zurich: EVZ-Verlag, 1970), pp. 171–83. A discussion of Traugott's critique, which basically agrees with his negative evaluation of the character and abilities of Rink, is provided by Lewis White Beck, "Kant on Education," in *Essays on Kant and Hume* (New Haven and London: Yale University Press, 1978), esp. pp. 194–7. The matter is also discussed briefly by Ted Humphrey, *What Real Progress Has Metaphysics Made in Germany since the Time of Leibniz and Wolff?*, p. 13.

5 See de Vleeschauwer, "La Cinderella de Kant," p. 108; Lehmann, Ak 20:483.

6 On these points I am largely following H.J. de Vleeschauwer, *The Development of Kantian Thought*, trans. A. R. C. Duncan (London: Thomas Nelson and Sons, 1962), pp. 161–2.

7 Jakob Sigismund Beck (1761–1840), a commentator on Kant's philosophy, is best known for his *Einzig möglicher Standpunkt, aus welchem die Kritische Philosophie beurteilt werden muss* (1796) (*The Single Possible Standpoint from which the Critical Philosophy Must Be Judged*). As the title suggests, the work is an attempt to provide a unifying "standpoint" for interpreting the *Critique* that will make it possible to avoid the misunderstandings (particularly concerning the radical dualism between sensibility and understanding) to which Kant's own exposition in the *Critique* had supposedly left him vulnerable. But though attempting only to clarify Kant, Beck actually exerted a significant influence on the development of post-Kantian thought. In his discussion of *Progress*, de Vleeschauwer has maintained that Kant was completely converted to Beck's approach and, accordingly, began an endeavor continued in the *Opus postumum* to reformulate the critical philosophy in such a way as to meet the criticisms of the new generation of philosophers, including thinkers such as Salomon Maimon (1754–1800) and Johann Gottlieb Fichte (1762–1814). See *The Development of Kantian Thought*, p. 157,

and *La Déduction transcendentale dans l'oeuvre de Kant*, vol. III, pp. 467–9. This would seem to be somewhat of an exaggeration, however, since, as noted above, the basic idea (though not the terminology) is already in place in the second edition Transcendental Deduction, where Kant states that "of all representations *combination* [*Verbindung*] is the only one which cannot be given through objects" (B 130).

8 For a useful discussion of this topic, see Lewis White Beck, "Five Concepts of Freedom in Kant," in *Philosophical Analysis and Reconstruction*, a Festschrift to Stephan Körner edited by J. T. Srzednick, (Dordrecht: Martinus Nijhoff, 1987), pp. 35–51.

9 On this point see Lewis White Beck, *A Commentary on Kant's "Critique of Practical Reason"* (Chicago: University of Chicago Press, 1960), pp. 207–8. Kant himself returns to the distinction between autonomy and autocracy in the *Metaphysics of Morals* (Ak 6:383).

What real progress has metaphysics made in Germany since the time of Leibniz and Wolff?

1 A crafty king of Corinth, Sisyphus was condemned in Hades to the futile task of pushing a large stone up a hill. Whenever he neared the top, it fell from his grasp and rolled to the bottom again.

2 The term *sinnlich* may refer, with systematic ambiguity, either to the object of sensation, the sensible, or to the subject's capacity for sensing it. In the latter case (with Hatfield, p. 46 above), we render it by 'sensory' (as in 'extra-sensory perception'). For *Sinnlichkeit* we follow custom by adhering to 'sensibility'. The above distinction is explicitly made in Kant's Latin works (*sensualis/sensibilis*), and seems the more necessary here, in that the intent of the passage is clearly to deny that causality, for example, is a part of the subject's sensory endowment, rather than to affirm that it is an attribute of the nonsensible. See 20:267 below.

3 For references to ontology, see *Critique of Pure Reason*, A 247/B 303, A 845–6/B 873–4; *On a Discovery*, 8:190; and 20:286 below.

4 For philosophy as a doctrine of wisdom, see *Critique of Practical Reason*, 5: 108–9, 130–1, 141, 163; *Opus Postumum*, 21:155–6, 22:38–9, 544–5; and *Proclamation*, 8:418, 421–2.

5 Earlier discussions of mathematics in relation to philosophy are to be found in *CPR*, A 160–2/B 199–202, A 712–38/B 740–66; *Metaphysical Foundations*, 4:470–9. See also *Op.Post.*, 22:544–5.

6 The antinomies, here briefly alluded to, are brought up again at 20:287–8 and 326–9 below. For the original arguments, see *CPR*, A 420–43/B 448–71, A 462–76/B 490–504, A 508–15/B 536–43.

7 The tangled skein of the "three stages" has been helpfully unravelled in Professor Allison's Introduction to this work (pp. 341–2 above). For a previous version, see *CPR*, A 761/B 789.

8 For earlier expositions of this celebrated distinction, see *CPR*, A 6–13/B 10–14, A 150–8/B 187–97; *Prolegomena*, 4:266–70; *On a Discovery*, 8:226–46.

9 For Kant's indebtedness to Hume, see *Prolegomena*, 4:260–2, 310–12.

10   The account of intuition here is essentially that given in *CPR*, A 42–55/B 59–79. See also B 160–1, and *Prolegomena*, 4:282.

11   The distinction between phenomena and noumena, the concept of intellectual intuition, and the doctrine of a double self, which are summarily set forth at this point, are all more fully expounded in the closing pages of the B version of the Transcendental Deduction (*CPR*, B 144–59).

12   For the ideality of space and time, see *CPR*, A 26–8/B 42–4, A 32–6/B 49–55; *Prolegomena*, 4:290–4.

13   The term *Apparenz* is used by Kant to distinguish the misleading appearance (*Anschein*) of ordinary objects, due to error or lack of judgment, from the sense in which every empirical object is an appearance (*Erscheinung*) of a by-definition inaccessible thing-in-itself. Appearances of the latter sort are not, for Kant, illusory, as they would be for a "dogmatic idealist," who denies the reality of an external world. Compare *CPR*, A 45–6/B 62–3, B 274, A 293–8/B 349–55. Notes 4 and 5 on p. 736 of Guyer & Wood's edition (Cambridge University Press, 1998) relate to this point. See also *Prolegomena*, 4:315, 375, and Friedman's note 54 above.

14   On idealism, see *CPR*, B 274–9, A 367–80; *Prolegomena*, 4:288–94, 374–5; and further remarks at 20:276 below.

15   The 'sensory self', or *sinnliche Ich*, might equally be called the 'sentient self'. It is that formal subject of consciousness, also attributable to animals, which in man is at least partially subordinate to powers of thought and will – the rational or logical self – whereby its attention is guided, its content monitored, and the like. To render this term as the 'sensible self' would imply it to be an object of the senses, a *Mich* rather than an *Ich*, and thus a target for empirical observation in inner sense. This is not, to say the least, a likely interpretation of Kant. Compare *CPR*, B 155–6 (on line 8, p. 259, of Guyer and Wood's edition, the text should read: "time, although *it* is not itself an object …"). See also their footnotes 42–4 on p. 727, and *CPR*, B 422–3.

16   Composition (*Zusammensetzung*) is Kant's late-period substitute for combination, synthesis, or unification of the manifold of sensory intuition under categories. Compare *CPR*, B 130, and Guyer and Wood's note 33 thereto, on p. 726; Kant's note at B 201; and 20:275–6 below.

17   For Kant's table of judgments, see *CPR*, A 76–83/B 102–9; also *Prolegomena*, 4:302–3.

18   The *salto mortale* of the circus acrobat, an image borrowed from Jacobi, is quite frequently alluded to in Kant's late writings. See, for example, *Tone*, 8:392, 398 (and note).

19   For Kant's theory of schematism, see *CPR*, A 137–47/B 176–87.

20   For a fuller discussion of experience, see *CPR*, A 85–114/B 117–29.

21   For a similar rejection of the Humean appeal to custom and association as a basis for the causal law, see *CPR*, A 112.

22   On the insufficiency of the principle of contradiction for the same purpose, compare *CPR*, A 150–3/B 189–90; *On a Discovery*, 8:193–8.

23   On noumena and their unsuitability as objects of knowledge, see *CPR*, A 235–60/B 294–315, A 286–9/B 342–6; *Prolegomena*, 4:314–17, 333.

24 For Kant's objections to the principle of sufficient reason, see *CPR*, A 783/B 811; *Prolegomena*, 4:270; *On a Discovery*, 8:193–8.

25 For earlier criticism of Leibniz and his followers, see *CPR*, A 270–6/B 326–32; *On a Discovery*, 8:219, 247–50.

26 On the infinite divisibility of space, see *CPR*, A 439/B 467, A 524–7/B 552–5; *Metaphysical Foundations*, 4:503–8; *On a Discovery*, 8:202–3, and Hatfield's note 36 above.

27 On the identity of indiscernibles, see *CPR*, A 272/B 328.

28 Pursuit of the unconditioned, and cosmological quandaries in regard to the infinitude of space and time, are the principal topic of the First Antinomy. See *CPR*, A 416–20/B 443–8, A 481–4/B 509–12, A 528–32/B 556–60; *On a Discovery*, 8:207.

29 For the additional antinomies concerning simple elements, freedom and determinism, and the necessary and the contingent, see *CPR*, A 426–43/B 454–71; *Prolegomena*, 4:338–48.

30 For earlier discussions of teleology in Nature, see *Critique of Judgment*, 5:192, 219, 397–400; and *First Introduction to CJ*, 20:217.

31 For the transcendent Ideas of God, Freedom, and Immortality, see *CPR*, B 395, note; *CPracR*, 5:132–5; *CJ*, 5:473–4.

32 On autocracy, see *Metaphysic of Morals*, 6:383.

33 On persuasion, belief and probability, compare *CPR*, A 774/B 802, A 820–3/B 848–51; *Prolegomena*, 4:369.

34 Kant's critique of rational theology is more fully expounded in *CPR*, A 567–642/B 595–670. Compare also his posthumously published *Lectures on the Philosophical Doctrine of Religion*, 28:1004–12 (translated in Wood and di Giovanni, eds., *Religion and Rational Theology*, Cambridge University Press, 1996).

35 For allusions to Spinozism, compare *CJ*, 5:393–4, 421, 440; *On a Discovery*, 8:224, note.

36 Archimedes of Syracuse (c. 287–212 B.C.) was the greatest mathematician of antiquity. His seesaw scheme for lifting the earth inspires a famous passage in Descartes' *Meditations* (II), which Kant may also be recalling at this point. See *Tone* 8:403 for a similar allusion.

37 On theosophy, compare *CJ*, 5:459–60.

38 The notion of an "anthropic" argument also occurs in *CJ*, 5:463.

39 For the "glory of God" as end of creation, compare *CPracR*, 5:131.

40 On psychology, both rational and empirical, see *CPR*, A 351–66, A 648–9/B 876–7; *CJ*, 5:461.

41 On body, soul, and spirit, see also *On a Discovery*, 8:249; *Proclamation*, 8:417.

42 On the immortality of the soul, see *CPR*, A 345f./B 403ff.; *CPracR*, 5:122–4; *CJ*, 5:473–4.

43 The Danaids were the daughters of Danaus, king of Argos. They murdered their husbands on the wedding night, and were condemned in Hades to the vain labor of carrying water in a sieve.

44 For references related to the analytic/synthetic distinction, see note 8 above.

45 On Plato as a mathematician, see *CJ*, 5:363–6; *Tone*, 8:391.

46 On possibility, see *CPR*, A 220–6/B 267–74; *CJ*, 5:466.

47 For references related to the antinomies, see note 6 above.

48 Fülleborn (1769–1803) had published in 1792 an account of recent discoveries in philosophy.

49 This is a Stoic term, used by Epictetus among others, to designate the sovereignty of the will. For the argument that follows, see *CPracR*, 5:53–7.

50 On the conflict of principles, see *CPracR*, 5:31–7, 57–62.

51 For Kant's critique of the ontological argument, see *CPR*, A 592–602/B 620–30. For Leibniz's version of it, see his *Philosophischen Schriften*, 4:295–6, 7:261.

On a recently prominent tone of superiority in philosophy

1 Kant is referring to the early monastic settlements in Egypt (also in Palestine and Syria) during the Third and Fourth centuries A.D. Following the example of St. Anthony, many monks became hermits or solitaries and enjoyed at least a reputation for philosophic virtue and wisdom. For an equally skeptical view of the movement, cf. E. Gibbon, *Decline and Fall of the Roman Empire*, chap. XXXVII.

2 The Tungus and the Buryats are peoples of eastern Siberia and northern Mongolia, respectively. Kant alludes to them elsewhere, e.g., in *Religion within the Boundaries of mere Reason*, Ak 6:176, and cf. the footnote thereto in *Religion and Rational Theology*, ed. A. Wood & G. di Giovanni, (Cambridge University Press, 1996), p. 469.

3 Jean-Étienne Montucla, author of a voluminous *Histoire des Mathématiques* (1758–1802), "the first history of mathematics worthy of the name."

4 It was this remark which precipitated the "mathematical dispute" with Reimarus (cf. below).

5 The Twelfth Legion, the Fulminata, bore the emblem of Jove's thunderbolt on their shields. In 172, during a losing battle with the Quadi, they were saved from defeat by a violent rainstorm.

6 The Emperor Julian's attempt, in 363 A.D., to put the Christians out of countenance by rebuilding the Jewish Temple, was defeated by mysterious outbreaks of fire, reputedly of supernatural origin. Cf. E. Gibbon, *Decline and Fall*, chap. XXIII.

7 Aristotle, from his birthplace, Stagira.

8 A hecatomb is a large sacrifice, of oxen, for example.

9 The death-defying leap of an acrobat. The term is used in a metaphorical sense by F. H. Jacobi for the leap of faith, and is presumably borrowed by Kant, both here and in *Religion within the Boundaries of Mere Reason*, Ak 6:121; cf. Wood & di Giovanni, p. 464.

10 The work referred to is J. G. Schlosser: *Platos Briefe über die syrakusanische Staatsrevolution, nebst einer historischen Einleitung und Anmerkung* (Königsberg: F. Nicolovius, 1795). Plato's letters, especially the famous seventh, have often been invoked to support an esoteric interpretation of his philosophy. Their authenticity has at times been doubted, but the majority are nowadays accepted as genuine.

11 The "fifth wheel to the coach," a proverbial phrase for something superfluous, is Kant's sarcastic gloss on what he may have taken for an allusion, by Schlosser, to the doctrine of a fifth essence. Schlosser objected to the vulgarity of Kant's language, but since he took it to be a "fourth wheel," it is doubtful whether either party knew what the other was talking about.

12 The quotations that follow are from Count Stolberg's *Auserlesene Gespräche des Platon* (Königsberg: Nicolovius, 1796).

13 The Veil of Isis, and the inscription on her temple, are several times referred to in Kant's writings, from *The Only Possible Basis for a Demonstration of the Existence of God*, Ak 2:151 to a celebrated footnote in the *Critique of Judgment*, Ak 5:317. The same imagery recurs in Schiller, Novalis, Schelling, and other authors of the period. Beethoven kept a framed copy of this inscription on his desk, and seems to have taken it from Schiller's essay *Die Sendung Moses*. As a devoted reader of Plutarch, he could, however, have equally well found it at source in the latter's *De Iside et Osiride, Moralia*, chap. 9 (354c). Essentially the same words are there recorded as appearing on the plinth of a statue of Athena (= Isis) at Saïs. (Cf. E. K. Borthwick, in *Music and Letters* 79 [1998], p. 270.)

14 Fontenelle wrote a *History of Heathen Oracles*, which was translated into German by Gottsched. Kant is probably quoting (loosely) from the latter.

Proclamation of the imminent conclusion of a treaty of perpetual peace in philosophy

1 Cicero, *De natura deorum*, II, 160: "Sus vero quid habet praeter escam? Cui quidem ne putesceret animam ipsam pro sale datum dicit esse Chrysippus." Cf. *De finibus*, V, 38, and earlier citations in Varro; *De re rustica*, II, 4, 10, Plutarch, *Quaest. conv.*, V, 10, 3; and others. The saying is also attributed to Cleanthes, who preceded Chrysippus (c. 279–206 B.C.) as head of the early Stoa.

2 A sidelong reference to the title of Schlosser's ill-fated reply to Kant's previous attack.

3 Posidonius (c. 135–51 B.C.) was a leading figure in the middle Stoa; Pompey (106–48 B.C.) was the Roman general who joined Julius Caesar and Crassus in the First Triumvirate.

4 Venetian theriac is, or was, an antidote for venomous bites. Kant is poking fun at Schlosser's weakness for probabilistic arguments, and his overreliance on quotations.

5 Kant here quotes an epigram by the Göttingen mathematician Abraham Gotthelf Kästner – one of three that were later published in the Göttinger Musenalmanach *Poetische Blumenlese für das Jahr 1797* (Göttingen, 1797), p. 100. The original is entitled *Vom ewigen Frieden* (On Perpetual Peace) and runs:

> Auf ewig' ist der Krieg vermieden,
> Befolgt man, was der Weise spricht;
> Dann halten alle Menschen Frieden,
> Allein die Philosophen nicht.

The "sage" is quite probably Kant himself, whose tract on *Perpetual Peace* had appeared in 1795, and who had already sought Kästner's advice during his own earlier quarrel with Eberhard in 1790. Kästner was no Kantian, but the two were on friendly terms, and the older man's judgment was much respected by Kant. For another allusion to this epigram, and for further details of the Kant–Kästner relationship, cf. *Opus postumum*, ed. E. Förster and M. Rosen (Cambridge University Press, 1993), pp. 83, 267–8.

6   Alluding, perhaps, to *John* 8:44.

Glossary

German–English

Abhängigkeit	dependency
Abmessung	dimension
Absonderung	separation
Abstechung	prominence
Abteilung	section
Abwiegung	weighing
Abwürdigung	demotion
Abziehung	derivation
Ähnlichkeit	similarity
Ahnung	intimation
Allgemeinheit	universality
Anerschaffung	implantation
Angelegenheit	matter, affair
Angemessenheit	appropriateness
Anmassung	pretense, presumption, arrogance
Annehmung	assumption
Anschauung	intuition
Anwendbarkeit	applicability, appropriateness
Anziehung	attraction
Apparenz	apparency
Armseligkeit	puerility
aufburden	ascribe
Auffassung	apprehension
Aufgabe	task, problem
Aufhebung	removal (*remotio*)
Auflösung (-smittel)	solution, solvent
Aufmerksamkeit	attention
Aufrichtigkeit	sincerity
Aufschub	deferment, postponement
Ausdehnung	expansion, extension
Ausführlichkeit	copiousness, elaboration
Auslegung	account
Aussöhnung	reconciliation
ausweichen	evade

500

Bebung	tremor, vibration
Bedenkung (-lichkeit)	scrupulous attention, hesitation
Bedeutung	meaning
Bedingung	condition
Befugnis	legitimacy
Begebenheit	event, occurrence
Begreiflichkeit	comprehensibility
Begriff	concept
Beharrlichkcit	perdurance, persistence
Behauptung	assertion, claim, teaching
Behutsamkeit	cautiousness
Benehmen	mode of conduct
Beobachtung	observation
Berichtigung	correction
Berückung	deception
Berührung	contact, contiguity
Beschaffenheit	constitution, property
Beschäftigung	preoccupation
Bescheidenheit	modesty, unpretentiousness
Beschleunigung	acceleration
Beschwerlichkeit	fatigue
Bestandstück	constituent
Bestätigung	confirmation
Bestimmtheit, Bestimmung	determinacy, determination
Bestrebung	striving
Beurteilung	judgment
Bewandtnis	case, matter, situation
Bewegung	motion
Beweisung	demonstration, proof
Bewerbung	advocacy
Bewusstsein	consciousness
Beziehung	relation
Billigkeit	fairness, justice
blasericht	vesicular
Blödsichtigkeit	dim-sightedness
Brauchbarkeit	usefulness
Bündigkeit	cogency
Darstellung	presentation (*exhibitio*)
Dasein	existence
Dauer	duration, endurance
Deutlichkeit	clarity, distinctness

Dichtigkeit	density
Druck	pressure
Dunkelheit	darkness, obscurity
Durchdringung	penetration
Eigenschaft	property
Eigentümlichkeit	characteristic
Einbildung (-skraft)	imagination
Eindringung	penetration
Eindruck	impression
Eingebung	inspiration
Einhelligkeit	harmony, unanimity
Einrichtung	arrangement
Einschränkung	limitation, restriction
Einsicht	insight
Einteilung	division
Einwendung, Einwurf	objection
Eitelkeit	vanity
Empfänglichkeit	susceptibility
Empfindung	sensation
Endlichkeit	finitude
Endzweck	final end or purpose
Entfernung	distance
Entgegensetzung	opposition
Entgegenwirkung	counteraction
Erdichtung	fiction
Erfahrung	experience
Erfindung	discovery
Erhabenheit	sublimity
Erhebung	elevation
Erkenntnis (-vermögen)	cognition, knowledge
Erklärung	explanation
Erläuterung	elucidation
Ermangelung	lack, want
Erörterung	consideration
Erscheinung	appearance
Erstarrung	rigidification
Erteilung	imparting
Erwägung	consideration, reflection
Erwähnung	mention
Erweiterung	amplification, extension
Erwerbung	acquisition
erwidern	reply to
Erzeugung	creation

Fassungskraft	power of comprehension
Feder	spring
Fehler	error
Festigkeit	solidity
Flächenkraft	surface force
Flüssigkeit	fluidity
Fürwahrhalten	apprehension, assent
Gärung	fermentation
Gattung	species
Geberde	gesture
Gedächtnis	memory
Gegeneinanderstellung	comparison
Gegenstand	object
Gegenteil	opposite
Gegenwirkung	reaction
Gelehrsamkeit	learning
Gelingen	success
Gemächlichkeit	comfort, ease, indolence
Gemässheit	conformity
Gemeinschaft	community
Gemut	mind
gerathewohl	haphazardly
Gerüllkammer	junk closet
Geschwindigkeit	speed, velocity
Gesetzgebung	legislation
Gesetzmässigkeit	lawfulness, conformity to law
Gesinnung	disposition
Gestalt	figure, shape
Geständnis	admission
Gewandtheit	adroitness
Gewissheit	certainty
Gewohnheit	custom, habit
Gleichartigkeit	homogeneity, similarity
gleichförmig	uniform
gleichgeltend	equivalent
Gleichgewicht	equilibrium
Gleichgültigkeit	indifference
Gleichmässigkeit	proportion, regularity, symmetry
Glückseligkeit	felicity, happiness
gradlinig	rectilinear
Grenze	boundary, limit
Grösse	magnitude, quantity, size
Grundlage	basis, foundation

Gründlichkeit	profundity
Gültigkeit	validity
Habseligkeit	belongings
Halbmesser	radius
Haltbarkeit	tenability
herausklauben	extract
herleiten	derive
Hinaufsteigen	ascent
Hinweisung	allusion
hinzudichten	read into
Hinzukunft	addition
Hinzusetzung	appending
Hinzutuung	addition
Inbegriff	sum total
Kennzeichen	hallmark
Klebrigkeit	viscosity
Kleinode	jewel
Körper (-chen)	body, particle
Kraft	force
Kreditiv	credentials
Kreisbewegung	circular motion
krummlinig	curvilinear
Lage	position, situation
Leere	void
Lehrart	method
Lehrsatz	theorem
Leichtigkeit	ease, lightness
löcherig	porous
mannigfältig	manifold
Masse	mass, measure
Mattigkeit	dullness
Menge	aggregate
Merkmal	mark
Missdeutung	misunderstanding
Misstrauen	mistrust
Mitteilung	communication
Möglichkeit	possibility
Mutmassung	guess, surmise
Nachdenken	reflection
Nachforschung	inquiry
nähern	approach

Glossary

Naturanlage	natural predisposition
Naturanstalt	natural institution
Nichtzuunterscheidenheit	indiscernibility
Notwendigkeit	necessity
Obersatz	major premise
Ohnmacht	weakness
Ort	place
Probierstein	touchstone
Pünktlichkeit	exactitude
Raumesinhalt	volume
Rechtfertigung	defense, justification
Rechtmässigkeit	legitimacy
Regelmässigkeit	regularity
Reibung	friction
Richtung	direction
Ruhe	rest
Satz	principle, proposition
Scheidung	decomposition
Schein	illusion, semblance
Schlusssatz	conclusion
Schnelligkeit	rapidity
Schwankung	oscillation
Schwärmerei	enthusiasm, fanaticism
Schwere	gravity, weight
Schwierigkeit	difficulty
Seichtigkeit	shallowness
Selbstthätigkeit	self-activity, spontaneity
Sinnlichkeit	sensibility
Springfeder	spring
spröde	brittle
Starrheit	rigidity
Stetigkeit	constancy, continuity
Stoff	material
Stoss	impact
Streitigkeit	conflict, controversy
Tauglichkeit	fitness, suitability
Täuschung	deception
Teilbarkeit	divisibility
Trägheit	indolence, inertia
Trennung	separation
Trüglichkeit	delusiveness

Übereinstimmung	agreement, correspondence
Überredung	persuasion
Überschwänglichkeit	extravagance
übersinnlich	super-sensible
Überzeugung	conviction
unbedingt	unconditioned
Unbegreiflichkeit	incomprehensibility
Unbescheidenheit	insolence
unbildlich	unimageable
undeutlich	indistinct
Undurchdringlichkeit	impenetrability
Unentbehrlichkeit	indispensability
Unergründlichkeit	unfathomability
Ungereimtheit	absurdity
Ungrund	deficiency
Unkunde	incomprehension
Unsterblichkeit	immortality
Untauglichkeit	unsuitability
Unterlassung	omission
Unterschied (-scheidung)	difference, distinction
Untersuchung	inquiry
Unterweisung	discipline, teaching
unveränderlich	immutable, unalterable
Unvermeidlichkeit	unavoidability
Unvermögen	incapacity
Unverträglichkeit	inconsistency
Unzulänglichkeit	inadequacy
Unzulässigkeit	inadmissibility
Ursache	cause
ursprünglich	original
Urteilskraft	judgment
Verabsäumung	neglect
Veränderung	alteration, change
Veranstaltung	preparation
Verbindung	combination
Verbreitung	diffusion
Verdacht	suspicion
Verdrehung	distortion
Vereinigung	unification
Verfahren	procedure
Vergleichung	comparison
Vergünstigung	privilege
Verhältnis	relation

Verirrung	aberration, straying
Verkennung	misunderstanding
Verknüpfung	connection
Verlegenheit	quandary
Vermessenheit	audacity, presumption
Verminderung	diminution
Vermögen	capacity, power
Vermutung	supposition
Vernunft	reason
vernünfteln	finick up, quibble
Vernunftmässigkeit	rationality
Verschiebung	displacement
Verschiedenheit	difference
Verschlag	division, partition
Verstand	understanding
Verständlichkeit	intelligibility
Vertauschung	mistaking for
Verträglichkeit	sociability
Verwandtschaft	affinity
Verwechselung	confusion
verweisen	banish
Verwickelung	complication, entanglement
Verwirrung, Verworrenheit	confusion, confusedness
Verzichttuung	renunciation
Verzweiflung	despair
Vielheit	plurality
Vollkommenheit	perfection
Vollständigkeit	completeness
Voraussetzung	presupposition
Vorbedacht	forethought
Vorhersagung	prediction
vornehm	superior
Vorstellung	representation
Vorteil	advantage
Vorübung	preparatory exercise
Vorwurf	reproach
Wagschale	scale
Wahrhaftigkeit	truthfulness
Wahrheit	truth
Wahrnehmung	perception
Wahrsagergeist	prophetic spirit
Wahrscheinlichkeit	probability
Wechselwirkung	interaction

Weisheit (–slehre)	wisdom, doctrine of
Weitläufigkeit	expansiveness, prolixity
Weltkörper	heavenly body
Wesen	being, essence
Wichtigkeit	importance
Widerlegung	refutation
Widerspruch	contradiction
Widerstand	resistance
widerstreiten	oppose
Willkür	choice
Wirklichkeit	actuality, reality
Wirkung	action, effect
Wissenschaft	science
Wörterkram	verbiage
Wortkünstelei	verbal affectation
Zeitverspillerung	time wasting
Zergliederung	analysis, classification
Zernichtung	destruction
Zimmerung	carpentering
Zitterung	vibration
Zufälligkeit	contingency
Zufriedenheit	satisfaction (*acquiescentia*)
Zug	traction
Zugleichsein	simultaneity
Zulänglichkeit	adequacy
Zumutung	imputation
Zurechnungsfähigkeit	accountability
Zureichenden Grund, Satz des	principle of sufficient reason
Zurücklegung	traversal
Zurückstossung	repulsion
zurücktreiben	repel
Zurüstung	preparation
Zusammendrückung	compression
Zusammenfügung	conjoining, synthesis
Zusammenhang	cohesion, unity
Zusammensetzung	combination, composition, synthesis
Zusammenstellung	arrangement
Zusammenstimmung	agreement
Zuverlässigkeit	reliability
Zweckmässigkeit	purposiveness
Zweckverbindung	combination of purposes
Zweifellehre	doctrine of doubt, skepticism
Zwischenräume	interstices

English–German

absurdity	*Ungereimtheit*
acceleration	*Beschleunigung*
account	*Auslegung*
accountability	*Zurechnungsfähigkeit*
acquisition	*Erwerbung*
action	*Wirkung*
actuality	*Wirklichkeit*
addition	*Hinzukunft, Hinzutuung*
adequacy	*Zulänglichkeit*
admission	*Geständnis*
adroitness	*Gewandtheit*
advantage	*Vorteil*
advocacy	*Bewerbung*
affinity	*Verwandtschaft*
aggregate	*Menge*
agreement	*Übereinstimmung, Zusammenstimmung*
allusion	*Hinweisung*
alteration	*Veränderung*
amplification	*Erweiterung*
analysis	*Zergliederung*
apparency	*Apparenz*
appearance	*Erscheinung*
appending	*Hinzusetzung*
applicability	*Anwendbarkeit*
apprehension	*Auffassung, Fürwahrhalten*
approach	*nähern*
appropriateness	*Angemessenheit, Anwendbarkeit*
arrangement	*Einrichtung, Zusammenstellung*
arrogance	*Anmassung*
ascent	*Hinaufsteigen*
ascribe	*aufburden*
assent	*Fürwahrhalten*
assertion	*Behauptung*
assumption	*Annehmung*
attention	*Aufmerksamkeit*
attraction	*Anziehung*
audacity	*Vermessenheit*
banish	*verweisen*
basis	*Grundlage*
being	*Sein, Wesen*
belongings	*Habseligkeit*

body	*Körper*
boundary	*Grenze*
brittle	*spröde*
capacity	*Vermögen*
carpentering	*Zimmerung*
cause	*Ursache*
cautiousness	*Behutsamkeit*
certainty	*Gewissheit*
change	*Veränderung*
characteristic	*Eigentümlichkeit*
choice	*Willkür*
circular motion	*Kreisbewegung*
claim	*Behauptung*
clarity	*Deutlichkeit*
classification	*Zergliederung*
cogency	*Bündigkeit*
cognition	*Erkenntnis*
cohesion	*Zusammenhang*
combination	*Verbindung, Zusammensetzung*
comfort	*Gemächlichkeit*
communication	*Mitteilung*
community	*Gemeinschaft*
comparison	*Gegeneinanderstellung*
completeness	*Vollständigkeit*
composition	*Zusammensetzung*
comprehensibility	*Begreiflichkeit*
comprehension, power of	*Fassungskraft*
compression	*Zusammendrückung*
concept	*Begriff*
conclusion	*Schlusssatz*
condition	*Bedingung*
conduct	*Benehmen*
confirmation	*Bestätigung*
conflict	*Streitigkeit*
conformity	*Gemässheit*
confusion (mistake)	*Vertauschung, Verwechselung*
confusedness (disorder)	*Verwirrung, Verworrenheit*
conjoining	*Zusammenfügung*
connection	*Verknüpfung*
consciousness	*Bewusstsein*
consideration	*Erörterung, Erwägung*
constancy	*Stetigkeit*
constituent	*Bestandstuck*

constitution	*Beschaffenheit*
contact	*Berührung*
contingency	*Zufälligkeit*
continuity	*Stetigkeit*
contradiction	*Widerspruch, Widerstreit*
controversy	*Streitigkeit*
conviction	*Überzeugung*
copiousness	*Ausführlichkeit*
correction	*Berichtigung*
correspondence	*Übereinstimmung*
counteraction	*Entgegenwirkung*
creation	*Erzeugung*
credentials	*Kreditiv*
curvilinear	*krummlinig*
custom	*Gewohnheit*
darkness	*Dunkelheit*
deception	*Berückung, Täuschung*
decomposition	*Scheidung*
defense	*Rechtfertigung*
deferment	*Aufschub*
deficiency	*Ungrund*
delusiveness	*Trüglichkeit*
demonstration	*Beweis, Beweisung*
demotion	*Abwürdigung*
density	*Dichtigkeit*
dependency	*Abhängigkeit*
derivation	*Abziehung, Herleitung*
despair	*Verzweiflung*
destruction	*Zernichtung*
determinacy, determination	*Bestimmung*
difference	*Unterschied, Verschiedenheit*
difficulty	*Schwierigkeit*
diffusion	*Verbreitung*
dimension	*Abmessung*
diminution	*Verminderung*
dim-sightedness	*Blödsichtigkeit*
direction	*Richtung*
discipline	*Unterweisung*
discovery	*Erfindung*
displacement	*Verschiebung*
disposition	*Gesinnung*
distance	*Entfernung*
distinction	*Unterscheidung*

distinctness	*Deutlichkeit*
distortion	*Verdrehung*
divisibility	*Teilbarkeit*
division	*Einteilung, Verschlag*
doubt, doctrine of	*Zweifellehre*
dullness	*Mattigkeit*
duration	*Dauer*
ease	*Gemächlichkeit, Leichtigkeit*
effect	*Wirkung*
elaboration	*Ausführlichkeit*
elevation	*Erhebung*
elucidation	*Erläuterung*
endurance	*Dauer*
enthusiasm	*Schwärmerei*
equilibrium	*Gleichgewicht*
equivalent	*gleichgeltend*
error	*Fehler*
essence	*Wesen*
evade	*ausweichen*
event	*Begebenheit*
exactitude	*Pünktlichkeit*
existence	*Dasein*
expansion	*Ausdehnung*
expansiveness	*Weitläufigkeit*
experience	*Erfahrung*
explanation	*Erklärung*
extension	*Ausdehnung, Erweiterung*
extract	*herausklauben*
extravagant	*überschwänglich*
fairness	*Billigkeit*
fatigue	*Beschwerlichkeit*
felicity	*Glückseligkeit*
fermentation	*Gärung*
fiction	*Erdichtung*
figure	*Gestalt*
final end or purpose	*Endzweck*
finick (up)	*vernünfteln*
finitude	*Endlichkeit*
fitness	*Tauglichkeit*
fluidity	*Flüssigkeit*
force	*Kraft*

forethought	*Vorbedacht*
friction	*Reibung*
gesture	*Geberde*
gravity	*Schwere*
guess	*Mutmassung*
habit	*Gewohnheit*
hallmark	*Kennzeichen*
haphazardly	*gerathewohl*
happiness	*Glückseligkeit*
harmony	*Einhelligkeit*
heavenly body	*Weltkörper*
hesitation	*Bedenklichkeit*
homogeneity	*Gleichartigkeit*
illusion	*Schein*
imagination	*Einbildungskraft*
immortality	*Unsterblichkeit*
immutable	*unveränderlich*
impact	*Stoss*
imparting	*Erteilung*
impenetrability	*Undurchdringlichkeit*
implantation	*Anerschaffung*
importance	*Wichtigkeit*
impression	*Eindruck*
imputation	*Zumutung*
inadequacy	*Unzulänglichkeit*
inadmissibility	*Unzulässigkeit*
incapacity	*Unvermögen*
incomprehensibility	*Unbegreiflichkeit*
incomprehension	*Unkunde*
inconsistency	*Unverträglichkeit*
indifference	*Gleichgültigkeit*
indiscernibility	*Nichtzuunterscheidenheit*
indispensability	*Unentbehrlichkeit*
indistinct	*undeutlich*
indolence	*Gemächlichkeit*
inertia	*Trägheit*
inquiry	*Nachforschung, Untersuchung*
insight	*Einsicht*
insolence	*Unbescheidenheit*
inspiration	*Eingebung*

intelligibility	*Verständlichkeit*
interaction	*Wechselwirkung*
interstices	*Zwischenräume*
intimation	*Ahnung*
intuition	*Anschauung*
jewel	*Kleinod*
judgment	*Beurteilung, Urteilskraft*
junk closet	*Gerüllkammer*
justice	*Billigkeit*
justification	*Rechtfertigung*
knowledge	*Erkenntnis*
lack	*Ermangelung*
lawfulness	*Gesetzmässigkeit*
learning	*Gelehrsamkeit*
legislation	*Gesetzgebung*
legitimacy	*Befugnis, Rechtmässigkeit*
lightness	*Leichtigkeit*
limit	*Grenze*
limitation	*Einschränkung*
magnitude	*Grösse*
major premise	*Obersatz*
manifold	*mannigfältig*
mark	*Merkmal*
mass	*Masse*
material	*Stoff*
matter, affair	*Angelegenheit, Bewandtnis*
meaning	*Bedeutung*
measure	*Masse*
memory	*Gedächtnis*
mention	*Erwähnung*
method	*Lehrart*
mind	*Gemut*
mistrust	*Misstrauen*
misunderstanding	*Missdeutung, Verkennung*
modesty	*Bescheidenheit*
motion	*Bewegung*
natural institution	*Naturanstalt*
natural predisposition	*Naturanlage*

necessity	*Notwendigkeit*
neglect	*verabsäumen*
object	*Gegenstand*
objection	*Einwendung, Einwurf*
obscurity	*Dunkelheit*
observation	*Beobachtung*
occurrence	*Begebenheit*
omission	*Unterlassung*
opposite	*Gegenteil*
opposition	*Entgegensetzung*
original	*ursprünglich*
oscillation	*Schwankung*
particle	*Körperchen*
penetration	*Durchdringung, Eindringung*
perception	*Wahrnehmung*
perdurance	*Beharrlichkeit*
perfection	*Vollkommenheit*
persistence	*Beharrlichkeit*
persuasion	*Überredung*
place	*Ort*
plurality	*Vielheit*
porous	*löcherig*
position	*Lage*
possibility	*Möglichkeit*
postponement	*Aufschub*
power	*Vermögen*
prediction	*Vorhersagung*
preoccupation	*Beschäftigung*
preparation	*Veranstaltung, Zurüstung*
preparatory exercises	*Vorübung*
presentation	*Darstellung*
pressure	*Druck*
presumption, pretense	*Anmassung*
presupposition	*Voraussetzung*
principle	*Satz*
privilege	*Vergünstigung*
probability	*Wahrscheinlichkeit*
problem	*Aufgabe*
procedure	*Verfahrung*
profundity	*Gründlichkeit*
prolixity	*Weitläufigkeit*

prominence	*Abstechung*
proof	*Beweis, Beweisung*
property	*Beschaffenheit, Eigenschaft*
prophetic spirit	*Wahrsagergeist*
proportion	*Gleichmässigkeit*
proposition	*Satz*
puerility	*Armseligkeit*
purposiveness	*Zweckmässigkeit*
quandary	*Verlegenheit*
quantity	*Grösse*
radius	*Halbmesser*
rapidity	*Schnelligkeit*
rationality	*Vernunftmässigkeit*
reaction	*Gegenwirkung*
read into	*hinzudichten*
reality	*Wirklichkeit*
reason	*Vernunft*
reconciliation	*Aussöhnung*
rectilinear	*gradlinig*
reflection	*Erwägung, Nachdenken*
refutation	*Widerlegung*
regularity	*Gleichmässigkeit, Regelmässigkeit*
relation	*Beziehung, Verhältnis*
reliability	*Zuverlässigkeit*
removal (*remotio*)	*Aufhebung*
renunciation	*Verzichttuung*
repel	*zurücktreiben*
reply to	*erwidern*
representation	*Vorstellung*
reproach	*Vorwurf*
repulsion	*Zurückstossung*
resistance	*Widerstand*
rest	*Ruhe*
restriction	*Einschränkung*
rigidification	*Erstarrung*
rigidity	*Starrheit*
satisfaction (*acquiescentia*)	*Zufriedenheit*
scale	*Wagschale*
science	*Wissenschaft*
scrupulosity	*Bedenkung*

section	*Abteilung*
self-activity	*Selbstthätigkeit*
semblance	*Schein*
sensation	*Empfindung*
sensibility	*Sinnlichkeit*
separation	*Absonderung, Trennung*
shallowness	*Seichtigkeit*
shape	*Gestalt*
similarity	*Ähnlichkeit, Gleichartigkeit*
simultaneity	*Zugleichsein*
sincerity	*Aufrichtigkeit*
situation	*Bewandtnis, Lage*
sociability	*Verträglichkeit*
solidity	*Festigkeit*
solution, solvent	*Auflösung-smittel*
species	*Gattung*
speed	*Geschwindigkeit*
spring	*Feder, Springfeder*
straying	*Verirrung*
striving	*Bestrebung*
sublimity	*Erhabenheit*
success	*Gelingen*
sufficient reason, principle of	*Zureichenden Grund, Satz des*
suitability	*Tauglichkeit*
sum total	*Inbegriff*
superior	*vornehm*
super-sensible	*übersinnlich*
supposition	*Vermutung*
surface force	*Flächenkraft*
surmise	*Mutmassung*
susceptibility	*Empfänglichkeit*
suspicion	*Verdacht*
symmetry	*Gleichmässigkeit*
synthesis	*Zusammenfügung, Zusammensetzung*
task	*Aufgabe*
teaching	*Behauptung, Unterweisung*
tenability	*Haltbarkeit*
theorem	*Lehrsatz*
time wasting	*Zeitverspillerung*
touchstone	*Probierstein*
traction	*Zug*
traversal	*Zurücklegung*

tremor	*Bebung*
truth	*Wahrheit*
truthfulness	*Wahrhaftigkeit*
unalterable	*unveränderlich*
unavoidability	*Unvermeidlichkeit*
unconditioned	*unbedingt*
understanding	*Verstand*
unfathomable	*unergründlich*
unification	*Vereinigung*
uniform	*gleichförmig*
unimageable	*unbildlich*
unity	*Zusammenhang*
universality	*Allgemeinheit*
unpretentiousness	*Bescheidenheit*
unsuitability	*Untauglichkeit*
usefulness	*Brauchbarkeit*
validity	*Gültigkeit*
vanity	*Eitelkeit*
velocity	*Geschwindigkeit*
verbal affectation	*Wortkünstelei*
verbiage	*Wörterkram*
vesicular	*blasericht*
vibration	*Bebung, Zitterung*
viscosity	*Klebrigkeit*
void	*Leere*
volume	*Raumesinhalt*
want	*Ermangelung*
weakness	*Ohnmacht*
weighing	*Abwiegung*
weight	*Schwere*
wisdom, doctrine of	*Weisheitslehre*

Index of names

Index of subjects

CPSIA information can be obtained
at www.ICGtesting.com
Printed in the USA
LVHW022359260722
724418LV00004B/106